Smart Supply Chain Finance

"Professor Song Hua has been dedicating in supply chain finance and is the one of the authorities in this field. Based on deep theoretical thinking and wide practical research, Smart Supply Chain Finance conducted insightful research on the combination of finance technology and supply chain finance, with unique and profound understanding especially on avoiding supply chain finance risks and steady developing supply chain finance. This book is a must-read book in exploring the innovation and development of supply chain finance in China. I gladly recommend this book to you."

—Michael Steeman, *Professor at Windesheim University, Founder of European Supply Chain Finance Association*

Hua Song

Smart Supply Chain Finance

palgrave
macmillan

Hua Song
Renmin University of China
Beijing, China

Translation from the Chinese language edition: 智慧供应链金融 by Hua Song, © China Renmin University Press 2019. Published by China Renmin University Press. All Rights Reserved.

ISBN 978-981-16-5996-6 ISBN 978-981-16-5997-3 (eBook)
https://doi.org/10.1007/978-981-16-5997-3

This Palgrave Macmillan imprint is published by the registered company Springer Nature Singapore Pte Ltd.
The registered company address is: 152 Beach Road, #21-01/04 Gateway East, Singapore 189721, Singapore

Preface

The sunset shines on the curved lawn on the roof of the building across the street, making the green grass glow with a golden light. The sun, setting from the top of the hill in the west, overlooks the bustle and hustle city with its last smile and warmth. The square of the neighborhood is crowded with playful children and elderly dancers, marking that the spring of 2019 is coming to an end and the scorching summer will arrive soon. At this moment, a poetry named "Twilight Song" written by Xi Murong came to my mind and haunted me for a long time.

I love the wilderness at dusk
At this moment
All the colors have become silent
And darkness has not yet come
But in the lush forests on the hill
there is still a last trace of passion

I also like the life under the middle age
At this moment
All the stories have been formed
But the end has not yet come
I look back again with a smile
Seeking my heart that was confused and saddened

Writing is a process full of joy and sorrow. When it comes to the end of this book, relief and loss come to me at the same time, because, on the one hand, the happiness is that I can finally free myself from longtime thoughts, sleeplessness, and endless writing, just like a bird breaking out of its cage and rushing toward the boundless blue sky, but, on the other hand, the feeling is like losing something, a leaving friend or a fading dream. The most vivid memory of this yearlong writing was a day in February 2019 when I was living in Delray Beach, Florida. As usual, I woke up at 4:00 a.m. on February 13 and started writing. I was pondering over difficult questions and reveling in small discoveries during the writing about supply chain finance in agriculture. Sometimes I stared at the two happy swans in the small lake surrounded by the lawn in front of my window, and sometimes I meditated with soft music playing. Time passed slowly at this pace until 2:00 a.m. on February 14, when I put down my pen to go bed and suddenly realized that I should have taken a flight back to China on the afternoon of February 13. Later, I hastily booked a flight for the afternoon of February 14 in remorse, organized my luggage, and rushed to the airport. In retrospect, this scene has left me with a trace of fondness.

Passion, resentment, and doubt have been with me alternately for over a year since I started this book on the Lunar New Year's Eve, February 15, 2018. As the society called for and focused on the return of finance to the real economy in order to solve the difficulties and high costs of financing for SMEs, the government, industry, and enterprises began to explore innovative financial services to promote the development of industry and SMEs. In particular, the General Office of the State Council issued the *Guidance on Actively Promoting Supply Chain Innovation and Application* on October 13, 2017, which mentioned six key tasks including vigorously developing supply chain finance and enabling it to promote the growth of the real economy and effectively control risks. This was followed by the adoption of the newly revised *Law of the People's Republic of China on the Promotion of Small and Medium-sized Enterprises* on January 1, 2018, calling for the appropriate treatment of the relationship between the government and the market, the state and enterprises, the relationship between supporting SMEs and maintaining the principle of market fairness, and the relationship between supporting SMEs and their regulated development. Under this background, the whole society has given great expectation and attention to supply chain finance, resulting in supply chain finance, as a new and innovative finance has also developed by leaps and bounds in practice. As a theoretical researcher, I felt an urgent need to actively explore and research this rapidly evolving financial innovation to bring theory up to speed with these rapid practices. My resentment came from the misinterpretation of supply chain finance in real practice. I remembered that in a forum I mocked myself that the *Supply Chain Finance* (I wrote) published in 2015 had misled a batch of enterprises. Those who originally did not understand supply chain finance began to carry out "rogue supply chain finance" after reading the aforementioned book, that is, using their strong position in the industry to further extend billing period and further exploit suppliers in the name of supply chain finance. They not only deteriorated the business environment but also corrupted the business civilization. We should criticize and put an end to these behaviors, question some inordinate proposals in practice, and propose novel ideas. In 2019, as the whole society paid more attention to the development of MSMEs, especially how to effectively solve the problems of working capital and liquidity of MSMEs, a number of proposals kept emerging. Once watching the morning news, I saw some experts calling for commercial banks increasing medium- and long-term loans to SMEs and their tolerance for bad debts, and some even proposed to abolish acceptance bills. This made me ponder the feasibility of these proposals. Will these proposals help SMEs, or, on the contrary, eventually drag down commercial banks and core enterprises? What exactly is the fundamental solution to the financing difficulties of SMEs as well as liquidity? In addition, with the evolution of modern information and communication technology in recent years, some of the latest technology terms have been flooding the major financial forums, such as cloud computing, artificial intelligence, blockchain, and so on. One of the most frequent words is "enabling." At first glance, it was quite refreshing, but after a long time I couldn't help but wonder the relevance between these technologies and supply chain finance? Or, what do technologies enable finance actually and how does it enable finance? The exploration of the role of technology without combining the supply chain operation scenario is ultimately a daydream, down into a tool for capital speculation.

The abovementioned passion, resentment, and doubt intertwined and propelled the formation of the main line of this book. First, in my opinion, supply chain finance should be understood from both a narrow and a broad perspective. In a narrow sense, supply chain finance refers to short-term lending to specific SMEs in specific links based on supply chain operations, such as: finance based on accounts receivable and payable (standard factoring, reverse factoring, forfaiting, etc.), finance based on inventory (warehouse receipt pledge, inventory pledge, etc.), and finance based on advance payment (confirming storage financing, etc.). It can be regarded as a point-to-point (i.e., lender-to-borrower) relationship generated in a supply chain operation scenario. However, supply chain finance in a broad sense is not exclusively for specific SMEs, but for all the participants in the supply chain. In addition, the purpose of these supply chain finance activities is limited not only to financing but also to optimizing the capital flow in the whole supply chain through various financial means, so as to facilitate the supply chain operations, improve the efficiency of industrial operations, and ultimately improve industrial competitiveness. In this book, I believe that the perspective of broad supply chain finance is more suitable to reflect the requirements and trends of finance in aspect of serving the real economy. Based on this understanding, supply chain finance can not only be widely used in various segments such as industry, agriculture, commerce, and recycling economy in rich forms but also promote the innovation and reform of finance. In other words, the development of supply chain finance will definitely drive the development of financial supply chain after the former reaching a high level. Only the highly integrated development of supply chain finance and financial supply chain can lead the industry to run efficiently and smoothly. Second, the role of fintech should neither be overestimated nor be underestimated. Refusing overestimate means avoiding relying on technology totally, since not all risks in the operations of supply chain finance can be solved by applying a certain modern technology, and also a certain fintech can't be treated overoptimistically as the future of supply chain finance, such as blockchain-based supply chain finance. In fact, we need to make it clear that fintech in supply chain finance does not create credit, but only discovers and transmits credit. Not underestimating implies that when the driving force of supply chain finance shifts from core enterprises to network ecology, we should face up to the increasing demand for modern fintech to help realize objectification of interaction of underlying assets, end-business self-management, objectification of debt structure of capital end, and self-management of participants' credit. On this basis, this book argues that modern fintech is a convergent enabling system covering the perception layer, data layer, process layer, and model layer, which fully acts on all participants, all links and all activities of supply chain operations, in which fintech companies play the role of intermediary signals. Third, the sound development of supply chain finance requires systematic rules and regulations. Without regulation-backed safeguards, the profit-seeking nature of the economy will distort the normal business operations, thus increasing the number of cases of mutual violations and damages. This can result to, on the one hand, large enterprises bullying SMEs by extending the billing period and not paying when due, and, on the other hand, MSMEs defaulting and refusing to repay bank loans, and in turn to put press on the government (with the increase of bank loans of a certain enterprise, the government does not dare to allow the enterprises close down). Most frightening of all, if such malpractice spreads, enterprises will gradually "regard default as reasonable and bullying as customary," thereby undermining business civilization. According to this book, the fundamental solution to this problem should be considered from three aspects: The first aspect is to popularize electronic invoices and electronic documents to create a fast, low-cost, and efficient payment environment and to determine rights in the transactions. The second aspect is to limit payment delays, by strictly controlling the agreed payment terms in the upstream and downstream in order to prevent in advance the possible appropriation of SME funds, and establishing ex-post compensation mechanisms. The third aspect is to limit payment delays firstly from government departments, public institutions, and state-owned enterprises, thus bringing a positive impact on timely payments among private enterprises. Besides, timely payments to SMEs should be clearly defined as the social responsibility of large enterprises, especially listed ones, so as to establish a good business civilization.

The above purposes are what this book tries to achieve as the research result of the National Natural Science Foundation of China—*Research on the Impact of Internet-based Industrial Ecology on Supply Chain Finance Model and Efficiency (71872177)*. In completing this book, I would like to thank the National Natural Science Foundation of China. In addition, Mr. Huang Sheng, cofounder of UMARK, Mr. Cai Yujiang, cofounder of 10000link.com, and many other friends from business community provided extremely rich practical wisdom for this book. In particular, Mr. Huang Sheng helped me complete Chap. 6, Sect. 6.3, "Key Technologies Applied in Supply Chain Operations." During this period, my family was extremely supportive and helpful, allowing me to devote almost all of my time, including weekends and holidays, to my job or this book, so I owe the results to their consistent support. Ms. Fei Xiaoling and Ms. Zhang Ying of China Renmin University Press have done a lot of diligent work for the publication of this book. I would like to express my heartfelt thanks to them.

Supply chain finance is a growing and challenging research topic and field. In view of my limited ability, adding the rapid development of the field, there may be some errors and shortcomings in the book. I would like to welcome criticism and correction from all readers.

Beijing, China
May 3, 2019

Hua Song

Contents

List of Figures

List of Tables

CHAPTER 1

Supply Chain Finance Innovation: Origin and Evolution

1.1 Introduction

In recent years, supply chain finance, as a key mode of industry-finance integration, has drawn keen attention from both the business community and the academic community. Tier-2 suppliers are less involved in financial resources due to their long distance from the core enterprise. The difficulties and high costs of financing for SMEs have become major obstacles to the economic development of the whole society. Particularly, SMEs are also faced with working capital pressures due to the high percentage of accounts receivable with enterprises competitions intensified. Studies by the Global Supply Chain Finance Forum (GSCFF, 2015) showed that changes in international trade from 1978 to 2013 had led to a gradual shift in the settlement from the original L/Cs to open accounts, thus having put numerous small- and medium-sized suppliers under severe capital pressures (see Fig. 1.1). Similarly, according to the latest survey of Coface (2017) with respect to the payment status in Chinese SMEs, the ratio of open accounts remained as high as 78% in 2016, with the average billing period prolonged from 57 days in 2014 to 68 days in 2016, representing a growth margin of 19%. Among those companies surveyed, 68% said they had suffered delinquent payments from clients: 26.3% of them suffered an average delinquency period lasting for more than 90 days, and 15.9% even suffered an average delinquency period as long as more than 150 days. Due to their small scale, SMEs are more likely to be faced with cash flow

H. Song, *Smart Supply Chain Finance*,
https://doi.org/10.1007/978-981-16-5997-3_1

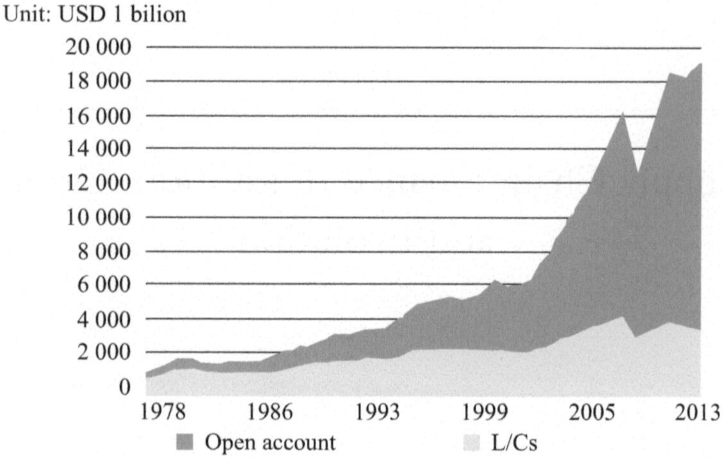

Fig. 1.1 Trends of open accounts and L/Cs in international trade, 1978–2013

stresses and capital breakdowns during production and operation than large companies; so how to invigorate their funds has become a major concern for SMEs. While SMEs are under financial pressures, the assets that need to be invigorated in the society as a whole are huge in sum. China's GDP was about RMB 86 trillion, and its total assets were five to seven times more than its GDP, in which movable assets accounted for 75%. As a result, total movable assets should be valued between RMB 350 and 500 trillion. The balance of RMB loans and foreign currency-denominated loans was about RMB 138 trillion, and the aggregate financing to the real economy (stock) was about RMB 190 trillion. Such a paradoxical phenomenon as described above clearly indicates the urgent need for innovative means to activate a large amount of industrial assets and effectively address the difficulties and high costs of financing for SMEs as well.

Given that supply chain finance, as an innovative model of industry-finance integrating commodity flows, physical flow, information flows, and capital flows, the supply chain has been developing rapidly. A report by McKinsey (2015) showed that the global revenues from supply chain finance businesses achieved an average annual growth rate of 20% from 2010 to 2014, and it could be expected that it would maintain a growth rate of over 15% in 2019. In terms of market size, it is indicated in the report by McKinsey (McKinsey, 2015) that as much as US$2 trillion of highly secured accounts payable were available for financing on a global basis. Global Business Intelligence (2016), a foreign research firm, noted that the global reverse factoring of such a supply chain finance product amounted to as much as US$400 billion. In addition, seen from the perspective of practices and theories, supply chain finance is not only huge in scale but also innovative in management and operation mode. The original bank-led trade finance and logistics finance have gradually turned to the supply chain finance innovation in which industrial enterprises play the leading role and the network ecology is to be even made the basis. Therefore, an interpretation will be given from a theoretical perspective in this chapter to how to understand the origin of supply chain finance and various stages in its evolution, the role that supply chain finance is to play for the sake of SMEs, and especially what the characteristics of supply chain finance are.

1.2 Emergence Background of Supply Chain Finance

Supply chain finance arises from the dilemma of SME financing process. Traditionally, enterprises may raise funds via two channels (i.e., internal financing and external financing). Internal financing, mainly including owner's equity, corporate retained earnings, and employee capital raising, is the financing channel most relied on by enterprises in their start-up period. However, as enterprises realize that internal financing is becoming insufficient to meet the needs of continuous expansion and growth, they gradually turn to external financing, which also help the enterprises to invest in new technologies and get higher returns. External financing mainly has two forms, that is, direct financing and indirect financing. Direct financing includes equity financing and corporate bond financing, while indirect financing mainly includes bank loans, discounting, and so on. Direct financing is prone to typical principal-agent issue unless the fund provider has direct knowledge of and control over the status of fund user. As a result, a prerequisite for direct financing is that the fund user must improve transparency of the operating conditions through information disclosure, audit, and so on, but this is relatively too costly for SMEs with small financing volumes. In addition, lower information transparency requires a higher-risk premium, so the SMEs that are able to meet their capital needs through direct financing tend to be those generating high returns (e.g., innovative technology SMEs), but it is difficult for most SMEs (Lin & Li, 2001).

Indirect financing means a kind of financing through financial institutions. In China, financial institutions mainly involved in indirect financing are commercial banks which screen financing targets through a series of screening methods rather than audits, with an aim to reduce information asymmetry at a lower cost. From another perspective, the financing process of SMEs may be considered as a sort of game between commercial banks and SMEs under the condition of asymmetric information (Wang, 2007). The risk-averse behaviors of commercial banks under information asymmetry raises the issue of credit rationing, which means that banks treat borrowers differently due to information asymmetry (Wang & Zhang, 2003). Specifically, as banks face excess demand for loans and are unable to identify a particular borrower risk, they carry out what is academically defined as "adverse selection." It means that banks ration loan to applicants at an interest rate that is below the competitive equilibrium rate but maximizes the banks' expected returns, instead of compensating for risk premium by raising the interest rates or screening borrowers through the interest rates. Even if an applicant is willing to accept a higher interest rate, the bank may refuse to grant loan to it at the time of rationing as the bank believes that the borrower's higher interest rate could still not cover the borrowing risk under information asymmetry and this kind of granting would lower the bank's average asset quality. In this case, banks may refuse high interest rates of borrowing at the risk of compromising their own interests, even if they have excess funds available for lending (Stiglitz & Weiss, 1981). Therefore, the core challenge to be addressed in providing financing services to SMEs is information asymmetry.

1.2.1 *Exploration of Traditional Lending Theories*

In response to the above SME information asymmetry, experts proposed corresponding lending solutions from the perspective of information collection based on traditional lending theories, the most typical of which is the soft and hard information theory proposed by Stein (2002). Hard information refers to the information that can be directly verified, such as the balance sheet, income statement, and cash flow statement of enterprises. The hard information is characterized by allowing the fund provider to understand and grasp the borrower's ability and credit directly through the verified information. Soft information refers to the information that cannot be directly and accurately verified by market participants other than the information provider, such as the management competence and character of an enterprise's managers. This type of information is difficult to quantify and transmit, and is held by familiar receivers within certain limits. On this basis, Berger and Udell (2002) proposed four approaches to address the information asymmetry between banks and enterprises, that is, financial-based lending, asset-based lending, credit scoring, and relational lending. The first three approaches are based on transactions, and there is a clear difference between them and the last approach, that is, relational lending. Relational lending relies more on soft information, or the long-term relationship that the borrower maintains with the bank (Boot & Thakor, 1994). Through this long-term relationship, the bank may have a better understanding of the borrower, thus increasing the likelihood of being granted loans by the borrower. Specifically, at the start of the relationship built between a bank and an enterprise, the bank requires a higher interest rate and a higher collateral requirement for a loan. As the bank-enterprise relationship deepens with the successful performance of previous loan contracts, the bank gradually lowers the interest rate and the collateral requirement for the enterprise, and may even provide loans without collateral for trusted enterprises. Therefore, the interest rate and collateral requirements are in inverse proportion to the tightness of the bank-enterprise relationship. From this, Berger and Udell (1995) explored the role of relational lending in SME financing. They also found that the length of time of such relation with the bank would affect lending rates and collateral requirements, as the relational lending based on long-term bank-enterprise relationship relies on the valuable information about the borrower's rating generated by the relationship to mitigate the issue of credit rationing resulting from the relatively high information asymmetry between banks and SMEs. In addition, a theoretical model built by Greenbaum et al. (1989) also found that the closer relation between a borrower and a particular fund provider would result in lower collateral requirements imposed by the fund provider.

However, the relational lending relying on bank-enterprise relationship also has limitations because most enterprise may not be able to repeatedly interact with banks to build a relationship of mutual trust. In addition, banks have little access to (much less direct involvement in) the actual production operations of enterprises, so they are unable to gain insight into the operating conditions of enterprises and the state of the industry, which leads to the persistence of information asymmetry.

1.2.2 Clustered Network Financing Theory

In addition to deeply studying the ways in which financial institutions may obtain real information about their financing targets more efficiently, some experts looked at the external environment in which SMEs operate. They tried to fill the "information gap" between SMEs and financial institutions by understanding how enterprises interact externally with other participants and with external environment, thus improving the financing outcomes of SMEs.

Apart from traditional approaches of lending from commercial banks, a financing with the help of the cluster where the SME is located is also an option. Porter (1990) considered a cluster as a group of enterprises that focus on a product as well as compete, cooperate, and interact dynamically with each other in a specific region. The cluster is characterized by agglomeration, proximity, and concentration. The enterprise clusters have a competitive advantage as they are composed of a group of independent and interrelated enterprises, which focus on a certain industry, carry out professional division of labor, and share and exchange related resources. This not only realizes efficient production and sale of products, but also generates knowledge accumulation and spillover benefits. It should be noted that the so-called collaborative advantage or complementary advantage among enterprises of a cluster is conditional on the commitment and trust in the relationship established through long-term cooperation (Huang & Chen, 2005). Compared to decentralization and randomness of sale and purchase markets, the enterprises of a cluster have geographical proximity, transaction repetitions, and industry linkages, which promote communication and coordination with, as well as interdependence and trust on, each other (DeWitt et al., 2006). This provides a basis for SMEs in a cluster to obtain financing by providing guaranties or personal commitments, or both (Long & Zhang, 2011).

Many scholars have explored the meanings of cluster network financing. In particular, Wang and An (2009) argued that cluster network financing was a unique method in which a number of SMEs in a cluster establish an alliance by means of equity or agreement to help each other to jointly reduce information asymmetry and lower financing costs. Kong and Feng (2009) said that cluster network financing was a mode of financing from financial institutions or financial markets that relies on the overall development and competitiveness of an industry cluster. Zhang (2010) pointed out that cluster network financing was in fact a mode of financing built on the industrial and agglomeration advantages of enterprises in a cluster.

Compared to individual enterprise financing, the cluster network financing is beneficial for both financial institutions and enterprises. For financial institutions, it offers the following advantages: First, it solves information asymmetry to a certain extent, because the operational and other information of each participant within a cluster is more easily disseminated and more easily accessed by financial institutions in a low-cost manner, especially the tacit knowledge that cannot be accessed in traditional lending, thanks to spillover effect of these information and knowledge generating from high-frequency interactions among enterprises and organizations within the cluster. Second, it reduces loan business costs of banks because it provides a platform for banks to grant credit to enterprises of a certain category or industry in bulk. Banks may establish applicable approval and risk control systems based on cluster characteristics, instead of having to review enterprises one by one. Besides, banks may have centralized access to the information required for granting loans, thus improving lending efficiency and reducing operational costs. Third, cluster network financing is less risky than traditional lending. On the one hand, as banks transform the lending risk of a single enterprise into the overall business risk of the cluster when they carry out cluster network financing, the solvency of the enterprise will be satisfactory as long as the cluster as a whole has good business conditions, so the risks faced by banks are reduced. On the other hand, the enterprises that remain within a cluster after long-time interaction are highly embedded in the cluster, resulting in high barriers for these enterprises to migrate from the cluster. In reality, these enterprises have relied heavily on the cluster to form a more efficient model of upstream and downstream collaboration and horizontal cooperation, and have built a relatively steady supply system and customer base, so they will not be willing to easily detach from the cluster. Assuming that an enterprise's reputation is at risk due to failure to repay loans on time, its credit within the cluster will likewise be reduced, and it will lose the competitive advantage that the cluster offers it. An expert who has studied Grameen Bank noted that the key to Grameen Bank's success was its requirement for setting a group of five farmers by the borrowing farmer.

The five farmers must be economically equivalent and familiar with social background and repayment ability of each other. According to its credit policy, if one farmer of the group fails to make repayments on time, the future credit line of the entire group will be negatively affected. As a result, the borrowing farmer will make every effort to repay the loan on time, while other group members will also supervise him/her or give necessary help to ensure his/her timely repayment (Wang, 2014). This research also illustrated the "embedding" advantage of cluster network financing.

For enterprises, cluster network financing offers the following advantages: (1) Credibility advantage. In a mature cluster, the enterprises that have demonstrated integrity in operations, production and contract enforcement over a long period of time are more likely to be certified in terms of credibility and therefore have a greater credibility advantage (Zhao et al., 2005). (2) Credit advantage. The existence of clusters facilitates the capital market to provide direct financing products for enterprises based on clusters, and the enterprises that have obtained capital market financing have a demonstration effect on the enterprises in the same clusters, leading to the spillover of credit resources (Du, 2004). (3) Collective rationality. When an enterprise in the cluster plays with other enterprises, it needs to consider the responses of other enterprises in the future game in response to the enterprise's actions in the previous rounds of game. Good competitive and cooperative relationships within the cluster, and the implementation of the reputation model, will allow them to avoid opportunistic behaviors and moral hazards (Gao, 2013). (4) Government support. Since industry clusters help improve the competitiveness of specific industries and the economic power of specific regions, governments tend to support them with financing policies. For example, Singh (2006) studied an Indian financing platform participated by the local government, SMEs, and financial institutions. The SMEs joining the platform pay membership fees on a regular basis, while the platform is responsible for approaching financial institutions, so as to obtain the financing required for the construction of infrastructure in the industrial park.

However, cluster network financing still has large limitations because this cluster-based financing behavior is rooted in unstructured or informal transaction networks. SMEs are able to obtain funds in this scenario thanks to the role of cluster credit (especially the understanding between enterprises within the cluster and interpersonal interactions due to blood ties) on reducing potential information asymmetries (Song & Wang, 2013). The drawback of this model is that it does not in fact reduce the default risk of a single SME, although it is beneficial for the fund providers to identify the status of the single SME by evaluating the cluster as a whole and its informal relationships with other enterprises in the same cluster. The operational status, capacity, and effectiveness of this single SME remain a "black box" for the fund providers. Especially under joint guarantee and joint lending (in practice, cluster network financing often uses mutual guarantees among cluster enterprises), if one enterprise in the network loses its credit, it will immediately trigger a chain reaction in the whole cluster network, leading to an "avalanche," that is, a collective passive loss of credit (Guo, 2012). In this regard, some scholars argued that too close informal relationships would bring social liabilities, instead of social capital (Hansen et al., 2001; Villena et al., 2011). Having identified the above-mentioned issues of cluster network financing, people began to explore whether there exists a network financing model based on close and formalized relationships to overcome the drawbacks of the cluster network financing model. This is the theoretical background from which supply chain finance emerged.

1.3 Early Stage of Supply Chain Finance

With the deepening of corporate practice, people gradually realized that supply chain operation had become an important strategy for enterprise development. The first awakening to the importance of supply chain management appeared in an article by Oliver and Webber (1992, p. 64) reproduced in an essay collection about supply chain management edited by Martin Christopher in 1992. According to the article: "Traditional management, which weighs the conflicting objectives of management functions (including purchasing, production, distribution, and sales), no longer works in industry chain, and therefore we now need a new perspective on management: supply chain management." Clearly, in this point of view the management activities of an enterprise were viewed as a whole. Since then, people increasingly realized that supply chain management was not only a coordination of functions within the enterprises but also a cooperative behavior between the enterprises (Stevens, 1989; Hesse & Rodrigue, 2004). The most representative of an array of perspectives is the concept of interfirm operation flow proposed by Stevens. He pointed out four phases of the operations of a firm, that is, decentralized activities, integrated functions, internal supply chain, and integrated flow of internal and external supply chain stakeholders. The core flows are commodity flow, logistics, information flow, and fund flow between enterprises. Commodity flow and logistics link different organizations together through business relationships; information flow facilitates information sharing and cooperation between organizations; and fund flow accelerates the movement of funds between organizations and reduces the cost of capital occupied. This concept gave birth to the preliminary supply chain finance, that is, trade finance and logistics finance.

1.3.1 *Trade Finance*

The discussion of trade finance began with the business practice of international trade finance. With the rapid growth of international trade, several core issues have been highlighted. First, the trade cycle is long and the payment collection is slow. Considering that international trade often uses sea transport, the entire transaction from order, shipment to settlement spans a long period of time. Second, the two parties to the transactions do not know each other, so in order to ensure the smooth completion of transactions, a third party needs to be involved in the payment process. Third, the amount of a single transaction is large and requires support in terms of financing. Based on this, international trade finance emerged and plays an important role (Auboin & Meier-Ewert, 2003). Statistics showed that more than 80% of international trade involved and used trade finance (Chauffour & Farole, 2009). According to Humphrey's (2009) classification, the main products of international trade finance include letters of credit (providing payment guarantees for exporters, or directly discounting letters of credit), trade credit (utilizing credits between parties to a transaction, including open accounts and prepayments), and buyer's credit (offering financial support to buyers not having sufficient funds to pay for goods).

Some scholars and organizations made adaption and innovation for the products of international trade finance in order to address the prolonged billing periods and financing that occurred between the upstream and downstream of the domestic supply chain. Structured trade finance, a combination of different products, was created to better meet the complex financial needs of supply chain companies. Structured trade finance is characterized by the combined use of multiple financing and settlement products, which not only meets the needs of enterprises, but also reduces bank risks (Xu et al., 2013). Having studied structured trade finance from different perspectives, many Chinese scholars believed that structured trade finance may facilitate trade between buyers and sellers, promote foreign trade and exports, ease the financial pressure of buyers and sellers, and complement traditional loan models to help enterprises cope with the financial pressure after the financial crisis. Under the structured trade finance model, products such as letters of credit, forward letters of credit, commitment financing, seller's credit, outward bill, inward bill, factoring, and forfaiting are used in combination according to the corporate needs and risk acceptance (SDB-CEIBS Research Group for Supply Chain Finance, 2009; Chen, 2014). The risks of trade finance mainly include performance risk, market risk of commodities, geographical risk, credit risk, business operation risk, and so on. In comparison to traditional lending, trade finance is more conducive to better risk assessment between trading partners and effective response to moral hazard after financing.

1.3.2 Logistics Finance

The prototype of logistics finance appeared in early human life. As far back as 2400 B.C., the circulating value of the grain produced in ancient Egypt gave rise to the "grain warehouse receipts" on the Mesopotamian plain, which not only served as a medium of circulation but also partially functioned as money. In Britain, "silver warehouse receipts" led to the creation of the British pound, as the earliest British liquid banknotes were based on silver warehouse receipts converted to one pound. With the evolution of finance, futures, and other industries, the early twentieth century saw the emergence of a "grain-backed" loan model in Czarist Russia, whereby Russian farmers pledged grain to banks to finance reproduction when the harvest was good but prices were low, and then repaid the loan to sell the grain when prices rebounded. Under this model, the banks could receive interests and the farmers could get more income from the sales of grain due to price rebound. This model of grain-back financing was the prototype of logistics finance (Hu & Liu, 2008). In 1916, the United States enacted the *US Warehousing Act of 1916* to establish a set of systematic laws and regulations on warehouse receipt pledges. The act made it clear that warehouse receipts could not only be used as collateral, but also be circulated in the market. The enactment of this act laid an important foundation for the subsequent widespread use of warehouse receipts as a financing model in U.S. agriculture to enhance agricultural production efficiency (Luo et al., 2002). Later, warehouse receipts were widely used for trading and pledging of commodities, which played an important role in balancing market prices and stabilizing price fluctuations.

The practice of logistics finance was based on warehouse receipts, which highlighted the key role played by warehousing in the overall finance. Therefore, "inventory financing" has long been the central object of study in foreign scholars' research on logistics finance. In early days, some scholars conducted descriptive studies on logistics finance. For example, Koch (1948) studied the past business models and control methods of logistics finance based on warehousing; Eisenstadt (1966) and Miller (1982) studied the progress of logistics finance in practice in the 1950s and 1970s, respectively. Subsequently, other scholars studied the models of logistics finance. For example, Lacroix and Varangis (1996) conducted a comparative study of logistics finance operations in the US and other developing countries and introduced the business models of logistics finance. Poe (1997) particularly studied asset-based financing operations in logistics finance and emphasized the key role of accounts receivable and inventories as collateral in logistics finance operations. Rutberg (2002) introduced the operational model of logistics finance taking United Parcel Service (UPS) as an example, and Fenmore (2004) studied the business model of order-based logistics finance. Buzacott and Zhang (2004) analyzed inventory management under the asset-backed financing model and combined collateral and production decisions. Bakker et al. (2004) dissected the principles and functions of inventory financing model adopted by SMEs in supply chain. Gertzof (1999) pointed out the advantages and characteristics of logistics finance business compared to other financing products and encouraged banks to actively expand this business. As practice-specific researches have increased, other scholars turned their attention to the risks involved in logistics finance and inventory finance. Wright (1988) argued that the key to risk control in inventory pledge business, which was classified into logistics finance, was how to assess the value of inventory and closely monitor it accurately, and pointed out the difficulty in assessment and monitoring of inventory value for financial institution, thus suggesting the need to introduce third-party logistics providers to participate in the business. Diercks (2004) also affirmed the importance of inventory monitoring in logistics finance and proposed a series of specific monitoring methods. Frye (2000) discovered that the risk of pledged loans arose mainly from the risk associated with price fluctuations of the pledges, while Coulter and Onumah (2002) explored how to ensure the smooth execution of pledged loan operations in developing countries and rural credit markets facing commodity fluctuations. Barsky and Catanach (2005) argued that the risk control of logistics finance should not adopt the traditional subject credit-based model of banks, but should adopt a flow-oriented risk control model covering the whole business chain of logistics finance. These two scholars also pointed out that the risks of logistics finance include process risk, environmental risk, IT risk, human risk, and basic structure risk. It is worth noting that, at a very early stage, foreign scholars have included logistics finance into the scope of supply chain finance and studied it as a form of supply chain finance.

In China, the study of logistics finance started with the concept of "commodity bank" in the planned economy. Early scholars such as Chen (1987) put forward the idea of constructing a commodity bank. At that time, the so-called commodity bank aimed to complete the transfer and exchange of commodities, in order to make the distribution of commodities more effectively. Although this concept is quite different from the current one, the idea of revitalizing the value "locked" in physical products is the same. As the concept of logistics has been accepted by more and more scholars, its connotation has also matured. For example, Yu and Feng (2003), Ren (2004), and Wang and Wang (2005) redefined the commodity bank as the organic combination and closed-loop operation of physical flow, fund flow and information flow of banks, and manufacturers and distributors through professional services provided by competent logistics companies, thus providing chattel pledge services that broke the geographical boundaries and ensuring access of cash-strapped businesses to a range of services, including financing. As pioneers who systematically proposed the concept of "logistics finance," Zou and Tang (2004) believed that logistics finance was the efficient use of fund flow and credit generated in the process of logistics operation, through the development, provision, and application of various financial products and financial services, and the effective synergy between them and commodity flow under the tandem of information flow. When thinking about logistics finance, Zou and Tang (2004) have taken into account a variety of financial service elements such as loans, insurance, investment, and securitization, so their definition of logistics finance was broad. In contrast, the concept of "financial logistics" proposed by Chen and Zhu (2005) considered that it referred to the integrated logistics services provided by third-party logistics companies, and the scope of such services included traditional logistics, warehousing, distribution processing, and financial services. This concept is closer to the current definition of logistics finance in a narrow sense by scholars. The logistics finance proposed by Zou and Tang (2004) and the financial logistics concept proposed by Chen and Zhu (2005) have set the conceptual boundary for the subsequent research on logistics finance. Nowadays, the commonly adopted definition of logistics finance comes from Li (2011). He believes that logistics finance is a variety of financial services, including financing, provided to enterprises in supply chain under the premise of in-depth cooperation between logistics enterprises and financial institutions. The core business of logistics finance is financing services provided for enterprises in supply chain through the closed-loop control of logistics, information flow and fund flow in the overall process based on accounts receivable, prepayments, and inventory generated under logistics. This definition has been recognized by a large number of scholars because it covers both the broad and narrow connotations of logistics finance.

Considering the existence of broad and narrow definitions of logistics, the discussion of logistics finance models was also divided into two groups. One group of scholars have studied how logistics is combined with banking financial services (e.g., financing and settlement), insurance financial services, and brokerage financial services (e.g., asset securitization and funds) according to the broad definition of logistics finance. In this regard, Zou and Tang (2004) and Yuan and Wang (2005) have made a more detailed research. Another group of scholars has focused their research on the way logistics is integrated with elements of banking services, including financing. Among this group of studies, the FTW model proposed by Luo et al. (2002) has set the stage for an array of subsequent studies. According to the FTW model defined by Luo et al. (2002), it is a comprehensive service platform covering credit integration and rebuilding, logistics and distribution, and e-commerce and traditional commerce for SMEs in the surrounding area, based on mobile commodity warehousing. Luo et al. (2002) noted that FTW models include credit model and guarantee model. Under credit model, logistics companies help cooperative enterprises obtain inventory pledge financing by virtue of their own credit, help banks grant credit, and assume supervisory functions, thus enhancing the financing efficiency of cooperative enterprises. Under guarantee model, logistics companies provide credit guarantee for enterprises in need of financing, or organize them to jointly and mutually guarantee each other, thus increasing the financing ability of enterprises. The FTW study gave a strong impetus to the research on logistics finance models in China (Zheng, 2004). After that, Chinese scholars expanded their study of logistics finance models based on FTW research. For example, Tang (2005) divided the logistics finance models into three models: advance payment model, warehouse receipt pledge model and confirming storage model. From the perspective of commercial banks, Chen (2008) pointed out that logistics finance may be divided into two models based on accounts receivable and inventory respectively, and the participants included not only financing enterprises and banks but also core enterprises and third-party logistics providers involved in supply chain. Song and Li (2009) believed that logistics finance included four models: logistics settlement model, logistics warehouse receipt model, logistics credit model, and integrated operation model. Among them, logistics settlement model covers payment collection, advance payment, and acceptance bill; logistics warehouse receipt model includes FTW and other derivative business models; logistics credit mode meant that logistics companies obtain credit from banks first, and then provide credit to financing enterprises; integrated operation model is to provide all the above three models of business and offer comprehensive financial services to clients.

1.4 Formation and Evolution of Supply Chain Finance

Along with the increasing research and in-depth practice of trade finance and logistics finance, supply chain finance has gradually been widely noticed and recognized. In the strict sense, supply chain finance is quite different from trade finance and logistics finance, although there are certain correlations: First, they differ in the way of combining industry and finance. Trade finance and logistics finance are both forms of industry-financing combination, but the deficiencies in combining corporate operations make them different from supply chain finance. Trade finance is the combination of commodity flow and fund flow, but in the process of combination the fund provider has relatively poor ability to manage and control logistics. Similarly, logistics finance is the combination of logistics activities and financial activities, but in the combination process, the fund provider knows little about the trade activities that occur between companies (Song, 2015). This makes it vulnerable to default risk because the fund provider does not have complete information about the SME's business. In the presence of moral hazard, opportunistic behavior may decrease the degree of risk control. To be precise, pure trade finance or logistics finance in practice is prone to fraudulent use of fictitious transactions or false logistics to obtain funds. Comparatively speaking, supply chain finance can avoid the above-mentioned problems, as it puts high emphasis on parallel control of commodity flow and logistics in carrying out financial activities, for this, and it is stronger than trade finance and logistics finance in terms of breadth and richness of information. Second, they differ in the scope of financial services. Under trade finance or logistics finance, financial services are usually generated for a transaction or movable asset, and are oriented to a single enterprise, while it is more difficult to cover the whole process of supply chain. In other words, the financial service activities cannot cover all links of supply chain. However, supply chain finance provides a broader range of financial services customized based on the overall business activities of supply chain, which are able to control all aspects of internal and external supply chain management from a systematic perspective. As a result, supply chain finance has a broader range of financial services. Considering the differences between supply chain finance and the previously emerged trade finance and logistics finance, theoretical and practical circles have begun to explore the meanings and features of supply chain finance.

1.4.1 Exploration of the Meaning of Supply Chain Finance

Supply chain finance is an innovation that stems from the intersection of supply chain and finance. Supply chain has always been regarded as one of the main elements of operation management. Many scholars have discussed the integration of physical flow and information flow in supply chain and have widely applied them in practice, but the fund flow in supply chain has been neglected for a long time. In recent years, the fund flow in supply chains began to attract the attention of more and more scholars (Pfohl & Gomm, 2009; Hofmann & Kotzab, 2010). Scholars pondered the possibility of coordinating the transport, information, and fund flows in supply chain to create value together. Timme and Williams-Timme (2000) earlier explored the meaning of supply chain finance, arguing that under supply chain finance some participants in the supply chain actively collaborate with financial service providers (banks, factoring companies, etc.) outside the supply chain in order to achieve the overall objectives of the supply chain, and take into account the physical flow, information flow, and fund flow within the supply chain as well as the supply operation process, other participants in the supply chain, and the status of all assets in the collaboration process. After that, many scholars who started to explore the meaning of supply chain finance have developed their own distinctive understanding of supply chain finance. Gelsomino et al. (2016) proposed the need to consider whether two elements are involved in each definition in order to distinguish between different categories of supply chain finance: first, the role played by financial institutions; second, the scope of supply chain finance, that is, whether it involves only reverse factoring, whether it involves inventory optimization in supply chain operations, and whether it covers fixed asset financing. The first element is to consider the role of financial institutions in supply chain finance. Some studies considered supply chain finance as a series of short-term funding solutions focusing on accounts receivable and payable in supply chain transactions provided by financial institutions, in which case the direct involvement of fund providers becomes a necessary element of supply chain finance. The second element is the scope of business involved in supply chain finance. Some studies considered supply chain finance not only as a series of short-term funding solutions but also simply as a factoring business and a service for buyer-to-supplier funding optimization (reverse factoring), while other studies argued that supply chain finance involves collaborative inventory management. Its management of inventory and accounts receivable and payable in supply chain operations implies that supply chain finance emphasizes the management of the entire working capital of the supply chain. Furthermore, some studies expanded the understanding of supply chain finance to include not only working capital management for the whole chain but also fixed asset financing (Gomm, 2010; Hofmann, 2005; Pfohl & Gomm, 2009). Currently, the representative definitions and understanding of supply chain finance are shown in Table 1.1:

Based on the above exploration of the meanings of supply chain, it can be seen that the supply chain finance has developed to a broader concept of financial services. First, financial activities are carried out for the specific business of industrial supply chain, which is based on industrial supply chain operations. On the one hand, finance serves industrial activities, and, on the other hand, different business characteristics and different participants will put forward differentiated value demands for financial services. Second, supply chain finance aims to optimize cash flow of the whole industry and shorten the cash flow cycle, thus allowing all stakeholders to achieve higher operating performance with lower cost of funds. Therefore, in this regard, supply chain finance not only involves financing and lending

Table 1.1 Definitions of the representative meanings of supply chain finance

Author	*Definition*	*Role of financial institutions*	*Reverse factoring only*	*Inventory optimization*	*Fixed asset financing*
Hofmann (2005)	Supply chain finance is the process of effectively planning, monitoring, and controlling financial resources between two or more organizations (including external service providers) in a supply chain for the joint purpose of value creation				Yes
Camerinelli (2009)	Supply chain finance is a series of products and services provided by financial institutions that facilitate the exchange of goods and information in the supply chain	Yes			
Pfohl and Gomm (2009)	Supply chain finance is the act of financial optimization and integration with clients, suppliers, and service providers to realize the value of all participating members of the supply chain			Yes	Yes
Gomm (2010)	Supply chain finance is a series of processes that optimize the financial structure and facilitate the fund flow in the supply chain			Yes	Yes

(*continued*)

Table 1.1 (continued)

Author	*Definition*	*Role of financial institutions*	*Reverse factoring only*	*Inventory optimization*	*Fixed asset financing*
Chen and Hu (2011)	Supply chain finance is an innovative financial solution that uses funds to create value by bridging banks with fund-starved companies in supply chain and reducing the supply-demand mismatch in fund flow	Yes			
Lamoureux and Evans (2011)	Supply chain finance is a fusion of technology and financial services that brings together global supply chain companies, suppliers, and financial institutions (especially technology service providers) who improve financial supply chain benefits by preventing damage cost shifting and improving the visualization, availability, delivery, and cost of funds of global supply chain participants	Yes			
Grosse-Ruyken et al. (2011)	Supply chain finance is an integrative approach that improves the visualization and control of fund-related processes in supply chain			Yes	

(*continued*)

Table 1.1 (continued)

Author	*Definition*	*Role of financial institutions*	*Reverse factoring only*	*Inventory optimization*	*Fixed asset financing*
Wuttke et al. (2013a)	Supply chain finance is a process of optimizing, planning, managing, and controlling the fund flow in order to promote the efficient operation of supply chain logistics.			Yes	
Wuttke et al. (2013b)	Supply chain finance is an automation solution that allows buyers to use reverse factoring to make flexible and transparent payments based on the entire supply chain	Yes	Yes		
More and Basu (2013)	Supply chain finance may be defined as the management, planning, and control of all processes related to transaction activities and funds among all supply chain stakeholders in a bid to improve working capital for all parties	Yes			

Source: Gelsomino, L. M., Mangiaracina, R., Perego, A., & Tumino, A. (2016). Supply chain finance: a literature review. *International Journal of Physical Distribution & Logistics Management, 46*(4), 348–366

but also includes financial service activities in a broader sense, even including the services jointly provided by financial institutions and technology service providers for industrial supply chains resulting from the synergy between various types of organizations. Third, supply chain finance has an active role of optimizing and developing the supply chain. Good supply chain financial services can not only solve the capital problem but even help the industry to build a more competitive supply chain system. Therefore, Supply chain finance is essentially a financial business carried out through the close cooperation of all parties involved in the supply chain and relying on supply chain operations (supply chain transactions, logistics, and information flow), which helps to accelerate the fund flow throughout the supply chain. The innovation and management of financial business also promotes the development of industrial supply chain in a more timely and effective manner.

1.4.2 *Evolution of Supply Chain Finance Practices*

Since supply chain finance has gained growing attention from both practical and theoretical circles, its operation model has evolved rapidly in recent years. As a result, different stages of development are formed. Specifically, the development stages and processes of supply chain finance, as well as their corresponding characteristics, need to be identified in two dimensions. The first dimension is the subjects involved in supply chain finance as well as the geographical scope, that is, the degree of diversity of the participants involved in supply chain finance activities. Some financial activities of supply chain may involve only a limited number of organizations and enterprises in supply chain, while others may involve multiple types and numbers of organizations or enterprises. Accordingly, financial activities are carried out simultaneously in different geographical areas on account of the large number and various types of organizations and enterprises that may be involved. The second dimension is the maturity and scope of activities of supply chain finance programs, which means whether the supply chain finance solution cover the business requirements of the whole supply chain process. Since supply chain operations include various processes and links such as procurement, production, distribution, sales, and returns, the maturity of supply chain finance programs will be higher if more characteristics of various businesses are taken into account in an integrated financial service solution. Based on the above two dimensions, four stages of the development of supply chain finance are formed at both practical and theoretical levels.

From the practice of supply chain finance, the four stages of the development of supply chain finance are supply chain finance driven by financial institutions, supply chain finance driven by industrial enterprises, supply chain finance driven by professional platforms, and supply chain finance driven by fintech (see Fig. 1.2).

The first stage is supply chain finance driven by financial institutions, which, strictly speaking, is about the use of trade finance and logistics finance. Under the first stage, the main drivers of supply chain finance are traditional financial institutions, such as commercial banks and factoring

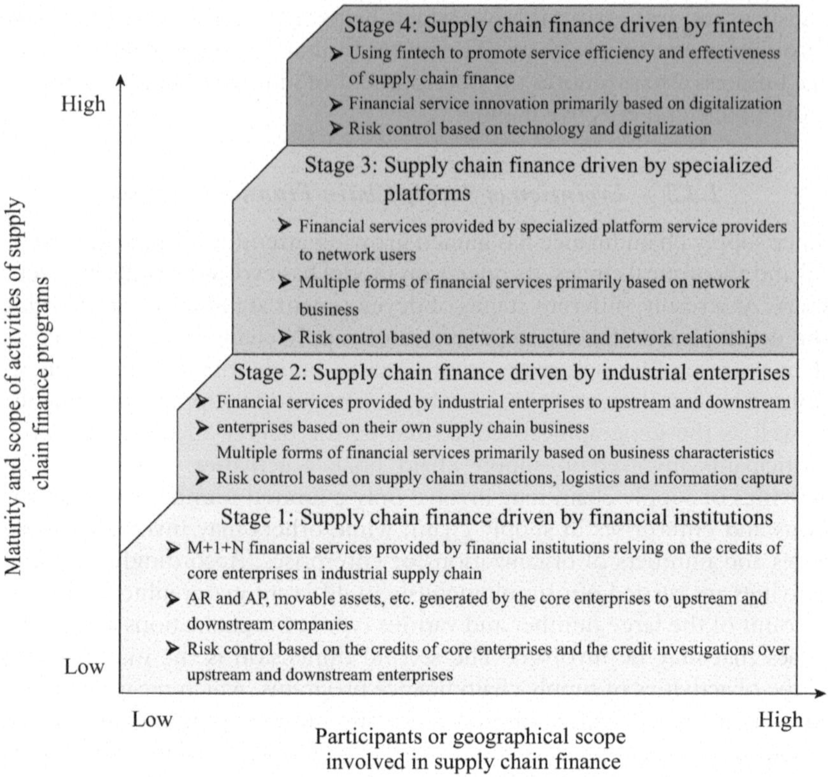

Fig. 1.2 Evolution of supply chain finance practices

companies. By combining with the core enterprises in industrial supply chain, financial institutions carry out financial services and control the corresponding financial risks. Specifically, the supply chain finance in the first stage mainly adopts "M + 1 + N" form: "1" means the core large enterprises in supply chain, "M" and "N" are, respectively, the suppliers and the customers of core large enterprises in industrial supply chain. "M + 1 + N" means that the financial institutions rely on the credit of the core large enterprises to develop financial services for M suppliers and N client in bulk. In terms of business forms at this stage, there are three main categories of financial services: (1) financial services based on accounts receivable or accounts payable, mainly including standard factoring, reverse factoring, reverse purchase, factoring pool financing, bill financing, and other products; (2) financial services based on inventory or movable assets, such as static mortgage and pledge, dynamic mortgage and pledge, standard warehouse receipt pledge, common warehouse receipt pledge, and other products; (3) financial services based on prepayment, including pre-shipment credit financing, confirming storage financing, and other products. The means of risk control at this stage is mainly based on the credit of core enterprises and the credit investigation of financial institutions over the upstream and downstream of core enterprises. From the perspective of supply chain operations, financial institutions acting as supply chain finance promoters or service providers are not really involved in business operations of supply chain, or, rather, they are not involved in the actual transactions and logistics of supply chain. Therefore, supply chain information is not directly obtained, monitored, and controlled by financial institutions.

The second stage is supply chain finance driven by industrial enterprises. Unlike the first stage, the drivers of financial services in suppler chain at this stage are not traditional financial institutions any more, but core industrial enterprises, such as manufacturers, distributors, or competitive third-party or fourth-party logistics providers in the industrial supply chain. They provide integrated financial services to their own suppliers or clients based on their own supply chain operation system. This stage presents a richer financial business forms, spanning from provision of guarantees by core enterprises to financial institutions, strategic supplier/client referrals, offering dynamic discounting to clients, and buyer or seller credit. It should be noted that the supply chain finance business at this stage may either require the cooperation of financial institutions (such as granting credit in a unified manner) or may be directly provided by the industrial core enterprises to the downstream clients with credit services, which is dynamic discounting in practice. Dynamic discounting is a low price or discount offered by the supplier to the buyer that provides flexibility in how and when the buyer pays the supplier in exchange for the purchased products or services (prime revenue). "Dynamic" refers to the fact that the buyer will enjoy a different discount rate depending on the period of payment; in other words, the earlier the payment, the larger is the discount. At this stage, risk control is mainly based on the trade flow, logistics, and information flow controlled by the core industrial enterprises. As core industrial enterprises are more knowledgeable about the businesses and operations of supply chains than traditional financial institutions, the financial activities based on supply chain business management are more likely to address information asymmetry and the corresponding moral hazard and opportunistic behavior, thus effectively controlling risks.

The third stage is supply chain finance driven by professional platforms. At this stage, the form of supply chain finance shifts away from the dominance of core enterprises and toward the roles of specialized platforms. This kind of platform-driven supply chain finance is different as below: First, the driver becomes the builders of the ecology and platforms, who, in a certain sense, are neither buyers/sellers of industrial operations nor financial institutions, but relatively independent third parties. Second, given that the drivers of supply chain finance are not the direct operators of supply chain business, the purpose of business process management is mainly to maintain the order of industrial supply chain operations, establish reasonable transaction and logistics rules, and carry out comprehensive value chain process management. Third, this stage focuses on the credit of the entire network ecology, instead of the credit of individual enterprises. The advent of supply chain finance driven by professional platforms is due to the following reasons: First, the second stage of supply chain operation and financial activities is promoted and managed by the leading core enterprises of the industry, whose service targets are often their direct upstream and downstream partners. This kind of "chain-based" supply chain finance cannot involve a wider range of participants, especially the integration and cooperation of those among the same industry (i.e., the cooperation between chain and chain). Second, besides the core leading enterprises, the industry has also some quasi-large enterprises and even medium-sized enterprises. These enterprises also have certain competitiveness in the industry, but they lack sufficient resources and ability to build a supply chain service system. They cooperate with financial institutions to provide financial services for their upstream and downstream clients. This backdrop has given birth to platform-driven supply chain finance, and, to some extent, professional platform-driven supply chain finance is more suitable to reflect the fairness and impartiality of financial services for MSMEs. On the one hand, the supply chain service platform is not controlled and managed by the core enterprises, so it is beneficial for each supply chain finance participant to participate more equally and understand the corresponding information. If the platform controlled by core enterprises is not reasonably regulated, it is easier to form a monopoly of industrial information by core enterprises, causing another form of information asymmetry. On the other hand, under the platform-driven supply chain finance, a large number of industrial enterprises, financial institutions, and other participants are integrated together through an independent and professional service platform, which can form the supply chain financial service market more effectively and avoid the suspicion that some core enterprises use the name of supply chain finance to exploit suppliers in essence. In view of the fact that the third stage of supply chain finance aggregates a large number of participants, therefore, its financial business has a high degree of integration. Apart from the high degree of integration between industrial activities and financial products, it also refers to the formation of a combined system of different financial products to serve the demands of industrial supply chain operations, such as the high degree of integration of various financial organizations and products including financing and lending, asset securitization, insurance, funds, and so on, and their mutual synergy to serve specific industrial scenarios. In terms of risk control and management, this stage is mainly based on the network structure and network relationships, that is, on the role of each organization or enterprise in the network, the role it plays and the marginal contribution it makes, while taking into account the status of mutual business transactions, so as to manage and control risks in an integrated manner. In a certain sense, this stage is easier than others to grasp the situation of SMEs and provide customized financial services, and its requirements for ecological management, especially the degree of information management, are more complex and arduous.

With the gradual advancement of the third stage of supply chain finance, the practice of supply chain finance in recent years has gradually evolved to the fourth stage, which is supply chain finance driven by fintech. Strictly speaking, the fourth stage is not completely different from the third stage, but a progression of the third stage. To put it differently, with the deepening of platform-driven supply chain finance, people naturally begin to focus on and emphasize the key role of fintech therein. Fintech refers to all technical innovations in the financial sector. With the help of these technologies, organizations and businesses are able to carry out financial services more efficiently, transparently, and reliably. This is evidenced by the fact that a growing number of professional technology platforms are driving supply chain finance services through integrated technologies including AI, blockchain, clouding, and big data. At this stage, its business development and risk control are not entirely based on business network structure or strong transaction relationship, but on gradual integration of digital information to promote supply chain finance. The emergence of this new form of supply chain finance leads to more efficient and effective financial operations on the one hand and gradually improves the openness (allowing more participants to get involved in supply chain finance business), balance (facilitating different organizations to obtain, analyze, and master the information and status of enterprises in a balanced way), and fairness (enabling supply chain finance to benefit enterprises of different nature and scale as well as the whole supply chain process, including green supply chain) of financial services on the other. This has become the latest trend in the practice of supply chain finance.

1.4.3 Evolution of Supply Chain Finance Theories

Parallel to the evolution of supply chain finance practices, the theoretical exploration of supply chain finance has also undergone an evolution from finance oriented, supply chain oriented, and network ecology oriented to fintech oriented (see Fig. 1.3).

Research on supply chain finance has long been classified by academics as finance-oriented research and supply chain-oriented research (Gelsomino et al., 2016). Most of the early supply chain finance research is finance

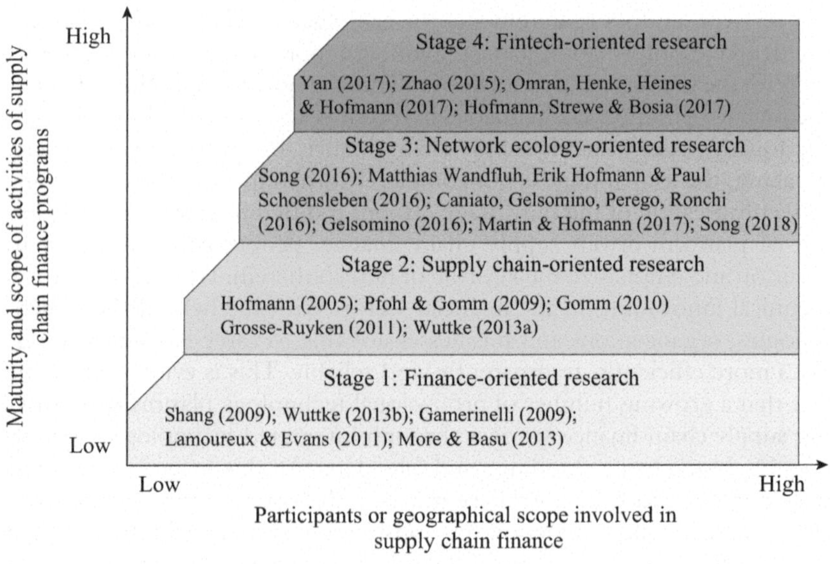

Fig. 1.3 Evolution of supply chain finance theories

oriented. Financial-oriented studies regard supply chain finance as a series of innovative financial solutions (Camerinelli, 2009; Chen & Hu, 2011). According to this point of view, financial institutions play a crucial role in supply chain finance. Another feature of finance-oriented research is that supply chain finance activities are viewed as a short-term financing process, or as a financing solution generated based on accounts receivable and payable. Lamoureux and Evans (2011) argued that the activities triggering supply chain finance are mainly events that occur in the trade process, such as order receiving, shipping, issuing bills, and due payments. Similarly, More and Basu (2013) thought that supply chain finance can be divided into three stages based on the activity process, namely pre-shipment financing, in-transit financing, and post-shipment financing. Among finance-oriented studies, other researchers saw supply chain finance more strictly as a buyer-driven solution regarding working capital, that is, reverse factoring (Wuttke et al., 2016). In addition, Kouvelis and Zhao (2017) studied the financing patterns in a situation where buyers and sellers in supply chain finance hold different credit ratings, and they concluded that in a supply chain consisting of suppliers and retailers, the supplier would charge zero interest rate to make the trade credit cheaper than bank loans, if the credit rating of the supplier exceeded a threshold. Otherwise, the supplier would charge a strictly positive interest rate. In such a situation, the combined use of trade credit and bank loans would be more consistent with inventory financing than trade credit. This threshold was influenced by the retailer's working capital position, the supplier's funding position, and the product's gross margin.

Unlike the previous stage, supply chain-oriented researches considered supply chain finance to be rooted in supply chain operations, that is, it reduces working capital requirements through inventory optimization throughout the supply chain, generates financing behaviors, or transfers working capital to supply chain participants who have access to funds at lower cost. For example, Pfohl and Gomm (2009) anchored the conceptual model of supply chain finance in the context of vendor-managed inventory (VMI). Randall and Theodore Farris (2009) analyzed the impact of inventory transfers between two supply chain participants on supply chain finance. It is worth mentioning that the study by Hoberg et al. (2017) used secondary data to analyze whether capital constraints have an impact on inventory management, that is, whether companies take into account the cost of capital when making inventory decisions. Their study found that financially constrained companies were not able to reduce inventories, while less financially constrained companies had lower inventories. The study revealed that, for now, capital constraints had not been taken into account in supply chain inventory management and decision-making. Another feature of supply chain-oriented research is the greater emphasis on the objects of financing (such as collateral and pledges). Gomm (2010) and Pfohl and Gomm (2009) suggested that supply chain finance was also applicable to fixed asset financing (financing payments for each production solution or joint investment in logistics assets). In addition, supply chain-oriented research considered financial institutions as the real drivers of supply chain financial business, which is unlike finance-oriented research which expands this scope. Since the supply chain-oriented research is based on financial services of supply chain operation and business objects, the main subjects to promote and develop the supply chain financial services may be the organizers of supply chain operation (including producers, distributors or third-party or fourth-party logistics providers). Financial institutions are not always the dominant players in supply chain finance, although they are also actively involved in the process.

In recent years, with the deepening of supply chain finance practices, theoretical researchers have gradually become aware of the potential problems of previous supply chain-oriented research. Previous supply chain-oriented studies put emphasis on financial services triggered by certain links of operations (e.g., inventory transfers) or assets (e.g., collateral and pledges), but neglected to analyze the conditions, scenarios, and innovative models for the development of supply chain finance from a whole supply chain perspective (Caniato et al., 2016). In addition, supply chain-oriented researches, while expanding the drivers of financial services, have not been able to clarify the role of professional platform companies or service providers (Song et al., 2018). Based on these understandings, supply chain finance research, since last year, began to shift to the third stage, namely network ecology-oriented research. The researches of this stage have three characteristics: First, they began to focus on the contextual factors that trigger supply chain finance, that is, which supply chain contexts give rise to supply chain finance behavior. Song et al. (2016) explored the impact of SMEs' supply chain network characteristics (strong and weak relations of SMEs in the business network) on financing, finding in particular that abundant weak relations are keys to SMEs' access to financing. Caniato et al. (2016) proposed that the degree of cooperation between enterprises in supply chain, the bargaining power, the degree of digitalization, and the attractiveness of financial services are all contributing factors to the successful implementation of supply chain finance solutions. Second, network ecology-oriented research explored the role of supply chain integration and the state of cooperation among supply chain participants for financing services. Successful implementation of supply chain finance requires, on the one hand, the realization of intra-enterprise synergies (between supply chain business department and finance department) for strategic integration of corporate finance and, on the other hand, the synergies between suppliers and buyers (including the information sharing and finance integration between buyers and suppliers). The achievement of good financing performance is subject to the simultaneous achievement of these two aspects (Wandfluh et al., 2016). However, the study by Wuttke et al. (2016) revealed that not all supply chain finance has a positive effect. The timing of supply chain finance and the positive and negative effects depend mainly on the payment terms and purchase volumes negotiated between buyers and sellers in the course of business. The larger the purchase volume and the longer the payment cycle, the greater is the need for early adoption of supply chain financial services. Third, ecology-oriented research clarified the driving role of professional service providers in supply chain finance. This was evidenced by the formal introduction of the concept of Financial Service Provider (FSP) in theoretical studies. Silvestro and Lustrato (2014) first proposed the role of FSPs in supply chain integration. Their study was a kind of descriptive analysis, rather than a discussion on services in supply chain finance, but they suggested that banks could play the role of service integrators. Later, Martin and Hofmann (2017) further analyzed the important role of financial service providers in supply chain finance, that is, financial service providers acted as intermediaries to resolve the mismatches existing between different supply chain participants and between financial institutions and commercial banks. They also pointed out that the financial service provider may be either a traditional bank, or more likely a new type of financial company or technology provider, and so on. By comparing the differences between new platform-based financial service providers and traditional commercial banks in the process of providing supply chain financial services for pre-trade, mid-trade, and post-trade risk control, Song et al. (2018) pointed out that financial service providers were more capable than traditional commercial banks of controlling pre-trade, mid-trade, and post-trade risks by monitoring the whole process of supply chain operations through trading information, networks, and processes. Those platform-based financial service providers were companies that directly engage in or organize supply chain operations.

With the advance of network ecology-oriented research, recently the key role played by fintech in the supply chain finance driven by network ecology has been gradually recognized, thus gradually evolving to the current fourth stage of research. It must be noted that research in this regard is just emerging and has not yet resulted in extensive findings, but some scholars have already raised interest in the role of new technologies in supply chain finance. For example, Yan (2017) studied the unique advantages that e-commerce B2B platforms have in using big data to control risk in the context of supply chain finance in China. Similarly, Zhao et al. (2015) argued that using big data, financial institutions would be easier to predict the failure rate of operations in supply chain finance. In addition, Omran et al. (2017) started their exploration on the use of blockchain in supply chain finance. Hofmann et al. (2017) further proposed the application of blockchain to reverse asset securitization in supply chain finance.

1.5 Structure and Content of This Book

From the above evolution of supply chain finance, on the one hand, we can see that the participants or geographical scope involved in supply chain finance are expanding. The participants involved in supply chain finance are becoming more and more diverse (not only borrowers and lenders, but all direct and indirect stakeholders involved in the operation of the supply chain are included in the scope of supply chain finance management), and with the help of technology, supply chain finance has also gradually crossed into the operation of supply chains and financial services in different regions and even in different countries. On the other hand, the maturity and scope of activities of supply chain finance are widening. It not only involves all the management and operation activities in supply chain operations, but also includes all the corresponding information elements, technology elements, and the integration of various financial activities. However, in spite of this evolution trend, there are still a lot of questions that need to be explored in the preliminary practice and theoretical research, including the following: How to understand the value realization of supply chain finance when it is gradually shifting from being driven by a single enterprise to being driven by a network platform? What characteristics should the network platform have in promoting the trend? In particular, with the development of financial technology, the current supply chain finance is increasingly characterized by intelligence, and what changes in supply chain operations are reflected by intelligence? What exactly is the role of technology in supply chain finance and how does it work? Based on these understandings, this book will explore the fintech-driven supply chain models and its financial innovation from a new perspective.

This book is the third one following the previously published *Supply Chain Finance* (China Renmin University Press, 2015) and *Internet Supply Chain Finance* (China Renmin University Press, 2017). All three books are based on industrial supply chain operations to explore financial services and innovation. In our opinion, supply chain finance is rooted in supply chain management and activities. Without industrial supply chain management, there will be no financial activity. If the industrial supply chain operations are separated from the real economy, finance will become a bubble and generate huge risks. In return, effective financial activities help the construction and smooth operations of industrial supply chain. Therefore, industry and finance are complementary and mutually reinforcing. The difference between this book and the previous two books lies in the focuses and the stages of supply chain finance explored. *Supply Chain Finance* published in 2015 put more emphasis on the innovation, operation, and the corresponding risk control of supply chain finance during the progress of shifting from traditional bank driven to industry core enterprise driven. *Internet Supply Chain Finance*, published in 2017, focused on the innovation of network platform-based supply chain finance. In this book, supply chain finance gradually began to move away from the supply chain finance dominated by industrial core enterprises to professional platform-driven supply chain finance in practice and theory, and in the process of this transformation the way of organizing supply chain activities and the mode of financial services have changed significantly. This book, on the basis of the previous two books, further explores the innovative operation of platform-based supply chain finance enabled by fintech, that is to say, exploring the innovative trend of supply chain finance, and even the future development direction after combining platform-based supply chain finance with fintech. To be specific, the book's exploration on supply chain finance has the following highlights: (1) Systematic analysis of the contribution of fintech development to the supply chain as well as financial services. Fintech has become a hot topic in industrial supply chain and financial services in recent years; however, what is the intelligence generated by fintech? How does it affect supply chain operations and financial activities, especially what is the goal and basic structure of technology enabling? These are all topics that need to be explored systematically. (2) When professional platform-driven supply chain finance is combined with fintech, what impact does it have on the meaning of supply chain finance products? In particular, what effect does it have on supply chain operations? In addition, how do professional platform of financial services companies interact with other participants or stakeholders in the supply chain to create value for customers? (3) The innovations of financial activities in the fourth stage of supply chain finance. In the past, our understanding of supply chain finance was often limited to the narrow act of financing. However, with the development of supply chain finance to a certain stage, it has gone beyond financing itself to some extent, but has increasingly integrated into various financial products and financial participants. In other words, finance itself has become the ecology supporting the industrial supply chain through innovation. Therefore, this book will also explore the role of financial ecology and elements in boosting the supply chain.

The subsequent parts of this book will be divided into nine chapters (see Fig. 1.4). Chapter 2 will explore supply chain finance from a financial

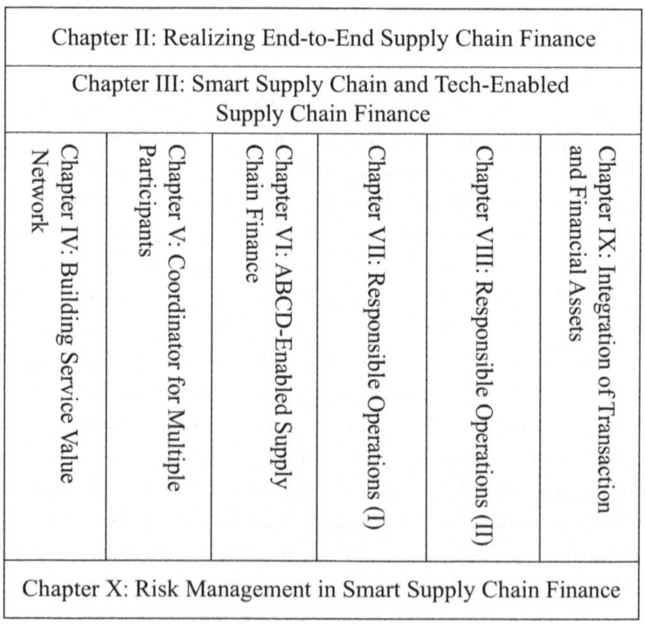

Fig. 1.4 Structure and content of the book

perspective, especially the direction and outreach of supply chain finance development from the perspective of cash flow cycle management. Chapter 3 will put emphasis on the definition of intelligence, as well as the meaning and the basic framework of intelligence supply chain finance. Chapters 4, 5, 6, 7 and 8 will systematically explore the elements of intelligence supply chain finance innovation, in which SMART (a five-dimensional model for realizing intelligence supply chain finance) is proposed. Chapters 4, 5, 6, 7, 8 and 9 will systematically explore the management of intelligence supply chain finance from the perspective of industrial risk management.

References

Auboin, M., & Meier-Ewert, M. (2003). *Improving the availability of trade finance during financial crises* (No. 2). WTO discussion paper.

Bakker, M. H., Udell, G. F., & Klapper, L. F. (2004). Financing small and medium-size enterprises with factoring: Global growth and its potential in Eastern Europe. World Bank Monograph, Washington DC.

Barsky, N. P., & Catanach, A. H., Jr. (2005). Evaluating business risks in the commercial lending decision. *Commercial Lending Review, 20*, 3.

Berger, A. N., & Udell, G. F. (1995). Relationship lending and lines of credit in small firm finance. *Journal of Business, 86*(3), 351–381.

Berger, A. N., & Udell, G. F. (2002). Small business credit availability and relationship lending: The importance of bank organizational structure. *The Economic Journal, 112*(477), 32–53.

Boot, A. W., & Thakor, A. V. (1994). Moral hazard and secured lending in an infinitely repeated credit market game. *International Economic Review, 35*, 899–920.

Buzacott, J. A., & Zhang, R. Q. (2004). Inventory management with asset-based financing. *Management Science, 50*(9), 1274–1292.

Camerinelli, E. (2009). Supply chain finance. *Journal of Payments Strategy & Systems, 3*(2), 114–128.

Caniato, F., Gelsomino, L. M., Perego, A., & Ronchi, S. (2016). Does finance solve the supply chain financing problem? *Supply Chain Management: An International Journal, 21*(5), 534–549.

Chauffour, J. P., & Farole, T. (2009). *Trade finance in crisis: Market adjustment or market failure*. Centre for Economic Policy Research, 119.

Chen, H. (1987). Vision for material bank [J]. *China Industrial Economy, 3*, 75–76.

Chen, S. Q. (2014). Banking service innovation in the FTA [J]. *China Finance, 3*, 15–17.

Chen, X., & Hu, C. (2011). The value of supply chain finance. In *Supply chain management-applications and simulations*. InTech.
Chen, X. F. (2008). *Theory of supply chain financial service innovation [M]*. Fudan University Press.
Chen, X. F., & Zhu, D. L. (2005). Financial service innovation of modern logistics—Financial logistics[J]. *Logistics Technology, 3*(4–5).
Coface. (2017). China corporate payment survey: The devil is in the detail. Retrieved January 30, 2017, from www.coface.com.cn/News-Publications-Events/Publications/China-corporate-payment-survey-the-devil-is-inthe-detail
Coulter, J., & Onumah, G. (2002). The role of warehouse receipt systems in enhanced commodity marketing and rural livelihoods in Africa. *Food Policy, 27*(4), 319–337.
DeWitt, T., Giunipero, L. C., & Melton, H. L. (2006). Clusters and supply chain management: The Amish experience. *International Journal of Physical Distribution & Logistics Management, 36*(4), 289–308.
Diercks, L. A. (2004). Identifying and managing troubled borrowers in asset-based lending scenarios. *Commercial Lending Review, 19*, 38.
Du, C. W. (2004). Industrial clusters and direct financing for SMEs [J]. *Management Observer, 9*, 33–34.
Eisenstadt, M. (1966). A finance company's approach to warehouse receipt loans. *New York Certified Public Accountant (pre-1986), 36*(000009), 661.
Fenmore, E. (2004). Making purchase-order financing work for you. *Secured Lender, 60*(2), 20–20.
Frye, J. (2000). Collateral damage: A source of systematic credit risk. *Risk, 13*(4), 91–94.
Gao, L. H. (2013). A review and outlook of domestic SME cluster financing [J]. *Economic System Reform, 1*, 88–92.
Gelsomino, L. M., Mangiaracina, R., Perego, A., & Tumino, A. (2016). Supply chain finance: A literature review. *International Journal of Physical Distribution & Logistics Management, 46*(4), 348–366.
Gertzof, M. (1999). The changing face of asset-based lending. *Commercial Lending Review, 15*, 52.
Global Business Intelligence. (2016). State of supply chain finance industry entering a new era of maturity. https://www.demica.com/library/gbi-2016-state-of-scf-april-21.pdf
Gomm, M. L. (2010). Supply chain finance: Applying finance theory to supply chain management to enhance finance in supply chains. *International Journal of Logistics: Research and Applications, 13*(2), 133–142.
Greenbaum, S. I., Kanatas, G., & Venezia, I. (1989). Equilibrium loan pricing under the bank-client relationship. *Journal of Banking & Finance, 13*(2), 221–235.

Grosse-Ruyken, P. T., Wagner, S. M., & Jönke, R. (2011). What is the right cash conversion cycle for your supply chain? *International Journal of Services and Operations Management, 10*(1), 13–29.

GSCFF (Global SCF Forum). (2015). Standard definitions for techniques of supply chain finance. https://www.abe-eba.eu/Repository.aspx?ID=f7855005-f9b1-4b7e-bc4a-36ece3c9eb3b

Guo, H. (2012). Problems and solutions of private capital lending—private lending crisis in Wenzhou as an example [J]. *People's Tribune: Midterm Journal, 1*, 85–87.

Hansen, M. T., Podolny, J. M., & Pfeffer, J. (2001). So many ties, so little time: A task contingency perspective on corporate social capital in organizations. In *Social capital of organizations* (pp. 21–57). Emerald Group Publishing Limited.

Hesse, M., & Rodrigue, J. P. (2004). The transport geography of logistics and freight distribution. *Journal of Transport Geography, 12*(3), 171–184.

Hoberg, K., Protopappa-Sieke, M., & Steinker, S. (2017). How do financial constraints and financing costs affect inventories? An empirical supply chain perspective. *International Journal of Physical Distribution & Logistics Management, 47*(6), 516–535.

Hofmann, E. (2005). Supply chain finance: Some conceptual insights. In *Beiträge Zu Beschaffung Und Logistik* (pp. 203–214). Springer Gabler.

Hofmann, E., & Kotzab, H. (2010). A supply chain-oriented approach of working capital management. *Journal of Business Logistics, 31*(2), 305–330.

Hofmann, E., Strewe, U. M., & Bosia, N. (2017). *Supply chain finance and blockchain technology: The case of reverse securitisation.* Springer.

Hu, Y., & Liu, S. W. (2008). An overview of discussion on logistics finance and its operation [J]. *Economic Theory and Economic Management, 2*, 75–79.

Huang, H. Y., & Chen, L. P. (2005). Structure of business clusters embedded in social networks and their advantages [J]. *Modern Management Science, 5*, 70–71.

Humphrey, J. (2009). Are exporters in Africa facing reduced availability of trade finance? *IDS Bulletin, 40*(5), 28–37.

Koch, A. R. (1948). Economic aspects of inventory and receivables financing. *Law and Contemporary Problems, 13*, 566.

Kong, L., & Feng, J. W. (2009). Cluster financing and innovation of SME financing mechanism in Yunnan [J]. *The Ideological Front, 35*(1), 92–97.

Kouvelis, P., & Zhao, W. (2017, December). Who should finance the supply chain? Impact of credit ratings on supply chain decisions. *Manufacturing & Service Operations Management, 20*(1), 19–35.

Lacroix, R., & Varangis, P. (1996). Using warehouse receipts in developing and transition economies. *Finance and Development, 33*, 36–39.

Lamoureux, J. F., & Evans, T. (2011). Supply chain finance: A new means to support the competitiveness and resilience of global value chains. https://ssrn.com/abstract=2179944 or https://doi.org/10.2139/ssrn.2179944

Li, Y. X. (2011). Risk assessment of supply chain finance [J]. *Journal of Central University of Finance & Economics, 10*, 36–41.

Lin, Y. F., & Li, Y. J. (2001). Development of SME financial institutions and SME financing [J]. *Economic Research Journal, 1*(10), 10–18.

Long, C., & Zhang, X. (2011). Cluster-based industrialization in China: Financing and performance. *Journal of International Economics, 84*(1), 112–123.

Luo, Q., Zhu, D. L., & Chen, B. M. (2002). Innovation in third-party logistics services: Preliminary exploration of financing warehouse and its operation mode [J]. *China Business and Market, 16*(2), 11–14.

Martin, J., & Hofmann, E. (2017). Involving financial service providers in supply chain finance practices: Company needs and service requirements. *Journal of Applied Accounting Research, 18*(1), 42–62.

McKinsey & Company. (2015). Supply-chain finance: The emergence of a new competitive landscape. https://www.mckinsey.com/industries/financial-services/our-insights/supply-chain-finance-the-emergence-of-a-new-competitive-landscape

Miller, R. A. (1982). Mas consultant's role asset-based financing. *The CPA Journal (pre-1986), 52*(000004), 24.

More, D., & Basu, P. (2013). Challenges of supply chain finance: A detailed study and a hierarchical model based on the experiences of an Indian firm. *Business Process Management Journal, 19*(4), 624–647.

Oliver, R. K., & Webber, M. D. (1992). Supply-chain management: Logistics catches up with strategy. In M. Christopher (Ed.), *Logistics: The strategic issues* (p. 64). Chapman and Hall.

Omran, Y., Henke, M., Heines, R., & Hofmann, E. (2017). Blockchain-driven supply chain finance: Towards a conceptual framework from a buyer perspective. IPSERA 2017: 26th annual conference of the International Purchasing and Supply Education and Research Association. Budapest, Hungary.

Pfohl, H. C., & Gomm, M. (2009). Supply chain finance: Optimizing financial flows in supply chains. *Logistics research, 1*(3–4), 149–161.

Poe, T. R. (1997). Subjective judgments and the asset-based lender. *Commercial Lending Review, 13*, 67.

Porter, M. E. (1990). *Competitive advantage of nations.* Free Press.

Randall, W. S., & Theodore Farris, M. (2009). Supply chain financing: Using cash-to-cash variables to strengthen the supply chain. *International Journal of Physical Distribution & Logistics Management, 39*(8), 669–689.

Ren, W. C. (2004). Conception and operation of material "bank" [J]. *Logistics & Material Handling, 10*, 017.

Rutberg, S. (2002). Financing the supply chain by piggy-backing on the massive distribution clout of united parcel service. *Secured Lender, 58*(3), 40–40.

SDB—CEIBS. (2009). *"Supply Chain Finance" Research Group: Supply chain finance [M].* Shanghai Far East Publishers.

Silvestro, R., & Lustrato, P. (2014). Integrating financial and physical supply chains: The role of banks in enabling supply chain integration. *International Journal of Operations & Production Management, 34*(3), 298–324.
Singh, D. (2006). *Financing export clusters-options and implications for strategy makers.* International Trade Centre UNCTAD.
Song, H. (2015). *Supply chain finance [M].* China Renmin University Press.
Song, H., & Wang, L. (2013). The impact of private and family firms' relational strength on financing performance in clusters. *Asia Pacific Journal of Management, 30*(3), 735–748.
Song, H., Yu, K., & Lu, Q. (2018). Financial service providers and banks' role in helping SMEs to access finance. *International Journal of Physical Distribution & Logistics Management, 1*, 29–42.
Song, Y., & Li, W. J. (2009). Logistics finance: Causes, development modes and risk prevention [J]. *South China Finance, 12*, 41–46.
Song, H., Yu, K., Ganguly, A., & Turson, R. (2016). Supply chain network, information sharing and SME credit quality. *Industrial Management & Data Systems, 116*(4), 740–758.
Stein, J. C. (2002). Information production and capital allocation: Decentralized versus hierarchical firms. *The Journal of Finance, 57*(5), 1891–1921.
Stevens, G. C. (1989). Integrating the supply chain. *International Journal of Physical Distribution & Materials Management, 19*(8), 3–8.
Stiglitz, J. E., & Weiss, A. (1981). Credit rationing in markets with imperfect information. *The American Economic Review, 71*(3), 393–410.
Tang, S. Y. (2005). Research on logistics finance practices [J]. *China Logistics & Purchasing, 2*, 18–21.
Timme, S. G., & Williams-Timme, C. (2000). The financial-SCM connection. *Supply Chain Management Review, 4*(2), 33–40.
Villena, V. H., Revilla, E., & Choi, T. Y. (2011). The dark side of buyer–supplier relationships: A social capital perspective. *Journal of Operations Management, 29*(6), 561–576.
Wandfluh, M., Hofmann, E., & Schoensleben, P. (2016). Financing buyer-supplier dyads: An empirical analysis on financial collaboration in the supply chain. *International Journal of Logistics Research and Applications, 19*(3), 1–18.
Wang, F. J., & An, G. J. (2009). Cluster financing: A new idea for SMEs to cope with financing dilemma under the financial crisis [J]. *China Finance, 21*, 33–34.
Wang, S. Z. (2007). Analysis of SME financing based on the perspective of "bank-enterprise game" [J]. *Journal of Nanjing University: Philosophy. Humanities. Social Sciences, 44*(6), 132–138.
Wang, W. (2014). Grameen Bank's micro-finance model and its inspirations for the development of rural micro-finance in China [J]. *Credit Reference, 32*(8), 90–92.

Wang, X., & Zhang, J. (2003). Bank credit rationing and SME lending [J]. *Economic Research Journal, 7*, 68–75.
Wang, Z., & Wang, Z. J. (2005). Financing warehouse and material bank [J]. *China Logistics & Purchasing, 2*, 28–30.
Wright, J. F. (1988). Accounting: Inventory-based lending. *Commercial Lending Review, 4*(3), 97–99.
Wuttke, D. A., Blome, C., & Henke, M. (2013a). Focusing the financial flow of supply chains: An empirical investigation of financial supply chain management. *International Journal of Production Economics, 145*(2), 773–789.
Wuttke, D.A., Blome, C., Foerstl, K., & Henke, M. (2013b). Managing the innovation adoption of supply chain finance—empirical evidence from six European case studies. *Journal of Business Logistics, 34*(2), 148–166.
Wuttke, D. A., Blome, C., Heese, H. S., & Protopappa-Sieke, M. (2016). Supply chain finance: Optimal introduction and adoption decisions. *International Journal of Production Economics, 178*, 72–81.
Xu, J. L., Li, J., & Ding, T. (2013). New model of export financing for SMEs—structured trade finance. *Financial Theory & Practice, 10*, 47–50.
Yan, H. (2017, July). Credit model of supply chain finance based on big data of E-commerce. In *Industrial Economics System and Industrial Security Engineering (IEIS'2017), 2017 4th International Conference on* (pp. 1–4). IEEE.
Yu, Y., & Feng, G. Z. (2003). Research on operation mode and risk control of material bank [J]. *Management Review, 15*(9), 45–50. (in Chinese).
Yuan, H., & Wang, W. (2005). Logistics finance—a new field of logistics services [J]. *China Logistics & Purchasing, 2*, 22–23.
Zhang, W. J. (2010). Cluster financing: Addressing the financing difficulty of SMEs in less developed areas—Discussion on the financing issues of ecological economic zone construction in Poyang Lake [J]. *Journal of Agro-Forestry Economics and Management, 09*(3), 70–73.
Zhao, Q., Deng, X. M., & Han, X. J. (2005). Analysis of innovation advantages of industrial clusters and its inspirations [J]. *Commercial Research, 8*, 70–72.
Zhao, X., Yeung, K. H., Huang, Q., & Song, X. (2015). Improving the predictability of business failure of supply chain finance clients by using external big data set. *Industrial Management & Data Systems, 115*(9), 1683–1703.
Zheng, S. Q. (2004). Financing warehouse—Third-party logistics bridge between banks and enterprises [J]. *The Theory and Practice of Finance and Economics, 25*(1), 43–45.
Zou, X. P., & Tang, Y. Q. (2004). A field requiring urgent attention: Logistics finance [J]. *Science & Technology Progress and Policy, 21*(11), 163–165.

CHAPTER 2

Realizing End-to-End Supply Chain Finance

2.1 Introduction

The essence of supply chain finance is about optimizing supply chain operations through financial services and activities, improving the financial performance of each participant in the supply chain, and ultimately enhancing the competitiveness of the entire supply chain. Therefore, in this sense, supply chain finance is about not only financing but also optimizing and improving the financial efficiency of the entire supply chain, helping all enterprises in the supply chain (including SMEs) to achieve best operational performance with minimum financial costs. This also means that the strategic, tactical, and operational decisions made by any manager in the supply chain will have an impact not only on financial costs and financial position of his/her own enterprise but also on financial positions of other enterprises, thus affecting the end-to-end financial efficiency of the entire supply chain. Timme and Williams-Timme (2003) said, "supply chain management will help to improve shareholder returns, however, few enterprises use it to manage the overall financial performance," treating the supply chain management as an opportunity to improve financial performance. The said overall financial performance consists of three points: First, we should not simply review an enterprise's book revenue and profit; otherwise it will make us ignore supply chain management. Second, as for supply chain management, strong cash flow is as important as profit. In this respect, how to maintain and accelerate cash flow is the core of supply chain management. Third, most enterprises

H. Song, *Smart Supply Chain Finance*,
https://doi.org/10.1007/978-981-16-5997-3_2

increase their competitiveness within the supply chain by improving capital efficiency and activating assets (Christopher & Holweg, 2011). The essence of supply chain and supply chain finance is evident from the above three points discussed by Christopher: first, enterprises in supply chain may get help to improve capital efficiency and accelerate cash flow; second, achieving end-to-end financial performance is necessary to achieve the competitiveness in supply chain, which means that not only the activities and capital efficiency of one enterprise can be optimized but also all related enterprises can reduce the overall cost of funds through effective means. Therefore, this chapter tries to explore how to understand that the essence of supply chain finance is optimizing end-to-end capital efficiency and capital flow and what specific role supply chain finance plays.

2.2 Impact of Supply Chain Management on Finance

An important financial objective for enterprises is to generate satisfactory returns on shareholders' equity (ROE). In fact, ROE is an indicator that measures the returns to equity investors and is used to evaluate the performance of corporate managers, namely profitability, asset management, and financial control. Fundamentally, a wide range of investors hold stocks for the basic purpose of making a good profit, so economic performance of an enterprise directly determines the amount and duration of investors' holdings of the enterprise's stocks. When analyzing ROE, the enterprise should consider the net investment and net investment value of shareholders. Assuming there are two enterprises, enterprise A has a profit of RMB 1 million and enterprise B has a profit of RMB 100 million, then enterprise B's profit seems larger than enterprise A's. However, if the net investment value of enterprise A is RMB 10 million, while that of enterprise B is RMB 10 billion, then enterprise A's ROE is 10% (1 million/10 million), while enterprise B's ROE is 1% (100 million/10 billion). Clearly, the shareholders of enterprise A will realize better returns. In addition to ROE, an enterprise's financial position and performance may be analyzed by comparing profits to the underlying assets, forming the return on assets (ROA). In reality, as a commonly accepted indicator of financial performance, ROA is used to compare management and performance among enterprises in the same industry and among enterprises in similar industries. Both ROE and ROA depend on the overall profitability of an enterprise, while the key to improving these two indicators is how effectively it conducts its operations and supply chain management.

Taking return on investment (ROI) as an example, an enterprise's ROI is equal to the ratio of profit to total investment. If an enterprise has a profit of RMB 600,000 and a total investment of RMB 5 million, the ROI will be 12%. From another perspective, the ROI calculation can also be expressed as follows:

$$\text{ROI} = \left(\frac{\text{Profit}}{\text{Revenue}} \times \frac{\text{Revenue}}{\text{Total Iinvestment}} \right) \times 100\%$$

Obviously, Profit/Revenue reflects the profitability of an enterprise, while Revenue/Total Investment reflects its yield on investments. In the above-mentioned example, if the enterprise's revenue is RMB 50 million, its profitability will be 1.2% (i.e., 60/5000 × 100%), while its yield on investments is 10 (i.e., 5000/500). A decline in any of these indicators will lead to a decline in ROI. For example, a decline in profit or an increase in total investment will lead to a decline in ROI if the revenue remains constant. Hence, it is critical for enterprises to improve profitability or enhance return on investment.

Supply chain management offers the opportunity to achieve these above goals. On the one hand, better effectiveness of supply chain services will drive stronger corporate profitability and vice versa. The effectiveness of supply chain services depends on whether enterprises can realize the value of clients and users in a timely and effective manner. On the other hand, the process and efficiency of supply chain can have an impact on the position of costs and assets. An inefficient supply chain not only drives up costs but also leads to a corresponding decrease in return on investment.

Figure 2.1 reflects the financial relationship between supply chain management and ROA. The effectiveness of supply chain services affects the sales level of enterprises, while the efficiency of supply chain process determines the total costs of enterprises. In addition, supply chain operation management also directly affects the assets of enterprises. Figure 2.1 shows that ROA is calculated by dividing profit by capital occupied or assets (profit/capital occupied). With a given level of capital occupied, a higher profit will generate a higher ROA and vice versa.

From the specific perspective of supply chain operations, an enterprise's cash and receivables are influenced by order cycles and cash-to-cash cycles. Order cycle, also generally known as delivery lead time, is the interval from preparation of ordered goods to receipt, which involves activities

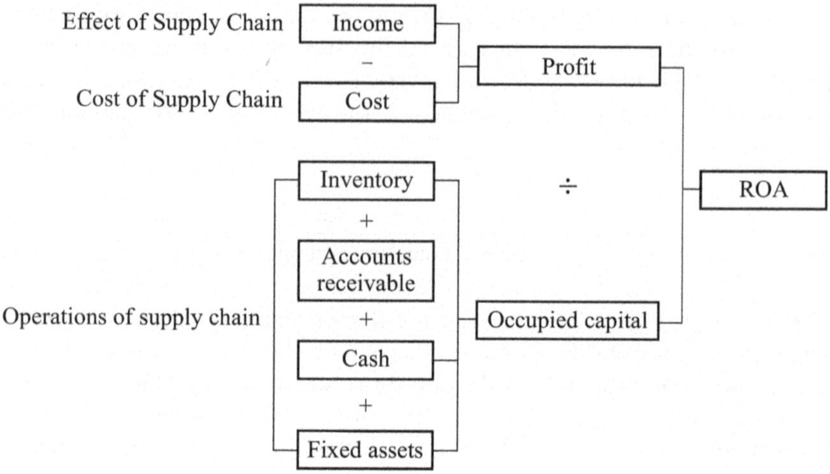

Fig. 2.1 Impact of supply chain on ROA

such as order preparation, order placing, order processing, supply as ordered, and order status tracking. Obviously, longer order cycles lead to larger receivables and higher cash consumption by an enterprise itself. Cash-to-cash cycle is a key tool and means used to measure and evaluate the performance of an enterprise's supply chain operations. Its basic concept is the cycle time of one unit of currency from raw material input to market value realization. This tool has a direct impact on how enterprises accelerate the management of cash flows and accounts receivable (see next section for details). In addition, reliability of supply and accuracy of information are also important in deciding the above two parameters, which will affect an enterprise's cash and receivables. Reliability of supply refers to the state of an enterprise's ability to adequately and efficiently serve its clients, and is often expressed in terms of order fulfillment rates and delivery timeliness. Higher order fulfillment rates and delivery timeliness will reduce accounts receivable and thus accelerate cash flow; conversely, an increase in accounts receivable will tighten the cash flow of an enterprise. The accuracy of the information is mainly reflected by the timely and accurate delivery of bills and documents, which obviously also has an impact on cash and accounts receivable. From the above analysis, it can be concluded that the efficiency and effectiveness of supply chain operations directly determine the amount of capital occupied.

Based on the above factors, an enterprise aspiring to improve ROA needs to achieve the above goals through better supply chain management, in addition to improving its own business capabilities. Possible approaches of supply chain management include effective network management, order management, inventory management, and transport management (see Fig. 2.2).

The impact of supply chain management on improving ROA is mainly reflected in the following aspects:

The first is network structure management. During supply chain operations, if a single enterprise takes on all assets and activities alone, its investment and capital occupied will be large, and also the operation will be poor and inefficient. Adding external service providers with more expertise and higher efficiency into the supply chain operations will result in lower supply chain costs and improved customer service efficiency for the enterprise itself. Especially in a highly uncertain market, this addition of external resources will produce more significant results (Kotabe & Mol, 2009). However, overuse of outsourcing may also drive up potential costs (Rossetti & Choi, 2005; Tsai et al., 2012). For example, a research of Tsai et al. showed that in logistics outsourcing services, relational risks (including supply-side opportunism, poor communication, lack of shared goals, and power asymmetry) would lead to

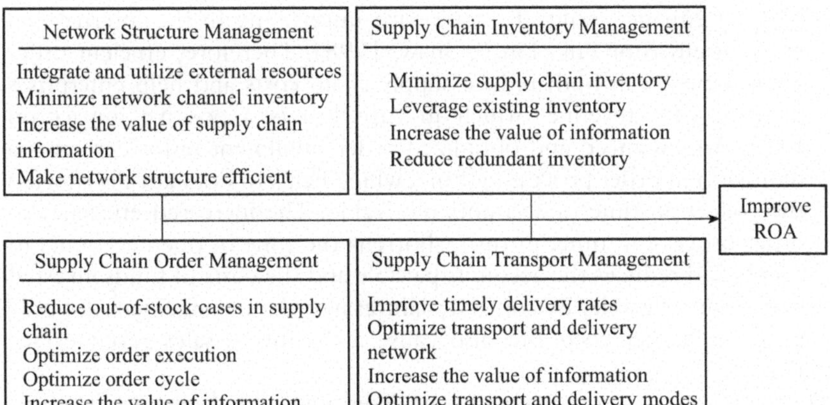

Fig. 2.2 ROA improvement with supply chain management

asset risks (including poorer employee utilization, information risk, internal governance costs, and dependency risk), which in turn would generate capacity risks (including deterioration of service performance, loss of control, blocked strategic development, and loss of capacity). Hence, a well-organized cooperative network can effectively utilize external resources while minimizing potential costs and risks, which is the key to improving ROA.

The second is supply chain inventory management. The lowering of inventory levels of all supply chain participants can reduce their capital occupied and improve capital efficiency. But, to achieve this goal, the supply chain participants must fully utilize the co-shared information at different levels and links, thus reducing forecast errors and increasing the frequency of collaboration (Ganesan et al., 2010). In addition, by effectively planning and setting up network structures (such as reducing unnecessary intermediary links), all participants in the supply chain can reduce inventory on the one hand and timely respond to market changes on the other. In this way, they will effectively reduce the capital investment in the supply chain and increase the sales revenue, thus ultimately increasing the overall ROA.

The third is order management. As a complex management process, it involves different activities and different service providers and depends on the interaction of various tasks, resources, and participants in the process. Order management aims, first, to deliver the right products and services to the right clients in the right place at the right time and, second, to enhance agility to cope with uncertainty in the internal and external environment (Lin & Shaw, 1998). Therefore, efficient order management can both reduce supply chain costs and help enterprises increase sales revenue, which in turn brings a positive impact on ROA. An enhanced and optimized order fulfillment ratio represents a reduction in order processing time, which helps to dramatically shorten the collection time of accounts receivable. The increased efficiency in order processing time, in turn, shortens the time of open accounts to clients and reduces the accounts payable and the costs of funds invested in accounts payable. By contrast, failures in order management not only result in higher costs but also cause a decline in sales revenue (see Fig. 2.3).

The fourth is transport management. The time of and changes in transport and delivery of goods have a significant impact on sales and inventory. Longer transport and delivery time means shorter client response

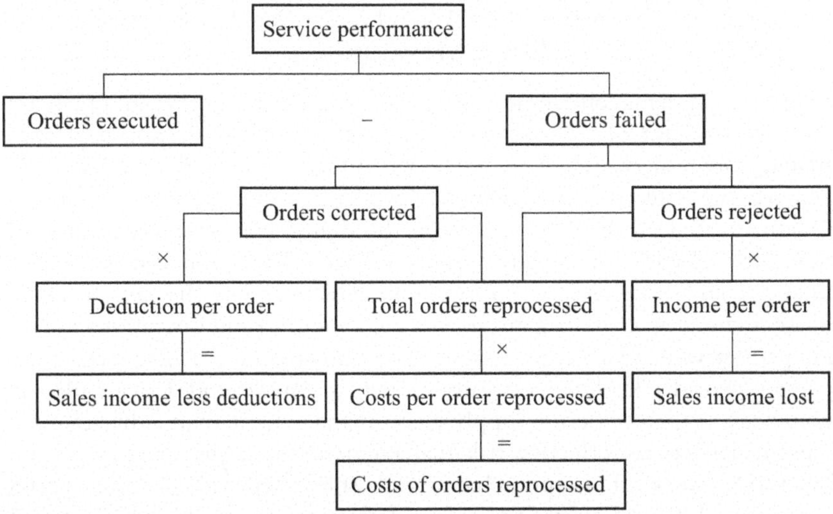

Fig. 2.3 Impact of order management on financial performance

time, which increases the likelihood of lagging sales. Similarly, goods under transport and delivery are in-transit inventory, and more in-transit inventory inevitably takes up a lot of capital, thus decreasing ROA. Therefore, optimizing the management of transport and delivery throughout the supply chain will also improve the financial position of the enterprises in the supply chain.

From the above analysis, it can be seen that in order to improve ROE or ROA, enterprises need to achieve effective end-to-end organization and management in the entire supply chain activities. When choosing alternatives for supply chain decisions, enterprises should refer to the changes and impacts of financial indicators such as net income, ROA and ROE, which are also the basic prerequisites for the development of supply chain finance. The reason is that inability to effectively manage the supply chain will inevitably lead to deterioration of their financial position, thus increasing the risk of carrying out supply chain finance; on the contrary, reasonable and effective supply chain activities not only boost ROA but also enable supply chain finance to help supply chain participants optimize their financial status, reduce financial costs, and accelerate cash flow.

2.3 Cash-to-Cash Cycle and Supply Chain Fund Management

Supply chain management involves an array of participants from upstream and downstream of the industry, and it refers to the organization and management of commodity, transport, information, and fund flows to achieve the effective movement of products from suppliers to clients (Mentzer et al., 2001). In particular, the digital era facilitates the use of new technologies, the timely capture of client data, and the sharing of financial and nonfinancial information, which makes the supply chain more focused on cross-organizational collaboration and operations to create greater value (Jain et al., 2010). The outstanding performance of the current world's leading companies, such as Apple and Coca-Cola, all comes from their superior supply chain management than other companies, which covers effective risk management of supply chain, declined inventory costs of supply chain, and shortened cash-to-cash cycles (Sheridan, 2000). Previous theories and practices on supply chain have put more emphasis on the optimization of operations, risk management, and inventory management, but have not particularly explored how to achieve the cash-to-cash cycle of the supply chain that affects cash flow.

2.3.1 Cash-to Cash-Cycle and Working Capital

The cash-to-cash cycle is deemed as one of the most important tools for evaluating supply chain performance of an enterprise. Its basic concept is measuring the cycle time of one unit of currency from raw material input to market value realization (Stewart, 1995). The meaning revealed by this tool spans the whole process of supply chain activities, including not only various operational activities within an enterprise (e.g., purchase, warehousing, production, distribution and other operations) but also external business behaviors (e.g., customer service). Its calculation can be done according to the revenue cycle generated by inventories. Some scholars believe that the cash-to-cash cycle helps enterprises to establish a good performance check tool or matrix that serves to optimize their supply chain logistics behavior and to establish an optimal business operation model (Slater, 2000). REL Consulting (2005) has surveyed the best companies in the world in terms of cash-to-cash cycle management (see Table 2.1). Currently, some leading enterprises have adopted the cash-to-cash cycle management with good results. These enterprises showed short,

Table 2.1 Companies with optimal cash-to-cash cycle (C2C) cycles in 2004

Company	*C2C*	*C2C change (%, compared to 2003)*	days sales outstanding (*DSO*)	days inventory held (*DIH*)	days payable outstanding (*DPO*)
Dell	-30	+1	33	3	66
Apple Computer	-25	+30	34	4	64
Regal Entertainment	-19	-17	7	1	27
Anadarko Petroleum	-17	-19	63	3	88
AMC Entertainment	-14	-23	8	0	22
Amerada Hess Corp.	-11	-157	48	13	72
DirectTV Group[a]	-8	-21	30	4	41
Yum Brands	-6	-14	8	3	17
Southwest Airlines	-4	-62	12	8	23
Burlington Resources	-4	+36	65	8	77
Continental Airlines	-3	-70	18	8	29
Brinker Int.	-2	-63	4	4	10
Maxtor	-2	N/A	41	22	65
Wendy's	-1	N/A	13	6	20
America West	-1	-90	17	9	27
Costco Wholesale	3	-56	3	28	27
7-Eleven	4	+103	6	9	10
Intuit	4	-41	18	0	14
Anheuser-Busch	5	+11	17	17	29
Marathon Oil	5	-45	23	15	33

[a]DirectTV Group is now a member of AT&T

or even negative, cash-to-cash cycles and achieved good operating performance.

What exactly is cash-to-cash cycle? Among the main definitions, Stewart defined it as "the cycle time of one unit of currency from raw material input to market value realization," while Moss and Stine (1993) considered it as the interval between the payment of cash for resaleable products and the resale of these products. Since then, another view was that "cash to cash cycle refers to the days requiring finance and support in an enterprise's operating cycle, while operating cycle can be regarded as the days used for inventory and product sales" (Gallinger, 1997), as a result of which the operating cycle became the standard for defining the concept of cash-to-cash cycle. On this basis, Pittiglio, Rabin, Todd, and McGrath and other scholars further developed the concept of cash-to-cash cycle. They considered it as the days between the time an enterprise pays money for raw materials and the time it earns revenue from product sales, which was expressed as the days to supply inventory plus the days to sell products, minus the average product payment cycle (Lancaster et al., 1998; Slater, 2000). Similarly, Schilling (1996) argued that "cash to cash cycle reflects the operating cycle of an enterprise and measures the time from the consumption of cash to purchase inventory for manufacturing activities to the receipt of cash through the sale of final products. Therefore, it may be expressed in days equal to the average inventory period plus the average time of obtaining revenue, minus the time of accounts payable." This definition is now widely accepted by the academic community. Based on this definition, some scholars further extended the concept of cash-to-cash cycle. Soenen (1993) thought that cash-to-cash cycle depends on a number of factors, including the days to pick up goods from suppliers, the days to produce and process final products, the days of inventory before sales, and the days to get money back from clients. Theodore Farris and Hutchison (2003) proposed the following formula for calculating cash-to-cash cycle:

$$\text{DIH}(\text{days inventory held}) = \frac{\text{Inventory value}(\text{RMB})}{\text{Cost of product sales}(\text{RMB})} \times 365$$

$$\text{DSO}(\text{days sales outstanding}) = \frac{\text{Accounts receivable}(\text{RMB})}{\text{Net sales proceeds}(\text{RMB})} \times 365$$

$$\text{DPO}(\text{days payables outstanding}) = \frac{\text{Accounts payable}(\text{RMB})}{\text{Cost of product sales}(\text{RMB})} \times 365$$

$$\text{C2C} = \text{DIH} + \text{DSO} - \text{DPO}$$

Wherein, net sales proceeds are net of discounts and returns on sales of goods.

The cash-to-cash cycle affects an enterprise's working capital directly. A longer cash-to-cash cycle causes a demand for more working capital. The relationship between working capital and cash-to-cash cycle is as follows:

$$\text{Working capital} = \text{Cash to cash cycle} \times \left(\frac{\text{Annual sales}}{365\text{days}}\right)$$

Assuming that a company has annual sales of RMB 5 billion and its inventory, accounts receivable and payable are shown in Fig. 2.4, then the

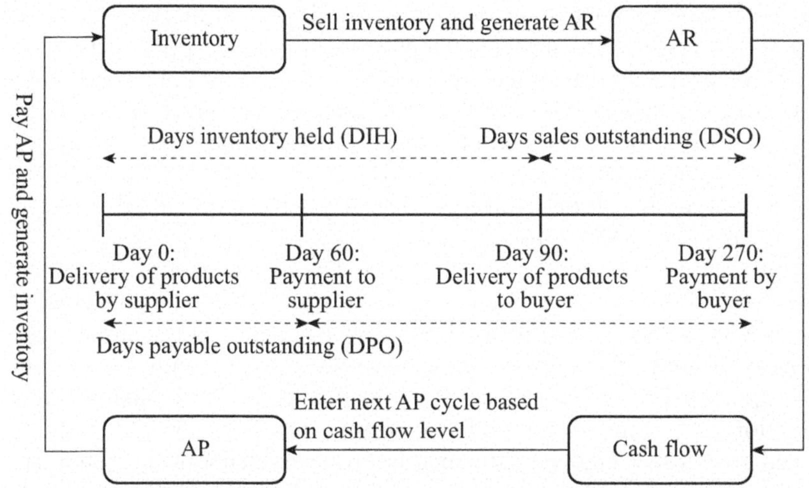

Fig. 2.4 Example of company X's cash-to-cash cycle

company's cash-to-cash cycle will be 210 days (90 + 180 - 60) and the working capital required will be RMB 2.877 billion.

In order to shorten the cash-to-cash cycle, enterprises should start with three elements. First, enterprises may extend the DPO by paying for costs of raw materials, inventory, salaries, and so on at the last minute or by partial payment rather than full payments to suppliers (Theodore Farris & Hutchison, 2003). Furthermore, the effective means to shorten the cash-to-cash cycle include reducing the frequency of external payments, but making full use of interest-free credit cards or lines of credit to make payments instead or not providing commitments to upstream enterprises until accounts payable are realized (Walz, 1999). The purpose of all these means is to control and manage cash payments. For example, if Company X extends its DPO to 80 days, the cash-to-cash cycle will be reduced to 190 days, and the required working capital will be decreased to RMB 2.603 billion.

Second, enterprises may shorten the production cycle and the DIH. As a criterion for measuring productivity, inventory generally has two forms: optimal inventory and excess inventory. The former means "the inventory that exactly meets the production demand," while the latter is "the inventory in excess of what is necessary for production demand" (Farris, 1996).

The latter can be further divided into "good" excess inventory that is prepared in response to strategic needs (e.g., to prevent price increases), and "bad" excess inventory that becomes a burden to the entire corporate system. To enhance cash-to-cash cycle management, enterprises must control excess inventory and adopt effective production and inventory strategies. For example, if Company X's DIH is shortened by 30 days, its cash-to-cash cycle will be reduced to 180 days, and its required working capital will fall to RMB 2.466 billion.

Third, enterprise may narrow the DSO. The management of accounts receivable is also an important element of cash-to-cash cycle management. The aim is mainly to control or limit cash payments and achieve rapid recovery of funds. Enterprises may achieve these goals mainly by encouraging quick payments and using discounts or incentives to maximize the collection of accounts receivable (Boardman & Ricci, 1985). Studies proved that lower sales performance is prone to delinquency (Stewart, 1995), so enterprises should claim interest on delinquent accounts and ask such clients to make immediate payments. Enterprises may also use electronic payments to speed up the collection of funds and, at the same time, offer some facilities to clients during their payment process (Walz, 1999), thus shortening the DSO. A narrowed DSO certainly reduces the working capital required by an enterprise. For example, if Company X's DSO is shortened by 60 days, the cash-to-cash cycle will be reduced to 120 days and the working capital required will be decreased to RMB 1.644 billion.

2.3.2 *Mingxi's SVC Model: C2C Management Practice*

Henan Mingxi Supply Chain Management Co., Ltd. (hereinafter referred to as "Mingxi") was founded in 2016 with a registered capital of RMB 10 million by Yuan Xianming, the former president of China Resources Henan Pharmaceutical Co. Ltd. Applying the idea of C2C management in supply chain, the company serves the upstream and downstream of pharmaceutical commercial enterprises to improve efficiency through cost savings, accelerate capital turnover, and create value for all parties. A management tool adopted by the company is the supply chain value creation (SVC) model. Based on the core concept of this model, the company uses the gross profit balancing tool to seamlessly connect with the existing ERP, e-commerce platforms, and banks. With the help of SVC system software, it adopts digital control to realize the conversion between financial cost and operating profit through supply chain finance. In addition, it achieves employee self-management by allowing employees to adjust varieties and check revenues by themselves, improving overall supply chain efficiency, and ultimately transforming business accounting from ex-post statistics to ex ante warning and control.

The SVC model was proposed because pharmaceutical circulation in China had been small in scale, scattered, and chaotic for a long time, while the national pharmaceutical reform in recent years, including two-invoice system (it means the first invoice of drug sold from pharmaceutical commercial companies to primary distributors, and the second invoice of drug sold from distributors to hospitals; the replacement of the common seven invoices and eight invoices with this two-invoice system aims to reduce profit exploitation in the distribution, and it is clearly stipulated that there should be no more than two primary distributors for each drug) and zero mark-up sales (China has implemented zero mark-up sales of drugs since July 1, 2017, which as a policy considered a key measure to separate hospitals and drugs) have changed the original situation of drug circulation, which has mangled profit margins of commercial enterprises. At present, most drug sales are driven by manufacturers, so most pharmaceutical commercial enterprises are actually distributors that rarely create value other than distribution, which inevitably leads to a strong upstream and downstream position and puts the value of Chinese pharmaceutical commercial enterprises to an acid test. Faced with this situation, Yuan Xianming, then president of China Resources Henan Pharmaceutical Co. Ltd., and his wife, Ms. Liu Aijuan, proposed the practice of balancing gross profit in 2008, in which the funds occupied by upstream and downstream were integrated into the profit accounting, so as to more accurately reflect the real dynamic profit of the company. And based on this, various variables in the gross profit balancing formula were adjusted to ensure the balanced development of the company's key indicators such as revenue, profit, and operating cash flow; externally, the structure of upstream and downstream clients were adjusted to find the best client structure. The introduction of the gross profit balancing concept has changed the traditional logical relationship in accounting. It transforms the traditional approach of evaluating enterprise's own operating performance by accounting into the method of completing the general principles of accounting by economics, expands the pure financial data into economic factor relationship, and integrates business, client relationship, and all circulation relationships of business into the accounting system of balanced gross profit. That is, all economic behaviors in commodity circulation have become basic factors in the balancing and control system. Therefore, the gross profit balancing tool allows the balanced development of the company, various clients, and internal indicators, thus creating continuous value for the company.

(1) Ideas of Gross Profit Balancing and Profit Creation in SVC Model

Nowadays, most of the researchers who study "profit" adopt the accounting profit method. According to the concept of tax law, accounting profit is equal to income minus expenses. Accounting statements or external reports are financial statements prepared in accordance with the *Accounting Standard for Business Enterprises of China* and are provided for external shareholders and governmental authorities to understand the enterprise's financial position. External statements are intended to be "hindsight" as a summary of an enterprise's operating results and do not dynamically reflect changes in business processes. The inevitable collection and payment behavior of enterprises in economic activities will lead to a large amount of accounts receivable and payable being occupied, which eats up huge profits of the enterprises. In addition, ERP systems currently used by most enterprises can only reflect the difference between the purchase price and the sales price of goods, without taking into account the cost of funds occupied by the upstream and downstream, and therefore does not truly reflect the cost of goods and the real value created for clients. Independent of the ERP systems, SVC system is a comprehensive and lean information system that has taken the funds occupied in upstream and downstream and variable costs into account through the concept of "balanced gross profit." SVC system surpasses the traditional financial mindsets and incorporates the financial settlement approach and the concept of time cost of fund occupation. Through systematic control, it finds the best balance point of fund occupation, helping enterprises improve net profit and cash flow with the same sales scale. SVC system fully applies GSP mindset (i.e., global thinking, supply chain thinking, Internet platform thinking). Through global thinking, it fully achieves the participation of all employees of the enterprise, especially transforming finance and human resources functions into profit creation center. Employees are fully motivated through performance linkage. Through supply chain thinking, it provides supply chain services of logistics, capital and cash flow for upstream and downstream clients to expand the enterprise's profit sources. With electronic trading and finance platforms for pharmaceuticals, it enhances the efficiency and broadens the profit sources of the enterprise.

The introduction of "balanced gross profit" concept has changed the traditional logical relationship in accounting. It transforms the traditional approach of evaluating enterprise's own operating performance by accounting into the method of completing the general principles of accounting by economics, expands the pure financial data into economic factor relationship, and integrates business, client relationship, and all circulation relationships of business into the accounting system of balanced gross profit. That is, all economic behaviors in commodity circulation have become basic factors in the balancing and control system.

The main factors affecting an enterprise's profit are sales volume, price and financial expenses, administrative expenses, and operating expenses, while SVC system focuses on variables that can be adjusted by the salesperson, such as price, volume, financial expenses, and operating expenses. Using SVC system, China Resources Henan Pharmaceutical Co. Ltd. explores improvements in business through continuous optimization of purchase, inventory, and sales process to improve the efficiency of working capital management, shorten the cash-to-cash cycle, and decrease the occupation of cash by operating activities. In the course of working capital management, it pays more attention to interconversion of financial cost and operating profit, fully considers the relationship between the adjustment of payment methods for purchases and billing periods and the change of purchase prices, and the adjustment of collection methods for sales and billing periods and the change of sales prices, and selects the optimal commercial terms according to the facts, in a bid to achieve the balance between financial cost and operating profit (see Fig. 2.5).

To be specific, SVC believes that in pharmaceutical circulation, enterprises need to calculate their business gross profit first when calculating pretax profit. The business gross profit is an enterprise's nominal gross profit, that is, the distribution gross profit of a pharmaceutical distribution enterprise, minus discounts (i.e., sales discounts and other expense-based discounts granted to clients in the course of operations), plus rebates from clients (including annual rebates, sales compensations, and other forms of rebates). Clearly, this gross profit calculation fully takes into account the various discount benefits from or to upstream and downstream clients in the operation of the enterprise. Next, SVC balances the gross profit on the basis of the calculated gross profit. Balance means subtracting the cost of occupied capital in the business gross profit. During supply chain operations, there are various forms of capital occupation; for example, if the drugs are stored in warehouse, there is bound to be capital occupied due

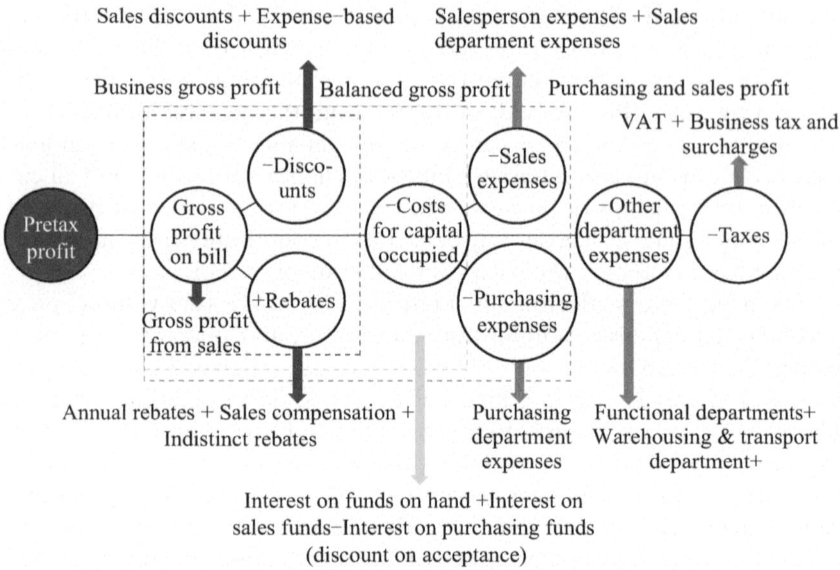

Fig. 2.5 Components of pretax profit as understood by SVC system

to the inventory, and, similarly, the extended billing period of upstream and downstream clients will also incur capital occupied. SVC proposes to consider all these capital occupied in the process of balancing the gross profit. On this basis, net profit of an enterprise is finally calculated by further deducting various expenses incurred in the sales or purchasing process, as well as the internal administrative expenses and taxes.

(2) Management of Balanced Gross Profit

In practice, in order to meet the different needs of business support and assessment and to reflect the differences in concerns and value creation of different business units, SVC has set up two formulas: balanced gross profit based on estimated sales and balanced gross profit based on actual sales. The former calculates the balanced gross profit that a business is expected to achieve and is used to find the key points of value optimization to support business decisions. The latter calculates the balanced gross profit achieved by the actual collection in the current period and is mainly used for assessment purpose. The two formulas have core indicators in common and also have differences.

Balanced gross profit based on estimated sales is the basic formula of balanced gross profit, which uses sales revenue as the basis to calculate the balanced gross profit expected to be realized on a product, not actually realized. The "balanced gross profit," including the gross profit from sales and finance costs, is used as a key reference formula among salespersons to guide their work. Moreover, the calculation results of this formula are used as the basis for setting annual budget KPI indicators for business departments, encouraging them to consider capital costs comprehensively in the sales and purchase processes, achieving the goal of controlling the indicators in advance and managing the budget effectively. The formula for balanced gross profit based on estimated sales is as follows:

$$\begin{aligned} &\textit{Balanced gross profit based on estimated sales} = \textit{Balanced gross profit based on estimated purchase} \\ &-\textit{Interest on sales funds}\left(\textit{estimated}\right) \end{aligned}$$

Wherein, *Balanced gross profit based on estimated purchase* = *Total gross profit from sales* + *Interest on purchase funds* + *Accepted discount on purchase*

$$\begin{aligned} &\textit{Total gross profit from sales} = \textit{Book gross profit on sales} + \textit{Upstream rebate}\left(\textit{excluding tax}\right) \\ &+\textit{Gross profit on refunds and additional payments} \end{aligned}$$

Balanced gross profit based on estimated sales may also be used as the "consolidated net profit" indicator on which the purchaser's bonus is based. To facilitate the understanding of the coherence of the formula, SVC presents the relevant formula settings and data sources, namely:

$$\textit{Consolidated net profit on estimated sales} = \begin{pmatrix} \textit{Balanced gross profit based on estimated sales} \\ -\textit{Total expenses} \times \left(1 - \textit{Valid tax rate}\right) \end{pmatrix}$$

Wherein, *Total expenses* = *Salary* + *Social insurance* + *Gasoline costs* + *Telephone bills* + *Rents* + *Daily expenses* + *Other expenses* + *Travel expenses* + *Freight costs* + *Other regional fees* + *Logistics fees* + *Business company fees* + *Sales management fees* + *Taxes and surcharges* + *Accepted discount on sales + Interest on deposits + Accepted discount on accounts receivable (sales) + Interest on rebates of accounts receivable but uncollected*

The meaning and calculation of the parameters in the formula are shown in Tables 2.2 and 2.3.

As for Mingxi SVC model, each parameter data is extracted through ERP system, and the balanced gross profit can be calculated by product, client, supplier, region, department, salesman, purchaser, and other different dimensions and levels.

The formula for balanced gross profit based on actual sales is based on the amount collected in current month to calculate the balanced gross profit actually realized. The final consolidated net profit calculated by this formula will be used as the basis for calculating the salesperson bonus. The formula for calculating balanced gross profit based on actual sales and the definitions of each parameter therein are as follows:

$$Consolidated\,net\,profit = \left(Balanced\,gross\,profit\,based\,on\,actual\,sales - Total\,expenses\right) \times \left(1 - Valid\,tax\,rate\right)$$

Wherein, *Balanced gross profit based on actual sales = Gross profit on collections + Upstream rebates (excluding taxes) + Interest on purchase funds + Accepted discount on purchase - Interest on sales funds*

$$\begin{aligned} Total\,expenses = {} & Salary + Social\,insurance + Daily\,expenses + Other\,expenses \\ & + Gasoline\,costs + Telephone\,bills + Rents + Travel\,expenses \\ & + Freight\,costs + Other\,regional\,fees + Logistics\,fees \\ & + Departmental\,expenses\,for\,sales\,department \\ & + Departmental\,overheads\,for\,sales\,department \\ & + Taxes\,and\,surcharges + Accepted\,discount\,on\,sales \\ & + Interest\,on\,deposits \end{aligned}$$

(3) Guidance of balanced gross profit model for supply chain business (Table 2.4)

The Mingxi SVC model aims to guide businesses better (including upstream purchasing business and downstream sales business) through the calculation of balanced gross profit, making each salesman focus not only on the difference between the purchase price and the sales price but also

Table 2.2 Definition of each parameter in balanced gross profit based on estimated sales

Serial no.	*Item*	*Definition/calculation*
1	Sales amount (taxes included)	Sales ledger in ERP
2	Book gross profit on sales (taxes excluded)	Sales price - Purchase price
3	Upstream rebates (taxes excluded)	All rebates in the rebate system
4	Gross profit on refunds and retroactive payments	Refunds and retroactive payments in purchase: refund and retroactive payments per package × quantity of products with price adjusted
5	Interest on purchase funds	=Σ Number of sales perproduct × purchase price × (payment days - 26) × daily interest rate
6	Accepted discount on purchase	=Σ Number of sales per product × purchase price × acceptance period × daily discount rate for acceptance (6%/12)
7	Interest on sales funds (estimated)	=ΣSales amount per product × credit period of downstream client × daily interest rate (7.2%/360)
8	Accepted discount on sales (estimated)	=Sales amount × acceptance period × daily interest rate (days of sales acceptance of customer basic information maintenance)
9	Salary, social insurance	Fixed expense, corresponding to each salesperson
10	Gasoline costs	Fixed expense, corresponding to each salesperson
11	Telephone bills	Fixed expense, corresponding to each salesperson
12	Daily expenses, other expenses	Actual expenses incurred, corresponding to each client
13	Travel expenses, freight costs	Actual expenses incurred, corresponding to each client
14	Logistics fees	Monthly sales amount × rate of logistics fees (based on the measured average rate the previous year)
15	Other regional expenses	The actual amount of expenses incurred within a region is apportioned among the departments within the region based on their sales for the month. Region is calculated separately by organizational structure department and region
16	Departmental expenses for sales department	The actual departmental operating expenses incurred by each department are calculated by organizational structure. The expense is apportioned within the department on the basis of each client's sales for the month

(*continued*)

Table 2.2 (continued)

Serial no.	*Item*	*Definition/calculation*
17	Departmental overheads for sales department	The actual departmental overheads and managers' salaries incurred by each department are calculated by organizational structure. The expense is apportioned based on each client's sales for the month in the region.
18	Taxes and surcharges	Gross profit on sales × VAT output rate per product × 10%
19	Interest on deposits	=Deposits × monthly interest rate
20	Interest on rebates of accounts receivable but uncollected (only for purchase department ledger)	=(Rebates receivable as of current month in the rebate system - rebate received) × 30 days × daily interest rate

Table 2.3 Other formulas in balanced gross profit based on estimated sales

Serial no.	*Item*	*Definition/calculation*
1	Gross profit margin on sales	=total gross profit on sales ÷ sales revenue
2	Balanced gross profit margin based on estimated purchase	=balanced gross profit based on estimated purchase ÷ sales revenue
3	Balanced gross profit margin based on estimated sales	=balanced gross profit based on estimated sales ÷ sales revenue
4	Estimated consolidated net profit margin	=estimated consolidated net profit ÷ sales revenue

on the capital occupied in the course of trading with upstream and downstream clients, thus improving the operation quality. Specifically, in the purchase process, SVC model sorts out various factors that affect net profit of products from purchase to payment, including purchase price, winning-bid price, upstream rebates, sales discounts, interest on upstream capital occupied, interest on downstream capital occupied, interest on inventory capital occupied, administrative expenses, sales expenses, business taxes and surcharges, and so on. Through these factors, the enterprise can improve its net profit margin of products in the purchase process based on the following factors: purchase price, upstream rebate, interest on upstream capital occupied, and interest on inventory capital occupied. The

Table 2.4 Meaning of each parameter in balanced gross profit based on actual sales

Serial no.	*Item*	*Meaning/calculation*
1	Gross profit on collections	Gross profit on open credits and cash collections in ERP
2	Upstream rebates (excluding taxes)	All rebates in the rebate system
3	Gross profit on refunds and retroactive payments	Refunds and retroactive payments in purchase: refund and retroactive payments per package × quantity of products with price adjusted
4	Interest on purchase funds	=ΣNumber of products collected in current month × purchase price × (payment days - 26) × daily interest rate
5	Accepted discount on purchase	=Number of products collected by salesmen × purchase price × months × monthly discount rate for acceptance (Months: number of months of acceptance negotiated in the agreement entered in the basic information of commodity)
6	Interest on sales funds	=Actual amount collected × (settlement date - outbound date) × daily interest rate
7	Accepted discount on sales	=Amount collected × days × daily interest rate (days = date of receipt of acceptance - due date of acceptance), accurate to days
8	Salary, social insurance	Fixed expense, corresponding to each salesperson
9	Gasoline costs	Fixed expense, corresponding to each salesperson
10	Telephone bills	Fixed expense, corresponding to each salesperson
11	Daily expenses, other expenses	Actual expenses incurred, corresponding to each client
12	Travel expenses, freight costs	Actual expenses incurred, corresponding to each client
13	Logistics fees	Monthly sales amount × rate of logistics fees (based on the measured average rate the previous year)
14	Sales amount (including taxes)	Sales ledger in ERP (for cost sharing)
15	Other regional expenses	The actual amount of expenses incurred within a region is apportioned among the departments within the region based on their sales for the month. Region is calculated separately by organizational structure department and region

(*continued*)

Table 2.4 (continued)

Serial no.	*Item*	*Meaning/calculation*
16	Departmental expenses for sales department	The actual departmental operating expenses incurred by each department are calculated by organizational structure. The expense is apportioned within the department on the basis of each client's sales for the month
17	Departmental overheads for sales department	The actual departmental overheads and managers' salaries incurred by each department are calculated by organizational structure. The expense is apportioned based on each client's sales for the month in the region
18	Taxes and surcharges	Gross profit on sales × VAT output rate per product × 10%
19	Interest on deposits	=Deposits × monthly interest rate

combined use of each factor to improve overall profitability, which is difficult to achieve quickly by traditional manual calculations, becomes easier through SVC model. The parameter value, target value, minimum value, and actual value are set in purchasing profit evaluation model. By adjusting the parameter values, the model provides guidance in the selection of product types and suppliers, determining the purchase price, payment time, and payment method. It sets the proportion of each type of products in the purchasing based on variable factors such as payment time and payment method for each type of products. This has the advantage of optimizing the payment structure of various upstream clients, reducing upstream advance payments, controlling the proportion of sales of low-margin products, and using all kinds of financial means such as acceptances to generate operating cash flow.

As for the whole sales process, the variable factors that affect net profit and cash flow from sales to collections include sales discounts, collection methods, collection days, and interest rates on funds. The SVC model can monitor profit forecasts for downstream clients and aggregates them layer by layer from the smallest accounting unit (commodity) to find the balance point of maximum profit and optimal cash flow. For example, (1) it may produce profit contribution analysis reports of downstream clients and guides salesmen to adjust the collection period and collection method and, ultimately, improve the consolidated net profit margin of products; (2) it guides salesmen to optimize and adjust the product portfolio of downstream clients by forecasting and monitoring the profitability of their products and replacing products with lower profitability in order to maximize the clients' contribution to the consolidated net profit; (3) it maximizes profits by paying early and seeking greater discounts, as long as the enterprise has sufficient cash flow; (4) it breaks down profit, cash flow, and other indicators to the smallest accounting unit in each profit center of the enterprise and monitors and directs them effectively.

The SVC model can also be used to optimize inventory management. By analyzing and monitoring the factors affecting cash generation in the inventory links, including safety inventory, quantity per purchase, arrival time, and days sales of inventory, with the help of gross profit balancing tools, it determines reasonable purchasing methods, lots, and quantities when negotiating with suppliers in order to reduce the inventory level and the capital occupied due to inventory.

In addition, the SVC model can also be used as one of the KPI indicators for salesmen, departments, regions, and other dimensions, and the consolidated net profit can be directly used as the base for calculating bonus. In order to decrease the capital occupation, control the financing quotas, reduce the loan interests, and improve the ROI, enterprises can consider the consolidated net profit margin (consolidated net profit ÷ actual collections), consolidated ROI (consolidated net profit ÷ (accounts receivable occupied + deposits - accounts payable occupied)), and EVA (consolidated ROI - WACC) in addition to the original sales revenue and gross profit in the performance assessment.

2.4 Collaborative Cash-to-Cash Cycle and Dynamic Discount

Although the cash-to-cash cycle improves the operational performance of certain enterprises, it does not improve the fund position of all supply chain participants, because a decrease in an enterprise's accounts receivable often means an increase in accounts payable of its counterparties or a lengthening of an enterprise's days payable outstanding inevitably ties up funds of other enterprises (Hong, 2015). Similarly, a decrease in DIH of an enterprise may be the result of an increase in costs or inventory of it counterparties. For instance, computer parts suppliers prefer high-frequency and low-volume delivery to improve their own service capabilities and sales performance, or even downstream computer operators adopt supplier-managed inventory instead of VMI (i.e., suppliers manage parts inventory and deliver parts according to actual downstream demand) to save costs and reduce fund pressure. In this case, the downstream computer operators have much shorter cash-to-cash cycles because the inventory of parts is managed by the suppliers. However, the upstream suppliers have longer cash-to-cash cycles and higher working capital, because the suppliers not only extend the DIH and increase the DSO but also bear inventory holding costs and increase operational risk and finance costs. Therefore, in order to optimize the working capital of the entire supply chain and improve the competitiveness of all supply chain participant, we need to explore the cash-to-cash cycle from a systematic perspective, not a single enterprise.

2.4.1 Definition of Collaborative Cash-to-Cash Cycle

(1) Collaborative Cash-to-Cash Cycle

The collaborative cash-to-cash cycle (CCCC) was proposed by Hofmann and Kotzab (2010), who pointed out that discussing the cash-to-cash cycle purely from the perspective of enterprises would only result in abuse of power and that shared value could only be achieved by shortening the cash-to-cash cycle from a systematic perspective. The CCCC is a comprehensive approach to shorten the cash-to-cash cycles and accelerate the cash flow from the collaboration among the various participants from a global perspective. In other words, the CCCC is not simply a summation of the cash-to-cash cycles of multiple enterprises, as this does not truly optimize the cash flow of the entire supply chain. In terms of supply chain operations, business activities involve supply-side external networks (i.e., supply sources), sale-side network relationships (i.e., final consumers), and multitier enterprises within the supply chain system (see Fig. 2.6). If the cash-to-cash cycle is managed only from the perspective of each enterprise, the cash flow acceleration throughout the supply chain will be difficult to achieve. Therefore, instead of simply calculating DSO, DPO, and DIH for each enterprise, the CCCC is a systematic calculation of the cash-to-cash cycle for the entire supply chain. Specifically, Hofmann and Kotzab (2010) argued that accounts receivable and accounts payable in the middle segment of a supply chain would not have a substantial impact on the whole supply chain, and, therefore, CCCC should be the DIH of each stage in the supply chain plus the DSO of the final segment minus the

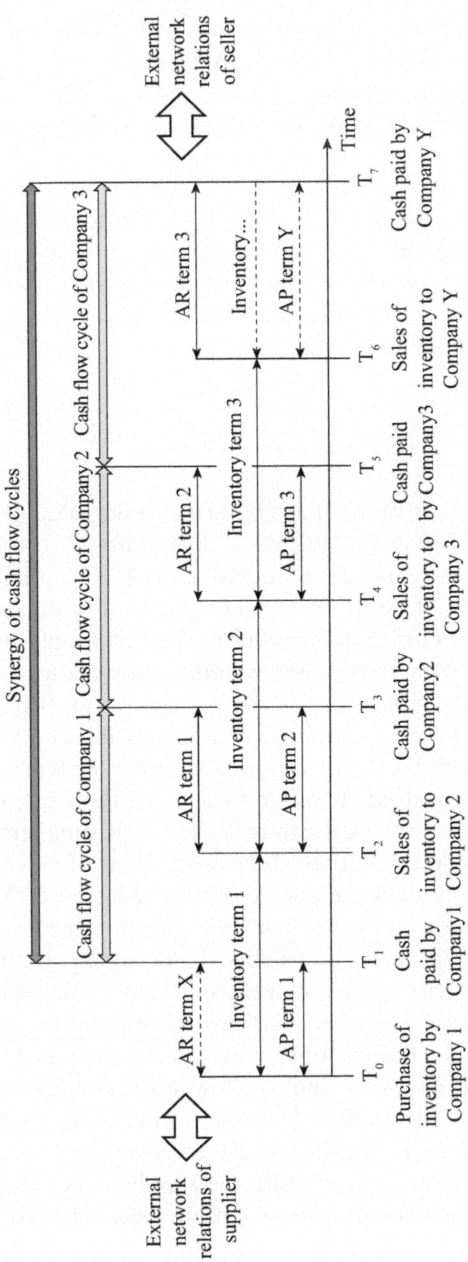

Fig. 2.6 Collaborative cash-to-cash cycle

DPO of the initial links. Taking Fig. 2.5 as an example, CCCC = DIH_1 + DIH_2 + DIH_3 + DSO_3 - DPO_1. Apparently, shortening the CCCC requires reducing the weighted average cost of funds of enterprises in the supply chain to achieve maximum economic added value or shareholder added value.

As an indicator of an enterprise's comprehensive cost of funds, the weighted average cost of funds (WACC) is the total cost of funds calculated by weighting the cost of funds of various long-term funds by the proportion of each type of capital in the enterprise's total capital. WACC requires involving shareholder and creditor factors (Ross & Jaffe, 2005). It is calculated by the following formula:

$$WACC = \frac{E}{E+D} \times i_E + \frac{D}{E+D} \times i_D (1-r)$$

Wherein, E is market value of assets, D is market value of debts, i_E is cost of assets, i_D is cost of debts, and r is cash tax rate.

As seen from the formula, reduction of WACC can be achieved either by decreasing cost of assets or by decreasing cost of debts, while decrease of cost of assets or cost of debts requires that the supply chain participants can fully balance their respective strengths and weaknesses to achieve efficient output systematically. Effective output was proposed based on Goldratt's Theory of Constraints, which basically implies that there are constraints or bottlenecks in an organizational system that need to be focused on and resolved in order to achieve the organization's system goals. When constraints exist externally (such as suppliers or clients), the organization should strengthen the management of external resources or activities, so as to enhance effective output (Mateen & More, 2013). In addition, achieving an effective compensation mechanism is also a key to reducing the cost of assets and debts. Under compensation mechanism, supply chain participants are compensated with corresponding benefits while implementing effective asset management for other participants (Yaqin et al., 2013). For example, when a client's cost of funding is lower than that of a supplier, the client is allowed to raise funds to pay the supplier in advance, which will reduce the overall cost of funding in supply chain. However, such early payment increases the cost of funds and expenses for the client, thus cutting the supplier's profit. In this case, the supply chain needs to set up a compensation mechanism to achieve advance payment from the client to the supplier without reducing the profit. The most typical way of this compensation mechanism is dynamic discount.

2.4.2 *Dynamic Discount under WACC Management*

(1) Definition and Process of Dynamic Discount

An increase of the discount rate or an extension of the permitted payment period will impose impact on cash flow. As one of the widespread tools currently used among enterprises for improving cash flow, discount management is a form of management that gives enterprises price concessions by encouraging them to pay earlier. Generally speaking, discount management involves the calculation of discount rates and discount utilization rates, of which discount rate is the ratio of the specified discount amount to the purchase volume (or net purchase volume), while discount utilization rate is the ratio of the actual discounted revenue to the specified discount amount (see Fig. 2.7 and the formula). For example, when a supplier enters into a contract with a downstream enterprise for RMB 10 million and agrees to an AP term of three months and a 2% discount rate for payment in the first month, the downstream enterprise actually pays RMB 12 million in advance in the first month. As per the formula, the total discount revenue should be RMB 200,000, but the actual discount revenue is RMB 120,000, so the discount utilization rate is 60%.

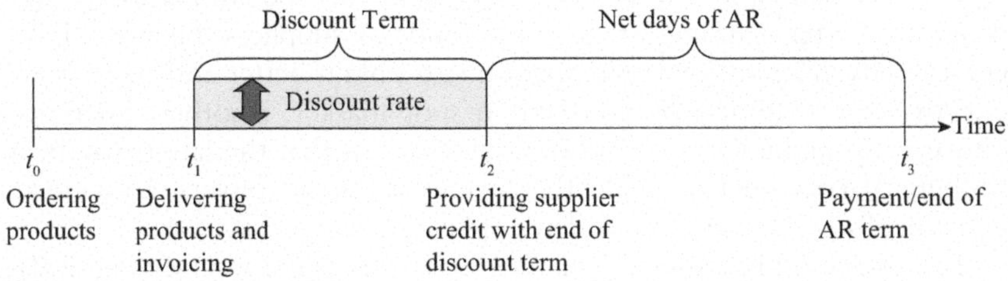

Fig. 2.7 Payment with discount

$$\textit{Discount rate} = \frac{\textit{Specified discount amount}}{\textit{Net purchase volume}} \times 100\%$$

$$\textit{Discount utilization rate} = \frac{\textit{Actual discounted revenue}}{\textit{Specified discount amount}} \times 100\%$$

Clearly, as far as enterprises are concerned, higher discount utilization rate as well as discount rate can be a good way to improve the cash flow and also benefit the downstream clients from discounting. However, this static discount has corresponding shortcomings: first, the discount rate and discount period are inflexible; second, the rules of discounting are unilaterally determined by suppliers without fully taking into account the discretion of downstream clients on their financial positions. For these reasons, dynamic discounting has nowadays become a key tool adopted by many enterprises in order to improve their cash-to-cash cycle (Gelsomino et al., 2016). Unlike the "use or abandon" principle of static discount, dynamic discount allows the buyers and sellers to jointly determine the terms of early payment and place those terms on a sliding scale (see Fig. 2.8). That is, under dynamic discount model, buyers have more flexibility in choosing how and when to pay suppliers in exchange for lower prices or discounts on the purchase of goods and services. "Dynamic" is the options to offer discounts to suppliers based on payment date. Generally speaking, the earlier the payment is made, the greater the discount will be. Dynamic discount facilitates buyers and sellers to initiate early payment discounts on an invoice-by-invoice basis. It allows buyers and sellers to view invoices through a web-based platform and select approved invoices for early payment. Dynamic discount offers the advantage of reducing the uncertainty of demand for operational assets and promotes better planning of incoming funds by suppliers. Likewise, buyers take advantage of dynamic discounts to obtain better and more cost-effective raw materials or products in spot market. Another difference between dynamic discount and static discount is that the latter may be a tool for partial buyers, while the former is for all buyers. Therefore, dynamic discounts are more widely applicable.

The operation process of dynamic discount is as follows (see Fig. 2.9): first, when the purchase order is received, the supplier sends the required products and electronic documents (via the Internet) to the buyer. The buyer acknowledges receipt and agrees to pay. Second, the buyer issues an early payment proposal (EPP) for both parties to determine the revised

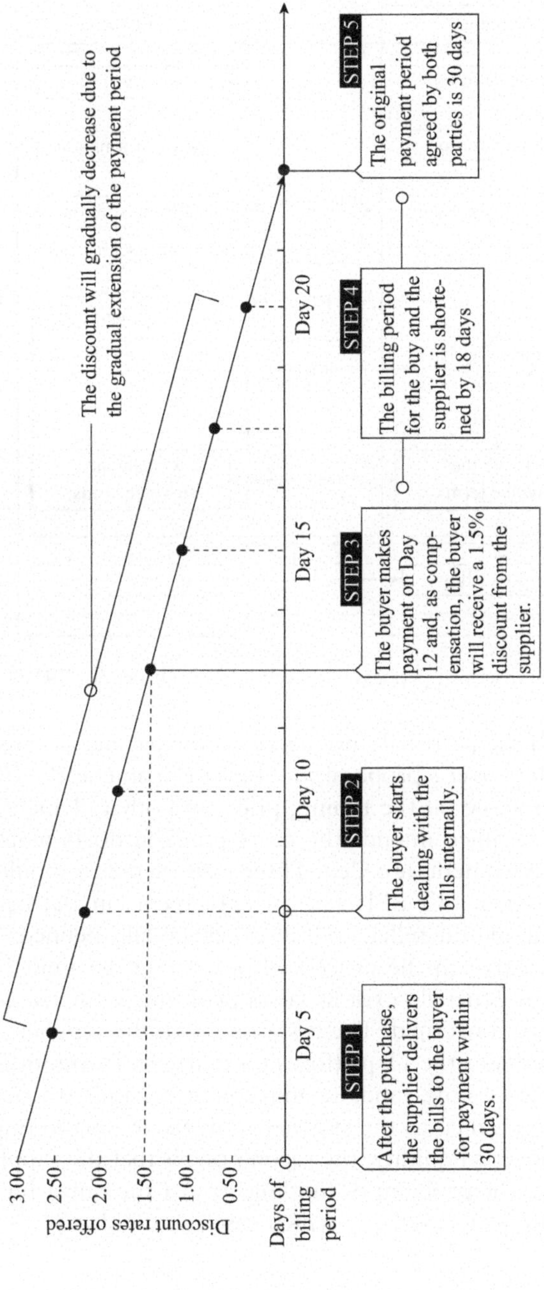

Fig. 2.8 Dynamic discount

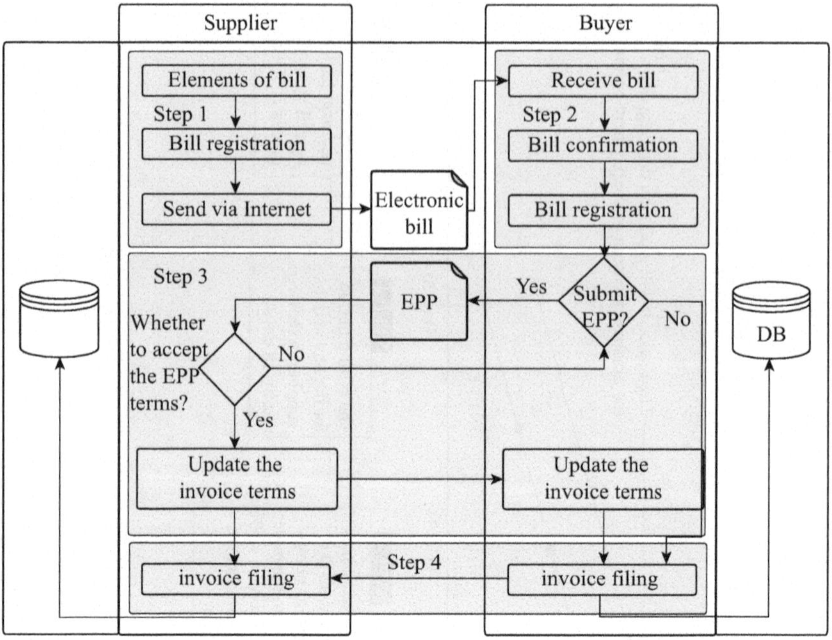

Fig. 2.9 Dynamic discount process. (Source: Gelsomino et al., 2016)

payment terms. If the parties do not agree on the payment terms and the supplier rejects the buyer's proposal, the buyer can amend the EPP again until both parties agree on the timing, price, and other elements of payment. Then the supplier amends the corresponding documents accordingly. Third, the documents are filed. Three main elements should be filed in dynamic discounts: (1) EPP, (2) an agreement on payment terms between the buyer and the seller, and (3) other specially defined elements. It is worth noting that in the process of promoting dynamic discounts, two configurations generally exist as far as platforms, systems, and funds paid in advance are concerned. The first one is that the supplier develops, provides, and maintains the IT platform for dynamic discounting, so that the buyer uses the existing funds to implement dynamic discounting or the funds paid in advance to the supplier in dynamic discounting mainly come from the buyer's liquidity; the second one is that the supplier helps the buyer to solve the problem of funding so that the buyer implements dynamic discounting smoothly, in which case the supplier plays the dual roles of dynamic discounting service provider or IT platform and financial service provider. The latter one involves the supply chain finance business. In practice, the two allocations are often mixed. If the first allocation appears alone, it requires the buyer to have sufficient funds, which not only increases the buyer's fund holdings but also indirectly raises the opportunity cost of the buyer's funds.

(2) Basic Model of Dynamic Discounting

Gelsomino et al. (2016) proposed a model of dynamic discounting, in which they argued that dynamic discounting is based on the buyer's credit being higher than the supplier's credit. That is, assuming that r_s is the supplier's financing cost per unit of currency per day (the cost of short-term debt compared to trade credit (i.e., discount)) and r_b is the buyer's financing cost per unit of currency per day, then the basic assumption of dynamic discounting is $r_b \leq r_s$. When the buyer decides to use dynamic discounts, it needs to raise liquidity to pay in advance. If the supplier delivers the products and the bills to the buyer every T days, the bill cycle time will be T. The bill specifies a payment deadline of G. When $t = 1$, T will be equal to G, so $t \in N[1; G]$, based on a year of 12 months and 30 days per month, or 360 days. When considering multiple suppliers or multiple operations, the nominal value of the bills over the cycle time is $N \times V(n)$, wherein $V(n)$ is the average value of each bill. t is equal to T/G, so all bills to be paid are NG/T, and that for one year is $360/T$.

If a dynamic discount is implemented, the payment will be realized dynamically before the payment deadline G, and the realized discount is both a gain for the buyer and a loss for the supplier. However, the early payment of the buyer will result in a financial cost, that is, the cost of funds for early payment. So for the buyer, the gains are Π_b = discount - capital cost; for the supplier, the gains are Π_s = capital cost savings - discount. After the supplier agrees to the buyer's EPP, the parties will determine the daily discount rate and the early payment time. The early payment time is $Ep(t) = G - t$. Assuming a daily discount rate of $dd(n,t)$ and a determined early payment time of t, the value of the discount paid by the buyer to the supplier is as follows:

$$dv(n,t) = v(n) \times \left(1 - dd(n,t) \times Ep(t)\right)$$

The maximum discounted price paid by the buyer to the supplier during the bill cycle time is as follows:

$$Nv(n) \times (1 - dd(n,t) \times Ep(t))$$

If the rate of early payment of the bill cycle *n* at time *t* is considered as *Θ(n,t)*, the total gains obtained by the buyer through the discount in one year is as follows:

$$\text{Discount} = \sum_{n=1}^{\frac{360}{T}} \sum_{t=1}^{G} \Theta(n,t) \times Nv(n,t) \times dd(n,t) \times Ep(t)$$

The gains obtained by the supplier from the buyer's early payment are:

$$fs(n,t) = dv(n,t) \times r_s \times Ep(t)$$

The total capital cost savings for one year are:

$$\text{Capital saved} = r_s \times \sum_{n=1}^{\frac{360}{T}} \sum_{t=1}^{G} DNV(n,t) \times Ep(t)$$

For buyers, the implementation of dynamic discounts requires a large amount of liquidity, and the use of capital necessarily involves costs, which may include both the opportunity cost of funds and the financing cost of funds. The opportunity cost of funds is the sunk cost or other costs incurred by the funds, which means that once the own funds are invested in dynamic discounts, they cannot be used in other areas. Assuming that the opportunity cost of funds is y_l, the total opportunity cost of funds will be liq × y_l. In addition to the opportunity cost of funds, when liquidity is not available, the buyer will incur financing cost $dv(n,t) \times r_b \times Ep(t)$. Assuming that *al (n.t)* is the difference between the liquidity owned by the buyer and the value of the discount that has occurred at point *t* of the bill cycle *n*, the buyer's financing cost will be

$$fc(n,t)=\begin{cases}0\text{当}al(n,t)-dv(n,t)\geq 0\\ dv(n,t)\times r_b\times Ep(t)\end{cases}$$

At this point, the buyer's total cost of funds for one year will be:

$$\text{Total cost of funds}=\sum_{n=1}^{\frac{360}{T}}\sum_{t=1}^{G}fc(n,t)+liq\times y_l$$

Dynamic discounting also involves the issue of discount rates. Assuming that the buyer finances the discount amount entirely through short-term debt, the minimum discount rate should ensure that the gains obtained by the supplier are greater than the cost of the discount, that is:

$$v\times(1-dd\times Ep)\times r_s\times Ep-v\times dd\times Ep\geq 0,\text{so}$$

$$dd_{\min}=\frac{r_s}{(1+r_s\times Ep)}$$

Similarly, the maximum discount rate should ensure that the buyer's gains are greater than the corresponding cost, that is:

$$v\times dd\times Ep-v\times(1-dd\times Ep)\times r_b\times Ep\geq 0,\text{so}$$

$$dd_{\max}=\frac{r_b}{(1+r_b\times Ep)}$$

It can be seen that the larger the difference between dd_{min} and dd_{max}, the more is room for judgment between buyers and sellers, and the higher is the room for dynamic discounts. To shorten the cash-to-cash cycle, upstream and downstream enterprises need to carefully consider their respective costs of funds, make reasonable decisions on the discount period and discount rate for purchase orders, and accelerate cash flow.

2.4.3 Demica's Dynamic Discount Service

Founded in 1990 and headquartered in London, UK, Demica Limited ("Demica") is a world-renowned provider of supply chain finance services that specifically provides working capital solutions for medium and large companies and banks. Its service platform of supply chain finance can run accounts receivable, inventory, and other asset-backed financial programs, and manage invoices one by one, accounts receivable securitization, invoice discounting functions, and supply chain financing for large enterprises. Its accounts receivable financing program allows multinational enterprises to achieve financing based on accounts receivable, determine qualified accounts receivable for financing, and maintain separate records, management reports, and financing calculations for each account receivable. It also offers supply chain financing solutions that enable clients to extend intraday accounts payable and obtain early payment discounts from suppliers, as well as enable suppliers obtain lower-cost financing and improve their profit margins. Demica's dynamic discount service platform connects large clients with small and medium-sized suppliers, making it easy for large clients that hold large amounts of cash to allow suppliers to choose dynamic discount options and pay them in advance. This reduces purchase costs for large clients on the one hand and facilitates small and medium-sized suppliers to obtain funds in a timely manner and accelerate cash flow on the other hand.

Demica's dynamic discount management is uniquely characterized by dynamic discount service based on billing period management. In other words, Demica not only provides the trading platform for dynamic discount management but is also able to propose optimized solutions and services based on billing period management. Based on this, suppliers can propose their expected level of working capital and the corresponding period, and Demica is able to promptly and effectively indicate when and at what discount rate dynamic discounts should be applied based on the determined working capital level and period (see Fig. 2.10). Besides, Demica combines dynamic discounting with supply chain financing in an effective manner. Once the request for dynamic discount and the corresponding discount rate is made and confirmed by the upstream small and medium-sized suppliers, Demica can also help its downstream clients to purchase the upstream products or services at a certain discounted price by connecting them with investors or financial institutions for financing.

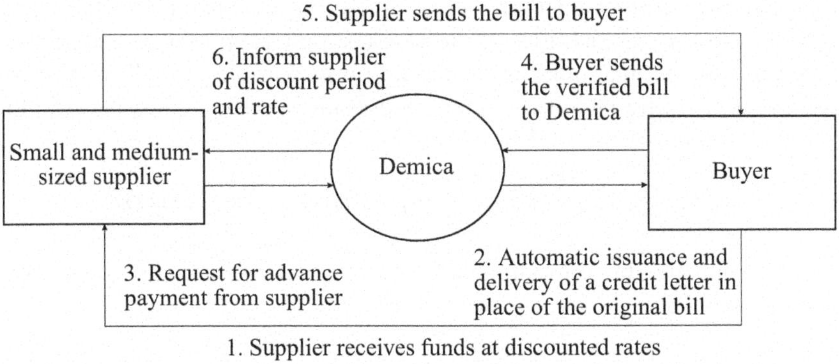

Fig. 2.10 Demica dynamic discount flowchart

2.5 Modified CCCC and End-to-End Supply Chain Finance

2.5.1 Definition of Modified CCCC

With more and more enterprises experiencing working capital shortages and liquidity shortages, it is becoming more difficult to obtain financing solely from external sources, so new tools should be put into use urgently for supply chain operations. Advance payment is one of the most key solutions to address the shortage of funds for SMEs. However, previous measurements of cash-to-cash cycle did not take into account advance payment, an element that plays a very crucial role in supply chain operations and services (Talonpoika et al., 2014). The modified cash-to-cash cycle incorporates advance payments into the calculation and management of the cash-to-cash cycle, thus providing a comprehensive view of the cash flow position and the efficiency of operations. The modified cash-to-cash cycle is calculated as follows:

$$mCCC = DIH + DSO - DPO - DAO,$$

Wherein, DAO (days advanced outstanding) = Amount advanced/ Sales × 100%

Similarly, when the cash-to-cash cycle is extended to the whole supply chain process, advance payments should also be included in the consideration of the CCCC. In other words, the modified CCCC is equal to the inventory at each link of the whole supply chain plus the accounts receivable at the final link, minus the accounts payable as well as advance payments at the initial links. Under a supply chain system consisting of (1) supplier, (2) processor, and (3) client:

$$mCCCC = DIH_1 + DIH_2 + DIH_3 + DSO_3 - DPO_1 - DAO_1$$

Based on the above-modified CCCC, the cost of funds for the whole supply chain is:

$$TC = INV \times \left[(1+c)^{d1} - 1\right] + AR \times \left[(1+c)^{d2} - 1\right] - AP \times \left[(1+c)^{d3} - 1\right] - AE \times \left[(1+c)^{d4} - 1\right]$$

Wherein, *INV* is days of inventory, *AR* is days of accounts receivable, *AP* is days of accounts payable, *AE* is days of advance payments, *c* is annualized interest rate on funds, *d1* = DIH/365, and *d2* = DSO/365, *d3* = DPO/365.

Efficient supply chain management is about achieving zero of mCCCC and minimizing total cost of funds. Achieving this goal requires intensive management in the following aspects (Randall & Theodore Farris, 2009): the first is to decrease days of inventory held in the whole supply chain, that is to minimize inventory from the perspective of the whole supply chain. The second is to turn client-side inventory into upstream-side inventory, thereby achieving a push-type timely delivery. The third is to reduce the days of accounts receivable across the supply chain. The fourth is to expand advance payments throughout the supply chain. Clearly, from the perspective of the modified CCCC, how to expand advance payments becomes a key factor in optimizing the industrial supply chain as well as accelerating working capital throughout the chain. To achieve this goal, solutions should to be sought from a perspective of end-to-end supply chain finance.

2.5.2 End-to-End Supply Chain Finance

End-to-end supply chain finance means that not only is the business of supply chain finance the financing in invoicing or product acceptance stage after the agreement on sale and purchase, but it also extends to the whole process of supply chain operation from the beginning of sourcing to the final payment.

Based on the time of the occurrence of supply chain finance (see Fig. 2.11), end-to-end supply chain finance business can be divided into sourcing finance, pre-shipment finance, in-transit finance, and post-shipment finance. Sourcing finance is a relatively special type of financial behavior, because, strictly speaking, no actual transaction is taking place between buyers and sellers at this point. This finance is performed on suppliers or their upstream clients in a bid to stabilize or develop strategic suppliers or optimize supply chain operations. Obviously, sourcing financing is based entirely on the trust partnership formed between buyers and sellers in long-term transactions, and is therefore relatively the riskiest. Once this trust relationship collapses or is challenged, the flow of funds may be disrupted, leading to increased risk. Pre-shipment finance allows suppliers to obtain funds from financial institutions based on buyers' purchase orders to meet their working capital needs before the products are shipped. This type of finance relies on purchase orders rather than bills and, therefore, has a higher credit risk. Pre-shipment finance is also based on the trust relationship formed between buyers and sellers. In-transit finance allows borrowers to obtain loans from financial institutions, and the loans are based on products or inventory in transit or in the course of

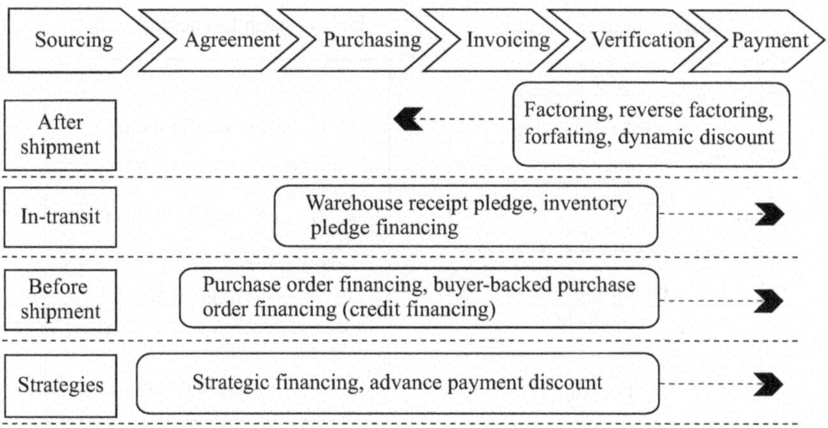

Fig. 2.11 End-to-end supply chain finance by time dimension

other logistics services. The risk control of in-transit finance is based on the products in logistics activities; therefore, the credit risk of this type of finance is weaker than that of pre-shipment finance and the interest rate is usually lower. Post-shipment finance allows borrowers to obtain working capital from financial institutions based on accounts receivable. This type of supply chain finance relies on bills, shipping orders, bills of lading, and so on, so the risk is also lower than that of pre-shipment finance and in-transit finance.

According to the availability of collateral (see Fig. 2.12), supply chain finance business can also be divided into arm's-length finance and relationship finance. Arm's-length finance is based on verifiable information or tangible collateral (such as bills, purchase orders, inventory, etc.), and, besides, it is regulated by laws. That is, in case of failure to perform the abovementioned acts, the corresponding rights can be reclaimed through laws. Therefore, the credit risk of arm's-length finance is more easily to be assessed from the angle of financial institutions. In contrast, relationship finance relies on a trust relationship established between the buyers and sellers, rather than a binding contractual relationship. Therefore, there is no tangible collateral under this finance as a guarantee for risk control. Usually such finance service providers are participants of the supply chain operations or platform service providers, who fully understand the credit status, transaction history, and supply chain operation capabilities of the

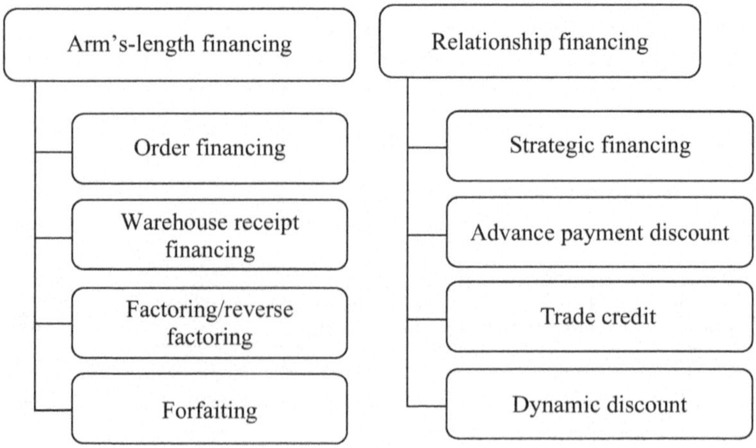

Fig. 2.12 End-to-end supply chain finance by collateral availability

borrowers. With this information, the lenders are able to assess the credit levels of the borrowers more accurately and thus make financing decisions.

2.5.3 End-to-End Supply Chain Finance Products

(1) Supply Chain Finance in Sourcing Stage

The main financial services in this phase include strategic financing and advance payment discount. Strategic financing is a kind of financial behavior for maintaining a good buyer-seller relationship in which one party offers funds to support the strategic investments or to enhance the competitiveness of products or business of counterparty. Strictly speaking, there is no actual purchase and sale between the buyer and the seller at this stage, but a long-term and stable partnership is formed, and a high level of trust is developed for each other. In this context, one party supports its partner's strategic investment or competitiveness by giving financial assistance to its counterparty, with the aim of obtaining priority in regards of the counterparty's competitive products or distribution support in the future, as well as further stabilizing and developing the strategic partnership (see Fig. 2.13). For instance, if a buyer wants to have priority in purchasing competitive technologies or products in the future, it may financially support the supplier's technological upgrade and thus lock in future orders. This type of financial product is used to secure future orders, production, or sales support. Under this type of finance, the credit provider and fund provider are the buyer, and the service is offered to the buyer's upstream and downstream partners.

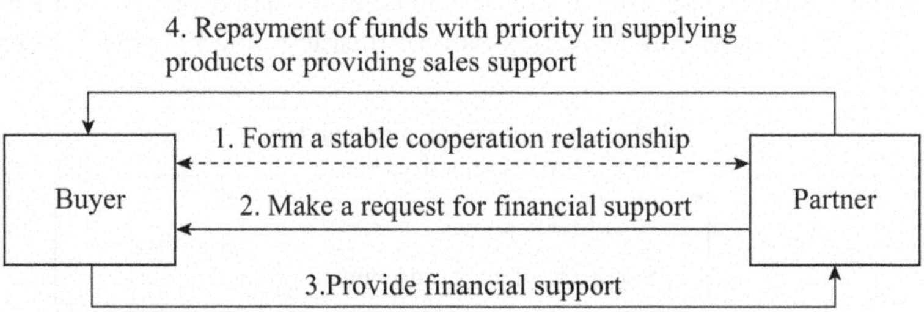

Fig. 2.13 Strategic financing

Advanced payment discount means that the buyer pays money in advance to the supplier in order to gain a discount at delivery in the future. The supplier's discount commitment provides an incentive for the buyer to pay in advance, thus relieving the supplier's working capital pressure. In turn, the buyer gains assurance of product supply by paying in advance (see Fig. 2.14). Strictly speaking, the buyer and the seller have not yet formed an actual purchase agreement at the advanced payment discount stage, but rather have entered into an intentional order to receive preferential pricing or operational support in the future. Advance payment discount differs from strategic finance as follows: in strategic finance, the buyer and the seller secure future orders, production, or sales support, and so is an expectation of future behavior, while advance payment discount secures intentional orders and are relatively more specific in its security. In addition, the financing objectives of the two are not exactly the same. The purpose of strategic finance is broader and can be considered as either a strategic action (e.g., enhancing the operational capacity of an enterprise) or a specific operational business (e.g., order locking), while the purpose of advance payment discount is to obtain supplies at a certain discount. The similarity between the two is that it is always the buyer who providers the credit and fund.

(2) Supply Chain Finance in Pre-shipment Phase

The main supply chain finance business in the pre-shipment phase mainly includes purchase order financing and buyer-backed purchase order financing. Purchase order financing is a kind of business in which a small or a medium-sized supplier applies to a financial institution, before the product is shipped, for funds required to purchase raw materials or production based on a buyer's purchase order, and the financial institution decides whether to provide funds to the supplier based on its credit level (see Fig. 2.15). Obviously, in this type of business, the provider of credit

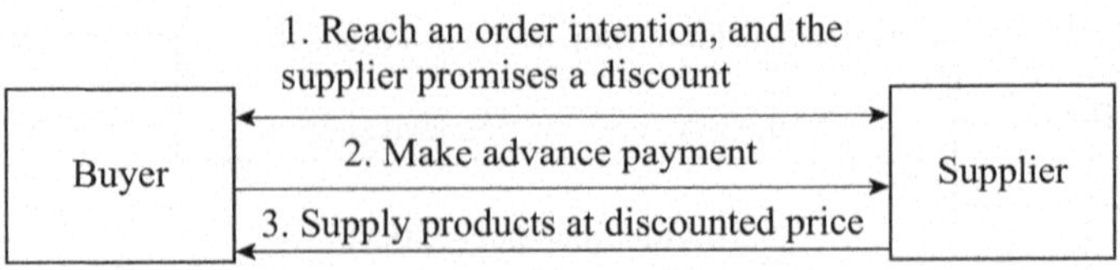

Fig. 2.14 Advanced payment discount

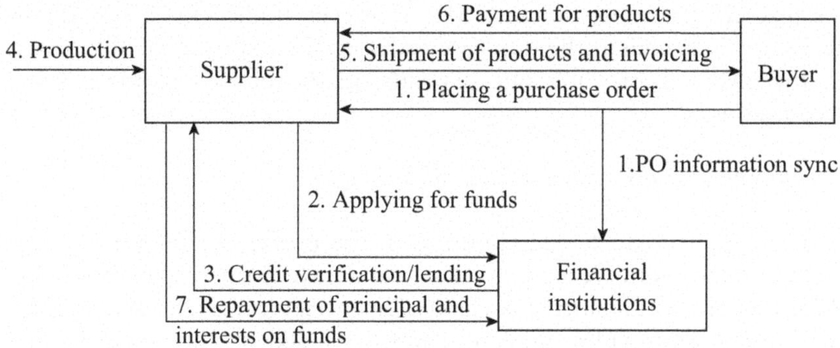

Fig. 2.15 Order financing

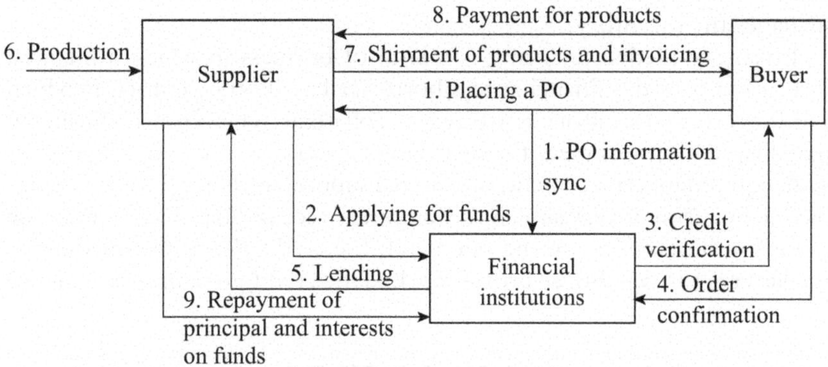

Fig. 2.16 Buyer-backed order financing

guarantee is the supplier, the provider of funds is a financial institution such as a bank, and the beneficiary of the financing is the supplier.

Buyer-backed purchase order financing, also known as credit financing, is also based on the buyer's purchase order and is provided by a financial institution to a supplier for the purposes of solving the supplier's financial needs in preparing products or production, or meeting the supplier's requirement for timely and full access to sales funds. It differs from pure purchase order financing as its credit provider is the buyer, not the supplier itself (see Fig. 2.16). Usually, in the absence of a buyer guarantee, the interest rate depends on the credit check and the credit rating assessed by the financial institution for the SME. However, under buyer-backed purchase order financing, the purchase order is initiated by a credible buyer, so the SME's borrowing rate depends on the buyer's reputation and credit rating.

(3) Supply Chain Finance in In-Transit Stage

The supply chain finance business in the process of shipping mainly includes warehouse receipt financing and inventory pledge financing. Warehouse receipt financing is a kind of financial business in which a financial institution provides funds to a supplier based on the pledged warehouse receipts in the warehouse. This type of business is secured by the warehouse receipts for inventory in operation (see Fig. 2.17). The provider of the credit guarantee is the third-party warehouse manager who manages the inventory.

Inventory pledge financing is a kind of business in which a financial institution provides financing to a borrower based on inventory, in which the borrower's inventory is treated as collateral. This form of financing may help enterprises meet their working capital needs for capacity expansion, equipment replacement, or material supply (see Fig. 2.18). Inventory pledge financing is very similar to warehouse receipt financing, but has the following differences: on the one hand, the credit guarantee provider of the latter is the warehouse provider, while the credit guarantee provider of

Fig. 2.17 Warehouse receipt financing

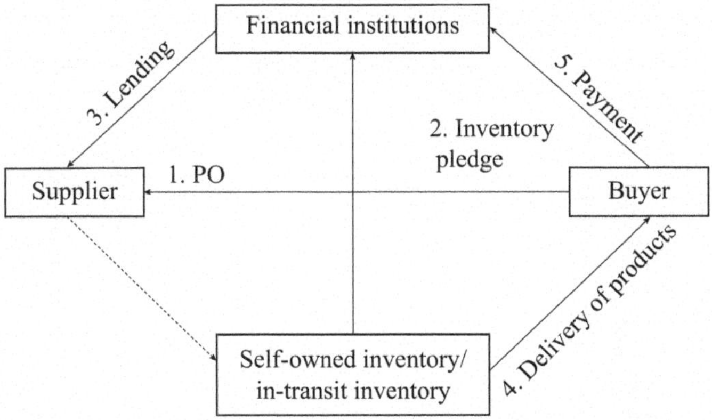

Fig. 2.18 Inventory pledge financing

the former is the borrower; on the other hand, the latter takes warehouse receipt as collateral, while the collateral of the former has a broader meaning, which may be the inventory formed in various forms of production (such as raw materials, inventory of semifinished goods, inventory of finished goods) and may also be the products in the way of logistics services (in-transit inventory).

(4) Supply Chain Finance in Post-shipment Stage

The post-shipment stage means that the products have been delivered from the supplier to the buyer and also invoice and bills of lading have been formed, thus the buyer and seller entering into a payable-receivable relationship. Based on the debt and claim relationship, an array of supply chain finance businesses has been generated, including standard factoring, reverse factoring, forfaiting, dynamic discounting, and other products. Factoring, also known as collection agency, is a comprehensive financial approach in which the seller assigns the present or future accounts receivable arising from the product sales/service contract concluded with the buyer to a factor, who provides a series of services such as financing, buyer credit assessment, sales account management, credit risk guarantee, and account collection (see Fig. 2.19). The collateral of supply chain finance business under the form of factoring is the commercial paper formed by the buyers and the seller; the provider of credit guarantee is the supplier;

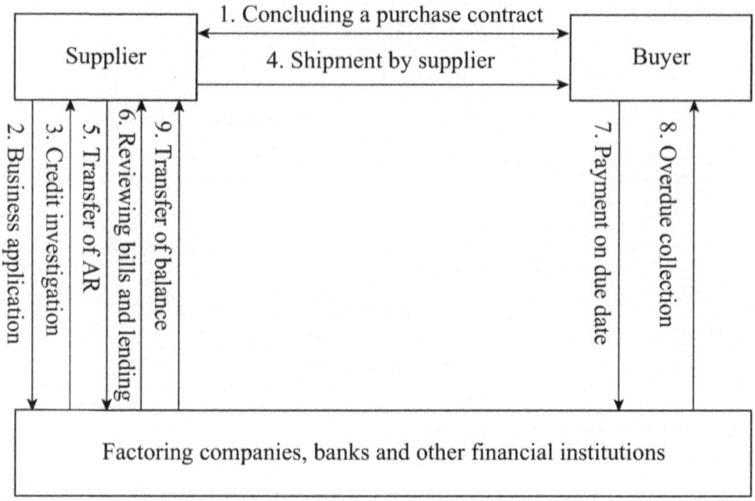

Fig. 2.19 Standard factoring

the financing provider is the financial institution; and the beneficiary of supply chain finance is the supplier.

Reverse factoring, also known as buyer's factoring, is a kind of factoring where the debtor (obligor) initiates the business application (see Fig. 2.20). Under the reverse factoring, differing from standard factoring, the factor performs risk assessment based on the buyer (core enterprise) rather than the supplier. In addition, since the factor knows the buyer better, it can select those accounts receivable for financing that the buyer has approved in advance to indicate agreement to pay, greatly reducing risk the factor bearing while making financing less costly for the supplier. Thus, in reverse factoring, the collateral for financing is the commercial paper provided by the buyer (core enterprise); the provider of credit guarantee is the buyer; and the beneficiary of supply chain finance is the supplier backed by the buyer.

Forfaiting, a supply chain finance product closely related to export trade, is a nonrecourse buyout by a bank or other financial institutions from an exporter of accounts receivable arising from the export of goods or services (see Fig. 2.21). Compared with other trade financing, the most significant feature of forfaiting is nonrecourse. In other words, by handling forfaiting, exporters can obtain 100% convenient and fast financing

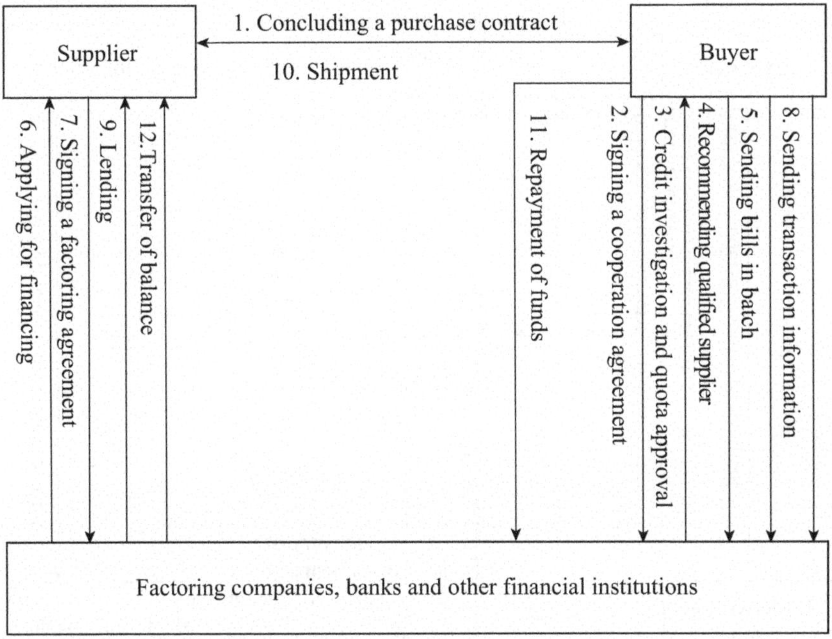

Fig. 2.20 Reverse factoring

from a bank for improving their asset-liability ratio without taking up the bank's credit lines. At the same time, exporters can also use it to effectively avoid interest rate risk, exchange rate risk, credit risk, and other risks. The differences between forfaiting and factoring are as follows: forfaiting is based on letters of credit, while factoring is a settlement without letters of credit; forfaiting bears more interbank risks, while factoring bears the risk of buyers' credit; factoring is often a coordinated service, including factoring account escrow and account collection, while forfaiting is purely involving financing.

As mentioned before, dynamic discount is a kind of transaction activity featuring financial attributes, in which the buyer can gain a dynamical price discount if it pays in advance within the agreed billing period, thus, both the buyer and the seller could benefit. Under the negotiated early payment period and the discounted price, the buyer can apply for financing from the financial institution to pay the supplier in advance, and, after a certain period of time, repays the funds to the financial institution

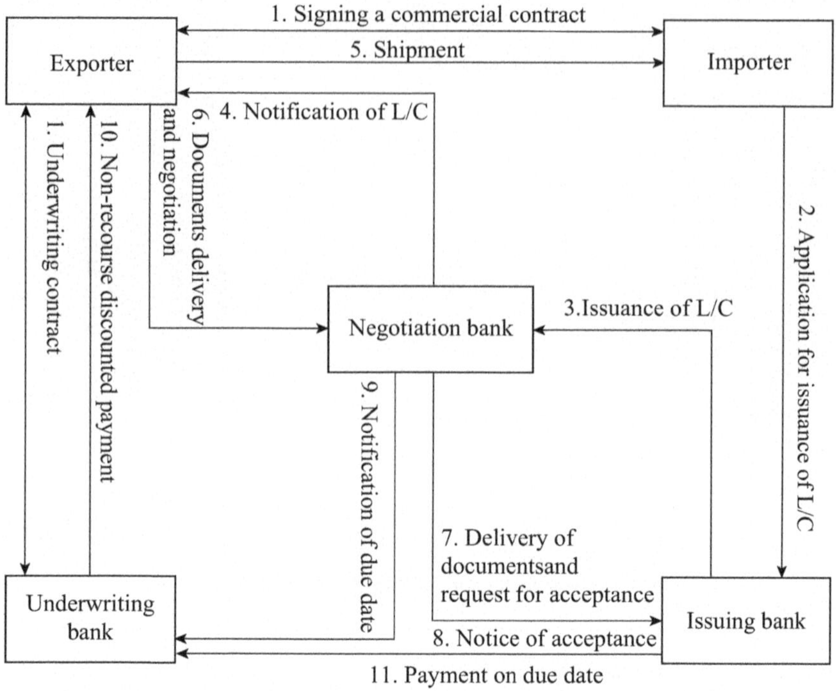

Fig. 2.21 Forfaiting

(see Fig. 2.22). In this case, the buyer's decision to apply for financing or not depends on the difference between the interest on the funds and the discount of early payment. If the discount is greater than the interest on the funds, the early payment through financing will be a better option. The provider of credit guarantee in this business is the supplier; the provider of financial benefits is the supplier if no financial institution is involved, or both the supplier and the financial institution if the financial institution is involved; the beneficiary is the buyer.

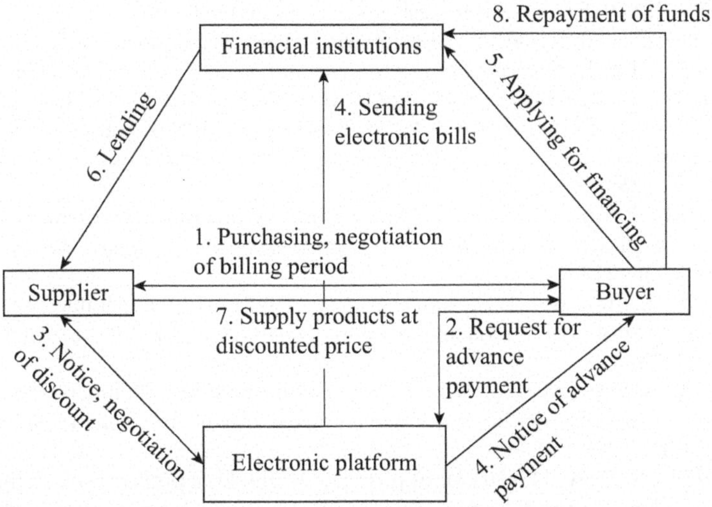

Fig. 2.22 Supply chain finance based on dynamic discount

References

Boardman, C. M., & Ricci, K. J. (1985). Defining selling terms: Economics of delaying payment–how does your industry compare? *Credit & Financial Management, 87*(3), 31–33.

Christopher, M., & Holweg, M. (2011). "Supply Chain 2.0": Managing supply chains in the era of turbulence. *International Journal of Physical Distribution & Logistics Management, 41*(1), 63–82.

Farris, M. T., II. (1996). Utilizing inventory flow models with suppliers. *Journal of Business Logistics, 17*(1), 35.

Gallinger, G. (1997). The current and quick ratios: Do they stand up to scrutiny. *Business Credit, 99*(5), 22–25.

Ganesan, S., Brown, S. P., Mariadoss, B. J., & Ho, H. (2010). Buffering and amplifying effects of relationship commitment in business-to-business relationships. *Journal of Marketing Research, 47*(2), 361–373.

Gelsomino, L. M., Mangiaracina, R., Perego, A., & Tumino, A. (2016). Supply chain finance: Modelling a dynamic discounting programme. *Journal of Advanced Management Science, 4*(4), 283–291.

Hofmann, E., & Kotzab, H. (2010). A supply chain-oriented approach of working capital management. *Journal of Business Logistics, 31*(2), 305–330. https://doi.org/10.1002/j.2158-1592.2010.tb00154.x

Hong, S.-J. (2015). Is cash-to-cash cycle appropriate to measure supply chain performance? Revenue In V. Kachitvichyanukul, K. Sethanan, & P. Golinska-Dawson (Eds.), *Toward sustainable operations of supply chain and logistics systems* (pp. 21–36). https://doi.org/10.1007/978-3-319-19006-8_2

Jain, J., Dangayach, G., Agarwal, G., & Banerjee, S. (2010). Supply chain management: Literature review and some issues. *Journal of Studies on Manufacturing, 1*(1), 11–25.

Kotabe, M., & Mol, M. J. (2009). Outsourcing and financial performance: A negative curvilinear effect. *Journal of Purchasing and Supply Management, 15*(4), 205–213.

Lancaster, C., Stevens, J. L., & Jennings, J. A. (1998). Corporate liquidity and the significance of earnings versus cash flow. *Journal of Applied Business Research, 14*, 27–38.

Lin, F.-R., & Shaw, M. J. (1998). Reengineering the order fulfillment process in supply chain networks. *International Journal of Flexible Manufacturing Systems, 10*(3), 197–229.

Mateen, A., & More, D. (2013). Applying TOC thinking process tools in managing challenges of supply chain finance: A case study. *International Journal of Services and Operations Management, 15*(4), 389. https://doi.org/10.1504/IJSOM.2013.054882

Mentzer, J. T., DeWitt, W., Keebler, J. S., Min, S., Nix, N. W., Smith, C. D., & Zacharia, Z. G. (2001). Defining supply chain management. *Journal of Business Logistics, 22*(2), 1–25.

Moss, J. D., & Stine, B. (1993). Cash conversion cycle and firm size: A study of retail firms. *Managerial Finance, 19*(8), 25–34.

Randall, W. S., & Theodore Farris, M. (2009). Supply chain financing: Using cash-to-cash variables to strengthen the supply chain. *International Journal of Physical Distribution & Logistics Management, 39*(8), 669–689. https://doi.org/10.1108/09600030910996314

REL Consultancy. (2005). REL 2005 Working Capital Survey. http://www.rel-consult.com/CFO

Ross & Jaffe, J. (2005). Corporate Finance, International Edition, 7th ed, McGraw-Hill, New York.

Rossetti, C., & Choi, T. Y. (2005). On the dark side of strategic sourcing: Experiences from the aerospace industry. *Academy of Management Perspectives, 19*(1), 46–60.

Schilling, G. (1996). Working capital's role in maintaining corporate liquidity. *TMA Journal, 16*(5), 4–7.

Sheridan, J. H. (2000). Now it's a job for the CEO. *Industry Week/IW, 249*(6), 22–27.

Slater, D. (2000). By the numbers. *CIO Magazine, 13*(10), 38.

Soenen, L. A. (1993). Cash conversion cycle and corporate profitability. *Journal of Cash Management, 13*, 53–53.

Stewart, G. (1995). Supply chain performance benchmarking study reveals keys to supply chain excellence. *Logistics Information Management, 8*(2), 38–44. https://doi.org/10.1108/09576059510085000

Talonpoika, A.-M., Monto, S., Pirttilä, M., & Kärri, T. (2014). Modifying the cash conversion cycle: Revealing concealed advance payments. *International Journal of Productivity and Performance Management, 63*(3), 341–353. https://doi.org/10.1108/IJPPM-12-2012-0130

Theodore Farris, M., & Hutchison, P. D. (2003). Measuring cash-to-cash performance. *The International Journal of Logistics Management, 14*(2), 83–92.

Timme, S. G., & Williams-Timme, C. (2003). The real cost of holding inventory. *Supply Chain Management Review, 7*(4), 30–37.

Tsai, M.-C., Lai, K., Lloyd, A. E., & Lin, H.-J. (2012). The dark side of logistics outsourcing–unraveling the potential risks leading to failed relationships. *Transportation Research Part E: Logistics and Transportation Review, 48*(1), 178–189.

Walz. (1999). On-line lecture. http://www.trinty.edu/dwalz/3301f99/sld160.htm

Yaqin D., Wenjie W., & Jiahao L. (2013). Supply chain financing coordination based on cash-to-cash cycle strategy[J]. *Finance and Accounting Monthly, 22*, 118–120. (in Chinese).

CHAPTER 3

Intelligent Supply Chain and Tech-Enabled Supply Chain Finance

3.1 Introduction

In recent years, along with the emergence of the Internet, IoT, cloud computing, big data, AI, and other technologies, the trend of supply chain operations and intelligent supply chain finance has vigorously led the development of supply chain. Given that the introduction of end-to-end supply chain finance is based on the full-process and seamless supply chain operation services, so any failure in the management of supply chain links, participants, or activities will pose a serious threat to the smooth development of end-to-end supply chain finance. Nowadays, the trend of supply chain and supply chain finance evolution is putting more and more demands on intelligence, as, on the one hand, the changing environment makes supply chain activities increasingly complex. Enterprises have long moved beyond the era of "atomistic" competition and have become active participants in supply chain networks that cover multiple businesses and relationships (Lambert & Cooper, 2000; Ben-Daya et al., 2017). With the global fragmentation of production, many supply chains are beginning to go national, or even global, and therefore the risks exposures have further expanded (Butner, 2010). Clients are also becoming more demanding in terms of product customization, product pricing, and service quality (Christopher, 2016). This, coupled with rapid technological changes and upgrade, has resulted in tighter production, shorter product cycles, and higher complexity in many industries (Levi et al., 2003). In order to

H. Song, *Smart Supply Chain Finance*,
https://doi.org/10.1007/978-981-16-5997-3_3

survive in such a complex environment, both enterprises and supply chains are required to build their resilience and risk mitigation capabilities and maintain the overall structural flexibility to quickly respond to the challenges posed by environmental uncertainty (Ben-Daya et al., 2017). All of these inevitably translate into higher demands for supply chains and the "intelligence" of supply chain finance (Butner, 2010). On the other hand, information and communications technologies (ICT) have a huge impact on the management behaviors of enterprises in the supply chain. For instance, along with the evolution of information technology, semiconductor technology, and other analytic technologies, modern supply chains start to take advantage of advanced technologies and the ecologic cooperation concept of "value co-creation" to achieve the seamless integration of data, information, physical objects, products, and business processes (Schuster, 2007), which allows enterprises to achieve a state of "intelligence" by managing their production and life in a more fine and dynamic way (Pan Honghua, 2012). This shapes an "intelligent supply chain" with proactive analysis and response functions similar to those of the human brain (Wu et al., 2016). The factories equipped with smart devices, as an example, can collaborate and manage orders in real time with global teams through intelligent analytics and a dynamic order management system that spans the entire value chain (Hessman, 2013). Undoubtedly, enterprises are able to use their resources more efficiently when embedded in a supply chain with intelligent storage, smart analysis, automatic alert, and contingency functions, which contributes to ensuring the enterprises' own flexibility and resilience capabilities, as well as maintaining the supply chain's precision and sensitivity. As a result, not only does the productivity of the enterprises increase (Wu et al., 2016), but the ability to control financial risk in the supply chain also increases.

Under the aforesaid context, this chapter will, first, from theoretical perspective, elaborate the definition of supply chain intelligence and its key elements. Based on the understanding and role of intelligence, this chapter will then explore the role of modern ICTs in enabling the asset side and the capital side in the operations of supply chain finance, as well as the overall framework for realizing intelligent supply chain finance. Given that framework and in combination with intelligent supply chain and financial services of CSJ and Xianyi supply chains, this chapter will analyze the enabling process of ICTs.

3.2 Intelligence of Supply Chain and Relevant Elements

Definition of Supply Chain Intelligence

With the development of ICTs, the intelligence of supply chain has increasingly become the key factor to industrial development. In academic researches, there are an array of terms related to intelligent supply chain, including "electronic supply chain management" (eSCM) (Le Tan et al., 2017; Liu et al., 2016; Akyuz & Rehan, 2009), "Business environmental intelligence" (Pinheiro et al., 2018; Lee et al., 2018; Koch et al., 2010), "IoT" (Tu et al., 2018; Lee et al., 2015; Ben-Daya et al., 2017; Fleisch, 2010; Papert & Pflaum, 2017), "industrial Internet of Thing" (Mouratidis & Diamantopoulou, 2018; Pease et al., 2018; Tao et al., 2017; Jeschke et al., 2017), "cyber-physical systems" (CPS) (Monostori, 2014; Lee et al., 2018; Babiceanu & Seker, 2016), "smart factory" (Lucke et al., 2008; Wang et al., 2016; Radziwon et al., 2014; Kang et al., 2016; Chen et al., 2018), "cloud manufacturing" (Fisher et al., 2018; Zhang et al., 2014; Wu et al., 2013), "big data analysis" (Chen et al., 2018; Wang et al., 2016; Yin & Kaynak, 2015; Lee et al., 2014), and "cloud computing" (Thoben et al., 2017; Lu, 2017; Wu et al., 2016; Low et al., 2011). In general, the development of modern ITCs has led to a paradigm shift in management in many areas, including supply chain management (Ben-Daya et al., 2017). For example, electronic commerce facilitates online transactions for traditional enterprises, while electronic supply chains go further than "transactions" by emphasizing the integration of supply chain operation processes (Akyuz & Rehan, 2009; Wu et al., 2016). Moreover, the IoT, a new information technology with a multibillion-dollar market potential (Gartner, 2014), further advances the integration of supply chains, connecting information systems and physical objects of enterprises (Ashton, 2009; Fleisch, 2010; Papert & Pflaum, 2017). By embedding physical objects with specific AIDC technologies, such as RFID tags, telematics modules, or sensor tags, physical objects are able to express themselves and act as information senders. As a result, physical objects have intelligent features, recognition, localization, communication, sensing, and logical thinking. The "passive" physical objects becomes "active" ones (Atzori et al., 2010; Haass et al., 2015; Papert et al., 2016; López et al., 2011; Thiesse & Buckel, 2015; Papert & Pflaum, 2017). The "communication" in the supply chain scenarios has also been raised to a new level, realizing the communication between "people" and "things" and independent coordination between "things and things." These interactions can be stored in devices or transferred among different entities in the supply chain (Ben-Daya et al., 2017). The concept of "Modern IoT" is now further enriched by the optimization and innovation of technologies such as GPS devices, smartphones, social networks, cloud computing, and data analysis. The common IoT is centered on "connection," but "objects" do not actually have "initiative." By adding a larger communication network to the "objects" and supplementing it with "brain response center" such as big data and cloud computing, the cyber-physical systems (CPS) are born. In reality, IoT provides a platform required to connect sensors, actuators, and production equipment (terminals) to CPS (Ben-Daya et al., 2017). CPS consists of machines, storage systems, and production equipment, in which the physical participants actively exchange information, trigger behaviors, and monitor each other through organic integration and deep collaboration of 3C (i.e., Computing, Communication, Control) technologies (Kagermann et al., 2013). In essence, CPS is equivalent to the industrial Internet, which is based on sensors, processors, actuators, information networks, cloud computing, and big data to map the real physical world into a virtual digital model. Through big data analysis based on advanced algorithms, the optimal decision data is fed back to the physical world so as to optimize the operational efficiency and improve the safety level of the physical world (Li et al., 2012). However, the application of CPS is not limited to industry, but may also be expanded to other production and life fields such as transportation, medical, agriculture, energy, and so on. Therefore, in terms of the scope of application, CPS covers the industrial Internet. Moreover, in the CPS or industrial Internet context, IoT platforms usually use cloud computing functions in external data centers, which led to the creation of the supply chain concept (Ben-Daya et al., 2017) and the development of smart factories in the industry 4.0. Of course, thanks to the gradual development of the above technologies and the gradual intelligence of "objects," our smart environment has been formed. A smart environment is an electronic environment that has sensing and feedback to a person. In other words, the aforementioned sensors, actuators, displays, and various computational and analytic elements are seamlessly embedded in operations to support daily operational activities (Weiser, 1999), making it easier and more natural for people to use this information and the intelligence hidden in the network behind these devices.

Clearly, the technological development process not only links the above terms but also pushes the depth and breadth of the "connection": from isolated RFID applications to local IoTs with greater interconnection, to industrial Internet or CPS built with big data and cloud computing based on IoTs, thus driving the realization of cloud manufacturing in smart factories and defining a wider "smart environment" (Wu et al., 2016). Following this development process, supply chain "intelligence" may also be defined as a new commercial system for interconnections that extends isolated, local, and single-enterprise applications to supply chain–wide smart systems. In this course, the IoTs, smart devices, and smart infrastructure are the underlying foundation of this smart system. With the construction of the underlying foundation, it realizes the interconnection of all things in the supply chain (people, things, and information systems), the digitization of the whole supply chain process, and the visualization of the supply chain operations, thus promoting the intelligence of overall decision-making, improving the operational efficiency and response speed of the supply chain, and ultimately better serving clients.

To be specific, the intelligent supply chain is different from both the traditional value chain of enterprises and the previous supply chain (Lazzarini et al., 2001). The enterprise value chain was first proposed by Porter (1985), who pointed out that "each enterprise is a collection of activities that design, produce, market, deliver, and support products. All of these activities represent the way in which it uses the value chain....The value chain reveals the total value, including value activities and margins. Value activities are the activities carried out by the enterprise that have corporate and technical uniqueness and are the basis for the production of valuable products for buyers. Margins are the difference between the total value and the total costs of carrying out the value activities". For the purpose of realizing the margins, enterprises obviously need to organize and manage value activities reasonably and effectively. Crossing the limits of a single enterprise, supply chain is a process that gathers upstream and downstream enterprises, organizes transactions vertically, and completes value creation level by level. It aims at achieving high industry performance through reasonable coordination, organization, and management of commodity, transport, information, and fund flows between upstream and downstream enterprises. To fulfill this aim, it is necessary to divide the supply chain into five major processes (planning, purchasing, production, distribution, and refund), and to define, measure, and implement supply chain operations from the three levels of supply chain division, configuration, and process, thus forming the SCOR Model. On the basis of supply chain, intelligent supply chain greatly expands the system structure and scope. With the help of Internet, IoT, and other emerging ICTs, it enables interaction between multiple parties and creates value through organic organization and combination of various industrial stakeholders or industrial clusters and based on commodity, transport, information, fund, knowledge and talent flows. As is clear from the above descriptions, intelligent supply chain or network chain crosses the single vertical supply chain and presents the characteristics of collaboration of multiple related industries or multiple same-level participants, different industries, enterprises, or geographically diverse organizations undertaking the corresponding value creation and delivery process according to the service demands, and finally forming the systematic value. Therefore, these three different "chains" are not substitutes for each other, but three different levels of value creation. Value chain is the creation of value activities at the enterprise level, supply chain is the creation of value activities at the sector level, and intelligent supply chain is the creation of value activities at the industry level. And certainly, from this perspective, intelligent supply chain is impossible without a good construction of enterprise value chain and supply chain.

Structural of Intelligence

As the physical world is transforming into an information system with sensors and micro devices connected by cables or wireless networks, the business models predominantly based on static information architecture are now facing a number of challenges after the advent of new ways of creating client value (Bughin et al., 2010). The deep integration of the digital world and physical world is likely to revolutionize the global supply chain. However, despite the current consensus on the huge potential of "intelligence" and "smart" and the relevant technological elements to support their development, there still lacks consensus on how to construct the relevant systems and how to realize the value after its construction (López et al., 2012). After summarizing previous researches, Butner (2010) and Wu et al. (2016) identified six distinctive features that an intelligent supply chain should have:

1. Instrumented: The information in supply chain operations must be generated by automated or sensing devices (e.g., RFID and tags).

Lacking effective ICT will lead to no access to information in the supply chain. Therefore, it should be the first feature of intelligent supply chain.

2. Interconnected: All participants, assets, information systems, and businesses in supply chain must be highly connected. Intelligent supply chain aims to form interrelated and interdependent network relationships among different participants, different businesses, and different elements through ICTs. Therefore, interconnection is another feature of intelligent supply chain.
3. Intelligent: With the help of ICTs, it is possible to achieve large-scale optimization of decision-making and improve supply chain performance. Intelligent supply chain aims to optimize the decision-making process through the information integration realized by ICTs, and effectively guide the supply chain operation toward the direction of high efficiency and high competitiveness.
4. Automated: The supply chain business processes can be driven by information technology equipment, instead of inefficient resources, especially manual operations. Frequent manual intervention in the supply chain often results in inefficiencies, as it not only prolongs the response time of the supply chain but also increases moral hazards and the possibility of information asymmetry and opportunistic behaviors.
5. Integrated: Intelligent supply chain boosts collaboration among various participants, including joint decision-making, investment in public systems, and information co-sharing.
6. Innovative: Intelligent supply chain fuels innovation and creates new value by providing integrated solutions or meeting existing value claims in new ways.

Development Elements of "Intelligent" Supply Chain

Information, among all critical resources, still plays a key role in supply chain management, as supply chain performance is often reflected in real-time collaboration and complex integration activities (Wu et al., 2016). Definitely, intelligent supply chains create new value mainly by innovating business model, improving business processes and reducing associated costs and risks (Chui et al., 2010). In fact, the aim of intelligent supply chains is to produce more information, smarter decisions, better processes, and more high-quality products (Wu et al., 2016). After considering the structural features of intelligence and emphasizing the key role of information in the whole intelligent supply chain management, it can be concluded that the development of intelligent supply chain are mainly focused on five elements (Wu et al., 2016). The first element is information in supply chain. As a crucial element for achieving an intelligent supply chain (Meindl & Chopra, 2013), a large number of studies have explored the types of information, improvement of information quality, timeliness of information, speed of information transmission, information accessibility, and information risk and protection. The second element is IT, which is how information is obtained and applied. It includes how the IoT and the Internet are used throughout supply chain operations (Masciari, 2012; Zelbst et al., 2012). The third is automation of supply chain processes, that is, how exactly ICT changes the operational processes of the supply chain, replacing inefficient manual activities and optimizing supply chain processes. The fourth is advanced analysis, that is, how to use big data to analyze the issues in the supply chain and provide a basis for supply chain optimization decisions based on big data analysis. The last element is supply chain integration and innovation, that is, how to highly integrate IT, advanced analysis, and process automation to drive supply chain upgrades. This integration involves three levels, namely culture integration at the organizational level, solution integration at the strategic system level, and practice integration at the operational level (Vallet-Bellmunt & Rivera-Torres, 2013). In addition to integration, current research explores innovations in intelligent supply chains, that is, innovations in products/services and processes driven by a high degree of information technology integration, such as the high-degree integration of online and offline supply chains (Wu et al., 2016), as well as the creation of complex adaptive systems, and so on (Wycisk et al., 2008). In fact, the above five development elements encompass all structural features of intelligent supply chain. For example, IT includes hardware devices (instrumented) and virtual network connections (interconnected), while technologies related to advanced analysis (including big data, cloud computing, edge computing, etc.) facilitate the development of "intelligence," and information in supply chain is indeed a basic requirement for "intelligence" (Wu et al., 2016).

Information in Supply Chain

In terms of information management in the supply chain, information is the "meaningful data" that can be interpreted to support decision-making, rather than the "meaningless" data (Detlor, 2010). These "meaningful data" are the essential assets for supply chain management (Chopra & Meindl, 2013). The current researches on supply chain information management focus on the management of demand (or order) information in the supply chain (Kumar & Pugazhendhi, 2012). In dynamic environments involving uncertainty and disruption, demand information is critical to the overall operations of supply chain (Mithas et al., 2011; Wu et al., 2016). Further, visibility of demand information can help to shorten delivery cycles, reduce associated costs, and improve responsiveness and effectiveness of decision-making (Handfield & Nichols, 2002). Other information involved in supply chain operations includes inventory, cost, pricing, transport, location, capacity, quality, and technical information (Pedroso & Nakano, 2009). With the development of intelligent supply chain, a large number of devices generate huge amounts of sensor data (Loher, 2012), and the transformation of such data into useful information requires a lot of resources. Therefore, in order to create an efficient intelligent supply chain, enterprises should think about the efficiency and effectiveness of information, that is, "what information is required for the overall cooperative operation of supply chain, and what useful information can be input to the supply chain or to specific partners" (Holmberg, 2000; Handfield & Nichols, 2002). The lack of a clear definition and location of information makes it difficult to transmit information in the supply chain and actually also makes it impossible to transform the data backlog of various smart devices as well as sensor facilities into valuable information resources (Wu et al., 2016). The importance of information quality is emphasized by Wang and Strong (1996) and Lee (2002), who argued that the information quality should be evaluated in two aspects: intrinsic requirements and contextual requirements. Intrinsic requirements refer to the objective properties of the information itself, mainly including accuracy, timeliness, consistency, and completeness of the information. Contextual requirements refer to the context in which the high-quality information is observed and used, including relevancy, value-added, quantity, believability, accessibility, and reputation of the data. Analysis using low-quality information may cause significant losses to enterprises, so supply chain managers who rely on big data for decision-making should perform Total Quality Management (TQM) of the data and the information derived from the data analysis. Similarly, Pedroso and Nakano (2009) believed that good information should have right type (useful and valuable), high quality (accuracy), accurate timing of transmission, timely or real-time delivery, easy access, and controlled sharing and privacy protection. In addition, the management of information in the supply chain involves the information sharing. Information becomes more critical in environments where demand is more uncertain. Therefore, there are numerous studies that point out that information sharing is a key factor in driving supply chain performance (Cachon & Fisher, 2000). Through adequate sharing of information, upstream and downstream enterprises in the supply chain are able to coordinate their behavior and planning more effectively and, as a result, create more efficient logistics and information flows (Damiani et al., 2011). The development of information technology has gradually reduced the cost of information sharing. In fact, the more challenging issue now is the "redundancy" existing during information sharing in supply chain, which again puts emphasis on the issue of "quality" and "quantity" of information sharing (Handfield & Nichols, 2002; Liker & Choi, 2004).

Information Technology

Since the required information is identified, it is then necessary to determine how it will be accessed and used, which involves the configuration of IT, as, after all, IT plays a pillar role in facilitating the information flow in supply chain (Wu et al., 2016). Indeed, IT is a booster of effective supply chain management (Ross, 2016), which plays a key role in helping supply chain reduce the challenges and risks associated with environmental uncertainty (Ben-Daya et al., 2017). IT strongly influences the essence of the supply chain and the structural setup of the supply chain. Due to its outstanding contribution in improving communication, information access, and transfer between internal and external supply chain nodes, IT not only facilitates the integration of various supply chain processes within an enterprise but also accelerates the operational integration of the enterprise with external suppliers and clients (Ben-Daya et al., 2017). As a result, the various supply chain nodes are also able to make more effective decisions, which in turn could improve the overall operational performance of the supply chain. In the development of intelligent supply chains, IoT is a very important infrastructure for the underlying framework. IoT is a dynamic global network infrastructure based on standard and interoperable communication protocols. Physical and virtual "things" therein have identities, physical properties, and virtual personalities, and are seamlessly integrated into information networks through intelligent interfaces (Xu et al., 2014). In short, the IoT connects the corporate information systems and physical objects (Ashton, 2009; Fleisch, 2010; Papert & Pflaum,

2017), achieving the integration of "virtual things" (information networks) and "physical things" (specific devices and specific contexts, etc.) and making them interact efficiently. IoT can be called a technological revolution in computing and communication that realizes our desire to communicate with anything, at any time, at any place, and through any medium (Atzori et al., 2010). The construction of IoT architecture requires the support of basic technologies and applications such as RFID technology, wireless sensor networks (WSN), middleware, cloud computing, and IoT application software (Lee & Lee, 2015). Specifically, as an NFC technology like Bluetooth, RFID is used for noncontact automatic identification. RFID automatically identifies the target object and obtains relevant data through RF signals without human intervention, and can work in all harsh environments. RFID technology can be used to identify objects moving at high speed and to identify multiple tags at the same time, which is fast and easy to operate. The combination of RFID technology with Internet and communication technologies can realize global tracking and information sharing of items and visualize the supply chain (Masciari, 2012).WSN is a distributed sensing network that is mainly used to monitor and track the status of different devices, such as location, movement, and temperature, and to identify and process these devices (Oudenhoven et al., 2012). Wireless sensor network has many types of sensors for detecting a wide variety of phenomena in the surrounding environment and can also interact with RFID tags (Lee & Lee, 2015). Middleware acts as an intermediary between RFID tags and applications, which means that a common set of application program interfaces (APIs) provided by middleware from the application side can connect to RFID readers and read the data of RFID tags. In short, middleware is a service-oriented software layer that allows software developers to communicate with different devices such as sensors, actuators, and RFID tags. Cloud computing is a distributed computing technology. As an Internet-based computing platform, it is based on sharing, demand, and easy scalability to obtain the required resources. Cloud computing is crucial to the development of IoT because the large amount of data generated by IoT devices requires processing and analysis using high-speed computers before timely and efficient decision-making (Lee & Lee, 2015). Currently, many IoT cloud platforms have emerged in the market, such as the domestic Aliyun, Baidu Cloud, Tencent Cloud, Huawei Cloud, and the well-known international Amazon AWS, Microsoft Azure, and Cisco IoT Cloudlock. The role of IoT cloud platforms is similar to that of middleware, aiming at connecting the IoT devices and IoT applications (i.e., the data generated by IoT devices is transferred to ERP systems and commercial intelligent software), thus providing timely reference to decision-makers. Finally, IoT applications are the interaction between devices and devices and between devices and people. Many applications constitute the interface between people and devices, and they present data in an intuitive way while identifying problems and providing solutions (Lee & Lee, 2015). Certainly, the positive effect of IoT on the overall operational efficiency and effectiveness of supply chain has been evidenced by numerous studies. Therefore, enterprises should actively embrace IoT technology and integrate IoT into all links of their supply chain to improve the effectiveness of their overall supply chain operations. However, the effectiveness of IoT technologies is greatly diminished by the inability of many enterprises to integrate them with other existing technologies and systems (Ericsson, 2019; Lee & Lee, 2015), and IoT has even become a "liability" for these enterprises. After all, the adoption of IoT technologies requires significant investments, which are often irreversible (Ericsson, 2019; Lee & Lee, 2015). In addition, the use of IoT in supply chain is still in its infancy and exploration phases, leaving a huge room for improvement (Witjaksono et al., 2018; Ryan & Watson, 2017). Therefore, there are also many challenges and obstacles for enterprises to optimize or even reorganize their supply chains using IoT, for which a comprehensive consideration is needed.

Process Automation

After digital integration of the entire supply chain process via IoT, it is necessary to automate the entire supply chain operations. Process automation refers to the automatic analysis of operational data or the automatic processing of physical devices or products (Wu et al., 2016). The integration of the network with the physical infrastructure not only makes machines and equipment smarter but also brings additional benefits to other facilities, industries, and assets with which they are economically connected (Kim & Heller, 2006). Generally, automation optimizes processes related to order fulfillment and other processes and contributes to the reduction of overall costs of supply chain operations (Wu et al., 2016). In fact, automation applications in supply chain are also embedded in such aspects as data analysis, manufacturing, purchasing, warehousing, distribution, and retails (Li et al., 2013; Trebilcock, 2013).

Advanced Analysis Technology

Business analysis is a process that combines mathematical techniques and functional knowledge to produce insights that can be implemented afterwards (Wu et al., 2016). Many scholars agree that analytics, the foundation of big data analysis, can help enterprise make better fact-based decisions to achieve the ultimate goal of driving strategy and improving performance (Waller & Fawcett, 2013). In fact, a study of Schoenherr and Speier-Pero (2015) also found that the main benefits that enterprises perceive from big data are more formal decision-making capabilities, improved supply chain efficiency, enhanced demand planning capabilities, reduced supply chain operation costs, and increased supply chain visibility. In terms of decision-making, plenty of studies focused on how big data improves the effectiveness, accuracy, and science of business decisions (Liang Hongbo, 2014; Provost & Fawcett, 2013; Brynjolfsson et al., 2011; Ye Bin et al., 2014; Liang Yan, 2014). And Brynjolfsson et al. (2011) also found that enterprises that call themselves data-driven ones make more objective evaluations of their financial and operational results, and also have higher productivity and profitability overall than their competitors. In terms of improved supply chain efficiency, the impact of big data analysis on supply chain efficiency is mainly through the efficient use of supply chain resources, data analysis, rational allocation of resources, and improved synergy across the supply chain (Yan, 2013; Wang, 2014). In terms of enhanced demand planning capabilities, data analysis allows enterprises to aggregate different aspects of data and analyze the demand for resources in each business segment, and to organize business activities more reasonably by taking into account the real needs of clients, which enables enterprises to not only innovate their business according to customer demand but also improve their ability to respond to challenges brought by changes in customer demand (Xiang, 2013; Liang Yan, 2014; Yan, 2013). In terms of reduced costs of supply chain operations, enterprises share information with upstream and downstream enterprises so that they can optimally arrange limited resources to maximize the benefits of resources (Xue, 2014; Yan, 2013). Advanced analysis is certainly essential to realize the value of big data. If big data is not parsed by analytics, it is just a pile of worthless "data" (Waller & Fawcett, 2013). Therefore, with IT development, supply chains will inevitably become one of the main sources of big data. In this regard, advanced analysis may become a decisive competitive asset for enterprises and supply chains, and may even become a core element for improving supply chain performance (Wu et al., 2016). From another perspective, analysis without big data as its object of study is at best a mathematical and statistical tool and application method, and does not have value and meaning for enterprises. Chae et al. (2014) analyzed the relationship between three capabilities (i.e., data management capabilities, the ability to use science and technology for planning, and performance management capabilities) for improving supply chain satisfaction and operational performance. After its empirical study of data collected from 537 production plants, it found that data management capabilities are a key driver of supply chain decision-making using analytics, and pointed out that before enterprises can use big data for analytic decision-making, they have to firstly develop the ability to manage big data.

Integration and Innovation in Intelligent Supply Chain

Supply chain management includes a series of processes such as design, purchasing, production, and distribution, and the participants of the supply chain play different roles in value creation. Supply chain management means coordinating all the participants and operational components to ensure the efficient operation of the supply chain (Wu et al., 2016). As competition increases and information technology evolves, the division of labor in the supply chain becomes more detailed and well defined. Therefore, the ability to combine effective supply chain practices with cross-organizational information sharing becomes the key to improving supply chain performance (Kumar & Pugazhendhi, 2012). Supplier integration (Danese et al., 2013) and reverse logistics integration (Cardoso et al., 2013), for example, are deemed as important strategies to improve the performance of supply chain operations. Of course, in addition to the integration of various processes in the supply chain, the integration of information technologies with other technologies, human resources, and organizational capabilities in supply chain operations to gain competitive advantage in the value creation process is also an important concern in the construction of intelligent supply chains (Carmichael et al., 2011).

In an intelligent supply chain, the effective interaction between integrated IT, advanced analysis technology, and process automation provides unprecedented opportunities to maximize supply chain surpluses (Wu et al., 2016). As mentioned earlier, big data itself does not have value until enterprises have the ability to use and analyze the data and apply it for process improvement (Waller & Fawcett, 2013). That is, enterprises and supply chains need to use information technology to collect, store, and manage large amounts of data and then turn it into timely, informed decisions through advanced analysis. Process automation assists in the implementation of the entire decision and ensures that it is implemented effectively. This is how the interactive value of the three elements can be realized, which is built on the seamless integration of the three elements mentioned above (Wu et al., 2016).

In addition to the integration of supply chain process and overall supply chain technologies, intelligent supply chain also puts forward higher requirements on the innovation of products, services, and operation process. Generally speaking, the intelligent supply chain changes the negative way of environmental response. Due to the improvement of "intelligence," the supply chain as a whole can make proactive and even early adaptation to the changes in the environment. As a result, the supply network has changed from a linear structure to a "complex adaptive system," which is considered to be able to adapt to environmental changes in a timely and proactive manner (Wycisk et al., 2008). This adaptive system actually has a positive effect on maintaining the stability and performance of the supply chain, while a stable supply chain contributes to collaborative innovation among participants (Modi & Mabert, 2010). Of course, the full integration and visualization requirements of intelligent supply chains also enhance the trust among the collaborating participants, which further increases the possibility of collaborative innovation among them and the performance of collaborative innovation. Apart from the enhanced partnership caused by intelligent supply chains, the developmental elements of intelligent supply chains are naturally themselves closely related to innovation (Waller & Fawcett, 2013). In fact, "big data" represents a new way of life, provides a new resource and capability, is a new technology, and brings a new way of thinking (Li & Xia, 2013), leading to lower cost thresholds, more business opportunities, and more likelihood to give rise to disruptive innovations (Ren, 2014). Concretely, in terms of enterprise business, Han (2013) pointed out that big data technology brings innovative ways to analyze existing business challenges and potential opportunities and that this new resource and analysis technology can also improve business operations in new ways; in terms of technology, Li and Long (2013) highlighted that big data helps reduce the cost and speed up the transformation of knowledge and that knowledge in the process of transformation boosts innovation in technology. In terms of the role of big data for supply chain innovation, Tan et al. (2015) argued that enterprises can use big data to gain new ideas or better understand customers, markets, and products. They also proposed an analytic framework based on graph technology to help enterprises integrate their own capability sets with those of other enterprises, so that they can enhance their supply chain innovation capabilities through better use of big data to gain an overall competitive advantage. China Resources Vanguard/P&G (China) (2014) also proposed that big data may not only change the way enterprises operate but also contribute to collaborative innovation in the supply chain. Jiang (2015) believed in the positive impact of big data on innovation of supply chain financial services. Thus, it can be seen that intelligent supply chain is not only the result of innovation under the use of information technology but also a catalyst and driver of innovation. It accelerates not only the innovative development of technologies but also the innovation of products, services, management, and operational processes (Evans & Annunziata, 2012).

3.3 ICT-Enabled Supply Chain Finance

Along with the intelligence of supply chain, especially the transformation of supply chain operations driven by ICT, supply chain financial activities also showed a high trend of integration with ICT. The increasingly efficient and smart financial activities based on supply chain operations gave rise to fintech. This requires exploring what intelligent supply chain finance means, the role and positioning of convergent ICT in supply chain finance, the issues that need to be addressed, and what are enabled.

Definition of Intelligent Supply Chain Finance

The intelligence trend of supply chain finance is just like that of supply chain, both originated from the efficient process of modern ICT for business reengineering. Convergent ICT (such as IoT, big data, cloud computing, AI, and blockchain), which is instrumented, interconnected, intelligent, automated, integrated, and innovative, drives the transformation of both supply chain operations and financial operations. With the comprehensive integration and innovation of information, IT, process automation, and analysis technology and activities, the two fields achieve a high degree of integration, resulting in intelligent decision-making, ecological participants, service-oriented activities, and visualized management of supply chain and financial activities, effectively solving the problems of information asymmetry and moral risk in industrial and financial activities, realizing the use of finance to promote the development of supply chain ecology, and achieving the expansion and value-adding of financial ecology by leveraging on supply chain operations (see Fig. 3.1). It should be noted that intelligent supply chain finance is a manifestation of fintech, and there is no standard definition of fintech as it is in the process of development. In March 2016, the Financial Stability Board (FSB), a leading global financial governance body, released the *FSB, Fintech: Describing the Landscape and a Framework for Analysis*, providing a preliminary definition of fintech for the first time from the perspective of an international organization and saying that fintech refers to business models, technology applications, processes, and products that have a significant impact on financial markets, institutions, and financial services as a result of financial innovation driven by emerging cutting-edge technologies such as big data, blockchain, cloud computing, and AI (FSB, 2016). At current stage, the Basel Committee on Banking Supervision classifies fintech into four categories: payment and settlement; deposit, loan, and capital raising; investment management; and market facilities. Supply chain finance is related to payment and settlement as well as deposit and loan business, so intelligent supply chain finance is one of the forms of fintech.

One of the characteristics of intelligent supply chain finance is the comprehensive use of convergent ICT in supply chain finance: a variety of ICTs with different functions are interrelated and organized into a system to fully enable supply chain finance activities. Relying on industrial supply chain operations, supply chain finance is a kind of management process

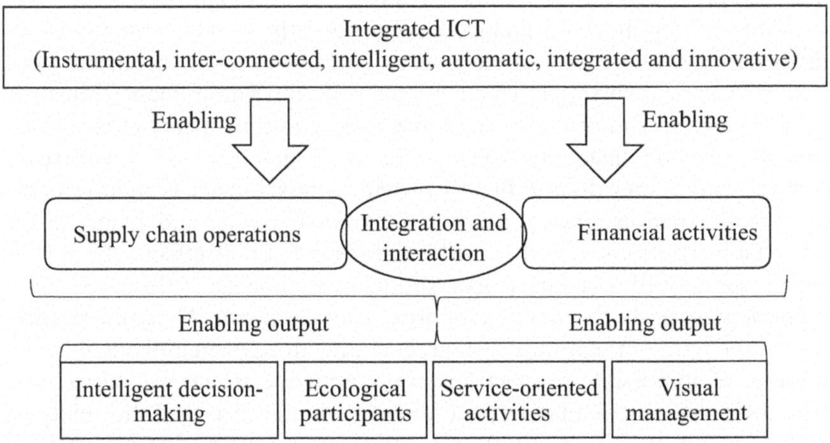

Fig. 3.1 Meaning of intelligent supply chain finance

integrating logistics operation, business operation, and financial management. It closely binds buyers, sellers, third-party logistics providers, and financial institutions in trade, realizing the role of revitalizing capital with supply chain logistics and pulling forward supply chain logistics with capital at the same time (Song, 2015). The realization of this process gives rise to different types and stages of supply chain finance operations. These different types or stages of supply chain finance operations can be distinguished by the structural, process, and information characteristics of the supply chain and finance (Blackman et al., 2013).

First of all, in terms of structural characteristics, traditional supply chain finance is financial businesses led by financial institutions. In other words, supply chain finance products are designed, provided, and managed by commercial banks or traditional financial institutions, which provide corresponding supply chain finance products based on the industrial supply chain of core enterprises and their credit. Such products include receivables and payables business (e.g., standard factoring, reverse factoring, reverse purchase, and bill pool financing), inventory business (e.g., warehouse receipt pledge and inventory financing), and prepayment business (e.g., confirming storage financing). In this context, traditional financial institutions such as banks do not directly participate in the process of supply chain operation, but are only participants in the industrial supply chain operations who provide funds and manage capital risks for enterprises therein. While at the stage of supply chain finance driven by industry leading enterprises (commonly known as supply chain finance 2.0 stage), the structure of supply chain finance changes greatly, in which supply chain financial services are promoted by core enterprises in the industry, who, based on their own supply chain system and combining financial institutions, upstream and downstream enterprises, and third-party service institutions, provide financing services for their upstream or downstream partners (note: they do not directly provide funds, but act as an intermediary of information service, playing the role of bridge and manager for financial institutions to control risks and provide funds effectively). From the perspective of social networks, supply chain finance at this stage has a high degree of both network density and centrality. Network density means the ratio of the number of direct connections of an individual to the number of all possible connections in the network, which is used to measure the proximity of an enterprise to network members and the ability to control resources (Scott, 2000). Centrality measures the degree to which an individual is at the center of the network and reflects the importance of the enterprise in the network. Or, to put it another way, this type of supply chain presents a tightly coupled condition, and in such a supply chain, the core enterprise, the provider of supply chain financial services, is at the center of the industrial supply chain operations. In this way, the core enterprises can adequately manage and control the entire business structure, and the corresponding risks relating to the capital entering the supply chain can be effectively unfolded and controlled. However, after the gradual progress of supply chain finance driven by industrial core enterprises, the corresponding limitations also emerge. First of all, not all enterprises are able to build supply chain financial service system, because only enterprises with strong resources and management ability can promote supply chain financial service on the basis of their own supply chain system which is relatively perfect. Most enterprises, especially SMEs, have not yet built their own supply chain system, so it is not possible for them to promote supply chain finance at this stage. Second, this second stage of supply chain finance only serve the first-tier suppliers or first-tier clients of core enterprises, and cannot realize the penetration of supply chain financial services into multitier suppliers or clients in the supply chain, that is, serving the N-level suppliers of suppliers, or the N-level clients of clients. This gives the birth of the third stage of supply chain finance, that is, the stage of supply chain finance driven by network platforms (also known as Internet supply chain finance (ISCF) or supply chain finance 3.0 stage; see *Internet Supply Chain Finance, Beijing: China Renmin University Press, 2017*). The structure formed at this stage is no longer a "chain-based" supply chain, but a platform, especially a virtual industrial cluster with the Internet as a technical means, that is, the collaboration and cooperation between industrial ecology and ecology (Song & Lu, 2017). This cooperation structure incorporates both vertical cooperation between different upstream and downstream links and horizontal cooperation between similar links, and oblique cooperation across regions and industries. Therefore, the structure tends to be loosely coupled on the one hand, with a low network density relative to the second stage, but, on the other hand, the organizers of supply chain finance are at a high degree of centrality, and the whole supply chain structure presents a highly organized mesh structure (Song & Yang, 2018). This kind of supply chain finance based on the ecology of network platform brings huge challenges in management. On the one hand, there is a wide range of participants, involving not only the direct upstream and downstream partners of enterprises, financial institutions and third parties, but also other direct or indirect participants; on the other hand, the business activities among various entities are very different, involving various business activities and financial behaviors. Therefore, this kind of supply chain finance driven by network platform is unsustainable, if not enabled, and supported by sound ICTs. This is one of the reasons that we need "intelligent" supply chain finance.

Second, as far as the process characteristics of supply chain finance are concerned, the supply chain finance driven by traditional financial institutions mainly focuses on the flow of funds, including whether the loans are used for the real borrowing intention and whether the borrower can return the funds and interest. However, as previously analyzed, financial institutions are not concerned with the transaction process and logistics process in the supply chain because they are not directly involved in supply chain activities, and they cannot really grasp the details of transactions and logistics. It is for this reason that banks and other financial institutions base their credit to enterprises mainly on financial statements and pledged assets. In the supply chain finance 2.0 stage, supply chain financial service providers mainly drive the flow of funds through the control of transaction flow and logistics. In other words, they provide corresponding financing services by intervening in and managing the transaction process of buyers and sellers, as well as the logistics operation process, and according to the characteristics of the business and the position and role of fund providers in the supply chain operation. At the stage of supply chain finance driven by network platform, the complexity of the network and the wide range of participants prevent financial service providers from directly intervening in all aspects of transactions and logistics operations. Therefore, they need strong capabilities in supply chain capacity management, demand management, customer relationship management, procurement, and supplier relationship management, service and distribution management, and capital management (Ellram et al., 2004), aiming to reduce the huge risks present in the network-driven supply chain finance. The formation of these capabilities necessarily requires the use of comprehensive modern ICTs to grasp the situation in the entire supply chain network in a comprehensive manner. Otherwise, the absence of any link and any activity management may bring great risks to financial activities.

Third, supply chain finance at different stages also varies in terms of the breadth and depth of information. At the bank-led supply chain finance stage, financial institutions mainly focus on financial information and enterprise credit to overcome the ex ante information asymmetry, and use collateral guarantee and post-loan risk control to overcome the ex post information asymmetry. In contrast, at the core enterprise-driven supply chain finance stage, ex ante information asymmetry is managed mainly by transaction information and borrowers' transaction credit, and ex post information asymmetry is reduced by embedding borrowers in the supply chain operation process and controlling their behaviors (Song & Lu, 2017). However, at the stage of network platform-driven supply chain finance, the breadth and depth of ex ante and ex post information are different. Ex ante information is not limited to direct transaction information and transaction credit. Considering that supply chain financial service providers are not directly involved in all supply chain operation activities, it is necessary to obtain more objective and extensive information with the help of various ICTs to portray the true transaction credit and information of the borrowers in order to fully understand their status. Likewise, ex post management also requires the acquisition and grasp of behavioral data, business data, and corresponding asset data of each participant. The acquisition, integration, analysis, and decision-making of these data require comprehensive ICTs. Only through the support of these ICTs can the persuasive effect (i.e., the increase in willingness to lend and borrow funds due to the increase in information accessibility) and informative effect (i.e., the increase in information accessibility accelerates the learning process among enterprises and helps lenders make reasonable investment decisions) and the likelihood of capital lending in supply chain finance be enhanced (Zhou et al., 2018).

Position of Convergent ICT in Supply Chain Finance

From the above analysis, it can be seen that with the evolution of supply chain finance, modern ICTs have become increasingly important and gradually becomes the core element of the innovative development of supply chain finance. However, we still need to explore what role the ICTs play in supply chain finance activities. An understanding of this issue requires looking at the evolution of management information systems theory in terms of the changes in information technology in management. Cecez-Kecmanovic et al. (2002), in discussing the role of management information systems, argued that from a historical perspective the development of information systems has gone through five stages. The first stage is the production model of information systems. At this stage, the function of information systems is to collect and process data and generate information, and the goal of information systems is to automate the processing of data and improve control. This view clearly regards information systems as an objective thing that generates data, or as a tool for managing activities. The second stage is the interactive model of information systems. At this stage, the information systems generate information by acquiring and processing expert knowledge and external data, and their role is to support and help users to achieve efficiency and effectiveness in decision-making. The information system needs to interact with the managers who are involved in decision making. The third stage is the networked model of organization-wide information systems (e.g., MIS and ERP). At this stage, information systems span across all levels of functions across the organization. Therefore, the role of information systems is to provide comprehensive support for organization-wide processes and cross-functional coordination to achieve competitiveness. However, the function of information systems at the third stage is still limited, which is mainly functional coordination and data integration within a single organization, but not effective integration of figures and information between organizations. In view of this, the fourth stage is the model of interorganizational information systems. At this stage, information systems go beyond organizational boundaries and need to interface, collaborate, and share and exchange information with external institutions and organizations. In this sense, information systems become more than just technology and require the adoption of strategic, cultural, political, and legal perspectives to facilitate the connection and integration of technology across organizations. Therefore, information systems theory at this stage adopts a socio-technical view (Cecez-Kecmanovic et al., 2002). Today, information systems have become a more important means of social interaction, reaching the fifth stage—information systems as a social system mediating social interaction. At this stage, information systems enable new ways of interacting, acquiring, communicating, sharing, and transferring information and knowledge between organizations and between people, and the quality and forms of interactions have undergone a dramatic change. From the process of evolution of management information systems, the function of modern ICTs has gone beyond the technology itself and embedded more deeply into the whole process of industrial supply chain operations, and it has promoted the long development of supply chain finance through the efficient interaction between organizations, activities, and links. In particular, the following points regarding modern ICT and the positioning and role of technology service providers in supply chain finance should be focused on.

First of all, it should be clear that ICT is a kind of convergent system in supply chain finance. That is to say, in order to make technologies serviceable in various stages or activities of supply chain finance, it is necessary to build a reasonable technologies system, in which various functions are interrelated and are able to interact with various business entities smoothly. This means that smart technologies need to be embedded in the scenarios of supply chain finance, and once detached from the scenarios of supply chain operational and financial activities (such as big data modeling without data sources, blockchain technology without application scenarios, and cloud computing platforms without solutions), they would not be able to achieve the "enabling" process. Furthermore, the process of enabling supply chain finance by technologies is differentiated rather than homogeneous. In other words, the enabling effect of ICT on supply chain finance is differentiated according to different businesses, because different businesses often involve different participants and different activities, and the problems solved and the goals that supply chain finance tries to achieve are not the same. Just like the end-to-end supply chain finance introduced in Chap. 2, in different stages of supply chain operation, the form of supply chain finance business, and the target and way of solving problems are also different. Therefore, the information and data required by the differentiated financial activities, as well as the requirements for risk control, are widely divergent. For example, in strategic financing, there is no real purchase and sale between the buyer and the seller, and the fund provider provides funds to the partner to support its strategic investment behavior for a future strategic relationship or to lock in a technology product in advance. Therefore, in this example, more attention is paid to the potential capability of the partner and its competitiveness in the industry or market. On the contrary, in warehouse receipt pledges, attention needs to be paid to whether the products corresponding to the warehouse receipts really exist, whether they have value, whether the stability of the value is strong, and so on. Because of the characteristics of this differentiated supply chain finance, different technical means and methods need to be applied to obtain the corresponding information and make corresponding analysis and decision. In addition, technology is a solution in the intelligent supply chain finance stage. Multiple types of technologies are organized into an organic infrastructure. On a unified technology service platform, multiple institutions collaborate and interact to form a solid multilateral ecosystem to guarantee the efficiency and security of financial services.

Second, in supply chain finance, the provider of technology services is not the creator of industrial credit, but the transmitter of industrial credit, or the intermediary of industrial credit. Credit is a kind of production and social relationship of mutual trust formed between and attached to economic participants, transaction behaviors, and commodity logistics. As per the explanation on Baidu Baike, "credit," from the legal point of view, has two meanings: the first one is a relationship between the parties, and credit exists whenever the rights and obligations of the parties under a "contract" are not delivered immediately but in the future; the second one is the rights and obligations of both parties according to the "contract." Wikipedia defines credit as a trust that allows one party to provide funds or resources to another party, in which the latter does not immediately repay the first party (thus creating a debt), but promises to repay or return those resources (or other materials of equal value) at a later date. Put another way, credit is a method that is formally reciprocal, legally enforceable, and extensible to a large group of unrelated persons. Clearly seen from these definitions, credit is a relationship of trust between trading parties that arises between them because of their trading behavior as well as time lags. From this perspective, the creators of credit are the participants in the supply chain operations, who generate value interactions (i.e., the generation, production, and transmission of the required value), the corresponding transaction processes, logistical activities, and financial transactions, and who, as a result of this operational process, assume the respective responsibilities and obligations as required. The technology service providers are simply making credit more transparent through convergent and systematic technological means, so as to effectively transfer credit among industry participants and between industry and financial institutions. This means that when various ICTs are applied to supply chain finance, technology needs to be understood from the perspective of industry supply chain participants or users, rather than taking for granted that fintech is the gravedigger that disrupts all business models or financial models. The realization of user value from the perspective of supply chain operations is exactly the value of technology for each participant and financial institution. In this sense, fintech is neither finance nor technology, nor even the fusion of finance and technology. Technology should be defined as a solution that integrates ICTs, customer insight, financial scenarios, and product operations to help supply chain participants and financial institutions adapt to the needs of smooth and effective supply chain operations.

Thirdly, the technology service providers in supply chain finance are not fund providers, but facilitators of funds flow. In supply chain finance, there are mutually synergistic and well-defined entities (Song, 2015), including the following: (1) supply chain participants (i.e., upstream and downstream enterprises that are related because of buying and selling behaviors, as well as other cooperative parties); (2) platform service providers (i.e., entities that provides necessary application or basis for risk takers or liquidity providers), who facilitate access to and integration of supply chain information and figures, allowing the corresponding participants to learn about the process and credit of supply chain transactions in an automatic and timely manner, and in fact, is also the technology service provider; (3) transaction risk managers (i.e., entities that, through the use of integrated data and information, carve out the credit of specific subjects and provide corresponding financial services based on the characteristics of supply chain operations). Liquidity providers are specific fund providers, which are also the ultimate loan risk takers. These entities generate different stages and types of supply chain finance operations through a high degree of cooperation. Among them, the technology service provider can facilitate the flow of funds in the supply chain by revealing risks for investors (including transaction risk managers or liquidity providers) to understand and manage risks through various ICTs. But the technology service provider is not a fund provider itself, while the real fund providers are banks, funds, and other licensed and financially regulated financial institutions.

Challenges in Constructing Intelligent Supply Chain Finance

Through the above analysis concerning the positioning of ICT and its service providers in supply chain finance, it can be seen that intelligent supply chain finance faces many challenges, which are the most urgent issues that need to be addressed in the current process of supply chain finance development. The effective correction of wrong behaviors is what makes the realization of intelligent supply chain finance possible. These challenges include the following.

First, all relevant sectors and enterprises focus on acquiring data about supply chain and financial activities through ICT in supply chain activities, but they do not realize the integration and correlation of the data across the entire process. With digitalization gaining more and more attention from the whole society, enterprises and governments have set the construction of big data as a key aspect of development in recent years. In particular, the online and digital management of supply chain finance has further become a cornerstone for the development of supply chain finance because of the complexity of business activities, the large number of entities involved and the high level of risks. The digital construction has reached a bottleneck over time in spite of its faster progress compared to the past. This is because there is no effective digital coordination and integration between enterprise departments, between enterprises, between enterprises and government departments, and between government departments, so that many vertical "chimneys" of big data have been formed. As a result, enterprises have not established a data warehouse for the whole supply chain business, and have not integrated the front-end business operation data and back-end management data. Although a huge database has been established, the data are just stacked and stored in a haphazard way, without being cleaned and correlated, and thus cannot have a practical effect on supply chain finance business and management. Furthermore, the industry has not effectively integrated the data between enterprises and geographic areas, which cannot be used to reflect the industry's supply chain business situation and establish an industry-wide credit system to guide the industry's development. Likewise, government departments do not effectively correlate the data of each other, leaving a vacuum and loophole in government regulation, and overshadowing the development of supply chain finance.

Second, enterprises and organizations have established the corresponding information system of big data, but it does not have a clear guiding effect on the frontline business. The diversification of information sources and information entities as well as the expansion of information surface has greatly increased the data stock of enterprises. Data itself does not have value, and and becomes valuable only when it is converted into information that can provide a reference for enterprises to make decisions. Therefore, the data and information collected by enterprises from multiple parties requires cleaning, organization, and integration to be transformed into real "visual" information, not just simply numbering the data. The challenge of "visualization" for enterprises also lies in managing data and information from a dynamic perspective, because the development of mobile Internet and the Internet not only drowns enterprises in a huge amount of data but also makes information and data flow into the enterprise data and information collectors (i.e., enterprise information collectors need to constantly aggregate data and receive data). This again poses the challenge of "visualizing data" (i.e., it requires constantly cleaning, aggregating and transforming data, so that relevant decision-makers can quickly understand the deeper meaning of the data). When transformed into timely information useful for supply chain finance decisions, data can not only guide existing activities but also forecast the future, thus better guiding the enterprise's strategic decisions on supply chain finance and taking appropriate risk prevention measures. Obviously, for realizing the above objectives, several specific problems in data analysis and management need to be solved: First, although many enterprises have carried out a variety of businesses such as supply chain finance and accumulated a certain amount of business data, but the business staff did not put forward an array of analysis and forecasting demands in terms of customer management, risk rating, and business scale forecasting, so the figures and data may become dead. Second, the lack of a risk assessment system to support the daily operation of financial business leads to unrealized analysis and prediction of customer behavior. Third, there is no KPI system designed for operation and management of financial business. Data support for supply chain finance business requires not only digitization but also the construction of the whole supply chain management system, or the establishment of the whole supply chain business architecture and information architecture. The vacancy of these two architectures may turn the digitization into a castle in the air. As we usually say, we should realize digitization and informatization driven by business, instead of relying solely on digitization and informatization to drive business development.

Third, the collection, cleaning, and analysis of data and information are not clearly "targeted." The use of figures and information must be for a specific business and a specific target, not a purposeless act. And different businesses and objects have different requirements for figures and information. The prerequisite for carrying out supply chain finance is certainly supply chain management. Finance is a financial behavior that comes with specific supply chain business and long-term stable relationship. Supply chain finance cannot generate financial activities right from the start. In particular, supply chain finance is first based on multifrequency business (supply chain operations and partnership building), and only after that can low-frequency activities (financing behavior) be generated. Based on this feature, in the construction of digitalization or information technology, we first need to collect, clean, and correlate the corresponding business data, analyze the multifrequency business and partners, and then further understand and analyze the possible financial needs and conditions behind, instead of analyzing who is the borrower, the amount of capital it needs, and the corresponding risks at the beginning. In addition, the requirements of digitalization for different links and activities in the supply chain vary widely, requiring careful study of the characteristics of the industry, the features of transactions in the business, and the laws governing the operation of products and businesses. In terms of the "targeted" data, we also need to clarify the target entities. On the one hand, the data will be different for different target entities involved in the supply chain activities. For example, platform companies in the supply chain, buyers and sellers directly engaged in supply chain operations, and financial institutions providing financial services have different requirements on the data collected and the analysis results. Therefore, we need to analyze data and information according to different target entities to facilitate them to make decisions. On the other hand, data collection and analysis must be limited to the participants or related parties in supply chain financial activities, and should not be extended to nonbusiness subjects. Some big data service providers boast that they can paint a picture of each person by various means, which not only violates the security regulations in respect of online privacy but also does not help to promote the effective development of supply chain finance. The essence of supply chain finance lies in the control of debt structure, which is a supply chain operation and financial activity based on the business itself. Data collection and analysis against business entities and related stakeholders should not only achieve data security management without infringing privacy, but also truly understand and grasp supply chain business operations and financial behaviors to effectively prevent risks.

Goals of ICT Enabling Supply Chain Finance

Having clarified the position of ICT in supply chain finance as well as the concerns and challenges, we need to further clarify what exactly convergent ICT enables supply chain finance. The understanding of this issue is still premised on the understanding of the essential characteristics of supply chain finance. The basic core elements of supply chain finance, a specific application form of enterprise micro-finance, can be summarized by a "scale" in essence (Song, 2017; see Fig. 3.2). The base of this scale is risk control and management. The key to any financial innovation is the control of risk from the market, credit, liquidity, and operations. The loss of risk control may cause significant losses to financial activities, while the key

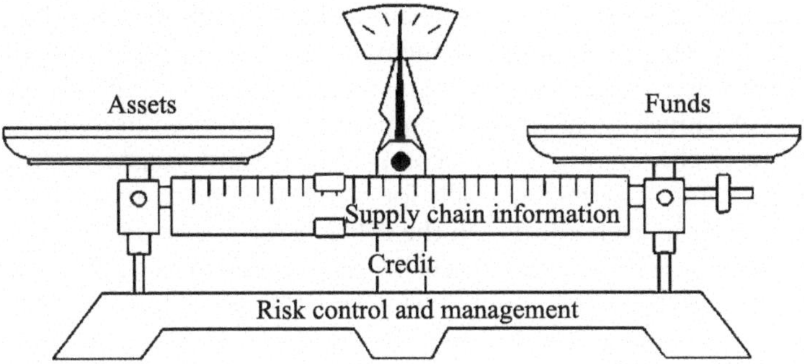

Fig. 3.2 Core elements of supply chain finance

to controlling risk is to grasp the information in the whole process of supply chain operations. Most of the risks in financial activities arise from information asymmetry, especially for the early stage of business and risky SMEs (Berger & Udell, 2006). Information asymmetry is prone to adverse selection and moral hazard, which can further impede SMEs' access to finance from financial institutions. As Brealey et al. state, "Venture capital markets cannot emerge when volume of information asymmetries exists and what's more, the supply of funds for poor projects excels that for good projects" (Brealey et al., 1977). Therefore, the pillar of supply chain finance (i.e., credit) can only be created by fully understanding and mastering the information of each link, entity, and activity therein. At one end of the scale are assets (i.e., the participants in the supply chain and the competitiveness of the business, and the value of fixed and current assets); at the other end are the funds (i.e., supply chain working capital characterized by volume, cycle, and interest rates). Supply chain finance is characterized by the establishment of good assets to dock funds, so as to achieve true combination of funds with assets. It helps the information of the whole process of supply chain to be transparent and accessible, and establishes effective corporate and industrial credit, thus effectively reducing the risks arising from information asymmetry. However, in reality, there are still many challenges in achieving this goal. On the one hand, the complexity of supply chain operations makes it very difficult to fully understand and capture the status of assets, especially as supply chain operations gradually move from a linear to a network structure. As mentioned by de Boer et al. (2015), supply chain networks often include two types of organizations: key members and supporting members. The key members are the core enterprises in the supply chain and all of their direct and indirect suppliers and clients. Supporting members are the third parties (logistics service providers) in the supply chain who provide assets, knowledge, and services. Obviously, in a supply chain network composed of multiple entities, it is very challenging to get a comprehensive and realistic understanding of the status of assets, especially for each business activity each product and each asset in each entity. On the other hand, the same complexity of supply chain operations makes it challenging to get an exact picture of the real use of funds in the supply chain and the possible risks, including whether the demand for funds is based on real trading relationship, whether the funds are under effective risk control level in each participant whether the entities use the funds reasonably among themselves, and whether the interest rate of the funds is in line with the real risk and business capacity of the borrower, and so on. These are difficult to achieve through traditional management means, and even if they can be achieved, they are often costly to operate. The answers to these questions are hard to obtain through traditional management tools, or often require high operational costs even if obtainable. Therefore, the goal of ICT enabling supply chain finance is to effectively make a significant impact on the assets and funds, promote the transparency, accessibility, and availability of information throughout the supply chain, and reduce the transaction costs of the entire supply chain operation as well as the operational costs of management and supervision.

Specifically, the impact of ICT enabling supply chain on assets is mainly reflected in "objective underlying interaction and autonomous end business." Objective underlying interaction refers to the real, detailed, and transparent reflection of supply chain transactions and operation activities, so as to realize the objectivity of the interaction between objects and objects and between people and objects, as well as the fine granularity risk management based on the authenticity of business background, and further activate the new economic value of the objects themselves. There are two layers of meaning herein. One is, how to realize the logical relationship management between objects and objects and between people and objects through ICT enabling, and then extrapolate to the relationship management between people and people. In the traditional supply chain finance operations, the risk control is mainly based on the understanding of the credit of "people" (i.e., a comprehensive portrayal of the financial status, asset status, and business status of the operating enterprise). This information is used to fully reflect the ability and operational stability of the enterprise itself, as well as the business relationship between the enterprise and other enterprises. However, with the growing complexity of supply chain operations and the increasing diversity of participating parties, even across industries, it has become difficult to investigate over and understand the credit and business relationships of all economic entities, and the marginal management costs are also increasing. Therefore, we need to use ICT to monitor and manage the business objects or targets (i.e., assets and the flow of assets in the supply chain) in a real-time and dynamic manner, so that the credit of the "objects" themselves can be established. Based on the credit relationship between "objects" and "objects in the flow," we further establish the relationship between "people and objects" (i.e., corporate credit corresponding to the operation of assets) or portray and reflect the capabilities and management status of enterprises in the entire supply chain based on the products and processes operated, and finally realize the management of the trust system between "people" and "people." In order to achieve this, we need, on the one hand, to pay attention to the relationship between objects and objects, as well as the relationship between people and objects (such as which enterprises need what objects at what time, how, and at what cost). Only by fully understanding the nature of objects can we understand the role of finance and the scenarios in which technology can be used. On the other hand, it is necessary to focus on what kind of ICT enabling is required for different object-to-object, people-to-object, and people-to-people relationships. In general, the object-to-object management requires the integration of dynamic digital memory, sensing, and communication capabilities to get access to all the necessary information throughout the supply chain and life cycle. The people-to-object management requires standardization to ensure that these different sources of information and solutions from different suppliers can not only coexist in one system but also communicate with each other and be highly integrated. The people-to-people interconnection refers to a good organizational ecology between people, where all stakeholders connect, interact, and cooperate with each other. Another important meaning of objective underlying interaction is the fine-granularity management of assets. By fine granularity, we mean that the management of asset status in supply chain finance management is based on the real status and information of each product and each activity, and their possible changes (rather than entirely based on the total products and all economic activities and on the probability and the law of large numbers) to control the corresponding risk. The aim of fine-granularity management is to truly understand the value changes and flow status of each product and activity and to develop and apply supply chain finance products and activities differently.

Autonomous end business means realizing autonomous at every stage and in every activity of supply chain operations and behavior-driven intelligent business of organizations. This goal also includes two layers of meaning. First, we should establish a scenario-based dynamic business model with autonomous configuration on demand. The operation previous process is a kind of synergistic process among fixed models, fixed subjects, and fixed elements, or the whole supply chain is an operation process among fixed cooperative subjects and according to the transaction and logistics methods established in advance. However, nowadays, this unchanging model has changed dramatically. First of all, the value demands of clients present a differentiated and variable situation. Put another way, different clients have different needs and value demands, and even the same client has dynamic changes in demands at different times and in different regions. Second, along with the gradual transformation of supply chain operations from single chain to network, the increasingly diversified participants show different resource and capacity status. Therefore, how to organize different participants to carry out differentiated supply chain operations according to the changing application scenarios in time and provide differentiated supply chain financial services based on this has now become an inevitable issue for the further development of supply chain finance. The solution to this issue certainly creates new requirements for ICT, resulting in the following contradictions: between the demand for industrial interconnection and the integration of heterogeneous information systems of stakeholders; between the demand for complex and diverse business management and the ability to develop and deploy rapid application services; and between the demand for diverse and highly concurrent application support and resource allocation. Until these contradictions and issue are effectively resolved or systematic ICT is built and enabled, supply chain finance cannot achieve networked, ecological, and intelligent development. Meanwhile, corresponding to the above issue, the autonomous end business also requires standardized, intensive, and platform-oriented intelligent cloud services. Lack of business standardization and integrated management of data and information among different participants, different links, and different elements in the supply chain may lead to the difficulty of sustainable supply chain finance due to information asymmetry. Obviously, the realization of this aspect also requires the timely identification of different stakeholders and their corresponding value claims with the help of systematic ICT, so as to carefully understand and analyze the characteristics of each industry and business, and discover the value of finance for the industry and business.

In addition to enabling the assets of supply chain, ICT also enables the funds, which is mainly manifested as "objective debt structure and autonomous participant credit." Debt structure refers to the debt relationship generated in the process of transaction and the structure of capital transaction formed by this relationship. A very important prerequisite for the effective and stable development of supply chain finance is the clarity of creditor-debtor relationship, as well as the matching of the capital structure with the business structure. The confusion or complexity of creditor-debtor relationships in the supply chain (such as joint guarantee loans), or the failure to match capital transactions with asset transactions, will certainly generate huge financial risks. Therefore, how to truly reflect the debt structure becomes the key to effective risk control in supply chain finance, which is the original meaning of objective debt structure. The realization of objective debt structure is based on three aspects of ICT-enabled management. The first aspect is the cross-checking of the business and asset authenticity background, that is, whether the creditor-debtor relationship is based on real business transactions. If the operational status of assets and the process of assets' transactions in different participants cannot be informed timely and effectively, the resulting debts and liabilities will be more risky. For this reason, the key to management lies in cross-verification and cross-validation of the authenticity and integrity of the debt structure with the help of ICT. The second aspect is the dynamic matching of various types of electronic documents (such as electronic orders, electronic packing list, electronic warehouse receipts, electronic waybills, electronic tax stamps, and electronic bills of lading) with logistics deliveries and accounts receivable. The asset security of supply chain finance also relies on standardized and electronic document management. Given that there are many participants and links involved in the operations of supply chain, the inability to reach business consensus or standards among different participants and links makes it difficult to ensure the safety of funds. In addition, the standardized documents should be safe and difficult to tamper with, while the delivery should be timely and transparent, which requires the use of ICT to achieve electronic. By electronic, we not only mean that documents are expressed in digital form but also mean that the management and transmission must be based on the

Internet to achieve real-time, synchronization, wide distribution, and transparency. Furthermore, the logistics delivery resulting from the transmission of electronic documents must be matched with the receivables in real time. The third aspect is the supply chain closed-loop discovery and seamless supervision and tracking of the entire circulation process. Based on the realization of the above two aspects, electronic documents management, debt management, asset management, and so on in the supply chain operation process need to achieve a closed loop, and all documents, assets, and relationships should be supervised and tracked. All of the above are essential elements to effectively prevent financial risks.

Autonomous participant credit refers to the objective and natural presentation of supply chain participants' credit in business and operational activities with the help of ICT. It encompasses three levels of meaning. The first level is the ability to objectively reflect the credit of participants through the business and financial activities of the supply chain. Supply chain business activities involve various processes, such as purchasing, production, distribution, inventory, and so on, while financial activities also involve debit and credit, reconciliation, payment, settlement, and other processes. With the help of ICT, the various processes can be effectively integrated and managed, and monitored in real time, allowing the entities involved in these activities to present their performance capability and credit objectively. The second level is the ability to use technology to objectively reflect the true credit of financial assets. In the supply chain financial activities, there are a large number of tradable financial assets with realistic price and future valuation, such as cash on hand, accounts receivable, notes receivable, loans, advances, other receivables, interests receivable, debt investment, equity investment, fund investment, and derivative financial assets. Ensuring the authenticity of these assets is the key to financial risk management, that is, the authenticity of the financial activities themselves and the authenticity of the financial activities with the corresponding business activities and assets. The achievement of this goal requires the use of ICT, such as IoT and blockchain. The third level is the ability to objectively reflect the credit of multilevel supply chain participants. In the past supply chain finance activities, core enterprises may better grasp the credit of upstream and downstream enterprises that have business relationship with them through directly management or control. However, as the scope of supply chain operation becomes more and more networked and ecological, the supply chain involves more and more diversified participants, and the supply chain extends to multiple levels (i.e., suppliers of suppliers and clients of clients). In this case, how to comprehensively grasp the credit of multilevel participants (i.e., to objectively, comprehensively, and completely reflect the credit of all participants in the supply chain) becomes a new issue. Obviously, the issue is difficult to address by relying on core enterprises to directly control the business, but need the help of ICT.

Financial Effect of Intelligent Supply Chain

After being energized by convergent ICT, especially for assets and funds, the supply chain and financial activities become truly "smart," boosting the effects of intelligence, ecologization, servicization, and visualization.

Supply chain decision intelligence refers to the ability to use all kinds of information and big data in the process of supply chain planning and financial decision-making to drive supply chain and financial decisions (from procurement decisions to manufacturing decisions, to delivery decisions, and, finally, to sales decisions) and the accompanying financial service decisions. Through the combination of big data and modeling tools, intelligent, and massive data analysis, supply chain financial decision intelligence can maximize the integration of supply chain information and client information, help to correctly assess the cost, time, quality, service, carbon emission, and other criteria in supply chain operations, achieve the best matching of logistics, transaction, and fund information, analyze the demand for funds in each business, and rationalize the financial business activities of supply chain based on the value demands of clients.

Supply chain service ecologization is the key for supply chain finance to move toward network platform. Ecosystem theory considers that numerous organizations and individuals are part of value creation, and they work together and organically cooperate to play different roles to drive the formation, development, deconstruction, and self-renewal of business networks. This ecological network structure results in a change in the way the supply chain is organized and behaves, from the original bilateral structure (dyadic), to trilateral structure (Andersson-Cederholm & Gyimóthy, 2010), and, finally, to a quadrilateral or a multilateral structure (Chakkol et al., 2014). The ecologization of supply chain means to look at the development of enterprises from the perspective of the whole industry: in addition to traditional upstream and downstream suppliers and clients, the ecosystem also includes other management organizations, industry associations, and other equivalent supply chains, which is to say, the ecosystem formed by the platform is a "small world," and the groups in the platform ecosystem will establish a virtuous cycle mechanism. This mechanism is expressed in the three dimensions proposed by Iansiti and Levien (2002). The first dimension is ecological robustness, that is, the ability of the cooperative network to cope with uncertainties and any sudden changes in the environment through synergy and cooperation among the participants involved. The second dimension is ecological productivity, that is, the ability to fully integrate their core elements through cooperation among the participants, continuously improving productivity over time, transmitting innovation, and jointly achieving higher efficiency and effectiveness. The third dimension is ecological niche creation, that is, the diversity of member roles in the ecosystem and the creativity that comes with it. Apparently, the realization of these three dimensions is conducive to the innovation and development of supply chain finance, reducing the risk of supply chain finance and promoting the optimization of industrial supply chain by supply chain finance.

The servitization of supply chain activities refers to the ability to effectively integrate various elements in supply chain operations to minimize the cost and maximize the value of element aggregation. This service-oriented management not only realizes effective supply chain planning (i.e., value management of supply chain operation), organization (supply chain coproduction management), coordination (supply chain knowledge management), and control (supply chain performance and risk management) through the combination of transaction, logistics, and fund flows but also brings new opportunities for enterprises and the whole supply chain through multiple elements, interaction, and aggregation, as well as contributes to supply chain innovation. This is mainly manifested in two aspects: first, supply chain participants achieve mutual service and value interaction, making the driver of innovation go from a single enterprise to the upstream and downstream synergy, and gradually to ecological openness; second, finance serves supply chain, and supply chain boosts finance, thus achieving asset-side and fund-side innovation.

The visualization of supply chain management refers to the use of information technology to collect, transfer, store, analyze, and process information about orders, logistics, and inventory and other related indicators in the supply chain and present them in a graphical way according to the needs of the supply chain. It mainly includes process visualization, warehouse visualization, logistics tracking management visualization, financial activity visualization, and risk management visualization. Connecting information of each node in the supply chain and breaking the bottleneck of information transmission allows each node enterprise to make full use of internal and external data, which undoubtedly strengthens the visualization of the supply chain. The visualization of supply chain further promotes the visualization of financial risk management in the supply chain. The visualization of financial risk management has the following benefits for business operations: (1) it provides a timely sense of what is happening in the real supply chain and facilitates enterprises to obtain and grasp first-hand information about the ongoing business process, what is happening, or what might happen; (2) it helps enterprises to plan the timing of actions in advance, that is, to set the rules of events as well as the principles of exceptions based on the analysis of strategic objectives of supply chain and the laws of supply chain financial operations; (3) it analyzes what is happening and allows enterprises to be able to effectively analyze the information and data acquired; (4) it determines the action plan so that, with the results of a graphical analysis based on business applications, enterprises know the resources and optimization tools they need to apply to adjust their supply chain operations and financial activities based on previously established business rules, exceptions, and other principles; (5) it implements the action plan and helps enterprises to identify specific measures to be adopted to achieve the adjustment and change of supply chain assets and financial processes.

3.4 GLP Supply Chain Finance Based on Industrial Scenario and Fintech

Based on subordinate business lines across logistics, food cold chain, FMCG, cross-border, and IoT, and targeting different industries, scenarios, and customer base, GLP Finance has formed a wide range of standard financial products, covering the production side, distribution side, sales side, logistics side, and other service sides of the industry (Fig. 3.3).

Standardized Financial Products under GLP Finance

Logistics Service: GLP Transport Loan and GLP E-Leasing

GLP Transport Loan and GLP E-Leasing are standardized supply chain financial products provided for logistics and transport enterprises and warehouse service enterprises. Based on scenarios of logistics industry,

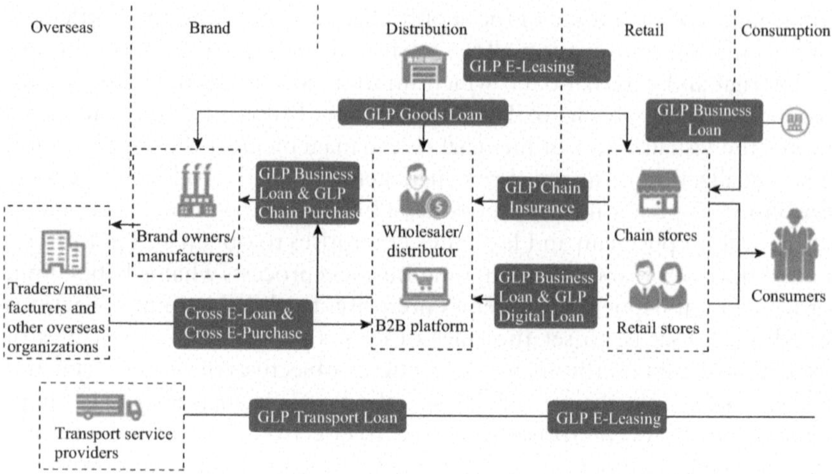

Fig. 3.3 Product map of GLP supply chain finance

GLP Finance can control the commodity flow and logistics transport with the help of data from core enterprises and core platforms and can provide financial service support to logistics platforms and core logistics enterprises through risk control based on big data (Fig. 3.4).

Cross-border Service: Cross-E Loan and Cross-E Purchase
The cross-border services of Cross-E Loan (see Fig. 3.5) and Cross-E Purchase (see Fig. 3.6) are divided into import business and export business, and mainly focus on customs clearance services and logistics services. These two types of data are relatively special. As far as the products for import and export are concerned, they need to be connected with the data of customs, forming verification of orders, payment slips, and waybills to ensure the authenticity of data. The difficulty lies in the analysis of the data and the control of the cargoes. With its resources in bonded warehouses and logistics, GLP Finance has formed a system for data analysis, logistics control, and cargo supervision. It controls risks through its systems and IOT devices.

Cold Chain Service: GLP Chain Purchase
GLP Chain Purchase about cold chain services manages the commodity flow and transport flow of the cold chain food trade chain based on the scenarios of food cold chain industry, with the help of the data of core

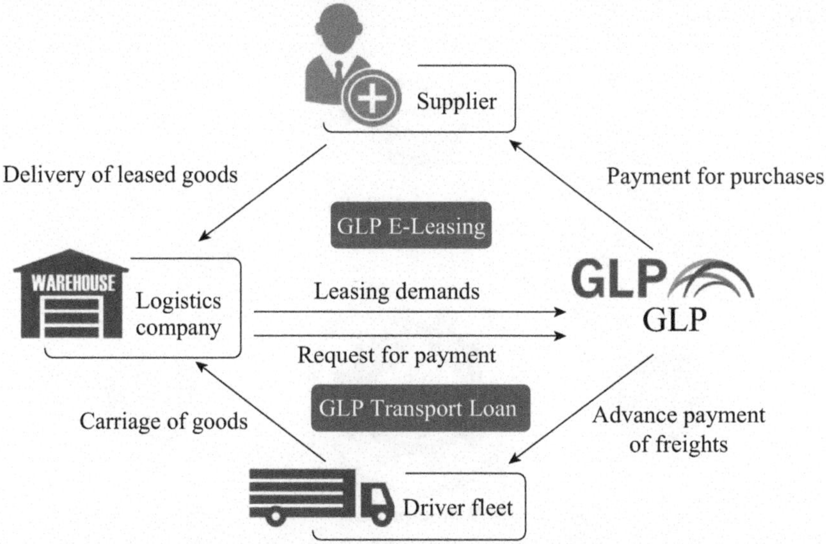

Fig. 3.4 Scenarios of GLP transport loan and GLP e-leasing

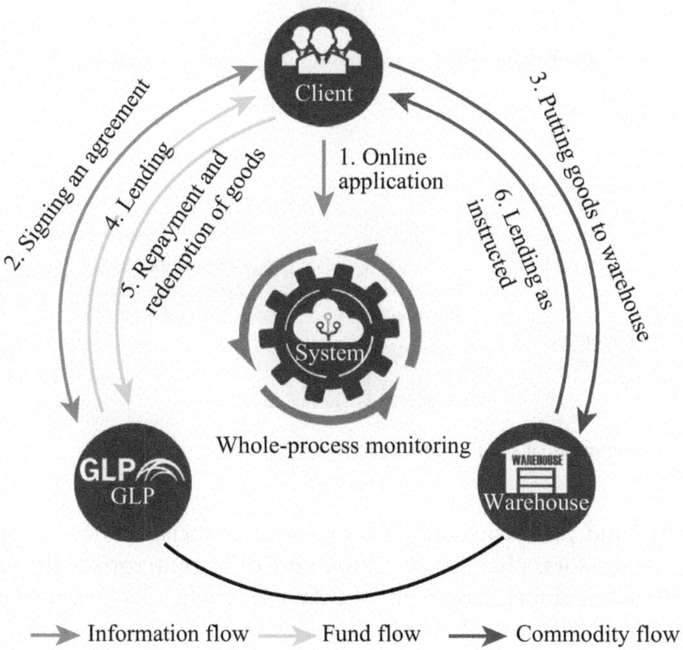

Fig. 3.5 Cross-e-loan process

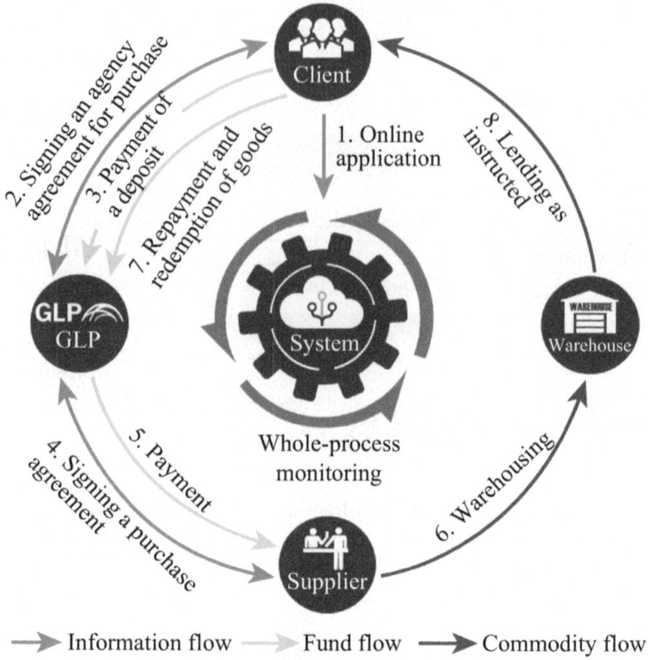

Fig. 3.6 Cross-e-purchase process

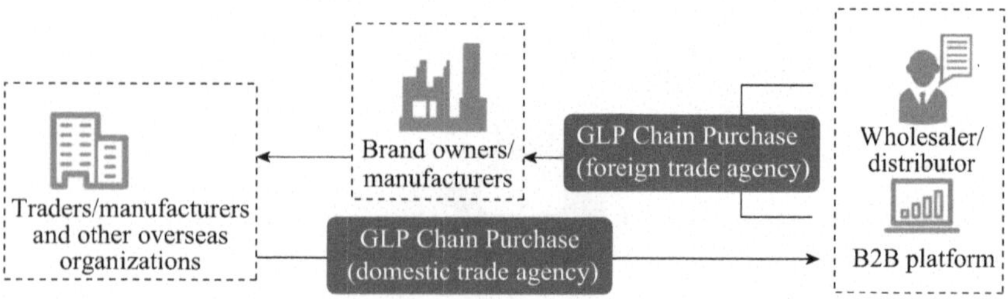

Fig. 3.7 Scenarios of GLP chain purchase

enterprises and platforms, and also provides financial service support for traders, processors, chain restaurants, and other enterprises through its risk control capability based on big data (see Fig. 3.7). After years of exploration, it has formed standardized and online operation procedures applicable to the whole product chain.

Trade Service: GLP Chain Insurance
Focusing on the trade sector, GLP Chain Insurance starts to track and control risks through industry data analysis and IoT devices based on standardized procedures, instead of previous lending model which was based on credits of core enterprises (see Fig. 3.8).

Supervised Warehouse: GLP Goods Loan
GLP has nearly 300 parks in China, with over trillions of dollars worth of goods. Based on its previous experience in supply chain finance regarding cargo pledge financing, GLP Finance has standardized and regulated its business rules and procedures, which is very important to promote the formation of standardized and regulated management for the entire industry.

GLP Goods Loan (see Fig. 3.9), born in this context, is a standardized product for enterprise owners who can apply for financing services through

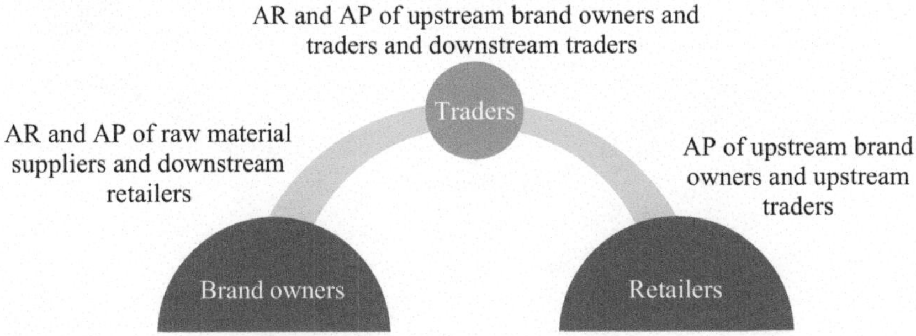

Fig. 3.8 Business scenarios of GLP chain insurance

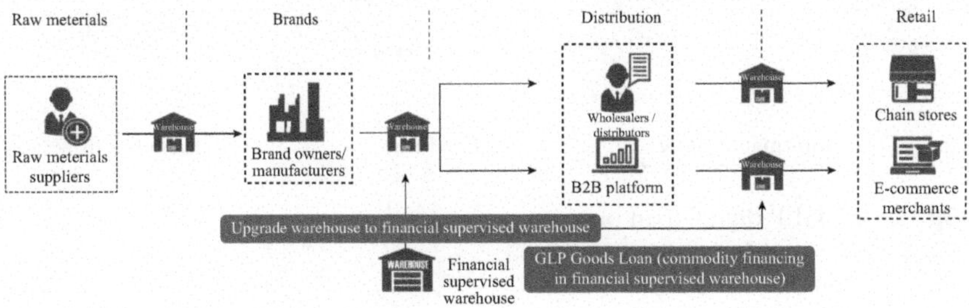

Fig. 3.9 Business scenarios of GLP goods loan

pledging of their goods. The formulation and implementation of the industry's financial regulation standards and procedures, as well as the establishment of a regulatory alliance and a pledge alliance, will lead to a healthier development of the industry.

Big Data + Scenario: GLP Business Loan and GLP Digital Loan

GLP Business Loan and GLP Digital Loan are products launched by GLP Finance based on data scenarios in logistics. GLP Business Loan is a credit product based on the data of SMEs in order placing and store opening and other possible entrusted payment scenarios, with an aim to offer funds to business operations. GLP Digital Loan is a financial product based on logistics scenarios combined with invoice data and mainly serves SMEs in those scenarios (see Fig. 3.10).

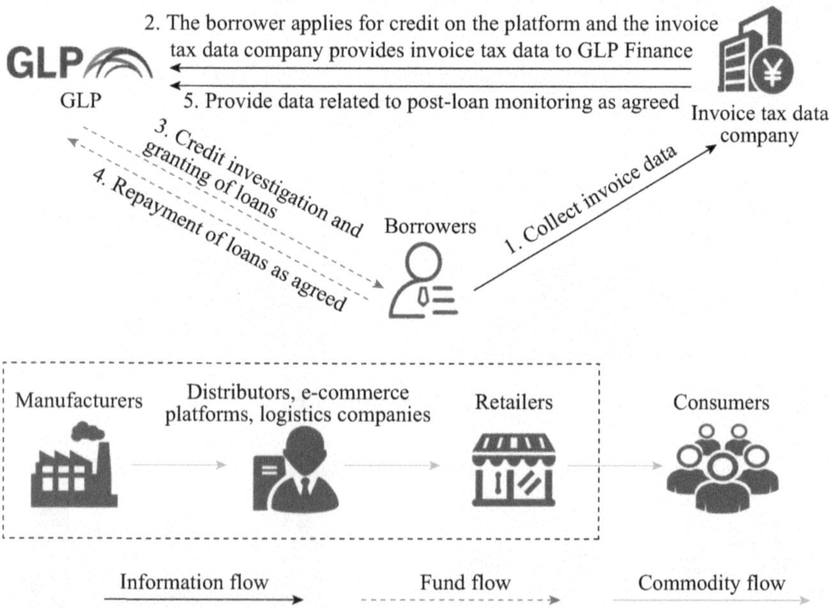

Fig. 3.10 GLP digital loan process

Advantages of GLP financial products

Full Online Operation

GLP standard financial products have now abandoned the traditional operation model, and have instead realized the online and modular operation of such products through the output of systems (combining with the services within GLP system, including the scenario services such as order management system (OMS), warehouse management system (WMS), and transportation management system (TMS), as well as property management and other diverse services) and standard data interfaces, improving the overall experience of customers who use financial products.

In addition to official website, app, WeChat mini program, and WeChat official account, GLP Finance also outputs standard data interfaces and application pages and then embeds them into the platforms of internal and external customers of the GLP system, allowing customers to apply for products without bothering to transfer information, which greatly improves the user experience.

At the loan granting and withdrawal stage, GLP Finance combines Internet technologies (OCR image recognition, AI, and other technologies) with standard data interfaces, as well as loan granting and utilization models. Through the data interfaces and the implementation of the models, the approval process has been greatly shortened to a few seconds. After passing the approval, users can immediately withdraw money online, which greatly improves the efficiency of capital flow.

As far as the account system is concerned, GLP Finance provides account management services, so users can manage and use the products through their own accounts, and also check information such as repayment plans, approval nodes, loan granted, and balance.

Meanwhile, the automatic clearing and settlement system developed by GLP Finance has realized various clearing and settlement functions such as fund transfer, real-time transfer, real-time automatic clearing, and so on, which improves user experience with risks controlled.

Risk Control Based on Big Data and Industry and Product Characteristics

Compared with traditional financial institutions (only paying attention to the local nodes of the industrial chain of enterprises), GLP Finance focuses on a large number of SMEs that are not served by the traditional financial institutions, with data often covering all scenarios of the entire industrial chain. As for data in different scenarios, GLP Finance integrates internal data (e.g., enterprise logistics cooperation data, inter-enterprise transaction data, and product data) and external data (e.g., customer data from industrial and commercial bureaus, public security bureaus, prosecutors' offices, courts, and credit agencies) to sort out the relationships between entities, thus finally forming a supply chain knowledge map of GLP Finance, which is applied to GLP Finance's business procedures. In addition, GLP Finance controls risks from several perspectives of borrowers, commodities, and partner platforms in a dynamic manner, while traditional financial institutions rely only on static corporate credit to grant loans to SMEs, which not only makes it difficult to reach most customers with insufficient credit records but also makes it difficult to monitor post-loan risks.

At present, based on the data in the scenarios and the relationship of related entities in the industry chain, GLP Finance has formed a corresponding supply chain knowledge map and a complete risk control model. The perspectives and breadth of data are most important for a data-based risk control model. The previous infrastructure construction allows GLP Finance to have data covering commodity flow, transport flow, information flow, and fund flow. Utilizing the data of these four flows, GLP Finance has designed risk control logic for different enterprises in different industries and nodes, which can be divided into pre-loan, loan-granting, and post-loan modules.

At the pre-loan stage, GLP Finance screens enterprises that submit loan applications to exclude high-risk ones. Fraud detection is also performed by accessing data such as credit records from the People's Bank of China and GLP Finance's internal and third-party blacklists. Then, GLP Finance uses anti-fraud models, credit rating models, and other big data models to make approval decisions on qualified customers and determine the loan terms. Also, before granting loans, the amounts and terms of loans are determined by relying on the big data model.

At the loan-granting stage, GLP Finance mainly focuses on data standardization, credit granting model, as well as credit line and interest rate evaluation model. First, GLP Finance standardizes multidimensional non-standardized data through crawlers and OCR technology, in addition to docking already-authorized data, to make it verifiable and quantitative. Second, GLP Finance has established a 360° credit evaluation model that covers the dimensions of industry access, SKU access, and company access and incorporates internal data from the system and external data from third parties, in order to complete the first review on applicants and directly reject the enterprises that do not meet the model criteria. GLP Finance's credit line and interest rate evaluation model can output the credit lines and interest rates that can be offered to customers by presetting a credit line and interest rate to assist the risk control personnel in making decisions. Loan application within approved credit lines can be approved directly through the risk control model. Furthermore, the credit line model outputs withdrawal approval conditions and a preset withdrawal approval model to assist in withdrawal review.

The post-loan monitoring platform is mainly supported by the risk warning model and the collection model. GLP Finance profiles customer business information based on multidimensional data sources in order to anticipate risks and safeguard funds in a timely manner. Currently, GLP Financial has formed certain industry standards for monitoring indicators for different industries.

Blockchain Technology in GLP Ecosystem

Building Service Provider System: Blockchain-based Asset and Funding Platform

1. From the perspective of the source of funds and assets, GLP Finance is both an asset provider and a fund provider. As an asset provider, GLP Finance provides high-quality assets for funds from banks, brokers, trust companies, and other institutions, and as a fund provider, GLP Finance provides funds to upstream and downstream enterprises and service providers in the industry.
2. GLP Finance builds a blockchain-based asset and funding platform.

   Leveraging the characteristics of supply chain logistics and financial services, and combining with the distributed, encrypting, tamper-evident and traceable features of blockchain, the underlying asset providers, investors, and other participants are allowed to jointly maintain the ledger, thus connecting the information silos of various participants in the supply chain, promoting the transparency of information, realizing the penetrating supervision of underlying assets, and enhancing the ability of risk discovery and control.
3. GLP Finance's asset and funding platform provides full-process asset management services to fund providers (see Fig. 3.11). First,

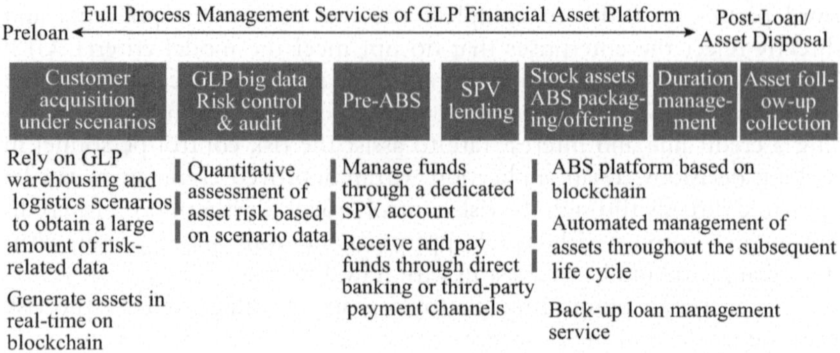

Fig. 3.11 "Full Process" management services of GLP financial asset platform

GLP Finance acquires customers in existing logistics, cargo, retail, and other scenarios through a variety of standardized financial products as described above. Compared with traditional asset providers, GLP Finance builds financial products suitable for industrial scenarios around its own industrial ecology, but these industrial scenarios have certain barriers to entry, so it is difficult for financial institutions themselves to replicate such scenarios. By building a platform, GLP Finance helps these institutions to invest their funds in these industrial scenarios and use their strong industrial and technological backgrounds to effectively reduce the risk of their assets.

4. At the same time, GLP Finance uses big data-based risk control to create the new models of supply chain finance. GLP Finance analyzes the data of upstream and downstream enterprises in the industry chain, and relies on its self-developed access model, anti-fraud model, credit rating model, risk pricing model, and risk warning model in the whole course of loan access, pre-loan, loan-granting, and post-loan stages to quantitatively assess asset risks and achieve strong control over assets. Through standardized financial products, GLP Finance synchronizes asset information to the blockchain in real time to prevent information from being tampered with and effectively guarantee the authenticity of data.
5. With the help of big data-based risk control system, GLP Finance provides pre-ABS services for customers' high-quality assets and lending services to SPVs. By incorporating data into the supply chain, GLP Finance provides real, accurate, and high-quality supply

chain financial assets and other value-added operation services to its partner fund providers. At the pre-ABS stage, GLP Finance manages the SPV accounts of its partner fund providers separately. Meanwhile, at the loan-granting stage, the funds are received and paid through direct bank-enterprise links or other third-party payment channels to ensure the orderly and safe flow of funds.

6. When customers are willing to package its stock of debt and issue ABS, GLP Finance uses its blockchain-based ABS platform to provide the customers with real-data-based, asset-penetrated, accurate cash flow analysis and an efficient management platform. At various stages of asset screening, product design, and product issuance, participants in the alliance chain input key asset and brokerage data into the blockchain to ensure that investors and partner fund providers can penetrate the underlying assets in real time. Meanwhile, as far as duration management is concerned, the customers perform real-time loan and post-loan monitoring through the investor service platform, obtain online asset service reports and other relevant broker performance documents, and monitor default indicators to penetrate broker-related risks. Once asset performance declines, GLP Finance also provides follow-up asset collection and other services and provides the customers with automatic life cycle management of asset to ensure the safety of customer funds.

Based on several major weaknesses of existing SMEs in the supply chain, GLP Finance has created a blockchain-based asset and funding platform (see Fig. 3.12). The platform connects standardized data based on standardized financial products on the asset side, and utilizes the tamper-evident nature of data on the blockchain to unite SMEs to write their core associated data on the chain. Furthermore, based on the data input into the chain in real time, the platform provides risk pricing, dynamic risk warning and monitoring of assets by means of big data and machine learning, helping financial institutions penetrate products and supervise underlying assets, realizing scientific "transfusion" based on actual operation data of SMEs and promoting healthy development of SMEs.

For example, take the alliance chain-based ABS platform built by GLP Finance.

GLP Finance leverages the advantages of blockchain technology such as smart contracts and data tamper-proofing to serve logistics and warehousing assets, supply chain financial assets, and other high-quality assets

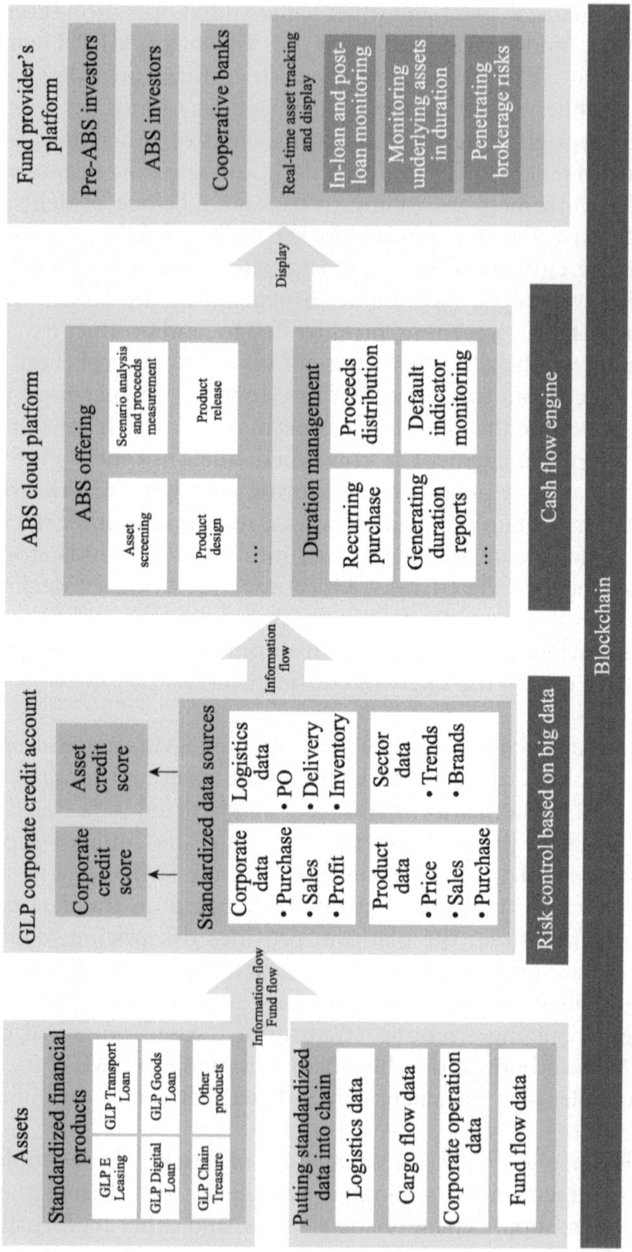

Fig. 3.12 GLP ABS platform

within and outside the GLP system. It attracts market capital by creating ABS products and other means. Using blockchain technology as a guarantee for risk control, each participant in the supply chain, such as asset provider, fund provider, and supervisor, is treated as each data node on the blockchain, thus penetrating the underlying assets at any time and ensuring that the fund provider can get knowledge of the underlying assets, the intermediary can control the risk of asset default in real time, and the supervisor can effectively utilize the financial levers, which greatly prevent systemic risks in advance.

During the asset portfolio construction, GLP Finance's blockchain-based ABS platform achieves real-time incorporation of loan and repayment information flow and cash flow into the chain, so as to achieve

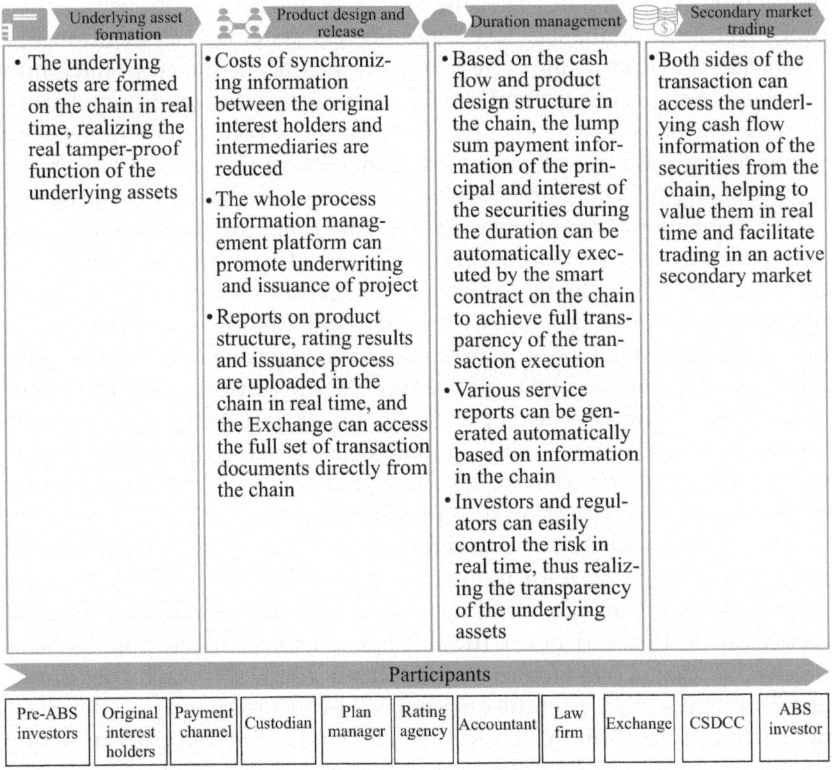

Fig. 3.13 ABS business process of GLP finance

authenticity and tamper resistance of the underlying assets. By deploying each participant as a verification node, each transaction in the blockchain management system requires consensus of all nodes before it can be incorporated into the chain, and it cannot be privately tampered with by a single party after being incorporated into the chain, thus ensuring the authenticity and integrity of the underlying loan and repayment data in the ABS service provider system.

At the product design and issuance stage, the transaction structure and rating results are confirmed by the rating agencies and brokers and then incorporated into the chain as a consensus on smart contracts. Meanwhile, exchanges can obtain the full set of transaction documents directly from the chain and incorporate the approval results into the chain to help strengthen regulation, and penetrate and control the underlying asset risks in real time. This provides a key innovative technical means to help regulators effectively use financial levers and prevent systemic risks in advance.

During the product life cycle, based on the cash flow incorporated into the chain at the first stage and the transaction structure incorporated into the chain at the second stage, the smart contract may automatically send the principal and interest payment information of the securities to investors, realizing full transparency of transaction execution and reducing the risk of manual operation errors. At the same time, the smart contract can automatically generate various service reports based on the information on the chain, thus helping investors and regulators to control the risks in real time and realize the underlying asset penetration. In addition, based on the real underlying asset and cash flows incorporated into the chain and relying on big data and quantitative models, the platform can achieve all-round quality control of asset portfolios, as well as more refined cash flow forecasting, asset portfolio pricing, and advance rating, helping both parties to the transaction to make real-time pricing and complete the transfer of ownership of securities on the chain in real time.

The blockchain-based asset and funding platform built by GLP Finance will provide a reference for industry standards in respect of supply chain finance, provide intelligent and data-based logistics services and financial services to SMEs, and boost the intelligent growth of the supply chain finance industry. GLP Finance will gradually connect to each core enterprise's system so that asset information will be incorporated into the chain upon asset production, which will help all kinds of investors to subscribe to assets through the ABS platform subsequently.

Building a Blockchain-based Credit Alliance

Currently, the corporate credit of SMEs cannot be effectively verified. In order to solve the problem of credit investigation over SMEs, a blockchain-based credit alliance has been built to increase credit for enterprises. Although the information construction of the logistics industry has made small achievements, the data of each enterprise is still like a single stand-alone silo. For financial institutions, it is difficult to verify the authenticity of the fragmented and scattered corporate data, and therefore difficult to provide loans to SMEs. GLP Finance has set up a corporate credit evaluation mechanism by taking advantage of scenarios and data, connecting core enterprises and platforms in its own ecosystem, as well as upstream and downstream enterprises extended by these enterprises. This mechanism connects all channels of the underlying data from production, transport, and warehousing to sales. GLP Finance also cooperates with an array of large logistic platforms, obtains all kinds of order information, transaction information, vehicle information, and location information thereon via system docking, and have more data control over the receivable information of borrowers thereon via data docking and information cross-verification. In this way, a practical and efficient data-based credit investigation model is formed.

Moreover, based on the corporate credit information within the GLP ecosystem, GLP Finance has built a blockchain-based credit alliance. Currently, the ones that partner up with GLP Finance include not only financial institutions but also core enterprises such as brand owners, core traders, and retailers. As a platform, GLP Finance forms a credit alliance system with a variety of institutions, including cooperative financial institutions, aiming to share credit data and address the needs of each institution in the alliance. Now, the credit alliance created by GLP Finance mainly relies on the risk control system in the GLP ecosystem.

The risk control system of the GLP credit alliance consists of two main parts:

1. Data supervision: GLP Finance uses co-shared data from enterprises within its own system to cross-verify and ensure credible scenarios through fund flow, industrial information flow, logistics information, and debt information (e.g., data from vehicle GPS service providers, as well as orders and logistics data from vehicle and cargo matching platform).

2. Offline supervision: This is a major difference between the GLP system and traditional financial institutions. The logistics parks within the GLP system and the various service points of the enterprises within the system are like tangible hands, and the shared routes and systems are used as the last gate for risk control. For example, all the gates of the GLP system's parks and warehouses have become gates of risk control by being equipped with new technologies.

For example, take the supervised warehouse built by GLP Finance (see Fig. 3.14).

GLP Finance's supervised warehouse evaluation standard system is a set of evaluation standards on supervised warehouses and operations established for a series of financial products such as cargo pledge financing. This standard system mainly serves financial institutions. Currently, as for movable asset pledge financing, the goods are nonstandardized assets. Although different evaluation and supervision exist for nonstandardized assets, a set of unified procedures regarding management and supervision can be sorted out as far as the procedures and infrastructure management are concerned, thus regulating the whole market and reducing risks. Financial institutions may grant loans under cargo pledge financing with reference to GLP Finance's supervised warehouse standards. The supervised warehouse scores may be used to classify and grade the entire

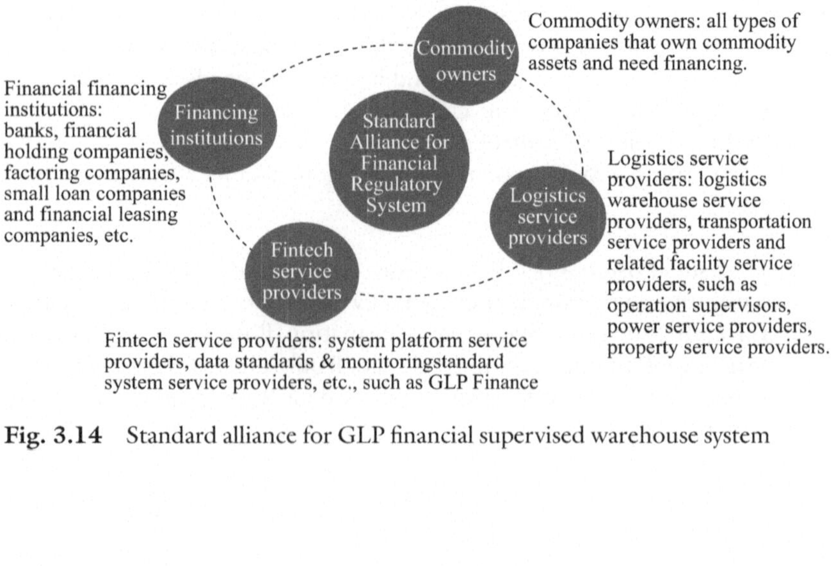

Fig. 3.14 Standard alliance for GLP financial supervised warehouse system

supervised warehouse system, thus supporting the business evaluation of financial institutions.

For the time being, there are many problems in the process of carrying out cargo pledge financing business: inconsistent warehouse standards, inconsistent operator (supervisor) evaluations, inconsistent system standards, and so on. All these problems have hindered the development of cargo pledge financing. Considering from the industry, GLP Finance centers its supply chain finance business on warehouses, refines the standards for supervised warehouse system from its business experience, and takes the lead in establishing an alliance of supervised warehouse system standards for serving all parties.

References

Akyuz, G. A., & Rehan, M. (2009). Requirements for forming an 'e-supply chain'. *International Journal of Production Research, 47*(12), 3265–3287.

Andersson-Cederholm, E., & Gyimóthy, S. (2010). The service triad: Modelling dialectic tensions in service encounters. *The Service Industries Journal, 30*(2), 265–280.

Ashton, K. (2009). That 'internet of things' thing. *RFID Journal, 22*(7), 97–114.

Atzori, L., Iera, A., & Morabito, G. (2010). The internet of things: A survey. *Computer Networks, 54*(15), 2787–2805.

Babiceanu, R. F., & Seker, R. (2016). Big Data and virtualization for manufacturing cyber-physical systems: A survey of the current status and future outlook. *Computers in Industry, 81*, 128–137.

Ben-Daya, M., Hassini, E., & Bahroun, Z. (2017). Internet of things and supply chain management: A literature review. *International Journal of Production Research*, 1–24.

Berger, A. N., & Udell, G. F. (2006). A more complete conceptual framework for SME finance. *Journal of Banking & Finance, 30*(11), 2945–2966.

Blackman, I. D., Holland, C. P., & Westcott, T. (2013). Motorola's global financial supply chain strategy. *Supply Chain Management: An International Journal, 18*(2), 132–147.

Brealey, R., Leland, H. E., & Pyle, D. H. (1977). Informational asymmetries, financial structure, and financial intermediation. *The Journal of Finance, 32*(2), 371–387.

Brynjolfsson, E., Hitt, L. M., & Kim, H. H. (2011). *Strength in numbers: How does data-driven decisionmaking affect firm performance?* SSRN: 1819486.

Bughin, J., Chui, M., & Manyika, J. (2010). Clouds, big data, and smart assets: Ten tech-enabled business trends to watch. *The McKinsey Quarterly, 56*(1), 75–86.

Butner, K. (2010). The smarter supply chain of the future. *Strategy & Leadership, 38*(1), 22–31. https://doi.org/10.1108/10878571011009859
Cachon, G. P., & Fisher, M. (2000). Supply chain inventory management and the value of shared information. *Management Science, 46*(8), 1032–1048.
Cardoso, S. R., Barbosa-Póvoa, A. P. F., & Relvas, S. (2013). Design and planning of supply chains with integration of reverse logistics activities under demand uncertainty. *European Journal of Operational Research, 226*(3), 436–451.
Carmichael, F., Palacios-Marques, D., & Gil-Pechuan, I. (2011). How to create information management capabilities through web 2.0. *The Service Industries Journal, 31*(10), 1613–1625.
Cecez-Kecmanovic, D., Janson, M., & Brown, A. (2002). The rationality framework for a critical study of information systems. *Journal of Information Technology, 17*(4), 215–227. https://doi.org/10.1080/02683960220000017752
Chae, B., Olson, D., & Sheu, C. (2014). The impact of supply chain analytics on operational performance: A resource-based view. *International Journal of Production Research, 52*(16), 4695–4710.
Chakkol, M., Johnson, M., Raja, J., & Raffoni, A. (2014). From goods to solutions: How does the content of an offering affect network configuration? *International Journal of Physical Distribution and Logistics Management, 44*(1/2), 132–154.
Chen, B., Wan, J., Shu, L., Li, P., Mukherjee, M., & Yin, B. (2018). Smart factory of industry 4.0: Key technologies, application case, and challenges. *IEEE Access, 6*, 6505–6519.
Chopra, S., & Meindl, P. (2013). *Supply chain management: Strategy, planning, and operation* (5th ed.). Pearson, Upper Saddle River, NJ.
Christopher, M. (2016). *Logistics & supply chain management*. Pearson UK.
Chui, M., Loffler, M., & Roberts, R. (2010). The internet of things. *McKinsey Quarterly* (2), 1–9.
Damiani, E., Frati, F., & Tchokpon, R. (2011). The role of information sharing in supply chain management: The securescm approach. *International Journal of Innovation and Technology Management, 8*(3), 455–467.
Danese, P., Romano, P., & Formentini, M. (2013). The impact of supply chain integration on responsiveness: The moderating effect of using an international supplier network. *Transportation Research Part E: Logistics and Transportation Review, 49*(1), 125–140.
de Boer, R., van Bergen, M., & Steeman, M. A. (2015). Supply chain finance, its practical relevance and strategic value, 1st ed, *The Supply Chain Finance Essential Knowledge Series*. Zwolle.
Detlor, B. (2010). Information management. *International Journal of Information Management, 30*, 103–108.
Ellram, L. M., Tate, W. L., & Billington, C. (2004). Understanding and managing the services supply chain. *The Journal of Supply Chain Management, 40*(4), 17–32.

Ericsson. (2019). Key technology choices for optimal massive IoT devices, ericsson.com

Evans, P. C., & Annunziata, M. (2012). Industrial internet: Pushing the boundaries. *General Electric Reports.*

Fisher, O., Watson, N., Porcu, L., Bacon, D., Rigley, M., & Gomes, R. L. (2018). Cloud manufacturing as a sustainable process manufacturing route. *Journal of Manufacturing Systems, 47*, 53–68.

Fleisch, E. (2010). What is the internet of things? An economic perspective. *Economics, Management, and Financial Markets, 5*(2), 125–157.

FSB. (2016). *Describing the landscape and a framework for analysis.*

Gartner, Gartner. (2014, 11 November). Says 4.9 Billion Connected "Things" Will Be in Use in 2015, Barcelona, Spain.

Haass, R., Dittmer, P., Veigt, M., & Lütjen, M. (2015). Reducing food losses and carbon emission by using autonomous control–A simulation study of the intelligent container. *International Journal of Production Economics, 164*, 400–408.

Han, R. (2013). Application and exploration of big data in enterprises [J]. *China Internet Week, 19.*

Handfield, R. B., & Nichols, E. L. (2002). *Supply chain redesign: Transforming supply chains into integrated value systems.* Ft Press.

Hessman, T. (2013). The dawn of the smart factory. *Industry Week, 14*, 14–19.

Holmberg, S. (2000). A systems perspective on supply chain measurements. *International Journal of Physical Distribution and Logistics Management, 30*(10), 847–868.

Iansiti, M., & Levien, R. (2002). *The new operational dynamics of business ecosystems: Implications for policy, operations and technology strategy.* Citeseer.

Jeschke, S., Brecher, C., Meisen, T., Özdemir, D., & Eschert, T. (2017). Industrial internet of things and cyber manufacturing systems. In *Industrial Internet of Things* (pp. 3–19). Springer.

Jiang, C. F. (2015). Innovation of supply chain financial services [J]. *China Business and Market, 1.*

Kagermann, H., Helbig, J., Hellinger, A., & Wahlster, W. (2013). *Recommendations for implementing the strategic initiative INDUSTRIE 4.0: Securing the future of German manufacturing industry; final report of the Industrie 4.0 Working Group.* Forschungsunion.

Kang, H. S., Lee, J. Y., Choi, S., Kim, H., Park, J. H., Son, J. Y., ... Do Noh, S. (2016). Smart manufacturing: Past research, present findings, and future directions. *International Journal of Precision Engineering and Manufacturing-Green Technology, 3*(1), 111–128.

Kim, S., & Heller, M. (2006). Emerging cyberinfrastructure: Challenges for the chemical process control community. *Computers & Chemical Engineering, 30*(10–12), 1497–1501.

Koch, M. T., Baars, H., Lasi, H., & Kemper, H. G. (2010). Manufacturing Execution Systems and Business Intelligence for Production Environments. In *AMCIS* (p. 436).

Kumar, R. S., & Pugazhendhi, S. (2012). Information sharing in supply chains: An overview. *Procedia Engineering, 38*, 2147–2154.

Lambert, D. M., & Cooper, M. C. (2000). Issues in supply chain management. *Industrial Marketing Management, 29*(1), 65–83.

Lazzarini, S., Chaddad, F., & Cook, M. (2001). Integrating supply chain and network analyses: The study of netchains. *Journal on Chain and Network Science, 1*(1), 7–22.

Le Tan, T., & Thi Dai Trang, D. (2017). Issues of implementing electronic supply chain management (E-SCM) in enterprise. *European Business & Management, 3*(5), 86–94.

Lee, H. L. (2002). Aligning supply chain strategies with product uncertainties. *California Management Review, 44*(3), 105–119.

Lee, I., & Lee, K. (2015). The Internet of Things (IoT): Applications, investments, and challenges for enterprises. *Business Horizons, 58*(4), 431–440.

Lee, J., Kao, H. A., & Yang, S. (2014). Service innovation and smart analytics for industry 4.0 and big data environment. *Procedia Cirp, 16*, 3–8.

Lee, J., Ardakani, H. D., Yang, S., & Bagheri, B. (2015). Industrial big data analytics and cyber-physical systems for future maintenance & service innovation. *Procedia Cirp, 38*, 3–7.

Lee, J., Davari, H., Singh, J., & Pandhare, V. (2018). Industrial Artificial Intelligence for industry 4.0-based manufacturing systems. *Manufacturing Letters, 18*, 20–23.

Levi, D. S., Kaminsky, P., & Levi, E. S. (2003). *Designing and managing the supply chain: Concepts, strategies, and case studies*. McGraw-Hill.

Li, R. F., Xie, Y., Li, R., & Li, L. (2012). A review of some key issues of information-physical convergence systems [J]. *Journal of Computer Research and Development, 49*(6), 1149–1161.

Li, W. L., & Xia, J. M. (2013). Innovation of business model based on "big data" [J]. *China Industrial Economics, 5*, 83–95.

Li, Y. Q., & Long, J. (2013). Research on innovation path of strategic emerging industries in big data era [J]. *Consumer Electronics Magazine, 14*, 173–174.

Li, J., Morrison, J., Zhang, M., Nakano, M., Biller, S., & Lennartson, B. (2013). Editorial: Automation in green manufacturing. *IEEE Transactions on Automation Science & Engineering, 10*(1), 1–4.

Liang Hongbo. (2014). Cloud logistics and big data change the logistics model. *China Circulation Economy, 28*(05), 41–45.

Liang Yan. (2014). A preliminary study on the development of supply chain financing business of Agricultural Bank in the era of big data. *Journal of Agricultural Bank of China Wuhan Training College, 03*: 28–31.

Liker, J. K., & Choi, T. Y. (2004). Building deep supplier relationships. *Harvard Business Review, 82*(12), 104–113.

Liu, Z., Prajogo, D., & Oke, A. (2016). Supply chain technologies: Linking adoption, utilization, and performance. *Journal of Supply Chain Management, 52*(4), 22–41.

Loher, S. (2012). Big data: Rise of the machines. *The New York Times*, December 31, p. B6.

López, T. S., Ranasinghe, D. C., Patkai, B., & McFarlane, D. (2011). Taxonomy, technology and applications of smart objects. *Information Systems Frontiers, 13*(2), 281–300.

López, T. S., Ranasinghe, D. C., Harrison, M., & McFarlane, D. (2012). Adding sense to the Internet of Things. *Personal and Ubiquitous Computing, 16*(3), 291–308.

Low, C., Chen, Y., & Wu, M. (2011). Understanding the determinants of cloud computing adoption. *Industrial Management & Data Systems.*

Lu, Y. (2017). Industry 4.0: A survey on technologies, applications and open research issues. *Journal of Industrial Information Integration, 6*, 1–10.

Lucke, D., Constantinescu, C., & Westkämper, E. (2008). Smart factory-a step towards the next generation of manufacturing. In *Manufacturing systems and technologies for the new frontier* (pp. 115–118). Springer.

Masciari, E. (2012). SMART: Stream monitoring enterprise activities by RFID tags. *Information Sciences, 195*, 25–44.

Meindl, P., & Chopra, S. (2013). *Supply chain management: Strategy, planning, and operation, 5/e.* Pearson Education India.

Mithas, S., Ramasubbu, N., & Sambamurthy, V. (2011). How information management capability influences firm performance. *MIS Quarterly, 35*(1), 237.

Modi, S. B., & Mabert, V. A. (2010). Exploring the relationship between efficient supply chain management and firm innovation: An archival search and analysis. *Journal of Supply Chain Management, 46*(4), 81–94.

Monostori, L. (2014). Cyber-physical production systems: Roots, expectations and R&D challenges. *Procedia Cirp, 17*, 9–13.

Mouratidis, H., & Diamantopoulou, V. (2018). A security analysis method for industrial Internet of things. *IEEE Transactions on Industrial Informatics, 14*(9), 4093–4100.

Oudenhoven, J., Vullers, R., & Van Schaijk, R. (2012). A review of the present situation and future developments of micro-batteries for wireless autonomous sensor systems. *International Journal of Energy Research, 36*(12), 1139–1150.

Pan Honghua. (2012). Intelligent supply chain management and application based on the Internet of Things. *China Logistics and Purchasing, 12*, 74–75. (in Chinese).

Papert, M., & Pflaum, A. (2017). Development of an ecosystem model for the realization of internet of things (IoT) services in supply chain management. *Electronic Markets, 27*(2), 175–189.

Papert, M., Rimpler, P., & Pflaum, A. (2016). Enhancing supply chain visibility in a pharmaceutical supply chain: Solutions based on automatic identification technology. *International Journal of Physical Distribution & Logistics Management, 46*(9), 859–884.

Pease, S. G., Trueman, R., Davies, C., Grosberg, J., Yau, K. H., Kaur, N., ... & West, A. (2018). An intelligent real-time cyber-physical toolset for energy and process prediction and optimisation in the future industrial Internet of Things. *Future Generation Computer Systems, 79*, 815–829.

Pedroso, M. C., & Nakano, D. (2009). Knowledge and information flows in supply chains: A study on pharmaceutical companies. *International Journal of Production Economics, 122*(1), 376–384.

Pinheiro, P., Macedo, M., Barbosa, R., Santos, R., & Novais, P. (2018, June). Multi-agent systems approach to industry 4.0: Enabling collaboration considering a blockchain for knowledge representation. In *International Conference on Practical Applications of Agents and Multi-Agent Systems* (pp. 149–160). Springer, Cham.

Porter, M. E. (1985). Competitive advantage: Creating and sustaining superior performance. *New York: FreePress, 43*, 214.

Provost, F., & Fawcett, T. (2013). Data science and its relationship to big data and data-driven decision making. *Big data, 1*(1), 51–59.

Radziwon, A., Bilberg, A., Bogers, M., & Madsen, E. S. (2014). The smart factory: exploring adaptive and flexible manufacturing solutions. *Procedia Engineering, 69*, 1184–1190.

Ren, G. J. (2014). Innovation and inspiration of business model based on "big data" [J]. *Modern Business Trade Industry, 2.*

Ross, A. D., Kuzu, K., & Li, W. (2016). Exploring supplier performance risk and the buyer's role using chance-constrained data envelopment analysis. *European Journal of Operational Research, 250*(3), 966–978.

Ryan, P., & Watson, R. (2017). Research challenges for the Internet of Things: What role can OR play? *System, 5*(1), 24.

Schoenherr, T., & Speier-Pero, C. (2015). Data science, predictive analytics, and big data in supply chain management: Current state and future potential. *Journal of Business Logistics, 36*(1), 120–132.

Schuster A. J. (2007). Intelligent Computing Everywhere. In Schuster A. J. (eds) *Intelligent Computing Everywhere.* Springer, London.

Scott, J. (2000). Points, lines and density. *Social Network Analysis: A handbook.* London: SAGE Publications, 67.

Song, H. (2015). *Supply chain finance (Second Edition) [M].* China Renmin University Press.

Song, H. (2017). *Internet supply chain finance [M].* China Renmin University Press.

Song, H., & Lu, Q. (2017). Innovation of supply chain finance model based on virtual industry cluster: Case study of SJET [J]. *China Industrial Economics, 5*, 172–192.

Song, H., & Yang, X. (2018). Study on impact of SMEs' competitiveness and network embeddedness on performance of supply chain finance[J]. *Chinese Journal of Management, 5*(4), 616.

Tan, K. H., Zhan, Y., Ji, G., Ye, F., & Chang, C. (2015). Harvesting big data to enhance supply chain innovation capabilities: An analytic infrastructure based on deduction graph. *International Journal of Production Economics, 165*, 223–233.

Tao, F., Cheng, J., & Qi, Q. (2017). IIHub: An industrial Internet-of-Things hub toward smart manufacturing based on cyber-physical system. *IEEE Transactions on Industrial Informatics, 14*(5), 2271–2280.

Thiesse, F., & Buckel, T. (2015). A comparison of RFID-based shelf replenishment policies in retail stores under suboptimal read rates. *International Journal of Production Economics, 159*, 126–136.

Thoben, K. D., Wiesner, S., & Wuest, T. (2017). "Industrie 4.0" and smart manufacturing-a review of research issues and application examples. *International Journal of Automation Technology, 11*(1), 4–16.

Trebilcock, B. (2013). Very cool automation. *Modern Materials Handling*, February, 42–45.

Tu, M., K. Lim, M., & Yang, M.-F. (2018). IoT-based production logistics and supply chain system – Part 2: IoT-based cyber-physical system: a framework and evaluation. *Industrial Management & Data Systems, 118*(1), 96–125.

Vallet-Bellmunt, T., & Rivera-Torres, P. (2013). Integration: Attitudes, patterns and practices. *Supply Chain Management: An International Journal, 18*(3), 308–323.

Waller, M. A., & Fawcett, S. E. (2013). Data science, predictive analytics, and big data: A revolution that will transform supply chain design and management. *Journal of Business Logistics, 34*(2), 77–84.

Wang, R. Y., & Strong, D. M. (1996). Beyond accuracy: What data quality means to data consumers. *Journal of Management Information Systems, 12*(4), 5–33.

Wang, X. L. (2014). Research on business and application scheme of open logistics platform under big data environment [J]. *Logistics Business Theory, 6*, 159–160.

Wang, S., Wan, J., Li, D., & Zhang, C. (2016). Implementing smart factory of Industrie 4.0: An outlook. *International Journal of Distributed Sensor Networks, 12*(1), 3159805.

Weiser, M. (1999). The computer for the 21st century. *ACM SIGMOBILE Mobile Computing and Communications Review, 3*(3), 3–11.

Witjaksono, G., Rabih, A. A. S., Yahya, N., & Alva, S. (2018). *IOT for agriculture: Food quality and safety*. IOP Publishing.

Wu, D., Greer, M. J., Rosen, D. W., & Schaefer, D. (2013). Cloud manufacturing: Strategic vision and state-of-the-art. *Journal of Manufacturing Systems, 32*(4), 564–579.

Wu, L., Yue, X., Jin, A., & Yen, D. C. (2016). Smart supply chain management: A review and implications for future research. *The International Journal of Logistics Management, 27*(2), 395–417.

Wycisk, C., McKelvey, B., & Hülsmann, M. (2008). "Smart parts" supply networks as complex adaptive systems: Analysis and implications. *International Journal of Physical Distribution and Logistics Management, 38*(2), 108–125.

Xiang, T. T. (2013). Technical support for e-supply chain finance [J]. *Electronic Test, 7X*, 245–246.

Xu, D.L., He, W., & Li, S. (2014). Internet of things in industries: A survey. *IEEE Transactions on Industrial Informatics, 10*(4), 2233–2243.

Xue, J. H. (2014). How to use big data in supply chain finance [J]. *China Forex, 18*, 36–37.

Yan, J. (2013). Research on impact of big data on development of courier industry [J]. *Logistics Technology, 24.*

Ye Bin, Huang Wenfu, & Yu Zhenhan. (2014). The application research of big data in logistics enterprises. *Logistics Technology, 33*(15), 22–24.

Yin, S., & Kaynak, O. (2015). Big data for modern industry: Challenges and trends [point of view]. *Proceedings of the IEEE, 103*(2), 143–146.

Zelbst, P. J., Green, K. W., Sower, V. E., & Reyes, P. M. (2012). Impact of RFID on manufacturing effectiveness and efficiency. *International Journal of Operations & Production Management, 32*(3), 329–350.

Zhang, L., Luo, Y., Tao, F., Li, B. H., Ren, L., Zhang, X., … Liu, Y. (2014). Cloud manufacturing: A new manufacturing paradigm. *Enterprise Information Systems, 8*(2), 167–187.

Zhou, Z., Xiao, S., Ho, Y.-C., & Tan, Y. (2018). The persuasive and informative effects of information disclosure: Evidence from an online supply chain finance market. *SSRN Electronic Journal, Lewis*, 1–35.

CHAPTER 4

Building Service Value Network: Foundation of Intelligent Supply Chain Finance

4.1 Introduction

The purpose of supply chain finance is to accelerate cash flow by helping participants obtain working capital effectively through supply chain operations and management, which requires the establishment of good interorganizational relationships and the formation of synergistic operation and service systems among each other. In particular, when supply chain finance is increasingly shifting from single financing to comprehensive financial services based on the network, the achievement of this goal further requires the effective organization of mutual service system among the interested parties, the effective control of increasingly complex risks with the help of ICT, the precise targeting of financial activities to specific organizations, the formation of comprehensive value, and, eventually, the formation of the overall competitiveness of the network (i.e., service value network (SVN)), which has become one of the characteristics of intelligent supply chain finance. In order to understand the characteristics, we must recognize that service is a complex variable in the servitization of supply chain. Studying the quantity of services alone cannot uncover the essence of servitization (T. Baines et al., 2017). According to many foreign studies, service-oriented strategies may not increase revenue and customer satisfaction, but instead pay extra costs. Moreover, inappropriate servitization transformation may cause enterprises to lose their strategic focus and result in organizational conflicts (Barnett et al., 2013; Kohtamäki et al., 2018), which is a phenomenon known as the "servitization paradox." Apparently, addressing the servitization paradox requires a new

H. Song, *Smart Supply Chain Finance*,
https://doi.org/10.1007/978-981-16-5997-3_4

understanding of services in the industrial operation process from the perspective of the way services are generated and the definition of service value. In fact, along with the continuous growth of industries and enterprises, people gradually realize that collaborative value creation is a new rule in the service sector. Customers are transformed from passive recipients of products or services to coproducers of services, and value is realized in the use of services by customers. A good interactive partnership among stakeholders is the keyword for competition in the service-oriented market (Adrodegari & Saccani, 2017). From this, we can see that exploring a collaborative value creation model that matches the supply chain service-oriented strategy is the basis for upgrading supply chain finance. However, the questions involved and need to be studied include the following: What is the logic of the service value network that facilitates the development of supply chain financial business? What are the differences in structure, process, and elements from the previous value chain and value shop? What are the supply chain services and financial products that embody the service value network, and what are the specific impacts of ICT on supply chain services? Why can these impacts facilitate financial activities?

4.2 From Value Chain and Value Shop to Service Value Network

The gradual shift in the driving force of economic development from manufacturing and production to services has become a common phenomenon. In particular, management-related research has found that traditional product manufacturing supply chains in the context of service-oriented production are no longer adapted to management practices. Scholars have begun to explore service-oriented supply chains (Ellram et al., 2004; De Waart & Kemper, 2004; Baltacioglu et al., 2007), a process known as "servitization" in operational management (Vandermerwe & Rada, 1988; T. S. Baines et al., 2009), or service-dominant logic in marketing services (Vargo & Lusch, 2004, 2008). Servitization is considered an operational model that creates a sustainable new competitive advantage when services are effectively integrated with production. Servitization is the process by which enterprises change and add value from providing products alone to providing both products and related services (Barnett et al., 2013). However, enterprises that adopt a servitization model do not simply shift from providing products to providing products and services or simply increasing the number of services, which is not the essence of servitization. Servitization should embody the characteristics of innovation. The implementation of a service-oriented strategy requires enterprises to rely on diverse networks of stakeholders and to adopt interrelated and interdependent value creation activities in achieving their goals. This is a process of continuous supplier-customer interaction (Kastalli & Van Looy, 2013; Martinez et al., 2010). The service-dominant logic is almost identical to the concept of servitization, except that the latter puts more emphasis on the service value creation process from the perspective of operation, while the former focuses more on the service value creation process from the interface between enterprises and customers. The service-dominant logic is relative to the previous product-dominant logic. The reason for the shift from product-dominant logic to service-dominant logic is that, on the one hand, the behavior of customers has changed significantly from being passive recipients of products or services to being participants in the product or service operation process who are able to actively participate in the collaborative creation of value (Vargo & Lusch, 2008). On the other hand, adopting a service-dominant logic is also necessary for enterprises to continuously improve their competitive advantage. More and more practices and researches prove that enterprises can enhance their competitive advantage through services. However, under a service-dominant logic, the parties to a transaction no longer exchange only materials and products, but services that are based on the integration of operant resources (Vargo & Lusch, 2008). Services are no longer products that can be exchanged directly, but rather products that are created in the process of customers' use of products and cocreated by service providers and customers. This fundamental change in business dominance requires enterprises to redefine the products and services they offer and to change the way they think and work. Therefore, how to provide products and services that satisfy customers by integrating operant resources inside and outside the enterprises, based on the effective use of operated resources, is the key to winning in the market competition. Some scholars (Basole & Rouse, 2008; Grönroos & Gummerus, 2014; Heinonen & Strandvik, 2015) even argued that the customers are the real value creator and that all activities of the enterprises are used to support the value creation process of the customers. Thus, it can be seen that both the theories of servitization and the theories of service-dominant logic have pointed out an important change in today's business model, which is centered on the fact that the way value is created is significantly different from the previous value chain and value shop (Blau et al., 2009; Fu et al., 2017; Li & Whalley, 2002; Song et al., 2018; Stabell & Fjeldstad, 1998).

4.2.1 *Logic of Value Chain*

The concept of value chain was first introduced by Michael Porter of Harvard University in 1985 in his book *Competitive Advantage*, in which he argued that "every firm is a collection of activities in the process of designing, producing, selling, delivering, and supporting its products. All these activities can be expressed in terms of a value chain" (Porter, 1985). In other words, the creation of value by an enterprise is a process through a series of activities. The value is achieved in the process from the initial input, to the production of intermediate products and finished products, and, finally, to the delivery to customers. Therefore, it is a continuous, end-to-end process between those activities. This value creation in the form of interacting and interrelated activities, or the realization of cost efficiency, is able to meet the needs of consumers or clients at the lowest costs and highest efficiency; or the realization of differentiation can differentiate competitiveness with unique products or forms (Porter & Millar, 1985). Obviously, according to the concept of value chain, the carrier of value is the materials and products created by the enterprises through a series of activities, which are used to meet the market demands. And the process of value creation is accomplished through a series of activities and the correlation between these activities (including primary and supporting activities). Put another way, organizational activities are synergistic through sequential dependencies (see Fig. 4.1). The dependencies of organizational activities are classified by Thompson (1967) into three categories: pool dependencies, sequential dependencies, and interdependencies. Sequential dependencies refer to the interrelationship of organizational activities as a front-back correlation, or a linear input-output relationship. In the terms of regulation or governance of value, the connection and coordination of activities is achieved through organizational management coordination or through organizational functions as well as management authority.

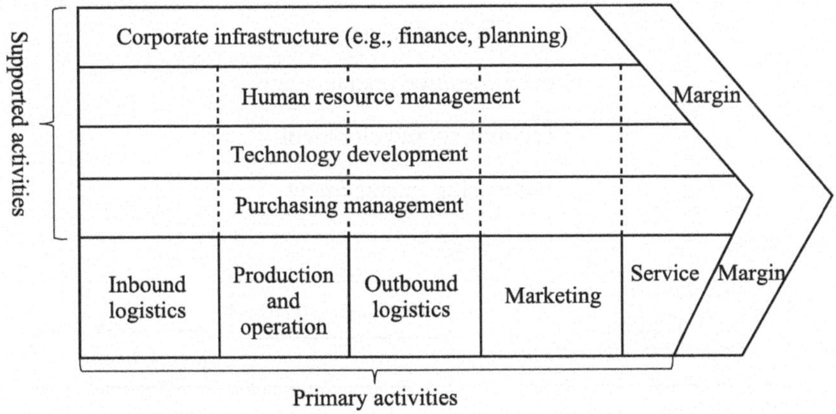

Fig. 4.1 Enterprise value chain

4.2.2 *Logic of Value Shop*

The concept of value shop was first introduced by Stabell and Fjeldstad (1998) and then enriched and developed into a widely accepted concept by Gottschalk (2007). With the expansion of related researches, this concept gradually evolved into value configuration (Sweet, 2001). The value shop or value configuration emphasizes the flexible selection and configuration of all resources and activities to meet customers' specific value requirements or to solve a specific problem they face. In this regard, the biggest difference between the value shop and the value chain lies in the fact that the enterprise organizes its resources and activities flexibly and according to the specific requirements of the customers, instead of performing all activities in a fixed order or manner to create value for the customers (see Fig. 4.2). Therefore, the customer needs to be addressed determine the "density" of value shop activities (Stabell & Fjeldstad, 1998). The value created by the value shop is determined by a combination of several factors. The first factor is the differentiated value claims of customers. The customers are active participants in the value shop, not passive recipients of products or services. In the context of the value shop, customers are involved in the value creation process. Only based on the differentiated claims of customers can the organizational allocation of resources and activities be targeted and truly create value. Or rather, the value realized in the value shop is unique to each particular customer, but

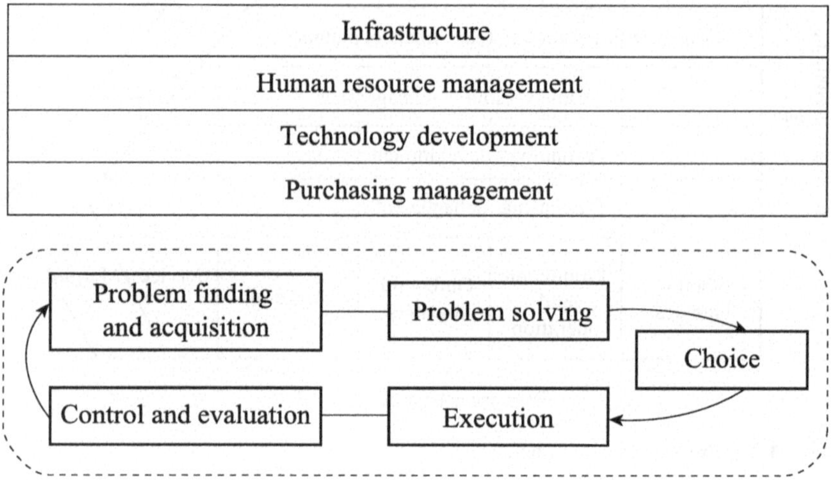

Fig. 4.2 Value shop. (Source: Stabell C.B. and Fjeldstad O.D. (Stabell & Fjeldstad, 1998))

not generic. Second, the realization of value in the value shop is based on intensive technology and knowledge, because the activity of providing services adapted to specific customer requirements requires flexible identification, coordination, organization, and allocation of external resources and capabilities, which places a strong and dynamic demand on the learning and management capabilities of the enterprises. Thus, the process of value creation is a highly technical, knowledge-intensive activity (Gottschalk, 2007). Third, the process of value creation is a circular and iterative approach. The value identification and creation of the value shop is the result of repeated communication and feedback between service providers and customers, which is not a single linear relationship. The enterprises constantly make ready corrections according to the changing requirements of customers and changes in the market, and organize flexibly so that the value is finally realized. Thus, the activities in the value field are a spiral of interaction (Stabell & Fjeldstad, 1998). Fourth, the value is presented by either value-added configuration or value capturing configuration (Sweet, 2001). Value-added configuration means that if a new feature or function can be added to an existing product or service and the customer is willing to pay for it, the value will be generated from adding the feature into the product or service system. For example, an enterprise provides installation and consulting services to customers who purchase products through e-commerce. Value capturing configuration is the process of capturing information about business procedures, transactions, or customers from users or sources and using this information to create value. For example, by analyzing data on customers' past purchase history or behavioral preferences, an enterprise can explore the real needs of customers and develop new products or services based on this knowledge. This way of presenting value is linked to the process of value creation. Through a continuous cycle of iteration, repeated communication and interaction with customers, enterprises help customers solve established problems while generating new inspiration or discoveries that drive the creation of new products or services.

4.2.3 Logic of Service Value Network

Service value network is a new approach to value creation, and can be described as a way to greatly expand the understanding of value and value creation scenarios based on value shop (Adrodegari & Saccani, 2017; Basole & Rouse, 2008; Blau et al., 2009; Lusch et al., 2010; Stabell & Fjeldstad, 1998; Sweet, 2001). Service value network refers to an intelligent business network based on stable, open, complementary, and alternative standardized service modules that delivers value to customers in an agile and continuous manner through a flexible and market-based portfolio of complex services and extensive use of information technologies (Blau et al., 2009). Service value network is different from virtual organization, which refers to a temporary network relationship formed by different independent enterprises to obtain complementary resources or benefits. Virtual organization puts emphasis on the complementary resources in the value creation process and the temporary interactions that may be terminated by the achievement of goals. The challenge of virtual organization is the issue of trust. In other words, the temporary interactions make the enterprises lack a deep understanding of each other, especially the control over cooperative behavior, which is prone to a lack of long-term awareness of cooperation. The service value network or intelligent business network goes beyond the concept of a virtual organization and intelligently uses modern ICT as a facilitator of interaction between network members and as a trigger for network agility. In other words, ICT allows enterprises to apply business procedures at any time in response to changing market or customer needs. In addition, as individual nodes in an intelligent business network, enterprises need to have specific capabilities in order to meet the specific requirements of value cocreation at any time (see Fig. 4.3). The modularized capabilities of network members can not only comply with the requirements of supply chain network synergy, but also well protect the competitiveness of network members themselves. Value creation may be impossible by relying on a single module, but requires sufficient synergy among all members to jointly complete the value creation process (Fu et al., 2017). Thus, the members in this service value network can form stable trust relationships with each other, which is unlike virtual organization. Specifically, the characteristics of this service value network can be identified from structure, procedure, and element:

First, in terms of structure, the service value network presents the characteristic of modularity. The creation of service value in the service value network is realized by many enterprises in collaboration, instead of a certain enterprise alone. In other words, the value is finally realized through the combination of various products or services. The modularity of services and the diversity of service providers are the characteristics of the service value network, that is, the final delivery of services is realized by a large number of service providers by means of modular combinations. On the one hand, these service modules can achieve agile supply by

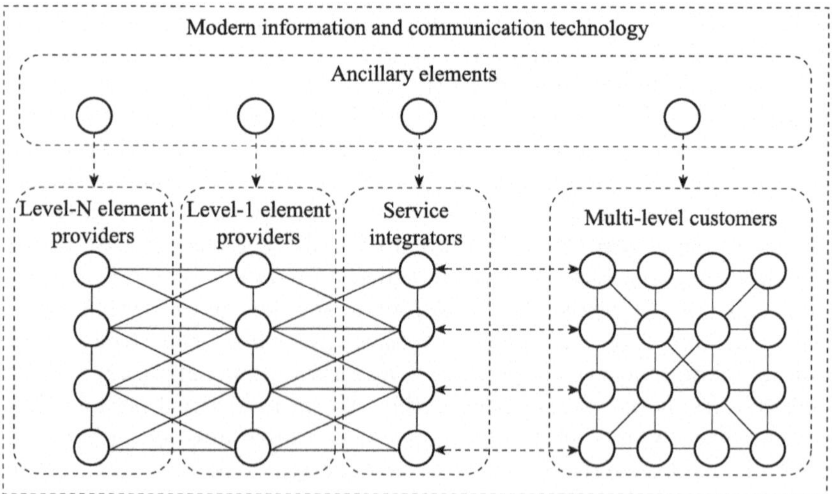

Fig. 4.3 Service value network

responding to the changing needs of the market or customers; on the other hand, they can serve other markets or customers with the help of the Internet and thus have open characteristics. Considering that different customers have different service requirements and value definitions, it is necessary to establish diverse service paths to realize the value demands of various customers (Turunen & Finne, 2014). In the traditional servitization process, there is a service paradox, which means the provision of high-quality services to customers does not necessarily improve business performance. This paradox arises because the continuous expansion of services blurs the business focus and makes interactions more complex and variable, resulting in dramatic cost increases and profit decreases (Gebauer et al., 2005). However, modular services can effectively solve the servitization paradox as a modular architecture contains numerous reusable and readily replaceable core elements (Tuunanen & Cassab, 2011) that flexibly support the simultaneous realization of economies of scale and scope (Thomas et al., 2014). Supply chain service providers can integrate services from many different service modules in a timely manner, reducing the complexity of the services offered, improving the value communication (Böttcher & Klingner, 2011), and optimizing the investments.

Second, in terms of process, value creation is achieved through a high degree of collaboration with customers. Same as the value shop, customers are also not passive service recipients in the service value network, but collaborative operators. In other words, customers are involved in the process of service production. However, the customer's involvement in the service value network is deeper than that in the service shop. The customers in the service shop acts as value proposers driving the communication and interaction between the two parties in order to make the services created by the suppliers more effective in realizing the variable value demands of the customers. But in the service network, on the one hand, the shared value between supply and demand based on the relationship economy is getting higher and higher. The participating parties work together to innovate the value that benefits everyone, or the participating parties get new opportunities and new markets to promote their own development in this process. On the other hand, the level of dependence between supply and demand is also getting higher. Both supply and demand are embedded in a complex network of business relationships, and each participating party provides the necessary capabilities, so the mutual value realization depends on the input and contribution of the partners. This collaboration system with a high degree of value sharing and dependency is also known as vested outsourcing (Vitasek & Manrodt, 2012), which has five characteristics. First, its business model is based on results rather than transactions. Put it another way, the business model is formed based on the shared vision and mission of all parties involved, rather than the aspirations of a particular enterprise itself. Second, it puts emphasis on "what" rather than "how." The respective tasks or activities undertaken by all parties are based on the objectives as well as the assignment of the tasks. Third, it clearly defines measurable expected outcomes. The service value network has good expected outcomes to measure and gauge performance for realizing the value. Fourth, it has an optimized pricing model to balance costs and benefits. This means that the service value network needs to establish a good pricing system and incentive system that, on the one hand, can enable all parties involved to be paid accordingly and enable each party to sustain robust development in the process of collaborative service operation and, on the other hand, can achieve maximum benefits and development at a reasonable cost. Fifth, its governance structure is based on insight rather than oversight. A good service value network must have a good governance mechanism that can regulate the responsibilities and obligations of each party as well as their corresponding behaviors, but such a mechanism should not be based on control and supervision, but should be able to guide the direction of collaborative value creation among all parties. Therefore, its governance mechanism is not a contract to regulate the behaviors of each party, but a kind of relationship governance.

Third, in terms of management element, a dynamic knowledge service pool is established. Given that the service value network serves customers by combining different service modules to form integrated solutions and create value collaboratively, it needs to form a good, mutually complementary, and continuously evolving resource knowledge system. Otherwise, if the integrated complementary resources and knowledge become substitutable after a period of time, the creativity of value will weaken and the partnership will disintegrate (Dyer et al., 2018). Lusch et al. (2007) also argued that the value network, like organisms, needs to continuously learn, evolve, and be ready to respond to the requirements of change, which is what makes them competitive. Clearly, this realization requires establishing the knowledge and capability pool dependencies. Pool dependency is a dependency pattern proposed by Thompson (1967), which refers to the fact that each part of the process makes a corresponding contribution to the whole. This dependency pattern is based on standardized work activities. Professional knowledge is integrated into an enterprise's activities through a set of rules, and the efficiency of the mechanism is ensured by effective communication (Holdt Christensen, 2007). In other words, the value network requires the establishment of a pool of knowledge and capabilities. The sharing of these knowledge and capabilities quickly promotes the formation of customized services and creates value. Moreover, when establishing this knowledge pool, a clear set of rules must be established to safeguard the rights and interests of knowledge and capability providers in the process of extracting and applying knowledge and capabilities, as well as to determine the methods of communication and the procedures for using knowledge and capabilities.

4.3 Intelligence and Realization of Service Value Network

From the above logic of the service value network, it can be seen that the participants in the service value network have diversity, including users in the industry, service integrators providing service integration and value delivery, and multilevel subservice providers offering services of each component within each module. Service value is generated jointly with the full synergy of all participants. ICT, on the one hand, enables service providers to reduce supply chain operating costs, increase productivity, and improve work flows and, on the other hand, facilitates access to, knowledge of, and processing of previously inaccessible information by customers (Basole & Rouse, 2008). The achievement of a high degree of convergence between ICT and service value creation ultimately boosts the intelligence of the service value network.

4.3.1 Meaning and Dimensions of Intelligence of Service Value Network

The service value network must be realized by using and leveraging borderless and interoperable ICTs. The lack of these ICTs may make the formation of the service value network difficult, because the rapid integration of services and the on-time realization of value require the openness of service or knowledge pool; otherwise, it is impossible to realize the efficiency of service creation. Based on this feature, we need to reconstruct the ICTs in the service value network to bridge the heterogeneous information systems of all participants in the supply chain, so as to truly realize the rapid interoperability and integration of resources and achieve the maximum density. Maximum density, as a theoretical concept, refers to a continuous set of resource presentation and integration. Maximum density is achieved when an enterprise is able to provide and integrate all the necessary resources to create value collaboratively in a given scenario at a given time and place (Lusch et al., 2010). In other words, maximum density reflects the efficiency of value network creation and operation. For example, when people use search engines to look up relevant information, they are able to quickly access information from all over the world to satisfy their desire to acquire specific knowledge, in which case the maximum density is achieved. Obviously, mobile information resources help to increase the maximum density, because if enterprises have timely and real-time access to the appropriate information, they can react quickly to combine services from the knowledge pool and thus create value. According to Lusch et al. (2010), the improvement of access to mobile information resources and the achievement of maximum density require reconfiguration of form, time, and field.

4.3.1.1 Form Reconfiguration

Form or structure refers to the arrangement of a series of elements to achieve the desired goals. For example, in the supply chain, the purpose of distributing products is accomplished by arranging and establishing elements such as factories, warehouses, and transports, and the system composed of such elements is the supply chain form. In the service value network, the realization of maximum density relies on the agility and adaptability of supply chain service value creation through embedding, scenario orientation, modularity, and reorganization of information forms (Lusch et al., 2010). Embedding reflects the ability of members in the network to communicate with each other in real time and share detailed information under the help of modern ICTs (Uzzi, 1997; Wu & Liu, 2009). For example, as the Internet hardware gradually shifts from large machines to portable ones, and even to smaller and more intelligent smart ones, the type of information access will become more and more specific and detailed, and the transmission of information will become more and more timely and transparent, so that the supply chain services can be flexibly and effectively adjusted according to the changing participants and changing customer value demands. Scenario orientation refers to the analysis and construction of information based on operational objectives of the supply chain. For example, in order to achieve full-process food safety tracking, we need to explore how to identify and manage operational activities in raw materials, packaging, production, distribution, and so on. Obviously, the realization of scenario orientation relies on information construction to analyze the activities that may arise in the value network from a full-cycle perspective. Lee et al. (1998) proposed the Scenario-based Object-oriented Hypermedia Design Methodology (SOHDM), that is, the informatization requires field analysis (including scenario diagrams to establish the boundaries of the system; event lists and scenario analysis to identify customer demands), goal modeling (establishing CRC cards, which are a standard collection of index cards, each of which represents a class; the class name is at the top, the class responsibilities are on the left, and the class collaboration relationships are on the right; the classes represent a collection of objects that abstractly model the design of the system, which can be a person, an item, or other; the class name is written at the top of the entire CRC card; the responsibilities include what this class knows about itself and how this information will be used, for example a person knows his or her phone number, address, gender, and other attributes, and knows his or her ability to speak and walk; this part is written on the left side of the CRC card; collaboration relationship refers to another class through which we get the information we want or achieve related operation; this part is written on the right side of the CRC card), review design (reviewing objects from CRC cards), guiding design (defining the nodes and connections of the informatization structure to be accessed), and implementation design (including user interface design and database logic design). Modularity refers to standardized components or architectures in the service value network, such as software and information services as components (Baldwin & Clark, 2003). Modular architecture facilitates many enterprises to outsource modules that do not have core competencies to specialized parties, and also enables more customization of the supply chain network value. This is one of the keys to service value network intelligence, because the service solutions required by customers are often customized to create unique value by integrating multiple information service components (Baldwin & Clark, 2003; Lusch et al., 2010). Reorganization refers to customer-driven process reconstruction through the decomposition and standardization of supply chain operations. Process reconstruction is the fundamental reanalysis and redesign of business processes and the management of related business changes in pursuit of performance (Hammer & Champy, 2009). Nowadays, with the continuous decomposition and standardization of supply chain operations and the change in information technology, customers are able to use ICTs to drive the self-fulfillment of service value. For example, once the order fulfillment process is broken down into standardized steps, customers can use Internet technology to configure and fulfill orders on their own, including using ICT for order verification, ordering products from suppliers, tracking the whereabouts of goods, automatic delivery of bill of lading, automatic invoicing, and more.

4.3.1.2 Time Reconfiguration

The intelligence of the service value network also involves a reconfiguration of the time in which the activities take place. The supply chain operation process often includes a series of activities, such as technical design, order placement, source finding, raw material inventory, production and operation, product inventory, distribution and delivery, after-sales service, and so on. Under the traditional business model, the above activities are a sequential process in time, that is, the realization of the previous link can trigger the occurrence of the next link, and each link is successively dependent. This sequential operation inevitably leads to the generation and management of information based on linear relationships. However, linear information management may result in inadequate and incomplete information due to time delay. For this reason, the realization of maximum density requires time reconfiguration. A key to time reconfiguration is concurrent working in supply chain operations, which is widely used in production and manufacturing (Sobek II et al., 1999) as well as system development (Lusch et al., 2010). Through synchronous working, cross-departmental works (including design, procurement, production, distribution, logistics, and after-sales service) are synchronously done mostly in phases as much as possible to avoid continuous changes in operations due to the subsequent needs of different departments. Synchronous working is able to respond to changes in the market quickly and achieve maximum density due to its synchronization (all activities are synchronized as much as possible), constraints (constraints are considered in advance and requirements of all parties are met synchronously), coordination (all parts of the supply chain are closely coordinated to achieve the best match of quality, cost, and time), and consistency (all activities are based on full communication and agreement of all parties). Of course, the realization of synchronous working requires the same systematic thinking to analyze the composition, process, and element changes of the whole service value network, and to design a comprehensive information strategy architecture based on scenarios, so as to avoid the duplication problems due to continuous iterations, overlapping problems due to parallel operations, and integration problems due to decomposition in synchronous working (Yassine & Braha, 2003). Another key to time reconfiguration is the real-time participation and zero-distance interaction of customers. In other words, customers can obtain upstream information in real time through ICTs and provide timely feedback on their value demands to service providers, and even participate in the whole supply chain operation process. In this way, the supply chain services will be more targeted, and value creation can be realized.

4.3.1.3 Field Reconfiguration

Field refers to the geographical area where the service value network occurs and where ownership is vested, that is, the space in which firms that collaborate and cooperate with each other are geographically distributed or controlled by ownership. Previously, geographically based clusters have been the main form of industrial development (DeWitt et al., 2006; Feldman et al., 2005; Morosini, 2004; Oinas, 2017), because such clusters offer external advantages of economy of scale such as technology and information spillovers, the provision of shared intermediate products and services, lower procurement and distribution costs, and the availability of specialized labor markets (Iammarino & McCann, 2006); as well as the ability to promote collective action among firms within the clusters (Schmitz, 1995) and lower barriers to entry, thereby increases the opportunities for firms to enter the market. Driven by information and network technologies and relying on the core competitiveness of each enterprise, the virtual clusters that break through the geographical limitation of specialized division of labor and overall collaboration, has gradually become the main way to realize service value network. Virtual clusters are also known as "e-business communities" or "b-Web communities." It is a kind of cluster that achieves cooperation and innovation, risk sharing, and common development in a virtual space by means of ICTs and using formal and informal contracts to make interrelated enterprises and organizations dependent on each other. This ICT-based virtual cluster enables the creation of service value to be realized collaboratively on a very large scale, thus configuring the field of the participants in the service value network. This field reconfiguration is not only adapted to simple, repetitive tasks but also to more complex creative activities such as new product research and development (Ganesan et al., 2005). In addition, field reconfiguration occurs not only in the spatial context but also in the context of ownership attribution. In the past, satisfying customer needs required the creation of material products and the transfer of titles to customers. However, the service value network puts more emphasis on taking the service as a unit of exchange and promotes the synergy between supply and demand through service delivery and value cocreation. Therefore, the realization of the service value network does not necessarily require titles of certain types of material products. On the contrary, its maximum density can be achieved through market-based behavior or collaboration. For example, you can lease the hardware and software of information system and cooperate with professional companies to jointly promote the information construction and management of service value network. Even some information service providers are deeply embedded in the customer supply chain system by providing hardware and systems for free, thus achieving common development by creating value and sharing value gains.

4.3.2 *Intelligent Platform Architecture of Service Value Network*

The realization of form, time, and field reconfiguration of the service value network requires a comprehensive and systematic construction of the information architecture of the service value network. Cenamor et al. (2017) proposed that the focus on specific elements in the servitization process should be shifted to the overall architectural design, leading to a platform-based digital servitization. In other words, the benefits are realized and the costs incurred in service provision are reduced by modularizing information and empowering new opportunities (Vendrell-Herrero et al., 2017). The realization of this goal requires a redefinition of the roles of the information front office and back-office in innovation of service-oriented information value. The back-office mainly establishes and coordinates the activities associated with the platform architecture and realizes the role of platform collaborator, while the front office mainly establishes and realizes the role of final service by combining various modules, that is, it plays the role of service builder. In addition, the back-office takes on the task of developing and designing standardized module blueprints to avoid the costs of constantly adapting development for different service scenarios, while the front office needs to explore opportunities to facilitate the development of new modules to rapidly capture and realize customer value, thus avoiding conflicts that make it difficult to achieve consistency due to interrelated goals (Smith & Lewis, 2011).

Specifically, this architecture consists of multilayer systems. Youseff et al. (2008) and Leimeister, Böhm, Riedl, and Krcmar (2010) proposed a multilayer architecture model for cloud computing in the value network scenario, including application, software environment, software infrastructure, software kernel, and hardware (see Fig. 4.4), reflecting a multilayer architecture from the front office to the back-office.

To be more specific, the cloud application layer is the most visible layer for the end users at the user interface. It is usually accessed through an Internet portal and builds the front office of the application that users interact with when using the cloud services. The services in the cloud application layer contain various service modules. Each user can select the corresponding individual service module according to its needs. Thus, this layer of the architecture can also be called Software-as-a-Service (SaaS).

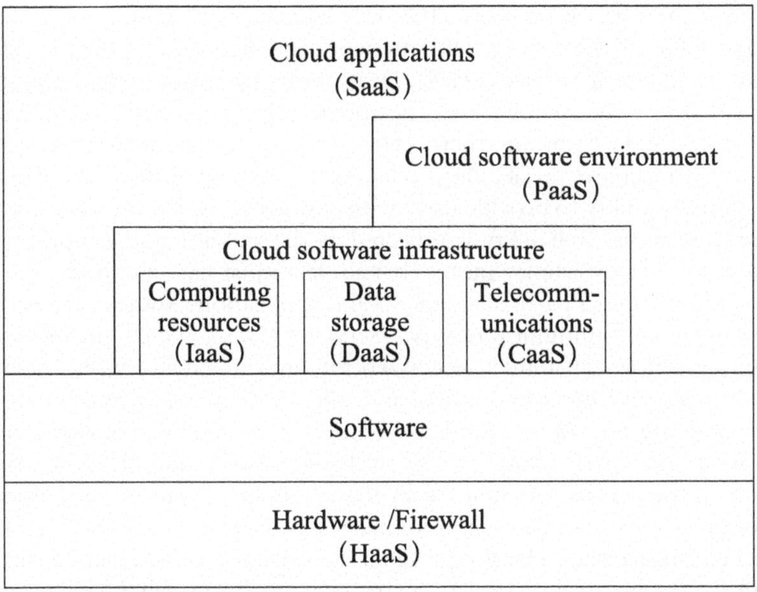

Fig. 4.4 Multilayer architecture model for cloud computing in value network scenario. (Source: Youseff et al. (2008))

The cloud software environment layer (also known as the software platform layer) provides the environment for the development of cloud application. This service architecture can also be called Platform-as-a-Service (PaaS). The software environment also provides a well-defined set of application programming interfaces (APIs) that allow platform participants to leverage the cloud services and interact with other cloud applications. However, in the absence of standards for application development, system development can only rely on the dedicated environment provided by the platform.

The infrastructure layer provides the resources for the above architecture. The services provided in this layer are usually distinguished as computing resources, data storage, and communication services. Computing resources are often referred to as Infrastructure-as-a-Service (IaaS). Leimeister, Böhm, Riedl, and Krcmar (2010) argued that virtual machine is a common form of providing computing resources to users, and they can be fully managed and configured to meet specific customer needs. Virtualization technologies can be deemed as supporting technologies for IaaS that allow data center providers to adjust resources on demand, thus utilizing their hardware more efficiently. Similar to computing resources, data storage in the service value network intelligence platform is called Data-Storage-as-a-Service (DaaS). DaaS allows users not only to remotely access data storage services with flexible requirements and also to access this stored data from anywhere. This service architecture requires data services to achieve availability, reliability, and consistency. Availability refers to the ability to provide users with easy access to remote data storage reading services. Reliability is reflected as the stability and continuity of data services. Consistency means that all data must have a consistent state when performing a particular analysis and application. Another infrastructure layer is Communications-as-a-Service (CaaS), which provides the communication capabilities necessary for high-quality services (such as network security, dedicated broadband, and network monitoring) to users, thus enabling the use of cloud technology in a collaborative cloud environment. Each participant can effectively establish communication groups based on the permissions granted by the administrator, using various messaging methods to enhance communication efficiency.

The software kernel layer represents the software management environment for the physical servers in the data center. It typically includes operating systems, hypervisors, monitoring systems, or cluster middleware.

At the bottom of the multilayer model of the value network is the actual physical hardware that forms the backbone of any cloud computing service. This hardware can either be built in-house or leased from a data center provider (i.e., acquired through outsourced services). This architecture is also known as Hardware-as-a-Service (HaaS).

Through the above five-layer architecture, an intelligent platform for the value network services is formed, thus realizing both the provision of comprehensive on-demand services according to customers' needs and the aforementioned form, time, and field reconfiguration. This provides a solid information foundation for the development of supply chain finance and risk management.

4.4 Intelligent Service Value Network and Supply Chain Finance

4.4.1 *Three Dimensions of the Effect of Intelligent Service Value Network*

The intelligent service value network consisting of the above five-layer architectures provides effective support for the development of supply chain finance. The effect of this support is mainly manifested in the reach, richness, and range, as proposed by Wells and Gobeli (2003). In their opinion, electronization and digitalization are based on these three dimensions. Through these dimensions, an integrated strategy is created. The intelligent service value network also needs to support and promote the development of supply chain finance through the establishment of these three dimensions. Specifically, the support of the intelligent service value network for supply chain finance is manifested in the following three dimensions.

First dimension is reach of financial resources. It means that financial institutions engaged in supply chain financial services reach their target customers quickly and effectively, so that the latter can know and use supply chain financial services in the process of interacting with service providers, while financial institutions can also get informed of the real state of supply chain operation of customers and their real financing demand in time. Customer reach has always been considered a key component of customer satisfaction, second only to service capability (Sureshchandar et al., 2002). One of the keys to the operation of supply chain finance is to know the authenticity of transactions. Only under the premise of timely and complete access to the real information and production and operation of customers and their upstream and downstream can financial services be both targeted and effective in preventing potential risks. Customers, as the targets of supply chain financial services, also needs to reach the service providers with the help of effective methods to understand what kind of support the service providers can give in financial activities and what clear value can be brought to them through these supports. Financial activities can only be effective and secure if both parties of the supply chain financial services can be effectively reached. Therefore, reachability is the basic requirement of supply chain financial services. The intelligent service value network promotes the reachability because ICT enables customers to reach service providers more effectively and creates a platform effect through frequent and direct interactions with service providers (Smedlund, 2012). Furthermore, with this intelligent platform, process integration and information integration are more direct and effective, thus enabling a more direct and effective grasp of the state of supply chain operations and the real information of each party in supply chain finance activities (Daugherty et al., 1995).

Second is richness of financial products. As another important impact on supply chain finance, the intelligent service value network can provide deep and customized supply chain financial services, thus enabling the information necessary for supply chain finance to be multidimensional. Through Haas, IaaS, DaaS, CaaS in the back-office, PaaS in the middle office, and SaaS in the front office, the intelligent platform architecture can quickly respond to the diverse value demands of customers and meet the various financial service demands arising from their daily operations. This on-demand service makes the relationship between supply and demand closer on the one hand and makes the business data obtained by service providers more diversified on the other, thus realizing the calibration among data. All these advantages provide a strong guarantee for effective implementation of supply chain finance and risk prevention. In addition, this intelligent platform composed of multilayer architectures can also promote the diversification of supply chain finance products and on-demand services. There are different types of financial services products in supply chain finance. As detailed in Chap. 2, supply chain finance presents diverse and differentiated products and services in different stages and under different collateral status. Therefore, how to quickly respond to the different features of customers' production and operation and provide appropriate services is a problem that needs to be addressed in the development of supply chain finance. The multilayer intelligent architecture consisting of front, middle, and back-offices also lay a foundation for providing differentiated financial services on demand.

Third is diversity of financial service participants. Connecting more participants and providing a wide range of diversified services is the basis of intelligent service value network to promote network-driven supply chain finance. From the perspective of the development trend of supply chain finance, the establishment of a collaborative supply chain finance network based on the division of labor among multiple participants is the main organizational approach. In the past, supply chain finance was mostly a business promoted by a single financial institution or organization, such as a bank providing standard factoring, reverse factoring, warehouse receipt pledge, and other businesses for core enterprises. However, along with the complexity of the supply chain business and the addition of more entities, it is difficult to rely on a single financial institution to serve the enterprises, because, on the one hand, one financial institution does not have the ability to fully meet the financial service needs of various enterprises and, on the other hand, one financial institution cannot effectively supervise and manage the global supply chain because of its capacity limitation. Likewise, the future supply chain finance will not be exactly driven by a certain monopolistic core enterprise itself, because although monopolistic core enterprises have strong negotiation power in the supply chain, they are not fully familiar with the operation and management of finance, especially how to manage and control risks through financial tools. In addition, the development of supply chain finance after maturity requires specialized ICT capabilities and the ability to connect multiple participants, which is more difficult for a single monopolistic core enterprise to achieve. More importantly, the supply chain finance system built by the monopolistic core enterprises is more prone to the existence of bullying behavior (i.e., wantonly delaying the supplier's billing period and then providing the so-called supply chain financial services to the supplier). Therefore, specialized and platform-driven supply chain finance should be the direction in the future. The realization of this direction requires an effective way to connect specialized organizations in different links, different fields, and different regions to provide global supply chain services and financial services. The intelligent service value network provides an open platform that, on the one hand, allows different organizations to effectively intervene and provide specialized services and, on the other hand, achieves a high degree of synergy to avoid inefficiencies and even operational risks arising from the previous supply chain links not being effectively connected.

4.4.2 Supply Chain Financial Business Based on Three Dimensions

Based on the above-mentioned three-dimensional effects of the intelligent service value network, different combinations are generated, which lead to different types of supply chain finance businesses. Several of these supply chain finance businesses are based on the interactive effects in the reach of financial resources and the richness of financial products with the help of intelligent ICT, thus resulting in three different states of information-based supply chain finance businesses (see Fig. 4.5).

In the first state, a higher reach of financial resources is achieved, but the richness of financial products is not deep enough, which is common in online supply chain financial business driven by banks. Usually, with the help of information technology, banks are able to directly and timely understand the basic status and lending behavior of customers, and realize online application, online credit investigation, online approval, and online loan repayment through the information technology-based system. From the standpoint of a financial institution, the direct access to customer information, especially the information about lending and borrowing, is achieved. However, this online supply chain financial business driven by financial institutions has certain limitations, that is, the lack of richness of

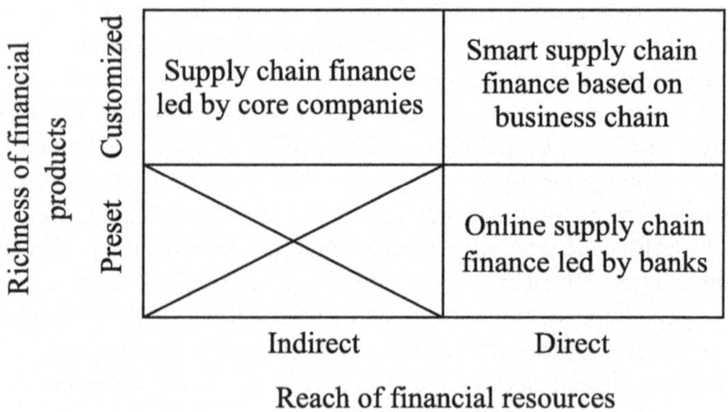

Fig. 4.5 Supply chain finance business based on reach and richness

information makes it impossible to provide customized supply chain financial products according to the differentiated capital needs of customers. Specifically, financial institutions cannot really obtain all kinds of business data and operation data from supply chain operations. Even if some financial institutions try to obtain all the data of supply chain operations by building their own B2B e-commerce platform, but the digital information obtained by such financial institutions cannot really penetrate into all links of the industrial supply chain and all upstream and downstream enterprises due to the nondirectional and targeted nature of their platform (i.e., it cannot fully adapt to the specific rules of industry operation and the special needs of corporate operation), coupled with the resistance of supply chain enterprises to base their data entirely on the platform of such financial institutions. In this case, the supply chain financial business driven by the financial institutions is merely the transformation from traditional business to online business (such as online standard factoring, online reverse factoring, etc.), but the financial institutions cannot customize financial service products according to the supply chain status of customers.

In the second state, financial institutions have abundant information about the supply chain business and a very deep understanding of customers; thus, they can provide a wide range of customized financial products according to the actual situation of supply chain customers, but the reachability to customers is low. This state is often seen in the supply chain finance business driven by core enterprises. In this state, financial institutions reach customers through a medium rather than directly, or they do not directly understand and grasp the status of customers' supply chain operations and the corresponding financial service needs. The participants who drive supply chain financial services are very familiar with the supply chain business by virtue of their position in the industrial supply chain and strong negotiation power, and they have a comprehensive grasp of the actual operation status and relevant information of the borrowers, so that they can effectively solve the operating funds required by the supply chain operation of their upstream and downstream enterprises. The core enterprises in the supply chain are the key to such supply chain financial services. Financial institutions can only rely on the core enterprises to provide the necessary funds to upstream and downstream enterprises and to effectively control risks. Financial institutions' unified credit granting and buyer's or seller's credit belong to the products and services in this state.

The third state is business chain-based intelligent supply chain finance, which is often kind of online supply chain finance, jointly driven by enterprises, financial institutions, and professional information service providers, and could achieve high reach of financial resources and high richness of customized financial products. In the operations and services of traditional supply chain, direct reach of financial resources and high richness of customized financial products cannot coexist, because it is difficult to achieve true integration and synergy between financial institutions and industrial enterprises. On the one hand, financial institutions do not understand the operations of industrial supply chain and the value of the figures and information generated by the operations. In particular, the vast majority of supply chain financial services serve MSMEs, whose financial information is often imperfect and data quality is low. In addition, with the transformation of supply chain operations from single value chain to value shop and eventually to service value network, the supply chain business activities become more and more complex and involve more and more entities. Therefore, only by truly grasping the status of its business operation and the status of MSMEs in the service value network can we know its position and capacity in the supply chain and judge the possible risks brought about by the financing behavior. And these are not the capabilities that traditional financial institutions have. On the other hand, most industrial enterprises (except for the leading core enterprises in various industries) are also less likely to truly and effectively incorporate financial institutions into their service value network, because their limited scale of operation and resources make them difficult to obtain the recognition and preferential support from the financial institutions. Specialized information service providers gather and integrate information and data by connecting industrial enterprises and financial institutions, thus filling the above-mentioned gap. These specialized information service providers can not only provide rich customized supply chain financial products for upstream and downstream customers of industrial enterprises according to the actual operations of industrial supply chain but also deliver effective information to financial institutions to strongly support them in risk control, thus realizing direct reach of financial resources.

In addition to the reach of financial resources and the richness of financial products, the diversity of financial participants is also a factor that deserves attention in the formation of intelligent supply chain financial business. If the reach and richness are taken as one dimension and the diversity of financial participants as another dimension, two forms of supply chain financial business are also generated (see Fig. 4.6). The first form is the above-mentioned intelligent supply chain finance based on business

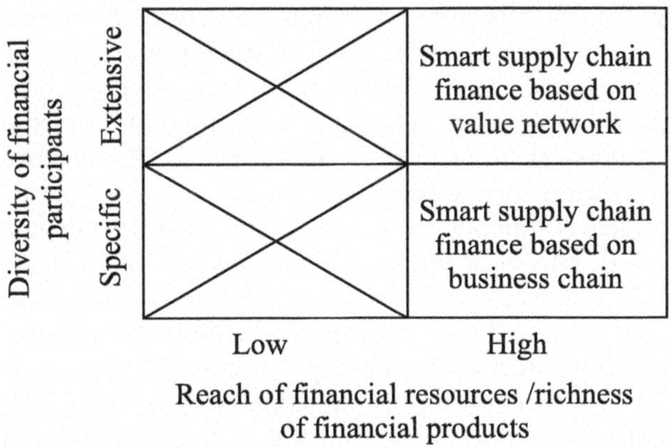

Fig. 4.6 Supply chain finance business based on reach, richness, and diversity

chain. As mentioned earlier, this type of supply chain finance is a business under the collaboration of cooperative enterprises, financial institutions, and professional information service providers. In terms of characteristics, this kind of financial service serves the upstream and downstream of cooperative enterprises. In other words, based on the self-owned business chain of cooperative enterprises, the professional information platform extracts, cleans, mines, and integrates the information of the business chain of cooperative enterprises and passes it to financial institutions so that they can assess the risks and finally finance the upstream and downstream customers of cooperative enterprises. The second form of supply chain finance is based on value network. Unlike the previous form, this type of supply chain finance not only has higher reach of financial resources and richness of financial products but also has higher diversity of financial participants, thus forming a wide business cooperation network. Specifically, first of all, the basis of this supply chain finance business is no longer the business chain of a particular enterprise, and the service targets are not entirely upstream and downstream customers of the cooperative enterprises but extend to the whole service value network, which means all the enterprises involved in the process of supply chain service may become its service targets. Second, the diversity of participants makes business data also become multidimensional, which is manifested by the increasingly diversified types of information data on the one hand and the diversity of sources of information data on the other. This multidimensional information data can realize cross-checking, which lays a solid foundation for effective financial risk control. Third, in terms of ICT deployment, the value network-based supply chain finance is also different from the business chain-based supply chain finance. In the former, ICT is deployed by specialized information service providers, whose role is mainly to connect, analyze, and deliver functions, that is, through its independently deployed cloud architecture to dock the information systems of cooperative enterprises and financial institutions, extract effective information data for analysis and calculation, and then provide the analysis and mining results of data to financial institutions for lending decisions. However, in the latter, the ICT multilayer architecture is embedded or contained in the service value network. The business behavior of all participants, the credit investigation, and risk control of financial institutions are naturally based on the ICT cloud architecture. In a sense, it does not have a strict process of system connection and data extraction, but forms the basis of risk control of financial institutions—credit management system—with the help of business activities and data on the cloud architecture.

4.5 Business Chain-Based Intelligent Supply Chain Finance Between LINO and OPPLE

The business chain-based intelligent supply chain finance aims to effectively connect the core enterprise, its upstream and downstream, as well as financial institutions, with the help of information service provider's information system service, to realize the connection of information data and smart management, and finally promote the smooth cooperation between finance and industry. Typical example of this finance is the supply chain finance business of OPPLE. As a core enterprise, OPPLE cooperates with LINO and financial institutions (Bank of Qingdao and Qingdao City Construction Investment (Group) Limited) to integrate the professional advantages of capital, business and technology as well as elements such as distribution channel network, transaction data and logistics business. Through the transaction records of the platform, it brings together industry and finance through the Internet, and develops the online supply chain finance business under "credit mode" for distributors and online reverse factoring business for suppliers.

4.5.1 Operations of OPPLE Sales-Side Supply Chain and Its Project Background

Established in 1996, OPPLE Lighting (referred to as "OPPLE") is a comprehensive lighting enterprise integrating R&D, production, sales, and services. It was officially listed on the main board of Shanghai Stock Exchange on August 19, 2016. The company has more than 6000 employees, with headquarters in Shanghai and multiple production bases in Zhongshan Industrial Park and Wujiang Industrial Park. OPPLE's products cover LED and traditional light sources, lamps and lanterns, electrical appliances, kitchen and bathroom ceiling products, and so on. In 2017, its total operating revenues exceeded RMB 6.9 billion, an increase of 27.03% over the same period in 2016. Its sales outlets reached 30,000, with more than 3000 distributors. OPPLE adopts a sales strategy guided by terminal prices. The inventory at each sales outlet shall not exceed 10% of the annual sales volume, and all outlets adopt the arrangement of production after order placement and 50% payment, as well as full payment before delivery, which allows the gross profit of the sales outlets to reach 50%. In addition, its customers are very stable due to its strong industry specialization and low substitutability. Many of its distributors have been cooperating for more than four to five years, and even some of them for more than ten years.

However, under the new competition, OPPLE still faces great challenges. The first challenge is how to help distributors accelerate cash flow and relieve capital pressure. The traditional sales model (i.e., OPPLE produces after receiving an order from a distributor and issues an invoice after delivery, according to which the distributor needs to make full payment) has caused huge financial pressure on the distributors. Also, as a manufacturer, OPPLE hopes to collect funds as early as possible for the purpose of reproduction reducing risks. This situation is more obvious for OPPLE's strategic partners. On the one hand, the strategic distributors want good financial support; on the other hand, OPPLE also hopes to stabilize the core distributors through financial arrangement and maintain their leading position in the industry. The second challenge lies in OPPLE's supply chain operations. OPPLE aims to integrate logistics, inventory, procurement, and financial data through the distributor interaction platform and to predict the sales speed of goods and arrange procurement more accurately through in-depth analysis and mining of the whole supply chain data. The third challenge is how to eliminate isolated islands of information and realize connection of data in OPPLE's internal systems, so as to improve management efficiency, boost finance and business integration, break the information barriers between finance and warehousing and logistics, and allow the finance department to see the logistics information of the whole process. Meanwhile, the business management process can be optimized through finance-related payable information, which greatly enhances the efficiency of OPPLE's internal supply chain and financial management. In response to the above challenges, OPPLE strives to enhance its competitiveness through supply chain informationization and financial services, stabilize downstream distributors, and promote the development of the supply chain at the sales end.

The adequate solution of the above challenges obviously cannot rely on OPPLE alone. OPPLE is equivalent to a core enterprise in the supply chain, so it has sufficient capital flow and good reputation. OPPLE can connect the data about its owned customer base and large-scale distributors with financial institutions' systems, making such data an important basis for financial institutions to grant credits. However, the realization of this goal requires the ability to build an information platform connecting financial institutions and to complete the structured integration of the information required for risk control by financial institutions. However, as a manufacturer, OPPLE have no such abilities. In addition, when building the system, it is also necessary to consider how to avoid business risks from business initiation, process design, and division of responsibilities and rights, to ensure no impact on OPPLE's existing business operations, and to guarantee information security from process design and system implementation. All these need professional enterprises to help OPPLE to realize. Based on the above, OPPLE has formed an intelligent supply chain finance based on the business chain in the form of multiparty cooperation with LINO, a professional information service provider, as well as Bank of Qingdao and Qingdao City Construction Investment (Group) Limited.

4.5.2 Three-Party Collaborative Sales Supply Chain Finance Model among LINO, OPPLE, and Financial Institutions

Founded in 2016, with headquarters and R&D center in Beijing and offices in Shanghai and Wuhan, Beijing LINO Financial Service Technology Co., Ltd. (hereinafter referred to as "LINO") specializes in consulting, implementation, and O&M of large and complex online supply chain finance plans. In the early stage of the project, LINO and financial institutions, with the cooperation of OPPLE, screened out OPPLE's high-quality distributors. OPPLE has a total of more than 3000 distributors, including core distributors, first-class distributors, and second-class distributors. Their capital needs are more urgent and the dropout rate is very low (i.e., dropping out of their class due to sales decline within three years). Specifically, those who achieve sales of more than RMB 5 million for three consecutive years from 2013 to 2015 are called core distributors. There are 50 customers in this class, their dropout rate is zero, their expected loan amount is about 10% of annual sales, and the annual interest rate is less than 7%. Those who achieve sales of RMB 2–5 million for three consecutive years are called first-class distributors. There are 69 customers in this class, and their dropout rate is zero, their expected loan amount is about 7% of annual sales, and their annual interest rate is less than 8.5%. Those with sales of RMB 0.3–2 million for three consecutive years are called second-class distributors. There are 1232 customers in this class, their dropout rate is 0.73%, their expected loan amount is about 5–7% of annual sales, and their annual interest rate is less than 10%. Obviously, these distributors are the core customers of OPPLE and the targets that supply chain finance serves.

After the core customers were identified, the construction of a three-party collaborative intelligent supply chain finance model was launched. First, LINO built an integrated online information platform to realize the connection between LINO platform and systems of financial institutions. At the same time, it opened the interface to the downstream distributors, so that they can access it online. In addition, the LINO platform was also effectively docked with OPPLE's business system to extract and integrate related data, thus realizing the interconnection among OPPLE, financial institutions, and distributors (see Fig. 4.7). Then, distributors who need funds signed contracts with OPPLE and financial institutions, thus realizing online financing based on the Internet. In this process, all parties have clear responsibilities and obligations. As a core enterprise, OPPLE is required to provide the historical transaction data and monthly incremental data of distributors and ensure that all data are true, accurate, and not false. In case of customer default, OPPLE assists the bank to reduce loss in terms of distributorship, rebates, inventory transfer, and so on and cooperates with the bank by completing the required works in the whole process of working capital loans. As an information service provider, LINO helps all parties to get the necessary service through the information architecture, thus ensuring the smooth and effective transmission of

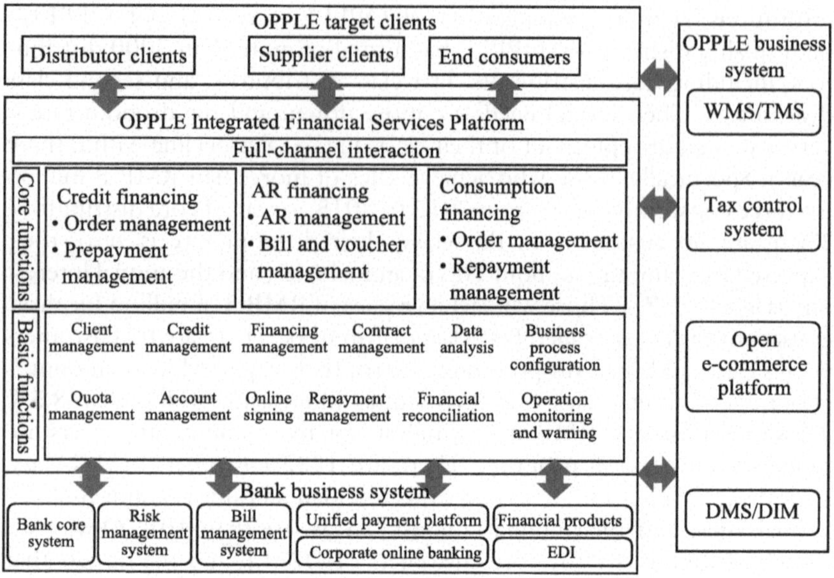

Fig. 4.7 Architecture of OPPLE/LINO supply chain finance information platform

information. With the help of financing platform, Qingdao Bank and OPPLE can see the payment, delivery, loan application, updates, and repayment status of distributors. Finally, the transparency of the whole process from pre-loan preparation, loan application, approval and loan granting, repayment, and post-loan management is achieved (see Fig. 4.8).

Considering the fact that the loan applications of customers are fully online process, financial institutions cannot consider the risks faced by small and medium-sized distributors on a case-by-case basis like traditional financing services. At the same time, the capital chain of such distributors is greatly affected by the overall market and environment. In the event of forcible picking-up of goods on due date or failure to pay for goods on due date due to poor operations, financial institutions would face credit default risks and losses. In response to this situation, OPPLE and financial institutions have designed the corresponding risk control measures. First of all, OPPLE maintains a good cooperative relationship and system docking with financial institutions. OPPLE transmits the sales data of its partner distributors in the past three years to the financial institutions, allowing

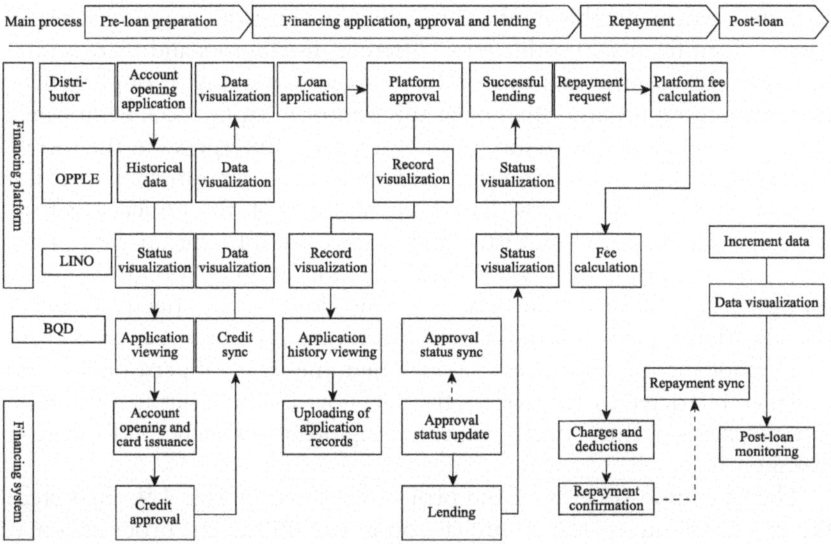

Fig. 4.8 Main operational activities of OPPLE/LINO supply chain finance

the financial institutions to determine their corresponding credit line after analyzing and judging the operating condition and ability of these distributors. Second, in view of the fact that those who apply for loans under the "credit model" are larger-scale high-quality distributors with better credit ratings, financial institutions and OPPLE pay more attention to their qualification. Only the distributors with more than three years of sales records in OPPLE can pass the approval of their credit lines. Moreover, thanks to the real-time interaction with the platform data, financial institutions can monitor the real and comprehensive transaction information and data of the distributors. As the transactions are repeated, these information and data will be accumulated and improved, as a result of which a set of life cycle business data system for dynamic monitoring is established. This is the basis for financial institutions to provide commercial credit loans to distributors. In addition, the amount of each loan under the "credit model" is generally small. Through this dynamic cycle of small loans, OPPLE and financial institutions can control the corresponding risks by the principle of large numbers. Under this model, financial institutions manage OPPLE's distributors by granting uniform credit to OPPLE and establishing a perfect risk control mechanism. For each relevant participant, this model can reduce the cost of designing separate supply chain financial products for different distributors and increase the number of customers in a short time in a geometric way through benchmarking and replicating. By seizing this opportunity, financial institutions are closely integrated with industrial enterprises. Enterprises in the supply chain can realize credit extension and transfer of risk variables with the help of financial institutions. Based on the Internet, the project has realized the integration of industry and finance by forming an ecosystem. Also, utilizing big data, it has realized the unification of commodity flow, transport flow, information flow, and fund flow, which effectively solves the risk control problems of financial institutions. As far as the risk control in the implementation process is concerned, the scope of personnel access to data is restricted by controlling the data flow and building an authorization mechanism, thus effectively preventing problems such as information leakage.

The operation process of the project is shown in Fig. 4.9. First step: When a distributor places a purchase order to OPPLE, the order information will be synchronized to the online collaborative supply chain platform built by LINO. Second step: OPPLE will also synchronize the

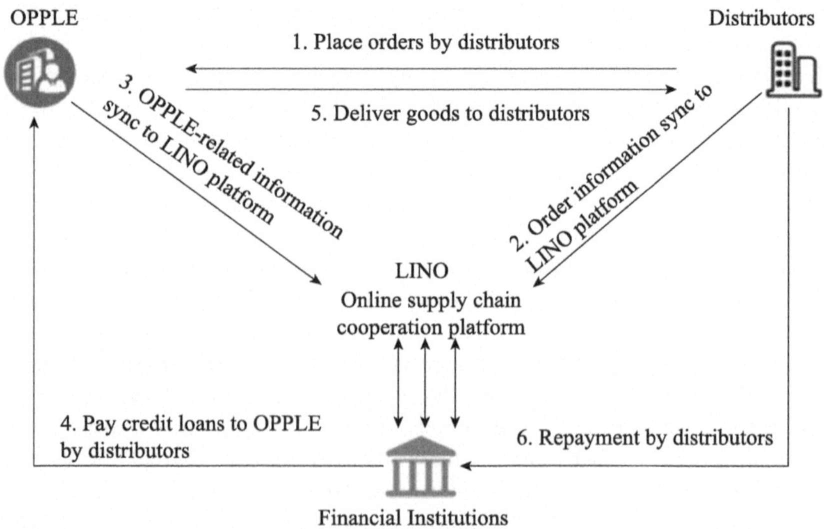

Fig. 4.9 OPPLE supply chain financial operation process

corresponding production and supply information to the LINO platform, thus enabling the cross-checking of order information and supply information. Third step: Based on the tripartite cooperation agreement, the financial institution will review the above information and qualification online and pay the credit loan of the distributor to OPPLE. Fourth step: The distributor completes the sales and repays the funds to the financial institution, thus closing the loan.

4.5.3 *Operational Performance of OPPLE's Sales-Side Supply Chain Finance*

As of October 2018, the project has approved a total of 1016 loans since the first business occurred on August 19, 2016, with a cumulative total loan amount of RMB 368,770,100, serving 280 distributors (mainly core and first-class distributors), with interest rates ranging from 6.5% to 9.5% per annum.

The project is an upgrade and iteration of traditional supply chain finance based on the Internet. By forming an ecosystem, it connects financial institutions, core enterprises, and distributors to achieve a win-win situation for all the three parties. This supply chain finance model optimizes the value of the supply chain. To be specific, the downstream distributors may obtain financing at a lower interest rate and without guarantee and collateral, which solves their problem of capital constraints in a timely and effective manner. OPPLE optimizes the business procedures, eases the tension between supply and demand, and realizes the interests of distributors while safeguarding its own interests. As an online platform, LINO deconstructs the value chain of core enterprises, strengthens the competitiveness of the procurement and supply system of downstream suppliers, and integrates it into the supply chain value system of core enterprises. Apart from changing the simple lending relationship, financial institutions can also better expand their business and realize risk-free income.

Obviously, this project mainly solves the financial needs of distributors, which has become a key direction of the B2B platform. With no need to provide collateral and guarantee, or complete procedures on-site, the distributors can achieve the timely arrival of funds through "online financing" function of the platform. In addition to convenience and high efficiency, the distributors can also enjoy the same preferential interest rates as large enterprises, greatly reducing interest expenses. Seen from the current operation, the project has some breakthrough achievements. On the one hand, there is a breakthrough in remote account opening for distributors. On the other hand, the whole process has been connected, so it takes only a few seconds to complete from the submission of loan application by customers to the release of loans.

4.5.4 Supply-Side Intelligent Supply Chain Finance

After the success of the sales-side supply chain finance, OPPLE, together with LINO, Bank of Qingdao, Bank of Shanghai, and other financial institutions, launched another online intelligent supply chain finance for suppliers in November 2018. The reason for extending to the supply side is that OPPLE needs to purchase a large amount of materials from suppliers in its production process, but the traditional procurement model also puts suppliers under huge financial pressure. As far as the procurement process is concerned, after OPPLE places an order to an upstream supplier, the latter produces and delivers products as per the order request. After the arrival of and inspection over the products at OPPLE, the supplier issues an invoice. Only after a period of billing period can the supplier collect the sales income. Therefore, it is obvious that the supplier faces a shortage of working capital for a longer period of time. Supply chain finance can help shorten the collection time of accounts receivable.

Based on the above considerations, the three parties worked together again to establish a financing solution for supplier accounts receivable with the procedures as detailed in Fig. 4.10. First, OPPLE signs a purchase agreement with a supplier, and the latter will provide products and invoices. Second, OPPLE synchronizes the accounts payable information to LINO's supply chain platform, and the supplier synchronizes the payment notice and the confirmation of the purchase terms and conditions to the platform. The information and data of both parties are checked and verified online. Third, the supplier that needs money can apply for loans on the platform and confirm the time of transferring accounts receivable and the accepted interest rate. Fourth, the bank makes discount financing to the supplier. Finally, OPPLE pays for the products to the supplier's account as per the billing period.

The implementation of the above model is beneficial to both OPPLE and the suppliers. From the perspective of OPPLE, it can improve its credit rating, establish a good image of integrity in the supply market, and can effectively reduce its payment pressure and procurement costs, thus

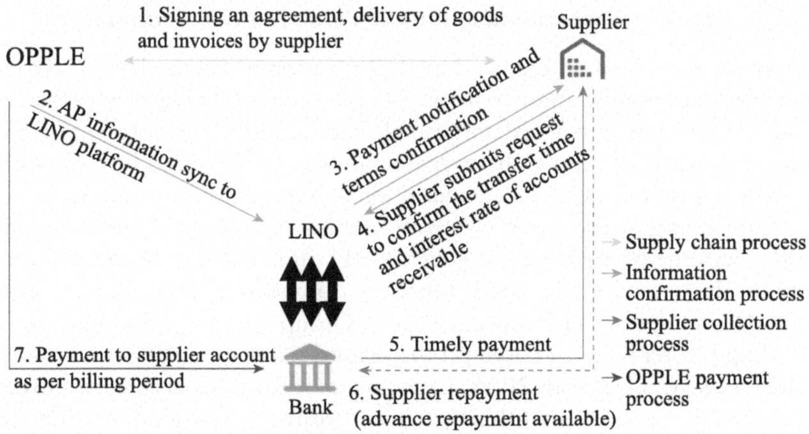

Fig. 4.10 OPPLE Supply-side online supply chain finance

saving money and enhance soft power. Moreover, with the online information and financial service platform built by LINO, OPPLE can systematically manage its upstream suppliers and greatly improve its operation efficiency. From the suppliers' point of view, the model greatly reduces their financing difficulty and financing costs, efficiently relieves their financial pressure and optimizes their cash flows, reduces the procurement costs and improves the market competitiveness of their products, and increases their business scale and efficiency and brings higher profits.

4.6 Ouyeel's Value Network-Based Intelligent Supply Chain Finance

Unlike the business chain-based intelligent supply chain finance, the value network-based intelligent supply chain finance effectively integrates multiple interest parties through a comprehensive information service platform, providing different parties with both a high-level reach of financial resource and richness of financial products. These in-depth and extensive supply chain financial services optimize the entire service value network. Its typical example is Ouyeel, a steel commodity supply chain network and financial service platform.

4.6.1 *Background of Ouyeel Value Network Platform*

As the first steelmakers engaged in B2B business in China, Baowu Group has been developing industrial supply chain for many years. www.bsteel.com.cn, which was invested and established in 2000, is a representative of the early stage of supply chain development. At that time, the platform provided whole-process electronic trading services for strategic large clients, including futures sales, electronic contracts, electronic bills of lading, and electronic payment, while covering JIT supply and other professional supply chain services. In 2013, for the purposes of meeting the demands of SMEs for spot steel products, Baowu Group set up the Shanghai Steel Trading Center in 2012 based on the second-party spot platform, baostar, which was established in 2006. Later, by increasing social steel resources, it gradually expanded to a third-party platform and provided clearing and trading services. Baowu Group also set up platforms such as Cai Gou Bao and Hua Gong Bao in 2011, with an aim to provide industrial products procurement and coal chemical products sales services for Baowu clients and public users.

Along the steel industry gradually entering the era of slight profits and the demand for industrial restructuring of urban steel mills, Baowu Group actively promoted the three strategies of transformation "from manufacturing to service, from steel to material, and from China to world." In February 2015, Baowu Group established Ouyeel Co., Ltd (referred as to "Ouyeel") by integrating internal and social resources. In 2015, the registered capital of Ouyeel was RMB 3.33 billion, and the shareholding structure was 49% by Baowu Group, 42.33% by Baosteel International, and 8.67% by Baosteel. In May 2017, Ouyeel completed its first round of equity opening to achieve mixed ownership reform. Six investors (including Ben Gang Group, Shougang Fund, Shagang Group, Mitsui & Co., GLP, and CITIC Trust) and 126 employees are selected to take a stake in Ouyeel, increasing its capital by approximately RMB 1 billion.

Ouyeel aimed to build a third-party service system integrating trading, storage, processing, transport, finance, data, technology, information, and other services and to realize the transformation from service-oriented manufacturing to production-oriented services. Specifically, Ouyeel has formed the architecture of multicategory and cross-regional commodity market services. Based on the supply chain covering various industrial fields such as raw fuels, ores, steel, home appliances, automobiles, and shipbuilding, as well as the connection of all links such as procurement, production, sales, processing, and logistics, Ouyeel has the ability to provide comprehensive solutions for industrial chain users, forming a basis for commodity market services that connect the full industrial chain and four flows. In addition, it ensures the authenticity and security of the whole-process transactions and services by using specialized and multilevel risk control means. The architecture of this platform mainly includes three layers (see Fig. 4.11): The first layer is a bulk trading service platform focused on the whole steel industry chain. The platform fosters the habit of online trading of steel mills and clients, promotes resource pooling, and thus optimizes production and sales activities. The second layer is an infrastructure service platform that integrates supply chain elements such as transport, warehousing, processing, and financial services. The platform allows transparent and efficient management and customized services for commodity logistics in the supply chain. The third layer is a credit system construction platform. Using the accumulated data from cloud services, it realizes the intelligence of resource allocation, improves the efficiency of resource utilization and builds a new type of ecosystem.

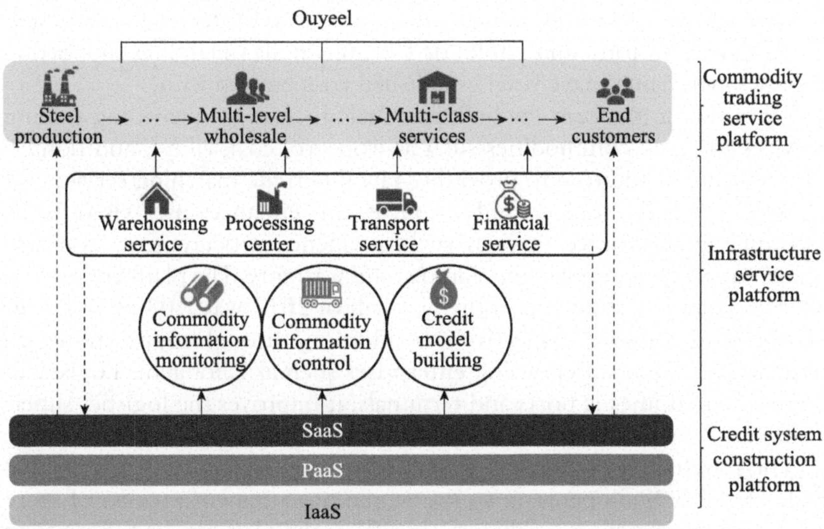

Fig. 4.11 Three-layer architecture of Ouyeel value network platform

4.6.2 *Ouyeel Commodity Trading Service Platform*

4.6.2.1 Functions of Ouyeel Trading Service

At present, Ouyeel has formed six e-commerce trading platforms for steel products, bulk raw fuels, spare parts, and construction machinery procurement, coal and chemical industry, recycling materials and cross-border business, basically forming a service platform architecture for all varieties, all processes, all regions, and all systems of the steel industry chain.

Abandoning the traditional model of purchasing raw materials and supplies to selling finished steel products, the trading platform for steel products reduces transaction costs and time and creates direct value for steel mills, suppliers and end users by setting standardized trading rules and online procurement and sales channels. The platform relies on the warehouse management system, BaoSaaS, to guarantee the authenticity and quality reliability of the sources of goods. In 2016, Ouyeel achieved the cumulative trading volume of 37.86 million tons, the cumulative transaction amount of RMB 64.56 billion, with a total of 55,000 users, compared with 5200 users in 2013. In the first half of 2017, a total of 60,915 users have registered, the average daily effective VM achieved more than 1.1 million tons, the effective VM of steel mills achieved 500,000 tons, the steel trading volume reached 5.5 million tons, the steel settlement volume reached 3.28 million tons, the transactions of steel mills accounted for 2.67 million tons, and a total of 179 steel mills (including supporting channel merchants) have been established cooperation with.

The trading platform for bulk raw fuels focuses on providing trading services for bulk commodities such as iron ore, coal, alloys, and nonferrous metals. In addition to providing raw fuel trade matching services for mines, steel mills, traders, and so on, it also enhances user viscosity by introducing innovative services such as agency procurement, consignment, supply chain exchange, bidding, and warranty. The platform's transaction volume in 2016 and in the first half of 2017 was 7.03 million tons and 3.46 million tons, respectively. In addition, through cooperation with large logistics and warehousing enterprises such as Zhongchu Logistic as well as large domestic ports and terminals, it improves the logistics supervision capacity and lays a foundation for expanding supply chain finance.

The purchasing platform is a comprehensive third-party platform that realizes the online operation of the whole procurement process of spare parts and construction machinery. In 2016, the platform had more than 30,000 registered suppliers and more than 300 purchaser clients, and the purchasing transaction volume reached RMB 43.3 billion. In the first half of 2017, the purchasing transaction volume was RMB 27.2 billion.

The chemical trading platform, established in 2011, is the earliest coal chemical third-party platform in China and the only coal chemical trading platform designated by China Coking Industry Association. By 2016, the platform had achieved rapid development, with more than 3000 registered users, nearly 50 trading sponsors, and more than 50 varieties of coal and petrochemicals. In 2016 and the first half of 2017, the trading volume of the platform reached 1.45 million tons and 1.04 million tons, respectively.

The trading platform for recycled materials provides enterprises professional and sincere service of full functions for online disposal of unused and waste materials. The platform strictly audits the transaction objects and transaction materials to ensure that the transaction process is fair, open, and just. The platform also helps manufacturing enterprises to build Internet-based systems for the disposal of recycled materials to achieve standardized, rapid and value-added sales and improve customer viscosity. In 2016 and the first half of 2017, the transaction amount of the platform was RMB 2.1 billion and RMB 1.55 billion, respectively. As of the first half of 2017, the platform has more than 9000 buyer users and more than 400 seller users.

The cross-border e-commerce platform aims to solve the problems in the import and export of steel and other bulk commodities and third country trade, and to promote the reform in the international trade. By integrating resources in the industrial chain, such as global steel mills, warehousing enterprises, processing centers, traders, and end users, the platform provides the clients in the global steel ecosystem with guarantee, matchmaking trade-off, finance, logistics, and other services for bulk commodities such as steel and related products and industrial products. The Ouyeel International Platform was launched on June 30, 2016, and reached 550,000 tons of trading volume in the same year, of which 60,000 tons were traded on an intermediary basis. Now, Ouyeel International Platform is actively building an overseas warehousing and logistics system, hoping to lay out warehousing networks in key regions such as Southeast Asia and South Asia through the cooperation with international industrial clients and to enhance the cross-border ability in bulk commodity logistics.

4.6.2.2 Value from Ouyeel's Trading Services

Based on the above-mentioned functions of trading services, Ouyeel brings the following values and benefits through capacity presales, warehouse receipts trading, unified purchasing and distribution, as well as matchmaking trade-off.

First, the long-tail benefits can be tapped. In the steel industry, there are some unpopular products with small trading volume (such as variety steel and nonstandard products). Due to the specific use, scattered transactions, and small scale, nobody cared about the production and operation of these products, resulting in little product benefit. However, Ouyeel's trading service platform brings together the demands and intentions of all kinds of participants, realizing the long-tail benefits through transparent transactions and enhancing the value of these products. For example, on Ouyeel's trading service platform, SPHC 6.0 (nonstandard product) is RMB100/ton higher than SPHC 3.0 (standard product).

Second, premium gains can be created. Ouyeel's trading service platform aims to effectively integrate all the participants in the steel supply chain and make them directly connected to steel producers, processors, and clients, thus shortening the supply chain and achieving direct sales of products to terminals/subterminals, helping steel mills increase profits and reduce purchasing costs of end users. For example, after steel mill A fully joined the platform, the hot rolled steel added value of RMB 110/ton, reflecting a premium gain.

Third, efficient online centralized control can be realized. Ouyeel's trading service platform can provide steel mills with an efficient sales model under online centralized control. By solving the routine works in the sales process via the platform, steel mill's personnel can focus on control, pricing, and sales analysis, effectively reducing the labor costs. After fully joining the platform, steel mill B has attracted hundreds of clients and the average client dispersion rate has improved from 50% to 30%.

Fourth, comprehensive data analysis can be realized. Covering the whole process and all aspects of the steel industry chain, Ouyeel's trading service platform achieves all-round data monitoring, grasps key points of sales, collects trading data, and analyzes downstream users' habits and market trends to make the best production plan and sales strategy. At present, Ouyeel provides major steelmakers *Monthly Reports for Trading Service of Ouyeel Platform* to analyze the product situation from different perspectives.

4.6.3 Ouyeel's Infrastructure Service Platform

The comprehensive supply chain services for the steel industry require functional infrastructures, including the services of warehousing, transport, processing, and building materials. Based on these infrastructures, Ouyeel built the corresponding service platforms.

The current social logistics resources are relatively scattered and in need of integration. Ouyeel Logistics is a fourth-party logistics platform that relies on the ability in integrating the logistics service providers and has built a supply chain logistics network rapidly and at a low cost by integrating resources in a relatively asset-light manner. In terms of warehousing service, Ouyeel builds a well-organized offline supply-side logistics network through four ways (i.e., agreement-based cooperation, management-based cooperation, capital-based franchising, and strategic cooperation), laying a solid foundation for reconstructing the credit system in the field of steel trading. On the basis of steel warehousing, Ouyeel is also actively expanding horizontally to warehousing for nonferrous metals and other bulk commodities, enhancing the warehousing capacity and value in the B2B field and creating the conditions for carrying out spot and futures trading, and providing financial services for nonferrous metals and other commodities. So far, Ouyeel Logistics has collaborated with Ouyeel's resources to carry out the layout of nonferrous metal warehouses, providing corresponding support for Shanghai to become international financial center and develop commodity futures trading. In 2016, Ouyeel Logistics actively promoted the "Thousand Warehouse Plan," which was designed to integrate 1000 social warehouses nationwide through the warehouse management system "Bao Ying Tong" so as to achieve the goal of covering the whole country. This goal was achieved in mid-June 2016. By the end of 2016, 208 warehouses have cooperated with Ouyeel.

In terms of transport service, through Yunbang Platform Ouyeel has integrated 1832 carriers and more than 25,000 transport vehicles, registered more than 4000 consignors, innovated special lines, and stores as well as other products, and actively expanded the market in Lecong Station and other regions. In 2016, the annual trading volume reached 17.41 million tons, with the average daily trading volume of over 65,000 tons. In the first half of 2017, the transaction volume of Yunbang Platform reached 11.34 million tons, the settlement volume reached 2.41 million tons, and the transaction volume of special lines reached 133,000 tons. Using the services of Yunbang Platform, the vehicle utilization rate and transport efficiency of carriers have been effectively improved. Through competitive bidding and other methods, the transport cost of consignors has been reduced and the response efficiency of carriers is greatly improved. By expanding the scale of carriers, Yunbang Platform allows the improvement in order acceptance rate of consignors. The current order response ratio is as high as 60%. In addition, with the help of Yunbang Platform, the transport cost of consignors is reduced by 20–30% compared with conventional lines.

The steel logistics process involves a large number of processing services. In the past, clients had to find social processors on their own, which made it costly and inefficient to manage. For this reason, Ouyeel has formed a specialized Gongbang Platform by integrating social and self-owned processors. The processing plants and single rolling mills integrated in the platform provide steel service providers, component manufacturers, and end users with a package of services for displaying, matchmaking, and trading in respect of processing capabilities, processed products, and processing needs. The platform's full-process processing services are initially for plate shearing and later extended to other varieties. This platform not only enables clients to log in through multiple channels and place orders conveniently but also seamlessly connects to the processing plant management systems. The processing process is under control, and the pain points of low efficiency, poor bargaining power, and difficulty of off-site delivery for clients looking for processing plants in different places are solved. Since its launch in January 2016, Baowu Group and other 247 social processing centers (including 216 processors and 31 single-rolling mills) have been integrated. In the first half of 2017, the warehousing scale of the warehouses cooperated with Bao Ying Tong reached 12 million tons (on a daily average basis), the processing transaction volume reached 2.84 million tons, and 2149 users completed their purchases.

Ouyeel's Jianbang Platform provides e-commerce as well as financial and logistics services for the vertical extension of the channels of building materials-based steel mills, and attracts users based on the first-hand resources of these steel mills. By setting up the central warehouses, laying the business systems, and establishing the cooperative franchises, the platform serves end users in the building materials supply chain such as building materials retail stores, projects, contractors, and farmers. Through products on Jianbang, Ouyeel improves the stickiness of various subproducts such as Ouyeel consignment, finance, and logistics, and promotes the mutual attraction between products to continuously expand the scope of services. As a "tentacle" to serve the end user farmers, Jianbang Platform provides cash register system for the franchised building materials retail stores by promoting "mobile terminal" service and obtains the terminal-based consumption data in real time, laying a solid foundation for the price index compilation and financing service.

4.6.4 Construction of Credit System Platform

Ouyeel's transaction service platforms and infrastructure platforms provide the basis for risk control of the industry chain. This is because these series of platforms not only effectively integrate all kinds of participants but also realize the data accumulation in the whole process. Through data mining, Ouyeel has established a corresponding credit system to support the development of industry and supply chain finance.

First, online verification is an effective means for controlling transaction risks. Through the warehouse management system and quality information system, Ouyeel performs online verification on suppliers' goods and provides clients with light and seal inspection services to ensure the authenticity and quality reliability of the goods and effectively reduce transaction risks. If the goods are shown as green light in the platform, which means the goods are real and the information of the owner is consistent, the client can buy them with confidence; if the goods are shown as red light, they are not allowed to buy; if the goods are shown as green seal, which means the quality information and ex-factory information are consistent, the goods have safe and reliable quality. Ouyeel uses Internet technology to monitor transaction risks in an effective manner and provides endorsement of credit for clients, thus ensuring an honest transaction environment and improving the experience satisfaction of clients.

Second, data are tradable and realizable assets. Ouyeel promotes the development and application of data-based credit products and provides support for supply chain financial services through mining data in respect of transaction behaviors. In the promotion of the product "Green Financing" (a supply chain financing service product with Internet attributes launched by Ouyeel in the second half of 2016, which is a comprehensive service carried out based on the principle of "small amount, high frequency and dispersion," combining Ouyeel's capacity and system construction in the fields of e-commerce, logistics, and finance, as well as its active exploration in the "consignment" business, and integrating information flow, transport flow, and capital flow), Ouyeel determines the credit lines of users based on the transaction behaviors and accumulated transaction data of clients in the e-commerce platform as well as other credit investigation methods and actively explores the establishment of Ouyeel credit sharing platform to realize the real-time calls of credit data.

Finally, efficient asset management capability is an important guarantee. Ouyeel integrates the resources of social warehouses through the output of coverage and management capability of warehouse management system as well as multilevel cooperation like capital-based franchising, creating conditions for the development of movable assets pledge and other financial services. In addition, Ouyeel builds the Shanghai Banking Chattel Mortgage Information Platform and the Free Trade Zone Bulk Commodity Warehouse Receipts Information Disclosure Platform with an aim to improve the credit enhancement ability of warehouse receipts through the service of disclosing warehouse receipts information. Shanghai Banking Chattel Mortgage Information Platform is mainly used to prevent the financing business risks in the banking industry, provides services such as MTM, and eventually forms the bulk commodity financial supervision service system covering the banking industry nationwide. The Free Trade Zone Bulk Commodity Warehouse Receipts Information Disclosure Platform serves bulk commodity transactions in the Free Trade Zone, with the goal of establishing a bonded warehouse receipt service system based on disclosed warehouse receipts to provide convenient and efficient bulk commodity financing in the Free Trade Zone.

4.6.5 Ouyeel's Supply Chain Financial Services

Benefitting from the three-layer architecture, Ouyeel Financial Services has developed inventory financing, factoring, pawning, and other self-managed financing services, and fully taps the credit resources of the industry chain to promote financial services products such as real estate mortgage financing as well as factory-trader-bank and bill financing, reaching financing amount of ¥ 20 billion. Ouyeel also built a bill pool to meet the invoicing needs of various clients, and actively expanded the external market of third-party payment to achieve the successful renewal of easternpay's license. By strengthening the connection with banks, Ouyeel actively implemented credit lines to effectively enhance fund-raising capacity and meet the funding needs of various clients in Ouyeel's systems.

Specifically, Ouyeel Finance, as the only Internet financial platform under Ouyeel, relying on the rich offline resources and financial resources of Baowu Group, uses financial methods to establish an industry chain-based financial service system around the entire steel industry chain, establishes cooperation with various financial institutions, forms all-round financial service clusters, and provides online payment, financing, investment and wealth management, asset management, and other financial products for manufacturers, bulk commodity trading platforms, traders, end users, and so on.

In terms of the form of supply chain financial services, Ouyeel Finance continuously improves its products according to the different needs of clients with respect to financing threshold and financing cost, and provides various channels and levels of financing products by means of the Internet. At present, the supply chain financial products mainly include credit-based financing (such as Ouyeel IOU, platform overdraft, etc.), supply chain-based financing (such as supplier financing, buyer financing, accounts receivable factoring, etc.), and chattel mortgage– and real estate mortgage–based financing (such as steel inventory pledge financing, bill financing, housing pawn, and auto pawn, etc.). With the credit system formed, Ouyeel's credit financing achieves multilevel penetration of credits. For example, based on the long-term good cooperation between Baowu Group and Great Wall Motor, Ouyeel Financial Service establishes the credits of Great Wall Motor on the basis of mining and analysis of the long-term transaction data, logistics data, and payment data of both parties. On this basis, Ouyeel Financial Service successfully completed the lending of RMB 79 million to Hebitian Moter Dies Co., Ltd. by assigning the receivables of the upstream supplier Hebitian Moter Dies Co., Ltd. from Great Wall Motor Group (see Fig. 4.12). Ouyeel IOU is a small loan product offered by Ouyeel Finance, which provides credit financing services for e-commerce platform companies. Ouyeel IOU can be used for online payment scenarios such as payment for goods, freight and handling fees, and warehousing fees.

In supply chain financing, Ouyeel provides various financial services to platform participants based on the debts generated by the business of those platforms. In chattel pledge, Ouyeel provides financing to companies in real time based on the movable assets managed by Ouyeel Cloud Warehouse. The key to chattel pledge is the ability to supervise the movable assets effectively and in real time. For the asset management of industry chain clients, Ouyeel provides a comprehensive solution of warehouse receipt registration, asset supervision, asset valuation, value warning, and asset disposal for bulk commodities. On the one hand, Ouyeel realizes the

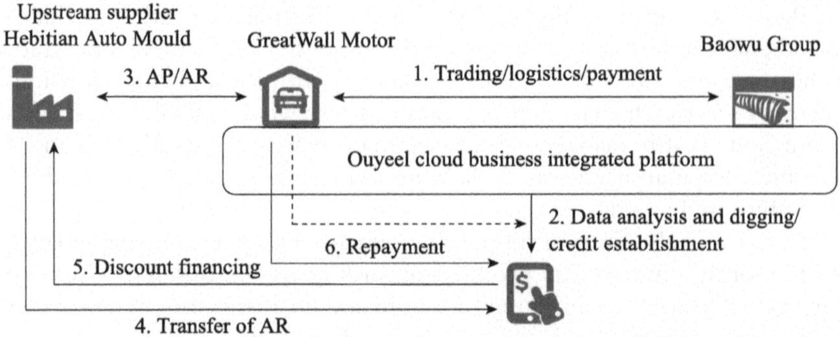

Fig. 4.12 Example of credit financing from Ouyeel financial services

physical management of bulk assets with the control system of "technical protection + manual protection" to ensure effective control of goods; and on the other hand, Ouyeel relies on professional value management model to realize dynamic value management of bulk assets and reduce market risks. Meanwhile, Ouyeel provides a shared and unified asset pledge registration platform to build up a risk defense line against repeated pledges.

References

Adrodegari, F., & Saccani, N. (2017). Business models for the service transformation of industrial firms. *The Service Industries Journal, 37*(1), 57–83.

Baines, T., Ziaee Bigdeli, A., Bustinza, O. F., Shi, V. G., Baldwin, J., & Ridgway, K. (2017). Servitization: Revisiting the state-of-the-art and research priorities. *International Journal of Operations & Production Management, 37*(2), 256–278.

Baines, T. S., Lightfoot, H. W., Benedettini, O., & Kay, J. M. (2009). The servitization of manufacturing: A review of literature and reflection on future challenges. *Journal of Manufacturing Technology Management, 20*(5), 547–567.

Baldwin, C. Y., & Clark, K. B. (2003). Managing in an age of modularity. *Managing in the Modular Age: Architectures, Networks, and Organizations, 149*, 84–93.

Baltacioglu, T., Ada, E., Kaplan, M. D., Yurt And, O., & Cem Kaplan, Y. (2007). A new framework for service supply chains. *The Service Industries Journal, 27*(2), 105–124.

Barnett, N. J., Parry, G., Saad, M., Newnes, L. B., & Goh, Y. M. (2013). Servitization: Is a paradigm shift in the business model and service enterprise required? *Strategic Change, 22*(3–4), 145–156.

Basole, R. C., & Rouse, W. B. (2008). Complexity of service value networks: Conceptualization and empirical investigation. *IBM Systems Journal, 47*(1), 53–70.

Blau, B., Kramer, J., Conte, T., & Dinther, C. van. (2009). Service value networks. *2009 IEEE Conference on Commerce and Enterprise Computing*, 194–201.

Böttcher, M., & Klingner, S. (2011). Providing a method for composing modular B2B services. *Journal of Business & Industrial Marketing, 26*(5), 320–331.

Cenamor, J., Rönnberg Sjödin, D., & Parida, V. (2017). Adopting a platform approach in servitization: Leveraging the value of digitalization. *International Journal of Production Economics, 192*, 54–65.

Daugherty, P. J., Ellinger, A. E., & Rogers, D. S. (1995). Information accessibility: Customer responsiveness and enhanced performance. *International Journal of Physical Distribution & Logistics Management, 25*(1), 4–17.

De Waart, D., & Kemper, S. (2004). Five steps to service supply chain excellence. In *Newsletter of the Stanford Global Supply Chain Management Forum*, 10, (4).

DeWitt, T., Giunipero, L. C., & Melton, H. L. (2006). Clusters and supply chain management: The Amish experience. *International Journal of Physical Distribution & Logistics Management, 36*(4), 289–308.

Dyer, J. H., Singh, H., & Hesterly, W. S. (2018). The relational view revisited: A dynamic perspective on value creation and value capture. *Strategic Management Journal, 39*, 3140–3162.

Ellram, L. M., Tate, W. L., & Billington, C. (2004). Understanding and managing the services supply chain. *Journal of Supply Chain Management, 40*(3), 17–32.

Feldman, M., Francis, J., & Bercovitz, J. (2005). Creating a cluster while building a firm: Entrepreneurs and the formation of industrial clusters. *Regional Studies, 39*(1), 129–141.

Fu, W., Wang, Q., & Zhao, X. (2017). The influence of platform service innovation on value co-creation activities and the network effect. *Journal of Service Management, 28*(2), 348–388.

Ganesan, S., Malter, A. J., & Rindfleisch, A. (2005). Does distance still matter? Geographic proximity and new product development. *Journal of Marketing, 69*(4), 44–60.

Gebauer, H., Fleisch, E., & Friedli, T. (2005). Overcoming the service paradox in manufacturing companies. *European Management Journal, 23*(1), 14–26.

Gottschalk, P. (2007). How knowledge organisations work: The value shop configuration. *International Journal of Services and Standards, 3*(4), 402–412.

Grönroos, C., & Gummerus, J. (2014). The service revolution and its marketing implications: Service logic vs service-dominant logic. *Managing Service Quality: An International Journal, 24*(3), 206–229.

Hammer, M., & Champy, J. (2009). *Reengineering the corporation: Manifesto for business revolution, A*. Zondervan.

Heinonen, K., & Strandvik, T. (2015). Customer-dominant logic: Foundations and implications. *Journal of Services Marketing, 29*(6/7), 472–484.

Holdt Christensen, P. (2007). Knowledge sharing: Moving away from the obsession with best practices. *Journal of Knowledge Management, 11*(1), 36–47.

Iammarino, S., & McCann, P. (2006). The structure and evolution of industrial clusters: Transactions, technology and knowledge spillovers. *Research Policy, 35*(7), 1018–1036.

Kastalli, I. V., & Van Looy, B. (2013). Servitization: Disentangling the impact of service business model innovation on manufacturing firm performance. *Journal of Operations Management, 31*(4), 169–180.

Kohtamäki, M., Rabetino, R., & Einola, S. (2018). Paradoxes in servitization. In M. Kohtamäki, T. Baines, R. Rabetino, & A. Z. Bigdeli (Eds.), *Practices and tools for servitization* (pp. 185–199). Springer International Publishing.

Lee, H., Lee, C., & Yoo, C. (1998). A scenario-based object-oriented methodology for developing hypermedia information systems. *Proceedings of the Thirty-First Hawaii International Conference on System Sciences, 2*, 47–56.

Leimeister, Stefanie, Böhm, Markus, Riedl, Christoph, & Krcmar, Helmut. (2010). The business perspective of cloud computing: Actors, roles and value networks. *ECIS 2010 Proceedings*, 56.

Li, F., & Whalley, J. (2002). Deconstruction of the telecommunications industry: From value chains to value networks. *Telecommunications Policy, 26*(9–10), 451–472.

Lusch, R. F., Vargo, S. L., & O'Brien, M. (2007). Competing through service: Insights from service-dominant logic. *Journal of Retailing, 83*(1), 5–18.

Lusch, R. F., Vargo, S. L., & Tanniru, M. (2010). Service, value networks and learning. *Journal of the Academy of Marketing Science, 38*(1), 19–31.

Martinez, V., Bastl, M., Kingston, J., & Evans, S. (2010). Challenges in transforming manufacturing organisations into product-service providers. *Journal of Manufacturing Technology Management, 21*(4), 449–469.

Morosini, P. (2004). Industrial clusters, knowledge integration and performance. *World Development, 32*(2), 305–326.

Oinas, P. (2017). *Proximity, distance and diversity: Issues on economic interaction and local development*. Routledge.

Porter, M. E. (1985). *Competitive advantage: Creating and sustaining superior performance* (Vol. 43, p. 214). FreePress.

Porter, M. E., & Millar, V. E. (1985). *How information gives you competitive advantage*.

Schmitz, H. (1995). Collective efficiency: Growth path for small-scale industry. *The Journal of Development Studies, 31*(4), 529–566.

Smedlund, A. (2012). Value cocreation in service platform business models. *Service Science, 4*(1), 79–88.

Smith, W. K., & Lewis, M. W. (2011). Toward a theory of paradox: A dynamic equilibrium model of organizing. *Academy of Management Review, 36*(2), 381–403.

Sobek, D. K., II, Ward, A. C., & Liker, J. K. (1999). Toyota's principles of set-based concurrent engineering. *MIT Sloan Management Review, 40*(2), 67.

Song, H., Lu, Q., Yu, K., & Qian, C. (2018). How do knowledge spillover and access in supply chain network enhance SMEs' credit quality? *Industrial Management & Data Systems, 19*, 274–291.

Stabell, C. B., & Fjeldstad, Ø. D. (1998). Configuring value for competitive advantage: On chains, shops, and networks. *Strategic Management Journal, 19*(5), 413–437.

Sureshchandar, G. S., Rajendran, C., & Anantharaman, R. N. (2002). The relationship between service quality and customer satisfaction – A factor specific approach. *Journal of Services Marketing, 16*(4), 363–379.

Sweet, P. (2001). Strategic value configuration logics and the "new" economy: A service economy revolution? *International Journal of Service Industry Management, 12*(1), 70–84.

Thomas, L. D. W., Autio, E., & Gann, D. M. (2014). Architectural leverage: Putting platforms in context. *Academy of Management Perspectives, 28*(2), 198–219.

Thompson, J. D. (1967). *Organizations in action: Social science bases of administrative theory*. McGraw-Hill.

Turunen, T., & Finne, M. (2014). The organisational environment's impact on the servitization of manufacturers. *European Management Journal, 32*(4), 603–615.

Tuunanen, T., & Cassab, H. (2011). Service process modularization: Reuse versus variation in service extensions. *Journal of Service Research, 14*(3), 340–354.

Uzzi, B. (1997). Social structure and competition in interfirm networks: The paradox of embeddedness. *Administrative Science Quarterly, 42*(1), 35.

Vandermerwe, S., & Rada, J. (1988). Servitization of business: Adding value by adding services. *European Management Journal, 6*(4), 314–324.

Vargo, S. L., & Lusch, R. F. (2004). Evolving to a new dominant logic for marketing. *Journal of Marketing, 68*(1), 1–17.

Vargo, S. L., & Lusch, R. F. (2008). Service-dominant logic: Continuing the evolution. *Journal of the Academy of Marketing Science, 36*(1), 1–10.

Vendrell-Herrero, F., Bustinza, O. F., Parry, G., & Georgantzis, N. (2017). Servitization, digitization and supply chain interdependency. *Industrial Marketing Management, 60*, 69–81.

Vitasek, K., & Manrodt, K. (2012). Vested outsourcing: A flexible framework for collaborative outsourcing. *Strategic Outsourcing: An International Journal, 5*(1), 4–14.

Wells, D., & Gobeli, D. H. (2003). The 3R framework: Improving e-strategy across reach, richness, and range. *Business Horizons, 46*(2), 5–14.

Wu, X., & Liu, X. (2009). Absorptive capacity, network embeddedness and local firm's knowledge acquisition in the Global Manufacturing Network. *International Journal of Technology Management, 46*(3–4), 326–343.

Yassine, A., & Braha, D. (2003). Complex concurrent engineering and the design structure matrix method. *Concurrent Engineering, 11*(3), 165–176.

Youseff, L., Butrico, M., & Da Silva, D. (2008). *Toward a unified ontology of cloud computing* (pp. 1–10). IEEE.

CHAPTER 5

Coordinator for Multiple Participants: A Booster of Intelligent Supply Chain Finance

5.1 Introduction

As the scenario of supply chain finance increasingly shifts from a single business or sequential chain to a service value network, the participants become more diverse and multilayered, involving not only the buyers and sellers in the transactions but also other stakeholders, including various financial institutions, service providers (e.g., third-party logistics providers), as well as institutions regulating and managing the transaction process, industry associations, and government departments. Such a huge number of participants involved in the operations of the service value network inevitably leads to complex interaction activities with different nature. Therefore, defining the roles and functions of each participant in the supply chain is a tricky task in the organization of supply chain finance. In particular, as the supply chain activities become increasingly multilayered, all transaction activities are carried out in a decentralized, sequential, or synchronized manner, which makes the organization and management of supply chain finance even more difficult. Under the scenario of service value network, all participants act as independent clusters with equal status that realize loosely coupled cooperation through behavioral interaction and value cocreation, instead of the core enterprises in the 2.0 era that provided supply chain financial services by controlling all upstream and downstream businesses. For this reason, no specific enterprise in the network can realize the global control of all transaction details. For example,

H. Song, *Smart Supply Chain Finance*,
https://doi.org/10.1007/978-981-16-5997-3_5

the transaction and logistics behavior between the suppliers and the sub-suppliers of the suppliers cannot be directly interfered with by the downstream service providers, and even the business behaviors between the multitier upstream enterprises are completely out of the control of a specific enterprise. Especially in the era of industrial Internet, the processes of production, operation, and organization is based on virtualized industrial clusters, instead of the previous geographical clusters. As a result, the scope and space of business cooperation has been greatly expanded and presents a complex state. In addition, supply chain business activities or matters are increasingly diversified accordingly under the scenario of service value network, including not only supply chain business activities such as technology, design, agreement, procurement, production, marketing, distribution, and refund, and various differentiated financial activities such as payment, settlement, tax refund, insurance, and investment, but also the great changes in the meanings and extensions of commodity flow, transport flow, and fund flow emphasized in supply chain management. For this regard, on the one hand, the inherent expression of these elements presents a misalignment of time and space. For example, in the process of trading and buying, different counterparties and different products may use different trading forms (e.g., local production for nationwide trading and seasonal production for all-year-round trading). On the other hand, various matching relationships appear among the four flows. Sometimes, there is a separation between the commodity flow and transport flow (e.g., logistic behavior is followed by trading behavior) and a misalignment between trading flow and fund flow (e.g., prepaid procurement, i.e., procurement behavior occurs after fund flow). Because of such complicated business activities, coupled with the participation of multiple subjects, the problem of information asymmetry becomes increasingly prominent in the era of service value network, thus making the risk of carrying out supply chain finance grow geometrically. Therefore, the orderly development of supply chain finance requires organizational innovation, which means that the specialized organizations (i.e., fintech companies) can solve the above problems and promote the development of supply chain finance driven by service value network. This chapter will first explore the basis for the emergence of such specialized organizations and the specific roles they play in the service value network from a theoretical perspective, and then analyze the current Chinese market of supply chain finance and the different modes of cooperation between such specialized organizations and other participants of the industrial supply chain.

5.2 Signaling Theory and Its Challenges in Supply Chain Finance

An important prerequisite for financial decision-making is the completeness and symmetry of information. Once information asymmetry arises between the borrower and the lender, any borrowing and lending behavior will have significant risks. Traditional economic theory assumes that all decisions are based on complete information, in which case people are rational. However, in reality, information is often incomplete and asymmetric as some is private. In particular, information asymmetry exists between the information owners and decision-makers (Stiglitz, 2002). This asymmetry leads to adverse selection and moral hazard, which become an important source of social transaction costs (Williamson, 1973). According to Stiglitz (2000), two types of information asymmetries require special attention, namely quality-related information and intention-related information. The former refers to the fact that one party does not know the actual situation of the other party, while the latter refers to the fact that one party does not know the behaviors and behavioral intentions of the other party. The asymmetry in these two types of information is particularly typical in financial lending. On the one hand, the fund provider is not fully aware of the actual situation of the SMEs, especially those in the start-up phase, whose business stability and investment returns are uncertain and whose actual development potential is difficult to judge directly. On the other hand, the business behaviors of SMEs is also difficult to be directly known to the capital providers. In particular, in the absence of complete financial statements, fund providers have no way to understand the actual operating status of the SMEs, including their real intention to use the funds. Therefore, these situations often lead to more serious information asymmetries, which is also the reason why it is difficult for financial institutions to provide lending to SMEs. Eliminating, and reducing the degree of, asymmetries in these two types of information requires a means to speed up the transmission of information. This means is the basic logic of signaling theory. Spence (1978) explored the role of education as a signal in his study of the labor market. Considering the difficulty for employers to know information about the quality of candidates, the candidates show their quality through their educational credentials. The information asymmetry is reduced in such a way. Kirmani and Rao (2000) proposed a basic model of signaling theory in which they identified two types of firms, namely high-quality firms and low-quality firms.

Each firm can choose to transmit or not to transmit signals. If it transmits signals, it can obtain high returns; otherwise, it can only obtain low returns. Likewise, financial markets have many means to serve as signals. For example, a firm's debt (Ross, 1973), dividends (Bhattacharya, 1979), and so on are signals that reflect its quality. Only high-quality firms are able to pay interest and dividends over time, while low-quality firms are unable to afford such payments for a long run. These signals influence the perception of external observers (e.g., lenders and investors) about the quality of the firms. Thus, signals have become a key tool to reduce information asymmetry in financial markets. However, who are the signal senders and signal receivers, what kind of signals should be transmitted, and the environment in which they are transmitted are important issues that still need to be explored.

Development of Traditional Signaling Theory

The traditional exploration of signaling theory revolves around the subjects, content, and process of signaling (see Fig. 5.1). The subjects refer to the signal sender and the receiver. The former is the subject who transmits the signal and receives the benefit, while the latter is the decision-maker who observes the quality of the senders by obtaining the signal. The content is the transmitted signal itself, which is the carrier reflecting the quality of the information. The process refers to the receiver's feedback to the sender after obtaining the signal and the overall signal transmission environment.

The research on signal senders constitutes a key aspect of signaling theory. As insiders, signal senders know the information about themselves (Spence, 1978), their products (Kirmani & Rao, 2000), or their organizations (Ross, 1973) that is not known to others. The research focuses on the traits, motivations, and behaviors of signal senders. The research on

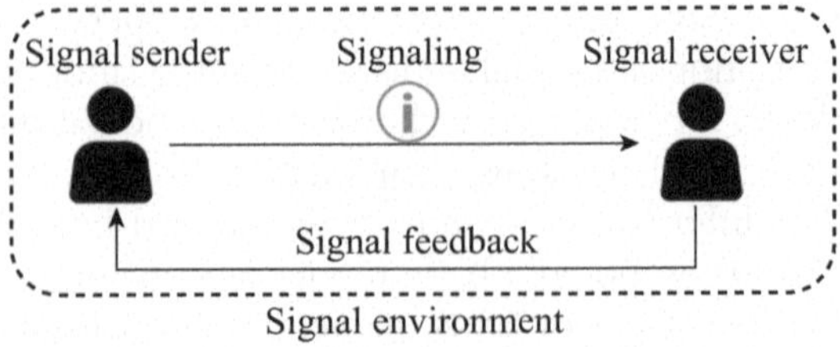

Fig. 5.1 Overall research framework of signaling theory

traits is exploring the kinds of people who deliver high-quality signals. Signals in market trading can be both positive and negative. The signal sender will decide what signals to pass on to outsiders. A dishonest signal sender will choose to deceive and pass the wrong signal to the receiver, thus benefiting itself on the basis of the receiver's loss. An honest signaler will deliver high-quality signals to the receiver, allowing the observer or receiver to make the right decision. Therefore, what kind of signal sender is regarded as honest is a topic to be explored by theoretical experts. Some scholars argued that honest signal senders can truthfully reflect unobservable signals (Arthurs et al., 2009; Ndofor & Levitas, 2004). According to some studies, the appointment of reputable directors by a firm can send a signal about compliance to investors (Certo et al., 2001). In other studies, the current and past behavioral performance has been used to define honest signaling, which means the honesty of signals sent by a firm depends on the status of historical results of past signals (Heil & Robertson, 1991a; Connelly et al., 2011). A sender will be considered as honest in the present if he has a reputation for sending high-quality signals in the past (Heil & Robertson, 1991a). Another focus of research on signal senders is their motivation to send signals. Some management research argued that whether a signal sender sends honest or deceptive signals depends on the differential costs of high- and low-quality signals (Ndofor & Levitas, 2004). For example, Westphal and Zajac (2001) explored an array of firms that indicated that they would purchase stock again in the future but actually did not end up purchasing. This separation between the original plan and the subsequent actual behavior is called decoupling, and a long-term state of decoupling gives rise to a reputation for dishonesty. Therefore, based on the research on signal senders, signaling theory suggests that incentives are key to facilitating the sending of high-quality information. Signal senders will send true signals only if they can bring good incentives or rewards to themselves by sending true signals. For example, signals about how the CEO reacts to the quality of the firm under the incentive of attempting to influence the stock price can more or less give prediction of the performance status of the firm (Westphal & Zajac, 2001). The signal sending behavior (i.e., when and at what frequency a signal sender chooses to send a signal) has also been one of the theoretical research concerns. For example, Janney and Folta (2003, 2006) found that signal senders would send fewer signals over time. For this reason, Connelly et al. (2011) argued that the future research needs to explore how signal sends balance the frequency of signaling as well as the timing of signaling (i.e., balancing the results of faster or slower signal changes) and the effect of different frequencies of signaling during the interaction of all parties on the signal display process.

In addition to the research on signal senders, the signals themselves are also of interest to economic and management experts. Research on the signals themselves has focused on signal quality (i.e., the classification and different qualities of signals). Some studies have classified signals based on whether they are observable or not. In other words, some signals may be more easily recognized by the receiver or observer than others. Thus, signals are classified as "strong" or "weak" (Gulati & Higgins, 2003). According to Julien et al. (2004), if a SME is in a strong relationship network, it will reflect a strong signal because it has common language, habits, and good complementary knowledge with other enterprises. However, if an SME is in a weak relationship network, it will reflect a weak signal, which is often harder to capture and interpret. Ramaswami et al. (2010) have defined signal strength and visibility (or clarity) from a theoretical perspective. Signal strength refers to the degree of importance or significance for a given signal recipient, which means that the more important the signal is for the receiver, the higher the quality of the signal will be. In a study, Heil and Robertson (1991b) suggested that an important quality of signals is signal aggressiveness, that is, the extent to which the signals sent threaten the survival and growth of the signal receiver. For example, a competitor's price reduction may threaten the operation and development of other peers. Such aggressive signals can affect the way the receiver interprets and applies the signals. Signal visibility refers to the degree to which a signal can be observed. Observable or clear signals can be easily identified and applied by the observer without large bias. One of the quality issues associated with these two types of signals is signal fit, that is, whether the signal sent is what the receiver cannot observe. If the signal sent reflects important states and information about the sender that the receiver or observer cannot obtain on their own, the signal can be regarded as having a good fit. Thus, signal fit is an important dimension reflecting signal quality, and can reduce many problems arising from information asymmetry. Apart from signal fit, signal frequency and consistency are also two dimensions that reflect signal quality. Signal frequency reveals the fact that sending more frequent and sufficient observable signals will lead to higher quality and efficacy of such signals (Janney & Folta, 2003). Especially in the dynamic market environment, information is constantly generated and changed due to the complexity and dynamics of the market, while the previous information and signals may become lagged or even present a completely different state as the environment changes. Therefore, only continuous sending of observable signals can gradually reduce the degree of information asymmetry. Signal consistency indicates that the signals reflecting a single thing are identical and do not present differentiated or even contradictory information (Heil & Robertson, 1991b). For example, judgments of a firm's capabilities can be made by observing factors such as the technical level of its products as well as its competitive behavior, market position, or supply chain management capabilities, but any one of the above signals should consistently reflect the state of the firm's capabilities. If the signals reflecting the same thing are inconsistent, the usefulness of the signals decreases, which not only fails to reduce information asymmetry but may increase it due to the complexity of the information. Therefore, signal consistency is also an important indication of signal quality (Fischer & Reuber, 2007). In other studies of signal quality, researchers have classified signals from a motivational perspective. The signals are classified as intent, camouflage, and need signals (Connelly et al., 2011). Intent signal is a signal that is deliberately sent by the sender in order to fulfill his/her intention, or to prompt a response from the receiver. For example, a company consciously provides financial statements to a financial institution in order to obtain a loan, in which case the financial statements are an intent signal. Camouflage signal is a signal released by the sender with an aim to disguise his/her vulnerabilities or bad characteristics, or to distract the attention of the receiver or the observer. For example, Song et al. (2017) found in their research on supply chain safety management of Chinese food firms that the firms facing the domestic market generally choose to build reputation to highlight their food quality and safety, thus disguising the weak side of their external supply chain management. Need signal is a signal that the receiver needs to consider. For example, when all branches of a group express a need for funds or resources, the head office will decide which branch is the most urgent, and the signal in this case is a need signal.

The signal receiver is the individual or organization that receives, interprets, and applies the signal in order to make decisions. Research in signaling theory posits that signal senders and signal receivers are two parties with potential conflict, which means the realization of benefits for the signal sender may require considerations of the receiver. Therefore, signaling does occur in such a way that the sender obtains a benefit from the receiver that would not otherwise arise (Connelly et al., 2011). Signal receivers must be individuals or organizations that provide benefits to the sender, including shareholders (Certo et al., 2001), creditors (Elliott et al., 2009), or customers (Basuroy et al., 2006). According to theoretical studies, the efficiency of signaling depends in part on the characteristics of the signal receiver. The first characteristic is the signal attention of the receiver, that is, the degree of attention of the receiver to observe the environment to obtain the signal. If the receiver is not searching for the signal or does not know what signal to search for, the signaling will be ineffective. For example, a study by Gulati and Higgins (2003) showed that the salience of signals from start-ups is highly dependent on the extent to which the receivers are focusing on the IPO market. Similarly, environmental monitoring is important as far as obtaining weak signals is concerned, as such signals are difficult to capture unless consciously sought by the receivers (Ilmola & Kuusi, 2006). The second characteristic is signal expertise of receivers, or the ability of signal receivers to accurately interpret signals, which relies on the experience accumulated by managers over time (Heil & Robertson, 1991b). If the receiver can effectively understand and apply the signal, the signal will play a key role, thus mitigating the information asymmetry problem; conversely, if the signal sent by the sender cannot be effectively interpreted by the receiver, or is even misinterpreted, it will not reduce transaction costs, and also increase potential risks. A major key to the signal expertise of receivers is their ability to comprehensively parse signals (Connelly et al., 2011), as the signals received by receivers are often complex and discrete, or the presence of one signal suggests the presence of the next. In such cases, the signal receivers should have the ability to organize this series of discrete signals and dissect the overall clear meaning (Rindova, Ferrier, Wiltbank, & Basdeo, 2002). The third characteristic is the definition of the signal field by receivers, that is, how the signal receivers define the signal source of its attention. Whether the signal is effectively received and used by the receiver also depends on the fields to which the receiver gives attention. For example, according to a study conducted by Heil and Robertson (1991b), signal interpretation tends to be most direct and effective when the receiver is in the same strategic cluster as the sender, because competitors in the same field tend to be attentive to the states of each other and are therefore able to interpret the signals from each other in a quick and effective manner. On the contrary, if the signals are sent by new entrants in different industries and strategic clusters, the receiver often fails to interpret and apply and tends to ignore such signals.

In the study of signaling theory, feedback from the receiver to the sender and the environment are also important factors deserving attention. Given the existence of information asymmetry, a two-way signal display is often required (Connelly et al., 2011). On the one hand, the signal receiver obtains valid signals from the sender to reduce the high transaction costs caused by information asymmetry; on the other hand, the signal sender also obtains feedback from the receiver on the signals to understand what is most stable and reliable in the signals that have been sent, what signals the receiver pays attention to, and how the receiver interprets the signals. According to the feedback, the signal sender makes subsequent adjustments to continuously enhance the quality and stability of the signals (Gulati & Higgins, 2003). In studies of feedback and environment, some scholars suggested that the costs for sending signals are an important factor in the effect of signaling (Rao et al., 2018), because there is a single point of inflection for signals in the initial establishment of signaling theory. In other words, the signals above the point of inflection are able to reduce information asymmetry and those below will exacerbate it. For example, Spence (1978), in his study of labor markets, argued that educational credentials are the inflection point of signals. However, in real organizational environments, signals tend to be continuous without a single point of inflection. In the labor market, for example, when job seekers consider whether to take a job in an organization, they often use employer interactions as a signal of how they will be treated once hired (Walker et al., 2013). There, the costs for sending signals vary with the continuum set. The efficiency of signals may increase at a decreasing rate when the costs for sending signals increase (Rao et al., 2018). In addition to the costs for sending signals, another factor that is overlooked is the costs for penalizing the sender, which is a form of negative feedback from the receiver (Gammoh et al., 2006). This negative feedback can often take many forms. In the case of interorganizational cooperation, for example, once the receiver discovers that the sender has sent false or erroneous signals, it can terminate their cooperative relationship, delay the cooperation (i.e., maintain the existing cooperation without initiating a new one), seek a third party to impose punishment, or inform others of the sender's dishonest signaling behavior. To this end, building a robust signaling environment requires an understanding of the best way to handle negative signals, the significance of signal priority, and the role of signal (feedback) in the signaling process (Taj, 2016).

Challenges of Traditional Signaling Theory in Supply Chain Finance Scenarios

By exploring the above issues, traditional signaling theory tries to address the high transaction costs caused by information asymmetry. However, traditional signaling theory still faces many challenges under the scenarios of supply chain finance.

First, from the perspective of signal senders, a majority of supply chain financial services are targeted at SMEs, which have a small scale of operation, unstable business model, and short business history. Therefore, SMEs that desire to be recognized as honest signal senders must build reputation and trust (Deelmann & Loos, 2002), which will take a long time to develop. In the short term, financial institutions are less likely to identify SMEs as honest or dishonest in their financial lending. Despite the extensive credit investigations made by financial institutions before lending decisions, the lack of valid financial statements and assets for collateral and pledging, as well as the short operating history of most SMEs, make it a significant challenge for financial institutions to obtain credit data. In particular, when the operation environment is highly uncertain, the SMEs' past operating performance cannot reflect their current or future growth potential, making it difficult for lenders to judge their reputation and build trust. Moreover, this status may lead the lenders to overlook high-quality SMEs that use countersignaling. As a further development of signaling theory, countersignaling was originally proposed by Feltovich et al. (2001, 2002), who argued that high-quality firms may show their high quality through countersignaling, instead of sending signals. Taking the job market as an example, they classified student job seekers into three types and two sets of signals, namely high ability, medium ability, and low ability, as well as endogenous (e.g., GPA) and exogenous (e.g., sealed letters of recommendation) signals. Both endogenous and exogenous signals have shortcomings. On the one hand, high-ability and medium-ability students have good GPAs, while low-ability students have poor GPAs, but GPA as a signal cannot distinguish between high-ability students and medium-ability students; on the other hand, high-ability students generally have excellent letters of recommendation, low-ability students have poor letters of recommendation, while medium-ability students do not know whether they have good or poor letters of recommendation. Therefore, letters of recommendation as a signal cannot distinguish between medium-ability students and low-ability students. Even the combination of these two signals is still not effective in distinguishing high ability students from the lucky medium-ability students. In this situation, they argued that the student job applicants with three different ability can be effectively distinguished through countersignaling. Under certain scenarios, high-ability students can distinguish themselves by only providing excellent letter of recommendation from medium-ability students who provide both GPA and letter of recommendation. Medium-ability job seekers are afraid to not provide GPA because they do not know the contents of their letters of recommendation. This theory is also present in the financial lending market. There are also endogenous (e.g., financial statements, assets for collateral, and pledge) and exogenous (e.g., competitive abilities and business models) signals that reflect the true status of the borrowers. However, given the confounding effect of endogenous signals (i.e., lenders cannot distinguish the authenticity of financial statements), high-quality SMEs may only rely on their exogenous signals to demonstrate their strengths, which is why some companies may use rhetorical signals (e.g., press releases, prototypes of new products, and appointing well-known managers) to obtain the appropriate resources (Steigenberger & Wilhelm, 2018). However, supply chain financial activities are different from venture capital activities. The latter only provides capital and professional knowledge and experience to help the invested company make more profits, which is a high-risk and high-reward business pursuing long-term profits, while the former aims to solve the short-term working capital of SMEs. The lender receives reasonable interests through loans, while the borrower uses the loans to solve operational liquidity. For this regard, ensuring the safety of each and every loan is the primary concern of the lender. Rather than relying exclusively on rhetorical signals to determine the quality of an SME, financial institutions, as lenders, use more objective exogenous signals (i.e., product competitiveness, technological capabilities) to identify the actual status of the borrowers. Such objective exogenous signals are often a natural reflection of their long-term operations. Therefore, it is more difficult for SMEs to demonstrate their honesty and high quality through their own signaling or nonsignaling behavior. In this case, the inability of financial institutions to distinguish between high- and medium-quality or even poor-quality SMEs results in, on the one hand, the potential loss of truly high-quality SMEs that use countersignaling and, on the other hand, higher default rates arising from indiscriminately higher lending costs (e.g., requiring all SMEs to provide collateral) or the inability to discern the quality and honesty of SMEs.

Second, from the perspective of the signals themselves, the signal fit (i.e., how to achieve a perfect fit between intent signals and need signals) is also a great challenge for supply chain finance. Generally speaking, SMEs have their own private information about their true lending purposes and operational capabilities, and so on, among which some are favorable and some may be negative. SMEs tend to send favorable information and hide negative information in order to obtain loans, although financial institutions, as lenders, often need comprehensive information to make lending decisions. Therefore, signal fit becomes the key to facilitate the supply chain finance business. The achievement of signal fit requires that the signals themselves objectively present meaningful and nonartificial information created by the supply chain participants (Connelly et al., 2011), rather than information or signals deliberately transmitted by SMEs. The meaningful and nonartificial signals should be of two characteristics. First, they are partially controlled by the SMEs (Podolny, 1993). In other words, although these signals are reflected by the behaviors of SMEs, the evaluation and transmission of such signals are carried out by other parties, as a result of which the SMEs have only partial control over such signals. For example, the service capacity, logistics capacity, and production capacity demonstrated by the SMEs in supply chain operations are their own operational behaviors, but the evaluation of their capacity levels is conducted by customers or other stakeholders. Thanks to the relative objectivity, or the impossibility to be embellished or selectively transmitted by SMEs, such signals are easily trusted and accepted by lenders. As Pollock and Gulati (2007) said, "many features that actors only partially control can often be used as signals." Second, they are scenario-based or completely uncontrollable signals for SMEs. In other words, such signals are simply completely objective reflections of the scenarios and business relationships in which the SMEs survive and thrive, which do not change with the conscious choices of the SMEs. For example, the operation networks and interorganizational relationships of the SMEs fall into the scope of completely uncontrollable signals (Plummer et al., 2016; J. Wu et al., 2017; Posthuma et al., 2018). In particular, the business networks and relationships the SMEs form with other participants in supply chain finance are often not established and maintained in a short term, and are therefore better able to indicate their quality and future expectations (Gulati & Higgins, 2003). Obviously, the signals with the above two characteristics circumvent the instability and unreliability of the previous signals and allow lenders to evaluate the actual status and quality of SMEs in a more comprehensive and objective manner. However, such signals are naturally generated in the process of supply chain operations, which financial institutions, as peripheral participants therein, cannot directly observe, obtain, and evaluate. For this, how to practically learn about, obtain, and apply the objective signals has been an urgent issue for the development of supply chain finance.

Third, from the perspective of signal receivers, traditional signaling theory is more concerned with the receivers' observation and analysis ability (i.e., effectively receive and deconstruct the signals sent by the senders), This problem becomes more complicated in supply chain finance. When most MSMEs lack working capital and send signals to financial institutions for loans, even if they are willing to bear high interest rates, the financial institutions will limit credit rationing or even dare not lend money. This case is not exactly the same as traditional credit rationing. Credit rationing was first introduced by Stiglitz and Weiss (1981), who analyzed the credit rationing phenomenon from an information structure perspective and provided a typical conclusion that adverse selection under incomplete information may lead to credit rationing as a long-run equilibrium phenomenon. After that, Bester and Hellwig (1987) added the credit rationing caused by the ex post moral hazards of borrowers. Specifically, information asymmetry exists in the lending market, which is reflected by the fact that, on the one hand, borrowers have the private information about whether they have ability to repay on time before lending, and, on the other hand, lenders are unable to determine the borrowers' default risk before lending based on the information about their past defaults, asset status, and loan purpose. Similarly, the lenders do not have full control over the borrowers' use and repayment of the loans after lending. The possibility of risky behavior on the part of the borrowers may expose the lenders to the risk of loan default. Thus, the expected profitability of lenders depends not only on the interest rates on loans but also on the magnitude of the loan risks. The independence between lending risk and interest rate will not result in the problem of credit rationing as the lenders can increase profits by raising the interest rate. Nevertheless, when lacking valid information related to borrowers, lenders may face two dilemmas by unilaterally increasing interest rates: first, truly low-risk borrowers may exit the financing market due to high interest rates; second, high-risk borrowers are induced to choose riskier investment projects, which will heighten default rates. These above reasons lead to lenders' reluctance to approve all borrowers' loan applications even if the borrowers accept high interest rates. In traditional credit rationing theory, lenders are reluctant to lend money because they lack pre-loan and post-loan information about the borrowers or because information asymmetry is caused by the scarcity of information. However, the current credit market is facing the problem of information overload. In particular, the development of modern ICT makes it easier, faster, and cheaper than ever to generate, obtain, and transmit information (Johnson, 2001), but today's information asymmetries arise less from information scarcity and more from the fog created by overloaded information and data (Shenk, 1997; Wallis, 2003). Even if financial institutions are not deterred by the sheer volume of information, they need to decide how to allocate their limited attention among the various sources of information. In this process, lenders typically need to process irrelevant, unclear, and inaccurate data in order to find the information they need. As a result, the cost of processing signals for lenders rises significantly, with the result that lenders may be reluctant to lend money due to the high cost of screening, mining, and applying signals, even if the SME conveys valid signals and bears a certain interest rate. Therefore, supply chain finance has not only the challenge of signal sending cost but also the challenge of signal processing cost for signal receivers. Both factors may hinder the effective transmission and reception of signals, resulting in the generation of information asymmetry.

Fourth, in terms of signal feedback and environmental factors, traditional signaling theory defines feedback as a response of the receiver to the signals sent by the sender. Behind this theory is the definition of both parties independently, that is, the sender of the signal is the party that needs access to resources and, therefore, transmits signals about the inability to observe on its own to the other party, while the receiver is the party that provides resources and receives and analyze the signals. However, in supply chain finance, financial institutions as lenders are not exactly passive receivers who receive and analyze signals, while they often take the initiative to collect and explore all kinds of information about the borrowers in order to effectively assess the potential risks. In other words, strictly speaking, there is no pure "receiver" in supply chain finance. The borrower and lender have interactive behaviors in the borrowing and lending decision process. Apart from receiving information from the borrower, the decision-maker also explores all kinds of information actively and makes decisions based on the comprehensive analysis of these two types of information. In addition, the traditional signaling theory proposes a penalty cost, which means the sender who sends a wrong signal will suffer a penalty from the receiver of the signal. In supply chain finance, financial institutions, as lenders, also have "penalty costs", which can take two forms. The first one is the loss from wrong decisions due to the receiver's failure to effectively analyze the signals, which is also called default or bad debts in financial lending. The second one is the opportunity cost arising from the receiver's failure to effectively identify high-quality SMEs (especially high-quality SMEs that use countersignaling). Although not identical in nature, both types of penalty costs lead to stagnation in financial lending.

5.3 Signal Intermediaries and Fintech Companies

Based on the above analysis, it can be seen that specialized organizations or institutions are needed in supply chain finance to filter, integrate, and transmit signals to promote the effective and smooth flow of signals between SMEs and financial institutions, reduce information asymmetry, and achieve effective financial behavior. The importance of the existence of fintech companies also lies in the use of signals to link SMEs and financial institutions in the supply chain to achieve a reasonable and effective docking of supply chain operations and financial resources.

Characteristics of Fintech Companies

Signal intermediaries are also called information intermediaries in information economics. Rose (2012) said: "an information intermediary is an independent, profit-maximizing economic information processing system that performs its activities (i.e., information acquisition, processing, and dissemination) on behalf of other agents requiring information." Other scholars considered an information intermediary as an entity that promotes the exchange of information between buyers and sellers by creating and integrating information and transmitting it to buyers or potential buyers (Caillaud & Jullien, 2001). According to all these definitions, information is apparently something objective that exists in abundance and the role of an information or signal intermediary is to gather and deconstruct information according to predetermined customer requirements in order to meet the specific needs of the customer (Womack, 2002). Seen from these definitions, the signal intermediary has several important characteristics:

First, the signal intermediary identifies and gathers useful information. In the state of information overload or information fog, information is not scarce, but here is a large amount of redundancy, and the sources of information are complex and multiple. Some easily available signals may be high volume but low quality, while some high-quality signals may be less easily available. Therefore, the information intermediary should be able to identify what is a valid signal and have the ability and access to gather the information that needs to be obtained.

Second, the information intermediary filters out the information unnecessary for customers. The role of signal intermediaries is their ability to know what kind of information the both parties need, so as to collect and process information in a targeted manner. This often requires the signal intermediary to be familiar with the state of the both parties, as well as the characteristics of their business transactions and their specific needs for information; otherwise, it would be difficult to identify effective, high-quality signals to the requester, as well as to filter out nonabsolute signals.

Third, the information intermediary processes information in a structured manner. According to Kauffman et al. (2000), signal intermediaries should have both intangible and tangible capabilities. The former is the skill and know-how to access intangible resources (e.g., knowing what models and methods to use to effectively analyze data and information), while the latter is the ability to replicate physical structures to serve customers (e.g., the ability of stock agents to effectively connect customers to exchanges using programs, networks, or databases). Both capabilities allow the structured information to be served to customers.

Obviously, the characteristics of signal intermediaries in supply chain finance is exactly the role that fintech companies need to provide. As mentioned earlier, because of the obvious overload of information in supply chain finance involving diversified participants, diversified assets, and diversified activities, as well as the difficulty for financial institutions as receivers to agree with the signals transmitted by SMEs, professional independent institutions are badly needed to collect, analyze, screen, and transmit structured information, thus promoting the transmission of real and valid information between SMEs and financial institutions, reducing information asymmetry and boosting financial activities. Of course, we should further explore what kind of financial institutions will need signal intermediary services from fintech companies, what kind of information or signals fintech companies deal with as signal intermediaries, and what benefits such intermediary services will bring to supply chain finance.

Financial Institutions Requiring Signal Intermediary Services from Fintech Companies

The exploration of the question of what kind of financial institutions will cooperate with fintech companies, who acting as signal intermediaries, is related to the value intention of financial institutions. Value attention framework was developed by Dodds and Monroe (1985), who argued that a person's or a firm's willingness to express a behavior is directly influenced by the perceived value of the consequences of the behavior, or that the value an organization expects determines the actions it takes. Value attention framework puts an emphasis on the relationship between expected costs, quality, and benefits, which can be said as a comparison between the value expected to be gained from it and the cost of implementation. From a value perspective, the expected value is the overall evaluation of the product utility given by the customer based on what he or she receives or is given (Zeithaml, 1988). Specifically, this evaluation relates to the functionality, reliability, and usefulness of the information (Diniz et al., 2005). Functionality refers to whether the services provided contribute to the customer's strategy and decision-making. The biggest challenge encountered by financial institutions in the supply chain finance activities is that they do not know the actual state of SMEs, especially the quality-related signals that are difficult to observe directly. In addition, financial institutions do not accept unsolicited signals from SMEs based on their idea that the lending motives of SMEs are not pure. Therefore, the value of signal intermediaries may be high if they can help financial institutions to obtain hard-to-observe signals about the quality of SMEs. Reliability refers to the inherent stability of the signals provided, meaning that different sources of information, as well as signals obtained at different points of time, can help financial institutions judge the quality of SMEs in a stable and consistent manner. Usefulness means that the signals or information provided by the signal intermediaries can be processed, customized, and visualized in a timely manner according to the requirements of the financial institutions. Obviously, the higher the expectation of functionality, reliability, and usefulness, the more willing financial institutions are to work with fintech companies to obtain signals from intermediaries as a basis for their financial lending decisions.

Another key factor included in the value attention framework of financial institutions is the costs or considerations. There are three types of costs that financial institutions need to bear. The first is the cost for signal sending. Higher costs of sending may lead to lower likelihood that the financial institution will get high-quality signals. The second type is the processing costs. Higher costs of analyzing and parsing signals by the financial institutions themselves may lead to higher degree of information asymmetry. The third type is the opportunity costs as penalty, or the costs of losing high-quality SMEs. Therefore, the cooperation between financial institutions and signal intermediaries also depends on the ability of fintech companies to help financial institutions reduce these costs or considerations. Fintech companies should not only lower the costs of sending structured and high-quality signals but also help financial institutions effectively reduce the actual costs of processing signals and effectively acquire high-quality SMEs. In addition, the benefits that fintech companies receive for their services are also related to the costs of financial institutions. Given that bridging the information exchange between the sender and receiver of signals reduces the degree of information asymmetry, the signal intermediary needs to charge a fee to the beneficiary of the information (i.e., the financial institution) to cover the effort done. In other words, the service of the signal intermediaries is not free, but requires the beneficiary to pay for it to restrict others from getting it for free and to cover the costs incurred by the signal intermediaries in processing the signals. However, this fee needs to be much lower than the gains from increased information symmetry. When the fee decreases with the marginal increase in the beneficiary's gain from information, or is even zero, the impetus for financial institutions to cooperate with fintech companies will increase.

Signals that Fintech Companies Deal with as Signal Intermediaries

The information or signals collected, processed, dealt with, and presented by fintech companies are the key contents of their signal intermediary services. The neediness of financial institutions for signal intermediaries lies in the fact that such information is not easily observable, accessible, and processed in terms of access and management, and significantly differs from the density of information obtained by financial institutions through traditional credit investigations. Considering the specificity of SME lending, any information that SMEs can control, select, and process on their own cannot be trusted by financial institutions. Therefore, fintech companies act as information intermediaries to handle those information resources that are not under the control of SMEs. More specifically, there are three types of information or signals that fintech companies deal with. The first type is the information completely out of the control of the SMEs and objectively presented from their operations, which is primarily represented by network signals made up of the business relationships of the SMEs. Today's connected economy highly values interorganizational relationships, and these relationships can provide signals for organizations to better identify and respond to changes in their environment and relationships (Posthuma et al., 2018). A study by Ozmel et al. (2013) argues that in the absence of other forms of signals, network signals are often the best way to reduce adverse selection. For example, the relationship between the start-up company and the venture capital, as well as the relationship of other firms are effective ways to prove the quality of the start-up company. Such network signals become important information for information intermediaries not only because relationships take a long time to build (Gulati & Higgins, 2003) but also because structural and relational embedding in networks provides a wealth of information and signals (J. Wu et al., 2017). Structural embedding reflects an SME's position in the business network, and a good position in the network helps it to have more necessary resources (Zaheer & Bell, 2005). Relational embedding measures a firm's ability to identify and use resources (Ebers & Maurer, 2014). Furthermore, shared networks provide explicit and implicit proof of identity for the participants therein, promoting mutual trust (Fischer & Reuber, 2007; Lampe et al., 2007). In other words, the shared business transactions and exchanges promote awareness and synergy among transacting parties, reduce the cost of connectivity, and facilitate trust building.

The second type of signals that fintech companies deal with is unconscious behavior information. Although the behaviors are made by the SMEs, this information is presented naturally. Therefore, this behavior information is not selected, processed, and transmitted by SMEs and can be used as one of the bases for decision-making by financial institutions. This type of signals and information consist of objectively presented information or third-party-owned information. The former reflects some natural behaviors of SMEs or other behaviors reflected in their business environment. For example, in a study of investment banks, Balvers et al. (1988) found that how an investment bank chooses an audit firm can be viewed as a signal of the investment bank's reputation. The investment bank's choice of audit firm reflects two major signals: a reduction in its uncertainty of returns and a reputation for intrinsic cooperation. Some scholars even thought that negative reports of firms are also a signal, such as negative events occurring in other similar firms or the attitude of firms toward negative events (Maslach et al., 2018). Objectively presented information from the unconscious of SMEs is also present in supply chain finance, including their strategic behavior, compliance with contracts or attitude toward opportunism, and reaction to crisis events. Third-party-owned signals refer to those obtained from other institutions than the SMEs. SME financing faces a particularly noisy signaling environment, especially when a large number of SMEs apply for financing, and the role that third parties play lies in their ability to release information about the potential of the SMEs (Plummer et al., 2016). As founded by Islam et al. (2018), the ability of SMEs to gain the recognition of reputable government research institutions is an important signal. Therefore, if possible, the third-party-owned information collected, processed, collated, and delivered by fintech companies is undoubtedly also an important basis for supply chain finance decisions.

The third type of signals that fintech companies deal with is those partly under the control of the SMEs. Although the behavior is a conscious act of the SME, the evaluation of its behavior is made by an independent organization. In other words, this type of information is sent by the SME, but the selection of this information and the evaluation of its quality is not under the control of the SME. This type of signals is represented by the dynamic and operational capabilities of the SMEs in the supply chain. From a resource-based viewpoint, capabilities are an overall state that a firm possesses to outperform its competitors and maintain its market position (Prahalad, 2000), which are classified as dynamic capability and operational capability (S. J. Wu et al., 2010; Helfat & Winter, 2011). Dynamic capability reflects a firm's ability to use its resources for a specific purpose and is directly reflected in "how you change the way you operate" (Helfat & Winter, 2011). Sharma et al. (2016), for example, argued that a firm's product innovation is a signal. In fact, a stronger innovation ability of an SME in supply chain finance implies a lower probability of default (Hsu et al., 2015). Operational capability reflects a firm's ability to perform its daily operations, that is, "how to operate more efficiently" (Helfat & Winter, 2011). It is expressed as how effectively a firm can improve its business capabilities with other firms. Specifically, the ability of the SMEs to continuously improve supply chain operations (e.g., quality improvement, process improvement, and financial cost control) and the ability to continuously explore supply chain business (e.g., using new methods and means to improve efficiency) indirectly reflect their quality, so these information are intermediary signals that fintech companies can explore.

Benefits That the Intermediary Services Bring to Supply Chain Finance

Thanks to the role of signal intermediaries, the marginal cost of information is almost zero, and the cost of information reconfiguration is also very low. Especially under the ICT context, this low cost of information reconfiguration achieves an economy of scale in information gathering and configuration (Womack, 2002). Just as a specific type of information producer can satisfy the demand of an entire market, a signal intermediary can also satisfy the information demand of an entire customer base, thus realizing an economy of scale in information services. In the supply chain finance scenario, such an economy of scale is mainly manifested in the possibility of scaling up the SMEs and their capital through the information intermediary services of fintech companies. On the one hand, the effective information gathering and identification service provided by fintech companies makes SMEs with real value become customers of supply chain financial services, as a result of which more and more supply chain financial services benefit eligible SMEs and the potential demand for supply chain financial services from SMEs is tapped. For example, based on the information they have, fintech companies can inform SMEs of the credit limits they can obtain from financial institutions and assist them in optimizing their industrial capital flows. On the other hand, the reduction of effective information sending cost, operation cost, and penalty cost by fintech companies prompt more financial institutions to join the ranks of supply chain financial services, and the effective mitigation of adverse selection and moral hazard problems arising from information asymmetry by fintech companies makes the capital cost for lending fall. The economy of scale in these two aspects achieves the matching scale between supply and demand in terms of SMEs and capital as well as high value-added services (Bhargava & Choudhary, 2004).

Another type of benefit that can be achieved by fintech companies is the economy of scope, that is, the simultaneous development of diversity in SMEs and finance. On the one hand, financial institutions are well positioned to identify different types of SMEs through the information intermediary services of fintech companies, which not only enables them to differentiate low-quality SMEs and reduce overdue and default rates but also allows them to provide targeted financial services by applying different risk control tools to high-quality and medium-high-quality SMEs that use countersignaling. On the other hand, the fintech companies acting as information intermediaries can also enrich the resources of capital, because they can bring more nonbank financial institutions into the scope of supply chain finance and provide appropriate financial services. For example, fintech companies can also provide comprehensive and effective information to insurance companies, so as to better integrate insurance into supply chain financial services and reduce the comprehensive risk of supply chain financial services.

5.4 Types of Supply Chain Finance Organization

Seen from the above theoretical analysis, in addition to SMEs, network ecological service providers, and banks providing financial services, the development of supply chain finance also needs to be driven by specialized fintech companies that assist in collection, cleaning, mining, structuring, and transmission of unobservable information to reduce information asymmetry through signal intermediary services and control adverse selection and moral hazard in financial lending. Specifically, fintech companies have transaction data, logistics data, and aggregated data, and deliver the integrated data to investors to make appropriate decisions. It organically organizes various economic actors (including supply chain buyers and sellers, third-party logistics service providers, financial institutions, and all other related institutions) to engage in supply chain finance activities. Its role is to verify data, integrate data, analyze data, and present data to facilitate the smooth implementation of financial activities in the supply chain (Song, 2015). From the current forms of cooperation between fintech companies and other participants, several ways of organizing intelligent supply chain finance have been formed.

Type I of Intelligent Supply Chain Finance

This type of supply chain finance organization is more specific and is characterized by a specific core enterprise as the network ecological organizer of supply chain services. In other words, the enterprise constructs a service value network, embeds a large number of SMEs in the network, organizes production operations, and manages the entire network, thus facilitating the exchange of purchase orders, bills, payables, and other documents between buyers and sellers in the supply chain as well as financial institutions. Meanwhile, the core enterprise itself is a participant that is directly engaged in supply chain production operations. More importantly, the signal intermediary service of fintech companies is also initiated and formed by that core enterprise, or the construction of the fintech companies is based on the resources and capabilities invested by the core enterprise. Fintech companies specialize in information collection, cleansing, mining, and analysis and, based on data parsing, provide the structured information to other institutions affiliated to the core enterprise to inform financial services decisions. In addition, the core enterprise also participates directly or partially in the funding of supply chain finance. In other words, some or all of the funds to provide financing services to SMEs come from the licensed financial institutions affiliated to the core enterprise. For example, when a core enterprise has licenses for factoring, micro-financing, payment, and trust, its licensed institutions can provide financial services such as financing to SMEs (see Fig. 5.2).

This type of supply chain finance organization is generally promoted by large core enterprises with strong resource capacity for the following reasons: first, given their own huge supply chain business volume, such enterprises have enough business space for carrying out supply chain financial services. Otherwise, if the business scale is small and the counterparties are specific, it is difficult to organize a perfect value network ecosystem, and the value of engaging in financial activities decreases at this time. Second, such enterprises have good resources and talents to form a fintech

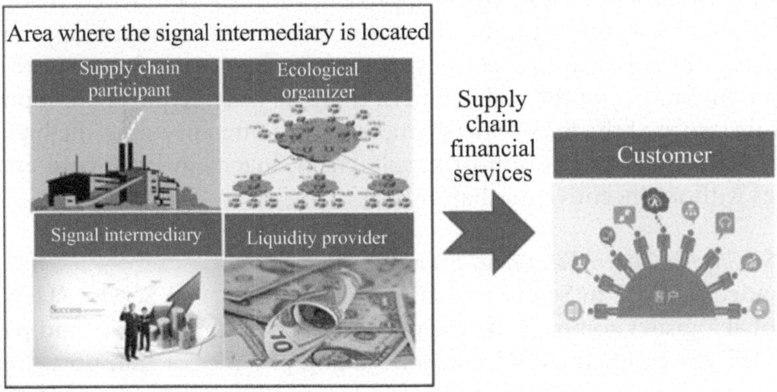

Fig. 5.2 Type I of intelligent supply chain finance organization

company, to develop and utilize various ICT technologies, to transform the business in the supply chain network ecosystem into figures, and to select, clean, and integrate the figures to support decisions on supply chain financial service. Third, such enterprises are also capable enough to engage in financial services and, at the same time obtain qualifications or licenses to engage in corresponding financial service activities. The advantage of this type of organization is that, in theory, the docking of resources is relatively strong, as the formation of the entire supply chain network and business is driven by the core enterprises and the docking of financial resources is done within the system. In addition, from the perspective of signal intermediary, the acquisition and processing of information signals are more convenient and effective. However, the biggest challenge of this type of organization lies in two aspects: first, all the resources are controlled by the core enterprises themselves, so the composition of the whole supply chain finance system is relatively closed, and it cannot effectively and reasonably integrate with external resources, nor can it expand the business to customers outside the system. Second, all signal acquisition and resource allocation are done within the system, which may lead to the increase of management cost within the enterprise system. In other words, the acquisition and allocation of information or resources could have been done in a market way, but it is changed to internal management control, which often generates a lot of administrative costs for internal negotiation, communication, and coordination. For instance, the confirmation of business authority by each branch of the enterprise required for the development of supply chain finance may be solved through the distribution of benefits under the market-based approach, but may be resisted by other departments or firms under the internalized management approach. Similarly, the risk management of supply chain finance needs to ensure the closure of funds, and the realization of this goal often requires the support and assistance of the finance department, which often becomes the biggest resistance to the promotion of supply chain finance in large core enterprises without incentive mechanisms.

UPS's Supply Chain Financial Services

Founded in 1907 in Seattle, Washington, United Parcel Service (UPS) is a global logistics company. As the world's largest express carrier and package delivery company, UPS is also a leading provider of transport, logistics, capital, and e-commerce services. In 2000, UPS acquired First International Bancorp to create UPS Capital, a company specializing in supply chain financial services. In the same year, UPS formed Kabbage.com, a platform specializing in information technology services and signal intermediary services, which has developed a range of supply chain finance services based on UPS's full-service logistics business for its customers. UPS's supply chain financial business currently includes UPS Capital Cargo Financing, Global Asset-Based Lending, Small Business Financing, and cash on delivery (COD) Payment Option. These supply chain financial products are featured by the logistics services provided by UPS itself, the establishment of a supply chain logistics platform and an information platform, and the funding from its own finance company (i.e., UPS Capital).

UPS Capital Cargo Financing

This service is strictly goods-in-transit financing, mainly for U.S. importers. Generally speaking, when importers purchase goods from overseas suppliers, they need a lot of money; however, they often go through a cycle of tens of days from the formation of a bill of lading from the supplier to the receipt of the goods by the importer. In addition, when the importer sells goods to downstream customers, it also takes a long time to receive payment for the goods. As a result, the importers face a shortage of funds for dozens of days, resulting in their inability to operate effectively and normally.

In response to this problem, UPS Capital has launched the Capital Cargo Financing (see Fig. 5.3). Importers and overseas suppliers need to form a close business relationship with UPS Logistics. On the basis of a purchase agreement, buyers and sellers outsource their global logistics operations to UPS Logistics, forming a guarantee for goods in transit. Based on this, UPS Capital finances the importer to make payments to the

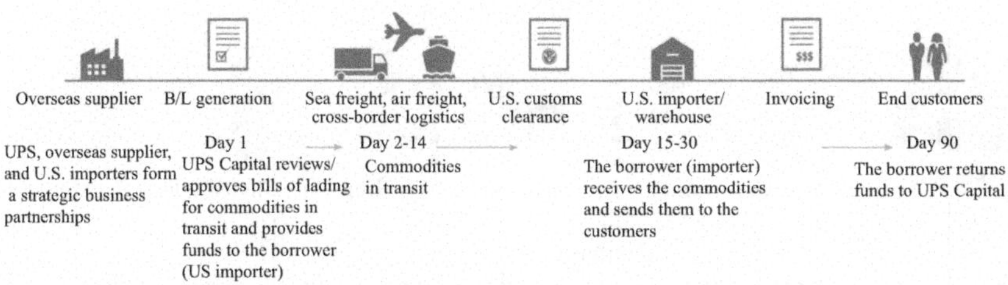

Fig. 5.3 UPS Capital's cargo financing

overseas suppliers. UPS Logistics then assumes the global logistics operations for the goods. When the importer needs to further sell the goods to downstream customers, the importer should first transmit the sales and distribution information to UPS Logistics and UPS Capital, and then send it to the importer's customers to form an invoice. Next, the importer returns the funds and interests to UPS Capital. This service is a fully unsecured credit facility, with a financing size typically ranging from US$300,000 to US$1.5 million and a payment term of up to 90 days.

Global Asset-Based Lending

UPS Global Asset-Based Lending is targeted toward U.S. companies engaged in global sourcing operations. Traditional supply chain finance is based only on local pledges of accounts receivable or warehouse receipts, which situation is difficult to adapt to global supply chain operations. In particular, along with today's globalization, many multinational companies often need to engage in procurement in multiple countries, creating a global inventory and in-transit inventory. Therefore, using the UPS global logistics service network, UPS Capital provides inventory financing services for global supply chain operations (see Fig. 5.4). To be specific, multinational companies form a comprehensive strategic cooperation with UPS and authorize UPS Logistics to provide end-to-end supply chain

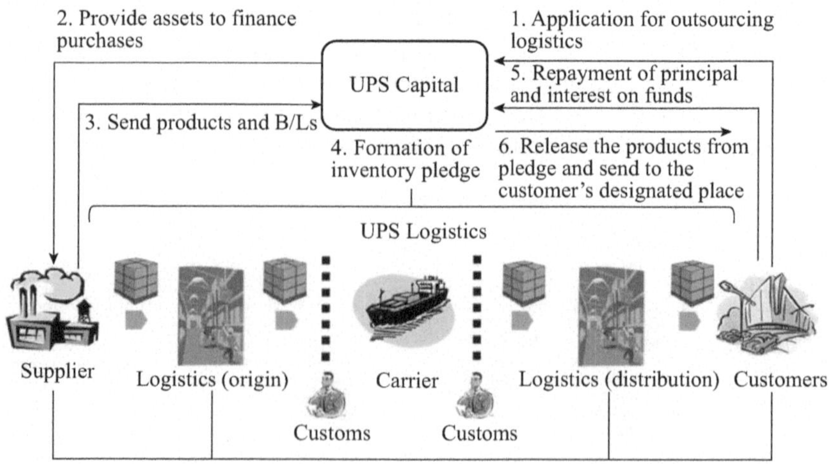

Fig. 5.4 UPS Capital's global asset-based lending

logistics services (i.e., from origin logistics, through customs clearance, customs declaration, customs clearance, to the logistics at place of sales). On this basis, multinational companies applies to UPS for financing. All inventory in transit, inventory at origin, and inventory at place of sales are pledged as collateral after UPS provides financing to the designated foreign supplier, who delivers the goods or bill of lading to UPS. Only when the customer returns the principal and interest on the funds to UPS Capital does UPS Capital notify UPS Logistics to release the collateral and deliver to the customer's designated place. Despite serving only U.S.-based companies engaged in global sourcing, this service has an annual turnover of US$10 million or more. UPS Capital can finance up to 50% of the customer's inventory and 85% of its accounts payable.

Small Business Financing

Small Business Financing is a supply chain financial service offered by UPS specifically for SMEs to address their needs for working capital, with financing amounts typically ranging from US$2000 to US$250,000. The specific operation process of this service is as follows (see Fig. 5.5). First, the small company outsources its logistics operations to UPS Logistics and registers an account on Kabbage.com to upload its basic business information. Based on the business information and other information, Kabbage reviews the small company's credit and notifies it of the financing amount

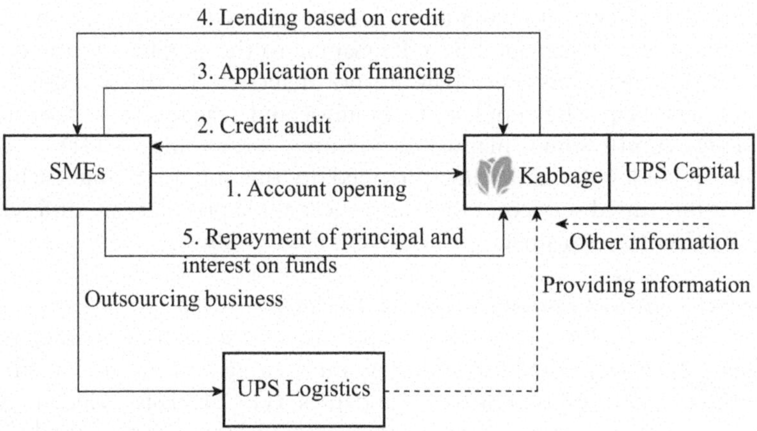

Fig. 5.5 UPS Capital's small business financing

it may receive. When a need for money arises, the small company submits a request through Kabbage.com, which provides money that is appropriate based on the credit rating. Finally, the small company repays the principal and interest on the money. This service meets the temporary working capital needs of small companies through access to and analysis of their information. In general, this service offered by UPS Capital requires small companies to have an annual operating volume of US$100,000 or more.

COD. Payment Option

COD Payment Option is designed for the cash on delivery used by the suppliers when selling goods to the buyers. In foreign trade, COD is a settlement method in which the importer pays after the exporter ships the goods and is actually an open-account transaction or deferred payment. This method of settlement gives the buyers relative flexibility, but puts the suppliers under a great challenge because the buyers pay for the goods after a certain period of time, during which the suppliers may face a shortage of working capital. To this end, UPS Capital offers three cash-on-delivery options: COD Secure Service, COD Automated Service, and COD Direct Service (see Fig. 5.6). All these three services are predicated on the supplier's opening an account with UPS and outsourcing its operations to UPS Logistics. On this basis, UPS Capital helps the supplier optimize its cash flow and maintain its customer base. Specifically, if UPS Capital finds through information that a supplier is very high quality, it can provide COD. Secure Service, which guarantees the supplier a specified amount of money in any situation. COD Automated Services are one type of financial service provided by UPS Capital to the suppliers in the event that the suppliers' customer bills are not defective. In this service, UPS Capital also helps the suppliers to monitor and manage their cash flow, reducing cumbersome manual accounting processing. COD Direct Service includes the financing provided to the suppliers, but excludes other value-added services. Obviously, these three products are differentiated services for customers with different credit ratings.

Transfar's Supply Chain and Financial Services

Established in 1986, Transfar Group covers such sectors as intelligent logistics, tech city, chemical industry, modern agriculture and financial investment, and hastwo listed companies (i.e., Transfar Zhilian and Wynca), seven national high-tech enterprises, and two national-level technology centers. In addition to the lack of intelligent and digital

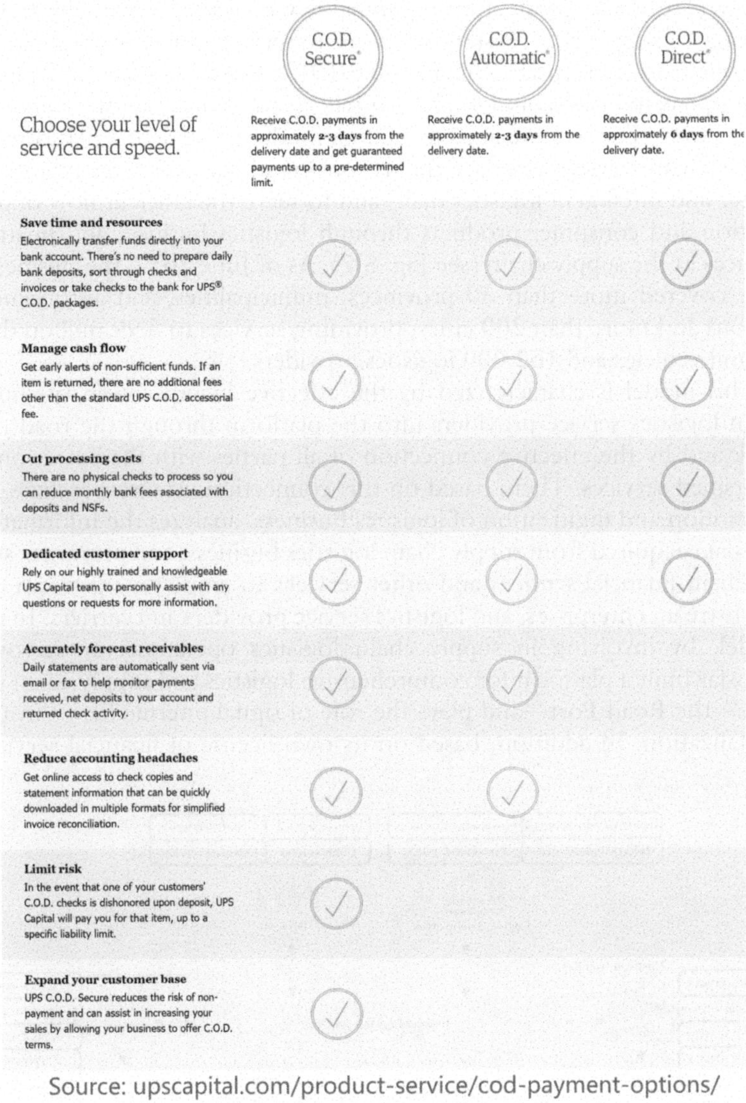

Choose your level of service and speed.

	C.O.D. Secure®	C.O.D. Automatic®	C.O.D. Direct®
	Receive C.O.D. payments in approximately **2-3 days** from the delivery date and get guaranteed payments up to a pre-determined limit.	Receive C.O.D. payments in approximately **2-3 days** from the delivery date.	Receive C.O.D. payments in approximately **6 days** from the delivery date.
Save time and resources Electronically transfer funds directly into your bank account. There's no need to prepare daily bank deposits, sort through checks and invoices or take checks to the bank for UPS® C.O.D. packages.	✓	✓	✓
Manage cash flow Get early alerts of non-sufficient funds. If an item is returned, there are no additional fees other than the standard UPS C.O.D. accessorial fee.	✓	✓	✓
Cut processing costs There are no physical checks to process so you can reduce monthly bank fees associated with deposits and NSFs.	✓	✓	✓
Dedicated customer support Rely on our highly trained and knowledgeable UPS Capital team to personally assist with any questions or requests for more information.	✓	✓	✓
Accurately forecast receivables Daily statements are automatically sent via email or fax to help monitor payments received, net deposits to your account and returned check activity.	✓	✓	
Reduce accounting headaches Get online access to check copies and statement information that can be quickly downloaded in multiple formats for simplified invoice reconciliation.	✓	✓	
Limit risk In the event that one of your customers' C.O.D. checks is dishonored upon deposit, UPS Capital will pay you for that item, up to a specific liability limit.	✓		
Expand your customer base UPS C.O.D. Secure reduces the risk of non-payment and can assist in increasing your sales by allowing your business to offer C.O.D. terms.	✓		

Source: upscapital.com/product-service/cod-payment-options/

Fig. 5.6 UPS Capital's three different forms of COD. payment option

infrastructure and production equipment, China now essentially lacks a package of supply chain system solutions to serve Chinese manufacturing. For this reason, Transfar Zhilian (002010), a listed company of Transfar Group, created tf56.com by taking intelligent logistics supply chain as its entry point. The website aims to build a modern and digital platform for supply chain services based on the national road networks (urban logistics center and intelligent logistics mall) and to serve the efficient flow of production and consumer products through logistics business and financial services in the supply chain (see Fig. 5.7). As of June 2017, the businesses have covered more than 30 provinces, municipalities, and autonomous regions and more than 200 cities, providing services to 3.99 million drivers and vehicles and 162,000 logistics providers.

This model is characterized by the effective incorporation of supply chain logistics service providers into the platform through the road network and by the effective connection of all parties with the provision of diversified services. Then, based on this connection, Transfar realizes the promotion and digitization of logistics business, analyzes the information and data acquired from supply chain logistics business, and promotes supply chain financial services and other services to empower upstream and downstream enterprises, and logistics service providers and carriers. In this model, by involving in supply chain logistics operations on its own, Transfar built a platform for comprehensive logistics and supply chain services—the Road Port—and plays the role of signal intermediary through digitalization. In addition, based on its own license of financial services,

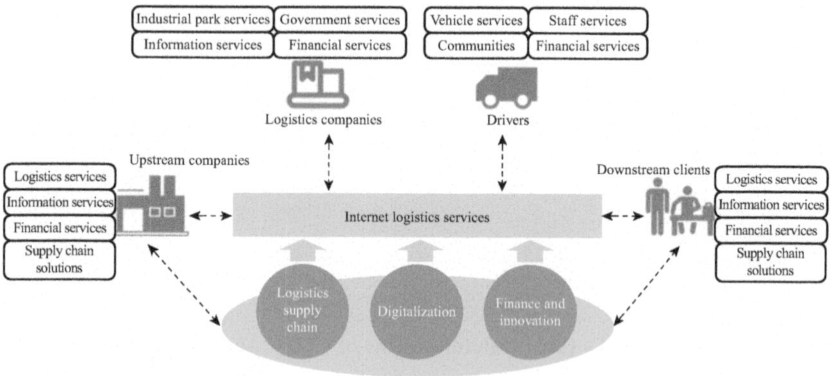

Fig. 5.7 Transfar's supply chain network service system

Transfar provides corresponding financial services to eligible supply chain participants by combining its own capability and external financial institutions.

Service Network System Based on Road Port

Transfar Group's Road Port aims to "make the platform serve the third-party logistics providers and the third-party logistics providers serve the cargo-owners" devotes itself to solving the domestic situation of "small, scattered, disorganized, poor and many" logistics operations. It provides the following services.

The platform of standardized infrastructure services provides standardized parking, operation, and office sites for small and medium-sized enterprises and individual drivers through park planning, design, and construction, solves their problems in parking, operations, offices, and warehouses through integrated management and resource sharing, and reduces the investment in infrastructure construction for them. In addition to hardware services, the platform also provides supporting software services for logistics enterprises. In particular, the platform provides one-stop supporting services such as license issuance, tax payment, three certificate verifications, network connection, finance, insurance, and vehicle repair and maintenance for small and medium-sized logistics enterprises and individual drivers joined in the platform by connecting transport management department, taxation department, industry and commerce department, security department, as well as banks, insurance companies, China Telecom, China Post, vehicle repair, and maintenance enterprises.

A national cargo distribution network has been built based on the interconnection of distribution centers and warehouses.

The distribution business is an integral part of Transfar's network, linking the roads and ports and forming an interconnected trunk line and distribution network. By building nationwide distribution centers and outlets, developing and operating transportation routes, laying out a national network for cargo circulation, and formulating unified service standards and price systems, the platform "Road Port" helps build urban logistics centers, devotes itself to gathering cargo sources in urban logistics, provides integrated logistics services integrating distribution, transportation, and delivery for customers inside and outside the platform, and focuses on solving the problem of the last mile in logistics. With nationwide unified products, service standards, systems, and prices, the platform promotes the interconnection between roads and ports and support the ecological layout of Transfar network.

Transfar's Internet-based Logistics Business

In addition to building the infrastructure of supply chain logistics, Transfar also focuses on the end-to-end intelligent dispatching service of "trunk line + urban distribution," and has developed two Internet-based logistics platforms, "LUJING" and "EHD," in an attempt to realize the accurate matching of supply and demand of logistics services.

As a transport capacity dispatching and command system in Transfar's network, LUJING offers controlled, efficient, stable, and matching capacity resources and achieves interconnection between ports and harbors with shared shuttles as the carrier. It provides members with a logistics information trading platform for network-wide information dissemination, network-wide information dispatching (based on LBS), and network-wide information matching. It has developed its own "One Card" online payment system to ensure transaction security. LUJING has become the first logistics trading platform that has integrated comprehensive services including shipping, distribution, parking, accommodation, catering, maintenance, payment, group purchase, settlement, billing management, and marketing support to realize all-scenario services.

In terms of the shared shuttle, its platform-based concept is to build a shared shuttle transport system connecting urban logistics centers to promote the efficient circulation of goods in relevant cities. Based on the big data about the transport flow of goods, the shared shuttle works with distribution departments to jointly plan national transport trunk and feeder routes, builds a rich pool of transport capacity for trunk and feeder routes through self-built fleets and procurement of social fleets and vehicles, provides stable and reliable high-quality transport services for platform customers with standardized products and dispatching systems, and promotes cost reduction and efficiency increase in the industry through the sharing of high-quality transport products.

Road Kangaroo uses the Internet-based intelligent dispatching technology to innovate the social sharing mode of machine hanging and implements the drop-and-pull transport services nationwide for the purpose of significant reduction of vehicle idling rate and waiting time. Road Kangaroo provides reliable and high-quality transport capacity support for shared shuttle and platform customers.

EHD is an urban logistics service platform built by Transfar for goods collection in "the first kilometer" and distribution in "the last kilometer." It is committed to connecting social storage and transport resources through technologies, building a national urban distribution network, and providing one-stop urban logistics solutions for enterprises, as discussed in the following: (1) warehousing and distribution integration: it builds warehouses flexibly, which operate efficiently according to customers' needs, and provides customers with guaranteed warehousing and distribution services through professional and intelligent management mode; (2) fleet joining: it gathers social transport capacity and individual drivers, provides them with professional training, information management, and value-added services, and provides stable sources of goods for high-quality fleets; (3) urban partner: it provides city franchise business for logistics companies, 3PLs, fleets, and so on to share high-quality resources and revenue.

Transfar's Intelligent Information System and Data Services
The core of supply chain services and financial services is the information technology and the control of supply chain data. Therefore, Transfar has established the corresponding supply chain logistics information systems to provide various data services, which include the following.

Transfar Cloud Warehouse is a professional SaaS platform based on cloud deployment, also known as OWMS. The platform helps cargo owners and warehouses improve management efficiency through operation strategies, order transactions, and intelligent equipment applications, realizes network-wide multi-warehouse cooperation and dispatching through order management, and creates a unified entrance by linking social warehouses, thus providing customers with a nationwide co-shared multilevel warehouse network.

Transfar Chain Cloud is an one-stop intelligent logistics management platform, also known as TMS, which integrates cargo landing, distribution, delivery, trunk transport, financial settlement, and information management and connects with distribution centers, special routes, and outlets in logistics parks. It is a logistics management SaaS platform that can be adapted to multiple scenarios and can also coordinate multiple transport routes. The integration of Transfar Chain Cloud and Road Port integrates the smaller and scattered dedicated transport capacities, while the combination of the regional network of distribution centers and the exclusive network of trunk routes creates a national scale effect, which forms a huge capacity pool, expands cargo channels, improves the informationization of logistics enterprises, and enhances their comprehensive competitiveness.

In order to improve the management and operation capabilities of the logistics parks that have joined it, Transfar has created an O2O operation and service platform for parks, also known as PMS, which improves the user experience of O2O consumption, increases the added value of logistics parks, and improves the management and operation capabilities of the parks by providing park management and one-stop park online services.

Whale Eye is an open transport capacity dispatching platform based on big data algorithm and technology application. With the help of big data, cloud computing, IOT, and other technologies, this platform, built for trunk drivers and cargo owners, can cover every link and scenario of trunk logistics transactions and optimize the efficiency of trunk logistics turnover with intelligent algorithms on the whole. The intelligent car management function of Whale Eye combines AI, user tags, and user vehicles' demands on usage scenarios, and is able to tag and combine vehicles in the platform to quickly form virtual fleets and push them to dispatchers. Through it, enterprise customers can conveniently dispatch and quickly build their own virtual fleets, and complete accurate dispatching and maintenance of virtual fleet communities within the platform; dock cargo sources with the platform through the open API interface for cargo sources and orders. The optimization of each model and algorithm of the Whale Eye system relies on the log data and feature data of people, vehicles, and goods in LUJING platform, the applications within the system are based on the models and calculations of Whale Eye, and the business data generated can be fed back and trained by Whale Eye AI.

Wind Leopard System is the "intelligent brain of urban distribution" driven by advanced technology in terms of urban distribution. Based on technological advantages, Transfar tries to achieve full transparency of urban distribution process, improve transport efficiency, and effectively reduce transport costs and risks. Meanwhile, the system carries out intelligent pricing, intelligent scheduling, intelligent dispatching, and common delivery through algorithms and optimizes delivery efficiency, costs, and experience through calculations. Last but not least, the system returns the retained big data to the data center, which, after analysis and processing, can analyze and predict the future to achieve an efficient city distribution system where goods are not yet moved, vehicles are firstly prepared, and warehouses are ready.

Transfar's Supply Chain Finance

The logistics and transport industry consists of a large proportion of SMEs and is characterized by high capital costs but low capital utilization efficiency. According to the estimation of Logistics Finance Professional Committee under China Federation of Logistics and Purchasing (CFLP), the demand for financing and loans from logistics enterprises in China is more than three trillion yuan per year, and less than 10% of that demand is met by traditional financial institutions. In terms of freight advances alone, there is an annual financing demand of about trillion yuan, but less than 5% of this demand is obtained by way of bank loans.

Transfar Finance originates from logistics and serves logistics. It has obtained third-party payment license, factoring license, leasing license, and insurance brokerage license. With big data-based credit as the driver, Transfar Finance offers integrated industrial and financial services to small and medium-sized logistics enterprises/cargo owners in the logistics industry. The types of financial business defined by Transfar Finance include freight factoring, installment purchase/financial leasing, petrol fee/toll fee advance, supply chain IOU, insurance and wealth management for logistics companies and drivers, and inventory/warehouse receipt finance and confirming storage financing for cargo owners.

Freight factoring is an important product in Transfar's supply chain financial services, which is named YUNYIRONG (see Fig. 5.8). As a financial product based on freight discount for 3PLs and small and medium-sized dedicated logistics companies and fleets inside and outside the system, it has the advantages of high credit limit, low interest rate, long term, pure credit, and convenient repayment. The specific business process of the product is as follows: First, the upstream cargo owner signs a logistics service contract with the logistics company and generates the corresponding accounts receivable. Second, Transfar's own information system is used to analyze and recommend a white list of customers who can provide supply chain financial services. Third, Transfar's factoring company makes further due diligence on the logistics company, grants credit, and signs contracts. Fourth, the logistics company transfers the accounts receivable in its hands, while the upstream cargo owner confirms its rights. Fifth, Transfar's factoring company lends money to the logistics company. Finally, the upstream cargo owner pays for the goods when due and the logistics company repays the money (actually the upstream cargo owner repays the money directly to the factoring company under the confirmed right condition). The above-mentioned digital information-based

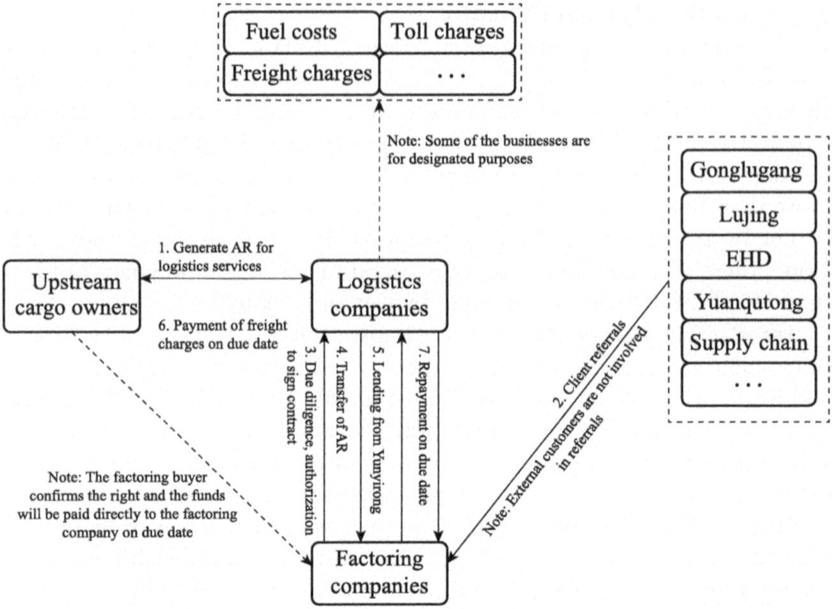

Fig. 5.8 Basic process of Transfar's YUNYIRONG

supply chain finance not only allows finance to serve the logistics industry effectively but also promotes the effective provision of financial services according to the business development status of enterprises. For example, a fleet-based logistics company in Hangzhou (a large downstream carrier of SF Express) obtained a credit line of RMB 10 million from Transfar's factoring company in August 2017. But in mid-November 2017, after being informed through the data operation of GPS system that the rapid growth of the company's business volume during Double 11 period led to a high pressure of advances, the factoring company was promptly added a temporary credit line of RMB 4 million for the company as freight advances during the peak periods of Double 11 and Double 12 shopping carnivals, which maximally met the financing needs of the customer. At the same time, relying on the platform advantages of Transfar Zhilian, the factoring company coordinated the deployment of 300 square meters of repair space and 18 staff dormitories, which solved a major problem in the company's operation and development (Fig. 5.9).

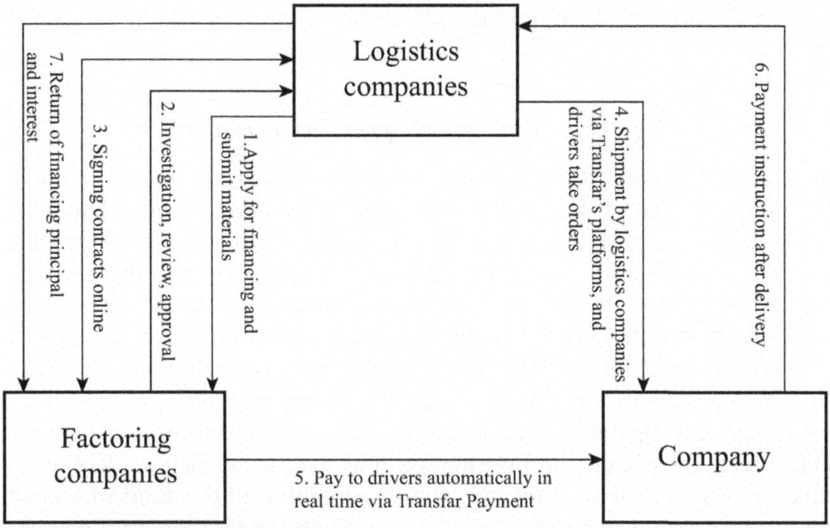

Fig. 5.9 Transfar's IOU note

Another major feature among Transfar's supply chain finance products is Transfar IOU, which is targeted at small and micro logistics enterprises and is jointly created with Transfar's intercity capacity dispatching and command platform "LUJING." Based on the advantages of flexible operation and convenient use, this product helps SMEs solve the problem of freight advance. The specific process is as follows: First, the logistics company cooperates with Transfar, puts forward its financing needs and submits relevant materials. Second, Transfar conducts due diligence and audit of the logistics company based on its digital information platform and gives approval results. Third, according to the credit approval result, the logistics company signs a cooperation agreement with Transfar's factoring company. Fourth, the logistics company ships the goods through Transfar's platform and the driver accepts the order. Fifth, based on these transport operations, Transfar's factoring company pays the funds to the driver through its payment system. Sixth, after completion of the transport, the driver sends a payment instruction to the logistics company. Finally, the logistics company returns the principal and interest to Transfar's factoring company. Apparently, Transfar IOU provides fast financing with no collateral and no guarantee only by virtue of its good transaction record on

LUJING, and pays the freight directly online after the credit investigation is approved.

Type II of Intelligent Supply Chain Finance

In terms of organization method, there are similarities and differences between this type of supply chain finance and the previous one. The similarity lies in the fact that the core enterprises are supply chain business participants and both the supply chain service platform and the financial technology system for information data mining, analysis, and integration are built. The difference is that the funding comes from external financial institutions (see Fig. 5.10). This method of organizing supply chain finance is also more suitable for large core enterprises, because only good resources and capabilities can organize the supply chain service platform and effectively obtain the information and data from each subject, each link and each element. However, the shortcoming of this kind of service platform is that how to effectively connect with financial institutions has become a great challenge for the enterprises, because the fund providers are external independent financial institutions. In response to this challenge, the core enterprises need to set up a specialized signal intermediary (i.e., fintech company).

The goals that fintech companies under this type aim to achieve differ somewhat from those under the first type. Fintech companies under the first type simply aim to acquire, analyze, mine, and integrate business

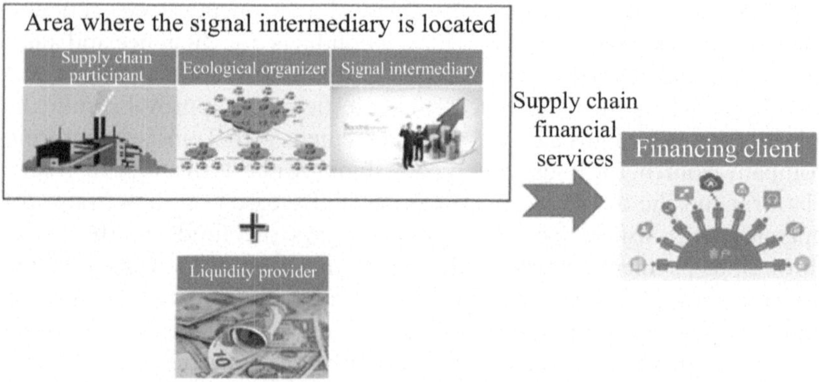

Fig. 5.10 Type II of intelligent supply chain finance organization

information so that the information can be delivered to other departments of the enterprise in a timely manner to support supply chain finance decisions. Therefore, the concern for fintech companies in this case is whether the information obtained is comprehensive, timely, and helpful for decision analysis (i.e., effectiveness issues), and does not raise questions about the legitimacy of the companies themselves (i.e., whether the work of fintech companies is trustworthy and its existence is reliable). But fintech companies under the second type have to face not only effectiveness issues but also legitimacy issues (i.e., how to convince external independent financial institutions to agree on the quality of intermediary signals). Considering that financial technology in this case is driven by supply chain business creators and service platform builders, its impartiality and honesty can easily be questioned and challenged by independent financial institutions. To address this issue, the signal intermediaries need to prove their legitimacy based on their own supply chain operation system in two ways. The first way is to help financial institutions effectively obtain and clarify the objective implicit information of core enterprises and realize the vertical integration of supply chain information and signals. The strong bargaining power of core enterprises in the supply chain leads to an unbalanced power contrast between supply party and demand party, and, therefore, it is easy to cause information asymmetry. For example, in the supply chain operation, the core large enterprises often do not confirm the right to the transaction, so how to determine the accounts receivables and payable, as well as the usage status of the products in the core enterprises, becomes a service that signal intermediaries need to provide (i.e., to help financial institutions understand the real business information of the core enterprises). In addition, how to realize the penetration of core enterprises' assets throughout the supply chain is an important service that signal intermediaries need to provide to financial institutions (i.e., objectively reflect the multilevel supply chain structure, status, and operation of core enterprises). The second way is to achieve the aggregation of information signals from multiple core enterprises through fintech companies in order to achieve horizontal integration of signals. Another challenge for financial institutions is that it is often difficult to obtain comprehensive structured information when dealing with multiple core enterprises in the same industry, and thus the cost of acquiring and processing information signals is high. If the fintech companies of core enterprises can help financial institutions to aggregate and process the integrated and objective signals, the recognition of these financial institutions will be easily obtained.

TCL's Supply Chain Finance

TCL's supply chain finance aims to solve the capital issues of multitier small and medium-sized suppliers of core enterprises. The difficulty and high costs of financing of SMEs is a major challenge in the industry today, and the suppliers at higher tiers face more serious challenges in financing. Generally speaking, traditional supply chain finance solves the capital problems of the first-tier upstream suppliers and downstream customers of core enterprises, that is, the account receivable and payable of direct suppliers and direct downstream customers. However, the first-tier upstream and downstream enterprises in the industrial supply chain (especially those transact with large core enterprises) do not necessarily lack working capital and are not in urgent need of financing because they have a certain scale. Even if the first-tier upstream and downstream enterprises lack money, they can easily obtain the services of financial institutions, such as standard factoring and reverse factoring, by virtue of the credit resources of the core enterprises. The industrial supply chain mostly involves N-tier suppliers and tends to be more and more SMEs as the number of tiers increases. As these SMEs are farther away from the core enterprises, it is difficult for financial institutions to effectively cover these N-tier suppliers and customers with financial services. In addition, financial institutions do not know the real operation status and performance status of these N-tier suppliers and customers, and even if they provide financial services, the interest rate is often high due to the considerations of risk control. In order to solve this problem, TCL has built a supply chain service platform and financial technology system, JDH, based on its own industrial supply chain, which works with financial institutions to effectively solve the problem of accounts receivable from N-tier suppliers.

JDH is an Internet-based platform under TCL Group that provides accounts receivable information services for enterprises, and its operator is Simple Hui Information Technology (Zhuhai) Co., Ltd., a wholly owned holding company of TCL Group. The main purpose of setting up JDH is to build a communication bridge of accounts receivable information and help SMEs to obtain accounts receivable financing more conveniently from financial institutions, so as to solve the financing problems of SMEs. In simple terms, the platform includes roles such as core enterprises, suppliers (from tier 1 to tier N), and fund providers. The core enterprise confirms its suppliers' accounts payable in the platform, thus forming a debt document—"golden bill." According to their own needs, the holders of the golden bill can flexibly transfer the bills in the platform, and can also apply for financing from the fund provider (see Fig. 5.11).

The basic process of this model is as follows: when TCL and the first-tier supplier sign the purchase cooperation agreement, TCL confirms the right online and forms a debt document—the golden bill. After the first-tier supplier gets the golden bill, it can request payment from TCL when due. At any time before the payment deadline, the first-tier supplier can also split the golden bill and transfer it to a second-tier supplier. After the second-tier supplier gets the split golden bill, it has three choices: (1) hold the golden bill and request payment from TCL when due; (2) further split the golden bill and transfer it to a third-tier supplier; (3) apply for financing to a financial institution, which pays the second-tier suppliers in advance, and after the golden bill is due TCL pays the funds to the bank account.

Obviously, although this model benefits TCL's multitier suppliers, financial institutions and other stakeholders are unable to recognize the legitimacy of the platform. This is because the platform uses a traditional centralized approach to store the circulation and transaction data of golden bills. The problems that arise in this situation are how enterprises can trust the platform, how suppliers can trust the core enterprise, and how fund providers can trust the core enterprises and the platform. The solution to these problems requires a technical means to seamlessly transfer the credits of core enterprises along their supply chain. Blockchain has

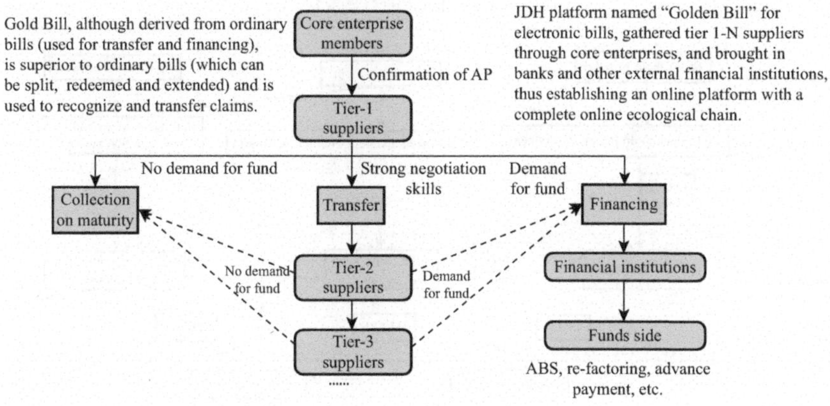

Fig. 5.11 Supply chain finance of TCL JDH platform

the technical features of distributed storage, tamper-evident, and traceability, which provides the possibility for the credits of core enterprises to be transferred within the supply chain system.

Considering the information sensitivity in their industry, financial institutions need a system that can be controlled autonomously, which public chains cannot do. Therefore, JDH's blockchain project is more suitable to choose a consortium blockchain. JDH serves as the foundation and is responsible for the membership issues and authorization of consortium members, and multiple core companies as well as financial institutions form a consortium to jointly maintain the blockchain ledger. JDH's blockchain project has chosen the world's most influential open-source consortium blockchain, namely the Hyperledger project under the Linux Foundation, as the underlying technical architecture, and is jointly developed by TCL Fintech and Shenzhen Tiannong Technology. The system architecture is as follows (see Fig. 5.12):

Layer 1: Source data layer. JDH platform is used as the source data layer to generate transaction data.

Layer 2: Data interface layer. JDH platform interacts with the transit system, which forwards the data and makes the data enter the chain. This

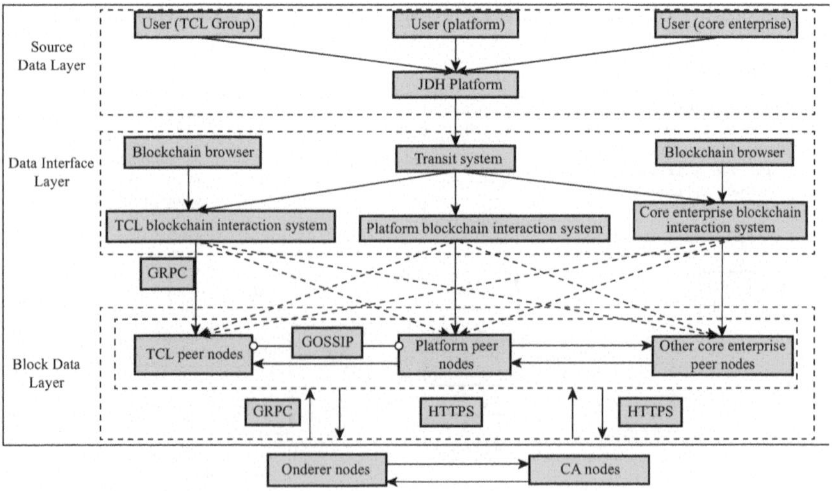

Fig. 5.12 TCL JDH architecture

layer does personalized development according to the application scenarios of JDH platform, shielding the upper-layer applications from the dependence on the underlying blockchain.

Layer 3: Data storage layer. It is the core of blockchain and is implemented by standard fabric architecture. Multiple peer nodes store block data, which can be individually deployed locally in the core enterprises. Order node is responsible for verifying, consenting, and packaging all transactions, and then informing peer nodes to put them into the chain. CA node is responsible for access authentication of all nodes.

The procedures for putting transactions into the chain are as follows:

Step 1: After a core enterprise opens an account in the blockchain system, the system automatically generates the enterprise's secret key, public key, and private key. The private key is stored in the local node of the core enterprise and kept by the core enterprise itself. The public key is stored publicly on the blockchain (if the account has been opened, the first step can be skipped).

Step 2: The enterprise completes the right confirmation or transfer of accounts receivable via the JDH platform, and the system saves the data in the central database.

Step 3: Combining AES and RSA encryption algorithms, the transaction data is automatically put into the chain after the signature and encryption are completed. Each node keeps the same copy of the data.

Step 4: The enterprise can view the transaction information, rights, and interests in respect of golden bills in the local node of the blockchain.

JDH supported by the above architecture brings great value to all stakeholders in the supply chain. Specifically, SMEs can enjoy the following benefits. First is efficient rights confirmation. The biggest drawback of traditional commercial factoring is the difficulty of buyers in confirming their rights. JDH allows core companies to take the initiative to confirm their rights on the platform. Second is low financing cost. The platform is docked with multiple financing channels. The borrowers do not need to provide collateral or guarantee, and the funding providers determine the financing rate based on the credits of the borrowers, so the interest rate is lower. Third is high financing efficiency. The whole life cycle of accounts receivable from the opening, transfer, financing to collection of the golden bills is operated online. Fourth is the splitable and extendable characteristics. The biggest drawback of traditional commercial bill is that it cannot be split and the term cannot be changed. The amount and term of bills held by enterprises cannot match the amount and term of accounts payable by their downstream suppliers, so the enterprises can only pledge their assets to banks and reissue bills to suppliers. The cumbersome procedures lead to inefficiency and low resource utilization. The golden bills can be flexibly split and matched in terms of amount and term, making the transfer of assets flexible and efficient and allowing enterprises to finance on demand and save financing costs.

With the help of JDH platform, the core enterprises can manage the enterprises in their industrial chain in a penetrating way and refine the management of suppliers. The costs of the SMEs in the chain are eventually converted into the costs of the core enterprises, so cost reduction and efficiency increase must start from the entire industry chain. Thanks to the benefits obtained by the SMEs on the JDH platform, the stability of the entire supply chain will be enhanced, suppliers will be more sticky to the core enterprises, and the ability of the core enterprises to control suppliers will be improved. While managing their own cash flow, the core enterprises, based on their position as masters of the supply chain, guarantee the health of the cash flow of the entire industry chain, allowing the surrounding enterprises to develop together.

The benefits obtained by the funding providers are as follows: First, they can reduce the cost for customer acquisition. JDH concentrates high-quality industrial resources, core enterprises, and industrial customers, so banks, factoring companies, P2P lenders, and other funding providers can use the platform to obtain a large number of customers, as a result of which the cost for customer acquisition is reduced. Second, they can reduce the risk of funding. JDH realizes the direct connection of the ERP systems of core enterprises, owns the original operation data of the enterprises, brings together information flow, fund flow and other aspects of information, and provides real and reliable risk control data for financial institutions. In addition, financial institutions can get rid of the disadvantages of credit investigation on a single enterprise in the past, and instead implement risk control over the entire industry chain, and put the focus of risk control on the inter-enterprise trade link.

CSCC's Supply Chain Finance

Zhongqi Yunlian (Beijing) Financial Information Service Co., Ltd. (referred to as "CSCC") was established in Beijing in May 2015 by CRRC as the initiator, together with some state-owned and private enterprises such as CRCC, SINOMACH, and Kingdee, after the approval of the SASAC. In November 2016, the capital increase gave 23 shareholders, including 11 central enterprises (namely, CRRC, CRCC, SINOMACH, CASC, CSIC, Ansteel, CHINALCO, COSCO Shipping, China Merchants Group, CEEC, and China Railway Material Group Co., Ltd.), 6 local state-owned enterprises (namely, Beijing Shougang Co., Ltd., BAIC Group, Shanghai Jiushi Corporation, ITG, Yuntianhua, and Zijin Mining), 2 financial institutions (namely, Industrial and Commercial Bank of China, Postal Savings Bank of China), and 4 private enterprises (namely, Kingdee, Zidesen, Beijing Hualian Group, and Yunding Assets). Currently, CRRC is the largest shareholder, holding 22.22% of its shares. CSCC's supply chain finance is the same as TCL's in that it also penetrates the credits of core enterprises into the supply chain in order to solve the fund dilemma of SMEs in multitier supply chains. However, one thing different from TCL is the realization of horizontal linkage of multiple core enterprises, thus effectively linking multiple core enterprises and providing comprehensive supply chain financial services to SMEs through the analysis of information and data and participation of financial institutions.

Basic Concept of CSCC's Supply Chain Financial Services

The concept of supply chain financial services proposed by CSCC is "open, free, co-shared and win-win." It hopes to build a free online information platform based on financial technologies to realize the effective connection between the assets of enterprises in the supply chain and the funds of financial institutions. The specific principles are as follows:

Gather industrial resources and allow large enterprises to become the protagonists in supply chain finance. First, CSCC provides a free supply chain finance platform for large enterprises, allowing them to independently decide the specific division of their own credit among member units, the financing cost of SMEs in the industry chain (instead of being priced by financial institutions), and whether to convert their own high-quality credit into value gains. Second, through the CSCC platform, large enterprises grasp the transaction data of multitier suppliers in the industry chain, clearly understand how their own credit is transferred to the end enterprises, and finely manage the supply chain. Third, large enterprises become the main decision-makers who outsource specific business operations to CSCC for free, thus fully enjoying the shared results and eliminating the investment and operation costs of building their own platforms.

Mobilize financial resources and build a new scenario of supply chain finance. In the process of traditional supply chain finance, financial institutions receive different demands from large enterprises, which reduces their enthusiasm. In addition, the lack of transaction data in many SMEs makes it impossible for financial institutions to carry out credit assessment and risk pricing, and causes supply chain finance to become a retail business similar to "peer-to-peer." By attracting China Postal Savings Bank and Industrial and Commercial Bank of China as shareholders, CSCC makes banks to grant credit only to the core large enterprises, which in turn transfer their own credit to upstream and downstream enterprises based on real transactions. This approach allows SMEs in the supply chain to share the credit of large enterprises. The capital risk exposure of SMEs in the supply chain is shifted from banks to the core enterprises, and the core enterprises, as risk-takers, will also gain the corresponding risk premium. On the one hand, banks improve their efficiency and reduce the risk of bad debts in supply chain finance; on the other hand, banks change their supply chain finance business from "retail" to "wholesale" and obtain the financial benefits of many large enterprises' industrial chain resources in bulk, thus realizing a win-win situation with large enterprises.

Create an "N+N+N" supply chain finance sharing platform and explore new models of financial services. CSCC attempts to bring online all the traditional offline supply chain financial services that require a lot of manpower and material resources, complete the business that used to be done in days instantly and reconstruct new scenarios of supply chain financial services. While providing free platform services for enterprises, CSCC insists on obtaining resources from core enterprises and returning revenue to them, so that enterprises are both the resource providers and the biggest beneficiaries of the platform. Specifically, CSCC innovates an all-online supply chain financial platform model of "N banks + N core enterprises + N upstream and downstream enterprises." CSCC's third-party service model is different from both the industrial supply chain finance model set up by some enterprise groups and the transaction supply chain finance model established by banks and other financial institutions. Compared with some platforms self-built by enterprise groups, this platform has the following characteristics: First, it is not limited to the supply chain of a single core enterprise and has obvious comparative advantages in capital. Second, it is asset-rich and risk-diversified, which is conducive to meeting the practical requirements of regulators on capital risk prevention and investment diversity. Third, it has the advantage of scale and can provide a full package of solutions for enterprise users. As far as the bank-enterprise platforms self-built by banks are concerned, despite the bank's advantages in funding, payment and settlement, and financial expertise, large enterprises and the enterprises in their supply chains are restricted by the credit facilities after joining these platforms. The inability of other financial institutions to join makes large enterprises to be tied to only one bank, leading to significant liquidity risk.

CSCC's Supply Chain Finance Operating Model

In the current credit system, core enterprises often obtain high credit lines from banks due to their strong capabilities, rich assets, and low risk degree. However, their countless financing channels, low financing costs, strong position in the supply chain, and low capital pressure have led to most of the credit granted to core enterprises by banks and other financial institutions being idle. In contrast, the majority of SMEs in the supply chain have difficulties in obtaining financing and high financing costs due to their small scale, slow development, and lack of credit accumulation. These core large enterprises coexist with upstream and downstream enterprises in the supply chain, so the core enterprises in fact bear some of the high financing costs of the vast number of SMEs due to the value transmission effect. This mismatch between the capital demand of enterprises and the capital supply of financial institutions has prevented a large amount of bank funds from being safely invested in the real industry.

In order to fully revitalize the credit lines and supporting funds offered to core enterprises by banks and other financial institutions, and to bring into play the leading position and high-quality credit of core enterprises in the real economy, CSCC launched a product based on strict compliance with the national legal framework—"Cloud Credit" (similar to an electronic payment commitment letter that can be split, transferred, and financed), which provides a new option for settlement of accounts receivable and payable between enterprises. This product realizes the circulation of the credit lines of core enterprises and fast financing of SMEs, allowing end enterprises in the industry chain, which were beyond the reach of traditional finance, to enjoy the high-quality credit of core enterprises, giving full play to the long-tail effect brought by Internet finance, and benefiting the majority of SMEs in the upstream and downstream of the industry chain.

After the core enterprise obtain cloud credit lines from banks and other contributors, it conducts risk assessment based on the scale, operation status, development direction, market orientation, and other information of its subsidiaries. Upon verification by the CSCC platform, the core enterprise allocates and sets the maximum cloud credit lines available to its subsidiaries in the platform. The total cloud credit lines it can allocate is the bank credit lines obtained by the core enterprise. The core enterprise pays the supplier with the cloud credit lines. The suppliers who receive the cloud credit lines have three options: (1) continue to hold such cloud credit lines in part or in full; (2) apply for factor financing to the platform in part or in full; (3) continue to pay other enterprises in part or in full with such cloud credit lines, so as to realize the wide application among industry chain enterprises (see Fig. 5.13).

Through the splitting and circulation by suppliers, the cloud credit lines quickly flow to more SMEs in the supply chain, clearing the triangular debts between enterprises for free and reducing the supply chain transaction costs. At the same time, suppliers can also use their cloud credit lines for financing by submitting contracts and invoices to the platform to achieve efficient and low-cost financing within two hours of T+0. The factoring company of the CSCC platform assigns the corresponding cloud credit lines in the form of commercial factoring of accounts receivable and transfers the cloud credit lines to banks and financial institutions by means of refactoring to obtain loans. In this process, the factoring company only charges an annualized handling fee of 2000ths of the loans, but does not

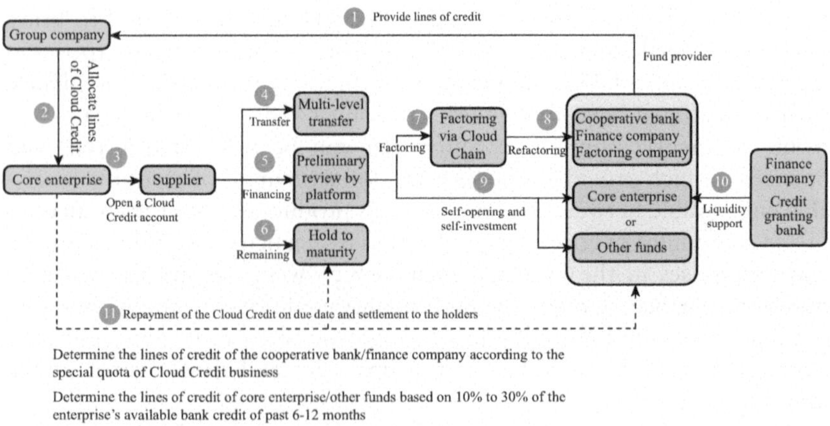

Fig. 5.13 CSCC's supply chain finance model

charge a spread. In this way, bank moneys are introduced to SMEs at the end of the industry chain in a safe, convenient, and efficient manner. If a core enterprise has sufficient funds to provide self-financing services for small suppliers with its own funds or its own finance company and other credit lines, then upon expiration of the cloud credit lines the core enterprise may transfer funds equal to the such credit lines to the bank, which will divide and transfer the funds to the bank accounts of the different entities that ultimately hold the cloud credit lines.

Concretely, cloud credit has the following distinguishing features:

First, all users complete registration, real-name authentication, and account opening on the platform. The application, receipt, splitting, transfer, and payment of cloud credit lines are free of charge. The platform charges an annualized fee of 2000ths of the financed amount only when the supplier uses the cloud credit lines to finance.

Second, cloud credit = silver ticket (reliable) + commercial paper (free payment) + cash (split at will) + trackability. (1) Easy to operate: enterprises complete the whole registration, receipt, payment, transfer, and even financing online in the platform. (2) Easy to split: After each supplier receives the cloud credit line, it can be split at will and free of charge on its own for circulation or financing purpose, making cloud credit highly flexible similar to cash. Easy to finance: Any supplier who receives a cloud credit line can realize same-day financing only through providing the contract and invoice with the buyer online.

Third, CSCC aims to create an industrial network for serving enterprises in the industrial chain. Through the services, it can obtain real information of accounts receivable and accounts payable between SMEs and core enterprises, and connect with independent financial institutions to realize the penetration of financial resources into the whole supply chain.

Fourth, considering that the financing business of this platform is characterized by small and high frequency and similar single business cost, CSCC established a financial workshop in Binhai, Tianjin, transformed the back-end processing of the business into an assembly line model, adopted a standardized and industrialized process, significantly reduced the operation cost of this platform with the help of task pools, ordered grabbing and piecework wages, and built a supply chain finance center for large enterprises to share.

Type III of Intelligent Supply Chain Finance

This type of supply chain finance organization is very different from the first two types. Enterprises that can engage in the first two types of supply chain financial services are often large core enterprises, which have sufficient resources and capabilities to build platforms and data services, and also have enough supply chain business to support platform services and financial services. However, this third type of supply chain finance is organized differently because the information intermediaries here are fintech companies specializing in data analysis and management, and they also act as organizers of ecological networks, which can effectively link up various participants in the industrial supply chain to carry out supply chain operations. By effectively organizing, serving, and managing the supply chain, they can make the original supply chain better coordinated, reduce transaction costs, and improve the operational efficiency of the industrial supply chain. In addition, with the help of their linked networks, they obtain objective data and information about SMEs from each node, and effectively transmit the screened and analyzed data to independent financial institutions for the purpose of supporting financial institutions to provide financing services to SMEs (see Fig. 5.14).

This kind of organization, as promoter of supply chain finance, realizes its value in two aspects. On the one hand, the organization links a large number of enterprises in the industry, which were originally decentralized and isolated from each other, to create mutual synergy, thus optimizing the industrial supply chain, improving the efficiency of industrial operation, and reducing the transaction costs caused by the original small, scattered, and chaotic situation of the industry. On the other hand, thanks to the linkage and synergy, the organization can better access industrial data and conduct data mining and analysis, so as to optimize decisions for the industry, especially supply chain financial service decisions. However, the challenge faced by the organization is how to effectively organize the established enterprises in the industry to intervene and participate in the ecological network it has built. The organization is not a participant in supply chain operations, so the legitimacy of its existence is easily challenged by other companies or institutions. This questioning of legitimacy comes from both industrial enterprises and fund providers. In order to enter the industry and gain acceptance of its legitimacy by other players, the organization can adopt two approaches. One approach is to completely change the transaction model of the industrial supply chain and

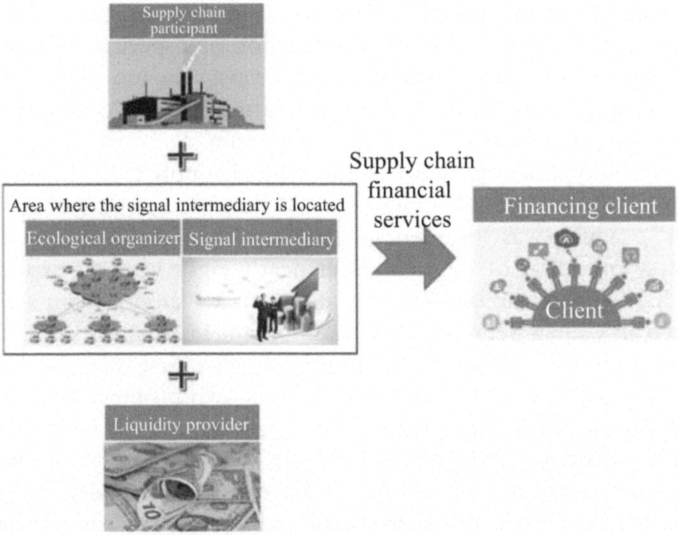

Fig. 5.14 Type II of intelligent supply chain finance organization

achieve the extreme simplification of the transaction structure. This approach is often disruptive and requires long-term accumulation of resources and capacities, and it is difficult to achieve without sufficient capital and resources. Especially in the state of industrial supply chain, this approach has great challenges because the transaction structure of industrial supply chain is specific (i.e., both participants and customers in the industrial supply chain are specific), so it is difficult to completely change the formed steady transaction structure in the short term. The other approach is revision and optimization, that is, the organization may become an organizer of network ecology by integrating transaction, logistics, and information flow based on the original supply chain transaction structure, optimizing inefficient and ineffective links, improving the synergistic effect among industrial supply chain players, and reducing the transaction cost of the whole industrial supply chain as well as the ownership cost of participants. The legitimacy challenge for this type of organization also comes from the fund providers, that is, financial institutions. Solving this problem requires that this organization has the ability to process, integrate, and transmit signals across multiple enterprises, layers, and elements, which, respectively, means: the ability to collect, analyze, and transmit signals from multiple enterprises and to cross-check them; the ability to understand not only the information of a specific enterprise but also the signals of the whole supply chain, or even the industry; the ability to aggregate and cross-check the information about commodity flow, transport flow, and fund flow in the supply chain.

One of the typical enterprises of this type of supply chain finance organization is Autozi Lianhe E-Commerce (Beijing) Co., Ltd. (referred to as "Autozi"), which was founded in 2010 by Dr. Zhang Houqi, former global vice president of Lenovo. After nearly eight years of exploration, Autozi has become the largest cloud platform for supply chain service of auto parts in China. Seen from its development history, the company has gone through two stages of development. The first stage is the self-operation stage, in which Autozi launched its own business, built an auto parts supply chain platform from scratch, and optimized the platform by gaining an in-depth understanding of the various links of the industry from buying, stocking, and selling to delivery. The second stage is open stage, in which Autozi moves from the self-operated mode to the open mode, continuously consolidates the parts supply chain business, and gradually expands into upstream and downstream of the industry chain. It no longer intervenes in transactions, but focuses on building a cloud platform for the auto industry chain. At present, Autozi has set up more than 20 branches nationwide, with business covering nearly 30 provinces. The wearing parts business is directly connected to first-tier manufacturers at home and abroad, covering original parts, branded parts, and customized parts. The model parts business is rapidly advancing in many core cities, covering mainstream models and mainstream categories. The tire business is rapidly integrating high-quality suppliers across the country.

Basic Situation of Industrial Supply Chain for Auto Aftermarket in China

As of September 2018, the vehicles owned by Chinese people reached 235 million, up more than 10% compared to 2017, and is expected to surpass the US (approximately 300 million) by 2020. In 2018, China's auto aftermarket reached RMB 1.3 trillion, an increase of over 20% year-on-year, making it the second largest market in the world after the US (US$241 billion). Meanwhile, the average age of vehicles in China exceeded five years in 2018. According to the development experience of developed countries, once the age of vehicles exceeds five years, the auto aftermarket will enter a period of rapid growth. It can be seen that China's auto aftermarket has huge potential for growth. However, the current auto aftermarket is too small, scattered, and chaotic.

The traditional authorization system is severely monopolized, and the circulation market is very confusing

Owing to several historical reasons, a kind of serious monopoly of auto parts and technology has existed in China for many years. OEMs supply auto parts and provide repair technology to authorized institutions only such as 4S stores and cooperative repair stores, resulting in very high prices for products and services within the authorization system. Under this circumstance, the parts-to-whole price ratio even approached 10 (e.g., that ratio of Mercedes-Benz GLK models reached 8.3 in October 2017). More than 400,000 independent repair enterprises exist in the independent aftermarket outside the authorization system, but their service levels are uneven. Since the overall industry is in monopoly situation, these enterprises cannot get the OEM parts from the formal channels, but only purchase other brand parts through n-tier agents. Worse, the market is flooded with counterfeit and fake poor-quality parts, resulting in the quality of parts not being guaranteed and the circulation market very confusing.

The industry suffers from a low level of informationization and relatively inefficient transactions.

The informationization infrastructure of the auto parts industry is weak. Most of the dealers and auto repair shops adopt traditional business model and lack informationized ERP system. The level of Internet knowledge of the relevant employees is low, and it is difficult for them to accept the online procurement, sales and settlement methods due to the ingrained old habits. The sales process in auto parts industry is still stuck in the mode of "customers placing orders by phone and salesmen taking orders and shipping manually," which has low efficiency and high error rate and highly depends on the personal ability of front-end salesmen. As far as the settlement method is concerned, there is a widespread delay in payment and lack of uniform standards, and payments are collected by manual phone calls and visits. Stores and inventory are managed manually without the support of information technology system, resulting in low efficiency and errors. The analysis of inventory and businesses as well as standardized and data-driven management of employees is even less possible.

With the auto aftermarket supply chain developing toward Internet and intelligence, payment and settlement, billing period, financing, and other difficulties have become the key problems restricting the development of auto parts B2B platforms. Currently, there are about 440,000 auto repair shops in China's auto aftermarket. In the traditional offline model, many auto repair shops have the habit of settling payments after a billing period. However, most auto parts B2B platforms use online payment and cash on delivery as the main settlement method, which has no way to solve the online billing problem of enterprises. Moreover, auto repair shops have small and high-frequency payments and settlements in actual business scenarios, while the original corporate banking for online payment is too inefficient to meet the demand of auto repair shops for quick payment. At the same time, some repair shops hope that the online payment periods can be flexible and are willing to bear certain interest costs for deferred financing after maturity.

Autozi's Supply Chain Service Platform
In 2018, Autozi upgraded its business model by upholding the core concept of "openness, connection and empowerment," focused on building an industrial online platform and devoted itself to realizing the online closed loop of "commodity flow, fund flow and transport flow" in the automotive industry chain. In terms of parts supply chain, Autozi rapidly expanded nationwide through regional layout. In terms of repair stations, Autozi has established a matrix consisting of five major services for car owners, including new car, used car, insurance, repair, and rescue. The ultimate goal is to provide quality SaaS services for each participant in the industry chain, realize the online interconnection of offline participants in the industry chain, and gradually establish a new ecosystem of the automotive aftermarket (see Fig. 5.15).

Trading Cloud Platform
Autozi provides an integrated platform for online trading and online management for all participants in the industry chain. The trading cloud platform that is continuously iterated supports accurate search, VIN code identification, online order placement, and online payment. The platform is open to the whole industry and supports seamless interface between social ERPs and the platform, realizing the integration of supply chain transactions and online management and avoiding secondary data entry. It continues to invest hundreds of people and tens of millions of dollars to establish an industry parts database, covering hundreds of vehicle brands and tens of thousands of models, realizing SKUs of ten million parts data, and providing wearing parts, model parts, original parts, and brand parts.

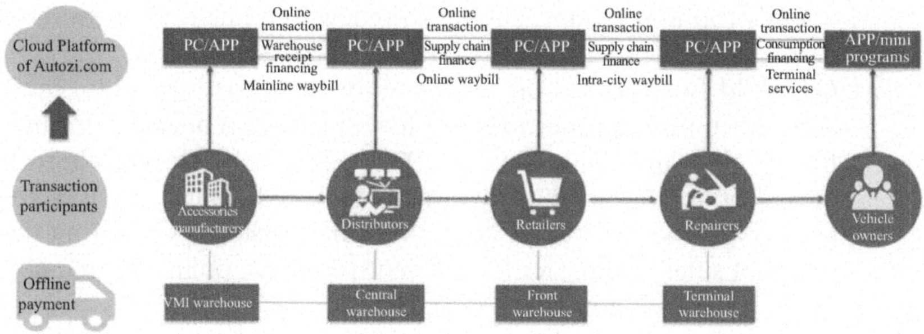

Fig. 5.15 Supply chain service framework of Autozi.com

Finance Cloud Platform

Based on different business scenarios, Autozi has built the industry-leading supply chain finance cloud platform—QTFIN.com. Utilizing digital technologies (DT) and Internet technologies (IT), both the external credit data and internal business data of e-commerce companies/core enterprises and their upstream and downstream clients are transformed into credit assets. Credit data is generated for SMEs in the industry chain based on real transaction orders. It has created a controlled supply chain transaction scenario focusing on each link of the industry chain and serve the transaction parties in the upstream and downstream of the industry chain. The platform continues to iterate and upgrade its supply chain finance products (e.g., credit financing, waybill financing, warehouse receipt financing, and bill financing). As the transaction volume rises, a large number of fund providers and nonbank institutions are attracted in to sign contracts. Currently, the platform is actively introducing trust funds and ABS to continuously reduce the cost of funds. At the same time, the platform will further improve the risk control model based on big data and blockchain technology to create an "online + offline" defense system for risk control. Specific financial products are as follows:

(1) Warehouse receipt financing: Based on Autozi's supply chain business scenarios, the platform provides a financial product for warehouse receipts—Warehouse Receipt Financing. The service mainly targets FMCG products featured by standardization, high turnover, hard currency, such as engine oils, batteries, and tires of the

world's top 500 brands, aiming to relieve the financial pressure of parts manufacturers and distributors.

(2) QT Gold Loan: Based on the scenarios of Autozi's retail business and distribution business, the platform provides a financial product for downstream supply chain—"QT Gold Loan." Through fintech means, it provides innovative and efficient financial services for retailers, auto repair shops and other small businesses, meeting the needs of small businesses for efficient payment, online billing, and deferred financing in a one-stop manner.

(3) QT Installment: Based on the scenarios of Autozi's car owner business, the platform provides a consumer installment product—"QT Installment." Aiming at the whole life cycle of vehicle use by car owners, it unites with financial institutions to provide financial services to meet the consumer installment needs of car owners for new cars, used cars, rental cars, insurance, and maintenance.

Autozi's finance cloud platform has solved online financing for multiple scenarios in the first stage, devotes itself to solving intelligent risk control over the transactions between industry chain participants in the second stage, and aims to become a payment and settlement platform among enterprises in the third stage (see Fig. 5.16).

Logistic Cloud Platform

Through the Internet, Autozi's logistics cloud platform connects distributors, logistics companies, and auto repair shops, realizes electronic, online, and transparent waybills, provides safe, efficient and hassle-free cargo undertaking, transport, and payment services, and provides innovative online payment tools and online financial products that fit the business scenarios, thus completely solving the problem of receiving and paying by logistics companies on behalf of their clients and protecting transactions in the industry chain (see Fig. 5.17). In particular, TUOFUBAO is an online payment tool integrated in the logistics cloud platform. Based on the quick payment via Ping An Bank account, this tool provides users with safe, fast, and efficient payment services.

Car Owner Platform

The platform sets up a connection between repair shops and car owners, provides owner-oriented consumer installment services, and improves the overall profitability of repair shops (see Fig. 5.18).

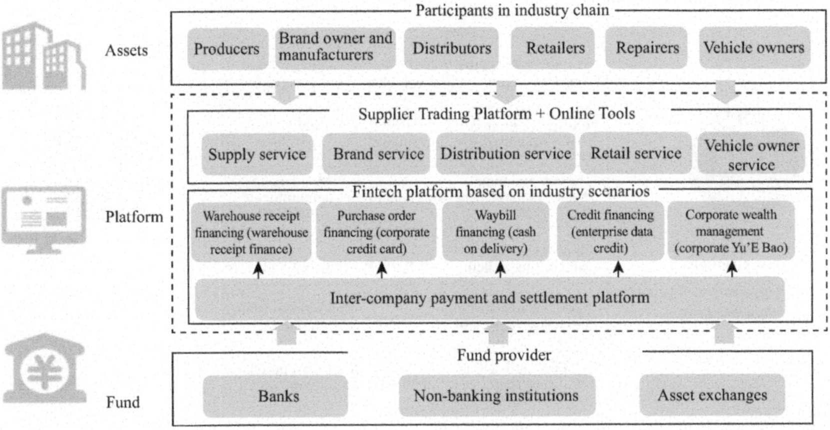

Fig. 5.16 Supply chain financial service framework of Autozi.com

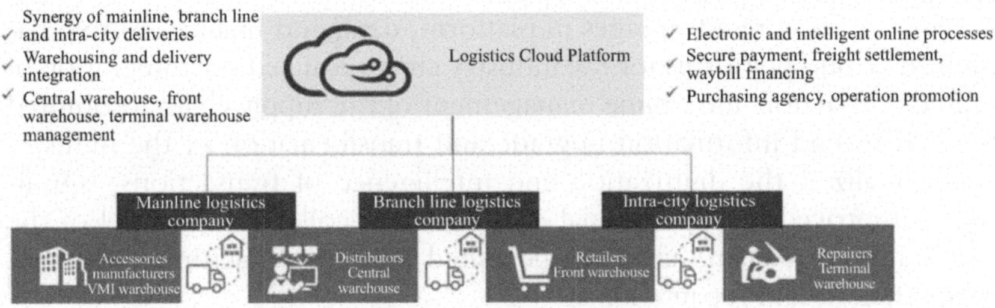

Fig. 5.17 Logistics cloud platform framework of Autozi.com

Centered on the repair scenarios, Autozi's car owner platform effectively improves the income of repair shops, enhances their stickiness and recognition of the platform, further expands their business, and fully empowers them. Autozi has formed a service matrix of "new car + used car + insurance + repair + rescue," which helps to upgrade its service capability. At the same time, the platform provides selected parts supply to high-quality repair shops with the help of selected high-quality parts supply from parts suppliers. Through the way of "parts supply in left hand + car owner service in right hand," the platform aims to become the first brand of repair in the automotive aftermarket.

Fig. 5.18 Car owner service platform framework of Autozi.com

Value Realization of Autozi's Supply Chain
Relying on its core advantages in platform, data, and finance, Autozi has built the cloud platforms for the industry chain, realized the integration of online transaction and online management of the supply chain, promoted the end-to-end information upgrade and transformation of the industry chain, realized the digitization and intelligence of transactions, significantly improved the operational efficiency and collaboration level of the whole industry chain, and fully benefited parts manufacturers, distributors, retailers, and repair shops:

Benefits for Parts Manufacturers
Autozi provides online marketing and distribution management for parts manufacturers, constructs an intelligent supply chain, visualizes sales data of each node and inventory data of warehouses at all levels in real time, and guides them to achieve more accurate replenishment and production. Autozi provides bill financing service for upstream suppliers and warehouse receipt financing service for downstream distributors, thus solving the capital turnover problems of all parties. It also connects manufacturers' ERP with supply chain platforms to realize the integration of transactions and online management, and relies on logistics cloud platform to provide perfect logistics management services.

Benefits for Parts Distributors and Retailers

Autozi allows parts distributors to obtain more cost-effective parts through centralized procurement, and to use online sales to capture more sales opportunities. Based on online transaction orders, it provides supply chain financial services for upstream and downstream parties to improve the efficiency of capital turnover; provides an integrated platform for supply chain transactions and online management to avoid secondary data entry; provides parts data query tools to achieve accurate matching of model and parts.

Benefits for Repair Shops and 4S Stores

Autozi provides repair shops with diverse, fast, excellent, money-saving, and accurate parts supply chain services; develops professional auto repair ERPs and connects them with supply chain platforms so as to improve the standardized management of repair and maintenance shops; provides an online platform for visualization of technical services to realize technical sharing of experts; provides consumer financial services such as whole car installment, repair and maintenance installment, and insurance installment to car owner consumers; establishes a car owner service platform to bring in more car owner service needs and improve profitability for repair shops.

Type IV of Intelligent Supply Chain Finance

This type of supply chain finance organization is driven by pure signal intermediaries in association with other participants. More specifically, the companies engaged in signal intermediary services are completely independent external organizations that connect industrial supply chain participants and ecological service organizers on the one hand and external financial institutions on the other. They promote the development of supply chain finance through information and signal services (see Fig. 5.19). Such companies face the greatest challenges because they are neither involved in specific business operations nor do they organize the ecosystem of supply chain services provided within the industry. Therefore, strictly speaking, they are independent fintech companies. In order to form good partnerships with industrial enterprises or industrial service platforms and engage in signal intermediary services, such companies need to go down to the bottom of their customers' supply chains and help industrial participants or other enterprises to informatize and digitize their industrial supply chains or supply chain financial activities, so as to better

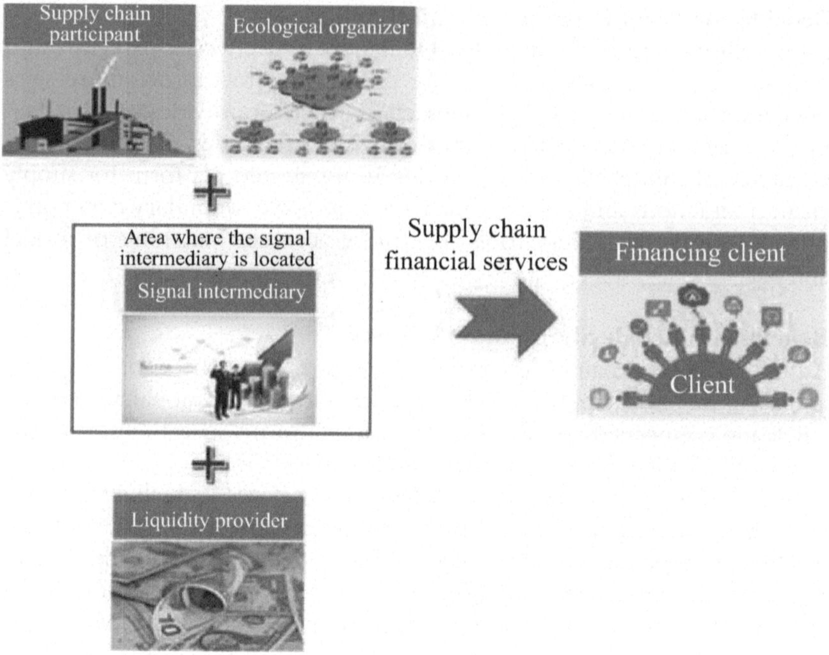

Fig. 5.19 Type IV of intelligent supply chain finance organization

process, present, and deliver objective information. Meanwhile, such companies need to be able to help financial institutions use information and communication technology to effectively connect to industrial enterprises and realize the timeliness, integration, and twinning of information and signals. Timeliness refers to zero delay in receiving information and signals by financial institutions. This means that the information of any industrial supply chain and the corresponding financial activities (payment, settlement, etc.) can be sent to financial institutions in real time, thus becoming effective and timely support for lending and borrowing decisions. Integration refers to the ability to corroborate and match the information about transaction, logistics, and fund generated among different enterprises in the industrial supply chain. Twinning refers to the ability to integrate different methods and advanced analysis to achieve future mapping based on real-time and historical data. In other words, it is able to not only effectively retrace the past financial lending behavior and decision performance but also realize the prediction of the next financial decision, thus realizing the full-cycle management of financial activities.

There are plenty of specialized fintech companies acting as this type of signal intermediary, of which LINO is one of the typical ones. Founded in 2014, with its headquarters and R&D center in Beijing, LINO is dedicated in providing financial service solutions based on supply chain information integration for enterprises and financial institutions. The information technology-based products provided by LINO mainly include EASYSCF (a supply chain financing service platform), SCCS (an integrated supply chain collaborative management system), Exchange Gateway (an electronic data exchange gateway), DMS (an information system for distributor network management), and E-Business Suite (an e-commerce platform). Based on the above products, LINO mainly provides related services to leading companies in medical, manufacturing and retail industries, as well as financial institutions. Relying on its Internet platforms and technical service capabilities, LINO collaborates with high-quality customers to design and develop integrated and systematic industrial supply chain finance solutions. The main sectors it serves and the corresponding information intermediary services are discussed in the following text.

Supply Chain Finance and Information Service Solutions for the Medical Industry

LINO's supply chain financial service solutions for the medical industry are designed to solve the current problem of suppliers concerning accounts receivable from hospitals. The medical industry suffers from an imbalance in negotiating power between buyers and sellers, resulting in the challenges of weak negotiating power, large accounts receivable and insufficient cash flow for most suppliers except for a portion of strong suppliers. In particular, delinquent payments of hospitals have become the norm under the influence of such policies as two-invoice system (which means the first invoice of drug sold from pharmaceutical commercial companies to primary distributors and the second invoice of drug sold from distributors to hospitals; the replacement of the common seven invoices and eight invoices with this two-invoice system aims to reduce profit exploitation in the distribution, and it is clearly stipulated that there should be no more than two primary distributors for each drug) and zero mark-up sales (China has implemented zero mark-up sales of drugs since 2017, which is a policy considered as a key measure to separate hospitals and drugs). Addressing this problem relies on supply chain finance which can optimize the accounts receivable and payable of both sellers and buyers. However, there are two problems that need to be solved for the realization of supply chain finance. The first problem is how to effectively integrate the information of upstream and downstream parties (i.e., suppliers' bills, distribution inventory, and financial reconciliation, and hospitals' recognition of accounts payable and online reconciliation). If the information of upstream and downstream parties cannot be integrated, it is difficult to reflect the real transaction status of suppliers and hospitals. The second problem is how the objective information that has been integrated can be effectively transmitted to financial institutions, allowing them to effectively control risks. To this end, LINO hopes to help the upstream and downstream parties in the medical industry to realize their online supply chain activities and deliver the mined and integrated information to financial institutions in real time, thus promoting its supply chain finance business (see Fig. 5.20).

Supply Chain Finance and Information Service Solutions for Procurement and Distribution in the Manufacturing Industry
This signal intermediary service focuses on financial services provided to manufacturing companies for their supply chains of procurement and distribution. Considering a large number of strategic suppliers and customers, who are the core resources, the manufacturing companies need to effectively embed these upstream and downstream parties into their supply chains and, at the same time, provide operating funds for upstream and downstream parties to promote the development of production

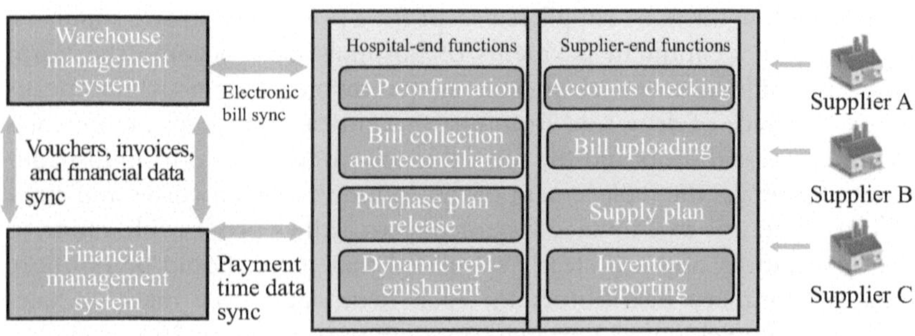

Fig. 5.20 Financial information service solution of LINO pharmaceutical supply chain

operations. However, most manufacturing companies, on the one hand, face the problem of insufficient IT talents and lack of data integration and application capabilities (i.e., how to establish an information technology platform to effectively extract relevant information, screen qualify suppliers and customers, and promote upstream online cash pledge financing and online factoring, as well as downstream online order financing and online cash pledge financing) and, on the other hand, face the problem of how to interface with financial institutions' risk control systems (i.e., converting the business data into a form that financial institutions can understand and accept). In response to these problems, LINO provides corresponding technical and digital solutions as well as comprehensive signal intermediary services, whose technical framework is shown in Fig. 5.21.

Supply Chain Finance and information Service Solutions for Fourth-Party Logistics
These solutions form a service platform for upstream and downstream transaction management by LINO for logistics transportation and park management, which is also called the fourth-party logistics financial service platform. It is a comprehensive service platform integrating logistics

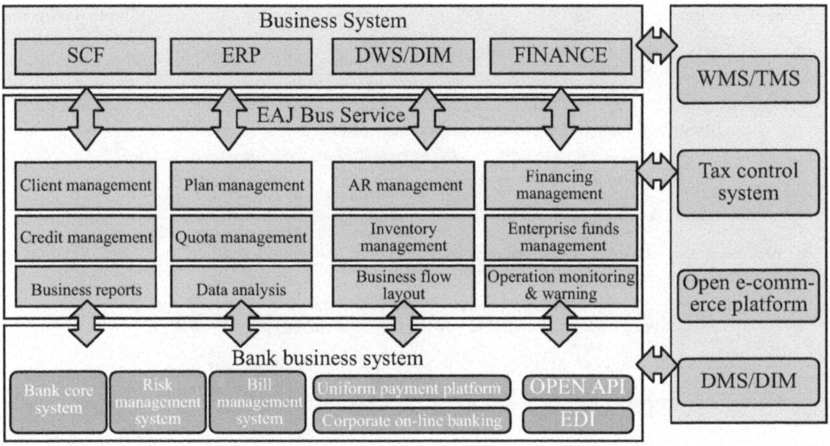

Fig. 5.21 Financial information service solution of LINO manufacturing supply chain

transportation management, park operation management, online transaction, and financing service (see Fig. 5.22).

Type V of Intelligent Supply Chain Finance

The signal intermediaries in this type of supply chain finance organization are neither the core enterprises of industrial supply chain, nor the organizers of industrial network ecosystem or specialized independent fintech companies, but the fintech companies driven and developed by the financial institutions. Industrial enterprises are the participants of supply chain operations and also establish the corresponding ecological network of supply chain services. However, the acquisition, analysis, and transmission of information and figures are handled by the companies established by the financial institutions themselves. Based on the objective and comprehensive digital information, financial institutions provide supply chain financial services to the upstream and downstream parties of industrial enterprises. The reason why financial institutions build their own fintech companies engaged in signal intermediary services is that, despite the strong reputation and credibility of industrial core enterprises, financial

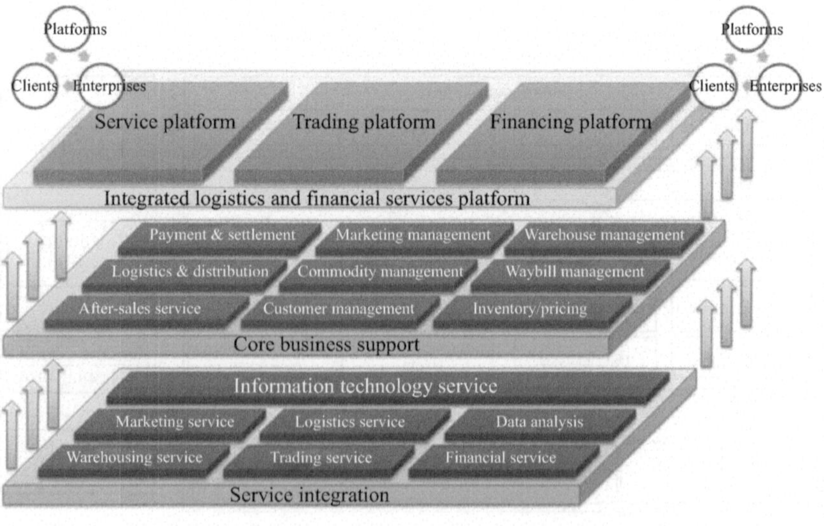

Fig. 5.22 Financial information service solution of LINO fourth-party logistics supply chain

institutions do not fully grasp the business transactions and real transaction status between core enterprises and their upstream suppliers or downstream clients, and therefore bear potential credit risks. For the purpose of grasping the real transaction information of core enterprises, financial institutions need to use ICT to effectively obtain complete and objective information about the transaction process to support their credit decisions and also to accumulate credits of core enterprises as well as their upstream suppliers and downstream clients (see Fig. 5.23).

The success of this type of organization, in addition to data mining and analysis, requires financial institution-led fintech companies to achieve breakthroughs in two aspects. First, since core enterprises are participants in supply chain operations and builders of supply chain service network ecosystem, fintech companies need to collaborate with core enterprises to realize standardization of supply chain business activities and electronicization of documents in order to effectively obtain complete supply chain business information. This standardization and electronization is beneficial not only for financial institutions to understand and grasp the supply chain process and business status but also for financial institutions to realize the validation of transaction data from multiple sources to objectively reflect the truth of transactions and assets. Second, because the industrial supply chain service network platform is built by industrial core enterprises, all the original data of supply chain operations are occurring and stored on the network platform. In this regard, how to use ICT to achieve real-time synchronization of supply chain business information, or to

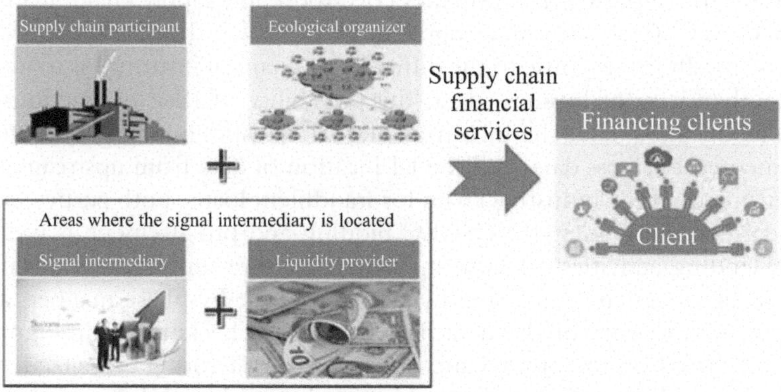

Fig. 5.23 Type V of intelligent supply chain finance organization

achieve synchronization and parallelization of supply chain operation figures, is also a problem that fintech companies need to solve.

Nowadays, this type of supply chain finance organization is used by an array of financial institutions. For example, DBS Bank and Standard Chartered have joined forces with Ripple, a technology company, to apply blockchain technology to supply chain financial business. They have used smart contracts and technology for point-to-point cross-border transactions to automate processes and improve security. A typical example in China is yzw.cn created by China State Construction E-Commerce Co., Ltd. and China Merchants Bank. China State Construction Engineering Group Co., Ltd. (referred to as "CSCEC") is one of the professional real estate operation and construction company group in China, with a series of construction products ranging from research and development of products and technologies, survey and design, project contracting, real estate development, equipment manufacturing, and property management. A large number of suppliers exist in the supply chain operations of the construction industry, and they all face high costs, opaque processes, and high risks of financing. For this reason, China State Construction E-Commerce Co., Ltd., a branch of CSCEC, and China Merchants Bank have joined hands to launch the intelligent supply chain finance based on centralized bidding and procurement. The companies affiliated to CSCEC are all participants in the construction supply chain. Based on yzw.cn, a network platform for industrial supply chain services built by China State Construction E-Commerce Co., Ltd., the fintech department of China Merchants Bank has used blockchain to build a real-time parallel digital platform, through which it provides corresponding supply chain financial services to CSCEC's winning suppliers.

Specifically, in response to the difficulty of financial institutions to judge the authenticity of business data, the possibility of false transactions in various business data, the inconvenience of statistics and aggregation of fragmented business data, and the falsification of data from upstream and downstream of the industrial chain for fraudulent loans, both parties, first, standardize the process for CSCEC bidding and procurement as well as bank lending activities, so as to manage the entire supply chain business and financial activities in a step-by-step and phase-by-phase manner, and ensure the integrity of the data flow and cross-checking of the figures. Second, based on the blockchain, online reverse factoring is realized (see Fig. 5.24). The platform adopts Hyperledger Fabric V1.1 consortium bockchain, which enables the transaction data of each procurement

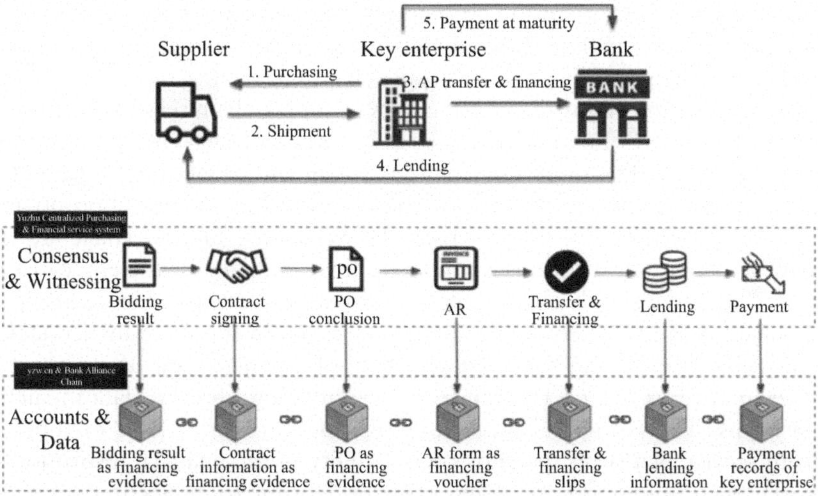

Fig. 5.24 Smart supply chain finance between CSCEC and China Merchants Bank

section to be written into the distributed ledger jointly maintained by core enterprises and financial institutions in real time, realize traceability of each transaction, eliminate the modification of transaction data, and enhance the credibility of transaction data. By importing all valid financing business-related data in advance, the platform allows supply chain data to be documented and enables closed-loop inquiries from tender documents to bid-winning notices, contracts, orders/output sheets, and accounts receivable to ensure that the data is real and valid. The platform supports CSCEC and China Merchants Bank to follow up the progress of financing in real time to ensure their smooth business operations. Up to now, the platform has processed data of 136 valid transactions with a total financing amount of RMB 205.6 million.

Type VI of Intelligent Supply Chain Finance

This type of supply chain finance is completely led by financial institutions. Financial institutions build their own supply chain service network platform, effectively integrate all supply chain participants into the supply chain network, mine and analyze the information and data accumulated in supply chain services, and provide financing and carry out supply chain financial services by restoring and judging the authenticity of the transaction process and profiling the credit level of each participant (see Fig. 5.25).

The advantage of this type of supply chain finance organization is that financial institutions, as the constructors of supply chain service platform, can more directly obtain the business information of each enterprise in the supply chain, and through information mining and profiling they can better understand the credit level of these enterprises, design appropriate financial products, and control risks. However, the biggest challenge is that the financial institutions cannot be fully recognized by the enterprises in the industrial supply chain since they do not directly participate in supply chain operations, or even indirectly engaged in supply chain services. Especially, considering the confidentiality of business data, these enterprises may even put up resistance to accumulating business data in such platforms. Therefore, the successful construction of this kind of supply chain service platforms depends on the ability of the financial institutions to play their unique functions and really bring value to these enterprises in the industrial supply chain and solve the pain points in the supply chain operations before including them into the platform. To be specific, financial institutions may start from two approaches to successfully become an ecological network platform for supply chain services. The first is to become a provider of capital and financial solutions for global supply chain operations; the second is to become a provider of financial service solutions for industry supply chain. The former means to help industrial enterprises solve the problem of higher transaction and management costs arising from different currencies, different trade practices and rules, and

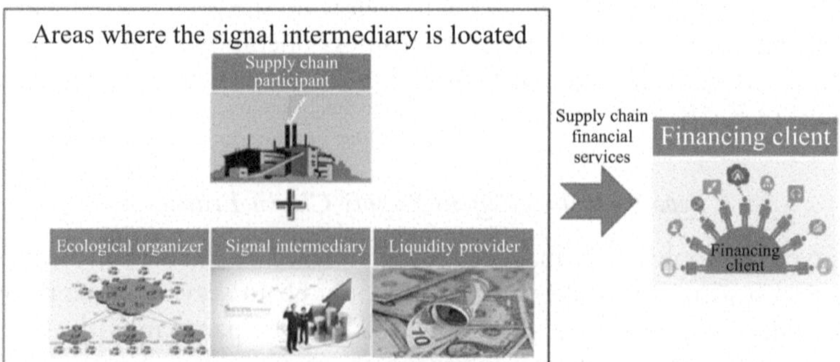

Fig. 5.25 Type VI of intelligent supply chain finance organization

different financial systems in the course of global supply chain operations in different countries and regions. One typical example of this type of supply chain finance organization is HSBC (Song, 2015). The latter refers to the need for financial institutions to reach out to industries or sectors to develop financial service solutions that fit the industry rules.

References

Arthurs, J. D., Busenitz, L. W., Hoskisson, R. E., & Johnson, R. A. (2009). Signaling and initial public offerings: The use and impact of the lockup period. *Journal of Business Venturing, 24*(4), 360–372.

Balvers, R. J., McDonald, B., & Miller, R. E. (1988). Underpricing of new issues and the choice of auditor as a signal of investment banker reputation. *Accounting Review*, 605–622.

Basuroy, S., Desai, K. K., & Talukdar, D. (2006). An empirical investigation of signaling in the motion picture industry. *Journal of Marketing Research, 43*(2), 287–295.

Bester, H., & Hellwig, M. (1987). Moral hazard and equilibrium credit rationing: An overview of the issues. In *Agency theory, information, and incentives* (pp. 135–166). Springer.

Bhargava, H. K., & Choudhary, V. (2004). Economics of an information intermediary with aggregation benefits. *Information Systems Research, 15*(1), 22–36.

Bhattacharya, S. (1979). An exploration of nondissipative dividend-signaling structures. *Journal of Financial and Quantitative Analysis, 14*(4), 667–668.

Caillaud, B., & Jullien, B. (2001). Competing cybermediaries. *European Economic Review, 45*(4–6), 797–808.

Certo, S. T., Daily, C. M., & Dalton, D. R. (2001). Signaling firm value through board structure: An investigation of initial public offerings. *Entrepreneurship Theory and Practice, 26*(2), 33–50.

Connelly, B. L., Certo, S. T., Ireland, R. D., & Reutzel, C. R. (2011). Signaling Theory: A Review and Assessment. *Journal of Management, 37*(1), 39–67.

Deelmann, T., & Loos, P. (2002). Trust economy: aspects of reputation and trust building for SMEs in e-business. *AMCIS 2002 Proceedings*, 302.

Diniz, E., Porto, R. M., & Adachi, T. (2005). Internet banking in Brazil: Evaluation of functionality, reliability and usability. *The Electronic Journal of Information Systems Evaluation, 8*(1), 41–50.

Dodds, W. B., & Monroe, K. B. (1985). The effect of brand and price information on subjective product evaluations. *ACR North American Advances.*

Ebers, M., & Maurer, I. (2014). Connections count: How relational embeddedness and relational empowerment foster absorptive capacity. *Research Policy, 43*(2), 318–332.

Elliott, W. B., Prevost, A. K., & Rao, R. P. (2009). The announcement impact of seasoned equity offerings on bondholder wealth. *Journal of Banking & Finance, 33*(8), 1472–1480.

Feltovich, N., Harbaugh, R., & To, T. (2001). *Signaling and Countersignaling: A Theory of Understatement.*

Feltovich, N., Harbaugh, R., & To, T. (2002). Too Cool for School? Signalling and Countersignalling. *The RAND Journal of Economics, 33*(4), 630.

Fischer, E., & Reuber, R. (2007). The Good, the Bad, and the Unfamiliar: The Challenges of Reputation Formation Facing New Firms. *Entrepreneurship Theory and Practice, 31*(1), 53–75.

Gammoh, B. S., Voss, K. E., & Chakraborty, G. (2006). Consumer evaluation of brand alliance signals. *Psychology & Marketing, 23*(6), 465–486.

Gulati, R., & Higgins, M. C. (2003). Which ties matter when? The contingent effects of interorganizational partnerships on IPO success. *Strategic Management Journal, 24*(2), 127–144.

Heil, O., & Robertson, T. S. (1991a). Toward a theory of competitive market signaling: A research agenda. *Strategic Management Journal, 12*(6), 403–418.

Heil, O., & Robertson, T. S. (1991b). Toward a theory of competitive market signaling: A research agenda. *Strategic Management Journal, 12*(6), 403–418.

Helfat, C. E., & Winter, S. G. (2011). Untangling Dynamic and Operational Capabilities: Strategy for the (N)ever-Changing World. *Strategic Management Journal, 32*(11), 1243–1250.

Hsu, P.-H., Lee, H.-H., Liu, A. Z., & Zhang, Z. (2015). Corporate innovation, default risk, and bond pricing. *Journal of Corporate Finance, 35*, 329–344.

Ilmola, L., & Kuusi, O. (2006). Filters of weak signals hinder foresight: Monitoring weak signals efficiently in corporate decision-making. *Futures, 38*(8), 908–924.

Islam, M., Fremeth, A., & Marcus, A. (2018). Signaling by early stage startups: US government research grants and venture capital funding. *Journal of Business Venturing, 33*(1), 35–51.

Janney, J. J., & Folta, T. B. (2003). Signaling through private equity placements and its impact on the valuation of biotechnology firms. *Journal of Business Venturing, 18*(3), 361–380.

Janney, J. J., & Folta, T. B. (2006). Moderating effects of investor experience on the signaling value of private equity placements. *Journal of Business Venturing, 21*(1), 27–44.

Johnson, E. J. (2001). Digitizing consumer research. *Journal of Consumer Research, 28*(2), 331–336.

Julien, P.-A., Andriambeloson, E., & Ramangalahy, C. (2004). Networks, weak signals and technological innovations among SMEs in the land-based transportation equipment sector. *Entrepreneurship & Regional Development, 16*(4), 251–269.

Kauffman, R. J., Subramani, M., & Wood, C. A. (2000). *Analyzing information intermediaries in electronic brokerage*. 10-pp. IEEE.
Kirmani, A., & Rao, A. R. (2000). No Pain, No Gain: A Critical Review of the Literature on Signaling Unobservable Product Quality. *Journal of Marketing, 64*(2), 66–79.
Lampe, C. A., Ellison, N., & Steinfield, C. (2007). *A familiar face (book): profile elements as signals in an online social network*. 435–444. ACM.
Maslach, D., Branzei, O., Rerup, C., & Zbaracki, M. J. (2018). Noise as Signal in Learning from Rare Events. *Organization Science, 29*(2), 225–246.
Ndofor, H. A., & Levitas, E. (2004). Signaling the strategic value of knowledge. *Journal of Management, 30*(5), 685–702.
Ozmel, U., Reuer, J. J., & Gulati, R. (2013). Signals across Multiple Networks: How Venture Capital and Alliance Networks Affect Interorganizational Collaboration. *Academy of Management Journal, 56*(3), 852–866.
Plummer, L. A., Allison, T. H., & Connelly, B. L. (2016). Better Together? Signaling Interactions in New Venture Pursuit of Initial External Capital. *Academy of Management Journal, 59*(5), 1585–1604.
Podolny, J. M. (1993). A Status-Based Model of Market Competition. *American Journal of Sociology, 98*(4), 829–872.
Pollock, T. G., & Gulati, R. (2007). Standing out from the crowd: the visibility-enhancing effects of IPO-related signals on alliance formation by entrepreneurial firms. *Strategic Organization, 5*(4), 339–372.
Posthuma, R. A., Flores, G. L., Barlow, M. A., & Dworkin, J. B. (2018). Social signaling and interorganizational relationships: Lessons learned from the professional sports industry. *Business Horizons*.
Prahalad, C. (2000). The Core Competence of the Corporation. In *Strategic Learning in a Knowledge Economy* (pp. 3–22).
Ramaswami, A., Dreher, G. F., Bretz, R., & Wiethoff, C. (2010). Gender, mentoring, and career success: The importance of organizational context. *Personnel Psychology, 63*(2), 385–405.
Rao, S., Lee, K. B., Connelly, B., & Iyengar, D. (2018). Return time leniency in online retail: a signaling theory perspective on buying outcomes. *Decision Sciences, 49*(2), 275–305.
Rose, F. (2012). *The economics, concept, and design of information intermediaries: A theoretic approach*. Springer Science & Business Media.
Ross, S. A. (1973). The economic theory of agency: The principal's problem. *The American Economic Review, 63*(2), 134–139.
Sharma, P., Davcik, N. S., & Pillai, K. G. (2016). Product innovation as a mediator in the impact of R&D expenditure and brand equity on marketing performance. *Journal of Business Research, 69*(12), 5662–5669.
Shenk, D. (1997). *Data smog: Surviving the information glut*. HarperCollins Publishers.

Song, H., Turson, R., Ganguly, A., & Yu, K. (2017). Evaluating the effects of supply chain quality management on food firms' performance: The mediating role of food certification and reputation. *International Journal of Operations & Production Management, 37*(10), 1541–1562.
Song, H. (2015). *Supply chain finance (secondedition) [M]*. China Renmin University Press.
Spence, M. (1978). Job market signaling. In *Uncertainty in Economics* (pp. 281–306). Elsevier.
Steigenberger, N., & Wilhelm, H. (2018). Extending Signaling Theory to Rhetorical Signals: Evidence from Crowdfunding. *Organization Science, 29*(3), 529–546.
Stiglitz, J. E. (2000). The contributions of the economics of information to twentieth century economics. *The Quarterly Journal of Economics, 115*(4), 1441–1478.
Stiglitz, J. E. (2002). Information and the Change in the Paradigm in Economics. *American Economic Review, 92*(3), 460–501.
Stiglitz, J. E., & Weiss, A. (1981). Credit Rationing in Markets with Imperfect Information. *The American Economic Review, 71*(3), 393–410.
Taj, S. A. (2016). Application of signaling theory in management research: Addressing major gaps in theory. *European Management Journal, 34*(4), 338–348.
Walker, H. J., Bauer, T. N., Cole, M. S., Bernerth, J. B., Feild, H. S., & Short, J. C. (2013). Is this how I will be treated? Reducing uncertainty through recruitment interactions. *Academy of Management Journal, 56*(5), 1325–1347.
Wallis, J. (2003). Information-saturated yet ignorant: information mediation as social empowerment in the knowledge economy. *Library Review, 52*(8), 369–372.
Westphal, J. D., & Zajac, E. J. (2001). Decoupling policy from practice: The case of stock repurchase programs. *Administrative Science Quarterly, 46*(2), 202–228.
Williamson, O. E. (1973). Markets and hierarchies: Some elementary considerations. *The American Economic Review, 63*(2), 316–325.
Womack, R. (2002). Information intermediaries and optimal information distribution. *Library & Information Science Research, 24*(2), 129–155.
Wu, J., Li, H., Zheng, H., & Xu, Y. (2017). Signaling in joint venture capital: a social network perspective. *Industrial Management & Data Systems, 117*(10), 2340–2363.
Wu, S. J., Melnyk, S. A., & Flynn, B. B. (2010). Operational Capabilities: The Secret Ingredient: Operational Capabilities. *Decision Sciences, 41*(4), 721–754.
Zeithaml, V. A. (1988). Consumer perceptions of price, quality, and value: A means-end model and synthesis of evidence. *The Journal of Marketing, 1*, 2–22.

CHAPTER 6

ABCD-Enabled Supply Chain Finance: Intelligent Elements

6.1 Introduction

The steady development of supply chain finance cannot be achieved without supply chain informatization. A lack of sound supply chain informatization may make financial activities risky, thus hindering the effective flow of funds among supply chain participants. Dating back to the 1970s, the emergence of electronic data interchange (EDI) as the first generation of supply chain information platform solved the cross-system information exchange. As a new method of business processing through computers, it exchanges and processes information from trade, transportation, insurance, banking, and customs industries in an internationally recognized standard format between the various departments, companies, and enterprises and completes the entire trade-related business process through computer communication networks (Iacovou et al., 1995; Premkumar et al., 1994). With the establishment of the concept of supply chain management in the 1980s, the collaboration between upstream and downstream enterprises became an important topic of concern for enterprises. More and more researches began to focus on information exchange and information integration between organizations (i.e., how to transfer the corresponding transaction information and logistics information to partners, so as to achieve both information sharing and effective integration of information from different sources and forms to support decision-making in supply chain business systems) (H.L. Lee et al., 2000; H.L. Lee &

H. Song, *Smart Supply Chain Finance*,
https://doi.org/10.1007/978-981-16-5997-3_6

Whang, 2000; Z. Yu et al., 2001). In particular, with the introduction of the bullwhip effect in supply chain operations in the 1990s (H.L. Lee et al., 1997a, 1997b), both theoretical researchers and actual managers gradually recognized the need for not only a system for sharing information among organizations but also a platform for integrating information to achieve synergy. In other words, information integration can be used to produce a good facilitation effect on supply chain operations and effectively suppress the bullwhip effect. For example, effective sharing and integration of information in supplier-managed inventory can achieve optimization of supply chain inventories (Angulo et al., 2004), or achieve efficient continuous replenishment between buyers and sellers (Raghunathan & Yeh, 2001). In the twenty-first century, with the emergence and continuous improvement of ERP, WMS, TMS, and other information systems, demand-oriented supply chain operations have gradually received more and more attention from scholars and enterprises. In particular, pull supply chain and push-pull supply chain have been the accepted forms of supply chain operations (Vakharia, 2002). Now, however, the development of information and network technology has put the demand for informationization and transformation of the supply chain in a new challenge. The emergence of new technologies such as A (AI), B (blockchain), C (cloud computing), and D (big data mining) also have provided new inspiration and solutions for enterprises and supply chain executors, in addition to constantly bringing impact and influence to enterprises. In addition, supply chain informatization has been pushed to a new step. The intelligent supply chain, which was regarded as unattainable by supply chain executors in the past, has actually been realized, providing a strong support to promote the development of supply chain finance.

6.2 Integrated ABCD Framework for Enabling the Whole Process of Supply Chain Operations

As a booster of effective supply chain management (Ross et al., 2016), modern ICT plays an important role in helping supply chains reduce the challenges and risks associated with environmental uncertainty (Ben-Daya et al., 2017). ICT has a substantial impact on the substance and the structural setup of supply chains. Thanks to its prominent contribution in improving communication, access, and transfer of information between various nodes of the internal and external supply chains, ICT not only allows the integration of the various processes of the internal supply chain within an enterprise but also accelerates the operational integration of the enterprise with external suppliers and customers (Ben-Daya et al., 2017). As a result, each node of the supply chain is also able to make more effective decisions, which in turn improves the overall operational performance of the supply chain. In addition to the direct impetus to the development of the entire supply chain, the increased efficiency of supply chain operations also provides a solid foundation for the effective access to working capital for the various participants in the supply chain. On the one hand, advanced ICT enables the aggregation of information and figures between partners. In particular, a platform-based supply chain can reduce information asymmetry, increase information transparency, and realize effective tracking of supply chain assets, thus creating a persuasive effect on the fund providers. On the other hand, comprehensive and all-round information and figures also lay the foundation for anticipating and preventing risks in supply chain operations. Better disclosure of borrowers' credit helps supply chain participants identify and manage various subjective and objective potential risks in supply chain finance at an early stage, generating an informative effect and enhancing the confidence of financial institutions in SME lending (Z. Zhou et al., 2018).

However, the above goals are not easy to achieve. On the one hand, the rapid development and widespread use of ICT in various industries has led to a large amount of data being generated in each activity of supply chain. In particular, supply chain operations involve multiple participants and multiple processes. Each participant and process, from R&D, design, procurement, production, inventory, distribution to sales and returns, generates huge amounts of information and data. According to the International Data Corporation (IDC), the growth of digital data in the medical industry alone will be as much as 40 trillion gigabytes by 2020. The sheer volume of data not only provides enormous opportunities for commercial organizations to use it effectively to make business decisions but also presents enormous challenges (Forward Industry Research Institute, 2017). On the other hand, although the current corporate information systems, such as ERP, WMS, TMS, and CRM, can effectively help an individual enterprise achieve a high degree of informatization and digitization, once the business crosses the boundary of such corporate systems and reaches upstream and downstream partners, an array of information silos may emerge because of the different structures of the information systems of each other. In this case, the business communication between these information silos still relies on traditional offline modes, which inevitably produce another "distortion" of information and data. This "distortion" may be discrepancies or errors caused by insufficient skills or inconsistent rules, or falsification caused by human moral hazard. All these phenomena bring great challenges to supply chain operations and supply chain finance. Therefore, solving the above problems and realizing the performance of supply chain operations and finance require systematic technology tools to realize the digital management of transaction and asset information throughout the whole process and all aspects of supply chain operations. This is the essence of integrated ABCD.

6.2.1 *Meaning and Framework of Integrated ABCD*

The convergence of ABCD has two meanings. The first meaning is that all kinds of modern ICT are interrelated as a whole. ABCD not only refers to AI, blockchain, cloud computing, and big data, but also includes the interrelated and differentiated roles played by these technological tools at different stages, in different processes, and under different conditions. No single ICT can work alone. The role is played through the interconnection and cooperation between them. The second meaning is that these interrelated technologies work together in the supply chain business and application scenarios to realize the interaction and mutual promotion between technology and business. In other words, ICT needs to be embedded in the supply chain operation scenarios, and the supply chain scenarios drive the development of ICT. On the one hand, the converged ICT can help all participants effectively assess the value of supply chain operations; on the other hand, the supply chain's requirement for value creation further boosts the development of the integrated ABCD. Specifically, the integrated ABCD is based on a four-layer ICT architecture for the whole supply chain process (see Fig. 6.1). The technologies located in the sensing layer (e.g., RFID, M2M (machine-to-machine/man), IoT, AI) are used to acquire basic data from each process of the supply chain. The data acquired by the sensing layer is passed to the data layer. The data layer uses mobile edge computing, fog computing, cloud computing, and other technologies to integrate, mine, and analyze the supply chain data and make decisions based on the data and information that have been mined and analyzed. The decision results are transmitted to the process layer, which is the third layer. The process layer is responsible for the circulation of electronic credentials such as supply chain bills and vouchers, as well as the blockchain technology and management based on the above electronic credentials. The electronic credentials and management information are

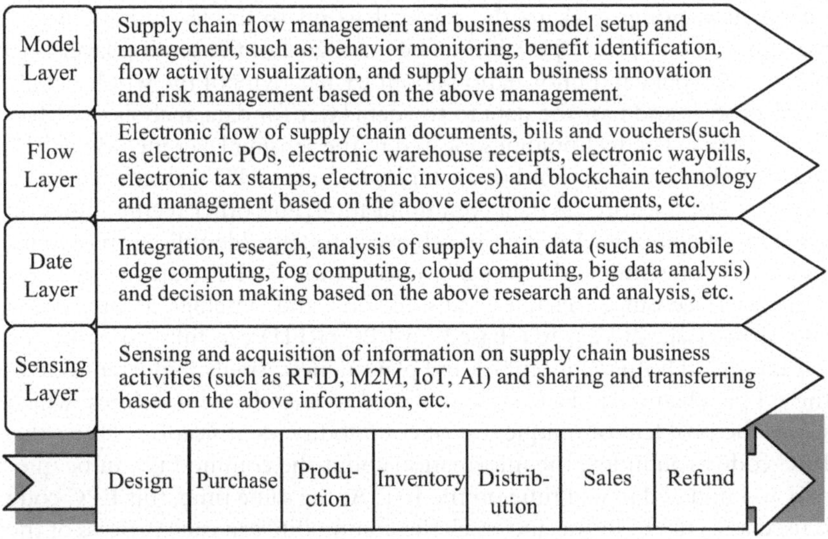

Fig. 6.1 Four-layer architecture for the integrated ABCD

sent to the model layer for further value assessment and value creation (e.g., behavior monitoring, benefit identification, and graphical presentation of activities), supply chain process management and risk management, and supply chain business establishment and innovation. The results of value creation are eventually fed back to the bottom layer of supply chain business in the form of data requests, so that the sensing layer can recapture business information based on the latest data requests

1. Sensing Layer

The sensing layer is the foundation of the supply chain technology architecture, and is the lowest-level technology to realize the intelligent supply chain. The sensing layer usually plays the role of digital twin, which is used to perceive the physical world and digitize the physical world. The ID, Sensor, IoT, edge computing AI, and cloud AI technologies used to realize the digital twin guarantee trustworthy ID, trustworthy transmission, trustworthy identification, and so on. These digital technologies reconfigure and model the physical world completely into a digital world, while most of the human activities and interactions in the supply chain take place in the digital world, with only a small amount of decision-guiding information going back to the physical world to guide equipment and machines to complete operations. The main goal of the sensing layer is to obtain basic data and information about each activity of the whole supply chain process and pass the data to the data layer for data analysis (A. Khan et al., 2017). The technologies located in the sensing layer include RFID, M2M, IoT, AI, and so on. For example, IoT uses RFID, electronic product code (EPC), wireless data communication, and other technologies on the basis of computer Internet to achieve automatic identification of items and interconnection and sharing of information. IoT is featured by comprehensive sensing, reliable transmission, and intelligent processing (R. Khan et al., 2012). IoT based on EPC/RFID can fully combine the advantages of both technologies and play an increasingly important role in the supply chain. The EPC system is used to encode commodities, which solves the problem of uniqueness of commodity identification. Using this EPC code as an index, the information about the commodity can be queried and updated in real time on the IoT. At the same time, this EPC code is used as a clue to locate and track the commodities in each process of the supply chain. RFID technology also has another function. When the electronic tag enters the transmitting antenna working area, it will generate induction current. At this time, the electronic tag gets energy and is activated to send its own code and other information through the built-in tag transmitting antenna to the back-end main system for relevant processing (Wang Man & Shao Feng, 2011).

2. Data Layer

The data layer processes and analyzes the data obtained from the sensing layer and makes decisions based on the analysis results. Big data analysis, for example, describes methods for collecting, managing, and analyzing large amounts of data. Supply chain operations have undergone a big change with the support of big data. As defined by McKinsey and Company, big data is "a data set that exceeds the capacity of typical database software and tools to capture, store, manage, and analyze data." This data set presents the 4V characteristics of big data, that is, large volume, wide variety, high velocity, and huge value (Katal et al., 2013; Robak et al., 2013). In fact, data is divided into two main categories: business data (often manually involved or extracted from operational data, which exists in WMS, TMS, and other systems) and operational data (often collected by devices, including timing data, video, images, and audio). It is difficult to achieve any of the first three of the 4V characteristics with business data alone. Traditional data analysis systems cannot achieve the fourth characteristic. The addition of operational data is what holds the promise of achieving the 4V. Edge/fog computing tends to deal with local data analysis, while the cloud computing is for global coordination. Supply chain cloud platform is an information platform based on cloud computing application model, big data, and communication network technology to provide network sharing service of supply chain product information, technology, equipment, and other data. In the cloud platform, all node enterprises, management agencies, and so on are integrated into a centralized pool of resources. The information requests from each process of the supply chain rely on the processing abilities of big data for accurate control of the processes, intelligent support for decision-making, and in-depth sharing of information. (Wu et al., 2013). Cloud computing simplifies and improves the efficiency of data processing within the supply chain, making all processes of the supply chain more transparent and facilitating collaboration between partners (Jun & Wei, 2011). Another related technology is edge computing, where data processing occurs at the edge of the network, rather than entirely in the cloud. Edge computing can address issues such as delay, limited battery life of mobile devices, bandwidth costs, security, and privacy in supply chain operations (Shi et al., 2016; Shi & Dustdar, 2016). Cloud manufacturing is an example of adopting edge computing and cloud computing for the integration and centralized production management of manufacturing resources through intelligent search technology on a cloud platform (B.-H. Li et al., 2010; Xu, 2012; L. Zhang et al., 2014). With the help of cloud manufacturing, customers can request resources to meet production demands through the cloud service platform throughout the entire life cycle of product development and design, manufacturing, testing, and management, thus completing supply chain operations quickly and efficiently (B. Li & Li, 2017).

3. Process Layer

The process layer that connects the data layer and model layer mainly aims at the electronic circulation of supply chain documents, bills, and vouchers using technologies such as blockchain. As a peer-to-peer network (Iansiti & Lakhani, 2017), the blockchain is a distributed database that is jointly participated and maintained by multiple parties and is continuously growing. The core of blockchain is to establish trust relationships among the parties through distributed consensus mechanisms, time-series untamperable cryptography, and distributed data storage (Weber et al., 2016) and to program and manipulate data using smart contracts to achieve value interconnection (Jiang Dongdong et al., 2017; Li Xiao et al., 2017). Digital bill is a new presentation form of bills developed by combining blockchain technology and the attributes, regulations, and market of bills. Completely different from the technical architecture of the existing electronic bill system, digital bills have four core advantages. First, no intermediary is required to transmit the value of bills. In traditional bill transactions, intermediaries often use information gaps for matching transactions. However, after realizing peer-to-peer transactions with the help of blockchain, the intermediaries will lose their intermediary function and need to reposition their identity. Second, the risk of the bill market can be effectively prevented. Thanks to the nonfalsifiable timestamp and the openness of the whole network, blockchain does not have the phenomenon of reneging after transaction, thus avoiding the problems of "multiple sales of single bill" and asynchronous payment and endorsement of electric bills. Third, the system construction and data storage do not require a central server, which eliminates the development cost of central server and access system, reduces the maintenance and optimization cost of the system in the traditional mode, and reduces the risk brought by the centralization of the system. Fourth, the market order can be standardized and the cost of supervision can be reduced. Blockchain data are linked back-and-forth to form a timestamp that cannot be tampered with, making the cost of supervision greatly reduced. A completely transparent data management system offers a trustworthy tracing path, and a common constraint code for regulatory rules can be established in the chain to achieve full coverage and hard control of regulatory policies.

4. Model Layer

The model layer is mainly used for the management of supply chain processes and the establishment, innovation, and risk management of supply chain finance models. With the help of ICT, the whole supply chain can react quickly in the rapidly changing market environment, so the supply chain's responsiveness to the market is improved. With the ongoing development of ICT, some innovative elements began to penetrate into the operations of the supply chain, which not only made the supply chain operations increasingly intelligent and efficient but also led to dramatic changes in the operation models, risk management, and control of the supply chain (Giannakis & Louis, 2011). The application of ICT is based on the operations and management in the entire supply chain process, mainly in design, procurement, production, inventory, distribution, sales, and returns. Core enterprises of the supply chain must be able to effectively coordinate the competition and cooperation among nodes, as well as coordinate internal capabilities and external resources, so that each participant can achieve its own development based on the benefits of the entire supply chain and deliver integrated services in a timely and effective manner. ICT contributes to the informationization of the supply chain operation process and allows companies to know the status of the supply chain operations and ensure the correctness of information in a timely manner.

The impact of integrated ABCD on the supply chain operation model is reflected in three main aspects. First, by applying IoT, AI, additive manufacturing, and other technologies to the production process, it pushes forward intelligent upgrading of production equipment, process transformation, and basic data sharing. In addition, with the help of edge computing, fog computing, and cloud computing, it builds and pushes the development and utilization of industrial big data, which contributes to the intelligent transformation of manufacturing industry and fosters the formation of an industrial ecosystem of open, co-sharing, and collaborative intelligent manufacturing supply chain. Second, it uses the Internet to collect customers' changing value demands and respond to personalized needs, boosting the flexible transformation of key processes such as design and development, manufacturing, and supply chain management, and realizing the innovation of the service model and business model of C2B2M personalized products. Third, enterprises collaborate closely with various processes in the industrial chain through the Internet, promote comprehensive interconnection of production, quality control, and operation management systems, and implement new models such as crowdsourced design and R&D and network-based manufacturing. Fourth, by building a network-based collaborative manufacturing public service platform, it clusters innovation resources, production capacities, and market demands and builds connection with financial services to enhance the ability in serving SMEs.

6.2.2 *Functions Fulfilled by the Integrated ABCD*

The above-integrated ABCD architecture improves the visibility, transparency, traceability, and credibility of supply chain operations, thus improving the efficiency of supply chain operations and providing a good environment and foundation for the development of supply chain finance. Specifically speaking, the integrated ABCD brings the following changes to supply chain operations.

First change is visibility. Visualization of supply chain management refers to the use of information technologies to collect, transfer, store, analyze, and process the information of order, logistics, and inventory indicators in the supply chain and then present it in a graphical way according to the needs of the supply chain. It mainly includes processing visualization, warehouse visualization, logistics tracking and management visualization, and application visualization (Guo Renzheng, 2015). By connecting the information of each node in the supply chain and overcoming the obstacles of information transmission, it allows each node enterprise in the supply chain to make full use of internal and external data, which undoubtedly increases the visibility of the supply chain. In turn, the supply chain visualization further promotes the management visualization. In addition, ICT allows real-time monitoring and remote access to transport flow, commodity flow, fund flow, and information flow in the supply chain (Caridi et al., 2014). Visualization is reflected in multiple aspects of the supply chain, such as inventory management visualization (A.N. Zhang et al., 2011), risk visualization (M.-C. Yu & Goh, 2014), and visualization of interaction and collaboration with former partners (Williams et al., 2013).

Second change is transparency. Transparency means that ICT gives enterprises access to information about the components of supply chain products, names of suppliers, locations of facilities, relevant certifications, and so on, thus leading to the co-sharing of necessary relevant information about products in the supply chain among all stakeholders and without losses, interference, delays, and distortions (Trienekens et al., 2012). Transparency is the key to supply chain management and allows the supply chain to present a high degree of accountability. Thanks to this transparency in the supply chain, enterprises are able to know the performance of their partners from raw material procurement to delivery. The achievement of greater transparency in the supply chain relies on the development of comprehensive ICTs to offer open communication and shared information to all participants at every stage of the process from order to delivery, thus ultimately realizing virtual supply chain management (Gunasekaran & Ngai, 2004). It is worth adding that while traditional centralized systems can also provide visibility and transparency, the drawback is that they suffer from a single point of trust failure. Given that external parties view information in this single point system, problems may arise if this single point system maliciously tampers with the data. For this reason, a distributed co-sharing ledger can be applied to ensure the transparency of data only to the relevant participants, or transparency degree options can be used to safeguard the privacy of business data.

Third change is traceability. Traceability refers to the ability to identify and track the history, application, or location of entities and processes through records throughout the supply chain (including all stages of production, processing, and distribution) (Bechini et al., 2008; W. Zhou & Piramuthu, 2015). In practice, the goal of traceability can be achieved if enterprises keep records of suppliers and customers and exchange all information throughout the supply chain. For each component or each production batch of products, they must can be traced and tracked. Specifically, tracing means identifying the source of an entity based on the supply chain, while tracking means following the path of an entity from the supplier to the consumer in the supply chain (Bollen et al., 2006). According to W. Zhou and Piramuthu (2015), supply chain traceability is divided into three levels: the first level is the traceability of physical flows (i.e., the status of all products or assets in the supply chain operations can be effectively traced and tracked); the second level is the traceability of business processes (i.e., the process of business operations and their decisions can be traced and tracked); and the third level is the traceability of performance (i.e., the performance of all stages of supply chain operations as well as the global performance can be traced and tracked). Choudhury (1997) suggests that there are three types of information systems to achieve traceability: centralized system, multilateral system, and electronic peer-to-peer system. Among them, the increasing feasibility of B2B collaboration based on a peer-to-peer (P2P) approach reduces the need for centralized exchange and makes electronic dialogue more and more attractive. This electronic P2P system is the characteristic of the integrated ABCD, that is, it can change all the physical objects and processes in the supply chain from the managed objects to the elements that actively and equally participate in the supply chain operations, and these elements are verified against human actions, not only to avoid human errors and moral risks but also to effectively and comprehensively trace the status of assets, processes, and performance.

Fourth change is credibility. Currently, most RFID-based supply chain traceability systems are based on the use of a centralized system with government departments or third-party organizations to achieve supply chain information transparency. But these centralized organizations are totally nontransparent and users can never know the internal details of transactions, which possibly leads to information fraud and information distortion among supply chain participants. Thanks to the integrated ABCD, especially blockchain, traceability systems eliminate the need for centralized organizations and provide an information platform that is open, transparent, neutral, reliable, and secure for all participants of the supply chain (Tian, 2016).

With the integrated ABCD, data can be initially acquired from activities of the whole supply chain process, gradually transmitted from the sensing layer to the data layer, process layer, and model layer, and finally fed back to each activity of the whole supply chain process in the form of new data requests, thus achieving the visibility, transparency, traceability, and credibility of the supply chain, which facilitates more effective decision-making at each node and promoting the intelligence of the supply chain. Specifically, reengineering of supply chain process and management is realized by the integrated ABCD (see Fig. 6.2). First, as far as offline business execution is concerned, it determines the operation tasks to be performed

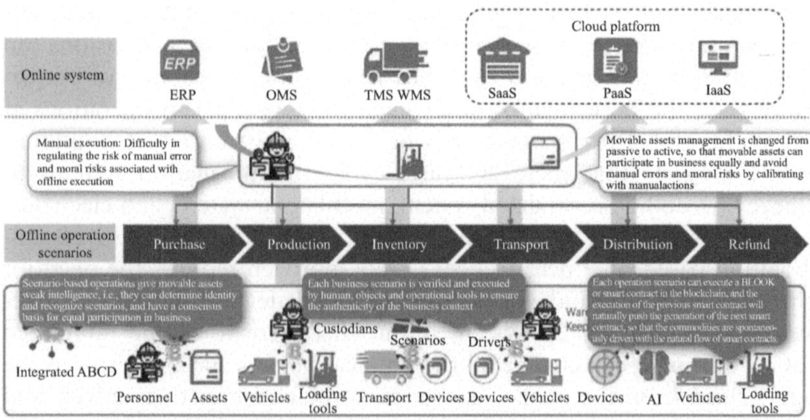

Fig. 6.2 Full supply chain enabled by the integrated ABCD

according to the business rules and distributes such tasks, and ensures that online operators can perform accurately and effectively offline by constraining offline operators. Second, it combines various types of ICTs to establish a scenario-based multimode consensus blockchain for offline operators. The consensus verification result of the tasks is a pass or certificate that truly describes assets, operations, people, and time. All online systems can smoothly carry out decision-making based on the enabled supply chain assets or business, and establish an efficient business collaboration system among enterprises directly with the intelligent chattels or business as the entrance.

6.2.3 *Paths for Achieving the Integrated ABCD*

The establishment and application of the integrated ABCD system requires systematic paths and approaches. In general, the adoption of any ICT needs to be combined with specific supply chain scenarios and needs, which means there is a need to systematically analyze the optimization and adjustment items of industrial supply chains, or the supply chain system that requires to be set up. The supply chain system includes complex business activities, which can usually be analyzed from three perspectives, namely business value, business process, and system architecture (Liu & Jia, 2010). The perspective of business value reveals how economic value is created and delivered in a network. The perspective of business process describes the process of value creation in a business process. The perspective of system architecture reflects the systems that support the business process (Gordijn et al., 2001). Analysis from these three perspectives allows the creation of a systematic and the integrated ABCD from the process of business model and technology development interaction (see Fig. 6.3).

First, the value creation is analyzed. Based on the three perspectives of industrial supply chain, value creation resolves the elements of supply chain value creation. These elements of value creation include actor, market segment, value activity, value object, value port, value interface, and value exchange. Specifically, actor refers to an independent economic organization or an individual. The actors in the supply chain creates profit by implementing value activities. Market segment refer to specific submarkets with the same attributes, which are decomposed from the whole market. Value activity reflects the process of adding value, which is implemented by the actors. Value object is the final objects created and consumed

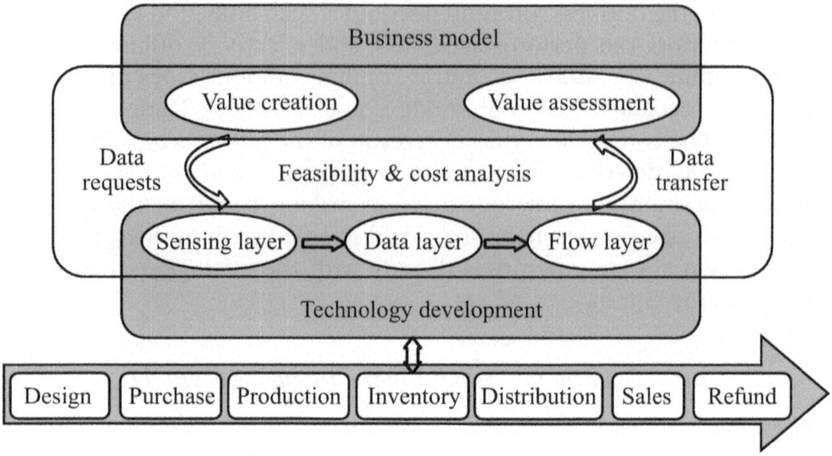

Fig. 6.3 Path for realizing the integrated ABCD system

through value activities, which includes products, services, assets, funds, and so on. Value port refers to an area where the actor provides or acquires the value object. Value interface reflects the boundary of providing or receiving business services. Value exchange reflects one or more transactions of value objects facilitated by connecting two value ports. The importance of analyzing value from these elements is because only by fully understanding the details of these value-creating activities can we break down the supply chain activities between individual actors into standardized scenarios.

Second, the demands for data and technology service are put forward based on the analysis of value creation. Upon fully understanding and recognizing the offline supply chain scenarios, the corresponding demands for data service and technology service are put forward, which include the establishment of traceability degree, status, storage situation, transportation status, occurrence location, and other elements of the application scenarios. The demands for data and technology service often take into account the requirements of the sensing layer, the data layer, and the process layer. It should be seen that the sensing layer is not essentially about sensor-based collection, but about application services for the corresponding scenarios constituted by the combination of the Internet of things and the Internet of people. In essence, the core idea of the sensing layer is to incorporate those objects that are originally managed by people, so that the sensing layer, with the technical support of AI, can intervene in the management of the system together with people who originally dominate the whole process. In this way, the overall ability in data and business management is enhanced. More management points, data collection points, and points involved in operational collaboration will naturally lead to an increase in the management effort of the business and a decrease in the difficulty of management. Similarly, the core idea of the data layer and process layer is that after defining the execution logic of the transaction contract according to the business rules, the corresponding instructions and standardized operations will be automatically triggered in the actual scenarios through IoT smart terminals, so that both people and things can ensure the execution of the contract according to their respective standards. At the same time, a valid document will be generated as bookkeeping credentials and returned for online storage, thus ensuring the authenticity of data sources on the chain and realizing multimode peer-to-peer consensus of people and things as well as effective decision-making.

Third, feasibility and costs are clarified based on the analysis of the demands for the corresponding data and technical services. This is a key element in building an integrated ABCD system. Feasibility analysis aims to clarify how to secure resources and capabilities to achieve the required technologies and services (i.e., whether the corresponding technology system can be established by effective means, the corresponding data can be acquired, and the authenticity, timeliness, and security of the data can be guaranteed). The cost analysis aims to explore the cost of applying ICTs and using data to support effective supply chain operations. Excessive building and applying costs will inevitably limit the diffusion and use of ICTs. The necessary prerequisite for the integrated ABCD (i.e., convergent ICT) to effectively enable supply chain activities is that the marginal cost of ICTs decreases or even goes to zero as the number of service scenarios and users increases.

Finally, the value that the integrated ABCD brings to the supply chain is judged. In judging the performance generated by ICT-enabled supply chain, both economic cost or transaction cost reduction and market opportunity creation are included. It is worth noting that the judgment of costs and opportunities vary among different participants in the supply chain. The judgment may tell who is the beneficiary of the integrated ABCD after the same use of ICT and who is more willing to pay for this kind of ICT construction and data services.

6.3 Key Technologies Applied in Supply Chain Operations

As mentioned earlier, the integrated ABCD is based on a four-tier ICT architecture for the whole process of supply chain operations (see Fig. 6.1). These layers apply the following five key technologies from the bottom-up: IoT, edge computing, cloud computing, AI, and blockchain technology. In terms of ICT in the sensing layer, IoT technology is used to acquire the basic data collected by devices in each process of the supply chain. The data acquired by the sensing layer is passed to the data layer, and the information required for subsequent analysis is sent to the cloud after data processing such as noise reduction, dimension reduction, and feature extraction using mobile edge computing near the device terminals. The cloud computing technology is used to integrate, mine, and analyze the supply chain data and make decisions based on the data and information that have been mined and analyzed. The data from the data layer needs to be analyzed and decision models based on the data need to be constructed so as to reliably assist decision-makers in their decision-making. The decision results are transmitted to the third layer, the process layer. The process layer is responsible for the electronic circulation of supply chain documents, bills, and vouchers, as well as the blockchain technology and management based on the above electronic credentials. Meanwhile, blockchain technology also serves for sharing and accessing data information, providing a reliable and on-demand shared data source for the process layer of each participant in the supply chain. Electronic credentials and management information as the output results of the process layer are transmitted to the model layer for further value assessment and value creation (e.g., behavior monitoring, benefit confirmation, and graphical presentation of process activities) for supply chain process management and risk management, as well as supply chain business establishment and innovation. The value creation results are finally fed back to the lower supply chain business in the form of data requests.

Specifically, the sensing layer reacquires business information based on the latest data requests. The data layer analyzes and refines new data characteristics based on new data requests and adjusts data sharing rules to share new data. The process layer adapts and evolves processes based on changes in data requests. The evolution of each layer is repeatedly iterated in the process of supply chain operations, which leads to the adaptive adjustment of each layer therein, forms a complete closed loop of supply chain operation feedback and evolution from data collection, data processing, process setting to model updating, and finally improves the overall efficiency of supply chain operations. Moreover, the application of IoT and edge computing has gradually moved the data collection and analysis process from the information stage of data collection based on devices to the digital stage of data collection and analysis based on data requests. The use of AI and cloud computing has completely changed the device-based data collection in the supply chain into digital processes and models, allowing most of the activities and interactions in the whole process of supply chain operations to take place in digital processes. Only a small amount of decision information is fed back to supply chain devices to direct such devices and machines to complete operations.

6.3.1 IoT Technology in the Intelligent Supply Chain

Broadly speaking, IoT refers to a huge network formed by using various information sensing devices and protocols (i.e., RFID (RFID + Internet), infrared sensors, GPS, laser scanners, gas sensors, etc.) to collect information in real time from any object or process that needs to be monitored, connected, and interacted with, and combining such information with the Internet. IoT aims to achieve object-to-object, object-to-person, and object-to-network connections to facilitate identification, management and control. IoT is mainly applied in the sensing layer of the integrated ABCD architecture for the data collection of devices involved in each process of the supply chain. Just like the nerve endings in the supply chain operation system of the integrated ABCD, the sensing layer plays two roles. The first is data collection and sharing. It collects all the valuable data from the devices in real time and shares it to the upper data layer for further data refinement. The devices may also need to share their real-time data directly to other participants according to the consensus result of the process among the participants. The second role is to drive the devices to react accordingly and execute instructions based on the decisions made at process layer.

In order to guarantee the reliability and credibility of the process of supply chain operations, the devices must address the two challenges. The first is the reliability of data. Reliability refers not only to the elimination of human interference and risk of tampering with the data collected by the devices but also to the need for the receiver of the data to have sufficient data preprocessing capabilities (such as fast caching and data compression) to process in parallel the high-frequency data streams generated from the high-frequency sensors, as well as to the consideration of the heterogeneity of the data itself. The second challenge is the identity-based access control of device data. In the process of data and instruction interaction between devices and the upper data layer and process layer of the supply chain, how to ensure that the device data is not tampered with during transmission, how to make the instructions issued to the devices reliably verified at or near the devices, and how different participants can access the device data according to the access control rules predefined by the process, all require unified identity management of devices through IoT. With IoT identity management, each device within the IoT is given a unique recognizable identity, and based on this, the relationship between the device and the user, owner, and leaser, and so on is further managed within the supply chain operation framework. The device and the interacting party can verify the identity and access control authority of each other to ensure that the device data flows credibly and securely from the sensing layer to the process layer during supply chain operations, while the instructions for devices flow credibly and securely from the process layer to the sensing layer. The credibility for the flow of the device data and instructions refers to the ability of the receiver to verify the authenticity of the data and instructions through the identity mechanism and ensure that the data and instructions have not been tampered with. The security for the flow of the device data and instructions refers to the use of data protection technology such as encryption to ensure that it is not intercepted and decrypted by unauthorized third parties during the transmission process. Currently, the preprocessing of device data is mainly achieved through edge computing technologies. The main research direction for data protection and reliable identity management of devices focuses on embedded hardware security modules (HSMs), whose main concept is to uniquely identify a device (such as a sensor) by physically embedding a hardware module with an inaccessible and unique private key for encryption, decryption, and signature, and to encrypt and sign its output data on demand through this module.

6.3.2 *AI Technology in the Intelligent Supply Chain*

IoT allows the quantification and collection of direct data for the sensing layer in supply chain operations, while AI makes the collection of data for the sensing layer in supply chain operations more intelligent. Currently, AI is applied in the following four aspects in the sensing layer.

First, AI converts the data collected from the sensors into the required information. For example, the video images captured by the IoT sensors of logistics vehicles can identify the identity of the vehicle driver through AI image recognition technology. For another example, the inspector confirms the product safety inspection by voice, and the AI voice recognition system verifies the product information with the inspector's electronic signature, which is then written to the database.

Second, AI monitors and analyzes the data collected from the sensors in real time. For example, the possible existence of internal air bubbles in finished steel products is a defect, and ultrasonic flaw detection technology is one of the effective ways to detect internal air bubbles in steel. By analyzing the vibration images returned by the vibration sensors during the ultrasonic penetration of the finished steel products, AI can give real-time alerts to the finished steel products with potential defects and improve the efficiency of quality inspection.

Third, AI realizes human-computer interaction and collect interaction information in the sensing layer. For example, the vehicle driver can interact with AI through voice recognition system during driving to know the real-time temperature and humidity of cold chain transport.

Fourth, AI automatically identifies and maps physical assets in the physical world against digital information of the participants, so that the feedback from the sensing layer triggers the update of the digital projection of the physical assets in the ledgers of the participants initiated by the model layer and the process layer. For example, in the case of goods transportation, AI image recognition technology uses vehicle images to identify the unique ID (e.g., license plate number) of an inbound vehicle, and the process layer triggers a series of processes including goods acceptance after the vehicle arrives at in the warehouse. The recognition and analysis of images, video, and audio are often done in real time at the edge based on their response time requirements, while modeling for large amounts of data training often relies on cloud computing.

6.3.3 *Edge Computing Technology in the Intelligent Supply Chain*

Edge computing is the use of an open platform that integrates core capabilities in network, computing, storage, and application, on the side close to the devices or data sources to provide the nearest-end services. With applications initiated at the edge, edge computing meets the industry's basic needs for real-time business, application intelligence, security, and privacy protection by generating faster network service responses. Specifically for the integrated ABCD architecture of supply chain operations, edge computing is mainly used to bridge the data preprocessing process between the sensing layer and the data layer. Edge computing plays a pivotal role in data preprocessing execution, secure deployment and update of data processing procedures, and reliable sharing of data between the devices.

In terms of data preprocessing execution, the data layer usually requires data features that are refined from the original data. For example, the data layer requires correlation analysis of every five-minute average data from multiple sensors. Transferring sensor data directly to the cloud and computing at the data layer would result in wasted network bandwidth and excessive latency. As far as supply chain is concerned, sensors (e.g., on-board temperature and humidity sensors in vehicles) typically collect data first to an on-board data gateway device, followed by a gateway device with greater data storage and computing power that sends the data to the cloud data layer. Therefore, by running customized edge computing applications on a local gateway device close to the device, preprocessing the data as required for a specific analysis scenario and uploading the processed data features or abstracts to the data layer, the computational load on the data layer can be significantly reduced.

Moreover, the gateway close to the device related to supply chain operations use edge computing technology to enable data preprocessing between the sensing layer and the data layer, and dynamically receive automated deployment and updates based on changes in data requests at the process layer, thus simplifying the response of the data layer and the sensing layer to data model updates at the model layer and process layer, and enhancing the flexibility of data processing at the data layer.

In addition, by configuring the abovementioned identity management module, edging computing can also achieve identity-based access control to securely manage the deployment and updates of edge computing applications at the device gateway. The device gateway is also able to verify the legitimacy of the identity of the deployer of the edge computing applications through the identity management module.

Furthermore, edge computing also allows secure data sharing among multiple parties. A participant can access a specified edge computing service deployed on the gateway of the device through the authorization of the device owner. The process can support two-way authentication, that is, the device can verify the legitimacy of the participant's authorization signature, and pushes the specified edge computing results to the participants and signs the results after the verification. The participant receives the calculation results and verifies the signature of the device gateway to determine the authenticity of the data. This method helps to reduce the trust cost of data sharing.

Specifically, the device data users don't need or have access to the original data of the device, but can obtain the data processing results based on authorized access to designated edge computing services, which reduces the risk of data privacy leakage for the device owners. At the same time, the verification mechanism based on the identity management module is introduced to the devices so that the data users can verify the authenticity of the received data.

6.3.4 Cloud Computing Technology in Intelligent Supply Chain

As mentioned above, IoT and edge computing are functionally used mainly in data collection and data preprocessing of devices. The data necessary for decision-making in supply chain operations, however, cannot usually be provided by a single sensor, but may require intensive aggregation, fusion, and feature extraction of data from a large number of devices involved in the entire supply chain operations, and may also require iterative model training of data from a large number of devices. Cloud computing, with its advantages in parallelism and extensibility, is well suited for these scenarios. Let's talk about it specifically under the integrated ABCD framework. As far as the analysis of historical transaction data is concerned, the adoption of cloud computing services can accelerate the extraction of features from financial data of historical transactions and build financial models, so as to create a value model for analysis needs in terms of risk control of supply chain finance and supply chain optimization. For example, risk control model is created on sensitive data such as overdue status and amounts of historical accounts receivable and payable of upstream and downstream enterprises in the supply chain. As for the large amount of operational data generated by supply chain devices, analyzing the data through cloud computing and big data can help upstream and downstream enterprises of the supply chain extract global characteristics of the supply chain from micro sensor data and build supply chain optimization models with a global perspective to optimize key activities of enterprises in the supply chain, such as raw material allocation, capacity scheduling, and delivery scheduling. In addition, cloud computing can analyze device data within the control scope of an enterprise. For example, the current maximum monthly capacity of an enterprise can be assessed through factors such as the production and maintenance periods of large machines and the correlation between device temperature sensor and failure rate. Another example is to assess the current available transport capacity of each logistics provider through factors such as their historical success rates, failure rates and current loads.

For the application of cloud computing in supply chain operations, special attention needs to be paid to how cloud computing can be used securely in the data layer, because the information contained in the data layer is distributed among the various participants of the supply chain, and how to share device data credibly among the various participants is a prerequisite for cloud computing to be used in the analysis scenarios of supply chain operations. As one of the feasible solutions, each participant can provide the required input data to the cloud computing task in an information-controlled manner through the edge computing service, thus ensuring that all input data involved in cloud computing has access authorization from each participant. Another more advanced solution is homomorphic encryption. Before the data is transmitted to the cloud computing service, each participant homomorphically encrypts the data, guaranteeing the invisibility of the data to other participants while still maintaining the computability of the data within the cloud computing environment. This second solution is suitable for data abstraction of highly sensitive and massive data involving multiple participants.

6.3.5 *Blockchain Technology in Supply Chain Operations*

In a narrow sense, blockchain is a chain-typed data structure that combines data blocks in a sequential manner according to chronological order, and also a distributed ledger that is cryptographically guaranteed to be tamper-proof and nonforgery. In a broad sense, blockchain is a new distributed infrastructure and computing paradigm that utilizes a data structure in the form of a blockchain to verify and store data, a consensus algorithm of distributed nodes to coordinate the execution of smart contracts and generate updated data, a cryptographic approach to ensure the security of data transmission and access, and a smart contract consisting of automated scripting codes to program and manipulate the data.

There are two common forms of blockchain: public blockchain and consortium blockchain. The biggest difference between them lies in identity and authority management. As for public blockchain, any node member can join the chain and obtain the same operation authorities. For consortium blockchain, specialized agencies audit, license, and issue certificates, and nodes with different identities have different operation authorities. Public blockchain is generally suitable for the scenarios with lower requirements in authority and identity management, while consortium blockchain can achieve perfect and reliable authority management and meet more diverse needs by designing different network topologies as per the business scenarios. Generally speaking, the consortium blockchain with authorization and identity management is more suitable for the characteristics of its various applications in supply chain networks. To be more specific, the consortium blockchain mainly consists of four technologies: shared ledger, smart contract, machine consensus, and authority privacy.

1. Shared Ledger

The shared ledger stores the transaction history and the post-transaction status of the assets in a chained structure. The hash of each block will be used as the data header for the next block and is chained together one after another in this way. Since each node and related party with access to the ledger holds the same ledger data, the hash checks can easily make the ledger data difficult to tamper with. The transaction history is stored in the ledger, and these transactions are signed by the transaction initiator, verified through some endorsement strategies, and written to the ledger after consensus.

2. Smart Contract

The smart contract describes the transaction rules and transaction processes in a multiparty collaboration. These rules and processes are deployed in the form of codes in the endorsement nodes of the relevant parties. The smart contract is executed by an internal and external event.

3. Machine Consensus

Machine consensus refers to the execution of the received transactions in the same order by each relevant node in the distributed network. These transactions are executed according to the logic represented by the smart contract, thus ultimately guaranteeing that the transaction records and results recorded in each ledger are consistent.

4. Authority Privacy
All persons, machines, objects, and institutions can join the consortium blockchain's network only if they are authorized to do so. Authority privacy guarantees proper visibility of the shared ledger, making it possible for only part of authorized persons to read and write the ledger, execute transactions, and view transaction history. At the same time, authority privacy can ensure that transactions are authentic, verifiable, traceable, nonrepudiation, and nondefeasible.

From the business perspective, the supply chain network can manage the shared processes, rules, and data more easily with the help of blockchain, as shown in Fig. 6.4, so as to step up the sharing, mutual trust, and value exchange among all participants in the supply chain network. From the legal perspective, the traceable, tamper-proof, nonrepudiation, and nonforgery transactions make people, enterprises, and things trust each

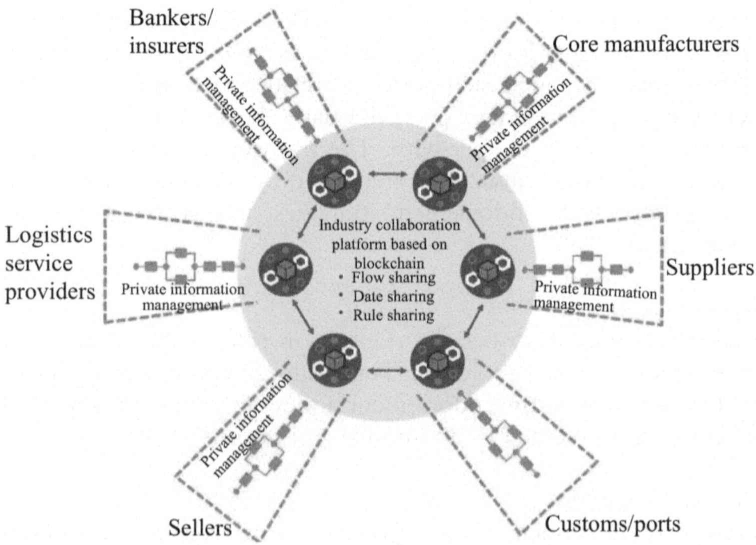

Fig. 6.4 Dual chain business network of blockchain + supply chain

other because of "connection," which will bring unprecedented organization and business model. When stepping in the blockchain as consortium nodes with review authority, regulators benefit from the visibility of relevant nodes within the consortium and can implement flexible regulation very easily. Introducing blockchain technology into the supply chain network can promote mutual trust-based sharing and value exchange within core enterprises (value chain of upstream and downstream data sharing from design, production, sales, and service to recycling) and among core enterprises (value chain based on production, operation, maintenance, and experience sharing). Trusted sharing of all kinds of related data can fully improve the design, production, service, and sales level of enterprises in the era of networked production.

Blockchain technology is mainly used in the process layer under the framework of supply chain operations. As mentioned above, the main goal of the process layer, which connects the data layer and the model layer, is to realize the electronic circulation of supply chain documents, bills, and vouchers using such technologies as blockchain. The full process of supply chain operations involves multiple participants, and the change of assets, rights in rem, and rights in goods between upstream and downstream enterprises in the supply chain as well as the traceable status of capital flow are recorded by the documents such as bills and vouchers endorsed by the credit of a large number of participants. Two major issues exist in the traditional bill management and recording model. One is how to verify the authenticity of the transaction by multiple parties; the other is how to share the data traceably and credibly such as bills generated during the transaction. As one of the effective solutions to both issues, a nonfalsifiable and consistent transaction process can be shared among participants to ensure the consistency, traceability, and verifiability of the execution status of the process and the records such as electronic bills generated on the multiparty ledger. Therefore, the multiple participants need to establish a distributed and trusted ledger in the supply chain operations. The key to trusted bill sharing and bill-based financing is the authenticity of the transaction to which the bill is related. In addition to the trusted sharing of the bill itself, the trusted sharing of the electronic bill also requires the simultaneous sharing of the execution status of the processes associated with the bill. The process, along with the related state that is traceable and verifiable by multiple parties, helps ensure the authenticity of the transactions. In addition, consistent smart contracts are used to detail each links for process execution and are executed by each participant. The results are written to their respective ledgers after consensus is reached on the contract execution results so as to ensure the consistency of the process execution status. Blockchain is a practical solution to achieve the above process. By establishing a supply chain operation network, each participant joins the network with a cryptographically verifiable identity and executes each link of the process by means of a smart contract. The bills generated in each link of the process are cryptographically signed and checked for consistency, and then written into their respective ledgers that are tamper-proof in chronological order, with an aim to ensure the verifiability of subsequent links, the legitimacy of the cryptographic signature, and the traceable causality between the process execution and the bill generated. This greatly reduces the trust cost among the participants arising from bill verification, improves the overall efficiency of process execution in the process layer, and accelerates the circulation of value.

6.4 Integrated ABCD and Intelligent Supply Chain Finance

The development of the integrated ABCD such as AI, IoT, big data, cloud computing, and blockchain has made the supply chain operations more efficient and transparent, laying a solid foundation for carrying out supply chain financial services on a large scale. Once the supply chain becomes intelligent, not only the real state of the competitiveness and operations of the supply chain can be reflected in a timely and effective manner but also the state and credit rating of each asset and each participant in the supply chain can be managed and reflected in real time, thus greatly reducing the financial lending default caused by information asymmetry. Meanwhile, the data finding, mining, and delivery functions played by the integrated ABCD directly provide a relatively perfect management environment for the corresponding supply chain financial products, which reduces the risks in financial services and taps potential opportunities for financial services. The typical application scenarios of such risk management and opportunity discovery cover the whole life cycle of supply chain financial services (see Fig. 6.5). In fact, different ICTs are used to support different stages of supply chain financial services, or different stages of supply chain finance require differentiated ICTs to support the corresponding services and decisions.

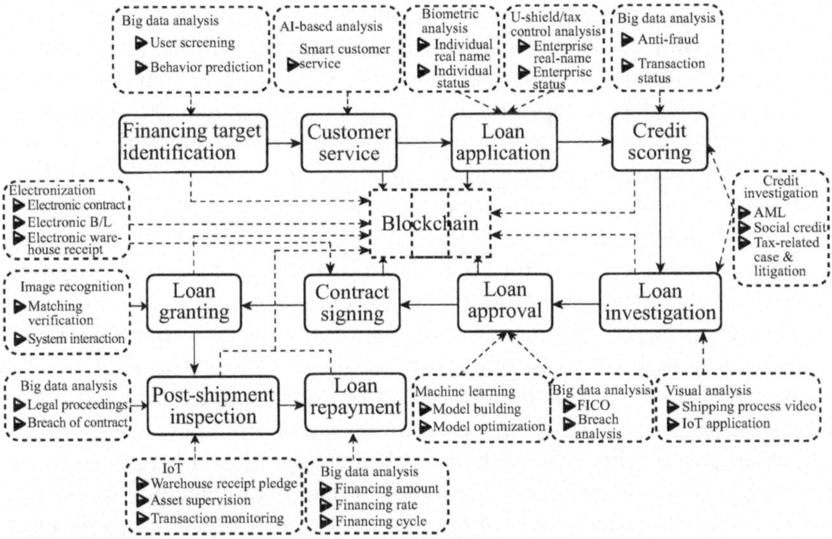

Fig. 6.5 Full cycle of supply chain finance served by the integrated ABCD

Specifically, according to the purpose of ICTs and the way they are integrated with supply chain finance activities, the integrated ABCD supports supply chain finance in three scenarios: advanced analytics of big data, smart monitoring and management, and electronic credentials and smart contracts.

6.4.1 *Advanced Analytics of Big Data and Intelligent Supply Chain Finance*

As today's world is driven by data, big data advanced analytics helps companies manage their operations faster and better, while also easing better decision-making for financial institutions to lend working capital and drive supply chain financial services. A study of IndustryARC (2018) points out that big data advanced analytics will be the most important application scenario in the supply chain sector, with the global data analysis market expected to reach US$96.06 billion by 2023, at a CAGR of 27%. Also according to Waller and Fawcett (2013), data science, predictive analysis, and big data will change the way supply chains are designed and managed. Big data in the supply chains mainly has four types: (1) Structured data mainly includes transaction data and time frame data. Nowadays, big data analysis is dominated by this type of data. However, limited by the form, this type of data still needs to be combined with more unstructured data, sensor data, and new types of data in order to improve the application value of this type data, although it can also play a role in predictive analysis itself. (2) Unstructured data mainly includes inventory data, social data, channel data, and customer service data. Based on the data classification in traditional information system, this type of data is shown as structured data, which is often used for analysis and prediction by comparing with historical data. However, the accuracy of the prediction and analysis results is relatively poor, so more unstructured inventory data needs to be incorporated for analysis to increase the accuracy. (3) Sensor data mainly includes RFID data, temperature data, QR code, and location data. The development of IoT will form new industries and build new logistics supply chains, while this type of data can bring huge business opportunities for supply chain finance. (4) New types of data mainly include map data, video data, image data, and sound data, and so on, which are often used for data visualization. These data help to further improve the quality of big data, enhance the timeliness of data, and also improve the accuracy of data analysis.

1. Data Quality in Supply Chain Finance Decision-Making

An important prerequisite for supporting supply chain finance decisions by the data acquired through the integrated ABCD is the high quality of data. Rather than effectively driving supply chain finance activities, low-quality data may increase the risk in lending funds. A study has shown that data quality problems would lead to tangible or intangible losses for companies. The usefulness of data is largely determined by its quality (Batini et al., 2015). In reality, the data on which companies base their decisions during big data analysis are often error-prone, so enterprises should highly value the quality of data when carrying out big data analysis (Hazen et al., 2014).

Despite the lack of a unified academic definition of high-quality data, there is consensus that multiple dimensions should be used in evaluating data quality (Ballou & Pazer, 1985; Wang & Strong, 1996; Cai & Zhu, 2015). Wang and Strong (1996) as well as Y.W. Lee et al. (2002) said that the evaluation of data quality should include two parts: intrinsic requirements and contextual requirements. Intrinsic requirements refer to the objective properties of the data, mainly including data accuracy, timeliness, consistency, and completeness. Contextual requirements means that the quality of data depends on the context where the data are observed and used, including relevancy, value-added, quantity (Wang & Strong, 1996), believability, accessibility, and reputation of the data (Y.W. Lee et al., 2002; Madnick et al., 2009). Decisions after the analysis of low-quality data may result in considerable losses to the enterprises, so supply chain managers who rely on big data to make decisions should pay as much attention to the quality of the data produced by the supply chain as to the quality of the products produced (Hazen et al., 2014). By giving examples of how the intrinsic requirements of data are reflected in the supply chain (see Table 6.1), Hazen et al. (2014) suggested that data should be managed for total quality.

2. Intelligent Supply Chain Finance Driven by Advanced Analytics of Big Data

Supply chain finance is a kind of management behavior and process that integrates transport flow, commodity flow, information flow, and capital flow, as well as an operation process that closely connecting sellers, buyers, third-party logistics, and financial institutions. Supply chain finance has the role of revitalizing the capital in the supply chain and stimulating the

Table 6.1 Examples of data quality evaluation in the supply chain

Evaluation aspects of data quality	*Description*	*Examples of application in the supply chain*
Accuracy	Are the data misreported?	The customer's address recorded in the CRM system should be the same as the address on his/her most recent order
Timeliness	Is the data updated in a timely manner?	Inventory levels at each retail store are accurately and timely reflected in the inventory management system
Consistency	Is the data presented in the same format?	All requested delivery dates are presented in DD/MM/YY format
Completeness	Is the required data complete?	The customer's address should include all information necessary to complete the shipment (e.g., name, street, city, country, and zip code)

Source: Hazen et al. (2014)

supply chain operations with capital (Song Hua, 2014). Since supply chain finance integrates the four flows of supply chain operations and completes the whole chain of closed operations, the impact of advanced analytics of big data on the healthy operations of supply chain finance will be more profound. The advanced analytics of high-quality big data achieved based on the integrated ABCD provides a complete solution for effective financial activities. Xiang Tingting (2013) pointed out that supply chain finance can enhance the interaction and synergy between the whole chain and third-party logistics providers and financial institutions, and make the whole transaction more visualized by introducing big data technology and using mature Internet and IT to build a platform to connect various participants in the operations of supply chain finance. In addition, it can also integrate transport flow, commodity flow, capital flow, and information flow generated from the business activities of relevant participants, and provide different online financing, settlement, investment, wealth management, and other comprehensive financial and value-added services according to the characteristics of different supply chains (Zhao et al., 2015).

More specifically, the operations of intelligent supply chain finance supported by advanced analytics of big data is characterized by the ability to profile the entity credit and transaction credit of each participant in the supply chain network in a comprehensive manner by acquiring and analyzing high-quality data and to effectively analyze and discover the destination of post-loan funds to help financial institutions efficiently locate target customers, speed up loan approval, offer appropriate financial service products, and give a digital support for risk control. Obviously, the realization of this goal requires the following capabilities for big data analysis. The first is the ability to reflect the full volume. Full volume means relationship analysis of all supply chains, not limited to a single supply chain. Usually in any supply chain network, companies have multiple downstream clients and upstream suppliers. The traditional supply chain finance model can only verify the transaction between an enterprise and the core enterprise, but this single transaction relationship does not easily reflect the overall transaction relationship and credit in the supply chain. Therefore, the new model carries out full-volume assessment of the characteristics of supply chain transactions through advanced analytics of big data. The second capability is closed loop, which means that the risk assessment based on advanced analytics of big data covers pre-loan review, mid-loan approval, and post-loan monitoring to realize the whole-process risk management. The third capability is accessibility, which means that SMEs can initiate applications and complete approvals and result feedback through a convenient portal in a simple and efficient manner.

6.4.2 *Smart Monitoring and Management and Intelligent Supply Chain Finance*

Physical assets are involved in many supply chain finance products, the most typical being inventory financing or stock financing. Inventory financing and accounts receivable financing are collectively known in the West as accounts receivable and inventory financing (ARIF), which is a commercial loan based on assets control. The combination of inventory and finance has a long history, which even dates back to the emergence of grain warehouse receipts in Mesopotamia in 2400 BC and the earliest circulating banknotes in England (which were a kind of redeemable silver mine warehouse receipts) (Chen Xiangfeng & Zhu Daoli, 2005). In the nineteenth century, with the development and maturity of the warehousing industry, logistics enterprises (in fact, most of them are warehousing enterprises) began to participate in inventory pledge business as a third party, which fundamentally changed the two-party relationship between banks and borrowing enterprises in the traditional pledge business. In the middle and late twentieth century, apart from the expanded scope of pledged goods, more crucially, the original static pledge was transformed into dynamic pledge with the participation of logistics enterprises, thus effectively supporting the operations of the enterprises. Afterward, inventory-based financing became an important form of supply chain finance (Buzacott & Zhang, 2004; Hofmann, 2009). However, among the great challenges faced by inventory or stock financing is the management of inventory or stock, that is, to ensure the real presence of physical assets. This real presence refers to not only the ability to achieve full-process seamless tracking and management of goods, real-time information of the location of assets and goods, logistics status and operation plans, and continuous real-time monitoring and collection of various environmental parameters and status data but also the ability to achieve unique correspondence and multimode consensus between physical assets and documents, form a complete mapping relationship with transaction flow, transport flow and fund flow, guarantee the authenticity of customer transaction management and assets, and ensure the true background and data of supply chain business.

The integrated ABCD allows managers to control and track the status of transactions and assets at any time and any place by acquiring asset information as well as environmental status in real-life supply chain scenarios in real time. As a result, the above objectives are achieved. Specifically speaking, IoT and AI allow chattels to autonomously and spontaneously drive the process of the supply chain business, while the multimode consensus verification performed offline ensures the authenticity of offline operations execution. Each link of the supply chain has a tamper-proof ledger consisting of electronic credentials and data of smart contract execution results. The integrated ABCD is an overall monitoring and management solution for supply chain assets and business management, of which three links, that is, scenario-based multimode consensus verification, confirmation of offline execution of smart contracts, and electronic credentials and ledger records, are the core of the technology implementation.

Based on key technologies in above three links, the effective development and application of supply chain finance is realized (see Fig. 6.6). The offline sensing technology confirms the authenticity of the business background of the supply chain and guarantees the credibility of the data source. While ensuring the transparency of supply chain information, data encryption storage and access authorization and audit can also guarantee that the key data of the enterprise will not be leaked to unauthorized parties in the supply chain. The platform of supply chain financial services conducts trade profiling of the entire supply chain process. In addition to offering innovative financial services to customers, on the one hand, it offers data authorization on demand to realize the closed loop of information, and, on the other hand, it monitors the flow of funds to realize the closed loop of funds. Moreover, the technical service platform can connect to other financial service platforms or application software systems, such as to the exchange system for bond financing plan and information disclosure, or to the financial institution system for providing underlying assets penetration management support to factoring/reverse factoring and virtual accounts, providing real and credible transaction background support and providing ABS support for supply chain finance. Enterprises announce their financing needs by listing their assets on the platform, and financial institutions select those assets on the platform. Following the two-way selection, both parties complete the financing transaction on the platform. The platform can also be connected with nonbank financial institutions, which greatly enriches the external financing channels of enterprises. The

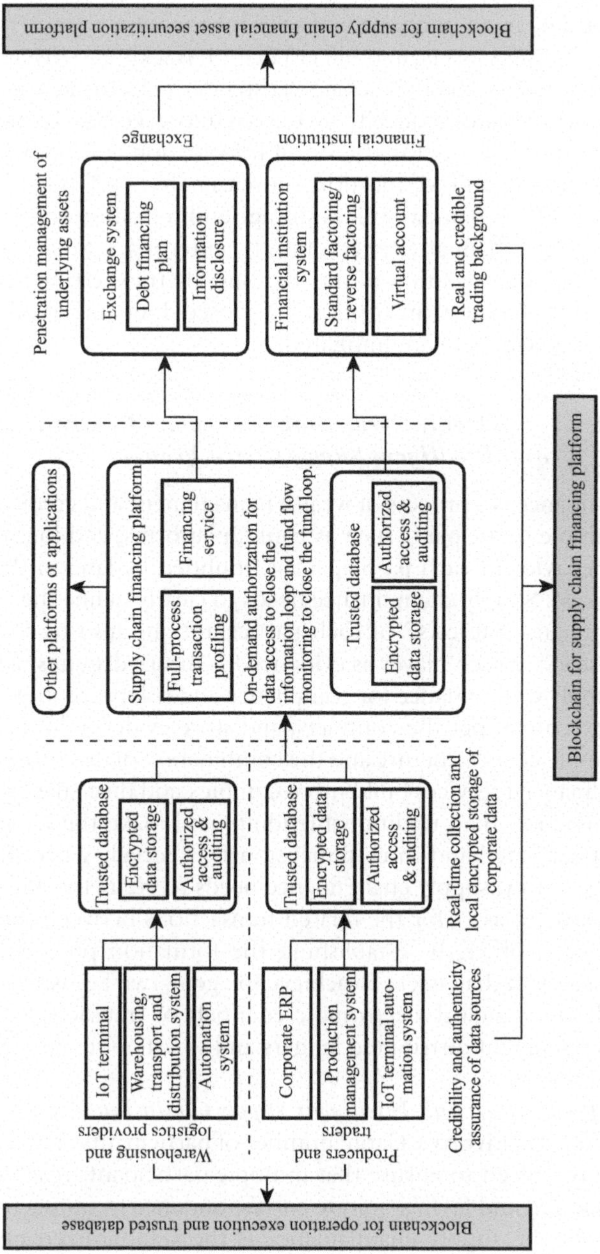

Fig. 6.6 Intelligent supply chain finance based on smart monitoring and management

whole-process data from purchase and sales information release, real-time monitoring of logistics assets, and bill circulation tracking to instant settlement is all recorded on the blockchain via standard electronic credentials, and such records are automatically processed and executed by the smart contracts. The problem of closed loop of information and trust is solved by offline execution and verification, nonfalsifiable and traceable data recorded on the blockchain, as well as storage and transmission of business data using the blockchain after encryption by enterprises. Smart contracts ensure the automatic execution of transactions. By transferring trade payments directly to financial institutions, a closed loop of credit loan is achieved and financial risks are mitigated.

6.4.3 Electronic Credentials and Smart Contracts and Intelligent Supply Chain Finance

Supply chain finance is a process of wealth management and credit creation involving multiple participants such as banks, platforms, and logistics providers. The behavior of each participant is bounded by laws in the whole financing process. Supply chain finance needs to clearly define the "responsibilities, rights and interests" of each participant and also to record the behavioral history of each player as evidence for future disputes. The basic strategy of supply chain finance for compliance and risk prevention is to act as per laws, execute as per the contracts, and store evidence in time. With the unique supply chain structure and the combination of inventory pledge, supply chain financial services build more complex and diversified scenarios for assets transaction than traditional lending, and make the credit structure more sophisticated and three-dimensional. Especially when the credit of participants is risky, supply chain finance needs to verify the authenticity and legitimacy of an asset for the related transactions between nodes that do not trust each other, by establishing the formation process and the transaction history of that asset. To achieve the goal, two key issues need to be addressed: (1) standard electronic credentials of transaction assets or activities; (2) intelligent distributed ledgers and smart contracts.

1. Electronic Credentials and Intelligent Supply Chain Finance

Supply chain finance involves a large number of participants. The first issue that needs to be solved to ensure that multiple participants reach consensus on a transaction and form a unique correspondence to transacted assets and activities in the supply chain finance is the standardized electronic credentials of transacted assets and activities, which is the basis for forming a consensus. This problem includes how to transform the transaction documents, warehouse receipts, and bills of lading in supply chain operations into standardized electronic credentials. Three progressive elements are covered: (1) the objects of supply chain operations, for example transactions, assets, chattels, and so on; (2) the credentials, that is, the form of contract formed in accordance with the commercial management and prescribed elements for securing transactions or assets; (3) electronization, that is, allowing multiple participants to manage the electronic contracts collaboratively and securely for the purpose of generating a management environment for efficient circulation.

Taking electronic warehouse receipts as an example, they correspond to inbound assets or products in supply chain operations, and such assets or products are objects in physical form. A warehouse receipt is a contract with legal effect formed in a recognized form for the abovementioned objects. According to the GB/T30332-2013 *Warehouse Receipt Fundamental Element and Form*, warehouse receipt is defined as a right certificate issued by the warehousing custodian in accordance with industry practice and the general principle of surface examination and appearance inspection over warehoused goods delivered by the depositor on the basis of the warehousing contract signed between them. From the fundamental elements of warehouse receipts, warehouse receipts must record the necessary elements to be valid in a legal sense. Article 386 of the *Contract Law of the People's Republic of China* provides that the warehouse receipt shall contain the following eight items: name and residence of the depositor; species, quantity, quality, packaging, number of pieces, and markings of warehoused goods; loss standards of warehoused goods; warehousing place; warehousing period; warehousing fees; insurance amount, period, and name of the insurer (if any); issuer, place of issuing, and date of issuing. The Supreme People's Court promulgated the *Interpretation on the Application of Laws in the Trial of Warehousing Contract Dispute Cases*, which stipulates in paragraph 5 that the warehouse receipts lacking the absolutely necessary items (such as name of depositor, species, and quantity of warehoused goods, warehousing place, and issuer) are invalid. This element characteristics make warehouse receipts become causeless credentials, which means that anyone can exercise the right in rem with the warehouse receipt alone, no other reasons and evidence are needed. Obviously, in addition to the warehouses, warehouse receipt services are also supported by the high level of operational processes, highly qualified operators and reliable risk management tools. The difference between chattels and warehouse receipts is shown in Table 6.2 (Yang Qinhe, 2019).

In addition to the change from chattels into standardized warehouse receipts with legal effect, another important change is electronization.

Table 6.2 Difference between chattels and warehouse receipts

No.	*Element*	*Chattels*	*Warehouse receipts*
1	Circulation method	Assignment, mortgage, pledge in physical form	Assignment and pledge by endorsement
2	Possession transfer method	Delivery	Delivery or endorsement and delivery
3	Pricing mechanism	The diversity of locations, delivery methods, acceptance methods, transaction units, and sizes of goods makes standardized pricing impossible. Per-order bargaining makes it difficult to develop fair prices	The elements of warehouse receipts that include the location of the goods, the delivery method, the acceptance method, and the unit and size of the transaction are formed in accordance with industry standards or practices, and therefore all the conditions for standardized fair pricing based on the payment method and wholesale size are in place, which leads to the location of issuing warehouse receipt easily becoming a pricing center
4	Circulation efficiency	Both parties to the transaction negotiate over the order of payment and delivery, the place of delivery, the method of acceptance, and the delivery procedures prior to each circulation. The goods shall be delivered several times from the producer to the final consumer at different delivery locations. Traditional, inefficient, and high-risk	The warehousing location, acceptance method, and payment agency are all recognized by all parties to the transaction, so the payment of one hand to deliver the warehouse receipt and the other hand to deliver the check (or letter of credit) can be achieved. The same warehouse receipt can be quickly delivered and changed hands many times by written endorsement only, and the efficiency is several times that of chattel

(*continued*)

Table 6.2 (continued)

No.	*Element*	*Chattels*	*Warehouse receipts*
5	Circulation costs	Acceptance and delivery of goods are required for each circulation, which consumes manpower and material resources and causes wear and tear at the same time	Only verification of warehouse receipts is required, allowing for single delivery and multiple circulations by endorsement
6	Credit basis	Seller's credit + buyer's credit (or additional credit from an independent warehousing provider)	Credit of an independent warehousing provider
7	Internationalization	Dependence on the construction and application of international standards for the goods themselves results in large differences among goods	China, the U.S., European countries, former colonial Asian, African, and Latin American countries have different legal basis for warehouse receipts and business practices, resulting in different levels of warehouse receipts business

Paper warehouse receipts have problems in forgery, alteration, and verification, and are not fast enough to circulate. Relying on technical development and legal support, electronic warehouse receipts can be generated, stored. and transmitted online. Most importantly, due to the basic commercial system as well as legislative and judicial basis of warehouse receipts, the issuers of electronic warehouse receipts that take legal possession of the goods can easily support the holders of electronic warehouse receipts to redeem the physical goods, get judicial and commercial protection from various countries, which is conducive to the full realization of online delivery of goods. The difference between paper warehouse receipts and electronic warehouse receipts is shown in Table 6.3 (Yang Qinhe, 2019).

The standard electronic credentials for supply chain transactions and assets greatly promote the development of supply chain finance, which is reflected in the cost reduction and efficiency improvement of carrying out supply chain transactions and chattel financing on the one hand and the transparency and security of supply chain financial activities on the other hand. For example, the development of standard electronic warehouse

Table 6.3 Difference between paper warehouse receipts and electronic warehouse receipts

No.	*Element*	*Paper warehouse receipt*	*Electronic warehouse receipt*
1	Media	Paper	Electronic media
2	Possession transfer method	Delivery or endorsement and delivery	Endorsement, transfer control, announcement/registration
3	Storage method	Traditionally, it is usually kept by a dedicated person and stored in a safe or locked cabinet managed by a specific department or person	It is stored on electronic media. Account password or digital certificate is required to obtain control and management rights
4	Verification method	Verify it in person at the warehouse or by phone or fax based on the seal and signature on the warehouse receipt	Verify it through digital signature and time stamp on the electronic warehouse receipt
5	Internal process	Time-consuming internal process. High probability of human error due to the use of manual calculations, multiple transmissions, and multiple summary calculations. Higher reliance on the competence and ethical level of the on-site personnel on duty. High possibility of cheating. Complexity and high cost of auditing	Set permissions in advance to shorten the online audit time. Add IoT-based automatic reading, counting and calculation, and technical verification. Lower reliance on the ability and moral level of the on-site personnel on duty. Lower possibility of error and cheating
6	Transmission	Slow transmission; high possibility of artificial alteration; large verification costs; no effective verification methods, more dependent on visual inspection and experience	Transmission through encrypted network, greatly reducing the transmission time; the generated warehouse receipts cannot be changed; artificial alteration is easy to find; verification based on password, reliable and convenient

(*continued*)

Table 6.3 (continued)

No.	*Element*	*Paper warehouse receipt*	*Electronic warehouse receipt*
7	Credit sources	Rely on the long-term accumulation of the warehouse itself	Warehouse's credit + independent third-party certification agency and professional commercial insurance
8	Sources and types of evidence	The holder provides the original warehouse receipt, warehousing contract, reserved traditional seal	A third-party depository and certification authority provides online depository evidences (including identity information, operation information, video information, warehouse receipt information, digital certificate information, etc.) and reserves corporate e-certificate and authorized personnel e-certificate
9	Legal basis	*Contract Law, Property Law, Security Law of the People's Republic of China* (some countries have *Warehouse Receipt Law* or *Personal Property Security Acts, Uniform Commercial Code*)	Electronic Signature Law, *Contract Law, Property Law, Security Law, UNCITRAL Model Law on Electronic Commerce*

receipts has prompted the shift of supply chain financial products from traditional chattel pledge to standard warehouse receipt pledge, which has resulted in significant changes in terms of pledges, elements of validity, public notice, specificity, operational process, circulation, rights and responsibilities, bona fide opposition, default disposal, and service conditions and levels (see Table 6.4). As judged from the above, electronic credentials are a basic tool for realizing intelligent supply chain finance, which promotes the standardization of transacted objects and the circulation and identification of those objects among multiple supply chain participants and regions, and strengthens the uniform, timely, and effective management of transaction activities and assets.

2. Distributed Ledgers/Smart Contracts and Intelligent Supply Chain Finance

Besides electronic credentials, the efficiency, fairness, and security of networked supply chain transactions require a technology that can arrange

Table 6.4 Difference between chattel pledge and electronic warehouse receipt pledge

No.	*Element*	*Chattel pledge*	*Electronic warehouse receipt pledge*	*Notes*
1	Pledges	Goods	Electronic warehouse receipts	The former uses chattels (i.e., goods) as pledges; the latter uses rights (i.e., warehouse receipts issued by the custodian after the goods are deposited in the warehouse) as pledges
2	Validity elements	Possession after transfer	Delivery by endorsement	In the former case, the goods are delivered to the pledgee (bank, etc.) for possession. Since most pledgees do not have the ability to take direct custody of the goods, but need to entrust a third-party supervisory company to take possession on their behalf, the facilities and costs for exclusively securing physical possession are higher. There is no simple and uniform sign of effective possession, and multiple evidences are required, such as all evidences in import, export, and deposit software. This poses greater difficulties and costs for the pledgee to prove. The pledgee is often found by the court to fail to validate the pledge due to incomplete evidence. In the latter case, the right to take delivery of the goods is transferred to the pledge by endorsement, bringing the electronic warehouse receipt under the control of the pledgee. Since its delivery and possession are most convenient, the warehouse receipt becomes the simplest and least costly mode to validate the pledge

(*continued*)

Table 6.4 (continued)

No.	*Element*	*Chattel pledge*	*Electronic warehouse receipt pledge*	*Notes*
3	Public notice	Possession after transfer	Delivery and registration	In the former case, public notice is given in the form of transfer and possession, but its public notice effect is actually weakened because most pledgees entrust a third-party supervisory company to take possession on their behalf. Only the principled public notice is made, and it is difficult to make specific public notice. In the latter case, the electronic warehouse receipts are under the control of the pledgee after endorsement, while the pledgee can also make the exact registration on the website www.zhongdengwang.org.cn or other platforms shared by the property owners if needed
4	Specificity	Unable or difficult to realize specificity	Able and easy to realize specificity	Most of the former are dynamic pledges and floating charges. Dynamic approval of inventory makes it difficult to specify the correspondence between specific goods and the owner at a certain point of time. Accordingly, the impossibility or difficulty in specificity leads to the registration of chattel pledges in substance difficult to set out the public goods, resulting in a substantial reduction in the role of public notice. The latter warehouse receipts detail the goods specification, brand, quantity, warehousing place, and other elements. Warehouse receipts are clearly numbered and managed; even the dynamic pledge can ensure that every single receipt corresponds to the goods and the holder's ownership

(*continued*)

Table 6.4 (continued)

No.	*Element*	*Chattel pledge*	*Electronic warehouse receipt pledge*	*Notes*
5	Operation process	Cumbersome	Simple and convenient	In the former case, a single business involves check and review notice, notice of price/adjustment of supervisory objects, notice of minimum limit, notice of pickup; output supervision method also requires a series of written materials such as consent to sublease letter, four books, three sheets, two forms, one chart, and inbound/outbound record book. After being confirmed and stamped by three parties, the order is delivered manually. The process of chattel pledge is numerous, tedious, and prone to errors. In the latter case, because it is a pledge of rights, the pledgee need not engage too much in the detailed process such as the custody of the goods under the warehouse receipt. The warehousing enterprise, as the custodian, performs the responsibility of sight payment. The change of warehouse receipt data and endorsement can be executed by giving instructions to the supporting warehouse receipt system

(*continued*)

Table 6.4 (continued)

No.	*Element*	*Chattel pledge*	*Electronic warehouse receipt pledge*	*Notes*
6	Circulation	Slow and high cost	Fast and low cost	The former is physical delivery and requires inspection and delivery of goods one by one during the circulation of goods. Each transaction incurs costs of inspection, point delivery, handling, and inbound/outbound storage. The latter is the circulation of warehouse receipts. Standardized and electronic warehouse receipts can become high-quality documentary assets in rem after certified underwriting. After a receipt and production of warehouse receipts, they can be circulated via endorsement for many times quickly. The transaction cost is much lower than the physical transaction and the transaction speed is more than ten times of the physical transaction

(*continued*)

Table 6.4 (continued)

No.	*Element*	*Chattel pledge*	*Electronic warehouse receipt pledge*	*Notes*
7	Rights and responsibilities	Complex	Clear and simple	The former pledge supervision agreement has individualized articles, and its recessive articles often infringe or fail to protect the legitimate rights and interests of the pledgee, or prevent the pledgee from having substantial control or possession of the rights in rem. The service mode is also based on non-standardized agreement. The latter has clear and explicit rights and responsibilities in law. As the warehouse receipt is a causeless instrument, the warehouse receipt service providers make sight payments to the warehouse receipt holders. If the goods in line with the recorded specifications, both parties can fully standardize the service criteria and legal rights and responsibilities after fulfilling the rights and responsibilities of the warehousing contract such as delivery in accordance with the specified quality and quantity, as well as the additional global standards of warehouse receipts

(*continued*)

Table 6.4 (continued)

No.	*Element*	*Chattel pledge*	*Electronic warehouse receipt pledge*	*Notes*
8	Bona fide opposition	Weak	Strong	In the former case, the pledgor delivers the physical goods to the pledgee. However, the pledgee's failure to take direct possession and custody of the goods as well as the unspecified inbound/outbound of the goods results in the pledgee having minimal control over the goods, thus exposing the risks. When a third-party dispute appears, judicial protection and priority of payment are not available from time to time due to the inability to prove the specific pledge relationship or the existence of defective rights. In the latter case, the warehouse receipt details the elements of goods. After endorsement and confirmation of the right, a convenient channel for public notice and warehouse receipt status inquiry is set up to fight against general claims as well as unregistered or post-registered mortgages. In addition, continuous warehouse receipt credit and ownership segregation or warehouse receipt holding and other operations can further protect the rights and interests of the pledgee or holder

(*continued*)

Table 6.4 (continued)

No.	*Element*	*Chattel pledge*	*Electronic warehouse receipt pledge*	*Notes*
9	Default disposal	Court proceedings, arbitration, and so on	Priority is given to commercial liquidation	In the former case, customer defaults are generally resolved through court proceedings, which are time-consuming and subject to various uncertainties or risks, and can seriously infringe on the actual interests of the pledgee. Chattel pledge nominally does not prohibit a negotiated liquidation, but because the pledgee often does not have substantial control, resulting in the pledgor having the upper hand and making it difficult to execute negotiated liquidation. In the latter case, as the control of assets under warehouse receipts is isolated from the pledgor, both parties control the goods through independent warehouse receipt service providers, allowing the preferred method of non-contentious negotiation. After a customer defaults, quick liquidation and payment can be realized through a third-party liquidation agency selected in advance. The convenient circulation of warehouse receipts is helpful for commercial disposal

(*continued*)

Table 6.4 (continued)

No.	*Element*	*Chattel pledge*	*Electronic warehouse receipt pledge*	*Notes*
10	Service conditions and level	Relatively low	Relatively high	The former applies to lower logistics infrastructure and lower levels of warehousing services. It is adopted as a last resort when the third party's logistics capacity is weak, so the financial institution is subject to higher risks accordingly. The latter can be advantageous only under the condition that the regional third-party public warehousing facilities are more popular, the security of the facilities is higher, and the warehousing company's warehouse receipt service capability is standardized

distributed ledgers based on the structure of participating nodes. In this way, data is no longer maintained by a single centralized institution, and agreements reached between multiple participants are nonfalsifiable, so that nodes cannot tamper with data according to the principles that benefit them. Ultimately, the asset transactions and transfers involved in the core functions of financing are automatically executed by machines when the relevant conditions are met, avoiding delays and moral risks caused by manual execution. This is also where blockchain plays a key role. Specifically, the roles played by blockchain have the following effects in promoting the development of supply chain finance:

First is the proof of credible data and real transactions. Based on the combination of blockchain, IoT, Internet, and supply chain scenario, all kinds of information and data can be obtained from the transaction network in real time. After the data of multiple participants are put into the chain, their authenticity and credibility are further guaranteed. On the one hand, these data are tamper-proof, noncopyable or traceable thanks to the technical characteristics of blockchain; on the other hand, the cross-verification of the multidimensional data (e.g., the matching of procurement data and logistics data, the cross-verification of inventory data and sales data, and the cross-checking of core enterprise data and downstream enterprise data) improves the validity and reliability of data and reduces the process conflicts caused by information asymmetry.

Second is the confirmation of rights in transactions. Through the automatic confirmation of the rights of chattels of each participant in the supply chain and the formation of nonfalsifiable rights ledgers, the existing difficulties in rights registration and rights realization are solved. Taking the rights of accounts receivable as an example, the docking with connects the ERP systems of core enterprises based on blockchain can realize real-time digital confirmation of rights, avoiding the delay of confirmation of rights in reality.

Third is smart contract. This is an automated operation tool for supply chain finance business execution, guaranteeing the automatic and mandatory transfer of goods, cargo rights, funds, and creditor's rights when conditions are met, guaranteeing the execution of other responsibilities and obligations stipulated in the contracts, addressing the low efficiency and high costs associated with manual operations, and solving the blockage (unwillingness to cooperate) and risks (losses caused by unintentional or intentional wrong operations) in manual operations.

Fourth is credit splitting. Supply chain finance aims to make financing cover all SMEs, but at present, the financing needs of a large number of second-tier and third-tier suppliers/dealers, and so on are still difficult to be met. For example, an auto manufacturer has more than 100,000 suppliers, but only 100 first-tier suppliers. The 100,000-plus downstream suppliers can hardly enjoy supply chain financial services. Supply chain finance only partially alleviates the issues of inconvenience and high costs of financing for SMEs. Blockchain uses tokens (equivalent to credits endorsed by the core enterprise) to split the credits of the core enterprise and pass it down tier by tier, so that the credits can penetrate the whole chain and cover the suppliers at each tier. The downstream suppliers who get the tokens can prove that they have cooperation with the core enterprise and can finance with the token.

In essence, this technology clearly creates an open, transparent, and tamper-proof mechanism that curbs human frailty (opportunism and moral hazard), fostering a fair, objective, and liable trading environment. The mechanism places multiple collaborating institutions in a context of mutual supervision, so that private collusion usually seen in the traditional model does not occur. Under this open and transparent mechanism, institutions that are trustworthy gain the consensus of participants. In continuous transactions, the authenticity of transactions and assets do not need to be repeatedly verified. The cross-verification of transactions generates "credit self-evidence" and "credit self-enhancement," which is not possible with traditional credit technology and transaction models.

6.5 Supply Chain Finance Based on Advanced Analytics of Big Data: CAINIAO and VZOOM

6.5.1 CAINIAO's Advance Payment Financing Based on Advanced Analytics

Cainiao Network Technology Co., Ltd. (hereinafter referred to as "CAINIAO") was founded in May 2013 by Alibaba Group in cooperation with Yintai Group, Fosun Group, Forchn Holding Group, STO Express, YTO Express, ZTO Express, and Yunda Express. CAINIAO aspires to be an innovative Internet technology enterprise based on Internet mindsets and technologies. Its vision is to build a data-driven logistics and supply chain platform based on social collaboration, provide open, shared, and socialized logistics infrastructure services, and strive to achieve the goal of 24-hour delivery within China and 72-hour delivery worldwide. Since its inception, CAINIAO has taken data as the core to open up the full-scale logistics chain involving cross-border transport, express delivery, warehouse-based distribution, and terminal delivery through social collaboration. By offering products connected with, empowered by or based on big data, and providing one-stop services such as integrated solutions of warehousing and distribution and cross-border worry-free logistics solutions, CAINIAO allows small and medium-sized merchants to focus on production, marketing, and operations, and helps logistics partners to improve service level, thus promoting cost reduction and efficiency, transformation, and innovation in the whole industry.

Currently, CAINIAO has joined hands with its partners to form the largest logistics ecosystem in China. CAINIAO runs a data system covering 70% of Chinese e-commerce parcel data, cooperates with 15 express companies accounting for over 90% of the national e-commerce express market share, works with more than 2 million express and warehousing-related employees, and provides cross-border logistics services covering

224 countries and regions in the world. In May 2016, CAINIAO set up the Supply Chain Finance Division specializing in providing logistics supply chain financial services. In September 2016, its official website of supply chain finance was launched for providing a complete supply chain + financing solution for merchants and logistics partners on e-commerce platforms, with products including inventory financing, advance payment financing, accounts receivable factoring, equipment financing, vehicle financing, and so on. As of March 30, 2017, nearly RMB 1.5 billion of loans were issued in total, and financing services were provided to 300 customers.

6.5.1.1 Case Background of CAINIAO's Advance Payment Financing

A branded appliance manufacturer (hereinafter referred to as "Manufacturer A") is a global technology group spanning consuming appliances, HVAC, robotics, and automatic systems, with sales of RMB 100 billion and net profits of RMB 10 billion in 2016, making it one of the largest and most complete appliance manufacturers in the world. Considering that the upstream supplier's raw material prices continue to pull up, Manufacturer A decided to increase the ex-factory price of its products from April 1, 2017.

An e-commerce company based in Shanghai (hereinafter referred to as "Company B") was established in 2013 and operates an official flagship store of a brand of microwave ovens in Tmall, with annual sales amounting to hundreds of millions of yuan, gross margin of 15%, and daily DIH of about 20 days. During the promotion festivals ("618" and "Double 11"), Company B purchased and stocked up a large amount of goods for business needs, resulting in a DIH of more than 40 days, and the financial pressure became obvious. In mid-March 2017, after being informed of an upcoming price adjustment by Manufacturer A, Company B needed to complete a purchase of RMB 18 million before Manufacturer A raised prices, in order to maintain its profits. But it lacked sufficient working capital. Traditional financial institutions could not meet Company B's urgent needs for money due to the long credit approval cycle.

Considering the imminent price increase of Manufacturer A, it became a problem to meet Company B's demand for funds for this purchase under the premise that its credit line of the existing inventory financing was basically exhausted. CAINIAO supply chain finance department, after thorough research and communication as well as analysis of Company B's operation data on Tmall, decided to provide the advance payment financing to Company B, which means that merchants can apply for short-term advance payment financing for purchasing funds to CINIAO supply chain finance platform based on the purchase and sales contracts signed with upstream manufacturers. The advance payment financing has the following features:

1. Higher credit line and earlier use of money. The credit line of advance payment financing is calculated based on a comprehensive assessment of the merchant's historical transaction data and overall business conditions, up to a maximum of RMB 30 million. The funds can be applied for as long as the merchant has reached a purchase agreement with an upstream manufacturer. The funds are designated for payment of goods under the order. Interest is charged on a daily basis and is repayable at any time.
2. Online operation with efficiency and convenience. CAONIAO realized the whole-process online operation of advance payment financing by relying on its order management system (BMS) and supply chain finance system (SCF). Procurement and financing are completed in one stop. After financing, merchants can continue to operate online processes such as product shipment and warehouse booking.
3. Safe and reliable financing base on confirmation by both parties. The manufacturers and merchants log into the system with different identities. Posting of goods and purchases are subject to review and confirmation by both parties to ensure the authenticity, validity, and compliance of orders and to avoid the risk of abnormal financing due to false orders initiated by either party.

6.5.1.2 *Implementation Process of CAINIAO's Advance Payment Financing*

The implementation process of CAINIAO's advance payment financing can be divided into four phases as below:

1. Business negotiation. Manufacturer A is a strategic partner of Alibaba Group and maintains good interaction and communication with both Tmall and CAINIAO. CAINIAO's supply chain finance business staff learned from their daily communication with Manufacturer A that it was planning to lift prices in April, and Company B was suffering from a lack of liquidity to complete its

purchase before the price increase. CAINIAO's supply chain finance business staff took the opportunity to introduce the "advance payment financing" to both Manufacturer A and Company B. CAINIAO proposed that Manufacturer A would only assume the responsibility of shipping the goods into the warehouse (i.e., guaranteeing the complete delivery of the goods under the order to CAINIAO's designated warehouse within the agreed time frame), but would not be required to provide repurchase guarantee. The parties agreed that March 30 would be the loan release date, and the subsequent process would be arranged based on this point.

2. Agreement conclusion. Given that four parties were involved in this cooperation (CAINIAO supply chain finance department, MYbank, Manufacturer A, and Company B), the legal, business, and risk control teams of all four parties participated in drafting the terms and conditions of the agreement. CAINIAO supply chain finance department assumed the responsibility of leading, communicating, coordinating, and integrating the demands of all parties on the basis of the original standard agreement. On March 29, the four-party agreement was officially signed.
3. Online operations. First, Manufacturer A published the goods information of this purchase in CAONIAO's BMS system and submitted it to MYbank for review. Upon approval, Company B initiated a purchase order in a total amount of RMB 18 million. After the purchase order was confirmed by Manufacturer A, the final credit review was done by MYbank, with a credit line of RMB 12 million (not exceeding 70% of the order price), which was displayed in the interface of Company B's SCF system in real time. Afterward, Company B applied to withdraw the funds. With the online signing of the *Loan Contract* and the *Maximum Pledge Contract*, the loan funds entered the escrow account opened by Company B in MYbank three minutes after the application for withdrawal and were transferred to the designated account of Manufacturer A instantly. At the same time, Company B transferred the self-paid amount (the remaining 30% of the order price) to the account of Manufacturer A. The online operation process was completed when Manufacturer A confirmed the receipt of money.
4. Shipping goods into the warehouse. After confirming the receipt of money, Manufacturer A started to prepare for shipment. At this point, Company B operated CAINIAO' BMS system again to book

a date for warehouse entry. Once the booking was done, the goods sent out by Manufacturer A would enter CAINIAO's warehouse for pledge supervision. Later on, as Company B continues to sell goods, the proceeds of sales could be used to repay the loan.

The basic process of CAINIAO advance payment financing is shown in Fig. 6.7.

6.5.1.3 Results of CAINIAO Advance Payment Financing

CAINIAO advance payment financing helped Company B solve its needs for a large amount of purchasing funds, and also allowed Manufacturer A to recover its money in advance, improving both DIH and DSO. Generally speaking, its supply chain financial products are characterized by the following:

1. Full-chain connection of information. Relying on CAINIAO's self-developed BMS system and SCF system, merchants and upstream manufacturers can complete the complex and scattered links such as publishing goods, placing purchase orders, applying for loans, settlement and payment, warehousing and distribution in one stop. After the advance payment financing expires, they can also apply for inventory financing. Theoretically, the financing period may be

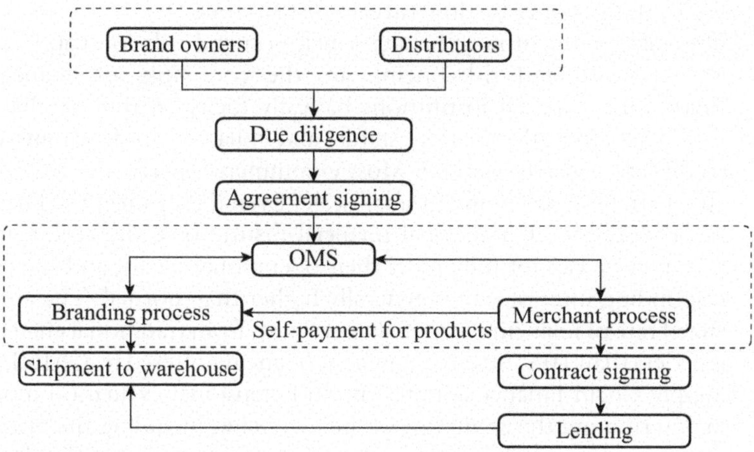

Fig. 6.7 Basic flow of CAINIAO advance payment financing

extended to nine months. Moreover, thanks to the natural symbiotic relationship between BMS system and SCF system, all the above links can be completed seamlessly and data can be pushed instantly and accurately. In the future, CAINIAO Supply Chain Finance also plans to use Aliyun's powerful cloud computing capability to integrate and analyze the data accumulated in the systems to form standardized data products and provide advice to merchants and manufacturers on strategic layout, business forecasting, resource allocation, and so on.

2. Win-win situation for upstream and downstream parties. The traditional advance payment financing products rely heavily on the core enterprises (i.e., upstream manufacturers), by basically transferring the credit risk of the merchants to the manufacturers. Therefore, the manufacturers need to provide strong guarantees for financing, such as repurchases, adjusted sales. These financing products are often difficult to promote on a large scale due to the greater risk borne by the manufacturers. Advance payment financing provided by CAINIAO Supply Chain Finance is based on CAINIAO's strong and controllable warehousing and supervision capabilities that can effectively control and dispose of the pledges by virtue of real-time monitoring of sales data on Alibaba's e-commerce platform. As a result, the operational and liability requirements for the manufacturers are greatly simplified and reduced, which spurs the widespread use of this product by downstream distributors.
3. Organic combination of financial inclusion and risk control. Credit line approval and risk pricing are the core links of financing. Traditional financial institutions basically focus on the merchant's own asset strength, financial status, and collateral to determine the credit line and interest rate. Most e-commerce merchants are operated with light assets and in small scale. Even if they meet the financing thresholds of traditional financial institutions, the credit lines they receive cannot fully meet their operational needs, and the corresponding interest rate is generally higher than normal. The annualized rate of financing for Tmall merchants from traditional channels is no less than 10%. Advance payment financing offered by CAINIAO Supply Chain Finance adopts a multidimensional evaluation model in determining the credit line of the merchant, including the historical transaction and logistics data of the merchant in Tmall and CAINIAO platform, the historical sales price of the purchased goods

in Tmall, and the credit performance records of the merchant. Meanwhile, the order itself is also one of the options for multidimensional evaluation. The merchant's assets, financial indicators and collateral are given significantly less, or even zero weight in the evaluation model. Risk pricing is also strictly based on the findings of the evaluation model, and is tiered according to the principle of "matching risks and returns."

6.5.2 VZOOM's Advanced Analytics for Supporting Supply Chain Financial Services

Shenzhen Vzoom Creditech Co., Ltd. (hereinafter referred to as "VZOOM") was established in 2014, headquartered in Shenzhen, with 18 branches in Beijing, Shanghai, Shandong, Jiangsu, Guangdong, and other regions. Its shareholders include state-owned enterprises, capital institutions, financial institutions, and so on. Since its establishment, VZOOM has established public platforms for tax and banking services in more than 20 provinces and cities in China, providing supply chain financial services for 20 million SMEs. Meanwhile, VZOOM has joined hands with tax bureaus and banks to create the first platform for fully automated approval of online financing based on enterprise credit, which promotes technological innovation in banking finance and provides SMEs with a fast and convenient financing channel. The overall strategy of VZOOM is to evaluate the overall credit of the enterprises through tax-related data (i.e., corporate credit scoring), develop a transaction-based credit model to evaluate the credit of supply chain transactions, jointly build an approval decision engine, and use invoice data to analyze the use and direction of loans. The overall business logic is as discussed in the following.

6.5.2.1 Data Basis

The core of this model is the tax data of enterprises. Given that tax collection, invoicing, and certification and other tax-related behaviors run through the entire life cycle of an enterprise, the tax data generated covers basic information, declaration and collection information, tax payment information, tax credit rating, supply chain information, and financial information of the enterprise. These data are strongly related to the enterprise's operations, which are both rich and objective, and therefore are the core basis for developing enterprise credit scoring model.

6.5.2.2 Establishing Enterprise Credit Scoring Model: Corporate Credit Scoring

Tax-related data are used to develop a corporate credit scoring model to classify customer risk levels. This new credit scoring model can be organically combined with the internal customer credit rating approaches usually adopted by commercial banks, or with some qualitative and quantitative indicators therein, in a bid to enhance the explanatory capacity of the model and make the model outputs more closely align with the bank's original risk appetite.

In the process of constructing independent variables for this credit scoring model, two principles are followed: first, deep understanding of the business meaning of tax-related data and scientific construction of indicators combined with expert experience; second, the principle of streamlining variables. The more independent variables are not necessarily betterl; the model just needs to determine the strong relevant variables by suitable methods.

Currently, the credit scoring model for micro and small enterprises in VZOOM interactive business has found some concise and explanatory independent variables with strong predictive power. Some examples of indicators are shown in Table 6.5.

Table 6.5 VZOOM evaluation indicators

Serial no.	*Indicator name*	
I. Interim report information		
1	Revenue growth for the last 6 months	U-shaped relationship with the probability of default
2	Dispersion coefficient of revenue for the last 12 months	Positive relationship with the probability of default
3	Total revenue for the last 12 months	Negative relationship with the probability of default
II. Certificate information		
4	Number of overdue payments for the last 12 months	Positive relationship with the probability of default
III. Supply chain indicators		
5	Percentage of overlapped purchases of top 10 upstream suppliers	Negative relationship with the probability of default
6	Number of overlapped downstream dealers	Negative relationship with the probability of default
7	...	

Bank risk modelers can use all the bank's data resources to create good and bad samples and combine expert experience and bank credit policies to boost the development of a tax data-based credit scoring model for the primary activities of supply chain finance, namely overall corporate risk assessment.

6.5.2.3 Credit Assessment Based on Supply Chain Relational Transactions

The results of transaction credit assessment can be used to screen out qualified downstream dealers. The so-called qualified downstream dealers are downstream customers with stable supply chain relationships and transaction credit or characteristics that meet the criteria jointly developed by business personnel, risk control personnel, and modeling technicians after full communication. For example, the criteria for qualified downstream deals may include the following:

1. Whether the supply relationship with the downstream dealer has lasted for three years
2. Whether the downstream dealer is always ranked in the top 10
3. Whether the downstream dealer's overlap over three years is up to standard
4. Whether the downstream dealer's transaction over the last 12 months has trended upward or fluctuated within ±30% of the average value

The following simple example (see Fig. 6.8) can give an explanation and illustration.

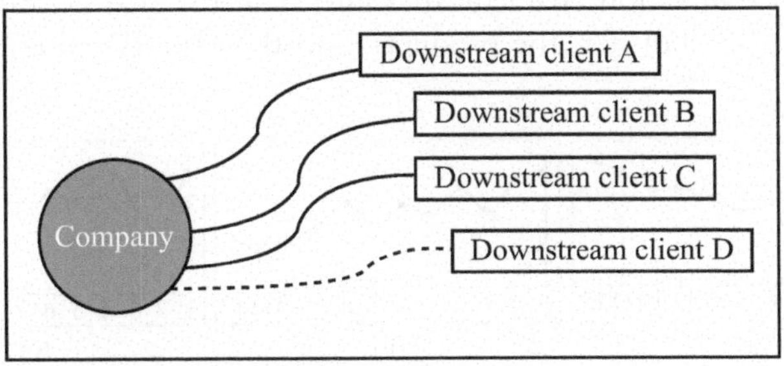

Fig. 6.8 Corporate business relationships

Figure 6.8 assumes that an enterprise has downstream dealers A, B, C, and D. By computing tax data, it is known that the downstream dealers A, B, and C have transaction relationship with the enterprise for more than three years, and all three dealers have been ranked among the top ten steadily in the past three years. Therefore, the downstream dealers A, B, and C are judged as stable customers. The downstream dealer D has business transactions with the enterprise for less than three years or accounts for a very low sales ratio of the enterprise, so it does not meet the criteria of stable supply chain relationship.

Further differentiation indicators are constructed for the downstream dealers A, B, and C to evaluate the transaction characteristics and determine whether they meet the ideal transaction characteristics criteria.

By aggregating the invoice information in the tax data, the monthly transaction amount of the enterprise with the downstream dealers A, B, and C for the past 12 months can be calculated. This accurate calculation based on invoice sales can reflect the real transactions between the enterprise and downstream dealers objectively. Three characteristic graphs may appear for the last 12 months of transactions (see Fig. 6.9).

Let us assume that the downstream dealer A has a stable upward trend, which is consistent with the characteristic (a); the downstream dealer B has a downward trading trend, which is consistent with the characteristic (b); and the downstream dealer C has a volatile trading, which is consistent with the characteristic (c). Obviously, the transactions with the downstream dealer A are the most ideal, and with the downstream dealer B is not ideal. The downstream dealer C may be qualified if the trading volatility is maintained within ±30%. In practice, it is possible to push forward one period to determine the trading characteristics more precisely. In other words, 24 months of transaction data are used for analysis, and the changes in transaction characteristics curves of the two cycles are compared with the industry, the products, and the experts' experience. The

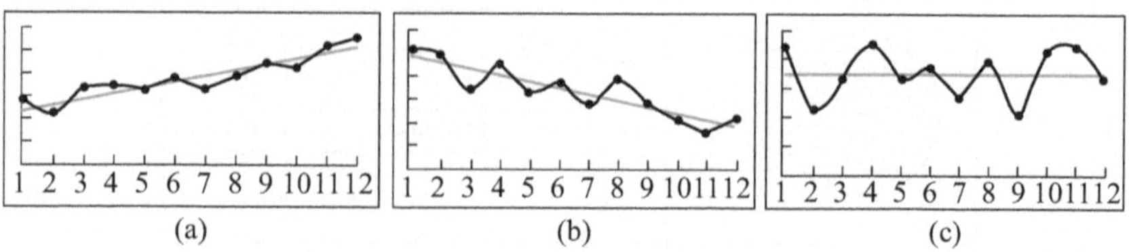

Fig. 6.9 Characteristics of corporate supply chain transactions

transaction credit is quantified from the perspective of stability, growth, and regularity of transactions to identify qualified dealers who meet the ideal criteria.

6.5.2.4 Determination of Credit Lines

A credit line is a line of credit based on the corporate credit and the transaction credit. In the above example, only the downstream suppliers A and C are qualified dealers, and their credits are determined as follows:

The first step is to calculate T. The value of T represents the average monthly transaction volume of the enterprise with the qualified dealers. The average monthly transaction volume between the enterprise and the downstream supplier A is expressed as t1, and the average monthly transaction volume between the enterprise and the downstream supplier C is expressed as t2, so T = t1 + t2.

The second step is to calculate the enterprise's average billing period P. The billing period P = 12 / accounts receivable turnover K. Accounts receivable turnover K = total sales revenue for the last 12 months/average accounts receivable for the last 12 months.

In general, the average accounts receivable in the calculation of accounts receivable turnover is obtained by adding the beginning amount and the ending amount and averaging it arithmetically. However, the arithmetic average results deviate from the actual situation for the companies subject to seasonal influences, so the interval average is used.

The third step is to calculate the value of the credit line.

The credit limit applied by the customer is indicated by L0.

Credit line 1(L1): L1 = T × P. L1 refers to the enlargement of the lender's average monthly transactions with qualified dealers by a factor of P, which is equivalent to the approximation of the entire liquidity/receivables lent by the lender to all qualified dealers.

Credit line 2 (L2): L2 = R × 0.4, where R is the average value of the accounts receivable on the enterprise's books in the past 12 months. Commercial banks usually require a chattel mortgage and pledge rate of 0.4.

Credit line 3 (L3): L3 = C/N, where C is the previous year's cost of main business and N is the working capital turnover, both of which can be calculated from the financial statement data in the tax data. L3 represents approximately the total amount of working capital of the enterprise.

The final determined credit line L = min (L0, L1, L2, L3). The final determined credit line is the minimum of the four values of L0, L1, L2, and L3, and usually the result should be L1.

6.5.2.5 *Post-Loan Monitoring Based on Invoices*

First, the analysis of purchase invoice data aims to monitor the usage and flow of loan funds. Through the analysis of purchase invoice data, the trade background and payment reasonableness of loan funds are verified to determine: first, the scope of counterparties for payment transactions (i.e., use the purchase invoice data to identify the transaction records between the enterprise and the counterparties to which the loan funds are paid); second, the reasonable range of loan payment amount. For example, if the monthly average purchase amount of Company A is calculated to be around RMB 2 million based on the purchase invoices, manual intervention must be reviewed whenever the loan payment amount excessively deviates from this value.

The monitoring of loan usage forms an important part of the closed-loop business risk system, which aims to ensure that credit loan funds are used for real production and operation as well as payment for upstream purchases. Currently, banks' review of loan usage based on purchase and sales contracts, invoices, and other materials usually only determine the compliance of loan usage in the form of "entrusted payment," but lack effective review of transaction background and reasonableness of payment. The analysis and calculation based on invoice data can make up for the shortcomings of the traditional review method, and can even greatly improve the efficiency and accuracy of monitoring through built-in early warning models.

Second is the tracking and analysis of sales invoice data—post-loan evaluation. By tracking the sales invoice data on an ongoing basis after the loan, it is possible to further evaluate whether the loan funds are effectively contributing to the supply capacity of downstream customers. The calculation based on the sales invoice data gives an indication of whether the supply transaction volume between the enterprise and a specific downstream customer is amplifying, so as to assess the performance of both parties in terms of transaction volume over the loan period.

6.5.2.6 *Basic Service Process*

Based on the advanced analysis logic of tax-related big data mentioned above, VZOOM has formed the basic business process of helping financial

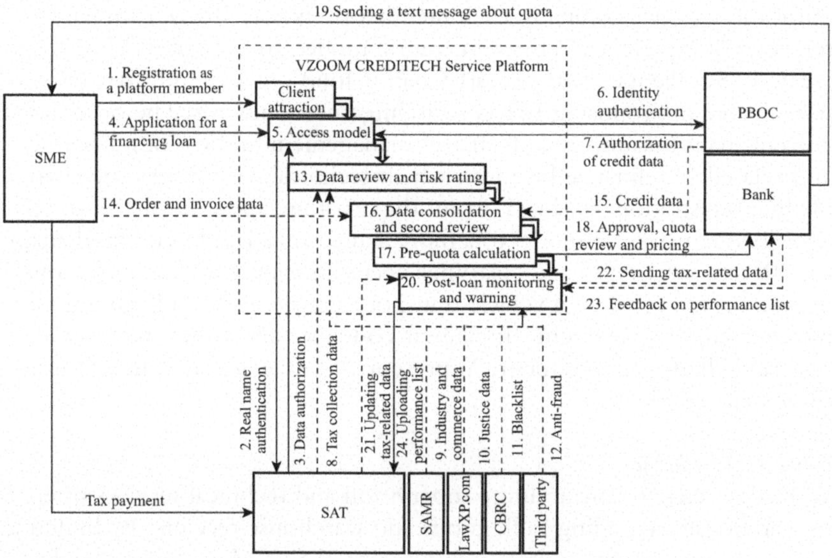

Fig. 6.10 VZOOM CREDITECH supply chain financial service flow

institutions carry out supply chain finance (see Fig. 6.10). First, small enterprises seeking supply chain financing register on the platform. Second, VZOOM acquires credit data, tax-related data, industrial and commercial data, judicial data, blacklist data, and so on. Based on this, VZOOM gives advice to financial institutions about the credit lines through advanced analysis. Third, VZOOM supports financial institutions' risk management through post-loan data analysis.

6.6 Supply Chain Financial Services Based on Supervision and Management: WSNCM

6.6.1 *Overview of WSNCM and Its Supply Chain Financial Asset Supervision Services*

Officially launching its business in 2016, WSNCM IOT Shanghai Co., Ltd. (hereinafter referred to as "WSNCM") has its headquarter and operation service center in the former Expo Macau Case Pavilion, Decheng Building, in Huangpu District, Shanghai. As an IoT technology innovation service company, each member of its core R&D team has over ten years of experience in the registration model. At present, WSNCM has created "SC-Piedge" and "Smart Chain Cloud" to IoT industry and has participated in proposing IoT core architecture standards. The company's current main business is IoT chattel management and operation services and related IoT finance business, which technically promotes the chattel pledge registration business from the existing spontaneous and self-described registration model to a more standardized and structured adapt to different asset types and customer needs and apply to four major business scenarios: intelligent vehicle transport management, bulk commodity warehousing management, intelligent container and pallet management, and fluid chattel management. At present, "SC-Piedge" has the following three main products:

6.6.1.1 W-Pledge

W-Pledge refers to the accurate supervision and technical services offered to warehouses regarding bulk goods and warehouse receipts. By building an IoT sensing system at the warehouse site, WSNCM perceives the physical state of goods and changes in goods value in real time and generates IoT warehouse receipts that guarantee uniqueness. By forming a dynamic warehouse receipt registration at the Credit Center of the People's Bank of China, the objective existence and unique registration of goods are ensured. W-Pledge App is used to restrain the legal and compliant operation of warehouse operators, while providing the first alarm and early warning of abnormal behavior for banks, supervisors, and warehouses.

Specifically, in terms of support for commodity pledge business systems, WSNCM achieves online and offline system docking and multilevel integration by fully aligning with the management requirements of banks and credit institutions. The main types of pledge business are the currently popular static goods pledge supervision and dynamic goods pledge supervision mode, where the dynamic goods pledge supervision mode includes fixed-amount goods control and chattel pledge financing support under approved inventory model. WSNCM uses IoT to support the entire goods supervision of inbound, outbound, replacement, and pledge release operations to achieve dynamic management of goods value, physical state, and storage environment, so as to achieve dynamic risk management. In addition, WSNCM also realizes the support of deterministic or general publicity under the unified registration method of security rights, thus supporting the financing business.

Fig. 6.11 Bulk commodity warehouse supervision system

WSNCM's bulk commodity warehouse supervision system (see Fig. 6.11) mainly includes the goods physical properties sensing subsystem, operational equipment management subsystem, abnormal behavior sensing subsystem, and cargo weight sensing subsystem. These subsystems can accurately sense changes in the weight and status of warehoused goods, sense the operation of machines in real time, detect mechanical operations by nonauthorized personnel, and monitor and track changes in the physical status of goods in real time, and so on. So in fact, WSNCM turns the flat scenarios into a three-dimensional space through the existing IoT and virtual reality means, turns the original flat coordinates into a three-dimensional spatial coordinates, and finally digitizes the goods and the warehouses in a complete way. After digitization, it is possible to get information of the physical properties of goods dynamically, and then, through the direct management of physical properties, it is possible to manage the dynamic goods value and risk changes of warehouse receipts accurately and fully in a certain warehouse in a continuous time period. The changes of goods value and risk status in this time period are dynamically matched and corrected with the goods control requirements (including goods control methods) of banks and financial institutions. At each moment, the restrictions and balance of credit line is determined and

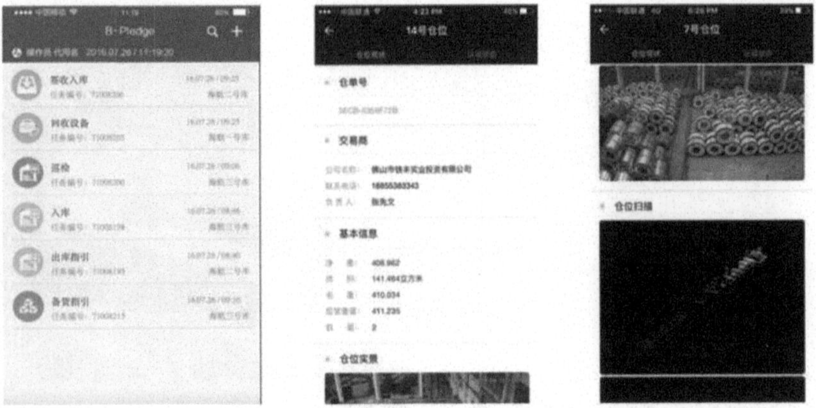

Fig. 6.12 Mobile application for warehouse receipt pledge risk management service

adjusted according to the risk relationship. Therefore, this is an automated on-site audit process. In addition, as shown in Fig. 6.12, WSNCM uses a warehouse risk management service app (for IOS and Android) to deliver the operation data of goods in time and to provide timely alarms in case of abnormalities, thus realizing the complete management process of goods (including warehouse receipts). Therefore, WSNCM can provide four types of services in respect of bulk commodities: supervision service, warehouse receipt management service, warehouse operation service, and alarm service.

In addition, under this management approach, the warehouse receipts supported by WSNCM evolve from a literal concept and a legal logical concept to a direct combination of physical relationships, that is, warehouse receipts with physical properties. These warehouse receipts have a one-to-one relationship with the physical object, and therefore have all the properties of the physical object and can be managed and traded. In view of this, by cooperating with the Credit Center of the People's Bank of China, WSNCM has launched the IoT chattel pledge registration service, with an aim to complete the registration of warehouse receipts in the registration system of the People's Bank of China through a warehouse receipt that can be clearly described, thus providing the deterministic or general publicity under the registration of security rights based on the physical object-based warehouse receipt.

6.6.1.2 V-Pledge

V-Pledge refers to the whole-vehicle supply chain management and pledge supervision data service provided by WSNCM. By realizing end-to-end smart management of the whole-vehicle supply chain and bridging the shortcomings of traditional manual management model such as untimely information transmission, inability to know the latest business status, lack of business authenticity background, and inability to discover the problems and track the business process autonomously, V-Pledge realizes the dynamic closed loop of the whole-vehicle supply chain and the automatic and intelligent operations under business scenarios, allows automatic and efficient human-machine intelligent collaboration, dynamic verification, and risk alarm of the entire supply chain process, as well as significantly lifts up the management efficiency and derivative service capabilities.

Unlike the management of goods properties and goods value for bulk commodities, WSNCM management of the automotive industry is a closed-loop management of the entire chain from the factory to the completion of sales, as shown in Fig. 6.13. The whole process from the vehicle leaving the factory to transport, in-transit storage, stock transfer, and vehicle sales realizes the automatic processing. All the documents from the vehicle outbound sheets, inbound warehouse receipts, and in-transit combined transport order to the sales lists and the final violation lists are automatically generated, automatically monitored, automatically cross-checked,

Fig. 6.13 Whole-process service of WSNCM vehicle supply chain

and automatically matched. The intermediate delivery operation process is all carried out in accordance with strict deterministic procedures. In the whole process, all the delivery links of different parties are self-integrated and handled in an integrated management way.

WSNCM combines V-Pledge vehicle supervision terminal device and the vehicles managed by it. This terminal device can be installed as software to provide services directly, without the need to attach any equipment in the vehicles. V-Pledge vehicle supervision terminal device has many technical advantages, including vehicle authenticity CA, intelligent working mode, business interactive operation, ultra-low power control, removal detection algorithm, independent battery power supply, and simple installation and removal.

On this basis, WSNCM's V-Pledge report big data service platform can view the following: the current and historical status of the vehicles managed (including location and trajectory); the business status of in-stock supervision, in-transit supervision, and out-warehousing supervision; the status of all tasks of operators, auditors, and drivers; messages and alarms; query services based on fields such as vehicles, dealers, documents, and tasks. The platform also supports the generation, query, export, and printing of reports and provides data interfaces to help customers integrate it into their ERP or other information management systems, and so on. Therefore, it can provide operation guidance and data services. Operation guidance means that operation instructions, operation notifications, and task notifications for the next chain can be precisely generated under comprehensive management and can be pushed to the relevant operators whose operations can be checked at the same time, that is, two-way checking and confirmation of objects or vehicles and people. Similarly, the V-Pledge App allows for binding and unbinding, delivery sign-off, alarm messages, application review, and status checking.

WSNCM's V-Pledge services effectively address a number of difficulties that currently exist in the automotive supply chain industry. First, it can effectively manage the assets in the enterprise supply chain, and predict and detect dealer irregularities and potential risks in a timely manner, so that the actual sales and inventory of dealers remain uniform and accurate with and OEM ledgers, and the assets can be seamlessly controlled in the full-process risk management. Second, it can optimize the funds in the automotive industry, urge dealers to redeem documents, and collect payments in a timely manner upon the occurrence of real car sales, and allow cross-region and cross-channel financial loans. Third, in terms of channel management it can include all parking points of dealers (including secondary network and secondary warehouses) into the management, detect private movement and privates sale of vehicles by dealers in a timely manner, help secondary network and secondary warehouse customers to obtain credit loans from banks more easily, as well as realize the confirmation of true information of vehicle sales, and so on. In addition to solving these difficulties, V-Pledge also solves problems related to many supply chain participants. For example, while helping OEMs with full-process monitoring and sales channel management, V-Pledge solves the problems of error-prone manual bookkeeping, high-cost in-stock supervision, and the potential for human moral hazard on the supervisory side, and helps banks solve the problems of lack of management tools for daily risks and difficulties in credit investigation of dealers' secondary networks and secondary warehouses. Therefore, thanks to V-Pledge services, WSNCM plays an important role in supporting the automotive supply chain financial services (see Fig. 6.14).

6.6.1.3 B-Pledge

B-Pledge refers to the seamless and real-time sensing services provided by WSNCM in the full process of supply chain, aiming to build an open joint R&D and experience plan for supply chain service providers, warehouse and logistics providers, financial institutions, and commodity producers and dealers. By providing intensive management based on standardized

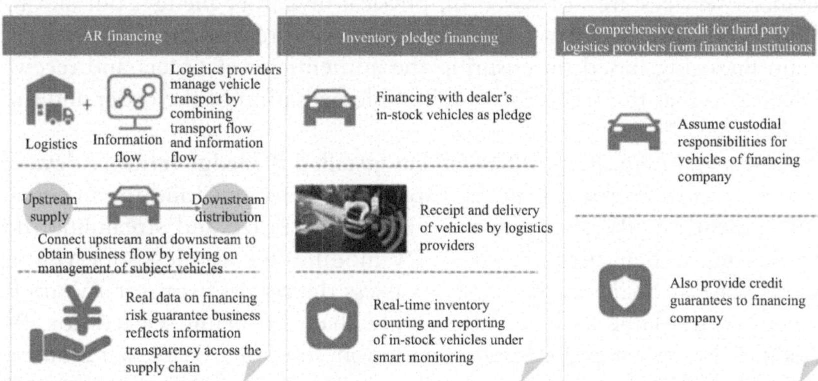

Fig. 6.14 WSNCM support for financial service business of automotive supply chain

pallets and containers, as well as automatic discovery and tracking services for the whole-process supply chain of commodities in storage, in transit, cross-border, and the last mile, B-Pledge realizes the dynamic closed loop of the supply chain and the automatic intelligent operations under business scenarios, allows automatic and efficient human-machine intelligent collaboration, dynamic verification, and risk alarm of the entire supply chain process, as well as significantly lifts up the management efficiency and derivative service capabilities. Meanwhile, B-Pledge ensures full-state awareness of the storage condition, safety condition, and brutal loading and unloading condition of commodities in the logistics and transport process.

The practical way for WSNCM to extend automotive management to other full supply chain management is to extend the management objects from the whole vehicles to the fine-grained pallets, containers, transit boxes and other logistics systems that can be managed in an intensive manner (including some raw materials, fast-consuming goods, electronic components, accessories). In addition to the same real-time services as for whole vehicles, B-Pledge also tracks cross-region operations, both domestic and overseas, to obtain full-chain information. The full supply chain management process includes the realization of risk and operation relationship, but more emphasis is placed on the validity of goods, that is, the management of cargo loss. WSNCM provides full supply chain management including supply chain services, warehouse management services and financial services for producers and traders. As the most core services, financial services are not based on physical inventory pledge, but aim to achieve risk measurement and early warning and reduce the risk of supply chain financing based on ensuring the authenticity of orders and receivables, as well as the reliability of full implementation of the order and the transaction.

As shown in Fig. 6.15, WSNCM has installed B-Pledge terminal device, sensing network device, B-Pledge App, and B-Pledge Cloud for an enterprise producing PV modules, aiming to standardize and streamline the whole supply chain process of solar PV modules for seamless supervision. Moreover, WSNCM allows banks to assess the risk of loans for PV modules as controllable and provides supply chain financing services for PV modules based on IoT-related supervision solution. From warehouses, logistics providers, ports, shipping companies, overseas ports to overseas logistics warehouses, WSNCM manages the complete process of PV modules from crating, inbound and outbound, waybill, departure, and sea bill

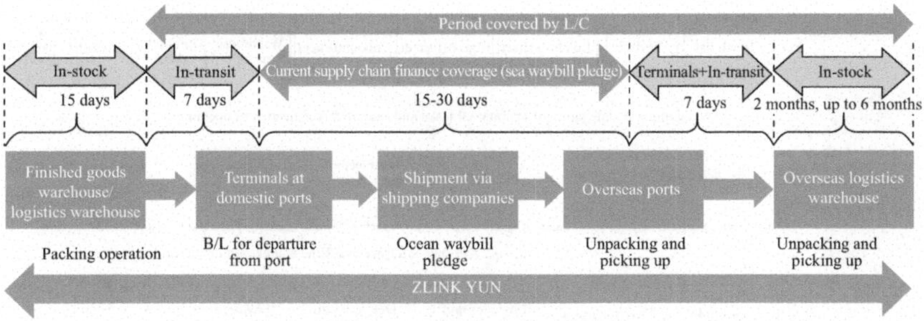

Fig. 6.15 Full cycle of PV modules under WSNCM supply chain financial service

to pickup and unpacking. After the whole chain management across departments, parties, operators, logistics providers, regions, and countries, all the original letters of credit and bills of lading are incorporated into the financial service package of banks. In other words, it incorporates orders, accounts receivable, advance payments, order deliveries, and all original letters of credit and bills of lading into the packaged services for detailed box-by-box and pallet-by-pallet management.

As a result, WSNCM's full-process supply chain management incorporates product crating, product inbound, product outbound, overseas warehouse transport, and box and pallet opening operations into the scope of supervision, substantially improving the efficiency and accuracy of supply chain operations. More importantly, errors are corrected in a timely and automatic manner. As a typical full process of supply chain finance based on the real business background for financing enterprises, it realizes the closed-loop and refined risk management of supply chain finance.

6.6.1.4 Smart Chain Cloud

In addition to the above three products of "SC-Piedge," another important technical service of WSNCM is the Smart Chain Cloud (see Fig. 6.16). Smart Chain Cloud changes the receiver of the original online system data from the operators to the WSNCM systems. Through IoT + blockchain model, WSNCM system on the one hand allows chattels to participate in business actively and equally and collaborates with operators in different business scenarios to verify the data (multimode consensus) and ensure the background authenticity of operations. On the other hand, WSNCM, through big data analysis, splits the operation instructions into

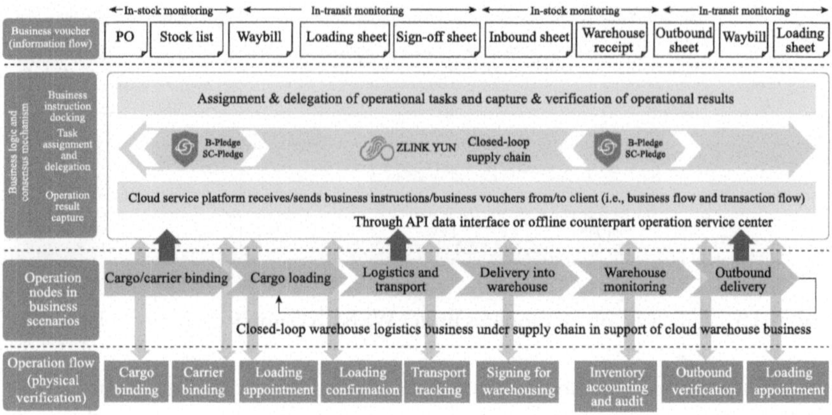

Fig. 6.16 Integrated ABCD consisting of WSNCM "Smart Chain Cloud" and "SC-Piedge"

standardized operation scenarios (such as outbound, loading, acceptance and unloading, inbound, stock transfer, and sales). The end of the chattel operation in a standard business scenario will naturally trigger the generation of the next business scenario, while the real business data will be uploaded to WSNCM online system (after checking the operation of operators and the status of goods, which cannot be tampered with).

As can be seen, the goal of Smart Chain Cloud is to ensure the authenticity of the business background, realize the automatic loop closure of the whole supply chain, stimulate the financial attributes of chattels, and make it possible and safe for financial institutions to provide liquid assets loan model to enterprises and supply chain financial products with chattels and supply chain business as the carrier.

6.6.2 Supply Chain Fintech Services Based on IoT + Blockchain between WSNCM and Zaokuang

Zaokuang Materials Group Co., Ltd. (hereinafter referred to as "Zaokuang"), a subsidiary of Shandong Energy Group Co., Ltd, a Fortune 500 company, is a global group with diversified development in commodities trading, logistics, finance, and investment. Zaokuang is committed to building a supply chain service ecosystem that integrates and optimizes the whole supply chain operations from raw materials to end user consumption. Zaokuang organizes, plans, coordinates, controls, and optimizes the "four flows" in the supply chain via various management means, and also provides supply chain management services that connect procurement, production, sales and settlement, in the supply chain. It reduces procurement costs by means of centralized procurement, factors accounts receivable of downstream enterprises through financial tools, uses electronic commercial bills, and relies on core supply chain enterprises to simplify the payment and settlement link of the entire supply chain, and reduces the financing costs of SMEs in the supply chain.

1. Accurate Control of Goods Using IoT to Ensure the Safety and Real Presence of Goods

The services provided by WSNCM for Zaokuang are based on the "SC-Piedge," which helps the latter to effectively monitor the pledged assets. Thanks to WSNCM's W-Pledge App or Web, the financial service providers on Zaokuang's supply chain service platform can see the geographic information, address, and precise indoor location of the enterprises' pledged chattels, and detect changes in various regulatory elements of pledged chattels (including weight, location, movement status, authorized area, contour and stacking shape, transaction and delivery operations, etc.) in real time. Different regulatory elements apply to different regulated chattels. At the same time, the system will generate a photo showing the activation of the supervision service as one of the bases of the initial supervision status. The system will package the information of the regulatory elements suitable for the pledged chattels together with the photo of the initial regulatory status to form an electronic certificate uniquely corresponding to the pledged chattels and record them in the blockchain ledgers. No changes in the physical state of these regulatory elements means that the pledged chattels have not been touched by anyone, in which case the goods certificate cannot be falsified.

After the chattel is pledged to the financial services institution, the regulatory alarm service will be activated. Once the system senses a change in the location, weight, shape, and contour of the pledged chattel, its movement status, transport and transaction delivery process, and other regulatory elements that are sufficient to change the value of the goods or pledge status without the permission of the financial services institution, an alarm will be sent. The financial services institution, the supervisor, and the warehouse manager can all receive the alarm information at the first time, and get the "live" parameters of that change captured by the system, which can be used to compare with the information and photos previously packaged. When the enterprise has repaid the loan to the financial service institution, the system will release the alarm service for the goods, and the enterprise can normally transport the goods from the warehouse.

In addition to supervising and managing the pledged assets, the WSNCM service system is also capable of effectively monitoring warehousing operations and behaviors. The centralized warehouse management system issues standardized operation instructions to warehouse managers in each warehouse, who is responsible for executing the corresponding goods in/outbound and lifting operations in accordance with the instructions. IoT terminals can monitor the compliance of warehouse operations in real time and verify the relevant goods through warehouse management workstations. Zaokuang's supply chain service platform can manage all its warehouses (including self-owned and cooperative warehouses) nationwide in a centralized off-site manner with unified and standardized operations. A complete business closed loop (in-stock—in-transit—in-stock) is formed for chattels from outbound warehousing, loading, transportation, unloading, and inbound warehousing, thus realizing the integration of customer warehousing and distribution.

2. Blockchain and IoT as the Architectural Foundation of the Supply Chain to Achieve Four Flows in One

Another important technology platform provided by WSNCM for Zaokuang is Smart Chain Cloud, which covers all business scenarios of in-stock supervision, in-transit transport, inbound and outbound storage, and goods delivery of the supply chain. By means of API data interface or offline operation service, Smart Chain Cloud service platform accepts business instructions from Zaokuang's supply chain service platform, returns business credentials (commodity flow and transaction flow), and sends the operation flow of each scenario to the app of frontline personnel for interaction of offline operation and confirmation of smart contract execution. After multimode consensus confirmation, a complete series of business documents (information flow) are formed and recorded on the blockchain ledger. The chattel automatically drives the business process and completes the integration of the four flows: information flow, fund flow, transport flow and commodity flow.

Through IoT + blockchain + supply chain management service, Zaokuang and WSNCM have cooperated to build practical application scenarios of intelligent supply chain ecosystem, and realized the application of supply chain service and intelligent finance in Wuxi Shuofang Stainless Steel Warehousing and Processing Center and Changzhou Liyang Copper Warehousing Center. They have transformed and upgraded the traditional local trade and financing method of buying and selling into a combined industry and financing model relying on the national service network of Zaokuang's supply chain service platform and WSNCM's IoT + blockchain technology. As a result, business efficiency has been improved across the board and supply chain finance risks have been significantly reduced. By the end of 2018, the two pilot centers have achieved sales of over RMB 1 billion and financing scale of over RMB 500 million through the platform. Combined with the market scale, it is expected that the two pilot centers will achieve a transaction volume of more than RMB 35 billion in the future.

6.7 Supply Chain Financial Services Based on Electronic Credentials: CWRE

China Warehouse Receipt Service Co., Ltd. (hereinafter referred to as "CWRE") is a national-level professional public service organization for spot warehouse receipts initiated by China's backbone logistics providers and financial institutions. CWR pioneered the whole-process financial outsourcing services in China such as spot electronic warehouse receipt authentication, quality inspection, endorsement, credit collection, and insurance and price protection. With two years of preparation, CWRE was initiated and incorporated in Qianhai, Shenzhen, by three founding shareholders (i.e., China Logistics Stock Limited, Shenzhen Tieyin Fund Management Enterprise (L.P.), and Shenzhen Linfeng Investment Holding Co., Ltd.) on October 14, 2014, with an initial registered capital of RMB 15.5 million. According to the provisions of the investment agreement, CWRE will continue to introduce representative domestic and foreign enterprises or institutions in the fields of technology, financial industry (insurance, futures), and credit, forming a diversified shareholder structure in order to enhance the credibility of its services.

China Financial Certification Authority (hereinafter referred to as "CFCA") is an integrated information security service organization based on electronic certification services, providing electronic certificates of electronic warehouse receipts and electronic information delivery security service.

Shenzhen Yinyan Financial Services Co., Ltd. is a financial information and financial logistics service company and is subordinate to Shenzhen Financial Electronic Settlement Center. The company provides professional technology services such as account opening and witness of warehouse receipt customers and credit investigation over warehouse receipts' ownership and transmission of financial certificates.

The warehouse receipt insurance is underwritten by a co-insurance body composed of PICC Property and Casualty Company Limited, Sunshine Property & Casualty Insurance Co., Ltd., and Ping An Property & Casualty Insurance Company of China Limited, of which PICC Property and Casualty Company Limited is the main insurer.

China Certification & Inspection Group is a third-party independent certification and inspection body licensed by the General Administration of Quality Supervision, Inspection and Quarantine of China (AQSIQ), accredited by the Certification and Accreditation Administration of the People's Republic of China (CNCA) and recognized by the China National Accreditation Service for Conformity Assessment (CNAS), and mainly specializes in "inspection, testing, accreditation and certification."

6.7.1 CWRE's International Warehouse Receipt Service System

Comprehensive services for international high-credit warehouse receipts aim at maintaining the convenience and safety of warehouse receipt trading and financing, and provides a package of basic support services for warehouse receipts such as authentication, quality inspection, credit investigation, and insurance and price protection for both sides of the transaction of warehouse receipt business. CWRE has attempted to set up a comprehensive service system of international warehouse receipts with high credit by incorporating the abovementioned service institutions and Chinese leading e-commerce platforms, spot trading houses, futures risk management subsidiaries, arbitration institutions, and so on, and has created "comprehensive services for international warehouse receipts with high credit" for financial institutions, logistics providers, and warehousing enterprises and cargo owners. On the basis of providing services of

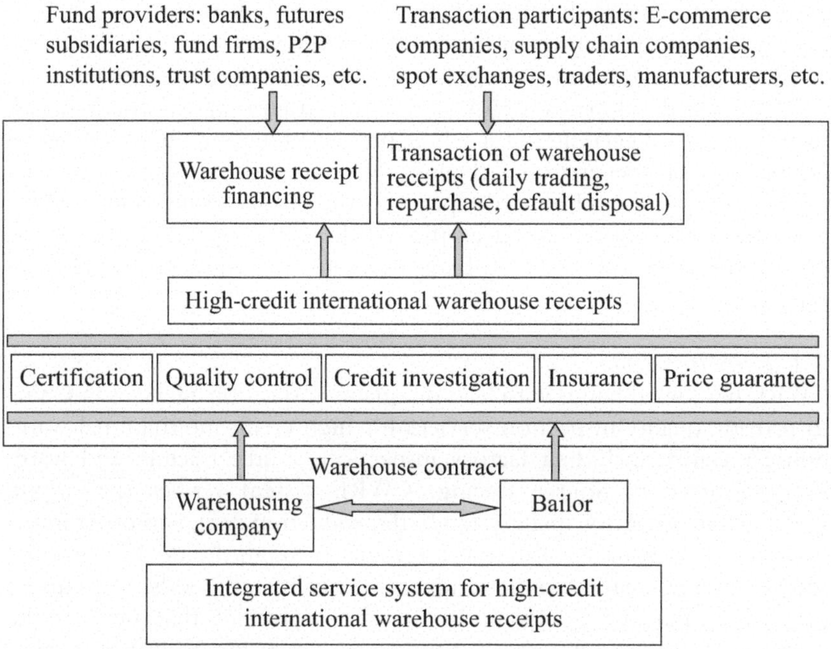

Fig. 6.17 CWRE integrated service system for electronic warehouse receipts

warehouse receipt certification, quality inspection, credit investigation, and insurance and price protection, and standardizing the national standards of warehouse receipt format, CWRE has played the role of a basic service supporter to promote the practical operations of international warehouse receipts (see Fig. 6.17).

1. Certification

Warehouse certification. CWRE has set up the certification standards of warehouses and cooperated with insurance companies to make comprehensive assessment on the management ability of warehouses, credit loss information and frequency of insured accidents, and so on by adopting the composite standards of logistics and insurance. At the same time, CWRE has united with professional certification agencies to electronically certify the warehouse infrastructure through the technical means of electronic encryption to ensure the authenticity and nonrepudiation of data collection, as well as the security of the transmission process.

Electronic warehouse receipt generation and duration certification. CWRE's self-developed warehouse receipt system supports the management and record keeping of the whole process of inbound booking, warehouse receipt generation, change of warehouse receipt duration information, and warehouse receipt payment, and allows financing institutions and cargo owners to check the warehouse receipts and inspect the goods remotely on a 24/7 basis through IoT devices installed in warehouses.

2. Quality Inspection

CWRE has joined hands with leading quality inspection agencies in China to provide quality inspection services for high-credit international warehouse receipts, including factory inspection, source tracing, and warehouse inspection. Source tracing: CWRE system verifies the origin, specification, quantity, quality standard, production date, and other information of goods under warehouse receipts through the docked product source tracing system to determine the quality of goods. Warehouse inspection: For the goods under warehouse receipt that need to be inspected in the warehouse, customers can apply for quality inspection online through CWRE system, and the quality inspection agency will send the staff to the warehouse site to take samples and then upload quality inspection reports through CWRE system. CWRE carries out electronic authentication for the sampling of warehouse inspection, uploading, and confirmation of quality inspection reports to ensure that the information is true, effective, and nonrepudiate.

3. Credit Investigation

CWRE has developed the indexes and evaluation system that are in line with the commercial characteristics of warehouse receipts. Based on the "CWRE Enterprise Credit System" with independent intellectual property rights, it provides the pioneering warehousing enterprise credit investigation and warehouse receipt credit investigation services in China, and supports real-time credit investigation and active credit investigation, thus meeting customers' needs for the latest information in this information era.

Warehousing enterprise credit investigation. The elements of warehousing enterprise credit investigation include basic information of enterprise, information of managers and personnel in important positions, financial status, operational status, warehousing facilities, warehousing management, litigation and negative information, insurance and historical claims, and so on.

Warehouse receipt credit investigation. The elements of warehouse receipt credit investigation include warehouse receipt elements, warehouse receipt endorsement records, property rights, quality inspections, warehouse premises, insurance, goods price and market and transaction scale, and so on.

4. Insurance

With the support of CWRE's high-credit international warehouse receipts certification and credit investigation services, as well as IoT technology and security devices deployed in the warehouse, PICC, the underwriter of customized warehouse receipt insurance, can complete pre-policy risk assessment, risk pricing, in-policy risk monitoring, and early warning and quickly determine liability and damages after the occurrence of an insured accident. CWRE's pioneering high-credit international warehouse receipt service system transforms chattels into standardized warehouse receipt information, providing the basis for upgrading traditional enterprise property insurance to the Internet-based insurance.

5. Price Protection

For the goods belonging to the underlying varieties of futures, CWRE formulates hedging programs by product as per market conditions or uses OTC options to provide price protection services in order to hedge the risk of depreciation of warehouse receipts caused by fluctuations in the price of goods. Compared with the warehouse receipts without price protection, the protected warehouse receipts can moderately improve the capital utilization rate and price risk resistance capacity when used as financing collateral.

6.7.2 CWRE's Service Support for Supply Chain Finance

CWRE has created a high-credit international warehouse receipt service system, which provides warehouse receipt certification, credit investigation, insurance, price protection, and other services. Logistics providers can effectively expand their supply chain financial business scale, avoid the risk of duplicate pledge and invalid pledge caused by their internal irregular operations, and carry out financial value-added services such as receiving goods and collecting payments or purchasing insurance, transferring pledge, and delivering goods on behalf of customers, so as to improve their market competitiveness. Banks and other financial institutions can avoid the risk of repeated pledge of warehouse receipts in the original pledge supervision business, improve the operational efficiency of pledge business, enhance the liquidity and safety of warehouse receipts cash-out, substantially increase the scale of supply chain financing, and reduce the bad debt rate. SMEs can improve financing efficiency and reduce costs by pledging the warehouse receipts, and solve financing difficulties caused by the lack of real properties.

1. Logistics and Warehousing Enterprises

Benefiting from the high-credit international warehouse receipt service system, logistics and warehousing enterprises are free from the scale limitation of their own credit in their financial logistics business and effectively expand their financial logistics service business scale, so that their business scale is only limited by their warehouse capacity, efficiency, and market reputation. At the same time, by effectively avoiding the risk of repeated pledges and invalid pledges caused by internal irregular operations, and effectively carrying out financial value-added services such as receiving goods, collecting payments, purchasing insurance, transferring pledge, and delivering goods on behalf of customers, CWRE effectively boosts the transformation and upgrading of warehousing enterprises to carry out high-end logistics business and improve their market competitiveness, which is an effective measure of logistics supply-side reform.

2. Financial Institutions

Thanks to the high-credit international warehouse receipt service system, banks completely avoid the risk of repeated pledge of warehouse receipts in the original pledge supervision business, as well as the technical risks of collusion between the low-level branch and logistics enterprises in forging warehouse receipts and the technical problem in auditing the authenticity of warehouse receipts by themselves, improve the operational efficiency of multilocation pledge supervision business as well as the liquidity and safety of warehouse receipt cash-out, significantly increase the scale of supply chain financing, and reduce the bad debt rate. In particular, the convenient and reliable endorsement of warehouse receipts and pledge transfer significantly reduces the rate of nonperforming loans of banks. Under compliant operations, the system will also form its own substitute funds for the institution's service system and provide an effective asset allocation and profit-making channel for the liquid funds of other participants (financial institutions, investment institutions, and traders).

Moreover, the trade financing services and products that the system can support include warehouse receipt pledge financing business (including both local and remote warehouse receipts), entrusted right of lading pledge issuance business, future right of lading pledge financing business, warehousing company guaranteed pledge financing business, confirming storage financing business, the combination of the above businesses, and the combination of factoring businesses, and so on.

3. Cargo Owners and Traders

With the help of the high-credit international warehouse receipt service system, cargo owners can improve financing efficiency, reduce costs, and increase the proportion of chattel pledged. The high-credit international warehouse receipt service system also supports cargo owners to choose suitable logistics and warehousing enterprises to store their pledged goods in multiple locations in order to be closer to the market areas and improve logistics efficiency. Cargo owners can entrust logistics and warehousing enterprises to collect goods or payment for goods or transfer pledge and deliver goods on their behalf. Besides, CWRE provides trading conditions for warehouse receipt assets and a platform for low-cost purchase and sale of bulk commodities.

The high-credit international warehouse receipt service system has the following important values for traders: First, it replaces physical transactions with warehouse receipt transfer, which greatly reduces the VAT and additional taxes arising from multiple transactions. Under the current mode of supply chain financing, if the fund provider adopts multiple physical transactions, it is necessary to issue invoices several times even if the goods are still in the same warehouse, and the VAT and additional taxes arising from each process must be borne by the fund provider. These taxes and fees become the "system cost" of the transactions. The high-credit international warehouse receipt service system replaces physical transactions with multiple endorsements of reliable warehouse receipts. Second, traders can efficiently and cost-effectively obtain bank pledges through court auction procedures within the system, and easily find counterparties for bulk commodities within the system to cash out the warehouse receipts. Third, financial asset companies, guarantee investment companies, short-term financial plans, and other legal institutions with high-liquidity capital allocation needs can choose as traders to trade and invest the warehouse receipts and enterprises that meet their own risk control standards and proceeds standards through the warehouse receipts transfer and assignment channels.

6.8 Blockchain-Based Intelligent Supply Chain Financial Services: E-VISIBLE, 33.cn

6.8.1 *Supply Chain Financial Services Supported by E-VISIBLE Blockchain*

Easy Visible Supply Chain Management Co., Ltd. (hereinafter referred to as "E-VISIBLE") was founded on June 23, 1997, with a registered capital of RMB 1.122 billion, and is one of the earliest listed companies in western China, with A-share code 600093. Supported by advanced technologies such as blockchain and IoT and oriented to customer needs, E-VISIBLE is dedicated to accelerating the capital turnover of SMEs and reducing transaction costs, and focuses on supply chain management and supply chain fintech services, covering three business segments: supply chain management, commercial factoring, and financial technology. Since 2016, E-VISIBLE has been committed to the R&D of "blockchain + supply chain finance" technology platform. Relying on the dual drive of technical innovation and model innovation, E-VISIBLE has joined hands with IBM Research-China to jointly develop the "E-VISIBLE Blockchain" platform. Since its launch in April 2017, the E-VISIBLE Blockchain platform has registered about 170 corporate clients online. As of July 31, 2018, the amount invested was nearly RMB 4.2 billion, and nearly 20 core enterprises involving pharmaceutical, chemical, manufacturing, bulk, logistics, aviation, real estate, and other industries were connected. Among them, the direct investment of financial institutions exceeded RMB 1 billion. E-VISIBLE Blockchain solution focuses on two core risk control logics in supply chain finance, namely “information closed loop” and “fund closed loop.” The platform uses blockchain as the underlying technology to profile the real trade background of both sides of the transaction in a nonfalsifiable way; provides visualized trade information, reflecting the fast speed and accuracy from purchase and sale information posting, real-time monitoring of cargo flow, and document transmission and tracking to settlement; supports diversified process designs such as open financing needs of two-way selection, lending, and repayment at any time; realizes the dedicated account management of financial institutions for trade loans and money recovery, in order to achieve the closed loop of funds. The solution also contains functions such as enterprise and user management, fund management, fund account service, electronic contract service, statement and report service, and notice service. Specifically, the solution proposed by the platform consists of four products: trusted data pool, supply chain trade system, supply chain financing platform, and E-VISIBLE receivables ABS management system (hereinafter referred to as “E-VISIBLE ABS”) (see Fig. 6.18).

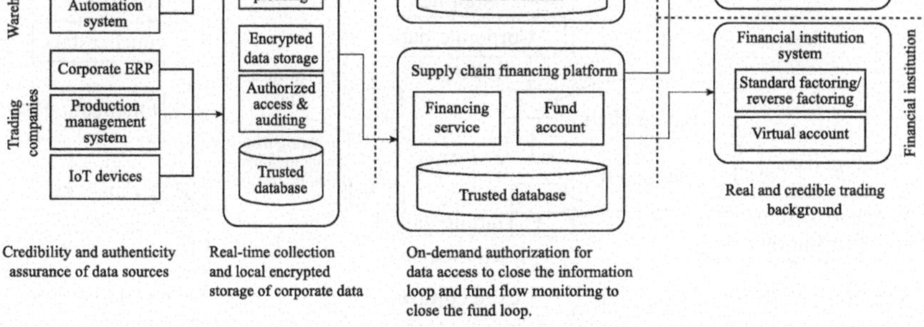

Fig. 6.18 Supply chain financial services architecture of E-VISIBLE blockchain

6.8.1.1 Trusted Data Pool and Supply Chain Trade System

The following issues exist in the industrial data transmission in the traditional supply chain. First, offline point-to-point information interaction between trade parties leads to discrepancies in reconciliation, redundant data, and low supply chain efficiency. Second, trade parties cannot prove themselves, which means they cannot prove the authenticity of transaction data to financial institutions and third parties, because the data are mostly for "self-use" and there is a possibility of tampering, so they cannot provide credit guarantee. Third, the data is not traceable, and all the transaction and financing data cannot be audited retroactively. Fourth, the data is misused, and all transaction and financing data are at risk of being leaked and misused.

For the purpose of addressing the above issues, E-VISIBLE has developed and designed a solution, that is, trusted data pool (see Fig. 6.19), which can help enterprises establish a data protection mechanism with clear ownership, credibility, and traceability based on blockchain technology. Three deployment methods are provided for enterprises to choose: public cloud-based SaaS service, private cloud deployment, and hardware and software all-in-one machine. Through real-time connection with the enterprise's trade system, production system, and ERP system, data is written in the form of blocks to the "trusted data pool" nodes under the enterprise's ownership, and the data is protected by encryption, while the data authorization access mechanism is also established through key management, so that the data is credible and traceable. The "trusted data

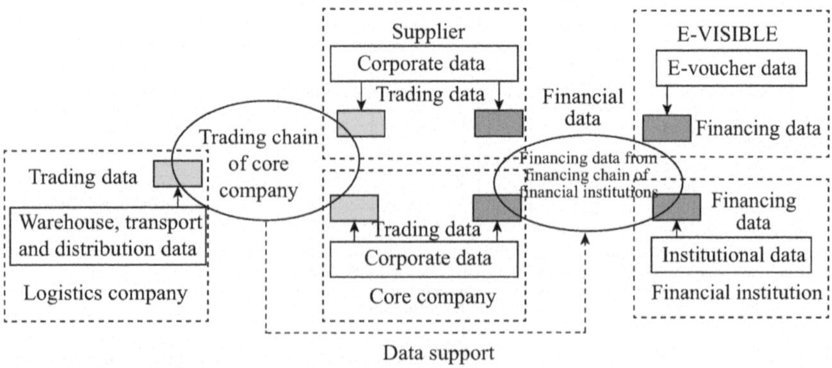

Fig. 6.19 E-VISIBLE data product solution

pool" with blockchain as the underlying technology can not only connect to diverse software applications but also realize cross-chain interactive reference in a block, and has the flexibility and extensibility of functional applications and connection modes.

E-VISIBLE trusted data pool embodies the following values: the platform and enterprise production data system are directly connected to realize real-time access to enterprise data, which data can be paired with trusted data pool data to complete the profiling of enterprise financial status in real time. Data is written to the blockchain, and all data is recorded on an enterprise-level blockchain distributed ledger to ensure the authenticity, security, and reliability. Data can only be used after authorization, and the enterprises as data owners can authorize all data usage separately. Data auditing is done on the blockchain because all data operations of the data pool are recorded on a separate enterprise-level blockchain distributed ledger, allowing data operation auditing at any time. A variety of data applications can be selected, and a variety of financial data can be used on the trusted data pool to profile, analyze, and apply financial big data to complete real-time enterprise data deposition, profiling, and value addition. Trusted data pool is the basic technical product of the whole traceable supply chain financial solution. Supply chain trade, supply chain financing, and E-VISIBLE ABS all use trusted data pool for data management and deposition.

The supply chain trade system based on trusted data pool, besides ensuring the authenticity and traceability of data, follows the supply chain trade business logic to sort out and manage the data and business processes, so as to realize the multiparty submission and confirmation, unified management, and presentation of data in the supply chain business and to provide convenience for business operations.

There are three main types of data access methods currently used by E-VISIBLE (see Table 6.6).

As can be seen, in terms of source data collection, contract and order data can be accessed from the enterprise ERP system by means of system docking and IoT device collection, and goods receiving data can be obtained from IoT devices (code sweeping, electronic weighting, etc.), thus ensuring the authenticity of the data source to the maximum extent. The authenticity of data source guarantees the application of blockchain technology in the trusted data pool, which solves the problem of authenticity of trade data required for business.

Table 6.6 Data access methods of E-VISIBLE

Scenario/mode	*Supplier access method*	*Core enterprise access method*	*Third-party data access*	*Typical clients*
Pharmaceutical	Supplier's ERP	Manual confirmation	—	Graded hospitals and their suppliers
Manufacturing company	Manual input	ERP and production management system, weighing system	—	Manufacturing companies of bulk commodities
Third-party data	Excel data uploading	ERP system	Logistics documents Warehousing, transport, and distribution system IoT data	Logistics companies Warehousing companies

The trusted data pool provides a variety of external access interfaces, which can develop data application web portals, and can also be docked and integrated with financial platforms (such as bank financing systems, financial transaction financing platforms, exchange systems, etc.) to realize external sharing of trusted data under the premise of authorization.

6.8.1.2 Supply Chain Financing Platform

The supply chain financing platform also uses blockchain as the underlying technology to portray the real trade background of both sides of the transaction in a nonfalsifiable way, provide visualized trade information, realize the special account management of financial institutions for the issuance and recovery of trade loans, and solve the problem of closed loop of funds, so as to realize the control and visibility of the whole process and improve the efficiency of trade and financing.

Utilizing the supply chain service model built on E-VISIBLE Blockchain platform, all parties involved in the supply chain, including core enterprises, upstream and downstream SMEs, banks, and other fund providers, can put the transport flow, commodity flow, fund flow, and information flow of the supply chain online, allowing the cross-checking and cross-verification among the "four flows," as well as the visibility, transparency, and nonfalsification of trade information and providing financial institutions with pre-loan and post-loan management functions. After the supplier releases financing demand on the platform, the financial institution will respond, the core enterprise will confirm the right, E-VISIBLE Blockchain will provide platform services, and the financial institution will provide loans for the supplier. This "four-flows-in-one" model effectively expands the low-risk loan granting of financial institutions, improves the capital turnover of suppliers, reduces the financing costs, and optimizes the procurement environment of core enterprises (see Fig. 6.20).

The platform shows trade contracts, orders, delivery orders, receipt orders, single settlement orders, settlement summaries, and other information. Through the "trade background form" on the platform, users can view the detailed data of each intermediate link. As the data can be viewed online and cross-checked by the "four flows," suppliers can greatly shorten the payment collection cycle from 90–180 days to 15 days, or even as fast as 1 day, which accelerates the supplier's own capital turnover and reduces the procurement cost of enterprises.

The application of blockchain technology in this supply chain service model solves the issue of data authenticity. Combined with the traceable cross-chain data access, both data credit and volume are increased. Based on the real trade data it obtains, financial institutions can grant credit to upstream suppliers based on the credit of core enterprises and provide

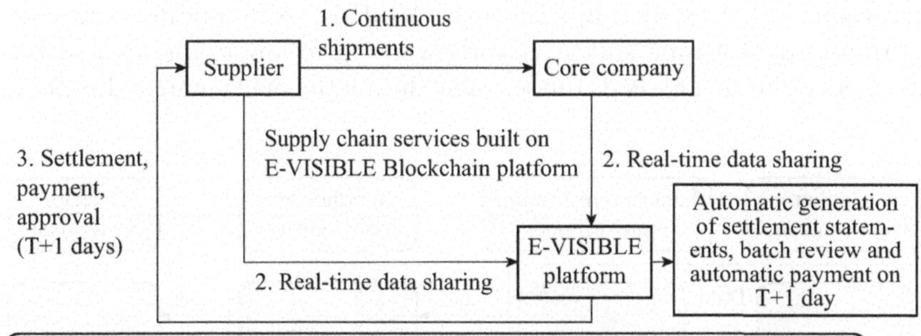

Fig. 6.20 E-VISIBLE supply chain financing service model

financing services to suppliers, which solves the problem of difficult financing for SMEs and also eases the payment pressure of core enterprises and revitalizes their funds.

6.8.1.3 E-VISIBLE ABS

Leveraging the advantages of blockchain data being tamper-proof and traceable, E-VISIBLE ABS effectively solves the problems of multiple links, complex processes, and low transparency of underlying assets in the ABS process.

1. Systems and Participants Involved in Accounts Receivable ABS

The process of ABS with accounts receivable as the underlying assets involves multiple participants and different systems. E-VISIBLE Blockchain is used to form the underlying assets, and then the asset management system E-VISIBLE ABS is used to manage the assets, and finally all relevant data is imported into the exchange to complete the ABS issuance and the information disclosure during the post-issuance period, as shown in Fig. 6.21.

2. Dynamic Assets Management

E-VISIBLE ABS manages the pooled assets through the data source, with the status and attributes of each asset corresponding to the accounts receivable in E-VISIBLE Blockchain. E-VISIBLE ABS monitors the asset attributes in real time and gives early warning to any single asset in the asset portfolio that exceeds the set value during the management duration.

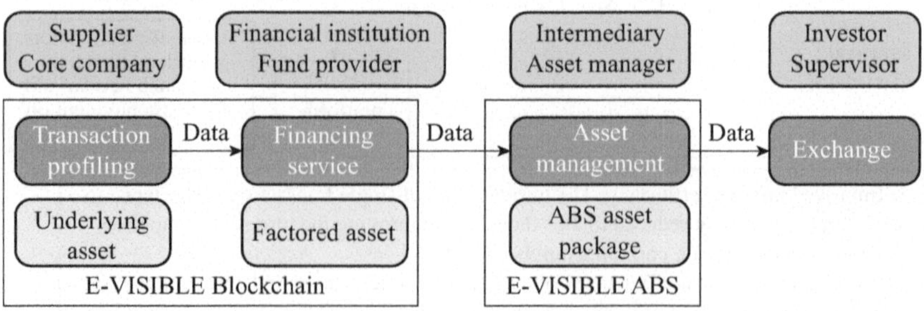

Fig. 6.21 E-VISIBLE solution for ABS products under dynamic asset management

Apart from the systematic management of all data from the source, all operations during the issuance period and the management duration are recorded by the system and uploaded to the chain, with the related attachments retained, so as to reduce the error rate arising from manual processing, achieve online collaboration across the chain, improve efficiency, and ensure operation visibility and data traceability. Through the analysis and cross-matching of asset data, the assets in the asset portfolio can be classified according to attributes and trends, and the health of the asset portfolio can be assessed. E-VISIBLE ABS solves the problems of nontransparent information and inadequate disclosure in the ABS process, and also effectively ensures the authenticity of the data of the assets themselves and the data of the asset management process to facilitate the value transfer and credit transfer of the whole process.

3. Full Information Disclosure and Penetration Management of Underlying Assets

E-VISIBLE ABS is mainly designed and developed as an assets management tool, but in fact it provides effective support for the full information disclosure and penetration management of the underlying assets, because it portrays the whole life cycle of asset formation, review, issuance, circulation, and maturity, and uses blockchain technology to guarantee authentic and tamper-proof data, so that the whole system realizes a closed loop of information and can accurately control the authenticity and risk of assets.

6.8.2 "HAIPIAOHUI" Bill Matching System between 33.cn and HAIPINGXIAN

Hangzhou Fuzamei Technology Co., Ltd. (hereinafter referred to as "33.cn") was founded in 2008, headquartered in Hangzhou, and has branches in Shanghai and Nanjing, with low latency and high-concurrency technology for deal-making systems. The company started the research and development of blockchain and smart contract in 2013. At present, the company's main business direction is blockchain bills, account receivable, advance payments, warehouse receipt pledges, points, exchanges, and so on 33.cn has officially launched blockchain projects in many Fortune 500 companies such as HNA HAIPINGXIAN, Midea Finance, and other power industry giants.

6.8.2.1 Background of HAIPIAOHUI

Developed by 33.cn, 33.cn Blockchain Bill Exchange is a bill trading system that uses blockchain technology to provide users with bill financing, bill investment, and debt transfer services. The entry, listing, withdrawal, and acceptance information of each bill is written into the blockchain, and investors can check the real, tamper-proof, and nonfalsifiable data at any time, and the transaction records can be preserved as evidence.

HAIPINGXIAN's bill matching system, "HAIPIAOHUI," is a bill exchange designed by 33.cn for HNA Group. Using blockchain technology, the system brings together the commercial bill information of enterprises and connects with various fund providers to effectively solve the financing problems of SMEs. The transactions between fund applicants and fund providers are completed on the highly credible blockchain, which makes the bill information, participant information, and transaction information on the smart contract tamper-proof and can easily solve the problem of credit deficiency of bill transactions.

6.8.2.2 33.cn Blockchain + Supply Chain Finance Solution

1. Introduction of System Functions

Registration and Login

Users register and log in with their cell phone number, email address, and user name. The system assigns private and public key addresses to them and binds the addresses to their accounts.

Real-Name Authentication, CA Authentication, and Corporate Credit Granting

Real-name authentication. Corporate user should first fill in the full name of the enterprise, license number, account bank, and other information, then the platform will randomly remit some money to the enterprise's account bank, and finally the enterprise should enter the amount of that money actually received by it into the platform's real-name authentication page. After the system confirms that the amount is correct, the enterprise will pass the real-name authentication. Future individual users can directly use the four elements (the name, the ID card number, a certain bank card, and the cell phone number reserved in bank) to complete the real-name authentication.

CA authentication. It is connected to the third-party digital certificate security management center. For users who have passed real-name authentication, CA authentication can be completed by private key signature. Finally, the user and public key are bound and written to the blockchain.

Corporate credit granting. The information platform grants an initial credit line based on the enterprise's information, credit rating, and other big data. The enterprise can obtain bill financing within this credit line. This credit line can be adjusted by HAIPINGXIAN at any time.

Bill Financing

1. Issuing and collecting bills via electronic commercial draft system (ECDS). The borrower collects bills through the ECDS.
2. Application for bill financing. The borrower provides the basic information of the bill and the screenshot from the ECDS, fills in the details of the bill financing and applies for money. The backend staff of the platform conducts primary review on the consistency of the bill information and financing details and the feasibility of financing.
3. Issuing digital bills by the platform. After the primary review, the platform will issue exclusive digital bills. Since the current business needs are not split, but directly endorsed and transferred in a single transaction, only one exclusive digital bill is issued for one bill. The digital bill will be sent to the borrower's account and displayed in the list of bills held by the borrower with the operation status of "Transferred."
4. Listing and transfer. After the borrower clicks "Transfer," the bill will be entered into the list of transferable bills for investors to select (if the borrower has a history of dishonesty, a deposit of 10% of the financing amount may be required in advance, which will be refunded after a successful transaction). This one exclusive digital bill will be sent via blockchain to the address agreed in the platform's smart contract.
5. Withdrawal of listing. If the borrower wants to give up the financing for his or her own reasons, he or she can find the bill in the list of transferable bills and click on "Withdrawal of listing." At this point, the exclusive digital bill will be returned to the borrower's account.

6. Delisting by platform. If an investor selects the bill, confirms the bank for receiving the bill, and clicks “Invest,” the digital settlement assets in the investor’s account equal to the amount financed by the bill will be sent to the address agreed in the platform smart contract.
7. Endorsement and transfer of the bill via ECDS. When the borrower finds the status of his/her bill as “Delisted” in the list of transferable bills, he/she can transfer the bill to the investor by endorsing it via ECDS.
8. Confirmation of the transfer of rights in the bill. When the investor finds the invested bill in the list of invested bills, the options available to him/her are “Receive Bill” and “Cancel Transaction.” “Receive Bill” is a confirmation that the bill is in your ECDS system and that you can execute the contract and complete the transaction. The reasons for “Cancel Transaction” include that the bill is not in line with the actual situation or the borrower has not transferred it for more than four hours, and the investor should provide screenshots to prove the reason. After the investor chooses to cancel the transaction, the platform will intervene to verify the transaction and, if true, will revoke the bill transaction and pursue liability accordingly.
9. Execution of smart contract. Digital settlement assets will be sent to the borrower and exclusive digital bills will be sent to the investor.
10. Bill write-off. Once the bill is due for acceptance, the investor should click “Accepted” under the bill in the list of bills held, thus confirming that the bill has been accepted. At this point, this one exclusive digital bill will be sent to the platform account, where it will be written off and will no longer be in circulation.

2. Technologies Implemented

Architecture of Blockchain Exchange

The blockchain exchange uses the Kubernetes scheduling system (see Fig. 6.22), which consists of a hardware layer, a virtual layer, a blockchain layer, an interface layer, a UI layer, a proxy layer, and a firewall. The back-end blockchain also uses the Kubernetes scheduling system to provide orchestration and management capabilities for heavily loaded containers. The orchestration capabilities of Kubernetes allow for the building of

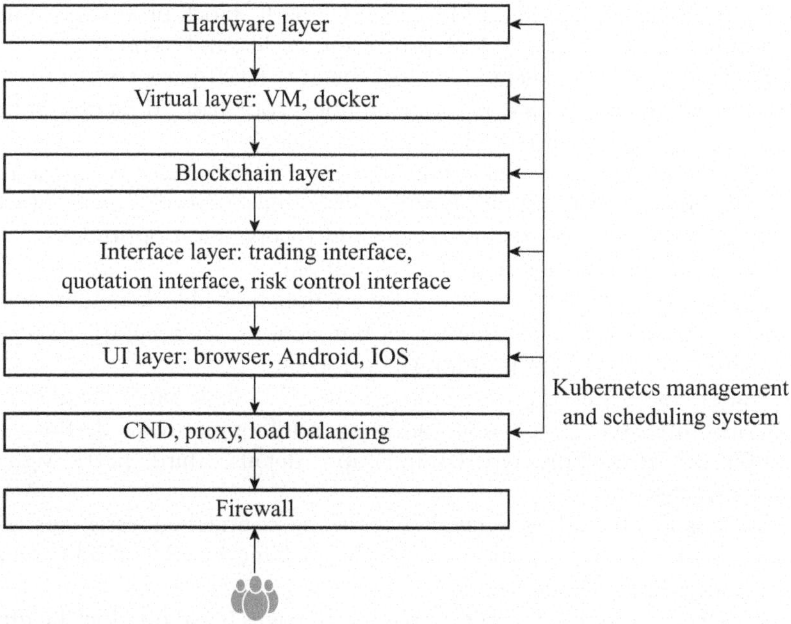

Fig. 6.22 HAIPINGXIAN blockchain exchange architecture

multicontainer application services, the scheduling or scaling of containers on clusters, and the management of their health status. The hardware layer provides the hardware facilities to run the blockchain. The virtual layer provides the underlying environment for blockchain development. The blockchain layer completes the blockchain development and operations. The interface layer completes the business logic of the system. The UI layer provides a user interface. The proxy layer optimizes the system operation speed and processing capability. The firewall provides security for the system.

Blockchain Browser

The blockchain browser provides block information query functions, including query and search for blocks, block details, operations, transaction records, transaction details, address list, bill information, and so on. The specific information that can be queried is as follows:

1. Block list page, including block height, hash, block producing time, number of transactions, block producing nodes, and so on
2. Block details page, including block height, hash, parent block hash, block producing nodes, random number, root hash, difficulty, time, block size, and transaction list within the block
3. Operation query page, including account operation records, operation time, bill acceptor, bill discount fee, discount rate; both parties of the transaction can filter records according to operation options such as entry, listing, withdrawal, and receipt of bills
4. Transaction list page, including transaction hash, block height, time stamp, transaction type, number of transactions, sending address, destination address, contract address, and so on
5. Transaction details page, including transaction hash, block height and hash, time stamp, contract address, sending address, destination address, transaction type, transaction details, third party signature, and so on
6. Address list, including general address and contract address; uers can check all related transaction records by clicking the address and entering the address detail page
7. Search engine, including jump to relevant pages based on block height, hash value, and public key address
8. Bill search, including search by bill number, acceptor, bill amount, and maturity date

3. Business Procedures

Bill Endorsement and Transfer Procedures

The bill endorsement and transfer system (see Figs. 6.23 and 6.24) realizes the circulation of blockchain digital assets and digital bills between enterprises. The specific endorsement and transfer procedures are as follows:

1. When an order is generated, the receiving company or borrower provides the goods to the goods recipient and then the goods recipient (i.e., the issuing company or acceptor) uses the draft to make payment.
2. When the draft is generated, the issuing company uploads the information and data of the commercial draft into the ECDS system, which is responsible for the issuance, receipt, and guarantee of the draft.

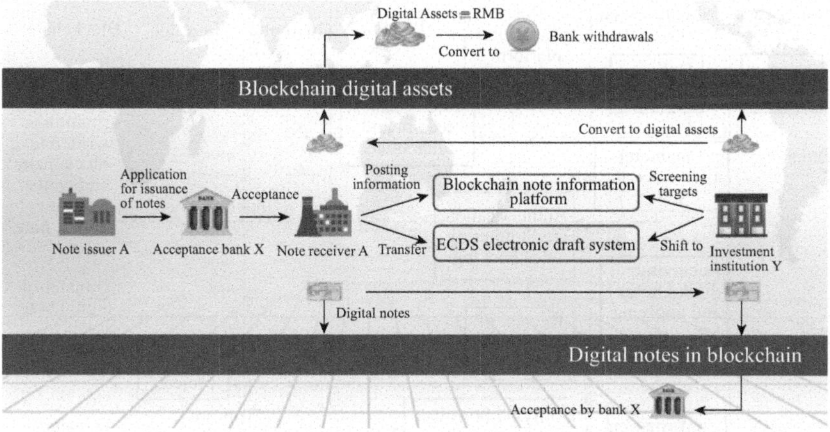

Fig. 6.23 PINGHAIXIAN bill endorsement and transfer process (1)

3. When the draft is successfully generated by the ECDS system, the issuing company applies for issuing the draft on the bill platform. The application information will be uploaded to guarantors (banks, non-bank financial institutions, factoring companies, P2P platforms, etc.) for their review.
4. After the review by the guarantor, the bill will be owned by the receiving company and can be exchanged for a blockchain digital bill or used for financing and trading. The information of this digital bill will be uploaded to the blockchain to generate the contract address of the digital bill.
5. The receiving company can post the bill information to the blockchain bill information platform or transfer it via the ECDS.
6. The investor can transfer funds to ECDS to obtain ownership of the digital bills or screen the underlying bills on the blockchain bill information platform. After making payments for the selected bills, the investor will be able to obtain ownership of the bills as well. When a fund provider selects a bill, the bill matching platform will receive the funds transferred by the fund provider and record it on the blockchain, while transferring the digital settlement assets to the smart contract address. The platform will also notify the receiving company that there is a new transaction waiting to be operated.

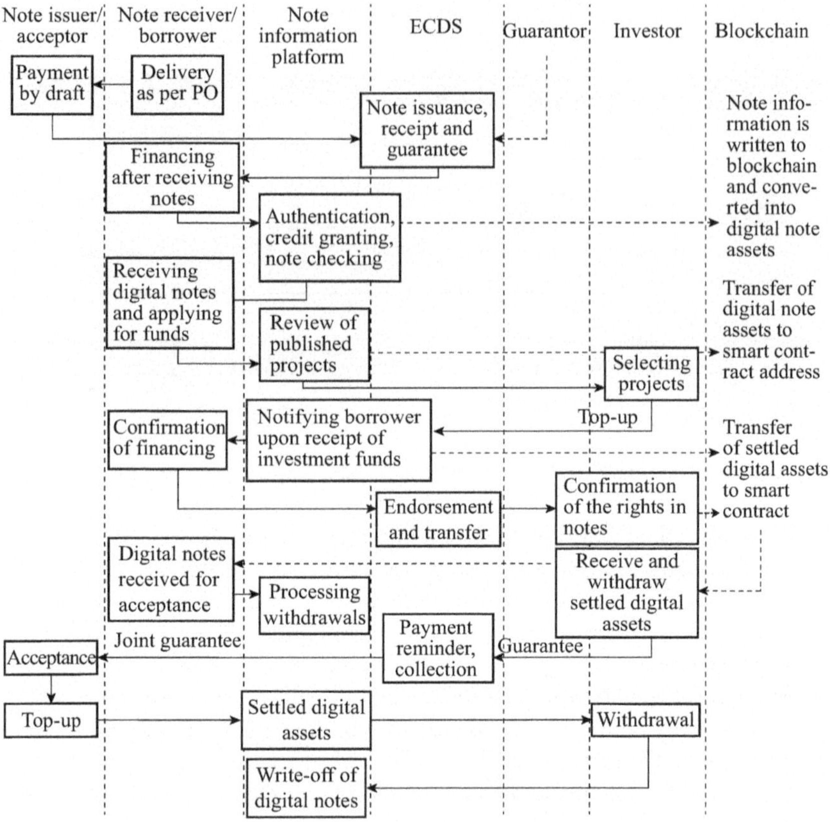

Fig. 6.24 PINGHAIXIAN bill endorsement and transfer process (2)

7. When the endorsement and transfer of the bill is completed and the investor confirms the bill, the blockchain back-end platform will execute the smart contract. The investor will receive the bill asset address and the issuing company will receive the fund asset address of the fund provider. Thus, the whole bill endorsement and transfer procedures are completed.
8. The blockchain digital bills can be accepted by a guarantor or a bank. The digital bills can be converted into RMB and withdrawn through a bank card.

Blockchain Smart Contract Execution Procedures

When a financing company uploads a digital bill held by it to the HAIPIAOHUI platform of HAIPINGXIAN, a secure bill address will be generated and stored in the blockchain. When an enterprise converts its liquidity into digital assets, a digital asset address will also be generated and stored in the blockchain. When two parties reach an agreement, the smart contract matching system of the blockchain will automatically execute by sending the financing company's bill address to the fund provider and the fund provider's asset address to the financing company. The smart contract system effectively solves the problem of whether to give the bill or the money first in the traditional bill endorsement. With the help of smart contract, both parties can complete the bill transaction without trust, thus creating the Alipay of the digital bill transaction industry (see Fig. 6.25).

6.8.2.3 *Issues That Need to be Addressed for Future Development*

1. Time Frame for Trading

The bill matching system is dedicated to providing corporate users with fast, convenient, and efficient transactions, but the advance payments from the fund providers need to be deposited in a trusted account, that is, the banking system, as a result of the transaction limits. HAIPIAOHUI has entered into a cooperation agreement with

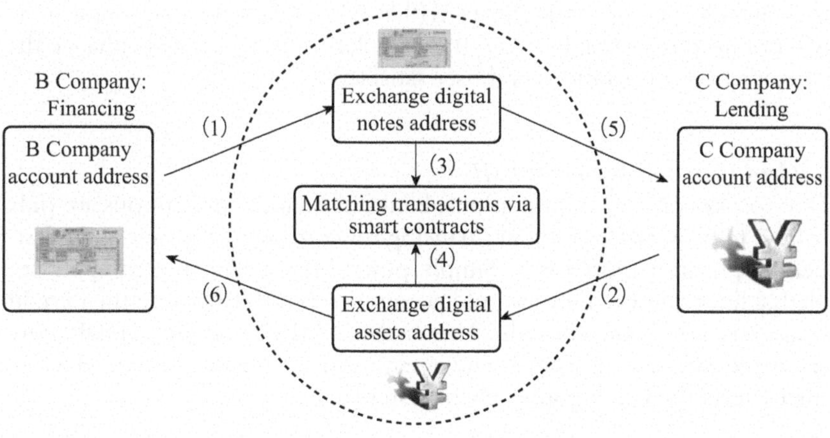

Fig. 6.25 Blockchain smart contract execution process in HAIPINGXIAN bill exchange

CITIC Bank to keep corporate funds safely in the CITIC account. Considering the working system of the bank, funds can only be processed during working hours on weekdays. If enterprises operate the funds in and out of the platform during nonworking days, the bank will delay the processing of these operation records, which makes it difficult for enterprises to operate conveniently.

The issuance of central bank digital currencies will effectively solve these problems. The central bank provides a national-level trusted platform where transactions of digital currencies can successfully overcome the shortcomings of manual processing of transaction operations. Each transaction is recorded, which reduces the tedious procedures of manual review and improves the efficiency of business-to-business bill endorsement.

2. Bill Synchronization in ECDS

In the HAIPIAOHUI platform, bill holders need to upload their bill information and pass the back-end review before they can enter the platform's trading system. When a transaction is completed, they still need to transfer the bill through the ECDS. The whole process of bill transfer involves multiple interactions with the ECDS, which weakens the user experience.

If ECDS can cooperate with the bill trading platform to synchronize the bill information with the HAIPIAOHUI platform, corporate users will not need to switch between the two platforms, which will enhance the convenience of operations and user satisfaction.

3. Credit Accumulation for SMEs

Due to risk control considerations, banks or financial institutions are only willing to provide factoring or financing for core enterprises and their first-tier suppliers in most cases. Simply put, SMEs are unable to apply for pledge financing even if they hold accounts receivable because their credit history is not good enough. This makes SMEs' working capital more restricted, their needs unmet, and their business volume limited, which in turn affects the whole supply chain system.

As one type of "trust machine," blockchain is traceable, highly consensual and tamper-proof. In the past, paper-based transaction records were not easily kept and publicly inspected. By using the identity authentication of digital signature, SMEs can effectively accumulate their credit points after recording their accounts receivable or payable on the blockchain, which solves the issue of insufficient credit for financing and improves the efficiency of capital turnover. This model makes the credit in the whole business system transmissible and traceable.

4. Splitting and Packaging of Accounts Receivable

The amount of accounts receivable varies widely among different enterprises within the supply chain system. Enterprises are subject to various objective restrictions when carrying out bill endorsement or accounts receivable pledge financing. One of the typical restrictions is that the bills cannot be split, resulting in second-tier suppliers, for example, no longer being able to use the good credit of the core enterprise for financing. However, blockchain can split or package the accounts payable of core enterprises to make payments, thus accelerating the liquidity of SMEs and reducing their financing costs.

The accounts receivable or payable can be considered as digital assets in the blockchain logic. The splitting and packaging of assets in an open and transparent manner with multiple witnesses is essentially the realization of credit circulation.

References

Angulo, A., Nachtmann, H., & Waller, M. A. (2004). Supply chain information sharing in a vendor managed inventory partnership. *Journal of Business Logistics, 25*(1), 101–120.

Ballou, D. P., & Pazer, H. L. (1985). Modeling data and process quality in multi-input, multi-output information systems. *Management Science, 31*(2), 150–162.

Batini, C., Rula, A., Scannapieco, M., & Viscusi, G. (2015). From data quality to big data quality. *Journal of Database Management, 26*(1), 60–82.

Bechini, A., Cimino, M. G. C. A., Marcelloni, F., & Tomasi, A. (2008). Patterns and technologies for enabling supply chain traceability through collaborative e-business. *Information and Software Technology, 50*(4), 342–359.

Ben-Daya, M., Hassini, E., & Bahroun, Z. (2017). Internet of things and supply chain management: A literature review. *International Journal of Production Research, 57*, 1–24.

Bollen, A. F., Riden, C. P., & Opara, L. U. (2006). Traceability in postharvest quality management. *International Journal of Postharvest Technology and Innovation, 1*(1), 93–105.

Buzacott, J. A., & Zhang, R. Q. (2004). Inventory management with asset-based financing. *Management Science, 50*(9), 1274–1292.

Cai, L., & Zhu, Y. (2015). The challenges of data quality and data quality assessment in the big data era. *Data Science Journal, 14*(0), 2.

Caridi, M., Moretto, A., Perego, A., & Tumino, A. (2014). The benefits of supply chain visibility: A value assessment model. *International Journal of Production Economics, 151*, 1–19.

Chen Xiangfeng & Zhu Daoli. (2005). Modern logistics financial service innovation-financial logistics. *Logistics Technology*, (03): 4–6+15.

Choudhury, V. (1997). Strategic choices in the development of interorganizational information systems. *Information Systems Research, 8*(1), 1–24.

Forward Industry Research Institute. (2017–2022). Global Health and Medical Big Data Industry Development Prospect Forecast and Investment Strategic Planning Analysis Report.

Giannakis, M., & Louis, M. (2011). A multi-agent based framework for supply chain risk management. *Journal of Purchasing and Supply Management, 17*(1), 23–31.

Gordijn, J., Akkermans, H., & Van Vliet, J. (2001). Designing and evaluating e-business models. *IEEE Intelligent Systems, 16*(4), 11–17.

Gunasekaran, A., & Ngai, E. W. T. (2004). Virtual supply-chain management. *Production Planning & Control, 15*(6), 584–595.

Guo Renzheng. (2015). Construction of visible intelligent supply chain. *Logistics Technology and Application, 20*(03), 87–88+90.

Hazen, B. T., Boone, C. A., Ezell, J. D., & Jones-Farmer, L. A. (2014). Data quality for data science, predictive analytics, and big data in supply chain management: An introduction to the problem and suggestions for research and applications. *International Journal of Production Economics, 154*, 72–80.

Hofmann, E. (2009). Inventory financing in supply chains: A logistics service provider-approach. *International Journal of Physical Distribution & Logistics Management, 39*(9), 716–740.

Iacovou, C. L., Benbasat, I., & Dexter, A. S. (1995). Electronic data interchange and small organizations: Adoption and impact of technology. *MIS Quarterly, 19*, 465–485.

Iansiti, M., & Lakhani, K. R. (2017). The truth about blockchain. *Harvard Business Review, 95*(1), 118–127.

IndustryARC. (2018). *Big data market with focus on supply chain management: Key trends, competitive landscape, geographic & end-user analysis (2012–2018).*

Jiang Dongdong, Shang Yulin, Tian Ye, & Lu Zenan. (2017). Construction of e-warehouse receipt circulation platform based on blockchain. *Journal of Xi'an Institute of Technology, 31*(06), 828–834.

Jun, C., & Wei, M. Y. (2011). The research of supply chain information collaboration based on cloud computing. *Procedia Environmental Sciences, 10*, 875–880.

Katal, A., Wazid, M., & Goudar, R. (2013). *Big data: Issues, challenges, tools and good practices* (pp. 404–409). IEEE.

Khan, A., Pohl, M., Bosse, S., Hart, S. W., & Turowski, K. (2017). *A holistic view of the IoT process from sensors to the business value.*

Khan, R., Khan, S. U., Zaheer, R., & Khan, S. (2012). Future internet: The internet of things architecture, possible applications and key challenges. *2012 10th International Conference on Frontiers of Information Technology*, 257–260.

Lee, H. L., Padmanabhan, V., & Whang, S. (1997a). Information distortion in a supply chain: The bullwhip effect. *Management Science, 43*(4), 546–558.

Lee, H. L., Padmanabhan, V., & Whang, S. (1997b). The bullwhip effect in supply chains. *Sloan Management Review, 38*, 93–102.

Lee, H. L., So, K. C., & Tang, C. S. (2000). The value of information sharing in a two-level supply chain. *Management Science, 46*(5), 626–643.

Lee, H. L., & Whang, S. (2000). Information sharing in a supply chain. *International Journal of Manufacturing Technology and Management, 1*(1), 79–93.

Lee, Y. W., Strong, D. M., Kahn, B. K., & Wang, R. Y. (2002). AIMQ: A methodology for information quality assessment. *Information & Management, 40*(2), 133–146.

Li, B., & Li, Y. (2017). Internet of things drives supply chain innovation: A research framework. *International Journal of Organizational Innovation, 9*(3), 71–92.

Li, B.-H., Zhang, L., Wang, S.-L., Tao, F., Cao, J., Jiang, X., Song, X., & Chai, X. (2010). Cloud manufacturing: A new service-oriented networked manufacturing model. *Computer Integrated Manufacturing Systems, 16*(1), 1–7.

Li Xiao, & Liu Zhenggang. (2017). Intelligent governance mechanism of supply chain based on blockchain technology. *China Circulation Economy, 31*(11), 34–44.

Liu, L., & Jia, W. (2010). *Business model for drug supply chain based on the internet of things* (pp. 982–986). IEEE.

Madnick, S. E., Wang, R. Y., Lee, Y. W., & Zhu, H. (2009). Overview and framework for data and information quality research. *Journal of Data and Information Quality, 1*(1), 1–22.

Premkumar, G., Ramamurthy, K., & Nilakanta, S. (1994). Implementation of electronic data interchange: An innovation diffusion perspective. *Journal of Management Information Systems, 11*(2), 157–186.

Raghunathan, S., & Yeh, A. B. (2001). Beyond EDI: Impact of continuous replenishment program (CRP) between a manufacturer and its retailers. *Information Systems Research, 12*(4), 406–419.

Robak, S., Franczyk, B., & Robak, M. (2013). *Applying big data and linked data concepts in supply chains management* (pp. 1215–1221). IEEE.

Ross, A. D., Kuzu, K., & Li, W. (2016). Exploring supplier performance risk and the buyer's role using chance-constrained data envelopment analysis. *European Journal of Operational Research, 250*(3), 966–978.

Shi, W., Cao, J., Zhang, Q., Li, Y., & Xu, L. (2016). Edge computing: Vision and challenges. *IEEE Internet of Things Journal, 3*(5), 637–646.

Shi, W., & Dustdar, S. (2016). The promise of edge computing. *Computer, 49*(5), 78–81.

Song Hua, Wang Lan, & Shi Xiaomeng. (2014). EVA-based supply chain financing model and performance measurement. *Contemporary Economic Management, 36*(05), 20–26.

Tian, F. (2016). *An agri-food supply chain traceability system for China based on RFID & blockchain technology* (pp. 1–6). IEEE.

Trienekens, J. H., Wognum, P. M., Beulens, A. J. M., & van der Vorst, J. G. A. J. (2012). Transparency in complex dynamic food supply chains. *Advanced Engineering Informatics, 26*(1), 55–65.

Vakharia, A. J. (2002). E-business and supply chain management. *Decision Sciences, 33*(4), 495–504.

Waller, M. A., & Fawcett, S. E. (2013). Data science, predictive analytics, and big data: A revolution that will transform supply chain design and management. *Journal of Business Logistics, 34*(2), 77–84.

Wang Man & Shao Feng. (2011). Research on the application and countermeasures of the internet of things in the supply chain. *Financial Innovation*, (5), 28–30.

Wang, R. Y., & Strong, D. M. (1996). Beyond accuracy: What data quality means to data consumers. *Journal of Management Information Systems, 12*(4), 5–33.

Weber, I., Xu, X., Riveret, R., Governatori, G., Ponomarev, A., & Mendling, J. (2016). *Untrusted business process monitoring and execution using blockchain* (pp. 329–347). Springer.

Williams, B. D., Roh, J., Tokar, T., & Swink, M. (2013). Leveraging supply chain visibility for responsiveness: The moderating role of internal integration. *Journal of Operations Management, 31*(7–8), 543–554.

Wu, Y., Cegielski, C. G., Hazen, B. T., & Hall, D. J. (2013). Cloud computing in support of supply chain information system infrastructure: Understanding when to go to the cloud. *Journal of Supply Chain Management, 49*(3), 25–41.

Xiang Tingting. (2013). The technical support of electronic supply chain finance. *Electronic Testing*, (14), 245–246.

Xu, X. (2012). From cloud computing to cloud manufacturing. *Robotics and Computer-Integrated Manufacturing, 28*(1), 75–86.

Yang Qinhe. (2019). What is the difference between chattels and warehouse receipts? Explain the difference between 3 perspective and 26 elements, CWRE, 2019-01-16.

Yu, M.-C., & Goh, M. (2014). A multi-objective approach to supply chain visibility and risk. *European Journal of Operational Research, 233*(1), 125–130.

Yu, Z., Yan, H., & Edwin Cheng, T. (2001). Benefits of information sharing with supply chain partnerships. *Industrial Management & Data Systems, 101*(3), 114–121.

Zhang, A. N., Goh, M., & Meng, F. (2011). Conceptual modelling for supply chain inventory visibility. *International Journal of Production Economics, 133*(2), 578–585.

Zhang, L., Luo, Y., Tao, F., Li, B. H., Ren, L., Zhang, X., Guo, H., Cheng, Y., Hu, A., & Liu, Y. (2014). Cloud manufacturing: A new manufacturing paradigm. *Enterprise Information Systems, 8*(2), 167–187.

Zhao, X., Yeung, K., Huang, Q., & Song, X. (2015). Improving the predictability of business failure of supply chain finance clients by using external big dataset. *Industrial Management & Data Systems, 115*(9), 1683–1703.

Zhou, W., & Piramuthu, S. (2015). IoT and supply chain traceability. In R. Doss, S. Piramuthu, & W. Zhou (Eds.), *Future network systems and security* (Vol. 523, pp. 156–165). 4th International Conference, FNSS 2018, Paris, France, July 9–11, 2018, Proceedings, Springer.

Zhou, Z., Xiao, S., Ho, Y.-C. (Chad), & Tan, Y. (2018). The persuasive and informative effects of information disclosure: Evidence from an online supply chain finance market. *SSRN Electronic Journal.*

CHAPTER 7

Responsible Operations (I): Sustainability of Intelligent Supply Chain Finance

7.1 Introduction

The intention of supply chain finance is to help high-quality SMEs solve the problems of financing difficulties and high financing costs by controlling the commodity flow, the logistics flow, and the information flow in the supply chain, to promote the rational allocation and circulation of funds among organizations through continuous and effective supply chain operations, and to further optimize the supply chain with the liquid funds, and finally to organize all supply chain stakeholders effectively to achieve a win-win situation and the goal of long-term sustainable development of enterprises, partners, industries, and society. Obviously, this goal implies the meaning of the social responsibility in the supply chain. Social responsibility in supply chain has been an important topic of interest in recent years in the industrial and academic circles, and its basic meaning is as follows: First, enterprises must be able to fulfill their social responsibility and incorporate socially responsible behaviors in their governance and management frameworks. Second, social responsibility is not an independent act of a certain enterprise, but needs to be spread across a wide range of partners. Therefore, the guidelines for social responsibility in supply chain refer to a holistic view of an enterprise's socially responsible behaviors. Enterprises are discouraged from just fulfilling their social responsibility by themselves while ignoring the impact on the ability of upstream and downstream partners to take social responsibility.

H. Song, *Smart Supply Chain Finance*,
https://doi.org/10.1007/978-981-16-5997-3_7

Despite a long history of exploring corporate social responsibility, the study of social responsibility in a supply chain context started less than two decades ago (Maloni & Brown, 2006). Poist (1989) was the first to suggest the need to consider social responsibility in the supply chain. Murphy and Poist (2002) concluded that although many enterprises have been slow to think and act socially, social responsibility is becoming increasingly important in the supply chain. Since then, social responsibility in supply chain has received widespread attention and exploration from both academia and industry (Carter & Jennings, 2002; Maloni & Brown, 2006; Carter & Rogers, 2008; Cruz, 2008; Andersen & Skjoett-Larsen, 2009; Salam, 2009; Spence & Bourlakis, 2009; Awaysheh & Klassen, 2010; Park-Poaps & Rees, 2010; Tate et al., 2010). According to the most typical points of view, social responsibility in supply chain is different from the previous corporate social responsibility (CSR, which refers to the integration of socially responsible behaviors into an enterprise's core values beyond the legal compliance basis to achieve better business interests) and corporate social watchdog (CSW, which refers to an enterprise's efforts to guide its partners or counterparties by setting standards and aligning them with the enterprise's values and expectations, but the full range of considerations and responses to issues in the supply chain beyond the narrow economic, technical, and legal requirements to achieve the social (and environmental) benefits as well as the traditional economic gains sought by each participant of that supply chain (Spence & Bourlakis, 2009). In general, social responsibility in supply chain has four characteristics: (1) social (environmental) benefits are realized throughout the chain; (2) all participants in the supply chain have legitimacy and the right to speak; (3) a true partnership can be formed between stakeholders; and (4) ethics are established through different ways of organizing the supply chain (Maloni & Brown, 2006; Spence & Bourlakis, 2009). Clearly, the first two points are concerned with supply chain sustainability, while the latter two look at social responsibility from the perspective of the environment and business civilization.

Social responsibility in supply chain is also the basis for the development of supply chain finance. On the one hand, supply chain finance should consider how it can more widely serve SMEs, especially the targets that are relatively difficult to reach in the past (the enterprises at the bottom of the pyramid), so that they can realize the economic benefits (i.e., flexible and low interest rates to obtain funds), as well as social and environmental benefits by virtue of equal, reasonable, and effective access to supply chain financial services, and finally sustainable development of supply chain finance is achieved. On the other hand, supply chain finance should consider how to organize and collaborate the business, especially to set up a reasonable operating system and environment so as to establish a system with business civilization. These are all key issues for the development of supply chain finance today. This chapter will mainly explore the former issue, that is, the sustainability of supply chain finance, while the next chapter will focus on exploring the environment and ethics of supply chain finance, that is, building the system and business civilization. First of all, this chapter will discuss the key factors of supply chain and supply chain finance, mainly from the perspective of sustainability. After that, operation models of sustainable supply chain finance will be explored by combining two most important areas for the future development of supply chain finance—agriculture and circular economy.

7.2 Sustainable Supply Chain and Sustainable Supply Chain Finance

Social and environmental concerns started independently of economic factors and gradually became a complete consideration system integrated with economic factors, resulting in the concerns of social responsibility in supply chain. The concept of sustainable supply chain (Carter & Liane Easton, 2011) evolved on this basis has gradually been integrated with supply chain finance, resulting in the sustainable supply chain finance (SSCF), which makes how to manage supply chain finance from a sustainable perspective and achieve sustainable development through supply chain finance a key direction of supply chain finance research nowadays.

7.2.1 *Sustainable Supply Chain Management*

The focus on supply chain sustainability began in a fragmented and piecemeal manner. Factors such as environment, diversity, and safety were studied independently rather than holistically in supply chain, and their initial exploration was not closely integrated with the economic factors. In fact, as early as the late 1990s and early 2000s, scholars have begun to explore the green factors in supply chain (Green et al., 1998; Walton et al., 1998; Beamon, 1999; Van Hoek, 1999; Bowen et al., 2001; Hall, 2001; Rao, 2002). For example, Bowen et al. (2001) were among the early scholars to propose the inclusion of environmental factors in procurement and supply.

Their research proposed a concept of green supply chain, which integrates environmental factors into the whole process of supply chain management (including product manufacturing, raw material procurement and selection, production, dedicated delivery of products to customers, and recycling at the end of the life cycle) (Srivastava, 2007). Subsequent researches began to expand from the single factor of environment to a triple bottom line in the supply chain domain, that is, environmental, social, and economic factors. The triple bottom line was originally introduced by the British scholar Elkington (1999), who argued that corporate social responsibility can be divided into three categories according to the areas of responsibility: economic responsibility, environmental responsibility, and social responsibility. Economic responsibility is the traditional corporate responsibility, mainly including increasing profits, tax liabilities, and dividends to shareholders and investors. Environmental responsibility is the protection of the environment. Social responsibility is the responsibility to other stakeholders in society. Based on this theoretical framework, many scholars have applied it to the field of supply chain and developed a holistic framework of sustainable supply chain (Carter & Rogers, 2008; Seuring & Müller, 2008; Pagell & Wu, 2009).

Carter and Rogers (2008) proposed that a sustainable supply chain is the strategic and systematic integration and fulfillment of an organization's social, environmental, and economic goals in the cross-organizational process, with a result that the long-term economic performance of this organization and its supply chain partners can be improved. Furthermore, they pointed out in their study that these three factors are closely related to the supply chain and that enterprises that implement sustainable supply chains are able to achieve higher economic performance than that consider a single factor or two factors. This is because supply chains that are able to integrate social and environmental resources or knowledge are difficult for competitors to imitate, thus creating a competitive advantage. These studies emphasized that the achievement of social and environmental goals should not completely exclude consideration of economic factors; otherwise, the economic benefits may be challenged by the high implementation costs. Therefore, sustainable supply chain requires simultaneous consideration of social, environmental, and economic factors and needs to be organized and managed rationally in terms of strategy, culture, risk management, and transparency (see Fig. 7.1).

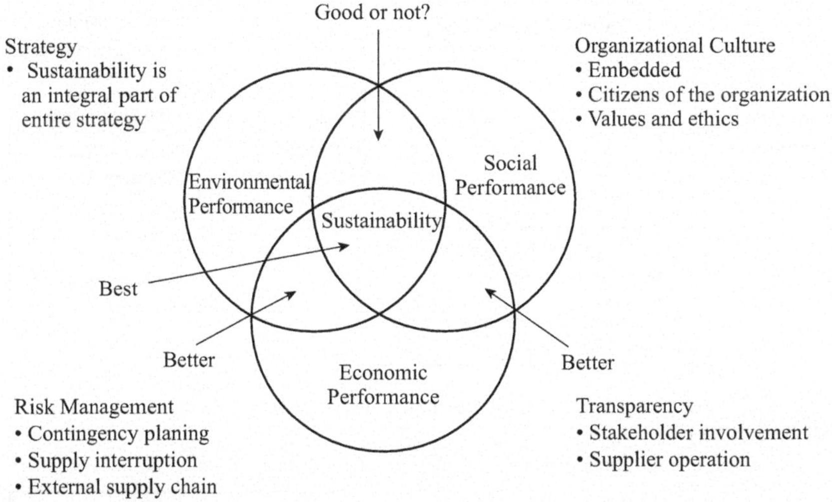

Fig. 7.1 Sustainable supply chain integration framework. (Source: Carter & Rogers, 2008)

Another typical literature that explores sustainable supply chains is the study by Seuring and Müller (2008), who presented a comprehensive framework based on a review of 191 literature from 1994 to 2007. By first exploring the factors that trigger enterprises to implement sustainable supply chains, the study argued that sustainable supply chains are implemented from three major sources of pressure and incentives, namely government, customers, and stakeholders. After receiving pressure and incentives from these three sources, the enterprises transmit them to their suppliers, thus driving two aspects of sustainable supply chain strategies, namely supplier risk and performance management (see Fig. 7.2) and supply chain management of sustainable products (see Fig. 7.3).

In terms of supplier relationship, Seuring and Müller (2008) concluded that there are several major barriers to sustainable supply chains, which, in order of importance, include high costs, coordination and complexity, and inadequate or lack of communication in the supply chains. However, the facilitating factors include communication, environmental and social management systems (e.g., ISO 14000 or SA8000), monitoring/evaluation/reporting/sanctions, training and education of procurement managers and suppliers, and integration of sustainability into the overall corporate

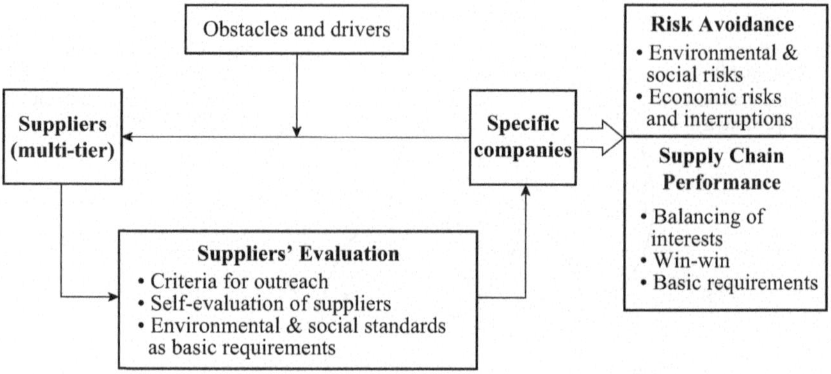

Fig. 7.2 Supplier risk and performance management. (Source: Seuring & Müller, 2008)

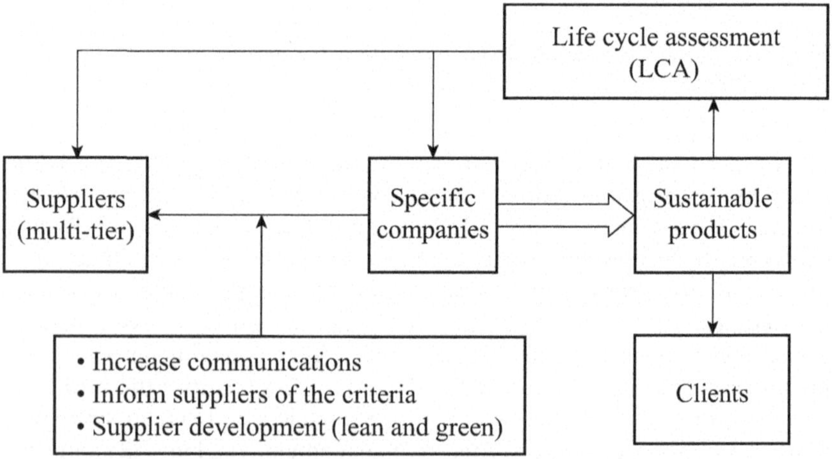

Fig. 7.3 Sustainable product supply chain management. (Source: Seuring & Müller, 2008)

strategy. From it, it is clear that communication is both a barrier and a facilitator. They believed that joint efforts between supply chain partners will reduce the costs of such communication. Another factor they considered important for sustainable supply chain development is the environmental and social management system (ISO14000, etc.), which is a guarantee to achieve the minimum requirements by monitoring and controlling corporate behaviors.

The third research on sustainable supply chains comes from Pagell and Wu (2009), who provided a framework to guide managers in developing sustainable supply chains based on their study of ten business cases. They argued that implementing a sustainable supply chain differs significantly in behaviors from business leaders who are simply engaged in the supply chain, and, therefore, developing a sustainable supply chain requires efforts in the following aspects (see Fig. 7.4): First aspect is commonality, awareness, and orientation. Adopting a sustainable supply chain requires integrating sustainability as a consensus throughout the supply chain system, especially by closely aligning the corresponding factors with business models, brands, and decisions. Second is continuity of suppliers. Sustainable supply chain leaders should strive to ensure that all of their partners stay in business so that they can thrive, reinvest, innovate, and grow. Therefore, enterprises use a number of effective incentives to help suppliers achieve sustainability, such as offering long-term contracts or helping suppliers obtain the resources necessary for their development. Some of the incentives used to help suppliers excel in sustainability issues are offering long-term contracts and access to resources for development, or paying above-market rates. In this case, buyers often demand more transparency

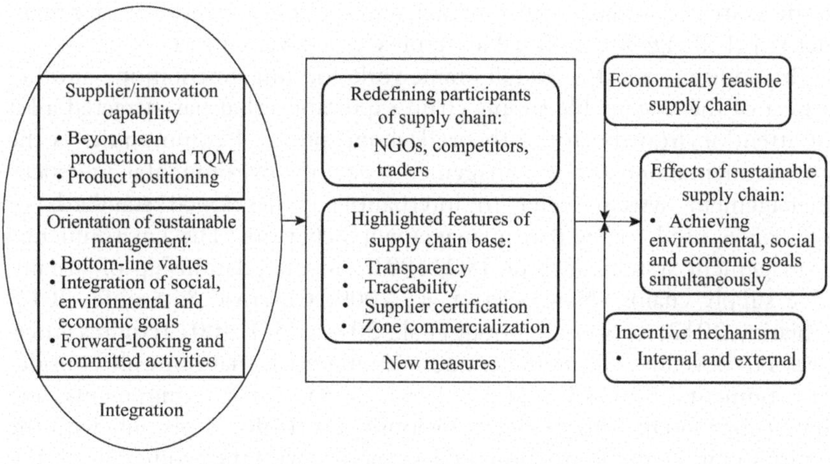

Fig. 7.4 Framework for sustainable supply chain management practices. (Source: Pagell & Wu, 2009)

in the chain, such as more detailed information about the capital flow. Sustainable supply chain leaders regard transparency as an important element of social responsibility, as it ensures that no participant of the chain is bullied. Third is redefinition of the supply chain and its participants. Sustainable supply chain leaders often work with external entities that the general business manager would ignore or view as adversaries, such as NGOs, local governments, and even competitors. Fourth is the practices of supply chain management. Sustainable supply chain leaders often link supplier selection and decisions to sustainability goals, work with suppliers to help achieve sustainability goals, or verify suppliers' social or environmental actions and results. Large buyers often request information directly from suppliers. In addition, another common characteristic of sustainable supply leaders is that they invest in human capital through a number of human resource policies, thereby increasing employee well-being and commitment to the organization. Fifth is the complex measurement. A striking finding of Pagell and Wu's (2009) study is that even though supply chain sustainability leaders struggle to measure the impact of their environmental and social activities, the complexity of measurement increases as sustainable supply chain practices are extended to suppliers. Their study found that some enterprises initially used life cycle analysis, but this method of measurement measured only environmental factors in the supply chain, without fully considering social factors. Therefore, how to measure economic, environmental, and social in a comprehensive manner is a challenge for sustainable supply chain development.

In addition to the overall framework for implementation, another aspect of the sustainable supply chain exploration that has attracted a lot of attention from both the theoretical and practical communities is the environmental and social management system. Environmental and social management systems refer to internationally developed standards or guidelines used to regulate management behaviors. The environmental management systems include ISO14001 and the relationship of sustainable supply chains (Nawrocka et al., 2009; Curkovic & Sroufe, 2011; Chiarini, 2012; de Sousa Jabbour et al., 2014). ISO14001 requires enterprises to develop and implement policies and goals that not only consider environmental factors but also reflect legal and other requirements, and reveal appropriate information. Obviously, ISO14001 deals only with the entire supply chain production process and not with the product itself. For this reason, ISO14001 also extends to processes that can be verified or certified. The implementation of the standard follows a five-step approach:

plan, implement, check, act, and continuously improve. These steps have a key contributing effect to the achievement of a sustainable supply chain, especially in terms of external supplier communication and management (Curkovic & Sroufe, 2011; Chiarini, 2012). Some studies have also pointed out that ISO14001 has a good role in promoting synergy with suppliers, but the achievement of this goal also requires synergy between different functions and departments within the organization. In other words, the coordination between internal and external supply chains is what makes ISO14001 truly effective (Nawrocka et al., 2009). Apart from ISO14001, another management system for sustainable supply chain development is SA8000, which is the acronym for Social Accountability 8000. As the world's first international standard on ethics, SA8000 aims to ensure that suppliers supply products that meet the requirements of social responsibility standards in terms of labor, health and safety, working hours, wages, and management systems, among others. Many studies have concluded that sustainable supply chains are feasible to implement in Tier 1 suppliers; however, as higher upstream tiers are reached, the implementation of social responsibility becomes challenging. In this case, SA8000 can help to reduce the information asymmetry that arises from the increasing number of supply tiers and to truly achieve a sustainable supply chain (Ciliberti et al., 2009). In recent years, another management system has been identified as a key one to drive sustainable supply chains, namely ISO 26000, published by the IOS in 2010. ISO 26000 transforms corporate social responsibility (CSR) into social responsibility, which means that the system is not only applicable to enterprises, but is adapted to all types of institutions and organizations. In this way, a wide range of stakeholders are included in the scope of sustainability. Furthermore, unlike ISO 9000, which focuses primarily on quality management, ISO 26000 offers a more comprehensive approach to the supply chain, including extended upstream and downstream involvement, as well as the integration of environmental approaches, such as recycling or life cycle assessment. Therefore, the adoption of the system will bring the recognition of the company by many stakeholders, thus forming and developing supply chain networks and partnerships (Castka & Balzarova, 2008).

From the above studies, it is evident that sustainable supply chains emphasize the continuous development of the entire supply chain network, with an aim to achieve balanced economic, social, and environmental development at the same time. However, the realization of this goal requires efforts in three aspects: (1) a wide range of stakeholders, especially a wide network of suppliers can be included and promoted as equally as possible, so as to jointly set sustainable goals and take desirable behaviors; (2) in the management process, the business activities of various participants can be communicated and collaborated, so that supply chain operations and behaviors can be transparent and traceable, and the risks and uncertainties can be effectively managed through such behaviors; (3) in terms of management elements, an effective culture and incentive system can be formed, so that each participant can obtain the corresponding resources and capabilities to achieve long-term development on the basis of following the triple bottom line.

7.2.2 Sustainable Supply Chain Finance

Following the intensive exploration of sustainable supply chains, sustainable supply chain finance has gradually attracted the interests of the practical and theoretical community at present (Perez, 2012; BSR, 2018; Liang et al., 2018; Tseng et al., 2018; Canto-Cuevas et al., 2019). Combining sustainable supply chain with financial services, sustainable supply chain finance aims to realize sustainable supply chain by using supply chain finance, and also drive the further development of supply chain finance through sustainable supply chain. According to a study (2018) by BSR, an international NGO, sustainable supply chain finance has created huge incentives for both buyers and sellers in the supply chains, while opening up new markets for financial institutions, which in turn will further transform the supply chain. The report showed that the current global 20% annual growth rate of the supply chain finance market, coupled with digitalization, has provided a huge chance for sustainable supply chain finance. The reason for this is that digitization allows any organization to easily access sustainability data and use it for supply chain finance operations. The report also estimated that sustainable supply chain finance may eventually cover one-third of all highly secure accounts payable suitable for financing globally, with a current market share of US$660 billion.

Sustainable supply chain finance can be understood from the perspectives of the extent to which sustainable supply chain performance is demonstrated and how difficult it is for the corresponding organization to intervene financially (see Fig. 7.5). A supply chain is a weblike structure consisting of a large number of suppliers, core companies and customers, in which a great deal of commodity flows, logistics flows, information flows, and capital flows occur. Supply chains often involve multiple levels or tiers

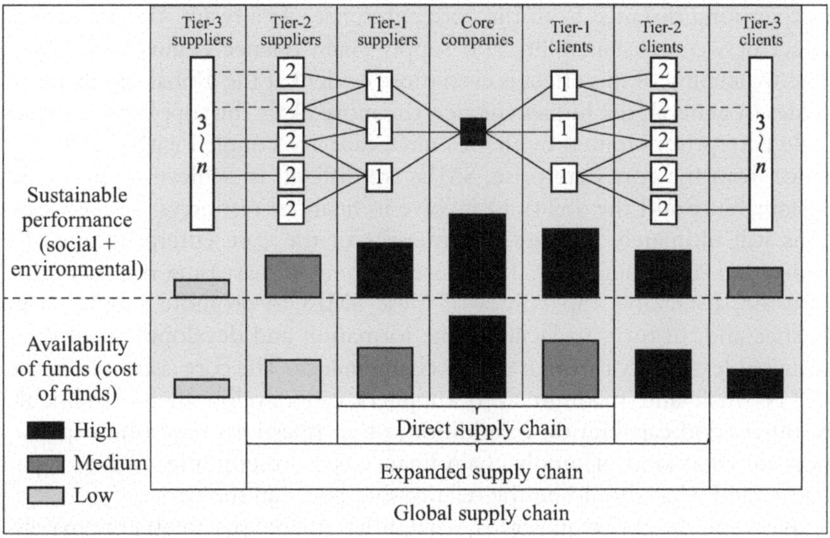

Fig. 7.5 Asymmetric distribution of sustainable risk and financial intervention in supply chain networks

(i.e., tier 1-n suppliers and customers), so from the perspective of a core enterprise, the supply chain structure can also be divided into three levels, that is, direct supply chain, extended supply chain, and global supply chain. The direct supply chain is composed of a core enterprise and its tier-1 upstream suppliers and downstream customers. Sustainability is easy to achieve, with environmental and social concerns to be driven by the core enterprise. In addition, the degree of involvement of tier-1 suppliers and tier-1 customers in financial resources is higher, because the core enterprises directly control the upstream and downstream business (directly engaged in procurement or distribution). In other words, it is easier to achieve supply chain finance and to form an interactive effect between supply chain sustainability and supply chain finance. The extended supply chain involves the tier-1 upstream suppliers and downstream customers a core enterprise. At this point, supply chain sustainability can still be achieved, due to the fact that the core enterprise can urge its tier-1 suppliers to follow the triple bottom-line principle with respect to their upstream suppliers and their purchasing practices; however, its power of control is clearly reduced. Tier-2 suppliers are less involved in financial resources due to their long distance from the core enterprise. As a result, the interactive effect between sustainability and supply chain finance begins to weaken. The weakening of this effect is even more evident at the global supply chain stage. In general, the higher the tier, the more likely the supplier is a small-scale enterprise. Limited by the resource capacity, coupled with the far distance from the core enterprise, SMEs are difficult to achieve supply chain sustainability and the ability to involve in financial resources is very weak. This will ultimately damage the interests of the core enterprise and the realization of sustainability. Therefore, there is an increasing need to cultivate the sustainable capabilities of these SMEs to promote supply chain finance and, in turn, to facilitate the formation and development of their sustainable capacity through supply chain finance. The core issue is how the tier-N small and medium-sized suppliers can develop their sustainable resources and capabilities. In addition, other questions requiring exploration are what kind of supply chain finance is corresponding to their capabilities and what should be the relationship between the two.

Based on the above questions, what differentiated sustainability capabilities need to be cultivated by tier-N SMEs can be explored from the perspective of Natural Resource-Based View (NRBV) and Social Resource-Based View (SRBV). NRBV is developed based on the Resource-Based View (RBV). Corporate RBV puts the internal factors and resources of an enterprise (including external environmental factors) as the basis for sustainable competitive advantage (Barney, 1995). As a new theory of corporate competitive advantages, NRBV proposes that the sustainable competitive advantages of an enterprise are based on its ability to achieve environmental friendliness in its business activities (Hart, 1995; Hart & Dowell, 2011). According to NRBV, the environmental behaviors that affect an enterprise's sustainable competitive advantages are classified into three categories: (1) pollution prevention behaviors; (2) product management behaviors; and (3) sustainable development behaviors. Pollution prevention behaviors mean minimizing waste emissions and achieving this goal throughout the life cycle. Product management behaviors mean exiting environmentally harmful operations in collaboration with stakeholders, redesigning the existing products to reduce the harms, or redesigning new products that reduce harms throughout the life cycle. Sustainable development behaviors refer to an enterprise's ongoing investment or long-term commitment to environmentally conscious strategies. NRBV not only gives the enterprise competitive advantages, but vitalizes the entire supply chain (Guang Shi et al., 2012; Mena et al., 2014; Song et al., 2017b).

Accordingly, supply chain operations and management capabilities are categorized into three: (1) maintaining and developing green in supply chain operations or production processes; (2) achieving green in supply chain business design; and (3) developing green supply chain awareness and strategies. Another new theory associated with the NRBV is the Social Resource-based View (SRBV), which argues that the sustainable competitiveness of enterprises depends not only on natural resources and other resources but also on social ability (Tate & Bals, 2018), which is defined as the ability to leverage internal and/or external stakeholder relationships to achieve reciprocal exchange objectives. This ability is mainly reflected in the 3Cs: Commitment (i.e., ethical and social commitment), Connection (synergy with a wide range of partners in a value network), and Consistency (building trust through consistency of behaviors). In fact, enterprises that form and possess the 3Cs are more likely to achieve the triple bottom line, and they are a prerequisite for establishing the triple bottom line goals and other competencies. As seen in the correlation between NRBV and SRBV, an increase in NRBV capabilities (i.e., pollution prevention behaviors, product management behaviors to sustainable development behaviors) will lead to a gradual change in SRBV competences (i.e., from commitment, to connection, to consistency). Therefore, the construction of the above three resources forms the elements of sustainable supply chain competitiveness (see Fig. 7.6).

In response to the capabilities developed based on SRBV and NRBV, supply chain finance becomes a key factor in investing and establishing sustainable supply chains. Different supply chain finance options have different costs, benefits, and scopes of cooperation and may be matched with different resource capabilities. All these form a sustainable supply chain finance system (see Fig. 7.7). As discussed in Chap. 2, supply chain finance offers a range of solutions and products with different relation attributes, involving post-shipment, in-transit, pre-shipment, and strategies, either market-based (e.g., order financing and warehouse receipt financing) or relationship-based (e.g., strategic financing, advance payment discounts, and credit facilities). Financial service products with different conditions apply to different SMEs' resource capabilities and sustainable supply chain capabilities, thus forming a good interaction. For instance, pollution prevention behaviors are associated with certain process innovations (e.g., like TQM, and personnel training and development). These sustainable supply chain capabilities can correspond to post-shipment or in-transit supply chain financial services, such as standard factoring, reverse

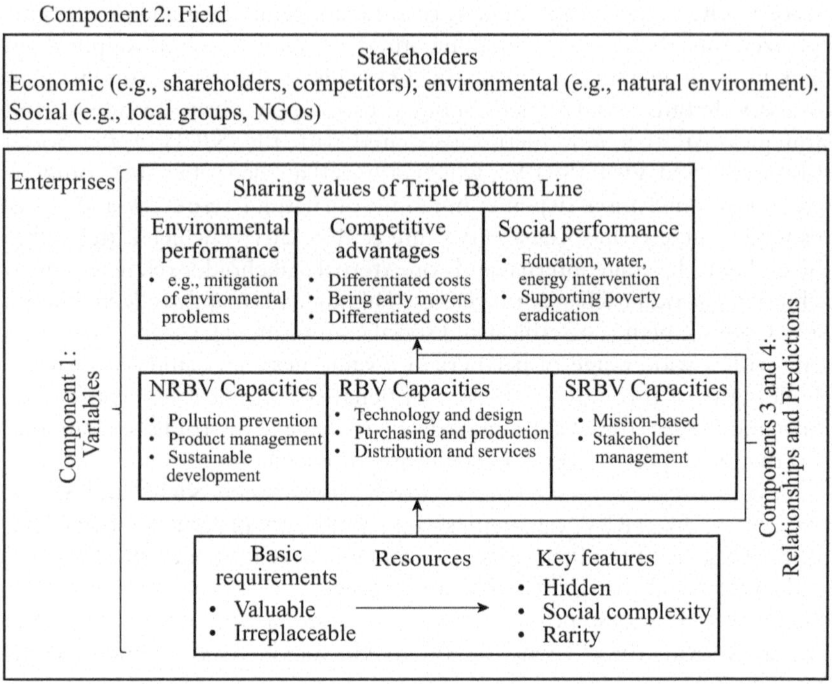

Fig. 7.6 Relations among RBV, NBRV, and SRBV. (Source: Tate & Bals, 2018)

factoring, inventory pledge, warehouse receipt pledge, and so on, so as to motivate tier-N suppliers to innovate processes and reinforce corresponding education and training in line with sustainability requirements. Similarly, product management behaviors (i.e., collaborative product design to achieve supply chain sustainability in terms of technology design) require suppliers to make a lot of technical investments, and the supply chain finance that matches them are pre-shipment financial services, such as order financing and credit financing, because specific business products have not been formed at this time, and financial support is needed in design and technology development. In the stage of sustainable development, sustainability is often integrated into the construction of the whole supply chain system as a strategy, or more stakeholders are included in the collaborative supply chain system in accordance with the goal of social benefits, so as to achieve social and environmental sustainability. A large

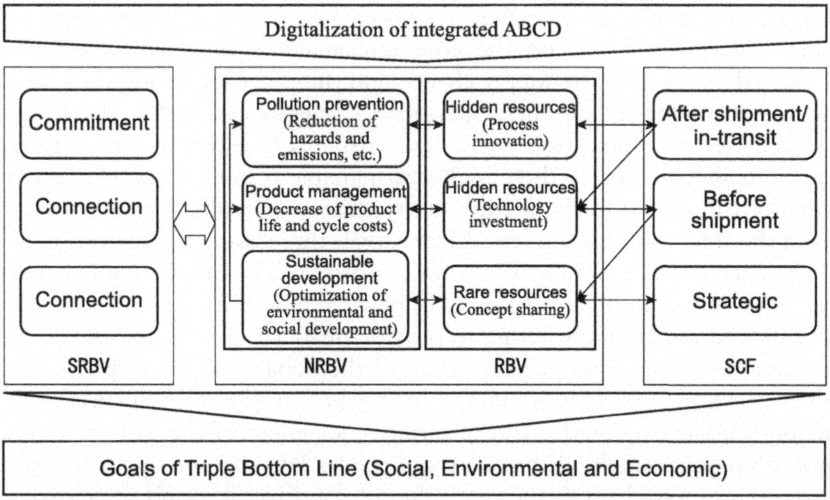

Fig. 7.7 Financial services framework for financial resource capacity under sustainable supply chain

amount of investment in fixed assets and factor inputs are required in this stage, which requires the use of some matching strategic financing businesses, or even supply chain finance for better achieving the above goals. Thus, it is clear that supply chain finance and supply chain sustainability are integrated and interact with each other. On the one hand, supply chain sustainability, with the help of modern ICT, is better translated into elements for assessing supply chain finance, thus facilitating the development and application of supply chain financial products (BSR, 2018). On the other hand, supply chain finance, also with the help of effective ICT, allows the continuous improvement of sustainability of all supply chain participants, ultimately achieving the triple bottom-line goals for social, environmental, and economic sustainability.

Specifically, supply chain finance plays two roles in the interaction with supply chain sustainability: (1) Motivator. Supply chain finance reflects whether an enterprise has achieved sustainable supply chain capabilities, thus positively or negatively motivating the enterprise to achieve the triple bottom line. In other words, the capabilities formed by the enterprises and their partners based on RBV, NRBV, and SRBV as well as their behaviors are used as input factors for supply chain finance decisions, and financial service providers (e.g., commercial banks) evaluate the competitiveness of such enterprises based on the commercial and sustainable capabilities reflected by them in the supply chains, and then provide financial services such as financing to help such enterprises accelerate cash flows. (2) Driver. As a driver for enterprises to achieve sustainable supply chains, supply chain finance is used to drive higher sustainable resource capabilities and achieve the shared goals of triple bottom line. The supply chain finance with the roles of motivator and driver reveals three issues for attention: (1) The characteristics and forms are not consistent. The supply chain finance with the role of motivator is a kind of reactive financial service. The financial institutions decide whether to provide financial services and the interest rates of financial service according to the behaviors of enterprises and their partners. Generally speaking, this type of supply chain finance tends to be transaction-based financial services; so, most of the in-transit and post-shipment supply chain financial services fall into this type. In contrast, the supply chain finance with the role of driver is a kind of proactive financial service. As an important resource input for enterprises and their partners to form sustainable capabilities, this type of supply chain finance tends to be relation-based financial services, typically along with low interest rates and based on trust formed by long-term partnership, since no actual transaction occurs and no product is formed when the financial service is provided. Strategic financing and pre-shipment financing are more often financial services with the driver role. (2) Both supply chain finance with motivator role and driver role need perfect ICT as support to form a good digital sustainability as well as performance management system. A sound performance evaluation and management system and a good digital system are required for reasonably evaluating who has sustainability and to what extent (Bai et al., 2012; Estampe et al., 2013). Without the support of this system and ICT, supply chain finance can neither make decisions nor determine whether and how it should support sustainable supply chain construction. (3) The roles of motivator and driver are not absolutely separated, but interact with each other and with sustainability practices. For example, the formation of pollution prevention behaviors and its capabilities may drive post-shipment and in-transit supply chain financial services, which not only stimulate the abovementioned behavior of enterprises but also drive the capabilities of the enterprise and its partners to further optimize product management. Similarly, good product management behaviors drive pre-shipment financial services, which in turn improve the overall sustainability capabilities and lead to a success in strategic financing, and so on and so forth. The above issues form intrinsic elements of sustainable supply chain finance.

7.3 Agricultural Supply Chain and Supply Chain Finance

As one of the key fields where sustainable supply chains and their financial services are applied, the sustainability of agricultural supply chains has been the focus of government, industry and society. According to the *Guidance on Actively Promoting Supply Chain Innovation and Application* issued by the General Office of the State Council in October 2017, "family farms, farmers' cooperatives, leading agricultural enterprises and agricultural socialized service organizations are encouraged to cooperate in establishing an agricultural supply chain system that integrates the production, processing, circulation and services of agricultural products." In addition, the *Guidance* also suggested "to step up the construction of agricultural supply chain information platform, integration of big data of all links such as agricultural production and operations, co-sharing of information relating to policy, market, science and technology, finance, insurance and other aspects, in a bid to improve the level of agricultural production technology and precision." However, given the decentralization and volatility of agricultural production and the diversity of operators, especially considering how to help a large number of farmers effectively join in the agricultural supply chains to achieve sustainable development beyond poverty elimination, organize agricultural productions in a logical manner to achieve green, organic, and orderly development, and optimize the structure, process, and services of agricultural supply chains, the use of ICT to empower agricultural supply chains and supply chain finance is a topic that currently requires intense exploration and innovation.

7.3.1 *Agricultural Supply Chain and Related Challenges*

7.3.1.1 Agricultural Supply Chain and Its Characteristics

Agricultural supply chain is a new approach of organization that creates industrial competitiveness by combining agriculture and supply chain. Internationally, there are many kinds of expressions, such as "agri-food supply chain," "agro-industrial supply chain," "agriculture supply chain," and sometimes "food supply chain." Generally, agricultural supply chain encompasses a wide range of "land-to-table" activities, including agricultural operations (e.g., land cultivation and land fertilization), production and handling, testing, packaging, warehousing, transport, distribution, and sales (Iakovou et al., 2012). Agricultural supply chains have the characteristics as shown in Fig. 7.8. First, they have various types of processes involved in the sustainable supply chain. Specifically, agricultural supply chains involve supply chain operations such as logistics, finance, technology, and various services, which can be specifically classified into five categories: (1) logistics and commodity flow; (2) capital flow; (3) information flow; (4) processing and disposal process; and (5) energy and natural resources (Tsolakis et al., 2014). Second, all these processes often involve various types of participants and stakeholders, which include public authorities and market stakeholders. The former mainly includes national government departments and related administrative authorities, regulatory authorities, and some international organizations. The latter include individual farmers and growers, agricultural cooperatives, farm machinery operators, agricultural cultivation and fertilizer companies, R&D institutions, agricultural processing companies, agricultural traders, logistics service providers, carriers, food stores, supermarket chains, and financial

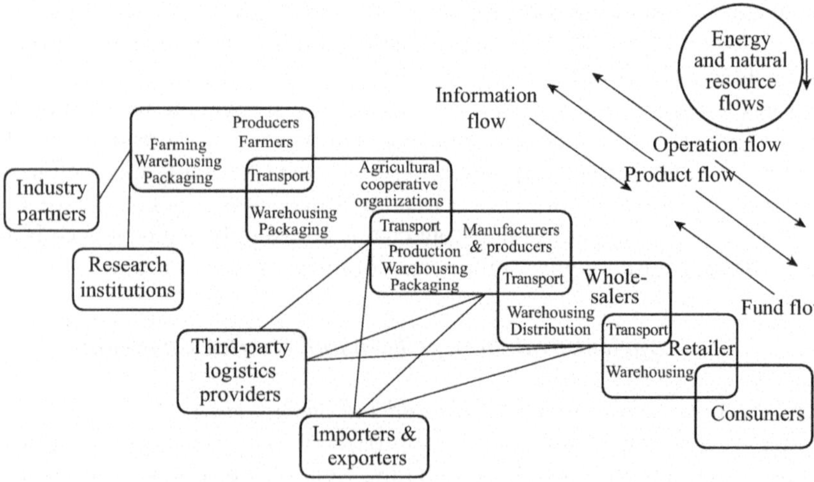

Fig. 7.8 Agricultural supply chain framework. (Source: Tsolakis et al., 2014)

institutions (Tsolakis et al., 2014). In recent years, some large agricultural production and operation companies (including some Internet companies) have started to enter the agricultural sector as new players. Third, agricultural supply chain requires some specific capabilities of participants because it has some unique elements compared with other industrial supply chains. According to Van Der Vorst (2006), agricultural supply chains have ten unique characteristics: (1) short life cycle of agricultural products; (2) highly differentiated products; (3) season nature of harvesting and production operations; (4) variability in the quality and quantity of agricultural products after processing; (5) specific requirements for transport, storage conditions, quality, and recycling of agricultural products; (6) the need to comply with national/international legislation, regulations, and directives regarding food safety and public health, and environmental requirements (e.g., carbon and water footprints); (7) the need for specific management attributes such as traceability and transparency; (8) the need for expensive technical equipment, as well as maintaining high efficiency and productivity, despite long production periods; (9) the complexity of operations; and (10) the presence of significant capacity constraints. Fifth, the agricultural supply chain will change with the changes in the external environment. A number of changes in agricultural environmental factors often have a dramatic impact on agricultural supply chains. These environmental factors include urbanization, the opening of domestic and international agricultural markets, the internationalization of agricultural products, and the food safety concerns.

7.3.1.2 Management Characteristics and Challenges of Agricultural Supply Chains

The above characteristics of agricultural supply chains lead to the characteristics and challenges in the management of agricultural supply chains that differ from those of supply chains in other industries.

First of all, in terms of organizational structure, agricultural supply chain differs from the supply chain of other industries, which has a trading network structure composed of many enterprises including even SMEs with the nature of legal persons. However, the initial producers in agricultural supply chains may be individual farmers or individual producers with the nature of natural persons, which makes management exceptionally complex. It is challenging to effectively communicate market information and requirements for production to such producers and to organize production rationally, because unlike legal persons with the necessary properties and registered capital for assuming the corresponding civil and economic responsibilities, individual natural persons are unable to achieve economized production and operations. Therefore, how to organize decentralized farmers into the supply chain and use modern ICT to achieve supply chain synergy has become a core issue in agricultural supply chains (Nilsson, 1998; Bijman et al., 2011; Parikh et al., 2007; Cechin et al., 2013). This issue is extremely serious in China, where agricultural production is characterized by the gathering of natural persons, and even the industrial enterprises therein have not formed an intensive organizational form. In terms of production, the per capita arable land area of farmers is insufficient. At current stage, the population engaged in agricultural production in China is 740 million, while the national arable land area is 1.8 billion mu, so the per capita arable land area is not only lower than that of developed countries such as the US, Canada, and France, but even lower than that of India. In terms of agricultural business, China has 30,000 traditional agricultural operators, and the vast majority of them have the same products and prices, which makes business difficult. In terms of markets, the current demand market is gradually becoming smaller, special, and refined, so the challenge is how to carry out agricultural production and operation in response to the diversified and changing demands. In addition to the abovementioned issues, another key feature of the agricultural supply chain in terms of organizational management is the large number of stakeholders, including not only agricultural producers but also numerous public sectors and various enterprises or organizations. Therefore, the success of effectively organizing and coordinating multiple stakeholders is what makes it possible to form agricultural supply chains and to truly reflect sustainable agricultural development (Dentoni et al., 2012; Peterson, 2013; Thiele et al.).

Second, in terms of business processes, the specificity of the products operated tends to complicate the management of processes. The safety management in agricultural supply chain is highly complex as agricultural product characteristics affect the transaction characteristics (the driving factors shaped by product characteristics may also affect the transaction characteristics) (Hobbs & Young, 2000). Based on the generally accepted classification of attributes of product quality and an extension of Stigler's (1961) information searching theory, Nelson (1970, 1974) and Darby and Karni (1973) have proposed three types of attributes of product quality: search attributes, experience attributes, and trust attributes. The search attributes refer to the information that consumers can obtain and evaluate before purchasing a product; the experience attributes refer to the inherent quality of a product that can only be known after consumers have purchased and used the product for a period of time; and the trust attributes refer to the information about a product that is remain unknown after consumers have purchased the product. Most agricultural products have only experience and trust attributes, which means that consumers cannot observe their quality before purchase or consumption, so they are exposed to "ex ante" uncertainty. This uncertainty may continue after the occurrence of an adverse event in an agricultural product. For example, the quality (defects) of a produce is not known unless the food-borne disease has occurred. If the consumers cannot determine the source of the disease, they are exposed to the "ex post" uncertainty (Antle, 1996). Besides, agricultural producers also face information asymmetries about food safety in the agricultural supply chain (Antle, 2001), because the raw materials (agricultural products) used by the produces also have only trust and experience attributes, and their quality is also uncertain. Especially in international trade, there is a high degree of risk and uncertainty due to the diversity of supply chain participants and geographical remoteness, both in terms of sourcing and sales. Therefore, the information asymmetry associated with the experience and trust attributes of the quality of agricultural products may result in moral hazards and adverse selection problems. In order to solve these issues in transactions, more and more agricultural enterprises adopt supply chains for vertical coordination and modern ICTs (such as RFID) to achieve traceability and transparency of agricultural products. However, business processes in the supply chain often involve capacity management (management of production and operation capacity of each participant in the industry), supplier management (management of farmers, land and planting, and agricultural materials and tools), customer management (management of market orders), logistics service management (logistics, warehousing, and distribution management of agricultural materials and products), and cash flow management (management of funds required for agricultural seeds, agricultural materials, agricultural tools, and funds settlement management, etc.). As a result, how to effectively manage these processes and how information technology plays a role in them becomes the key to the development of agricultural supply chains.

Third, in terms of services, agricultural supply chains need a full range of services to address the challenges faced in agricultural business. Salin (1998) argued that the reason why agricultural supply chains need to be supported by a full range of information services is that agricultural products are different in nature from industrial products. Industrial products can be classified into functional products and innovative products according to the nature of the products (Fisher, 1997). Functional products refer to the products with relatively stable and predictable demand, while innovative products present unstable demand and are more difficult to predict. The supply chains corresponding to the products of different nature are also different. The supply chain of functional products (i.e., lean supply chain) mainly focuses on cost control and reduction, regardless of the costs of production, transport, inventory, or information technology of the products. The supply chain of innovative products (i.e., agile supply chain) aim not at cost management but at maintaining sufficient flexibility and speed to respond quickly to changes in the market as well as to the changing needs of customers. However, agricultural products are more difficult to classify based on this criterion, because, on the one hand, agricultural products are highly variable, with some tending to be functional, such as grains and bulk materials, while others are innovative, such as cash crops, fresh produce, and so on. In particular, agricultural products that are perishable and difficult to preserve tend to be more time-sensitive (Salin, 1998; Shukla & Jharkharia, 2013). On the other hand, different final products even from the same source may have different natures. For example, raised cattle in livestock products may be sold to consumers both in fresh meat form and in canned form. Obviously, different forms of agricultural products also have different natures. The complexity in nature requires the organization process of the agricultural supply chain to both achieve low cost in the whole process of operations and facilitate the various stakeholders to respond quickly to changes in the market. Among the problems that need to be solved in practices, one is how to use an effective supply chain to vertically coordinate decentralized farms who cannot effectively correspond to the market, making them to quickly and efficiently produce agricultural products as per market demands, and thus effectively supplying agricultural products while safeguarding the farmers' own interests (Hobbs & Young, 2000). Another is how to make agricultural operators, agricultural technology service providers, and financial institutions to penetrate into the pre-, mid-, and post-production stages of agriculture to realize the full services with high-efficiency, low-cost, and controlled risk.

7.3.2 Agricultural Supply Chain Finance and Its Realization

7.3.2.1 Meaning and Characteristics of Agricultural Supply Chain Finance

Supply chain finance is a key tool in the process of achieving sustainable agricultural supply chain, especially in the construction of agricultural organizational structures, business processes, and industrial services. Effective financial activities can not only help the industry to form a good cooperative system but also effectively control the risks arising from the unique characteristics of the industry (Miller, 2011; Miller & Da Silva, 2007; Swamy, 2016). Agricultural supply chain, also known as agriculture supply chain finance, agriculture value chain finance, or agri-value chain finance, means the penetration of financial services into the agricultural supply chain, so as to provide all participants in the agricultural supply chain with opportunities to improve capital efficiency and payment, and strengthen the linkages between various parts and participants therein. Thus, agricultural supply chain finance is not a simple connection between, but a high-level integration of, finance and agricultural supply chains, with the aim of serving the development of the industry (Miller & Da Silva, 2007). Rather than being a development goal, agricultural supply chain finance is a means to achieve the goal of social, environmental, and economic sustainability in agriculture (Miller, 2011). The characteristics of agricultural supply chain finance can be understood in terms of the goals achieved, the types of products, and the financial service providers.

First, in terms of the goals achieved, agricultural supply chain finance helps to achieve efficiency and quality in the agricultural industry through the financial services activities as follows (Miller, 2011): identifying financing needs to strengthen the chain; tailoring financial services to the needs of the participants in the supply chain; helping operators to reduce costs by discounting payments and financing payments at the time of product sales; and using supply chain organization and knowledge to reduce the risks faced by the chain and its partners. As can be seen, the goal of agricultural supply chain finance is to achieve sustainable agricultural development, which includes the full realization of economic, social, and environmental goals. Specifically, the economic goal is to help agricultural participants, typically farmers, to obtain the funds required for agricultural production at low interest rates, thus improving the efficiency of the agricultural supply chain (Chen et al., 2015). The social objective is to promote supply chain finance to help agricultural production, allow farmers to better integrate into agricultural supply chain operations, give more dispersed farmers access to financial resources, achieve effective connection between agricultural production and the market, establish a long-term credit system, and realize a virtuous cycle among financial intermediaries, farmers, and the industrial chain (Quirós, 2007, pp. 52–54). The environmental goal is to reduce the risks in the agricultural production process and the synergistic risks among partners through the effective organization of activities in agricultural supply chain finance and to better achieve traceability of agricultural products.

Second, in terms of product types, agricultural supply chain finance often offers different business products when combined with different agricultural segments and elements. Wang et al. (2013) classified agricultural supply chain finance into upstream credit (order financing, accounts receivable financing, and warehouse financing), core enterprise credit (inventory financing, accounts receivable financing, and accounts payable financing), and downstream credit (accounts payable financing and advance payment financing) based on the service recipients. A study by Miller (2011) classified agricultural supply chain finance into product financing (trader credit, supplier financing, wholesaler financing, core enterprise financing), payable financing (trade receivable financing, factoring, forfaiting), asset collateral (warehouse receipt financing, repurchase agreements, financial leasing), risk transfer (insurance, forward contracts, futures), and financial enhancement (ABS, loan guarantees, joint venture finance) based on elements. In addition, van Bergen et al. (2018) classified financial services into hard tolling, soft tolling, and contract farming based on the degree of involvement of large enterprises in upstream farmers when engaging in agricultural supply chain finance. Hard tolling refers to the large enterprises' partial involvement in the production of upstream farmers and purchase of crops after harvest. This type of financing is usually suitable for the procurement of high-quality raw materials or the need to deal with problem-prone scenarios in crop production. Soft tolling refer to traditional fixed price delivery contracts. Contract farming refers to the large enterprises' involvement in the whole process of agricultural production, provision of financial services to farmers and full-process control of agricultural production. As clearly seen from the classification of types of agricultural supply chain finance, all financial services are providing financial services to farmers. Just as described in sustainable supply chain finance, some of these services are reactive financial services, meaning that they are provided after the formation of a procurement agreement or after the acquisition of agricultural products (including storage, warehouse receipts, etc.). Others are proactive financial services, which mean that they help farmers to finance their production capacity before a tangible purchase agreement is formed, such as order financing as mentioned by Wang et al. (2013) and contract farming as mentioned by van Bergen et al. (2018).

In terms of financial service providers, the long production cycles, seasonal fluctuations, high risks, high inventory, and susceptibility to lending risks in the agricultural supply chain make it difficult for traditional financial institutions to provide the necessary funds to agricultural enterprises, especially farmers (Wang et al., 2013). Therefore, large agricultural organizations or intermediaries can play an important role in facilitating agricultural supply chain finance. This role includes both a direct role, that is, directly helping upstream and downstream enterprises or individuals to obtain funds, and an indirect role, that is, acting as an intermediary or a bridge to induce financial institutions or other institutions to provide funds to farmers or other participants, and facilitating lending relationships between farmers and financial institutions (Miller, 2011). Obviously, these organizations and service providers need to better construct the agricultural supply chain service system in line with the characteristics of agricultural products and agriculture, so as to allow farmers and other agricultural participants to obtain financial resources in a low-cost and effective manner on the one hand and transmit the agricultural supply chain information to financial institutions to help them achieve traceability and transparency of agricultural supply chain operations and effectively control and reduce potential risks on the other.

The aforementioned characteristics of agricultural supply chain finance make its related financial services different from those in other industries, given not only the complexity of the agricultural supply chain, but also the unequal risk-reward nature of the financial services determined by the characteristics of agriculture. As Quirós (2007) pointed out, financial activities for the agricultural production present a situation of high risk, high demand and very low interest rate affordability. Therefore, the problem is how to build the agricultural supply chain to reduce potential risks and achieve information penetration and traceability in the agricultural supply chain. In addition, what kind of customized financial services can be provided by financial institutions according to the built supply chain system, and what kind of characteristics and management mechanisms different services should have are the next issues to be considered.

7.3.2.2 Key Elements of Agricultural Supply Chain Finance Decisions
The exploration of how to build agricultural supply chains or the key elements in building the agricultural supply chains to provide matching financial services should be combined with the characteristics of agricultural supply chains, so as to analyze the transaction costs caused by these problems and the possible ways to overcome them. From the perspective of transaction cost theory, the existence of transaction costs arises from bounded rationality and uncertainty.

(1) Bounded Rationality and the Organization of Agricultural Supply Chains

Bounded rationality was first proposed by Simon (1972), who pointed out the need to introduce incomplete information, the cost of processing information and some nontraditional objective functions of decision-makers into economic analysis. The decentralized and diverse players in agriculture spanning corporate enterprises, public institutions, and social organizations, as well as a large number of individual natural persons (farmers), so bounded rationality can be very pronounced and difficult to adapt to the needs of agricultural development (Parikh et al., 2007; Thiele et al., 2011). The fact is that decentralized farmers are less able to correctly grasp information about the whole chain, as well as the status of other organizations, due to the long supply chains of agricultural products, the large number and the different forms of participants. Besides, those farmers lack the ability to process useful information and use it effectively. The result of bounded rationality is information asymmetry. In other words, the decentralized individual farmer has no way of knowing the information necessary for the entire production operations, nor does he/she know which players in the industry are credible and whether the services offered are reasonably priced. This eventually creates a minority transaction problem (Williamson, 1973), meaning that some transaction processes are too exclusive or idiosyncratic, preventing the flow of information and resources, reducing the number of people involved in trading, causing the market to be dominated by a few, and ultimately leading to market failure. For example, a survey by Musshoff and Hirschauer (2011) found that 90% of farmers make decisions based on experience and, therefore, often do not have access to real information, resulting in higher transaction costs and capital costs due to the inability to identify or seek new lenders even when they encounter unreasonably high interest rates.

Therefore, the solution to this issue requires a reorganization by combining these decentralized individual farmers to generate collective behaviors. Only when collective behaviors are generated is it possible to reduce transaction costs, effectively involve in agricultural markets, and promote effective financial services (Markelova et al., 2009; Chen et al., 2015). However, such collective behaviors are not generated naturally, but require some intermediaries or governmental and nongovernmental departments to boost it (Chen et al., 2015).

In the exploration of the forms of intermediaries that promote collective behaviors, there are many studies that consider agricultural cooperatives as an effective organizational form (Ollila, 1994; Bijman et al., 2011; Cechin et al., 2013), because this cooperative form can help farmers achieve effective market coordination and reduce individual transaction costs in the market. Cechin et al. (2013) analyzed four factors why agricultural cooperatives trigger collective behaviors, namely market correspondence (better market correspondence will make the members to tend to behave collectively), nonhierarchy (no hierarchy in agricultural cooperatives felt by member will make them behave collectively), community orientation (a sense of belonging to a cooperative community will make them behave collectively), and democratization (a democratic atmosphere in agricultural cooperatives will make the members behave collectively).

In addition to traditional agricultural cooperatives, Nilsson (1998) also proposed a more advanced type of cooperative organization, which begins to extend to the back end of the industrial supply chain, and even includes agricultural cooperatives that cooperate with external parties. Based on this type of cooperative organizations, Thiele et al. (2011) proposed a concept of multistakeholders platform where different participants can share resources, improve understanding, build trust, define roles in collective behaviors, and participate in collective actions. Unlike the cooperative organization formed by farmers, which is a form of cooperative organization formed by the same type of participants, this platform is a gathering of different stakeholders. Therefore, multistakeholder platform refers to a platform with the ability to organically gather different participants in the agricultural supply chain (such as farmers, processors, distributors, third-party logistics providers, social organizations, governmental departments, etc.) to jointly overcome the transaction costs of agriculture and promote the development of the industry. From the above exploration, it is clear that the organization of agricultural supply chain is an important factor to overcome the information asymmetry and transaction costs of minority transaction problem arising from the bounded rationality. However, the degree of agricultural supply chain organization tends to be variable or a sequential set of development. Some may have relatively low degree of organization (e.g., cooperative forms among farmers), while others are highly organized (e.g., multistakeholder platform as proposed by Thiele et al.).

(2) Uncertainty and Discovery of Value in Agricultural Products

Transaction cost theory suggests that in addition to "human" factors such as bounded rationality and opportunism, another type of "transaction" factor that may lead to higher costs and market failure is uncertainty (Williamson, 1973). Uncertainty leads to transaction costs because if the environment is full of unpredictability and variability, both parties will incorporate this future uncertainty and complexity into the contract, which increases the bargaining cost of the contract and makes the transaction more difficult. In other words, the ex ante transaction cost rises. Moreover, uncertainty also drives up the cost of monitoring and managing counterparties after the transaction. Uncertainty is very significant in agriculture and consists mainly of uncertainty in agricultural products and in the prices or benefits. Uncertainty in agricultural products is mainly uncertainty in product quality and reliability (Hobbs & Young, 2000). The former refers to the fact that buyers are not clear about the specific quality and safety status of agricultural products before purchasing and during the operations/consumption (Song et al., 2017a), as most agricultural products only have experience and trust attributes, but no search attributes. This, coupled with natural characteristics such as perishability of agricultural products, makes the quality of agricultural products change very quickly. The uncertainty in reliability refers to the instability of the timing and quantity of the supply of agricultural products. The very large number of dispersed participants involved in agriculture, as well as the susceptibility of agricultural production to natural influences (susceptibility to natural factors and external environmental changes), hinder the supply at the agreed time and quantity (Borodin et al., 2016). In addition, the variability of agricultural markets, especially the safety consciousness of consumers and the changes in demand in international markets, may also have an impact on the supply of agricultural products (Shukla & Jharkharia, 2013). As far as agriculture is concerned, another type of uncertainty is that in prices or benefits (Hobbs & Young, 2000; Leat & Revoredo-Giha, 2013).

Long agricultural production cycles make it more difficult to determine the price before production. Agricultural production is also highly seasonal, resulting in high price volatility. Therefore, the difficulty in the implementation of agricultural supply chain finance is the difficulty in guaranteeing the self-reimbursement of returns and the high risks (Quirós, 2007). The above two types of uncertainty often result in information asymmetry, which also affects bounded rationality and ultimately gives rise to opportunism. Therefore, the possible reduction of transaction costs in agricultural supply chain finance services is predicated on the search for ways to reduce the uncertainty of agricultural products and their prices.

There are two ways to cope with the transaction costs resulting from the uncertainty generated by products and prices: (1) establishing quality standards and (2) achieving a fixed price or benefit guarantee, that is, value discovery. When faced with asymmetric information about the quality attributes of agricultural products, a signal is needed to show the quality status. According to a study by Fotopoulos and Krystallis (2003), an effective way to solve this problem is to establish quality labels as signals, the use of which can solve the adverse selection, improve the information obtained by consumers, and restore some of the market efficiency. Such quality labels are reflected in corporate quality assurance or standard setting (Westgren, 1999; Fotopoulos & Krystallis, 2003; Henson & Reardon, 2005; Botonaki et al., 2006). These standards are not necessarily government-established standards, but rather third-party or company-driven standards systems (Private Agri-food Standrad), whose role, on the one hand, is to transmit correct product information, improve customers' risk perception before purchase, and subsequently contribute to the refinement and development of the supply system. As Henson and Reardon (2005, p. 244) said: "Standards define and coordinate product and delivery attributes, and increase efficiency and reduce transaction costs. In turn, the implementation of these standards depends heavily on the organization of new purchase systems, including a shift from decentralized purchase to centralized supply system, from reliance on traditional wholesalers and spot markets to specialized/ dedicated wholesalers and designated suppliers as defined in contracts." On the other hand, as a way of guaranteeing the quality of agricultural products, the agricultural safety and quality certification system allows customers to understand the quality of products to a certain extent, thus increasing the percentage of informed quality, and helping to reduce the probability of low-quality products and inferior products in the agricultural markets. In response to price uncertainty, fixed-price mechanism, which refers to giving sellers a certain amount of premium as an incentive based on the open market price, is considered an effective solution (Miyata et al., 2009; Chen et al., 2015). In particular, some large enterprises transfer part of their marginal profits to farmers through bulk purchases, which can consolidate the relationship between buyers and sellers and ensure the safety of agricultural products (Vorley, 2007). The above analysis shows that value discovery is also an important path to help reduce uncertainty and thus transaction costs. A more improved value discovery mechanism can reduce more risks that may arise from agricultural supply chain finance and promote the sustainable development of the agricultural industry.

7.3.2.3 Overall Framework of Agricultural Supply Chain Finance and the Corresponding Financial Business

The two key factors (i.e., agricultural organization and value discovery that requires attention to address bounded rationality and uncertainty) influencing agricultural supply chain finance decisions generate four states in agricultural operations (four squares presenting different characteristics), which in turn determine the corresponding financial services (see Fig. 7.9).

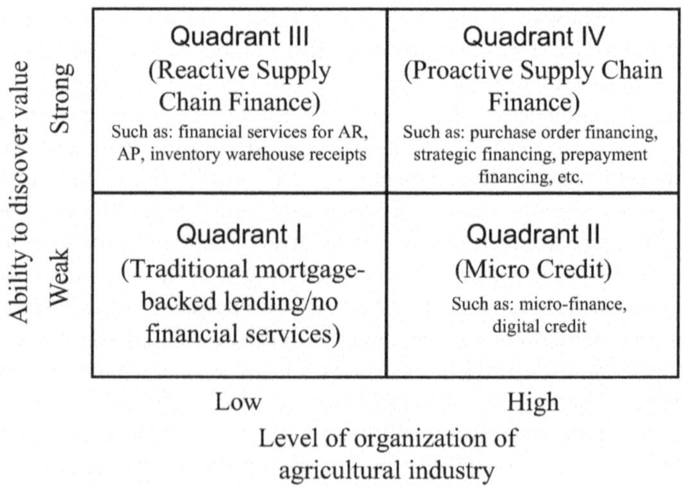

Fig. 7.9 Overall framework of agricultural supply chain finance

Quadrant I represents the state of traditional agriculture, which has not yet formed a supply chain system. On the one hand, the agricultural operations are less organized, and producers, processors, and distributors are not well coordinated, especially farmers as producers are not organized by effective means, so the transaction costs arising from bounded rationality are high. On the other hand, the low degree of value discovery implies a high degree of product and price uncertainty, and the resulting volatility makes the industry less resilient to risks. Financial behaviors based on the above characteristics are limited to traditional lending based on traditional collateral. In fact, financial organizations are unable to intervene in this state, because of the systemic risks resulting from the lack of organization and value discovery, combined with seasonal fluctuations and limited collateral. As a result, agricultural producers and operators are less likely to receive support from financial institutions.

Quadrant II represents a more unique state of the industry in which agriculture has a high degree of organization. In this state, some intermediaries are able to organize different participants in agricultural production, especially farmers, into associations that generate more collective behaviors and overcome opportunism and moral hazard due to human-related bounded rationality. However, the low degree of value discovery indicates the difficulty to correspond to the market and industry information asymmetry caused by uncertainty due to the inability to clearly manage product and price attributes. In other words, the transaction costs in this state are not caused by human factors, but by the attributes of the transaction. This state gives rise to micro-lending, an alternative to traditional finance or supply chain finance. As defined by Wikipedia, micro-lending is lending small amounts of money to people who lack collateral and have no permanent employees or no proven credit history, to support them in starting a business or escaping poverty. Micro-lending originated with the Grameen Bank, founded by Yunus in Bangladesh in 1983. Many studies have shown that the mechanism of modern micro-lending is based on familiarity with the local networks and the group effect of the farmer composition. On the one hand, if competing lenders and investors are able to understand local environment and are embedded in local networks where the balance between risk and return can be achieved, then funds will flow and realize better benefits than other forms of credit (Doran et al., 2009). On the other hand, group effects or collective behaviors motivate farmers who are borrowers to be more willing to repay the funds on time, because associative credit (i.e., a farmer's success in obtaining funds depends on the repayment status of other members of the network) makes each individual in the group more concerned with his or her wealth and social role in the group than with absolute individual wealth or income (Armendariz & Morduch, 2005; Kropp et al., 2009). Obviously, there are two bases for the implementation of micro-lending: (1) the effect of the network or group formed by individuals, that is, the collective behaviors that creates the necessary constraints on individuals; and (2) digitization, that is, digitally grasping the status of individuals in the economic network activity, thus effectively controlling the lending risks. It should be noted, however, that micro-lending, because it does not really penetrate into the operations of the industrial supply chain, and thus not achieve value discovery, is still subject to the possibility of default, especially during periods of economic volatility and downturn. The reason for this is that micro-lending generally supports the daily production activities or start-up behaviors of farmers, whose production operations are mostly primary and more competitive. In addition, the absence of collateral makes it easy to create multiple financing, which increases default (Ghosh, 2013; Khavul, 2010), especially when the network is not well organized or weak. This is why micro-lending places a strong emphasis on "short borrowing periods, small amounts, high frequency, and urgent needs of production operations," which is difficult to adapt to the financial needs of most agricultural supply chain operations.

Quadrant III is a category of agricultural supply chain finance, and the agricultural supply chain finance in this state mainly provides incentive-based financial services. Or rather, that is a kind of reactive supply chain finance. Financial financing is given according to the results of production and operation of producers or farmers, so that they can get the required funds in time and accelerate the flow of funds. This type of agriculture is characterized by the fact that agriculture is not very well organized, which means that the integration of industrial supply chain participants by intermediaries or service providers is not extensive enough, or the supply chain participants are relatively limited, without being able to effectively coordinate all the participants of different types, scales, and stages. However, the high degree of value discovery indicates that although the integration of supply chain participants is limited, the intermediary or service provider has a good grasp of business processes and markets, and can fully understand the whole process of production and operation of limited participants, and has a high control over market prices. In other words, the integration of supply chain is deep enough, albeit not extensive enough.

With an in-depth understanding of supply chain operations, intermediaries or service providers can carry out financial services based on agricultural supply chain business. These financial services are typical financial services based on the simultaneous and close integration of commodity flow, logistics flow and capital flow. To put it another way, financial activities are generated only after the formation of agricultural products procurement or even invoicing behavior (Song, 2015). Specifically, after specific procurement behavior of agricultural products, the corresponding business of inventory financing and warehouse receipt financing is provided to farmers or producers by controlling such elements as bills of lading, inventory, and in-transit inventory. Or, after invoicing, the financial services such as factoring, reverse factoring, forfaiting, and dynamic discounts are provided based on the accounts receivable. Such financial services provide incentives for farmers or producers to produce and operate in accordance with market rules and social contracts, and to produce competitive agricultural products. Once an upstream supplier fails to achieve its goals, the financing not only does not occur, but the buyer can impose reverse penalties by refusing to purchase or pay for the purchase. In terms of sustainability goals, these supply chain financial services can achieve organic production (pollution prevention) and product management in agriculture, but sustainability goals cannot be effectively achieved due to insufficient organization. From the perspective of supply chain finance risk control, the core of management lies in downstream control, that is, the ability to keep track of the state of the market, form good fixed prices and market orders, and have strong control over distribution logistics to ensure the quality of agricultural products during transport and inventory, and quickly respond to market demand for sales, logistics, and other services. The role played by ICT in this state is somewhat similar to that of reactive supply chain mentioned by Lee (2002), which means it has the ability to grasp demand patterns in a timely and accurate manner, and the ability to return orders to producers in a timely manner, and to quickly achieve effective linkage of logistics operations such as procurement, inventory, and transport with customer systems to achieve effective allocation and distribution of agricultural products in terms of quality, quantity, and price.

Quadrant IV represents the advanced state of agricultural supply chain finance, in which supply chain finance promotes sustainable development of the agricultural industry. Diversified and evolved supply chain finance activities can promote the full realization of the supply chain of the agricultural industry. On the one hand, it achieves a high degree of organization and really embeds the producers into the supply chain system effectively. Especially, it organizes the decentralized farmers into the industrial production process, so that they form groups with strong judgment and link with other stakeholders to form an interactive and mutual platform (Thiele et al., 2011) and generate the collaborative collective behaviors. On the other hand, value discovery is achieved, that is, the intermediaries or service providers are able to help set quality standards for agricultural products by deeply grasping the whole process (technology, production, logistics, marketing, services) and elements (land, production tools, agricultural seeds, storage, transport, etc.) of the industrial supply chain, generating fixed prices with premium nature with the help of branding, and transferring the marginal benefit from the market to the farmers. Clearly different from the traditional supply chain finance, the supply chain finance in this state makes the capital flow completely separate from the commodity flow and logistics flow, and the capital flow occurs before the commodity and logistics flows of agricultural products. In other words, before the actual purchase of agricultural products, supply chain finance provides money for the participants in the industrial supply chain, so that farmers can obtain various factors of agricultural production at low cost and engage in agricultural production according to predetermined rules and models. After the production is completed, the farmer sells to the intermediary or service provider to recover the funds at a reasonable or guaranteed price, which, after deducting the financing cost, are the benefit realized from the agricultural production operations. Obviously, this type of agricultural supply chain finance not only realizes the organic production and product management in the agricultural industry but also realizes the sustainable development of the industry and the sustainability of agriculture. The core of risk control of this type of supply chain finance is as follows: (1) accurate grasping of the market, which can realize branding based on the standardization of agricultural products and generate price premiums, thus boosting the production and distribution of agricultural products; (2) the ability to coordinate and integrate agricultural production, including that of production factors, as well as that of industrial production behaviors; (3) full use of the integrated ABCD (ICT) to realize digital agriculture and global collection of digital information of all participants, stages, and types of assets or activities in the agricultural industry. Therefore, the four-layer ICT explored in Chap. 6 should be comprehensively applied to all aspects of the agricultural industry.

The characteristics of financial services in the four states of agriculture are shown in Table 7.1.

Table 7.1 Characteristics of financial services in four states of agriculture

Category	*Traditional lending/no financial services*	*Micro-lending*	*Reactive supply chain finance*	*Progressive supply chain finance*
Industry characteristics	Supply chain capabilities	Well organized supply chain with weak value discovery capability	Less organized supply chain with strong value discovery capability	Well organized supply chain with strong value discovery capability
Service characteristics	Traditional	Based on group network	Financial services based on the grasp of commodity flow and logistics flow	Commodity flow, logistics flow, and capital flow are completely separated, and capital flow precedes commodity flow or logistics flow
Service forms	Collateral loans, secured loans	Micro-lending, digital credit	Factoring, reverse factoring, warehouse receipt pledge, inventory financing, and more	Order financing, strategic financing, advance payment financing, and so on
Risk control	Collateral, security	Industrial environment, group network, individual behavior	Market side, fixed price, distribution logistics	Accurate grasp of the market side, comprehensive coordination of industrial elements, comprehensive integration of industrial behaviors, and global digitalization
Role of ICT	Very weak	Grasping individuals' behaviors	Fast and accurate grasp of market/channel information	Establishment of a four-layer architecture of sensing, data, process, and model layers

7.3.3 *Micro-Lending Service: CD Finance's Micro-Lending and Ant Group's Trade Credit*

7.3.3.1 CD Finance's Micro-Lending[1]

CD Finance was formerly a micro-lending project for Qinling Mountains and Ta-pa Mountains jointly initiated by the World Bank and the China Western Human Resources Development Center in 1996 and transferred to the China Foundation for Poverty Alleviation (CFPA) in 1999. CD Finance Project Management Co., Ltd. was established in 2008 as an independent entity to take over the work related to micro-lending projects, with CFPA retaining a majority stake. In the past ten years, CFPA has maintained a growth rate that far exceeds that of similar institutions.

As of December 31, 2017, CD Finance has set up 258 branches in 21 provinces nationwide, with over 70% of them in national and provincial poverty-stricken counties and some others in less developed or earthquake-stricken counties. The total number of loans granted reached 2.07 million, totaling RMB 27.8 billion. Among them, in 2017 alone, CD Finance granted 410,000 loans with a total amount of RMB 8.6 billion, an increase of nearly 30% year-on-year, and the risk rate of loans larger than 30 days was only 0.94%. With its rapid development, CD Finance has been recognized as the largest and fastest-growing micro-lending institution for poverty alleviation in China. In 2017, CD Finance had 380,000 customers who were using its loans, 82.9% of whom were women, 89.5% of whom had only a junior high school education level or below, and 23.1% of whom were ethnic minorities (covering 52 ethnic minorities nationwide). The average amount of RMB 20,000 per loan has shown the distinctive features of CD Finance as a micro-lending institution serving rural low- and middle-income population.

(1) Basic Features of CD Finance's Micro-lending

CD Finance's customers have distinct characteristics that are in line with the international concept of micro-lending. Ninety-nine percent of CD Finance's customers are farmers, and half of them are poor

[1]Source: Luo Yu; Li Yan, "Boundary of Micro Finance: Case Study of CD Finance's Micro-lending," Journal of Central University of Finance and Economics, 2016, Issue 6; Zhao Meng, et al., "CD Finance in Transition: A Balanced Dance of Economic and Social Attributes," 2018, Case Library of Business School of Renmin University of China.

households that have been filed in the poverty alleviation office system. In terms of customer-level positioning, CD Finance serves low-income farmers who are very unlikely to obtain loans from financial institutions, which has little overlap with traditional financial institutions and other newly emerging profitable micro-finance companies. At present, rural credit cooperatives occupy the most dominant position in China's rural credit market, followed by agricultural banks and postal savings banks. However, these three major financial institutions face the problem of surging transaction costs when providing credit support to "rural areas, agriculture, and farmers." When the loan amount is below RMB 50,000, there is little possibility of profitability and therefore no further customer retention. Rural credit cooperatives, for example, provide credit services to 87,000 farmers, or about one-third of the country's farmers. There is still a significant portion of farmers who are excluded from financial services and have to rely on private lending. CD Finance serves a portion of the remaining two-thirds of farmers. CD Finance is actually not a competitor to other financial institutions in the rural financial market, but rather a complement to the existing financial system.

Currently, CD Finance has a per capita loan amount of RMB 10,000 and a published interest rate of 13.5% for a one-year loan (down to 12.5% for premium customers). The group lending service in the form of co-guarantee offers different loan limits for different levels of customers: after the first loan, the customer becomes a Level-1 customer. The customer will be automatically upgraded to Level-2 when he/she repay the loan on time and apply for a second loan. After repaying the second loan, the customer will be automatically upgraded to Level-3. The loan limit for Level-1 customers is RMB 10,000, that for Level-2 customers is RMB 12,000, and that for Level-3 customers is RMB 16,000. The maximum amount of personal credit loan is only RMB 50,000. The group loans are generally for a one-year period, and the farmers will repay the loan with ten equal monthly principal and interest payments starting from the third month, which spreads the farmers' repayment pressure evenly over the entire borrowing period.

CD Finance's main credit service is group co-guarantee loan, which is different from mainstream credit products in the following three aspects: First, no collateral is required. While traditional financial institutions focus on whether there is collateral or guarantee when approving loans, CD Finance serves nonprime customers of traditional financial institutions without collateral or public officials' guarantee. In response to such customer characteristics, the micro-lending products are designed with a philosophy of not looking at the customer's current assets, but trusting in the customer's future repayment ability and willingness to repay. Second, a co-guarantee approach is adopted. CD Finance's co-guarantee loans are based on the credit models of the international MFIs and adapted to the specific situation in China. Customers applying for a loan must first organize themselves into a co-guarantee group, and CD Finance does not interfere with the composition of the group at all. Usually, a group is composed of five persons who all have a need to borrow and are jointly and severally liable for repayment of the loan. The role of the group is obvious in the screening of creditworthy customers. Generally, the customers of a group are "acquaintances" such as neighbors, friends, or relatives (except immediate family members). A network of acquaintances is characterized by a full understanding of the backgrounds and personalities of each other, timely communication, abundant information, and high-quality information. Therefore, people with bad credit can be automatically and directly screened out in the process of forming a co-guarantee group. Third, the loans are mainly granted to women. Women are considered important customers because the micro-finance community generally believes that women are the core of the family and more eager for family stability, and they also have a higher level of integrity and a greater sense of responsibility and risk control for borrowing money.

(2) Risk Control Models of CD Finance's Micro-lending

CD Finance's risk control models are also significantly different from that of traditional financial institutions. Actually, co-guarantee is one of the risk control tools of micro-lending. The formation of co-guarantee group allows part of the risk control work to be done through the process of independent selection and mutual supervision by the group members. The co-guarantee group largely solves the work of pre-loan review, mid-loan monitoring, and post-loan processing for CD Finance. Utilizing the trust and moral constraints developed through interpersonal interactions in Chinese customary society, the co-guarantee group lending not only reduces the degree of information asymmetry, but also increases the cost of reputation damage in the event of default, thus reducing the problems of adverse selection and moral hazard common in lending activities.

CD Finance relies on a standardized set of loan operation procedures to control risk. CD Finance headquarters requires all branches to strictly follow its nationwide uniform operation procedures for farmer selection, information transmission, loan granting, fund collection, and risk monitoring. Credit specialists play a major role in micro-lending implementation. CD Finance's primary-level credit specialists are all local farmers and mostly married women aged 30 and above. The main selection requirements for credit specialists are that the candidates have integrity, no bad credit history, and extensive social contacts and that their village is in a location with easy access, high population density, and fast information flow, which makes it easy for them to travel and collect information. Primary-level credit specialists have a tough job. For example, a one-year co-guarantee loan of less than RMB 50,000 requires at least 12 visits by credit specialists, including 1 visit for investigation, 1 visit for loan granting, and 10 visits for money collection. Credit specialists have relatives in the surrounding villages and have knowledge of folk customs, economic conditions, and even family situations.

7.3.3.2 Ant Group's Trade Credit

MYbank is the first commercial bank in China whose core system is based on cloud computing architecture, initiated and established by Ant Group as the majority shareholder. As one of the first five private banks in China approved by the CBRC, MYbank was officially opened on June 25, 2015. With financial inclusion as its mission, MYbank hopes to use Internet technology, data, and channel innovation to help solve the problems of difficult access to financing and high financing costs for small and micro enterprises and individual entrepreneurs, as well as the lack of financial services in rural areas. As of August 2017, it has served a total of 4.173 million small and micro enterprises, issued a total of RMB 305.5 billion, with a loan balance of RMB 20,500 per customer and a bad loan rate of less than 1%.

MYbank's MY Loan, formerly known as Micro Loan, mainly solves the short-term, high-frequency, fast and urgent capital needs of small and micro enterprises, and self-employed people and farmers. As far as the basis on which the financial activities depend is concerned, MY Loan has built both in-system and out-of-system scenarios to master the business network status of micro and small enterprises as well as farmers and achieve a higher level of business organization. Specifically, the in-system scenarios mainly refer to an array of business scenarios established by Alibaba and Ant Group, including operation and sales-related scenarios, such as Taobao, Tmall, AliExpress, and 1688.com. These platforms can well reflect the trade status and business stability of small and micro enterprises or farmers. The second type of business scenarios are the financial service related scenarios, including Alipay, Yu'E Bao, Ant Credit Pay, Sesame Credit, Koubei and other products. In particular, Alipay is one of the important financial scenarios for MY Loan. The third type of scenarios are the logistics scenarios constructed by CAINIAO, which can reflect the operation status of small and micro enterprises or farmers. Based on the above three types of scenarios, the management basis of MY Loan is formed, that is, digital information from multiple sources. Through digital information mining and analysis, it can indirectly know and grasp the network status of small and micro enterprises, and realize good organization. Based on this network status, MYbank promotes its financial services based on the "310" model. The "310" model refers to 3 minutes' application, 1 second's loan granting, and 0 manual intervention in the whole process. The annualized interest rate of MY Loan is controlled at about 6%–12%, and, at the same time, borrowers are allowed to repay at any time and no more interest is charged for early repayment. In fact, many micro and small business operators lack continuity and stability in their business, so they do not borrow for a fixed period of six months or one year, nor can they agree on a rigid repayment time frame. MYbank's model is adapted to the business characteristics of these operators who may borrow and repay at any time. MYbank's loan customers use their loans for an average of 9.2 times a year, which adds up to nearly 90 days of use. A typical example of MY Loan using the in-system's scenarios to effectively grant loans is the "Shanghai Inspirational Lobster Brother," who is a young man selling lobsters on the street in Shanghai. After three years of starting his own business and sleeping only five hours a day, he needed some funds to meet temporary emergency needs such as stocking, and opened an Alipay collection code for this purpose. Since then, he has completed 2341 transactions and accumulated a credit line of RMB 38,000. After considering the scenario data, external data, and internal data, MYbank introduced the "More Collection & More Loans" business (see Fig. 7.10) to support the capital needs of young entrepreneurs.

The off-system scenario refers to Ant Group's cooperation with external platforms (including other e-commerce platforms, travel platforms, logistics platforms, O2O platforms, and platforms of banks and other financial institutions) to dock, connect, and integrate the digital information of each other for the purpose of fully grasping the credit status and business network status of loan applicants. In addition to facilitating the

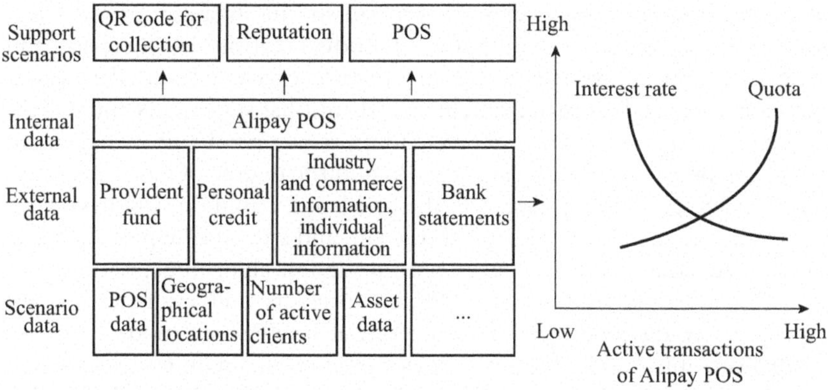

Fig. 7.10 Logic diagram of financial services (in-system scenarios) for a lobster restaurant in Shanghai

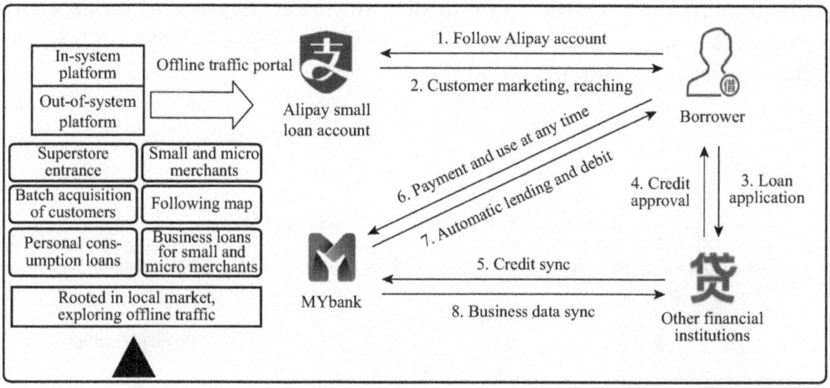

Fig. 7.11 ANT GROUP enabling micro credit (out-of-system scenarios)

provision of micro loans, MYbank can use MY Loan's technical capabilities to lower the cooperation threshold of partners and financial institutions, and provide more accurate and convenient financial services to customers through an open and enabling ecosystem (see Fig. 7.11). For example, MYbank brings 1 + 1 > 2 results through data cooperation and more accurate customer risk identification; solves the problem of data security and information isolation that institutions generally worry about by realizing data isolation of multiple institutions and customers in the platform; helps customers expand scenario-specific financial product features through flexible configurations of products, profit sharing ratios, and processes; and shows partners a full picture of capital and data assets through independent management of institutional statements and data.

The key to Ant Group's micro-lending risk control and management lies in the profiling of business networks and the degree of industrial organization achieved by big data. On the one hand, based on data from each platform scenario, external data, and so on, and with the help of statistical models, machine learning, deep learning, graph algorithms, natural language processing, and so on, MYbank predicts and evaluates various aspects of credit lending and uses artificial intelligence models for risk prediction, anti-fraud, account behavior prediction, credit evaluation, and value prediction. At present, MYbank has built at least 100 various prediction models for micro and small merchants. On the other hand, MYbank has formed a closed-loop whole process for credit management from data model to access, credit granting, pricing, asset management and post-loan management based on the establishment of various types of AI models and through the optimal use of various models, thus forming MYbank's intelligent risk control system (see Fig. 7.12).

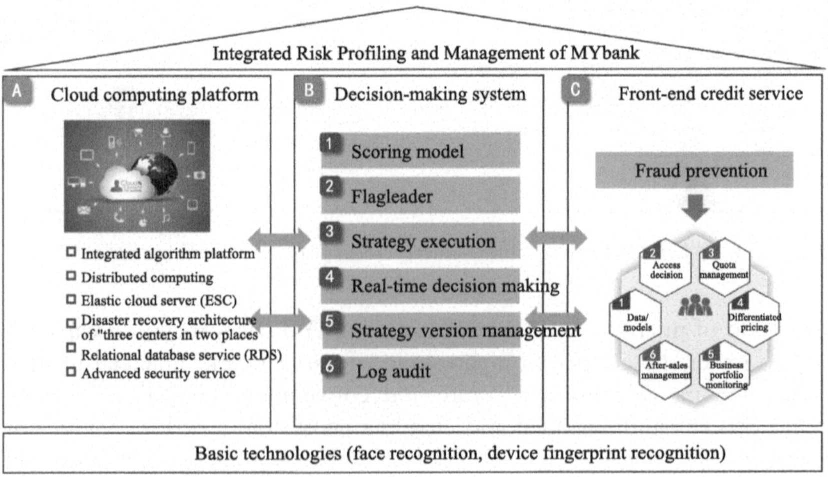

Fig. 7.12 Integrated risk management framework for micro credit in MYbank

7.3.4 Reactive Finance of Agricultural Supply Chain: ZM LOGISTICS—McCain Project's Agricultural Supply Chain and Financial Services

Founded in 1994, Shanghai Zhengming Logistics Co., Ltd. (referred to as "ZM LOGISTICS") has more than 600 cold chain transport vehicles, more than 50 special container transport vehicles, more than 300 vans and other transport vehicles, with a daily logistics volume of more than 15,000 tons, of which more than 5500 tons are cold chain logistics. The company is mainly engaged in general cargo (social cargo) transport, cold chain transport, interprovincial road passenger transport, freight forwarding, and so on. Since its establishment, ZM LOGISTICS has actively developed into various logistics fields, and has been transformed from a single transport-based carrier to a comprehensive third-party logistics enterprise, forming long-term, stable, and cooperative strategic alliances with an array of industrial enterprises. Its service network has spread from Shanghai and the surrounding areas of East China to the whole country, and has developed logistics partnerships with many overseas companies. Among plenty of customers, McCain is the core customer served by ZM LOGISTICS, which is located in Harbin and supplies French fries to McDonald's, KFC, and other fast food chains nationwide. ZM LOGISTICS has offered financial services for potato supply chain to farmers based on the partnership with McCain.

7.3.4.1 Challenges in Potato Sourcing

McCain's potatoes are mainly produced in the Hulunbeier region of Inner Mongolia. At the end of August and beginning of September every year, a large number of potatoes need to be transported to Harbin, which is McCain's potato base. Due to the short shelf life of potatoes, long transport distances and few transport vehicles, ZM LOGISTICS must have a high degree of transport expertise. Delayed transport of potatoes may lead to broken skins and spoilage, while McCain's refusal of the potatoes may result in a huge blow to the potato farmers' benefits. In addition, McCain faces many dilemmas during the souring season, which include the following:

1. Within one month of the annual potato sourcing season (mid-August to the end of September), McCain must complete the sourcing of 200,000 tons of potatoes. Each vehicle can carry 30–45 tons

of potatoes, so a total of 4500–5500 shipments are required, with an average of 150–200 shipments per day. Short-term and concentrated transport tasks are difficult to cope with.

2. McCain hires the fleets of dozens of suppliers in order to undertake the transport tasks. The large number of supplier fleets, the lack of unified vehicle scheduling, and the complex relationships between factories, farms, and fleets, coupled with inconsistent harvesting times at each farm, result in a waste of vehicle resources.
3. McCain's potato bases are located in Duolun, Lanqi, and Hulunbeier in Inner Mongolia, an average of more than 1000 km from the main production area. Potatoes are also breathing vegetables, and improper temperature control can affect potato quality. Quality control over long distances in transit is a challenge.
4. About 200 vehicles arrive in Harbin every day and wait in long lines in front of the factory for quality inspection before entering the factory and inbound procedures, which has caused road blockage, the prevalence of scalpers, serious queue jumping, and occasional incidents of potato theft, car oil theft, and tire theft. There are difficulties in coordinating the order of vehicles entering the factory, quality inspection and inbound procedures.
5. For the purpose of maintaining potato supply, McCain enters into purchase contracts with potato farmers in advance at the beginning of the year and pays 30% of the purchase price in the spring planting season to potato farmers. Once the transaction is completed, the potato farmers can receive full payment within a 60-day payment period based on documents regarding the quantity and identification of the grade. Potatoes are graded according to size, skin breakage, spoilage, sprouting, and other factors. First-grade potatoes are priced at RMB 1300–1500 per ton, and severely damaged potatoes are RMB 650–780 per ton. According to the overall calculation, McCain has to pay more than RMB 200 million for each sourcing season, causing pressure on its short-term fundraising and account processing.
6. In terms of sales of semifinished products, McCain's customers basically purchase according to their own purchasing plans at a certain time and quantity, resulting in a long backlog of McCain's semifinished products, some even for as long as two years, and a huge capital tied up in inventory.
7. In addition, McCain has high-quality requirements for potatoes, and starch and sugar content need to be controlled within certain

standards. Therefore, McCain needs to dispatch a lot of staff at any time during the growth process of potatoes to provide potato farmers with potato quality sampling. The quality inspection and control of potatoes also takes a lot of energy from McCain.

7.3.4.2 *Potato Supply Chain Service System Between ZM LOGISTICS and McCain*

In response to the above challenges, ZM LOGISTICS worked closely with McCain to effectively obtain specific information and plans for McCain's procurement. Based on this, ZM LOGISTICS sorted out the whole chain from potato seeds to French fries from the perspective of supply chain, and found out the uncoordinated and inefficient links and related stakeholders, and finally reconstructed a smoother and more efficient potato supply with a win-win result (see Fig. 7.13).

1. Planting Link: Advance Payment

The large payments to the farmers for the potato seeds and the relevant finished products has put McCain under financial pressure. In order to relieve McCain's financial constraints, ZM LOGISTICS agrees to make such payments on behalf of McCain for the potato planting and cultivation period on the premise of clarifying McCain's procurement plan and mutual cooperation. ZM LOGISTICS makes 20% advance payment to the potato farmers, and contracts the transport of the sourced potatoes after their maturity. After the potatoes are ripe, ZM LOGISTICS intervenes in

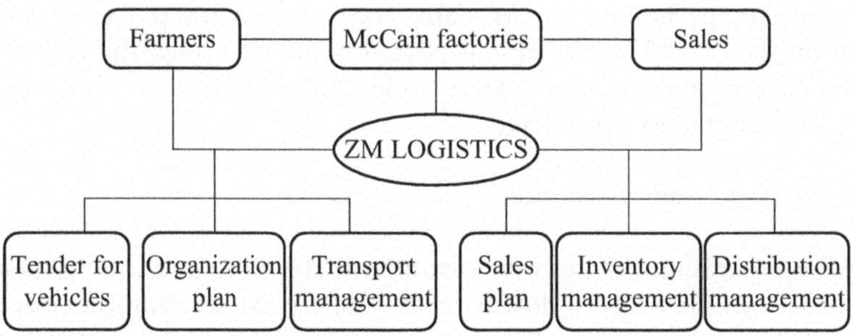

Fig. 7.13 Supply chain service system of ZM LOGISTICS—McCain Project

the "early quality" management of the potatoes, such as fresh transport and storage, thus penetrating the logistics service into the early stage of McCain's supply chain and expanding ZM LOGISTICS' supply chain service capability.

2. Purchasing Link: Vehicle Integration

In addition to penetrating the logistics service into the early stage of McCain's supply chain, ZM LOGISTICS embarked on the integration of potato transport vehicles as another important supply chain service. After McCain outsourced the transport and management of all potatoes to ZM LOGISTICS, ZM LOGISTICS has formed a professional transport team through tendering, rationalized transport plans and schedules, and ensured that vehicle needs are met. This approach not only allows effective management of multiple carriers and rationalization of pick-up, loading and transport plans but also eases the work intensity of operators to a certain extent, reducing the waiting time for each vehicle from 24 hours to less than 19 hours.

3. Receiving Link: Supply Chain Services and Financial Services

The potato sourcing process is a relatively tedious activity involving quality confirmation, payment for goods, warehousing, and so on. As for McCain, which is specialized in potato processing, these operations are more cumbersome and costly, so ZM LOGISTICS conducts quality acceptance, storage management, and other services on behalf of McCain, and carries out financial logistics activities based on pledge of goods in storage or in transit, undertakes to pay the remaining 80% of the purchasing price to the farmers for McCain, and shortens the payment period from 60 days to 15 days, helping potato farmers to solve the collection problem in a timely manner. Meanwhile, ZM LOGISTICS also relieves McCain's capital flow problem.

4. Sales Link: Trade Execution

After processing potatoes into semifinished French fries, McCain sells the processed products to downstream food companies, but as a processing company, McCain faces the challenges of distribution planning, inventory management, and accounts receivable period, and so on. ZM

LOGISTICS helps McCain in trade execution in the downstream links and solves McCain's problem of inventory backlog. Specifically, after clarifying McCain's sales plans with downstream companies, ZM LOGISTICS helps accelerate McCain's cash flow by promptly paying funds to McCain in exchange for the ownership to products. Then, ZM LOGISTICS sells these products on its own according to the purchase plans of downstream customers such as McDonald's and KFC. By virtue of the advantage of its own logistics network, ZM LOGISTICS achieves the integration of basic logistics businesses, and effectively ensures its own profitability with the purchase and sales price difference of semifinished products, while freeing up huge inventory occupancy capital and warehouse management expenses for McCain.

5. Warehousing Management of Finished Products (French Fries)

The management of finished goods is a key link of ZM LOGISTICS's supply chain management. Especially, if inventory is not effectively managed in the process of promoting supply chain financial services, huge risks may easily arise. ZM LOGISTICS uses the WMS system for the outbound, inbound, and inventory management of finished fries and executes standard warehousing management processes.

6. Mainline and Intercity Transport and Distribution of Finished Products

In addition to warehousing management, transport and distribution management is also an important part of supply chain operations. ZM LOGISTICS utilizes its national network resources and cold chain operation advantages to provide mainline transport services from Harbin factory to some cities in the eastern provinces and eastern China and urban distribution services in Harbin city and surrounding areas.

7.3.4.3 ZM LOGISTICS's Supply Chain Financial Services and Their Characteristics

Based on the setup of the above supply chain service system, ZM LOGISTICS penetrates into McCain's supply chain based on its partnership with McCain and its logistics, management and transport capabilities, especially those for potatoes, and provides supply chain financial services for the upstream and downstream links.

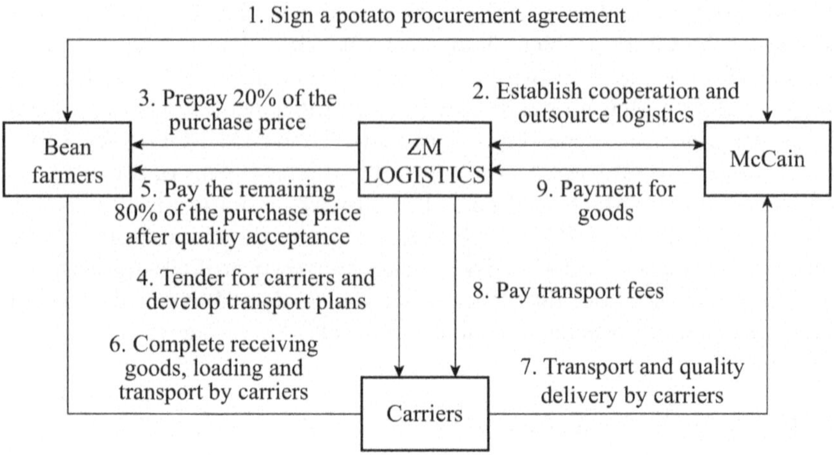

Fig. 7.14 Supply chain financial services for upstream procurement of ZM LOGISTICS

For the upstream links of the supply chain, ZM LOGISTICS provides the supply chain financial services as follows (see Fig. 7.14): (1) McCain signs potato sourcing agreements with potato farmers at the Hulunbeier base to determine the quantity, quality, and other sourcing parameters; (2) McCain forms a strategic partnership with and outsources the logistics to ZM LOGISTICS, and transmits the operation plan to ZM LOGISTICS; (3) ZM LOGISTICS makes an advance payment of 20% of the purchase price to the potato farmers under the condition that McCain's production and operation plan is clear; (4) ZM LOGISTICS tenders for carriers and decides the corresponding transport plans (capacity, timing, etc.) according to McCain's operation plan; (5) When the potatoes are ripe, ZM LOGISTICS conducts quality inspection on behalf of McCain and pays the remaining 80% of the purchase price to the potato farmers after inspection (financing service); (6) ZM LOGISTICS notifies the carriers to collect, load, and transport the goods according to the plan; (7) When the goods are delivered to the processing plant designated by McCain, ZM LOGISTICS conducts unloading and quality inspection and completes the logistics service; (8) ZM LOGISTICS pays the full transport fees to the carriers; (9) McCain makes full payment of the products to ZM LOGISTICS, completing the whole sourcing process.

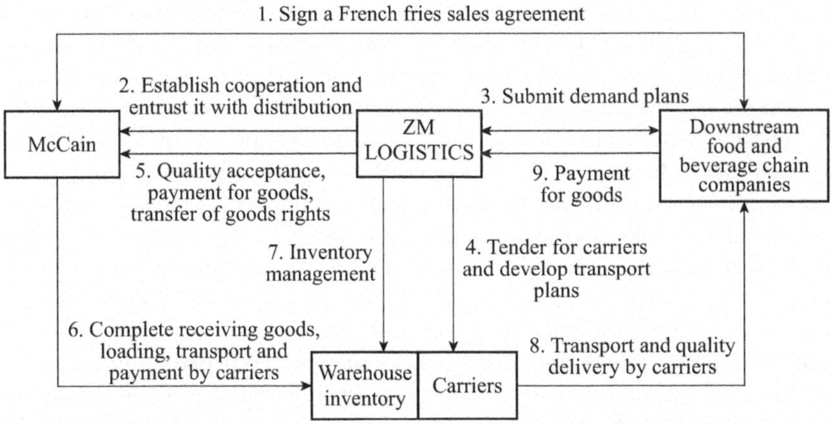

Fig. 7.15 Supply chain financial services for downstream distribution of ZM LOGISTICS

In addition to the supply chain financial services offered in the upstream souring process, ZM LOGISTICS further provides other supply chain financial services for McCain's sales process, with the basic process as below (see Fig. 7.15): (1) McCain signs the French fries sales agreements with its downstream food and catering enterprises (such as McDonald's, etc.); (2) McCain and ZM LOGISTICS form a strategic cooperation and sign a consignment distribution agreement; (3) downstream enterprises deliver the fries order plans to ZM LOGISTICS; (4) ZM LOGISTICS tenders for carriers based on the downstream enterprises' order plans and makes transport and distribution plans; (5) ZM LOGISTICS makes payments for the French fries after quality inspection in McCain's factory, in exchange for the ownership of the products from McCain; (6) ZM LOGISTICS organizes carriers to complete products receipt, loading, and transport to ZM LOGISTICS warehouse, and then pays transport fees to the carriers; (7) ZM LOGISTICS carries out inventory management to ensure the quality of the French fries in stock; (8) ZM LOGISTICS organizes carriers to deliver products to downstream enterprises as per the distribution plan and pays distribution fees; (9) downstream enterprises pay for the products to ZM LOGISTICS, thus completing the French fries distribution process.

In view of the above process of supply chain financial services provided by ZM LOGISTICS for the upstream sourcing links and the downstream distribution links, it can be concluded that the type of supply chain finance is based on McCain's clear business relationships. In other words, ZM LOGISTICS does not exist as a trader in the supply chain of potato or French fries industry, but plays the role of an intermediary facilitating organization or service provider through effective supply chain logistics services. Besides, from the perspective of ZM LOGISTICS, the partnership it has built with McCain allows ZM LOGISTICS to be fully notified of the business plans of upstream and downstream companies, and ZM LOGISTICS organizes carriers, arranges transport and distribution plans, and provides warehousing and inventory management services, so it plays a good value discovery function, control the possible risks in financial services, and curb the transaction costs arising from information asymmetry. From McCain's perspective, thanks to the outsourcing of supply chain logistics business to ZM LOGISTICS, it can effectively solve its own dilemma of capital shortage in supply chain operations, thus accelerating cash flow and make itself focusing on potato processing and customer relationship maintenance. In this regard, supply chain finance plays an incentive role.

7.3.5 *Proactive Agricultural Supply Chain Finance: Supply Chain Financial Services Between COFCO Trading and YANCHUAN FOUR APPLE*

7.3.5.1 *Key Elements for Building a Global Supply Chain for Agriculture*

The traditional agricultural supply chains have problems of scattered organizational structure, plenty of participants, weak synergy effect, complex process management, and many service elements involved. Therefore, the realization of overall synergy and global optimization of agricultural supply chain requires solving the obstacles existing in each link from the initial production side to the final market side (see Fig. 7.16).

Specifically, from the production side, the construction of a global agricultural supply chain needs to address three key issues: (1) The organization of decentralized farmers. As mentioned earlier, scattered individual farmers cannot effectively correspond to the requirements of industrial markets and are less able to resist external risks. Therefore, organizing scattered farmers in a market-oriented way becomes the key to building a global agricultural supply chain. In order to solve this problem, a related factor that needs attention is intensive use of planting land, which is more

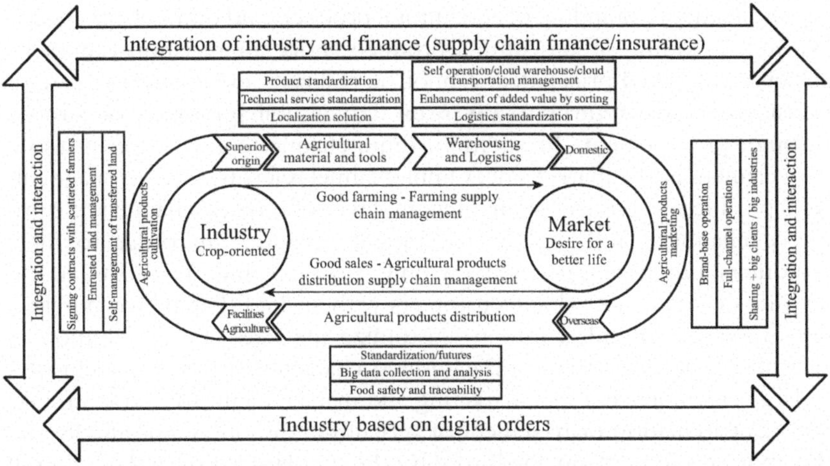

Fig. 7.16 Key elements in constructing a global supply chain for agriculture

typical in China. Only the realization of intensive use of planting land can truly solve the decentralization of farmers. (2) Timely and effective organization of external resources to provide agricultural producers and operators with appropriate seeds, production materials as well as tools on the basis of the preferred origin. Considering that agricultural production requires a large number of input factors, the competitiveness of input factors, as well as the timeliness and effectiveness of supply, will have a direct impact on the agricultural production process, not only in terms of labor productivity, but also in terms of the safety of agricultural products. The solution to this problem requires consideration of the standardization and safety of seeds, production materials and tools. In addition, the provision of relevant technical services and localized solutions for different regions, lands, and operation environments is also a core factor of the agricultural supply chain. (3) Standard and advanced logistics system. The natural attributes of agricultural products determine the level of logistics services and management, as well as the quality and safety of agricultural products. Therefore, the cold chain system, warehousing, transport, processing, and other operations are another facilitator or constraint for the construction of the supply chain at the production side.

From the market side, the agricultural supply chain needs to achieve the well-selling effect so as to ultimately protect the interests of farmers and various participants in the supply chain. To achieve this goal, two important factors deserve attention when constructing a global agricultural supply chain: (1) Branding of agricultural products and omni-channel sales. Without branding of agricultural products, price appreciation cannot be achieved, the fixed price effect cannot be realized, and enterprises cannot transfer marginal returns to upstream agricultural producers or farmers through procurement. In addition, omni-channel construction is also a core element at the market side. Omni-channel refers to the sale of agricultural products or services in an integrated way of physical channels, e-commerce channels, and mobile e-commerce channels in order to meet customers' purchasing needs at any time, any place and in any way, and to provide domestic and global customers with an undifferentiated purchasing experience. Besides, how to customize the sales and distribution of agricultural products to meet the business characteristics of large industries or large customers is also a marketing and management issue worth thinking. (2) Circulation management of agricultural products. Specifically, the distribution supply chain needs to solve the standardization and grading of agricultural products in terms of specifications. The failure to achieve this requirement makes it difficult to implement effective supply chain quality management, to use forward or futures markets, and to discover value. Moreover, big data analytics and safety traceability are important factors in distribution management. Big data analytics can help support effective planning and scheduling of distribution plans for agricultural products at different times, in different regions, and to different customers. Safety traceability management allows the visualization and transparency of agricultural product distribution, thus maximizing agricultural sustainability.

Having the key elements on the production side and market side, supply chain finance can play its role in all stages, empower each participant with more capabilities, accelerate the efficiency of capital in the whole industrial supply chain, and promote the full realization of agricultural modernization. The role of supply chain finance for agriculture is predicated on the integration and interaction of supply chain finance and agricultural digital orders. Optimization and change at the production and market sides of agriculture need to be transformed into a digital supply chain system, which means that, through the realization of the integrated ABCD, all links, participants, and activities in agriculture are formed into cross-checked digital information, thus achieving transparency, visualization, and traceability throughout the agricultural supply chain. Only after the entire agricultural supply chain is digitized can supply chain finance cover all aspects of agriculture and achieve full empowerment (INVERNIZZI, 2018). Likewise, only after the full penetration of supply chain financial services is realized can the agricultural supply chain be more solid and the sustainable agricultural development can be achieved.

7.3.5.2 COFCO Trading's Food Industry Supply Chain and Financial Services

As a first-tier subsidiary of China Oil and Foodstuffs Corporation, COFCO Trading Ltd. (referred to as "COFCO Trading") is the largest market-oriented grain distribution enterprise in China, a leading feed producer, an executor of the national grain macro-control policies, and an importer and exporter of wheat, corn, and other important agricultural products. The business scope mainly includes agricultural services, trading of food and feed ingredients, logistics services, feed products, and grain e-commerce trading. The varieties it deals with include wheat, corn, rice, mixed grains, beans, oil seeds, feed ingredients, and products, and so on.

COFCO Trading has 101 grain depots under its direct management, with a total storage capacity of 21.66 million tons, an annual port transit capacity of 18 million tons and a daily drying capacity of 67,000 tons. Its operation layout covers the main grain production and marketing areas in China, and it controls six major ports (namely, Beiliang Port, Jiangyin Port, Chenglingji Port, Fangcheng Port, Qingshan Port, and the new Xinsha Port of Dongguan under construction) and Chengdu Industrial Park and other key logistics nodes. Its "two horizontal and three vertical" grain logistics system is being built, including the Yangtze River and Xijiang River corridors, the maritime logistics corridor from Northeast ports to South China, the maritime logistics corridor from Northeast ports to East China, and the logistics corridor from Northeast production areas to inland distribution areas. Under COFCO Trading, there are specialized logistics operating companies such as Xinliang Shipping and COFCO Railway Transport, with an aim of forming a specialized logistics operation platform in terms of shipping, railroad, and container transport, and effectively integrating social resources to create a high-efficiency and low-cost logistics channels.

With the mission of "delivering food to the world and benefiting people all over the world" and the vision of becoming a "world-class grain distribution enterprise," COFCO Trading is committed to be an efficient bridge and bond between grain and oil producers and grain, oil and feed processors, provide high-quality planting and warehousing services to Chinese farmers, stable and reliable raw materials, technical support and solutions to processors, and safe and efficient feed products and services to the breeding industry.

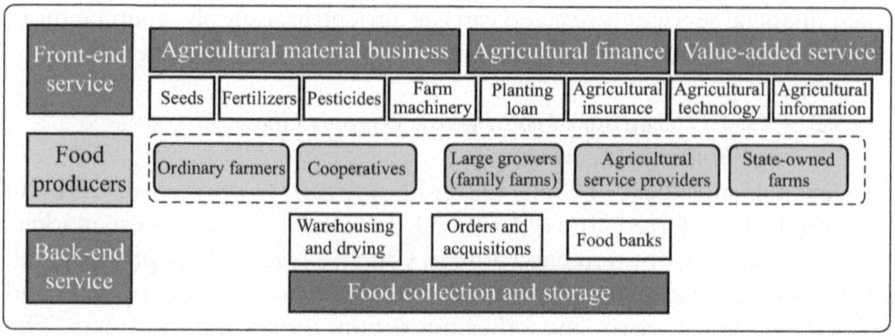

Fig. 7.17 Global graph of food production supply chain built by COFCO

(1) Supply Chain Construction at the Production Side of COFCO Trading

The basic idea of the supply chain construction at the production side of COFCO Trading is to integrate grain producers according to market demand and provide a package of solutions from front end to back end based on "4 categories and 11 services" (see Fig. 7.17). Integrating food producers means fully integrating all kinds of food producers, including ordinary farmers, cooperatives, family farms, agricultural service companies and state-owned farms, through supply chain organization. Four categories and 11 services refer to grain collection and storage services (providing storage and drying, ordering and grain banking services for all kinds of agricultural producers with its own storage and logistics resources), agricultural materials operation services (providing seeds, fertilizers, pesticides, and machinery services to agricultural producers in cooperation with external partners), agricultural financial services (providing planting loans and agricultural insurance services to agricultural producers in cooperation with external financial institutions), and value-added services (providing agricultural technical services and agricultural information services to agricultural producers with its own resources and external resources). Specifically, COFCO Trading has formed the following supply chain operation model at the production side around the above objectives.

A. Reinforcing cooperatives and establishing direct connections to the land. An important issue to be addressed in the agricultural production supply chain is how to integrate scattered farmers into synergistic business organizations, thereby enhancing competitiveness at the production side. To this end, COFCO formed a basis for cooperation with

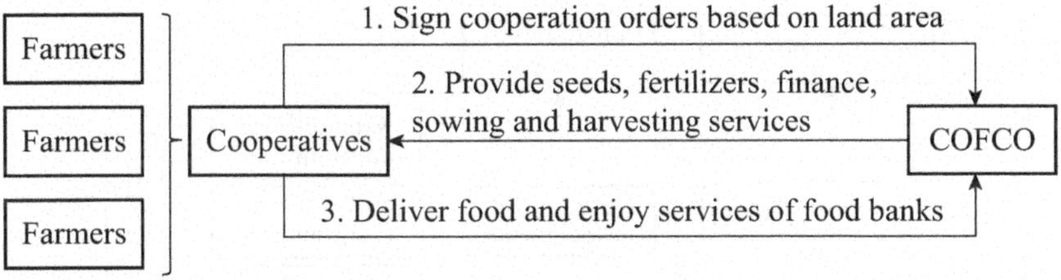

Fig. 7.18 Operation model (I) of COFCO TRADING production-side supply chain

itself in Ning'an, Heilongjiang Province, by directly helping farmers to establish and develop cooperatives (see Fig. 7.18). The specific process is as follows: Step 1—Research: COFCO conducts in-depth research on the relationship between cooperatives and farmers; Step 2—Publicity: COFCO educates each village about its agricultural services to gain the recognition of farmers and make them cooperate with COFCO voluntarily; Step 3—Promotion: Local governments set up cooperatives in the form of "one cooperative per village," equip them with institutions, personnel, members, ledgers, signatures and fingerprints, and complete information materials; members can be tracked, inquired, contacted, and served; Step 4—Service: COFCO signs order contracts with each cooperative and provides agricultural services in terms of agricultural materials, agricultural machinery, and finance according to the needs of the cooperative, and later recovers the ordered grain and provides food banking services.

B. Forming agricultural consortia. Another form of enhancing the competitiveness of agricultural production is large operating enterprises. For example, COFCO penetrates directly into the production chain by cooperating with agricultural production organizations. An advantage of doing so is that it can better arrange production through the resources of large operating organizations to counteract risks in grain production operations. To this end, COFCO Trading promotes the development of the agricultural production supply chain in the form of consortia in Baoxiang, Hebei Province (see Fig. 7.19). The specific division of work is as follows: COFCO Trading is responsible for order recovery; bringing together agricultural, financial, insurance, policy, and other resource support; and providing countryside warehousing

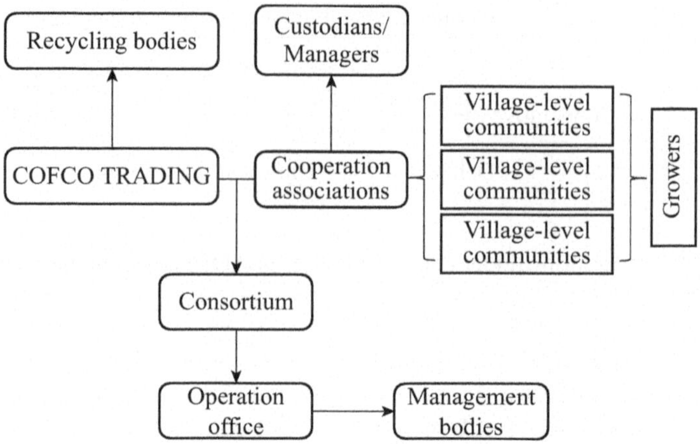

Fig. 7.19 Operation model (II) of COFCO TRADING production-side supply chain

facilities and some agricultural machinery support. The consortia are responsible for managing or transferring land and employing workers; setting planting plans, coordinating supervision and management; managing village-level societies and organizing order recovery. The village-level society is responsible for cultivation, planting, management, and harvesting, as well as management of planting personnel, and acts as temporary warehouse of crops.

C. Intervening in the whole agricultural production process through land integration. In solving the problem of land fragmentation in the agricultural production supply chain management, besides resorting to the methods of agricultural cooperatives or industrial consortia, COFCO now also directly solves the problem of land through various proven means for regions where integration cannot be achieved by the above methods in the short term, and then integrates other kinds of resources to empower the entire production supply chain. The typical implementation cases include Tongliao, Liaoning Province (see Fig. 7.20), with the following specific processes: (1) COFCO acquires land resources in the form of transfer, trusteeship, and lease, and applies for local government's agricultural policy qualification; (2) COFCO cooperates with third-party partners to invest in production

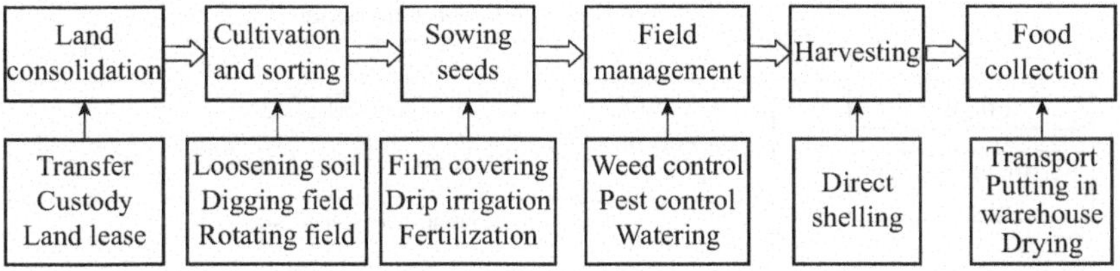

Fig. 7.20 Operation model (III) of COFCO TRADING production-side supply chain

factors such as farming materials, farm machinery, and farming tools to reduce planting costs and obtain farming guidance from seed companies, fertilizer companies, and farm machinery manufacturers; (3) COFCO joins with local farm machinery cooperatives to train grain depot workers to become capable grain growers and professional farm machinery operators to carry out field operations; (4) COFCO takes out planting insurance, and the grain is brought directly into COFCO grain depots after harvesting.

D. Seed-fertilizer-grain cycle operation model. This model is characterized by the cooperation with agricultural materials enterprises to build a common customer base. Agricultural materials are important input factors for agricultural production. Many agricultural materials enterprises have their own markets and customer bases, and although they can effectively help the production side by providing appropriate products, they are not competent for the production process and post-production management. Therefore, COFCO cooperates with agricultural material enterprises in order to jointly promote the formation of agricultural production supply chain, in which agricultural material enterprises play the advantage in preproduction, while COFCO plays the advantage of production and postproduction. Representative regions that carry out this type of model are Nenjiang, Suihua, and Kangjin in Heilongjiang Province and Songyuan in Jilin Province. The specific process is as follows (see Fig. 7.21): (1) COFCO cooperates with seed and fertilizer enterprises to expand their sales of agricultural materials, which can be sold by them to their customers or by COFCO to its customers. At the same time, COFCO provides agricultural services such as ordering, finance, agricultural machinery and grain

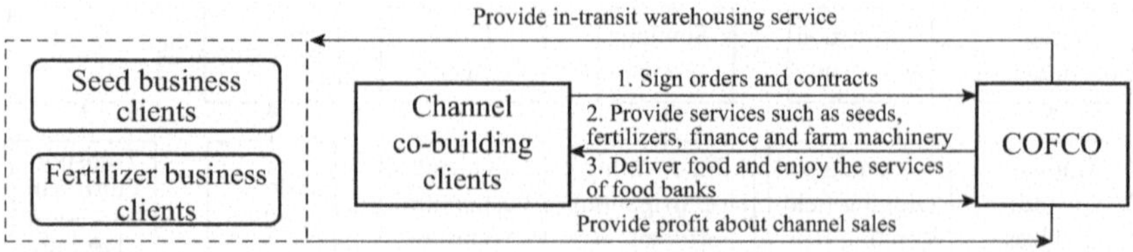

Fig. 7.21 Operation model (IV) of COFCO TRADING production-side supply chain

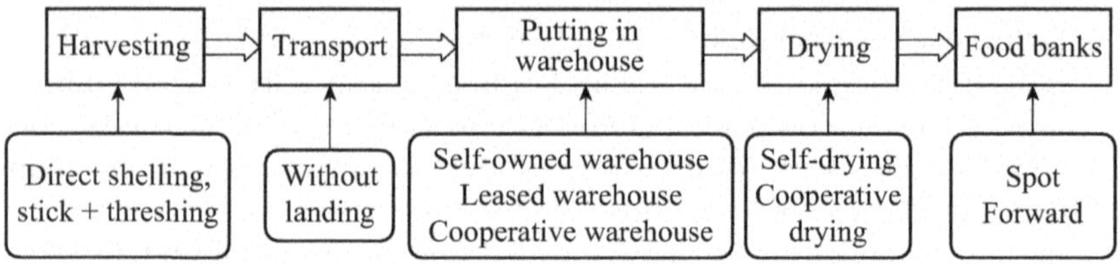

Fig. 7.22 Operation model (V) of COFCO TRADING production-side supply chain

banking; (2) Seed and fertilizer enterprises give part of their channel sales profits to COFCO, and COFCO shares profits with farmers in the harvest season to improve the order recovery rate; (3) COFCO plays the advantage in grain warehouse assets to provide agricultural storage and transit services for seed and fertilizer enterprises.

E. Cooperating with agricultural machinery owners or purchasing their own agricultural machinery to transport grain from the field to the COFCO grain depots in a no-landing mode. This model is mainly to help agricultural producers or farmers solve problems in grain harvesting. Grain harvesting often requires a large amount of agricultural machinery as well as specialized workers. Lack of timely supply of production resources or irregularities in operations may easily result in grain losses during harvesting. For this reason, COFCO cooperates with specialized harvesting machinery operators, or purchases its own farm machinery and hands it over to professionals to operate, while COFCO Acquisition provides follow-up services for farmers or producers, thus not only solving the problem of efficient harvesting of agricultural products but also providing good supply chain services for agricultural producers. The specific process (see Fig. 7.22) is as follows:

(1) COFCO controls the first link of postproduction logistics and transport of grain, and controls the logistics flow of grain; (2) grain is delivered to COFCO grain depots in a no-landing mode, which can avoid secondary handling, loss, and deterioration, and can improve farmers' income from grain sales; (3) docking to COFCO grain banks allows farmers to share the market opportunities arsing from market price fluctuations and sell grain at a reasonable price, while COFCO obtains the right to operate the grain in advance.

(2) Supply Chain Construction at the Market Side of COFCO Trading

In addition to constructing the production-side supply chain, how to build the market-side supply chain is also the key to the whole agricultural supply chain. To this end, COFCO and China Merchants Group have cooperated to build a one-stop comprehensive service platform for bulk agricultural grain—Liangdawang.com, aiming to establish an open, transparent, and liable grain e-commerce ecosystem by combining online trade and offline warehousing and logistics services (see Fig. 7.23). The traditional grain trading chain is relatively simple, but there are many circulation links, and the circulation and transaction costs of each link are high, which largely restricts the overall efficiency. Focusing on spot trading and based on the intermediate market, Liangdawang.com effectively connects

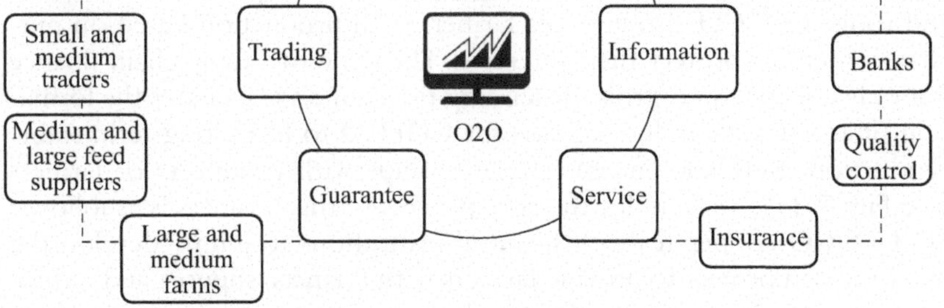

Fig. 7.23 Global graph of food sales supply chain built by COFCO

customers' actual delivery needs as well as their medium and forward trading hedging needs, providing a one-stop solution of "performance guarantee trading/settlement mode + risk management tools for trading + modern logistics service + supply chain financing" to promote the orderly and safe circulation of grain. At the same time, Liangdawang.com also provides various big data, including the data of future demand for grain varieties and quality, dynamic and real-time data of circulation direction, real price change data, nonstatistical inventory data, and so on, thus gradually forming a big data system in grain circulation and providing data support for national food security and grain policy formulation. Since its official operation in November 2015, Liangdawang.com has completed a total of 16,238 transactions as of August 2, 2017, with a transaction volume of 17.052 million tons and a transaction amount of RMB 35.3 billion. In 2017, 665 new traders were registered, and the total number of registered traders reached 5024.

(3) Agricultural Supply Chain Finance of COFCO

Based on the establishment of the above agricultural supply chain systems at the production and market sides, COFCO Trading has developed a series of empowering supply chain finance businesses. In other words, with the help of supply chain finance, it further promotes the construction of agricultural supply chains. At present, the specific supply chain finance businesses carried out by COFCO Trading include planting loan and grain bank in the agricultural production supply chain, as well as consignment loan and sales loan in the agricultural sales supply chain.

The planting loan is a business developed by COFCO in cooperation with financial institutions, designed to provide funds for operators or farmers at the production side for the purchase of agricultural materials and tools. COFCO also entrusts farmers with production based on purchase orders to protect their interests. This type of supply chain finance not only effectively controls the lending risks but also facilitates the formation of an effective industrial base for COFCO to form long-term stable production, purchase and sales relationships with producers or farmers (see Fig. 7.24). Specifically, the core process of this business is as follows: (1) COFCO cooperates with financial institutions to jointly develop the planting loan project to provide farmers with financial support and reduce capital costs; (2) the bank provides planting loans to farmers in the form

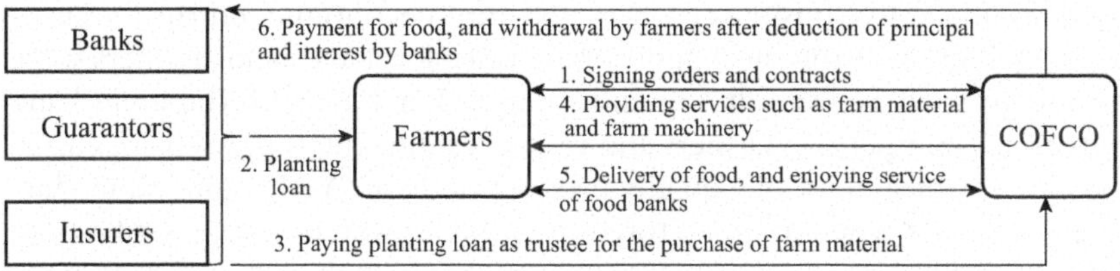

Fig. 7.24 COFCO production-side planting loan

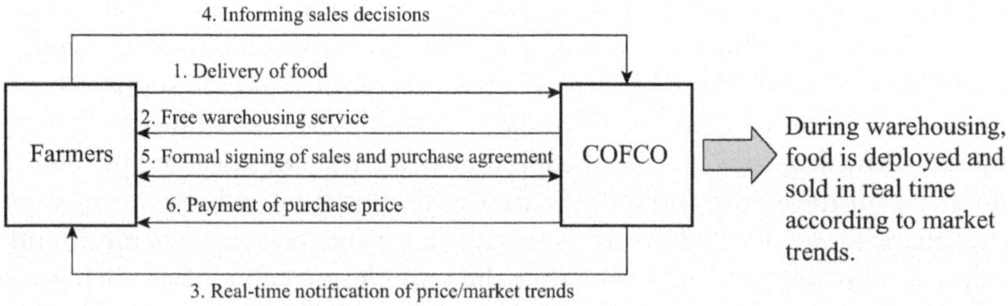

Fig. 7.25 COFCO food bank operations

of physical agricultural materials to prevent the loans from being used for other purposes and reduce the risks of bank; (3) COFCO provides farmers with services such as orders, agricultural materials, agricultural machinery, and grain banks to improve the stickiness with farmers and attract farmers to sell grain to COFCO, and finally COFCO makes the grain payments to the account designated by bank, so as to guarantee the financial security of the repayments to the bank.

Grain bank is a very innovative supply chain financial business developed by COFCO Trade. Agricultural product prices are highly volatile. Agricultural producers who choose to sell during the souring season when supply is large and prices are low face large financial losses, while those who choose to wait for future sales face storage problems. Agricultural products are difficult to store and vulnerable to natural factors. For addressing this situation, COFCO Trading innovatively uses its own warehousing and management resources and capabilities to provide farmers with free storage services to ensure grain quality. During the storage period, COFCO's system constantly reminds farmers of market prices and trends in real time. Farmers can promptly notify COFCO of targeted sales of their grain to COFCO when they think the price is right (see Fig. 7.25).

This innovative business ensures maximum economic returns for farmers to sell grain at the most appropriate price level and helps farmers solve problems such as grain drying and storage. For COFCO, the grain bank integrates competitive farmers and resources into the supply chain, ensuring the establishment of a quality production base. At the same time, during the period when grain is stored in COFCO warehouses, COFCO can deploy and sell grain in a timely manner based on the state of grain price fluctuations throughout the year as well as market trends, ensuring not only maximum economic benefits for the company itself, but also leveling out the negative impact of dramatic price fluctuations on other stakeholders. This type of business combined with the abovementioned supply chain services and planting loan realizes a unique kind of supply chain financial service, which is mainly characterized by the separation of commodity flow, logistics flow, and capital flow. In the common supply chain financial business, the three flows are often consistent, which means that the financial service behaviors (such as factoring, reverse factoring, and warehouse receipt pledge) arise after the completion of purchase behavior or logistics behavior. However, in the case of COFCO's grain bank, the financial behaviors occur up front (i.e., providing funds to help farmers with farm equipment or storage), while the actual purchase and transaction contracts occur at a future time. Similarly, the logistics flow and commodity flow are also separated, meaning that logistics occurs up front (during the period when COFCO helps farmers store grain on their behalf, grain is deployed and sold in a timely manner according to the rules of market changes to achieve year-round price leveling, thus maximizing economic and social effects), while the actual purchase, sale, or transaction contracts between COFCO and farmers occur in the future. On the one hand, this supply chain finance is clearly based on global supply chain optimization, that is, a long-term stable production collaboration relationship between farmers and COFCO. The separation of the three flows without the guarantee of such relationship would only generate risks. On the other hand, this supply chain finance also promotes the optimization of the industrial supply chain. The greater advantage is not in solving the problem of timely access to funds by farmers, but in achieving the consolidation and strengthening of the new production partnership through the act of financial services.

Consignment loan is primarily designed for consignment business among the principal customers. Usually, the customer consigns the grain at the market, and it is not until the grain is picked up by the customer

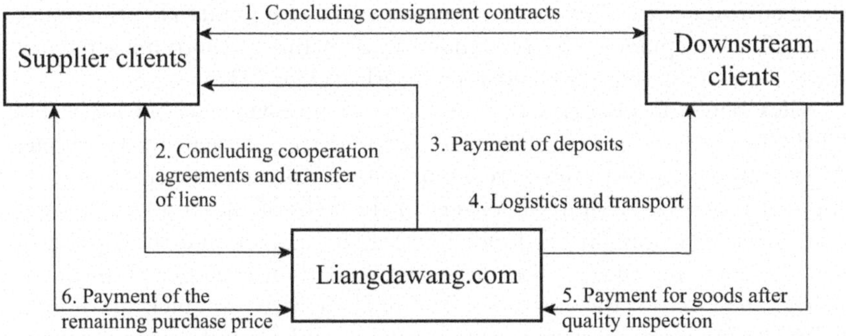

Fig. 7.26 COFCO consignment loan

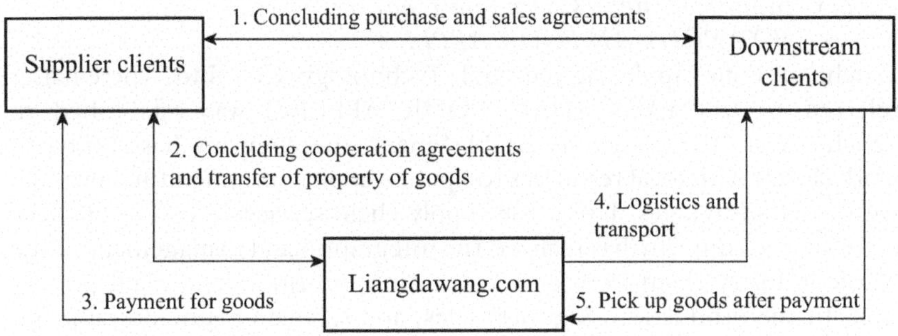

Fig. 7.27 COFCO sales loan

from the market that a real transaction takes place between both parties, resulting in accounts receivable and payable. Obviously, this business model takes up a lot of capital of the suppliers. On the one hand, they spend huge amounts of money on grain storage and logistics; on the other hand, during the period of grain storage, they are unable to obtain funds in a timely manner, which affects their next business activities. For this reason, COFCO has rolled out the consignment loan with the process as follows (see Fig. 7.26): (1) COFCO signs a cooperation agreement with the customer, thus enabling Liangdawang.com to obtain a lien (i.e., the right to manage the stored grain); (2) Liangdawang.com pays the customer a certain deposit to meet the funds necessary for its normal production and operations; (3) When downstream customers place demand orders for grain, Liangdawang.com organizes carriers to deliver grain to these customers; (4) Downstream customers pay for grain to Liangdawang.com after acceptance; (5) Liangdawang.com makes the remaining payment after deducting the deposit paid earlier (Fig. 7.27).

Sales loan is another type of sales supply chain finance service offered by COFCO to its customers, which is adapted to the agency sales model. After signing a grain sales agreement with a downstream customer, the supplier transfers the right of delivery or the right of sales to Liangdawang.com in order to obtain full funds in a timely manner, and the latter pays for the grain in advance. Liangdawang.com then organizes logistics to deliver the grain to the customer. The final payment and pick-up of grain by the downstream customer indicate the completion of the whole transaction process.

7.3.5.3 Industrial Supply Chain and Financial Service of YANCHUAN FOUR APPLE

Yanchuan Four Apple Agricultural Technology Co., Ltd. (hereinafter referred to as "YANCHUAN FOUR APPLE") was established in Yanchuan in 2016. Since its establishment, the company has chosen to work closely with local resources to operate apples, an agricultural product with local advantages. Using the supply chain services + ICT + financial services, the company has realized the integration and management of the whole industry chain from crop cultivation, nutrition, and plant protection, to the production, logistics, sales, and service of agricultural products. The first step in constructing agricultural supply chains is to organize an ecosystem, that is, how to integrate different participants involved in agricultural production into a symbiotic and cooperative system.

(1) Industrial Supply Chain Construction of YANCHUAN FOUR APPLE

The construction of YANCHUAN FOUR APPLE supply chain takes the organization of the market side as the first task, which is the basis for establishing a pull-type supply chain system. The planting base of YANCHUAN FOUR APPLE is located in Yanchuan County, Yan'an City, Shaanxi Province, at 36.8 degrees north latitude, with an average annual temperature of 10.6 °C, 2558 annual sunshine hours, and 185 frost-free days per year. The temperature difference between days and nights is large, and the annual precipitation is less than 500 mm. The area is a hilly and ravine terrain of the Loess Plateau, with a small flat surface, commonly known as "residual loess." The apple orchards have an altitude of 1100 meters, which is the best area to meet the ecological index of apples. Based on this, YANCHUAN FOUR APPLE has created the brand image of apples on the loess plateau in northern Shaanxi. Moreover, YANCHUAN FOUR APPLE has formed its brand story with the background culture of educated youth in Liangjia River, highlighting the simple personality of apples from "loess," and boosted the popularity of Yanchuan apples through various means, such as news media and e-commerce companies. With the convergence of the brand image and market orders, YANCHUAN FOUR APPLE promotes order-based agricultural production in reverse.

On the other hand, how to organically organize scattered farmers to engage in intensive production is also the key to the construction of agricultural supply chain. On the supply side, YANCHUAN FOUR APPLE realizes land trusteeship mainly by contracting with decentralized farmers. Its intensive planting and operations are based on the transfer of land and greenhouses. This approach allows the centralized management and service of production and operations but also enables the organization of decentralized farmers to enter the supply chain operations as agricultural workers, making them much more resilient to risks. In 2016, the first year since establishment, YANCHUAN FOUR APPLE contracted 28 farmers and managed the apples of about 300 mu. In that year, a severe hailstorm caused the farmers to face huge losses. When the farmers were looking at the hailstorm-hit apples, YANCHUAN FOUR APPLE decided to purchase all the apples from the contracted farmers to minimize their economic losses. About 700,000 pounds of apples were purchased, including the affected ones, resulting in a solid reputation and a sense of trust among the farmers. In 2017, the number of actively contracted farmers increased from 28 to 438, and the planting area under its management increased from 300 mu in 2016 to over 3000 mu, a ten-fold increase. In order to improve farmers' income, YANCHUAN FOUR APPLE has acquired all contracted farmers' apples, about 7.8 million catties, at a price of RMB 0.2~0.8/catty higher than the purchase price of that year. As of June 2018, the number of actively contracted farmers has increased to 761, and the managed planting area has reached 7825 mu, with the expected apple production of over 10,000 tons. At the same time, YANCHUAN FOUR APPLE has provided hundreds of jobs for local farmers. More than 500 people are employed daily during the apple harvesting season, which directly or indirectly provides jobs and financial support for poverty alleviation.

The construction of agricultural supply chain involves a large number of operators of production materials, while traditional operators of agricultural materials, agricultural tools, and pesticides are faced with the problem of how to directly connect with farmers, especially how to provide production materials adapted to the characteristics of production operations. YANCHUAN FOUR APPLE mainly realizes the synergistic operation of agricultural materials, agricultural tools, and pesticides by cooperating with some production materials operators, or docking with their business platforms. For example, in terms of pesticides, YANCHUAN FOUR APPLE has formed a strategic cooperation with Bayer, which provides pesticides and provides warranty services and guidance on application. In terms of fertilizers, YANCHUAN FOUR APPLE directly connects to SIMOCHEM's Modern Agriculture Platform (MAP), a platform built by SIMOCHEM Agriculture to integrate the resources of the whole industry chain and provide a full range of solutions, as well as seed, fertilizer, and medicine product packages, for large-scale farms. Based on in-depth cooperation with these companies, YANCHUAN FOUR APPLE provides the operators of agricultural materials, agricultural tools, and pesticides with direct sales and service channels to farmers, and also strengthens its own resource competitiveness.

Another important link in the agricultural products supply chain is logistics, which mainly includes logistics distribution and cold storage. The lack of good logistics service and assets support will put the agricultural products supply chain into a great challenge. In terms of distribution, YANCHUAN FOUR APPLE improves the quality of apple distribution services by cooperating with courier companies such as Yunda and SF, and strengthens inventory management by partnering with other third parties engaged in cold storage services.

Based on the above approach, a multiparty collaborative agricultural supply chain service platform is finally built.

(2) Integrated ABCD in Industrial Supply Chain of YANCHUAN FOUR APPLE

Upon establishing the organizational ecosystem of agricultural supply chain, the key to supply chain intelligence is how to ensure real-time, transparency, and traceability of the whole process of supply chain operations. Supply chain intelligence refers to the systematization of ICT tools to achieve the intelligence of supply chain operations, thereby innovating

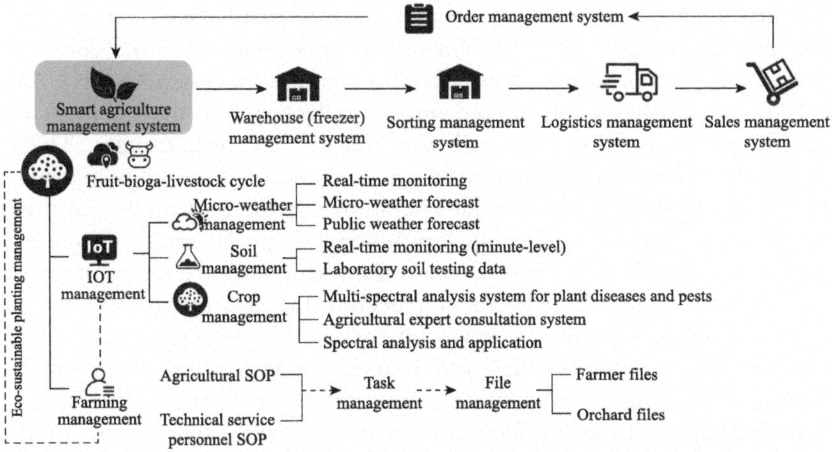

Fig. 7.28 ICT-enabled supply chain of YANCHUAN FOUR APPLE

business models and realizing value. Therefore, it is necessary to combine the problems that need to be solved in each link of the agricultural supply chain and adopt the corresponding ICT in a targeted manner. Specifically, the ICT application of YANCHUAN FOUR APPLE is focused on three aspects (see Fig. 7.28):

First aspect is informative and transparent agricultural management. The agricultural supply chain involves a large number of growers, so visualizing the scattered information about land and farmers on the system becomes a key part of intelligent management, and a prerequisite for organized production management including accurate and real-time technical services. The scattered information includes farmer files, planting management status, planting area, planting years, historical yields, estimated yields, and so on. Through the integration of self-built data and public data, YANCHUAN FOUR APPLE establishes corresponding big data for agricultural management, which can be updated and managed in real time through the Internet. Based on the big data analysis, mining and calculation, YANCHUAN FOUR APPLE provides technical services and implements planting management according to the condition of cooperative customers.

Second aspect is IoT-based farming and field management. Another key factor in agricultural supply chain intelligence is how to effectively implement field management. Agricultural production is susceptible to climate, geography, soil, and pests and diseases, so the lack of sound on-site management, or even preventive guidance, may lead to significant operational risks in supply chain. To address this situation, YANCHUAN FOUR APPLE has implemented on-site collection and management of agricultural production data with the help of IoT technologies. These technologies are used in three main aspects: micrometeorology management (i.e., providing agricultural operation guidance through real-time micrometeorological monitoring, combined with public weather forecasting), soil management (real-time soil monitoring and management), and pest monitoring and management (spectral analysis, monitoring, etc.). These various sensing nodes (environment, soil, image, etc.) and wireless communication networks deployed at agricultural production sites allow intelligent sensing, intelligent warning, intelligent control, intelligent analysis of agricultural production environment, and expert online guidance, thus realizing precise planting, visual management, and intelligent decision-making in agricultural production, and providing accurate data support for the efficient operations of all links in the industrial chain of apples and other agricultural products.

Third aspect is the informationization of the supply chain distribution operation process. The process of agricultural products circulation involves the safety traceability and management of agricultural products, which needs the support from the information of the whole process. One of the keys to the digitalization of agricultural product distribution is to establish standardized agricultural products and then realize the circulation. In this regard, YANCHUAN FOUR APPLE manages apples according to the standard ratings of apple futures trading market, so as to achieve the digitization of management standards in product circulation. In addition, the dynamic information of supply chain circulation and digital management of orders are also important elements for informationization. YANCHUAN FOUR APPLE is working with third parties to try to strengthen the intelligence in this aspect.

(3) Agricultural Supply Chain Finance of YANCHUAN FOUR APPLE

In addition to forming supply chain ecosystem and realizing intelligent supply chain operations, supply chain finance is also an important means for YANCHUAN FOUR APPLE to enhance industrial competitiveness. Farmers need money to purchase production materials, such as bags, fertilizers, pesticides, and so on, and also need insurance to ensure the safety of agricultural production. However, financial institutions are usually unable to provide effective financial services to farmers because of two reasons: first, farmers do not have sufficient assets as collateral and pledges, nor do they have the corresponding financial statements, resulting in their inability to obtain loans from financial institutions; second, considering the seasonality, volatility, and perishability of agricultural products, coupled with the inability to grasp the production and operation process of agricultural products, financial institutions are unable to directly grant credit to farmers. However, the big data obtained by YANCHUAN FOUR APPLE through the use of ICT can provide the basis for accurate service, whole process management, and risk control of financial institutions. First of all, the agricultural management system accumulates a large amount of information on farmers, land status, historical production, quality, delivery status, and so on, which makes it easier for financial institutions to more correctly assess the ability and credit of farmers and achieve ex ante management. In addition, IOT and its communication allow financial institutions to control the operation process in real time and achieve risk control during the process. By utilizing the standardized management, storage management, and order management information of apples, financial institutions can also better grasp the market conditions of agricultural products, thus realizing ex post management. Based on the above, YANCHUAN FOUR APPLE currently offers following two types of financial services by partnering with financial institutions: "Agriculture + Finance" and "Agriculture + Insurance."

"Agriculture + Finance" is a comprehensive production material financing service provided by YANCHUAN FOUR APPLE and Agricultural Bank of China (referred to as "ABC") for contracted farmers, aiming to solve the shortage of funds for farmers to purchase production materials, and also help production material suppliers to effectively connect with farmers to complete sales. The specific process is shown in Fig. 7.29: (1) YANCHUAN FOUR APPLE signs the purchase and sale agreement of apples with downstream customers and issues production plans to contracted farmers as per orders; (2) YANCHUAN FOUR APPLE provides a white list of contracted farmers and the corresponding data to ABC; (3) ABC provides the agriculture-oriented e-loans to qualified farmers, and the funds are paid to the agricultural production material suppliers cooperated by YANCHUAN FOUR APPLE through the planting technology service center; (4) The agricultural production material suppliers provide production materials to the contracted farmers and provide standardized

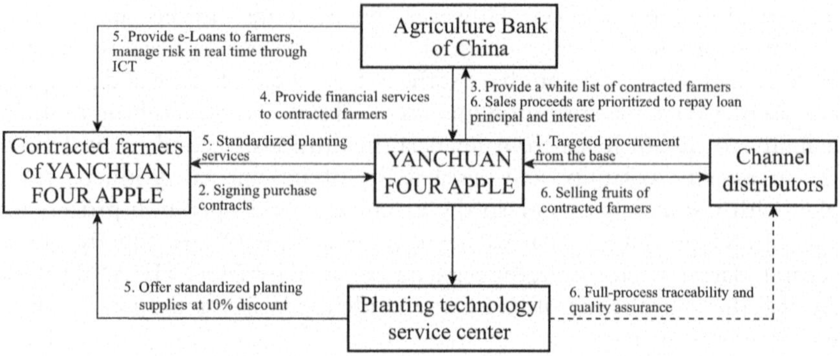

Fig. 7.29 ICT-supported "Agriculture + Finance" services of YANCHUAN FOUR APPLE

whole-process planting services in cooperation with YANCHUAN FOUR APPLE. The financial institution monitors the whole process in real time through the ICT system established by YANCHUAN FOUR APPLE to control the loan risk; (5) After the agricultural products are produced, they are sold to the downstream customers, and the sales proceeds are given priority to repay the principal and interest to the bank. It is worth highlighting that in consideration of reducing the interest burden arising from loans to farmers for the purchase of production materials (the current commercial annualized interest rate is 4%), YANCHUAN FOUR APPLE offers a 10% discount throughout the year when joining hands with production material suppliers to provide production material products, so as to offset the cost of borrowing for farmers and give them peace of mind in using bank funds and production materials.

"Agriculture + Insurance" is an insurance product provided by YANCHUAN FOUR APPLE and China Continent Insurance (referred to as "CCIC") for farmers, aiming to reduce the impact of natural disasters on agricultural production, stabilize the income of farmers, and promote agricultural and rural economic development. The specific process is shown in Fig. 7.30: (1) YANCHUAN FOUR APPLE provides the list of contracted farmers to CCIC; (2) after the application is approved, CCIC provides the corresponding insurance products to farmers; (3) CCIC implements supervision through IoT and Internet set up by YANCHUAN FOUR APPLE; (4) in the event of an insured accident, YANCHUAN FOUR APPLE will assist the farmer to complete the claim.

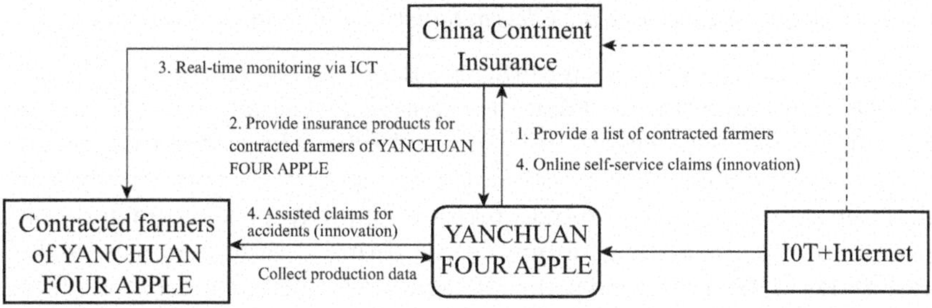

Fig. 7.30 ICT-supported "Agriculture + Insurance" services of YANCHUAN FOUR APPLE

As can be seen, the first step in the intelligence of an agricultural supply chain is to effectively integrate various stakeholders and organize customers into a large market. In the process of collaborative agricultural production, technical services for agricultural production, production material services and financial services need to be provided under the premise of safeguarding the interests of farmers. In addition, IoT and the Internet empower agricultural supply chain operations to achieve full visualization, transparency, real-time and traceability of farmers, agricultural products, and financial services.

7.4 Circular Economy and Supply Chain Finance

In recent years, circular economy, one of the topics of sustainable economic development, has received widespread attention from theoretical circles, practical circles, and policy-makers. The focus of the circular economy is to realize the reduction of resource consumption as well as availability and recyclability through a closed-loop production and operation system and effective management tools, and ultimately to achieve sustainable economic, social, and environmental development. Therefore, this strategy necessarily involves how the enterprises or participants therein can effectively coordinate among themselves to gradually evolve from reducing resource consumption to adjusting industrial structure and developing new technologies and management tools. In parallel, there is also a need to address the issue of how to adopt appropriate supply chain finance instruments to solve the working capital in the circular economy, to realize empowerment for the whole circular economy, and to promote the establishment and development of the circular economy.

7.4.1 *Meaning and Characteristics of Circular Economy*

The international exploration of the circular economy emerged in the late 1970s. Many studies argued that the theoretical exploration of the circular economy began with Pearce and Turner (1990), who introduced the linear and open-ended characteristics of contemporary economic systems by describing how natural resources provide inputs to production and consumption and affect the economy in the form of waste materials. Stahel and Reday (1976) analyzed some characteristics of circular economy from the perspective of industrial economy, and considered circular economy as a closed-loop industrial strategy, including waste prevention, job creation, resource efficiency, and dematerialization of industrial economy. Subsequently, a great deal of progress has occurred in the exploration of the circular economy. The modern understanding of the circular economy incorporates features and elements of many related concepts into the understanding of the closed-loop economy, including "cradle-to-cradle" (McDonough & Braungart, 2010), closed-loop and performance economies (Stahel, 2010), regenerative design (Lyle, 1996), and the blue economy (Pauli, 2010), among others. The most representative definition in industrial circles comes from the Ellen MacArthur Foundation (MacArthur, 2013), which argued that the circular economy goes beyond the waste management model and is redefining economic growth to focus on positive social benefits by moving away from economic activities that consume limited resources and redesigning economic systems that eliminate waste. With an emphasis on renewable resources, the circular economy establishes economic, social, and natural capital. According to the Foundation, the circular economy has three key principles: designing to eliminate waste and pollution; maintaining the use of products and raw materials; and regenerating natural systems. Moreover, as defined by academic circles, the circular economy is a regenerative system that minimizes resource inputs, waste emissions and energy leakage by slowing, closing, and narrowing material and energy circuits through durable design, maintenance, repair, reuse, remanufacturing, refurbishment, and recycling (Geissdoerfer et al., 2017). Another similar definition considers the circular economy as one in which the value of products and raw materials can be maintained, waste avoided, and resources in the economy can be kept when products reach the end of their life cycle (Geisendorf & Pietrulla, 2018). Circular economy was introduced in China in 1998 and adopted by the government in 2005 as a way to alleviate the contradiction between rapid economic growth and resource and energy shortages. As an important economic policy, the *Opinions of the State Council on Accelerating the Development of Circular Economy* clearly states that the goal of circular economy is to "reduce, reuse, and recycle" and points out that circular economy needs to be realized in all aspects of production, construction, distribution, and consumption. Yuan et al. (2008) argued that the key to the circular economy is to achieve a closed-loop flow of materials, raw materials, and energy in different stages of the economy. Obviously, regardless of the differences in the definitions of circular economy between China and foreign countries, the common points are as follows: (1) they both emphasize that the goal of the circular economy is to achieve pollution or waste reduction, product reuse, and resource or energy recycling; (2) they both consider circular economy as a closed-loop system, which requires end-to-end thinking for the overall design and management of the economic system.

The circular economy and sustainable development share many similarities, such as an emphasis on system transformation, multistakeholder integration, and sustainable development of society, and the former is an essential way to achieve the latter. However, in essence, these two concepts still have certain differences (Geissdoerfer et al., 2017), as follows: (1) The origins and goals of the concepts are different. The concept of sustainable development, which was proposed earlier, is based on people's concern for environmental and social issues, so the goals it pursued are more open and diversified. The concept of circular economy is proposed later and focuses more on the economic system. As some scholars have suggested, the circular economy is not simply an environmental strategy, but a strategy for sustainable economic development (Yuan et al., 2008), with a goal of developing a closed-loop economic system that minimizes input and wasted resources and truly realizes cycles of resources and energy. (2) The principle of realization and the beneficiaries are different. Sustainable development theory relies on the "triple bottom line" principle, that is, how to achieve economic, social, and environmental balance. Therefore, the beneficiaries of sustainable development are any stakeholder in society, and all stakeholders are equal in achieving development. The circular economy focuses on the economic principles, where the beneficiaries are, first of all, economic subjects, and subsequently other organizations or institutions whose environmental and social benefits are brought after the realization of the circular economy. In other words, the circular economy actually realizes the spillover of social and environmental benefits by taking the benefits of economic subjects as the original goal; (3) The agents or promoters are different. The agent or promoter of sustainable development is broader and can be any stakeholder in society. In other words, any individual or any organization can promote sustainable development. But the promoters of circular economy are mainly enterprises, industrial organizations, and governments. Obviously, the path to its realization involves direct subjects or direct affected ones in the economic system; (4) The time frame of change is different. Sustainable development is a long-term goal. Generally speaking, any society or organization eventually needs to achieve economic, social, and environmental balance, but the realization of this goal has no clear time frame in a strict sense, and is a long-term process that also requires constant adjustment and change. In contrast, the circular economy has the basic requirement that prescribed changes and adjustments must have been achieved in all parts of the economic system. In other words, there are clear thresholds for change; (5) The responsibility bearers and the interests to be taken into account are different. The bearer of sustainable development is any social person and social organization, so there is no specific responsible organization or institution specified. Also, the realization of sustainable development requires taking into account the interests of various stakeholders. On the contrary, the responsible parties for circular economy are mainly enterprises as well as regulatory bodies, which requires attention to the economic or financial capacity of enterprises and their impact on the environment.

7.4.2 Supply Chain Under Circular Economy and Its Key Elements

Given that enterprises are among the responsible parties of the circular economy, how to develop effective business models becomes an important way to realize the circular economy. Traditional business models are difficult to meet the requirements of the circular economy, so business development and economic systems need to be redefined from a new perspective (Planing, 2015; Witjes & Lozano, 2016; Lewandowski, 2016). The supply chain, as a management tool that coordinates and integrates the resources and capabilities of all parties, that breaks down the barriers and obstacles between links, and that integrates the flows of commodity, transport, information flow and fund, becomes a key tool to realize the circular economy (Zhu et al., 2010; Witjes & Lozano, 2016; Genovese et al., 2017). For example, Genovese et al. (2017), through a study of two case companies, pointed out that combining the principles of circular economy with sustainable supply chains is the best approach to achieve environmental goals. According to Witjes and Lozano (2016), traditional sustainability ignores the characteristics of the circular economy that uses waste as a resource input and acts as a bridge between production and consumption, so procurement activities in the supply chain need to be reexamined from a service system perspective. In other words, suppliers need to be selected in terms of technical and nontechnical requirements as well as sociocultural elements to develop the relationship between supply and demand. As can be seen, the reason why the supply chain is deemed an important approach to achieve the circular economy is that the goals to be achieved in circular economy are often based on adequate communication and synergy between multiple economic subjects. If upstream and downstream companies fail to develop a good sense of recycling as well as a culture among each other and to adjust their respective business rules and methods, the goal of recycling will be difficult to achieve (Witjes & Lozano, 2016). In addition, the closed-loop system emphasized by the circular economy needs to be realized with the help of the supply chain. Closed-loop means that all links from the first to the last are fully connected and operate smoothly and efficiently. The supply chain organically links synergistic multistakeholders in its structure, realizes multidimensional effective operation in its process, and fully integrates its elements, especially by establishing a corresponding product service system, all of which are fully compatible with the closed-loop requirements of the circular economy (Masi et al., 2017). It is worth mentioning that an important concept closely related to the supply chain in the circular economy is the green supply chain, which was introduced by the Manufacturing Research Institute of Michigan State University in 1996. The concept is based on environmental considerations in the design and operation of supply chains, which means complying with environmental requirements from the raw material procurement and product design stages, so as to avoid environmental hazards during the life and recycling period of products (Walton et al., 1998; Van Hoek, 1999; Zhu et al., 2005; Srivastava, 2007). Green supply chain is regarded as an important means to achieve an environmentally sustainable and circular economy. As a result, green supply chain and supply chain in the circular economy are explored and studied in parallel in most cases. Some studies argued that the two still have some differences although the overall goals are the same (Masi et al., 2017; Nasir et al., 2017; De Angelis et al., 2018). To some extent, the scope of supply chain under the circular economy is broader than that of green supply chain, which mainly considers environmental elements in the supply chain, while the former incorporates both environmental and social factors into the supply chain design. Moreover, green supply chain mainly focuses on the operation at the enterprise level, while circular supply chain considers various issues at the level of eco-industrial parks, government administration and society. Srivastava (2007) pointed out the lack of exploration of how management can contribute to economic and social development through rule making in green supply chains. Therefore, it can be concluded that the supply chain under the circular economy (defined by some scholars as circular supply chain) is an evolved or expanded green supply chain, because it integrates the requirements of the circular economy (i.e., 3Rs: Reduction, Reuse, Recycling) into the overall design and management of the supply chain, realizes the closed loop of forward and reverse supply chain operations by integrating the capabilities of stakeholders at all levels, and forms an overall system of commodity flow, logistics flow, information flow, and capital flow in the whole process from raw materials and manufacturing to final product consumption. Specifically, the levels of circular supply chain development can be distinguished from the scope and degree involved in supply chain operations (see Fig. 7.31).

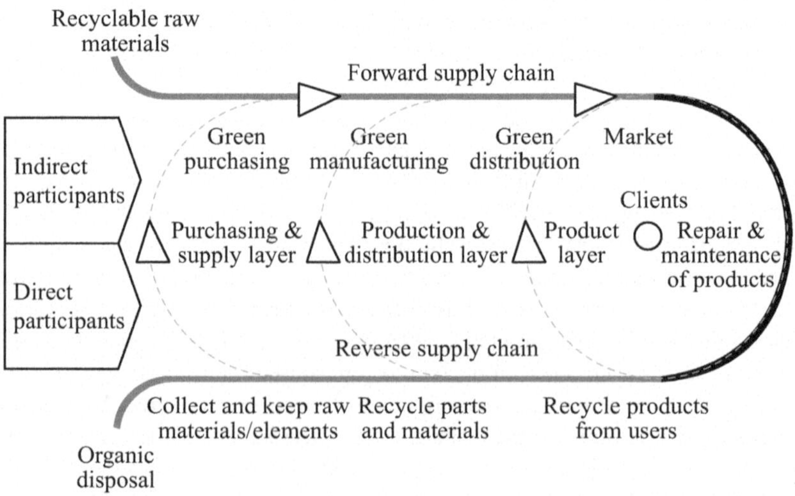

Fig. 7.31 Circular supply chain

(1) Degree of Circular Supply Chain Involvement

In terms of the extent involved, circular supply chains are divided into forward and reverse supply chains. Forward supply chain refers to the cooperative business behaviors between organizations from initial product design, procurement, production, distribution to sales to market customers. As a key aspect of circular supply chain management, forward supply chain ensures the sustainability of the supply chain system through green practices and management of the whole supply chain process. According to Green Jr. et al. (2012), such green management practices include internal environmental management, green information systems, green procurement, collaboration with customers, and ecological design, and so on. S.M. Lee et al. (2012) argued that the environmental sustainability in forward supply chain requires a full integration of corporate and operational strategies. Ninlawan et al. (2010) said that there are four important management elements in forward green supply chain management: green procurement, green manufacturing, green distribution, and green logistics. Green procurement is aimed at the supply side and refers to the ability of companies to select suppliers based on their environmental competence, technology, eco-design, environmental performance, development of environmentally friendly products, and ability to support the achievement of corporate environmental goals (Paulraj, 2011). Green manufacturing is a production process that converts inputs into outputs by reducing harmful substances, improving energy efficiency, and implementing the 3Rs to minimize wastes. Green distribution is a process of minimizing environmental damage in the distribution of finished goods by: reducing packaging; using "green" packaging materials; promoting recycling and reuse plans; working with suppliers to regulate packaging; encouraging and adopting recyclable packaging methods; minimizing material usage and time to open packaging; using recyclable pallet systems and saving energy in the warehouses. Green logistics is the intensification of logistics activities through effective management tools to reduce the negative environmental impact of transport and warehousing (Chin et al., 2015). Similarly, Planing (2015) pointed out the important links in a circular forward supply chain, including raw materials (arranging purified raw material flows to ensure that materials can be reused and put into the production process), product production (lower consumption and resources are consumed in remanufacturing compared to new product production), sales and service (the ability to extend the life cycle through repair, maintenance, and renovation), and customer (longer product life, or more efficient use of the product through shared consumption).

In addition to forward supply chain, reverse supply chain is also an important aspect of circular supply chain. Many scholars believe that reverse supply chain activities are a part of circular supply chain activities, which are closely related to forward supply chain, but there are still many differences. Forward logistics activities are more active and predictable, while reverse logistics are more passive and unpredictable (Tibben-Lembke & Rogers, 2002). Specifically, circular reverse supply chain activities include collection, inspection/splitting, reuse, reproduction, recycling, redistribution, and disposal of products or substances. Products are first brought to market using the conventional supply chain. Most products are used or consumed in their initial functional form, but the passage of time may result in the product having no usage or relative value to the initial users. At this moment, the products can be traded in the market once or more at lower prices, thus reentering the initial use and trade (Kokkinaki et al., 2000). It is worth pointing out that although the ownership of products keeps changing in this process, people still utilize the original function or original use value of the product, or rely on the original function for innovation in the purposes of use (namely, function recreation) until the original use value is completely exhausted. In this process, the role of reverse supply chain management is to promote and facilitate the conversion of products' use, in order to maximize the value of the products or part of the products on the basis of ensuring sustainable economic development, so that the resources used can be truly utilized. Of course, at some time in the future, when the use value of the products is completely exhausted, the products will enter the big reverse supply chain system and go to the stage of waste disposal. It can be seen that the reason why reverse supply chain becomes a special aspect of supply chain logistics management lies in the fact that its activities and management are greatly different forward logistics, and this difference also determines the special nature of information and supply chain management activities. First, the demand of reverse logistics is not from the active demand of customers, which brings greater uncertainty. Therefore, reverse logistics is more difficult to plan and forecast than forward logistics (Guide Jr et al., 2000). Second, reverse logistics is a multispecies transport from multiple points to a single point and cannot operate as a unit (Fleischmann et al., 1997). Third, the further processing of recycled materials that are transported from the starting point to the processing center is complex, and the accompanying difficulty in determining the final destination and transport routes makes logistics management difficult (Tibben-Lembke & Rogers, 2002). Fourth, compared to forward logistics, the costs of transportation, disposal, collection, sorting, reprocessing, and packaging are higher in reverse logistics activities (Tibben-Lembke & Rogers, 2002). Fifth, the tracking, control, and management of reverse logistics are more difficult to implement than in forward logistics, because current information technology and e-commerce take less account of the characteristics of reverse logistics operations (Rogers & Tibben-Lembke, 2001).

From the two aspects of supply chain operations under the circular economy mentioned above, it can be seen that the forward supply chain and the reverse supply chain are two wings of a circular supply chain. Although a pure emphasis on one aspect of green sustainability can also promote economic and social development, the closed-loop nature required by the circular economy will be challenged and the results will be somewhat limited. This is because a pure reverse supply chain without green sustainability of forward supply chain, even if it is implemented very well, still creates a huge challenge to the environment due to the excessive pressure of re-recovery, recycling, and redisposal. In particular, the collection and retention of raw materials or elements in the reverse supply chain (such as the transformation of waste steel products into elements such as the original liquid steel), and even the organic disposal of waste materials, are predicated on the green design and green procurement of products in the forward supply chain. By the same token, a forward supply chain lacking the cooperation of the reverse supply chain will also face challenges, because the reverse supply chain is the key to realizing the closed loop of circular economy. The high degree of integration between the two can not only realize recycling and reuse through the reverse supply chain but also realize low resource consumption with the help of green management activities in the forward supply chain. In addition, the high-degree integration of forward and reverse supply chains allows combining elements of the circular economy and creating new business models, that is, moving from the traditional product ownership model to a leasing and service-based supply chain strategy (De Angelis et al., 2018). The reason for this is that the realization of circular supply chains and the reduction of disposal of wastes or the waste of idle resources necessarily require a change from the traditional transaction model of ownership transfer to a new service model based on the sharing economy. Therefore, how to realize the combination of forward and reverse supply chains is one of the key issue of circular supply chain.

(2) Scope of Circular Supply Chain Involvement

Another key dimension of circular supply chain is the scope of supply chain synergy and integration. Although the circular economy is centered on an economic system, the circular supply chain covers a broader scope, instead of just focusing on a specific economic organization. Yuan et al. (2008) suggested that three levels of participants need to realize circular economy: (1) micro-level enterprises, who require or encourage the implementation of circular production; (2) meso-level eco-industrial networks, which means that different subjects or regional industries form a good environment and infrastructure to form an economic circular system; (3) macro-level management or policy departments, who promote the formation of eco-cities, eco-communities, or even eco-provinces. Clearly, circular supply chains often involve multiple and diverse stakeholders, and different stakeholders play differentiated roles to jointly promote the realization of circular economy.

First of all, the direct participants in the circular supply chain are often of multiple types, and the various participants are involved in different stages and roles in the circular supply chain (see Fig. 7.32). These

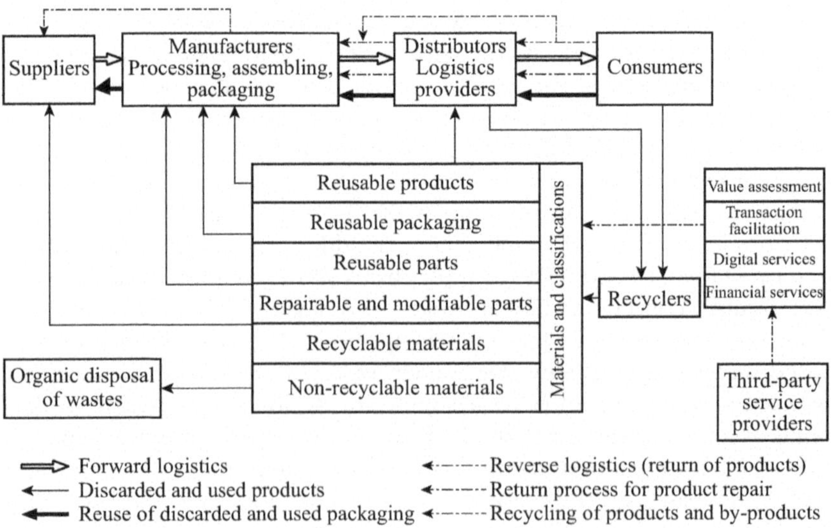

Fig. 7.32 Direct participants in circular supply chain

participants include the following: (1) Suppliers who supply raw materials or convert recyclables into raw materials. They constitute the input end of the circular supply chain. If these suppliers fail to go green or do not have the ability to dispose of waste materials in an environmentally friendly manner, supply chain sustainability will be greatly challenged; (2) Manufacturers engaged in the production and processing of products or the reproduction and processing of recyclables. They are directly engaged in the production process, and their capabilities directly determine the status of resource consumption and the degree of reusability or recyclability; (3) Distribution or logistics service providers engaged in the distribution of products or waste materials. They help realize the forward distribution and logistics of finished products and the reverse distribution and logistics of waste or recycled products. They play the role of creating time-space effect in the integrated circular supply chain; (4) Industrial customers or individual consumers. They are both the receiver and the creator of value of finished products. Their value demands for products or services drive the composition and management mode of circular supply chain; (5) Recycling operators. They effectively collect and aggregate waste or recyclables from industrial clients or consumers to form a certain scale effect, and classify the waste or recyclables by tests and put different categories of waste or recyclables into different channels for reprocessing or recycling; (6) Third-party service providers. Some unique service providers in the recycling supply chain operations play the role of value discovery and value promotion. The most typical participants in this category include value assessment service providers. Valuation of recyclables is a complex activity that involves not only assessing the financial value of the used item itself, but also determining the life cycle value from the perspective of the entire circular economy. The same waste material can be traded as second-hand goods or disposed of as raw materials, so it is important to assess the value and the impact of it on the environment from a holistic perspective. Another type of typical third parties is the platform service providers that promote transactions. They often recreate transaction value by building a platform, especially by using Internet technology to facilitate transactions of used and waste materials. Another type of typical third parties is the digital service providers. With the development of ICT, the importance of information technology and digitalization to the circular economy has become increasingly prominent. In particular, the circular economy involves closed-loop activities as well as multiple geographies and types of participants, so effective digital information management and services are critical to promoting the circular supply chain. Another important type of third parties are financial service providers. They provide customized financial services to economic agents in the circular economy and facilitate the smooth flow of funds in the supply chain.

Second, the indirect participants in the circular supply chain are also diverse and involve different institutions and organizations. In general, the first category of participants involved in the circular economy is the government regulators that directly affect the policy of circular economy development and the environment in which the supply chain operates. As noted by much of the literature studying China's circular economy (Zhijun & Nailing, 2007; Yuan et al., 2008; Geng & Doberstein, 2008), the development and promotion of the circular economy in enterprises, industrial parks, and cities and regions requires the regulators to effectively address institutional development, such as legal rules, operability principles, public participation, and the reference and application of advanced experiences. In addition, the regulators need to establish a scientific and effective evaluation system to obtain accurate information to improve circular economy guidelines. Another category of indirect participants is the communities or other nonprofit organizations, such as the Ellen MacArthur Foundation, which proposed the circular economy. Such organizations urge companies to establish and implement circular supply chains by promoting, guiding, and monitoring them in various ways. Therefore, this type of stakeholders is also a very important force in the construction and development of circular economy and its supply chain. The third type of indirect participants are enterprises or organizations in related industries that are closely related to the circular supply chain of the enterprises. The closed-loop nature required by circular economy inevitably covers various elements in the operations of the supply chain, such as the equipment for implementing effective waste disposal, the carriers or logistics standard tools for transporting and storing waste, the instrumentation for measuring product resource consumption or pollution, and so on. The design and production of these elements involve other industrial enterprises or institutions. Clearly, the circular supply chain cannot be fully realized without the cooperation and synergy of these associated organizations.

As seen above, the scope of direct and indirect stakeholders involved in the construction and development of circular supply chains also plays an important role in the supply chain. A narrower scope of stakeholders involved makes specific supply chain operations relatively easier to achieve and manage, with lower costs of communication and coordination among them. However, the broad integration of capabilities required by the circular economy will certainly be challenged. In contrast, a wider scope of stakeholders involved facilitates the integration of capabilities, but brings with it the problems of higher communication costs and difficulties in establishing mutual trust, which will ultimately pose challenges to the ultimate realization of the circular economy. For these reasons, how to address the issue of trust and communication cost while fully including all stakeholders is another key point for circular supply chains.

7.4.3 Circular Supply Chain Finance and Its Characteristics

Supply chain finance is an important issue in the development of circular economy. The ability of enterprises to effectively obtain finance, notably for green technologies, is crucial for achieving a circular economy (Pan et al., 2015; Masi et al., 2017). This is especially true for SMEs (Rizos et al., 2016). The solution to this problem goes beyond standardized market regulations or loans, but requires innovative financial services (Zhijun & Nailing, 2007; Geng & Doberstein, 2008). Supply chain finance is the most effective means of solving working capital in circular supply chains (Anca Iuliana Nicolae, 2018). However, the way in which supply chain finance is embedded in circular supply chains to play a differentiated role and prevent possible risks depends on the state of the circular supply chain. In fact, based on two key elements in the construction of circular supply chains, namely the degree of supply chain involvement (the degree of integration between forward and reverse supply chains) and the scope of supply chain involvement (the scope of stakeholder integration), circular supply chains present four different states (see Fig. 7.33). Each state makes the organization and management model of financial services highly heterogeneous due to its different supply chain characteristics.

Quadrant I is a relatively traditional state. Under this state, the circular supply chain has not been fully established, but only some initial efforts have been made and attention is beginning to be paid to it. Supply chain operations involve only simple green products and green production, and involve very limited participants. Under this state, circular supply chain finance has not really been developed, as financial activities have limited role in achieving economic circularity and the establishment of supply chain system. Financial activities only incorporate the greening factor of the enterprises on top of the traditional lending decision. Alternatively,

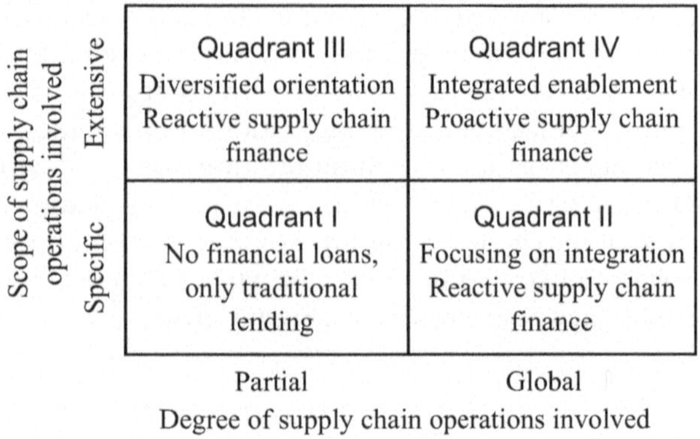

Fig. 7.33 Different forms of circular supply chain finance

financial activities under this state are no different from traditional lending decisions, and recyclability is only considered as an additional factor.

Quadrant II is a focused and integrated circular supply chain finance. This category is characterized by a deeper involvement in the circular supply chain, where the entire process of supply chain operation (from raw materials through manufacturing to finished goods) is managed effectively. Both forward and reverse supply chains are given attention, and the closed-loop requirement of circular economy is realized. However, the targets of management and control are more concentrated and limited. Comparatively, the targets of such circular supply chain integration tend to be direct counterparties, such as upstream or downstream enterprises of a particular enterprise. As a result, the integration of multiple capabilities as required by the circular economy is relatively limited. These characteristics lead to two major roles of supply chain finance: (1) supply chain finance plays an incentive role because the targets of supply chain financial services are more focused, mainly the partners with whom it deals. In other words, based on the degree of realization of circular economy of these partners, financial support is given to motivate these partners to take measures to realize circular economy. (2) Thanks to the strong closure of the circular supply chain, the financial products serve the whole process of supply chain operations completely. The organic connection between the financial products promotes the improvement of capital flow in the circular supply chain. In terms of risk control in supply chain finance, more attention is paid to the recyclable operation capability and the closure of the operating system in the partners' supply chain. In addition, the credit of the specific enterprise that drives the circular supply chain is also an element that financial institutions are more concerned about.

Quadrant III is a diversified circular supply chain finance. This category is characterized by a low level of involvement in the circular supply chain. In other words, the complete closed loop of the circular economy is not achieved, and only part of the supply chain operations may be involved, such as the reuse of waste materials, or green product production, and so on, but the whole circular supply chain system from raw materials to final products in the forward and reverse directions is not achieved. However, this type of circular supply chain integrates a wider range of stakeholders, which means that it can fully integrate the resource capabilities of all parties in a particular supply chain operation link. The financial activities generated by this type of circular supply chain also have two features: (1) Obvious targeted incentives. The targets of supply chain financial services are more diversified, so it is necessary to provide financial services adapted to the different links of economic agents in the circular supply chain operation; (2) The products are independent of each other because different targets have differentiated financial service needs in different states. In other words, each supply chain financial product exists for a specific state, and there is no interconnection between those products. From the perspective of risk control in supply chain finance, financial institutions are more concerned about the business or assets in a particular circular supply chain operation, because the status of the business and assets determines the ability of the enterprise for circular operation as well as the potential risks. Besides, the signal of specific enterprises (borrowers) in the network is also an important factor for risk control.

Quadrant IV is an integrated and empowering forward-looking supply chain finance, that is, a typical circular supply chain. On the one hand, it realizes all stages of the supply chain cycle and includes both forward and reverse supply chain systems with good closure; on the other hand, the resource capabilities of multiple stakeholders are well integrated. Corresponding to this kind of state, the role of supply chain finance is not only to stimulate but also to empower, that is, to further promote the realization of the circular goal through supply chain finance. In addition, the service targets of this type of supply chain finance are all the direct or indirect participants embedded in the circular supply chain. From the perspective of risk control in supply chain finance, this type of circular supply chain faces the problems of extensive business asset management and trust building as it involves various links and complex participants. Solving these problems requires the adoption of the integrated ABCD or convergent ICT to achieve visibility, transparency, traceability, and trust throughout the supply chain.

7.4.4 *Levi's Circular Supply Chain Finance Plan*

Levi Strauss & Co. is a U.S.-based private apparel company known globally for its Levi's brand of denim and jeans. In 2014, Levi Strauss partnered with the International Finance Corporation (IFC) under World Bank as well as GT Nexus, a supply chain financial service company, to start a circular supply chain finance plan aimed at supporting suppliers in developing countries to implement the circular economy. Under their Global Trade Supplier Finance (GTSF) plan, suppliers can obtain financing at competitive costs based on environmental, health and safety, and labor standards as set out in the Levi Strauss & Co.'s Terms of Engagement (TOE). A higher score on the recyclability index will result in a stronger financing offer for the suppliers. Moreover, the suppliers can improve their TOE scores to enhance the ease of financing from IFC and lower the interest rate.

The circular supply chain finance plan was developed by Levi Strauss in recognition of the fact that suppliers in developing countries often have difficulty applying for the necessary working capital for their operations. In particular, the cost for equipment and buildings during the investment phase of fixed infrastructure is high. The inability to obtain low-cost financing makes it impossible for many small and medium-sized suppliers to accommodate high-volume operations, thus losing many processing orders. Worse still, some enterprises have resorted to practices that endanger the working conditions of workers and the environment in order to save costs because they are unable to obtain financing effectively. Adding to the financial pressure is the lack of timely payments from downstream customers. The longer it takes for suppliers to receive payment, the more risks they assume and the more difficult it is to finance operations. This challenge has allowed customers who used to favor delayed payments to begin to see the benefits of advance payment. The effective supply chain finance promotes better fulfillment of the circular economy by small and medium-sized suppliers, thus achieving balanced economic, social, and environmental development from a long-term perspective, while stabilizing upstream and downstream supply-demand relationships and allowing downstream customers to obtain quality products at a lower cost.

Levi Strauss has developed TOE for the upstream supply chain. TOE focuses on three areas that affect the economic circular development, namely labor standards, health and safety standards, and environment standards. The labor standards provide factory managers, franchisees, and agents with regulations and guidance on how to use workers in the production process. There are three types of requirements, namely Zero Tolerance Violation (ZTV), Immediate Action (IA), and Continuous Improvement (CI). In addition, measures are set for different situations (including child labor, correctional labor, industry practices, legal requirements, ethical standards, working hours, payroll and benefits, common labor practices and unions, discrimination, community involvement, foreign migrant workers, accommodation, and permissions). The health and safety standards focus on how to safeguard health and safety during product manufacturing, mainly including regulations on chemical use, job restrictions, marking and labeling, and maintenance. Th environmental standards are its environmental concerns for supplier production, including global wastewater regulations, domestic wastewater regulations, biosolids management, waste management, prevention of stormwater pollution, and management of above-ground and underground wastewater.

Based on the above TOE, Levi Strauss provides circular supply chain financial services to suppliers with the following process (see Fig. 7.34):

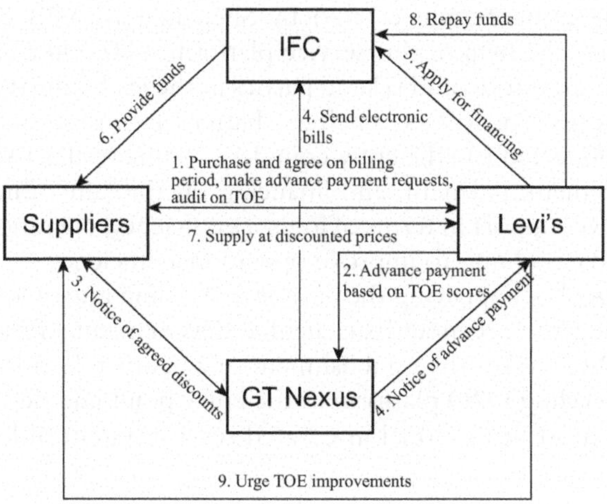

Fig. 7.34 Levi's circular supply chain finance flow

(1) Levi Strauss enters into a purchase agreement with the upstream supplier and agrees on the payment period. If the supplier wishes to pay in advance, he/she may submit a request to Levi Strauss. Levi Strauss audits the supplier's TOE; (2) Levi Strauss notifies GT Nexus of the terms (discount rate) to pay the supplier in advance based on the audited TOE score; (3) GT Nexus notifies the supplier of the agreed discount rate; (4) GT Nexus informs Levi Strauss of its advance payment agreement negotiated with the supplier; (5) Levi Strauss uses its credit to apply for financing from IFC; (6) IFC pays the specified amount of funds to the supplier within one to two days; (7) the supplier supplies to Levi Strauss at a discount; (8) Levi Strauss pays principal and interest to IFC when due; (9) Levi Strauss urges the supplier to improve the TOE core and uses it as the basis for the next supply chain financing decision. From the above process, it can be seen that, on the one hand, the circular supply chain finance plan developed by Levi Strauss stimulates sustainable and circular behaviors of suppliers and realizes a closed loop of circular supply chain operations; on the other hand, combined with the characteristics of industrial supply chain, Levi Strauss cooperates with GT Nexus and IFC to organically integrate dynamic discount and credit financing, which effectively relieves the financial pressure of suppliers and results in good effects.

7.4.5 *Circular Supply Chain Finance of BUYPB.CN*

BUYPB.CN is a comprehensive supply chain service platform focusing on lead recycling industry and created by Shenzhen BUYPB E-commerce Co., Ltd. With the help of this service platform, 600,000 electric bicycle repair shops/sales stores and related parties in the lead industry chain such as logistics service providers, smelters, battery factories, and agents are effectively connected to efficiently complete commercial activities such as trading, settlement, payment, and financing. At the same time, all parties can also receive support in terms of logistics efficiency, operation standardization, and data mining to improve operational efficiency.

With the goal of improving the harmless recycling rate of lead resources and promoting the green and sustainable development of industrial system, BUYPB.CN takes the establishment of a national lead battery circulation and recycling O2O platform as the entry point and devotes itself to building the most professional integrated service system of lead industry supply chain in China. Through the application of information and IoT technologies, the platform is deeply embedded in all nodes of the industry chain, achieving the visual management of the whole process of lead battery recycling and reuse, realizing the efficiency, reconstruction, and empowerment of the recycled lead industry chain, and initially creating a digital and intelligent ecosystem of the recycled lead industry.

In addition, BUYPB.CN also actively drives the formulation of standards for recycling and reuse of waste batteries and transfers hazardous waste products in the form of units through the promotion and application of "intelligent recycling bins" as well as related hardware and software, so as to help the participants in the industry greatly reduce logistics costs and improve the efficiency of recycling hazardous waste products, and finally promote the effectiveness and efficiency of the whole industry.

7.4.5.1 Product and Industry Background

Despite being an ancient metal, lead is mainly used in modern industry for anti-radiation materials, anti-corrosion materials, welding materials, lead-acid batteries, and so on; so, it is a strategic resource for national economic security. Lead-acid battery is a kind of chemical "power source" widely used in the world and has the advantages of stable voltage, safety, reliability, low price, wide scope of application, abundant raw materials, and high reuse and recycling rate. Especially in terms of voltage stability and low cost, lead-acid batteries are incomparable to other batteries. Both products for everyday consumption and professional communication equipment need lead-acid batteries, which mainly include power batteries, starter batteries, and fixed batteries.

At present, China consumes more than eight million tons of refined lead every year, of which only four million tons are recycled lead. Recycled lead will definitely become the mainstream in the future, and the "urban mine" of used batteries will become an important strategic resource. First of all, the wide use of lead-acid batteries result in the waste production of over eight million tons per year. If these used lead-acid batteries are disposed of illegally, they will cause serious and irreversible damage to the environment. Along with the introduction and implementation of relevant industrial and environmental protection policies and increasingly strict law enforcement in terms of environmental protection, China's recycled lead industry will usher in an unprecedented opportunity for standardized development. Second, the waste lead battery contains 74% lead, so they can be recycled and smelted into recycled lead, which has high reuse value. Besides, the energy consumption of the recycled lead is only 25.1%–31.4% of that of original lead, which also makes recycled lead have more obvious advantages in costs.

Before the intervention of BUYPB.CN in the lead industry, the traditional recycled lead industry as a whole was in a disorderly state, with the following major problems.

(1) "Black Box" of Information about the Waste Production Caused the Inability in Regulation

A large number of used lead batteries were illegally acquired, dismantled, and smelted, and sulfuric acid was dumped arbitrarily for a long time, causing great and irreversible pollution to the environment. Vicious cases occurred from time to time, threatening our living environment, damaging the image of governmental departments, and placing great pressure on the environmental protection departments. However, since the information about waste production was basically in the "black box" state, the environmental protection departments did not know where and how much is the output of waste products, whether they have been illegally acquired and disposed of, whether they would cause sudden and vicious environmental cases, and the source of waste production could not be managed and controlled. The increasing governance of environmental protection departments at all levels often treated the symptoms but could not fundamentally correct the industry chaos.

(2) Inability in Regulation Caused Disorder in the Industry

The lack of information about the waste production led to the inability of administrative supervision departments to grasp the "key points of rectification," which in turn caused the dilemma of "bad money drives out good" in the industry. Many individual retailers and small refineries reduced their production costs by illegal recycling and illegal disposal but at the cost of environment, and greatly squeezed the survival space of legal compliance enterprises by using unfair competition. As a result, regular smelters with standardized waste lead-acid battery recycling network system and legal qualification could only survive in the cracks, making the ratio of regular recycling and disposal less than 30%.

(3) Industry Information Asymmetry Caused Loss of Industry Efficiency

In the traditional waste logistics recycling system, most of the information transmission was diffuse, spontaneous, unorganized and verbal, and there was a great asymmetry, which brought about efficiency loss from two aspects:

On the one hand, the price regulation mechanism partially failed. For example, when the market demand of battery increases, an ideal price regulation mechanism will inform the source of raw materials (waste recycling) and quickly increase the supply of each tier by raising the price to quickly meet the market demand. However, small traders often take advantage of information to pursue the maximum self-interests, instead of raising the purchase price, thus leading to the failure of the price regulation mechanism.

On the other hand, the transaction costs were greatly increased. The information asymmetry makes it difficult to establish trust between both parties of the transactions, so both parties will increase their investment in transaction risk management, keeping transaction costs high.

(4) Poor Information Flow in the Industry Led to a Failure to Improve Supply Chain Efficiency

The lack of standardized and credible information flow channels in the industry led to confusion at all nodes of the industry chain. The overall lack of planning, organization, and coordination of the industry chain made it difficult to improve the efficiency of the industry supply chain.

Stores did not know who to sell to, what price was fair, and when they could come to recycle.

Recycling enterprises did not know where to recycle the used lead batteries, how many there were, and when they were available. Illegal vendors often took their advantage of daily streetwalking to firmly occupy the waste production terminals; whole legal and compliant enterprises were in a weak position due to their lack of effective channels of communication with stores and often faced the embarrassing situation of "lack of food."

Smelting enterprises did not know who would deliver, how much, and when. The stability of the supply of scrap lead batteries could not guarantee the procurement of raw materials. This caused great difficulties for the production planning of the enterprises and also led to the instability of the smelters' output and price, which subsequently affected the supply of raw materials for downstream lead battery manufacturers. There was a structural supply-demand conflict between the rate of lead ingot production in smelters and the demand of lead battery manufacturers, which greatly affected the supply chain efficiency.

(5) Lack of Industry Standards Led to Inefficient Industry Operations

From the perspective of recycled lead and its application development, all links in the recycling industry of used lead batteries (recycled lead raw materials), such as recycling, storage, transfer and settlement, lacked standardized processes and standards, and the costs of logistics flow, capital flow, and information flow were high and the efficiency loss was great, which led to the relatively low efficiency of the industry as a whole.

(6) Lack of Corporate Credit System Led to Financing Difficulties and Low Fund Utilization

On the one hand, most participants in the industry chain have weak qualifications and no collateral that meets the requirements, so they often could not obtain loans from financial institutions. On the other hand, the lack of good credit or credit intermediaries among the upstream and downstream enterprises in the industry chain has resulted in the repeated occupation of funds and low efficiency of fund utilization. All these factors made it difficult to improve the operational efficiency of the industry.

Therefore, the industry's challenges can be summarized as follows:

(a) Waste putters: Lack of price information, price takers who need funds.
(b) Stores: They have advantages in terms of service, but lack flexible pricing tools, face inventory capital pressure, and need to transport goods frequently.
(c) Qualified crude lead factories: Disadvantaged in cost and competition. Individual vendors raise the purchase price of used batteries and sell them to unqualified enterprises. These vendors have advantages in terms of cost, proximity to sources, and price flexibility, while the unqualified crude lead factories has the advantage of price in competing for the source of waste batteries (70 ~ 80%), which makes the qualified recycling enterprises and recycled lead enterprises to fall into the situation of "no business to do."
(d) Public welfare: Environmental pollution. The unqualified treatment plants dismantle randomly by manual means without antipollution

measures, acids are discharged randomly, surface corrosion is serious, and other wastes with no recycling value are discarded or land-filled at will, seriously polluting the environment.

(e) Industry regulation: Poor information sharing, lack of laws and regulations for recycling system; difficulty in joint management and regulation by multiple departments.

7.4.5.2 Construction of Circular Supply Chain of BUYPB.CN

In light of the current situation of the industry and the industry's problems, BUYPB.CN starts from the node of waste battery recycling and builds a green recycling supply chain service system according to the idea of "connection, empowerment and efficiency improvement," aiming to promote the optimization, transformation, and improvement of the supply chain in the lead recycling industry. The specific aspects are as follows:

First, BUYPB.CN brings together a large number of stores and recycling enterprises (which must be legally licensed) from offline to online platform through the Internet (see Fig. 7.35). After gathering stores, recycling companies, logistics companies, smelters, battery factories, and other related parties together to realize the information connection

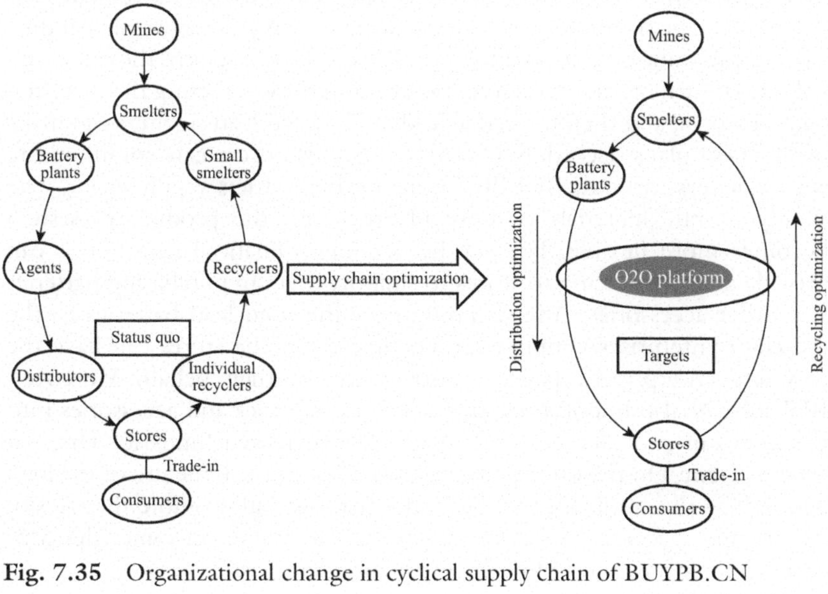

Fig. 7.35 Organizational change in cyclical supply chain of BUYPB.CN

among upstream and downstream enterprises, BUYPB.CN also removes excessive intermediate links to achieve price transparency, cost reduction, and efficiency improvement in the industry, and also establishes standardized systems for O2O recycling, temporary storage, transfer, as well as supervision.

Second, BUYPB.CN improves the recycling system from the perspectives of logistics and supply chain efficiency, and empowers enterprises through logistics and finance. On the one hand, BUYPB.CN can improve logistics efficiency by more than 30% by applying facilities and equipment for real-time tracking, path optimization, and advanced logistics to realize unitized operation of collection and transfer. Not only that, BUYPB.CN also uses RFID technology to track each SKU and directly hand the products over to the legal smelters to get standardized and harmless disposal, which can greatly save the time of handing over and transferring in each link. On the other hand, multidimensional data in respect of IOT, RFID sensing, GPS/LBS positioning, and network video/pictures provide credible evidences. The information of the whole transaction process is encrypted and stored by blockchain technology, which is nonrepudiation and tamper-proof. The authenticity of transaction settlement is also guaranteed by using blockchain smart contract.

Third, with the help of the data support and credit endorsement provided by the platform, the relevant participants can gradually realize industrial collaboration. For example, BUYPB.CN can grasp the recycling volume of each month in each region accurately by gathering the recycling data of stores, and then the crude lead and refined lead smelters can make production plans accordingly. Battery manufacturers can communicate with smelters through BUYPB.CN to optimize their supply chain. The supply of raw materials is more planned and the production system becomes more flexible. For another example, financial institutions can provide micro-financing to stores to support them in purchasing batteries and other accessories. After handing over the used lead batteries to the recycling enterprises within a certain time limit, the stores can have the recycling enterprises repay the borrowings on their behalf. Moreover, BUYPB.CN also imports relevant sellers of batteries and accessories into the platform and guides stores to use the borrowed funds for targeted procurement. On the one hand, the platform can track the use of the loan and reduce the credit risk; on the other hand, it can promote the sales of battery and accessories vendors and, at the same time, get some sales concessions for stores and reduce their procurement costs.

Based on the construction in the above three aspects, BUYPB.CN has basically formed the following abilities:

1. Transaction Matching

First of all, BUYPB.CN, as a waste lead battery O2O platform, connects the basic three parties, that is, the waste production parties (stores), the recycling parties (enterprises with recycling qualification), and the logistics service parties (subline and mainline logistics service providers), and has the ability to quickly matching transactions. As mentioned earlier, once an order is placed by a store, the platform will dispatch the order to the most suitable recycling enterprise and its cooperative logistics service enterprise (recycler) according to its algorithm and dispatch rules based on the location of the store. On this basis, the platform incorporates smelters, financial institutions, and professional service organizations, quickly connecting the supply and demand sides of products and services, and creating an ecosystem of recycled lead industry with diverse business forms, benign interactions, and continuous cycles.

2. Standard Setting

Purely solving the problem of information asymmetry is not enough to serve traditional industries well. The platform must go deep into the nodes of industrial operations, set up and promote the implementation of industry standards, so as to promote seamless integration among the participants of the industry chain and gradually realize industrial collaboration. Only in this way can it truly promote industrial structure optimization and efficiency improvement. Specifically the following:

(1) Transaction price standards. After collecting the prices from LME, Shanghai Futures Exchange, and smelters, BUYPB.CN automatically generates the guide prices for various regions and models of used batteries through the price model of the back-end system.
(2) Transaction settlement standards. Based on a comprehensive trade-off between efficiency and control, revenue and risk, BUYPB.CN provides a standard transaction and settlement process for all transaction in the platform, ensuring that all parties involved can both complete their transactions and settlements efficiently and effectively control their trading risks.

(3) Logistics service standards, which include those for hardware and software. In terms of software, BUYPB.CN has not only made clear requirements for service level, requiring the recycling needs of stores to be met in a limited time, and established an evaluation and assessment mechanism, but also put forward mandatory specifications for logistics handover process and requirements through the system. In terms of hardware, BUYPB.CN has designed intelligent recycling bins and set specifications and standards for recycling vehicles and loading equipment (including the application of IoT technology). The implementation of hardware standards has greatly improved the efficiency of recycling, storage, and transfer and the smooth connection of all links.

3. Operation Management

The operation management ability of BUYPB.CN is mainly reflected, as discussed in the following text.

First, the whole process is monitored visually. BUYPB.CN has created a powerful back-end system. From the time a store places an order in the system, the system can track the status of the whole process until the goods corresponding to the order are received by the smelter. With the help of this "clairvoyant," operators can master the status of any order nationwide, and when abnormalities or risk signs are found, they can call camera records, communicate by phone, or dispose of the order on site, depending on the situation, thus improving customer satisfaction, enhancing operation efficiency, and reducing operation risks.

Second, the behaviors of stores are guided. Through the establishment of operational mechanisms such as price guidance, point system, credit system, and activity operation, BUYPB.CN guides stores to be honest, trustworthy, and standardized, so that they can change from being highly arbitrary to being more planned, which will create favorable conditions for the increased planning and reduced volatility of the whole recycled lead supply chain.

Third, other participants are organized and coordinated. Relying on a powerful back-end system, BUYPB.CN organizes and coordinates recyclers, recycling enterprises, logistics service providers, and smelters to maximize the overall operational efficiency of the supply chain. For example, on the one hand, the system can make suggestions and guidance to recyclers on their recycling routes, and optimize the routes in real time after the addition of new orders, so as to improve the overall operational efficiency; on the other hand, through the establishment of assessment and monitoring mechanisms (monitoring of their locations and order completion), it can avoid the behavior of "picking orders" by recyclers to the detriment of the service level of stores. For another example, when a smelter is in urgent need of raw materials, BUYPB.CN can respond quickly and increase the recycling volume in the nearby area through price mechanism and operational measures.

4. Data Analysis

BUYPB.CN can automatically collect relevant data through various data sources, analyze them according to preset algorithmic models, and output the analysis results in response to the users' needs for scientific decision-making. For example, recyclers can use the RFM model provided by BUYPB.CN to analyze the reasonableness and loyalty of regular customers' transactions in their regions, so that they can take targeted measures to stimulate repeat transactions and avoid losing customers, and also reduce logistics costs appropriately. In addition, BUYPB.CN can also classify and manage customers according to the indicators such as absolute number of days of stopping transactions and transaction frequency.

5. Optimization and Coordination of the Whole Supply Chain

BUYPB.CN has connected through the industrial chains of recycled lead and its applications to achieve the goal of optimizing the industrial supply chain by improving the convenience of interaction, enhancing mutual trust, reducing transaction costs, strengthening the collaboration of procurement and sales plans at each node, and avoiding structural supply and demand imbalance as much as possible.

7.4.5.3 Circular Supply Chain Finance of BUYPB.CN

Based on the above lead recycling supply chain system, BUYPB.CN further establishes the supply chain services focusing on "recycling + supply chain finance." As an open third-party platform, based on 600,000 electric vehicle sales and repair stores, 400,000 auto sales and repair stores, and electric vehicle and auto parts sales platforms, BUYPB.CN uses the big data of stores and their transactions gathered, introduces banks, micro-finance companies, and other financial institutions into the platform, and provides them with credit information of each store, so that each participant on the platform can obtain financial services. CN uses the big data of stores and their transactions gathered by the platform to introduce banks, microfinance companies, and other financial institutions and provide them with credit information of each store, so that each participant on the platform can obtain financial services. At present, the supply chain financial services and products provided by BUYPB.CN include Huishoubao, Dingdanbao, and Refined Lead Bank.

Huishoubao mainly acts as an intermediary for payment and settlement arising from transactions between stores (i.e., operators engaged in the sales of new batteries and recycling of used lead batteries) and smelters. This financial product is designed to address the timely fund needs of the stores as well as the problem of the smelters whose timely payment is impossible due to its recycling production schedule that requires to use the recycled lead raw materials after a period of time. The specific operation process is as follows (see Fig. 7.36): (1) a smelter formulates the procurement plan for recycled lead through the O2O platform of BUYPB.CN; (2) BUYPB.CN places orders to stores through the platform; (3) the stores deliver recycled lead to BUYPB.CN, which picks up the goods and forms a certain storage; (4) BUYPB.CN, after obtaining credit from financial institutions, pays the funds to the stores; (5) after the smelter makes a delivery request, BUYPB.CN delivers the recycled lead to the smelter; (6) the smelter pays for the goods; (7) BUYPB.CN returns the principal and interest of the funds to the financial institution.

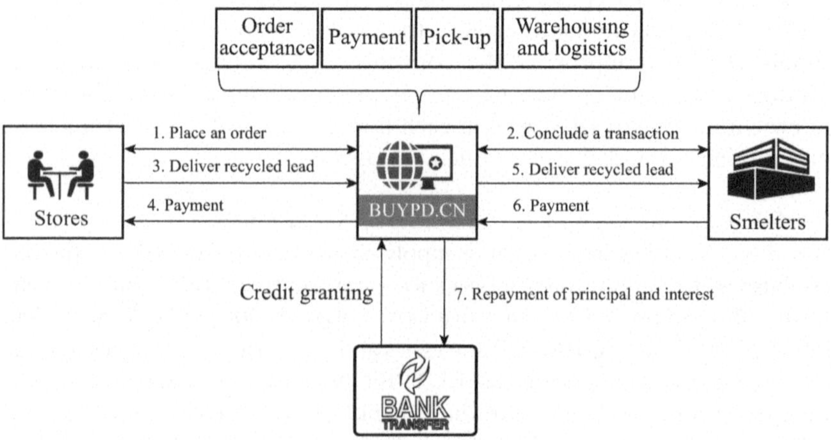

Fig. 7.36 Circular supply chain finance of BUYPB.CN—Huishoubao

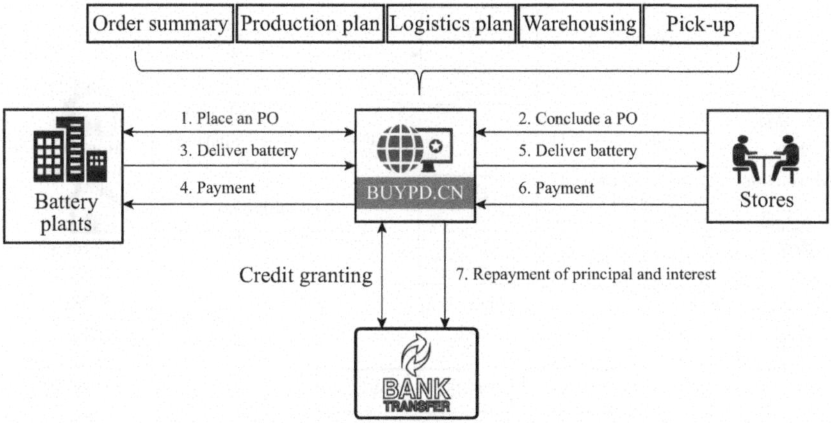

Fig. 7.37 Circular supply chain finance of BUYPB.CN—Dingdanbao

Dingdanbao differs from Huishoubao in that the latter is a financial service in the reverse supply chain, while the former is a financial service in the forward supply chain, aiming at solving the dilemma that stores need to pay funds to the battery factories in advance for ordering new batteries. The basic operation process is as follows (see Fig. 7.37): (1) a store places battery purchase orders through BUYPB.CN; (2) BUYPB. CN collects downstream purchase orders and places collection orders to battery factories; (3) the battery factories deliver new batteries to BUYPB.CN; (4) BUYPB.CN pays collection payments to the battery factories; (5) BUYPB.CN delivers the new batteries to the store; (6) the store pays the purchase price to BUYPB.CN; (7) BUYPB.CN returns the principal and interest of the funds to the financial institution to complete the transaction.

Refined Lead Bank is a warehouse receipt pledge business for financing customers (generally for stores, recycling enterprises, etc.). Recycled lead has a price fluctuation cycle within each year; therefore, recycling enterprises or stores do not want to sell immediately in order to get the most benefits, but wait for a period of time and sell when the price is reasonable, but they still need working capital for their business activities during this period of time. For this reason, BUYPB.CN offers a warehouse receipt pledge service. By transporting the refined lead, crude lead or used batteries to BUYPB.CN's designated supervised

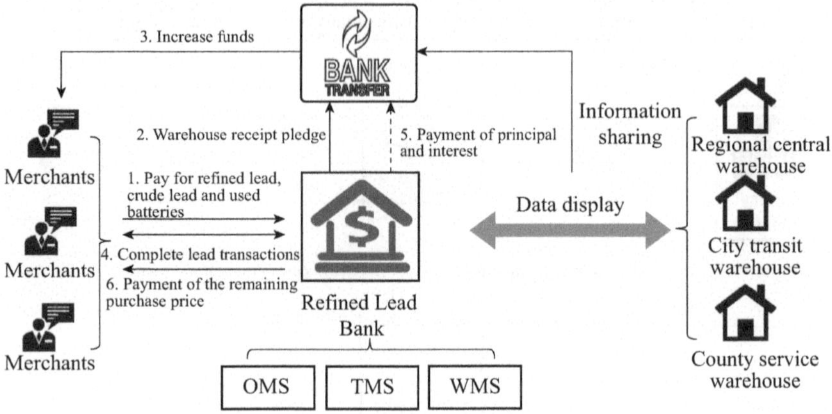

Fig. 7.38 Circular supply chain finance of BUYPB.CN—Refined Lead Bank

warehouses, the financing customers receive financing funds proportional to the total amount of incoming goods. Within a specified time, the financing customers completes the sale and repays the loan. The specific operation process is as follows (see Fig. 7.38): (1) a recycling enterprise delivers the recycled lead to the supervised warehouse designated by BUYPB.CN; (2) BUYPB.CN pledges the recycled lead warehouse receipt to the financial institution; (3) the financial institution grants a loan to the recycling enterprise based on the shared data; (4) the recycling enterprise completes the sales of recycled lead on BUYPB. CN in a certain period of time in the future; (5) the recycling enterprise repays the principal and interest to the financial institution through the BUYPB.CN account; (6) after deducting the principal and interest, the financial institution pays the remaining amount to the recycling enterprise's account to complete the transaction.

From the above supply chain financial services of BUYPB.CN, it is clear that the combination of Huishoubao, Dingdanbao, and Refined Lead Bank has realized the complete circular supply chain of lead and has organically connected all participants in the industry. This supply chain finance promotes the consolidation and development of the circular supply chain and plays a better empowering function. Meanwhile, the big data established by the platform and the use of blockchain technology have promoted the setting-up of information sharing and trust mechanisms among all participants and prevented potential financial risks.

References

Anca Iuliana Nicolae. (2018). Working capital financing in reverse supply chains—New perspectives (auto-financing). *Eurasian Journal of Economics and Finance, 6*(1), 35–46.

Andersen, M., & Skjoett-Larsen, T. (2009). Corporate social responsibility in global supply chains. *Supply Chain Management: An International Journal, 14*(2), 75–86.

Antle, J. M. (1996). Efficient food safety regulation in the food manufacturing sector. *American Journal of Agricultural Economics, 78*(5), 1242–1247.

Antle, J. M. (2001). Economic analysis of food safety. *Handbook of Agricultural Economics, 1*, 1083–1136.

Armendariz, B., & Morduch, J. (2005). *The economics of microfinance*. MIT Press.

Awaysheh, A., & Klassen, R. D. (2010). The impact of supply chain structure on the use of supplier socially responsible practices. *International Journal of Operations & Production Management, 30*(12), 1246–1268.

Bai, C., Sarkis, J., Wei, X., & Koh, L. (2012). Evaluating ecological sustainable performance measures for supply chain management. *Supply Chain Management: An International Journal, 17*(1), 78–92.

Barney, J. B. (1995). Looking inside for competitive advantage. *Academy of Management Perspectives, 9*(4), 49–61.

Beamon, B. M. (1999). Designing the green supply chain. *Logistics Information Management, 12*(4), 332–342.

Bijman, J., Muradian, R., & Cechin, A. (2011). Agricultural cooperatives and value chain coordination. *Value Chains, Social Inclusion and Economic Development: Contrasting Theories and Realities*, 82–101.

Borodin, V., Bourtembourg, J., Hnaien, F., & Labadie, N. (2016). Handling uncertainty in agricultural supply chain management: A state of the art. *European Journal of Operational Research, 254*(2), 348–359.

Botonaki, A., Polymeros, K., Tsakiridou, E., & Mattas, K. (2006). The role of food quality certification on consumers' food choices. *British Food Journal, 108*(2), 77–90.

Bowen, F. E., Cousins, P. D., Lamming, R. C., & Farukt, A. C. (2001). The role of supply management capabilities in green supply. *Production and Operations Management, 10*(2), 174–189.

BSR. (2018). *Win-win-win: The sustainable supply chain finance opportunity*. https://www.bsr.org/en/our-insights/report-view/win-win-win-the-sustainable-supply-chain-finance-opportunity

Canto-Cuevas, F.-J., Palacín-Sánchez, M.-J., & Di Pietro, F. (2019). Trade credit as a sustainable resource during an SME's life cycle. *Sustainability, 11*(3), 670.

Carter, C. R., & Jennings, M. M. (2002). Social responsibility and supply chain relationships. *Transportation Research Part E: Logistics and Transportation Review, 38*(1), 37–52.

Carter, C. R., & Liane Easton, P. (2011). Sustainable supply chain management: Evolution and future directions. *International Journal of Physical Distribution & Logistics Management, 41*(1), 46–62.
Carter, C. R., & Rogers, D. S. (2008). A framework of sustainable supply chain management: Moving toward new theory. *International Journal of Physical Distribution & Logistics Management, 38*(5), 360–387.
Castka, P., & Balzarova, M. A. (2008). ISO 26000 and supply chains—On the diffusion of the social responsibility standard. *International Journal of Production Economics, 111*(2), 274–286.
Cechin, A., Bijman, J., Pascucci, S., & Omta, O. (2013). Decomposing the member relationship in agricultural cooperatives: Implications for commitment. *Agribusiness, 29*(1), 39–61.
Chen, K. Z., Joshi, P. K., Cheng, E., & Birthal, P. S. (2015). Innovations in financing of Agri-food value chains in China and India: Lessons and policies for inclusive financing. *China Agricultural Economic Review, 7*(4), 616–640.
Chiarini, A. (2012). Designing an environmental sustainable supply chain through ISO 14001 standard. *Management of Environmental Quality: An International Journal, 24*(1), 16–33.
Chin, T. A., Tat, H. H., & Sulaiman, Z. (2015). Green supply chain management, environmental collaboration and sustainability performance. *Procedia CIRP, 26*, 695–699.
Ciliberti, F., de Groot, G., de Haan, J., & Pontrandolfo, P. (2009). Codes to coordinate supply chains: SMEs' experiences with SA8000. *Supply Chain Management: An International Journal, 14*(2), 117–127.
Cruz, J. M. (2008). Dynamics of supply chain networks with corporate social responsibility through integrated environmental decision-making. *European Journal of Operational Research, 184*(3), 1005–1031.
Curkovic, S., & Sroufe, R. (2011). Using ISO 14001 to promote a sustainable supply chain strategy. *Business Strategy and the Environment, 20*(2), 71–93.
Darby, M. R., & Karni, E. (1973). Free competition and the optimal amount of fraud. *The Journal of Law and Economics, 16*(1), 67–88.
De Angelis, R., Howard, M., & Miemczyk, J. (2018). Supply chain management and the circular economy: Towards the circular supply chain. *Production Planning & Control, 29*(6), 425–437.
de Sousa Jabbour, A. B. L., Jabbour, C. J. C., Latan, H., Teixeira, A. A., & de Oliveira, J. H. C. (2014). Quality management, environmental management maturity, green supply chain practices and green performance of Brazilian companies with ISO 14001 certification: Direct and indirect effects. *Transportation Research Part E: Logistics and Transportation Review, 67*, 39–51.
Dentoni, D., Hospes, O., & Ross, R. B. (2012). Managing wicked problems in agribusiness: The role of multi-stakeholder engagements in value creation: Editor's introduction. *International Food and Agribusiness Management Review, 15*(B), 1–12.

Doran, A., McFayden, N., & Vogel, R. C. (2009). The missing middle in agricultural finance: Relieving the capital constraint on smallholder groups and other agricultural SMEs. *Oxfam Policy and Practice: Agriculture, Food and Land, 9*(7), 65–118.

Elkington, J. (1999). Triple bottom-line reporting: Looking for balance. *AUSTRALIAN CPA, 69*, 18–21.

Estampe, D., Lamouri, S., Paris, J.-L., & Brahim-Djelloul, S. (2013). A framework for analysing supply chain performance evaluation models. *International Journal of Production Economics, 142*(2), 247–258.

Fisher, M. L. (1997). What is the right supply chain for your product? *Harvard Business Review, 75*, 105–117.

Fleischmann, M., Bloemhof-Ruwaard, J., Dekker, R., Van der Laan, E., van Nunen, J., & Van Wassenhove, L. (1997). Quantitative models for reverse logistics. *European Journal of Operational Research, 103*, 1–17.

Fotopoulos, C., & Krystallis, A. (2003). Quality labels as a marketing advantage: The case of the "PDO Zagora" apples in the Greek market. *European Journal of Marketing, 37*(10), 1350–1374.

Geisendorf, S., & Pietrulla, F. (2018). The circular economy and circular economic concepts-a literature analysis and redefinition. *Thunderbird International Business Review, 60*(5), 771–782.

Geissdoerfer, M., Savaget, P., Bocken, N. M. P., & Hultink, E. J. (2017). The circular economy—A new sustainability paradigm? *Journal of Cleaner Production, 143*, 757–768.

Geng, Y., & Doberstein, B. (2008). Developing the circular economy in China: Challenges and opportunities for achieving'leapfrog development'. *The International Journal of Sustainable Development & World Ecology, 15*(3), 231–239.

Genovese, A., Acquaye, A. A., Figueroa, A., & Koh, S. C. L. (2017). Sustainable supply chain management and the transition towards a circular economy: Evidence and some applications. *Omega, 66*, 344–357.

Ghosh, J. (2013). Microfinance and the challenge of financial inclusion for development. *Cambridge Journal of Economics, 37*(6), 1203–1219.

Green, K., Morton, B., & New, S. (1998). Green purchasing and supply policies: Do they improve companies' environmental performance? *Supply Chain Management: An International Journal, 3*(2), 89–95.

Green, K. W., Zelbst, P. J., Meacham, J., & Bhadauria, V. S. (2012). Green supply chain management practice: Impact on performance. *Supply Chain Management, 17*(3), 290–305.

Guang Shi, V., Lenny Koh, S., Baldwin, J., & Cucchiella, F. (2012). Natural resource based green supply chain management. *Supply Chain Management: An International Journal, 17*(1), 54–67.

Guide, V. D. R., Jr., Jayaraman, V., Srivastava, R., & Benton, W. (2000). Supply-chain management for recoverable manufacturing systems. *Interfaces, 30*(3), 125–142.

Hall, J. (2001). Environmental supply-chain innovation. *Greener Management International*, 105–120.
Hart, S. L. (1995). A natural-resource-based view of the firm. *Academy of Management Review, 20*(4), 986–1014.
Hart, S. L., & Dowell, G. (2011). Invited editorial: A natural-resource-based view of the firm: Fifteen years after. *Journal of Management, 37*(5), 1464–1479.
Henson, S., & Reardon, T. (2005). Private Agri-food standards: Implications for food policy and the Agri-food system. *Food Policy, 30*(3), 241–253.
Hobbs, J. E., & Young, L. M. (2000). Closer vertical co-ordination in Agri-food supply chains: A conceptual framework and some preliminary evidence. *Supply Chain Management: An International Journal, 5*(3), 131–143.
Iakovou, E., Vlachos, D., Achillas, C., & Anastasiadis, F. (2012). *A methodological framework for the design of green supply chains for the agrifood sector* (Vol. 184).
Invernizzi, M. G. (2018). *Supply chain finance as a sustainability enabler.*
Khavul, S. (2010). Microfinance: Creating opportunities for the poor? *Academy of Management Perspectives, 24*(3), 58–72.
Kokkinaki, A. I., Dekker, R., Van Nunen, J., & Pappis, C. (2000). *An exploratory study on electronic commerce for reverse logistics* (Vol. 1, pp. 10–17). Taylor & Francis.
Kropp, J. D., Turvey, C. G., Just, D. R., Kong, R., & Guo, P. (2009). Are the poor really more trustworthy? A micro-lending experiment. *Agricultural Finance Review, 69*(1), 67–87.
Leat, P., & Revoredo-Giha, C. (2013). Risk and resilience in Agri-food supply chains: The case of the ASDA PorkLink supply chain in Scotland. *Supply Chain Management: An International Journal, 18*(2), 219–231.
Lee, H. L. (2002). Aligning supply chain strategies with product uncertainties. *California Management Review, 44*(3), 105–119.
Lee, S. M., Tae Kim, S., & Choi, D. (2012). Green supply chain management and organizational performance. *Industrial Management & Data Systems, 112*(8), 1148–1180.
Lewandowski, M. (2016). Designing the business models for circular economy—Towards the conceptual framework. *Sustainability, 8*(1), 43.
Liang, X., Zhao, X., Wang, M., & Li, Z. (2018). Small and medium-sized enterprises sustainable supply chain financing decision based on triple bottom line theory. *Sustainability, 10*(11), 4242.
Lyle, J. T. (1996). *Regenerative design for sustainable development.* John Wiley & Sons.
MacArthur, E. (2013). Towards the circular economy. *Journal of Industrial Ecology*, 23–44.
Maloni, M. J., & Brown, M. E. (2006). Corporate social responsibility in the supply chain: An application in the food industry. *Journal of Business Ethics, 68*(1), 35–52.
Markelova, H., Meinzen-Dick, R., Hellin, J., & Dohrn, S. (2009). Collective action for smallholder market access. *Food Policy, 34*(1), 1–7.

Masi, D., Day, S., & Godsell, J. (2017). Supply chain configurations in the circular economy: A systematic literature review. *Sustainability, 9*(9), 1602.

McDonough, W., & Braungart, M. (2010). *Cradle to cradle: Remaking the way we make things*. North point press.

Mena, C., Terry, L. A., Williams, A., & Ellram, L. (2014). Causes of waste across multi-tier supply networks: Cases in the UK food sector. *International Journal of Production Economics, 152*, 144–158.

Miller, C. (2011). *Agricultural value chain finance strategy and design*. Food and Agriculture Organization.

Miller, C., & Da Silva, C. (2007). Value chain financing in agriculture. *Enterprise Development and Microfinance, 18*(2–3), 95–108.

Miyata, S., Minot, N., & Hu, D. (2009). Impact of contract farming on income: Linking small farmers, packers, and supermarkets in China. *World Development, 37*(11), 1781–1790.

Murphy, P. R., & Poist, R. F. (2002). Socially responsible logistics: An exploratory study. *Transportation Journal*, 23–35.

Musshoff, O., & Hirschauer, N. (2011). A behavioral economic analysis of bounded rationality in farm financing decisions: First empirical evidence. *Agricultural Finance Review, 71*(1), 62–83.

Nasir, M. H. A., Genovese, A., Acquaye, A. A., Koh, S. C. L., & Yamoah, F. (2017). Comparing linear and circular supply chains: A case study from the construction industry. *International Journal of Production Economics, 183*, 443–457.

Nawrocka, D., Brorson, T., & Lindhqvist, T. (2009). ISO 14001 in environmental supply chain practices. *Journal of Cleaner Production, 17*(16), 1435–1443.

Nelson, P. (1970). Information and consumer behavior. *Journal of Political Economy, 78*(2), 311–329.

Nelson, P. (1974). Advertising as information. *Journal of Political Economy, 82*(4), 729–754.

Nilsson, J. (1998). The emergence of new organizational models for agricultural cooperatives. *Swedish Journal of Agricultural Research, 28*, 39–48.

Ninlawan, C., Seksan, P., Tossapol, K., & Pilada, W. (2010). *The implementation of green supply chain management practices in electronics industry* (Vol. 3, pp. 17–19).

Ollila, P. (1994). Farmers' cooperatives as market coordinating institutions. *Annals of Public and Cooperative Economics, 65*(1), 81–102.

Pagell, M., & Wu, Z. (2009). Building a more complete theory of sustainable supply chain management using case studies of 10 exemplars. *Journal of Supply Chain Management, 45*(2), 37–56.

Pan, S.-Y., Du, M. A., Huang, I.-T., Liu, I.-H., Chang, E.-E., & Chiang, P.-C. (2015). Strategies on implementation of waste-to-energy (WTE) supply chain for circular economy system: A review. *Journal of Cleaner Production, 108*, 409–421.

Parikh, T. S., Patel, N., & Schwartzman, Y. (2007). *A survey of information systems reaching small producers in global agricultural value chains* (pp. 1–11). IEEE.
Park-Poaps, H., & Rees, K. (2010). Stakeholder forces of socially responsible supply chain management orientation. *Journal of Business Ethics, 92*(2), 305–322.
Pauli, G. A. (2010). *The blue economy: 10 years, 100 innovations, 100 million jobs.* Paradigm publications.
Paulraj, A. (2011). Understanding the relationships between internal resources and capabilities, sustainable supply management and organizational sustainability. *Journal of Supply Chain Management, 47*(1), 19–37.
Pearce, D. W., & Turner, R. K. (1990). *Economics of natural resources and the environment.* JHU Press.
Perez, G. (2012). *Sustainable supply chain financing: How financial institutions could enhance supply chain sustainability.*
Peterson, H. C. (2013). Fundamental principles of managing multi-stakeholder engagement. *International Food and Agribusiness Management Review, 16*(A), 11–22.
Planing, P. (2015). Business model innovation in a circular economy reasons for non-acceptance of circular business models. *Open Journal of Business Model Innovation, 1*(11).
Poist, R. F. (1989). Evolution of conceptual approaches to the design of logistics systems: A sequel. *Transportation Journal,* 35–39.
Quirós, R. (2007). *Agricultural value chain finance.* Food & Agriculture Org.
Rao, P. (2002). Greening the supply chain: A new initiative in South East Asia. *International Journal of Operations & Production Management, 22*(6), 632–655.
Rizos, V., Behrens, A., Van Der Gaast, W., Hofman, E., Ioannou, A., Kafyeke, T., … Hirschnitz-Garbers, M. (2016). Implementation of circular economy business models by small and medium-sized enterprises (SMEs): Barriers and enablers. *Sustainability, 8*(11), 1212.
Rogers, D. S., & Tibben-Lembke, R. (2001). An examination of reverse logistics practices. *Journal of Business Logistics, 22*(2), 129–148.
Salam, M. A. (2009). Retracted article: Corporate social responsibility in purchasing and supply chain. *Journal of Business Ethics, 85*(S2), 355–370. https://doi.org/10.1007/s10551-008-9733-0
Salin, V. (1998). Information technology in Agri-food supply chains. *The International Food and Agribusiness Management Review, 1*(3), 329–334.
Seuring, S., & Müller, M. (2008). From a literature review to a conceptual framework for sustainable supply chain management. *Journal of Cleaner Production, 16*(15), 1699–1710.
Shukla, M., & Jharkharia, S. (2013). Agri-fresh produce supply chain management: A state-of-the-art literature review. *International Journal of Operations & Production Management, 33*(2), 114–158.
Simon, H. A. (1972). Theories of bounded rationality. *Decision and Organization, 1*(1), 161–176.

Song H. (2015). *Supply Chain Finance*. China Renmin University Press. 1ed.
Song, H., Turson, R., Ganguly, A., & Yu, K. (2017a). Evaluating the effects of supply chain quality management on food firms' performance: The mediating role of food certification and reputation. *International Journal of Operations & Production Management, 37*(10), 1541–1562.
Song, H., Yu, K., & Zhang, S. (2017b). Green procurement, stakeholder satisfaction and operational performance. *The International Journal of Logistics Management, 28*(4), 1054–1077.
Spence, L., & Bourlakis, M. (2009). The evolution from corporate social responsibility to supply chain responsibility: The case of Waitrose. *Supply Chain Management: An International Journal, 14*(4), 291–302.
Srivastava, S. K. (2007). Green supply-chain management: A state-of-the-art literature review. *International Journal of Management Reviews, 9*(1), 53–80.
Stahel, W. R., & Reday, G. (1976). *The potential for substituting manpower for energy, report to the Commission of the European Communities.*
Stahel, W. (2010). *The performance economy*. Springer.
Stigler, G. J. (1961). The economics of information. *Journal of Political Economy, 69*(3), 213–225.
Swamy, V., & Dharani, M. (2016). Analyzing the agricultural value chain financing: Approaches and tools in India. *Agricultural Finance Review, 76*(2), 211–232.
Tate, W. L., & Bals, L. (2018). Achieving shared triple bottom line (TBL) value creation: Toward a social resource-based view (SRBV) of the firm. *Journal of Business Ethics, 152*(3), 803–826.
Tate, W. L., Ellram, L. M., & Kirchoff, J. F. (2010). corporate social responsibility reports: A thematic analysis related to supply chain management: Corporate social responsibility reports. *Journal of Supply Chain Management, 46*(1), 19–44.
Thiele, G., Devaux, A., Reinoso, I., Pico, H., Montesdeoca, F., Pumisacho, M., Andrade-Piedra, J., Velasco, C., Flores, P., Esprella, R., & Thomann, A. (2011). Multi-stakeholder platforms for linking small farmers to value chains: Evidence from the Andes. *International Journal of Agricultural Sustainability, 9*(3), 423–433.
Tibben-Lembke, R. S., & Rogers, D. S. (2002). Differences between forward and reverse logistics in a retail environment. *Supply Chain Management: An International Journal, 7*(5), 271–282.
Tseng, M.-L., Wu, K.-J., Hu, J., & Wang, C.-H. (2018). Decision-making model for sustainable supply chain finance under uncertainties. *International Journal of Production Economics, 205*, 30–36.
Tsolakis, N. K., Keramydas, C. A., Toka, A. K., Aidonis, D. A., & Iakovou, E. T. (2014). Agrifood supply chain management: A comprehensive hierarchical decision-making framework and a critical taxonomy. *Biosystems Engineering, 120*, 47–64.

van Bergen, M., Steeman, M., Reindorp, M., & Gelsomino, L. (2018). Supply chain finance schemes in the procurement of agricultural products. *Journal of Purchasing and Supply Management.*

Van Der Vorst, J. G. (2006). Performance measurement in Agri-food supply-chain networks. *Quantifying the Agri-Food Supply Chain*, 15–26.

Van Hoek, R. I. (1999). From reversed logistics to green supply chains. *Supply Chain Management: An International Journal, 4*(3), 129–135.

Vorley, B. (2007). Supermarkets and Agri-food supply chains in Europe: Partnership and protest. *Supermarkets and Agri-Food Supply Chains: Transformations in the Production and Consumption of Foods*, 243–267.

Walton, S. V., Handfield, R. B., & Melnyk, S. A. (1998). The green supply chain: Integrating suppliers into environmental management processes. *International Journal of Purchasing and Materials Management, 34*(1), 2–11.

Wang, T. R., Lan, Q. G., & Chu, Y. Z. (2013). *Supply chain financing model: Based on China's agricultural products supply chain* (Vol. 380, pp. 4417–4421). Trans Tech Publ.

Westgren, R. E. (1999). Delivering food safety, food quality, and sustainable production practices: The label rouge poultry system in France. *American Journal of Agricultural Economics, 81*(5), 1107–1111.

Williamson, O. E. (1973). Markets and hierarchies: Some elementary considerations. *The American Economic Review, 63*(2), 316–325.

Witjes, S., & Lozano, R. (2016). Towards a more circular economy: Proposing a framework linking sustainable public procurement and sustainable business models. *Resources, Conservation and Recycling, 112*, 37–44.

Yuan, Z., Bi, J., & Moriguichi, Y. (2008). The circular economy: A New development strategy in China. *Journal of Industrial Ecology, 10*(1–2), 4–8.

Zhijun, F., & Nailing, Y. (2007). Putting a circular economy into practice in China. *Sustainability Science, 2*(1), 95–101.

Zhu, Q., Geng, Y., & Lai, K. (2010). Circular economy practices among Chinese manufacturers varying in environmental-oriented supply chain cooperation and the performance implications. *Journal of Environmental Management, 91*(6), 1324–1331.

Zhu, Q., Sarkis, J., & Geng, Y. (2005). Green supply chain management in China: Pressures, practices and performance. *International Journal of Operations & Production Management, 25*(5), 449–468.

CHAPTER 8

Responsible Operations (II): Institutional Guarantee for Intelligent Supply Chain Finance

8.1 Introduction

Responsible supply chain finance, besides referring to the promotion of balanced economic, social, and environmental development through supply chain finance and the dynamic and interactive effects between supply chain finance and industrial supply chain, also reveals the construction of institutions in the operations and development of supply chain finance. From the perspective of institutional economics, institutions are socially constructed systems of rules designed by human beings to prescribe restrictions on the interactions of social actors (North, 1987). According to sociologist Scott (2008), institutions have three dimensions: regulation, norm, and cognition. The regulation is related to the rules promulgated by organizations that have legal authority or authority similar to legal authority, such as laws, policies, and regulations in society, which regulate behavior through rewards or punishments. This dimension is an institutional system of instrumental nature. The norm is related to social responsibilities, with a bias toward shared group values and social norms. This normative pressure is spread through mechanisms such as certificates and certifications. The cognition is related to socially constructed facts, which belong to the people's understanding of the external real world and is expressed in a metaphorical, symbolic or symbol system. The establishment of this system relies mainly on learning, that is, the identification with popular values and ideologies. According to institutional theory, the

H. Song, *Smart Supply Chain Finance*,
https://doi.org/10.1007/978-981-16-5997-3_8

above three dimensions of institutions exert pressure or motivation on organizations. On the one hand, the institution makes firms behave similarly, leading to the so-called isomorphism (DiMaggio & Powell, 1983); on the other hand, organizations in the environment with certain institutions can also develop institutional capital, thus increasing their use of resources (Oliver, 1991). Early institutional theories (Selznick, 1949, 1957) emphasized the influence of the environment on the organization, mainly in the form of isomorphic pressures, and asserted the unidirectional nature of this influence. Early institutional scholars believed that institutions are exogenous variables of organizations and enforce the compliance of organizations. In such a perspective, organizational behavior, organizational structure, and processes are shaped by institutions, while the organizations themselves have no agency. It emphasized that external institutions shape, penetrate, and constrain every aspect of the organization; and that the cultural environment determines how organizations are built, how they function, and how they are understood and evaluated. Along with the evolution of institutional theory and its empirical studies in different industries and organizational fields, certain scholars argued that organizations have agency. It is in an organization's own interest to have and be able to make choices about whether to avoid or control the environment in which it finds itself. The strategy school takes a more explicit view of institutions (Suchman, 1995), arguing that institutions are also an important resource that organizations can use to gain access to other resources. When faced with environmental pressures and expectations, organizations can adopt creative organizational design and find appropriate strategies and approaches to help them reduce the pressure of an unfavorable institutional environment or even benefit from a new institutional environment. However, the ultimate goal of both compliance and innovation is to gain legitimacy in the institutional environment.

The most critical issue in the institutional vision is legitimacy (Scott, 2008), which is the bridge between the organizations and the environment. In fact, the way to connect the organizations and the environment is the legitimacy mechanism. Legitimacy refers to "the general perception and assumption that an entity's behaviors are considered desirable, appropriate, and proper within a system of norms, values, beliefs, and definitions constructed by the society" (Suchman, 1995). The function of legitimacy is to help organizations gain recognition and support from the environment in which they operate and from other stakeholders. In the absence of such recognition, organizations cannot obtain the critical resources required to maintain basic operations. Therefore, the legitimacy obtained by an organization through appropriate activities is a necessary condition for its survival and growth. Dacin et al. (2007) pointed out that organizational legitimacy takes many forms, including investment legitimacy, market legitimacy, and social legitimacy. Investment legitimacy is primarily related to the organization's most directly interested parties, and it means that the organization's behaviors are recognized as valuable by the interested parties such as the board of directors, management, investors, or shareholders. Market legitimacy means that an organization's behaviors are primarily aimed at establishing or maintaining its rights or qualifications in a given market. This legitimacy is often judged on the basis of whether the organization is "doing the right thing," instead of whether it meets its own objectives. It reflects whether an organization can choose to obey established norms rather than the values of a particular group. Social legitimacy means that an organization's activities are widely known and taken for granted by different stakeholders. In Suchman's point of view, an organization and its actions will be taken for granted when stakeholders believe that there is no alternative to the organization.

From the above theories about institutions, it can be seen that institutions are a key factor acting on organizational behaviors, and even a key strategic resource that promotes the pursuit of legitimacy and increases the competitiveness of organizations in the society. The role of institutions in supply chain finance is also self-evident. In fact, the decisive factor for the sustainable development of supply chain finance is institutions rather than technologies. Although the effective means and commercial behaviors in supply chain finance have effectively solved the problem of credit rationing arising from information asymmetry and relieved the pressure of shortage of operating capital for the SMEs participating the industrial supply chain, commercial supply chain finance will eventually have a development bottleneck. In the absence of good social rules and institutional construction, even the most excellent supply chain finance operation and management system may incur huge social transaction costs due to the poor operating environment and immature system of rules. This situation will not only increase the risk and cost of supply chain finance implementation, but even hinder the benign development of supply chain finance due to poor business practices and culture, or, worse, result in the alienation of supply chain finance (the confusion of institutional system will cause a distorted understanding of legitimacy). For example, supply chain finance is originally intended to effectively solve the information asymmetry between borrowers and lenders through supply chain management and operations, and push forward the smooth capital flow between organizations by relying on the effective combination of commodity flow, logistics flow, and information flow, so as to finally realize the shortening of the collaborative cash flow cycle and create a win-win situation. However, in practice, some organizations or enterprises put the cart before the horse and regard supply chain finance as an effective means to delay the payment days of accounts receivable, or even regard supply chain finance as an important source of corporate profits. Merely for the purpose of obtaining supply chain finance profits, they wantonly extend the payment period for suppliers (Song, 2019), which only results in a worse business environment and creates a business culture and behavior of mutual harm and aggression. Therefore, the establishment and improvement of institutions is an important foundation for the realization of sustainable intelligent supply chain finance. To this end, this chapter will explore the institutionalization of supply chain finance from the perspective of institution building and with reference to international experience.

8.2 Restrictions on Payment Delay in Supply Chain Finance

Regulation is a series of mandatory rules for regulating behaviors, which includes a wide range of laws, regulations, rules, and so on. The mechanism of its role lies in "how it must be" (Scott, 2008). Given that supply chain finance is a kind of commercial and financial behavior, corresponding laws and regulations are inevitably needed as a guarantee to define the legal relationship, legal basis, and legal risks between enterprises. For example, China has enacted the *Real Right Law*, *Contract Law*, *Negotiable Instruments Law*, and *Guarantee Law* to define the responsibilities and obligations of each party and to compulsorily restrain and regulate the behaviors of each party. Beyond such laws and regulations, however, supply chain finance needs a crucial type of regulatory system that regulates the environment in which supply chain finance operates, allowing all parties to engage in sound supply chain operations and financial activities in a benign environment (Gloria, 2014). Currently, this type of regulatory system is an area that various countries are actively exploring. The exploration of such a type of regulatory system stems from the market structure inequity that naturally exists in supply chain finance, which is prone to loss of equity and market failure due to unilateral monopoly. Specifically, supply chain finance mostly exists in the business relationship between core enterprises and MSMEs, while the latter is naturally in a disadvantaged position in market negotiations, which is especially true for small and medium-sized suppliers. This position inequality always results in transaction inequality and also many unreasonable contractual patterns. If the unreasonable contractual patterns arising from this unequal position cannot be bound, the risks inherent in supply chain finance will be great.

The process of business transactions between enterprises often involves several payment methods, which include check, bank draft, commercial paper, cashier's check, remittance, entrusted collection, collection payment, credit card, and letter of credit. In terms of time of payment, they include cash on delivery (also known as COD), installment payment and agreed-time payment. COD refers to the payment when the supplier delivers the goods to the downstream customer, the customer inspects the goods, the goods are warehoused, and the transfer of ownership is completed. A special kind of COD also exists in supply chain operations, that is, Vendor Managed Inventory (VMI). VMI is a cooperative strategy to continuously improve inventory management by having the supplier manage inventory under a common agreement with the objective of obtaining the lowest cost for both the client and the supplier, and continuously monitoring the implementation of the agreement and amending the agreement. Under the VMI model, the actual transfer of ownership occurs when the downstream customer picks up goods from the supplier-managed inventory for use in the downstream production or sales operation, and this is when payment should be made. Installment payments are made to suppliers part by part, depending on the stage of business execution and whether or not the objectives of the different stages of execution are met, until full execution of the business. This type of payment is more commonly used in engineering projects. In actual commercial operations, the most common method is the agreed-time payment, which means that the buyer and the seller agree on payment period after the transaction is formed. Generally, the agreed period between enterprises in developed countries is usually 30 days, and sometimes that between SMEs and large enterprises is extended to 60 days (Tim & Sarongrat, 2017). Payment delay refers to the act of making payments beyond the agreed time, which not only violates business integrity but also causes great distress and bad debts to suppliers. In Western countries, the percentage of bad debts caused by payment delay to SMEs is typically between 6% and 8% (Tim & Sarongrat, 2017).

8.2.1 Status of Deferred Payments in Countries Worldwide

At present, countries worldwide are all facing challenges posed by payment delay. Plum, a firm specializing in communications, media, and technology consulting, has carried out a survey on payment delay in 11 countries in 2017 (Tim & Sarongrat, 2017), including Australia (AU), Brazil (BR), Canada (CA), France (FR), Germany (DE), Ireland (IE), Singapore (SG), South Africa (ZA), Spain (ES), the United Kingdom (UK), and the United States (US). The survey found that even today, payment delay is still a significant impediment to SME growth in these countries. The survey mainly examined three aspects of the current state of payment delay: (1) the severity of payment delay (2) whether large enterprises have a tendency to payment delay; and (3) the impact of payment delay on small and medium-sized suppliers. In terms of the severity of payment delay, the survey explored two forms of payment delay. One form is delayed payment of bills, which refers to the failure of an enterprise to honor bills when due, despite having agreed to issue them to suppliers; the other is delayed payment of overall accounts receivable, which is defined as the proportion of delayed payments of various terms or in various forms to overall accounts receivable. According to the results of this survey, the delays in bill issuance as a percentage of the total bills ranged from 7% to 18% in 11 countries (see Fig. 8.1). Likewise, the proportion of the delayed

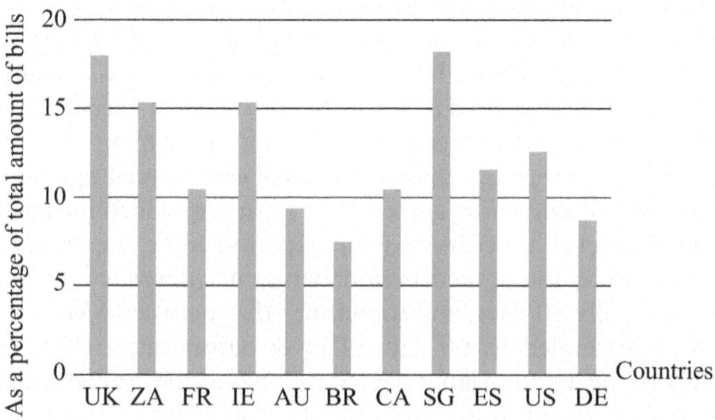

Fig. 8.1 Delayed payment of bills in 11 countries (Tim & Sarongrat, 2017). (Source: Tim and Sarongrat (2017))

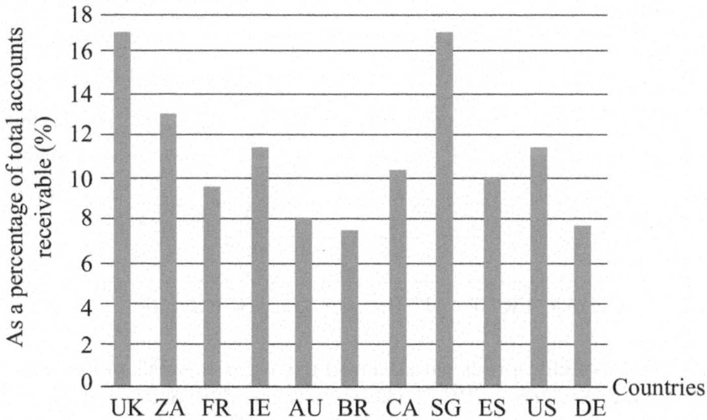

Fig. 8.2 Delayed payments as a percentage of total accounts receivable in 11 countries. (Source: Tim and Sarongrat (2017))

payments to the total accounts receivable of the surveyed companies ranged from 8% to 17% (see Fig. 8.2). The results showed that these two forms of payment delay are highly correlated and that payment delay has so far remained a problem of extremely high severity.

The fact that who causes payment delay is also one of the problems of current concern. The survey sorted out the types of enterprises that cause delays in payment of the accounts receivable of the SMEs in 11 countries and came up with the very surprising result that not all enterprises that have caused payment delay are large enterprises. All types of downstream enterprises use their dominant position in the industry to delay payments to upstream enterprises when they make payments for purchases (see Fig. 8.3). Even worse, when SMEs act as purchasers, they also sometimes infringe on the interests of their upstream SMEs. The results of this survey suggested that payment delay is a widespread social problem, which requires a rule to regulate the behavior of all enterprises, in addition to moral censure.

Another social issue studied in this survey is the negative impact of payment delay on small and medium-sized suppliers. Payment delays not only deteriorate business relationships but also exacerbate the cost and financial pressure on small and medium-sized upstream suppliers by increasing opportunity costs. Specifically, first of all, small and medium-sized suppliers need to spend a lot of time to recover overdue payments in a timely

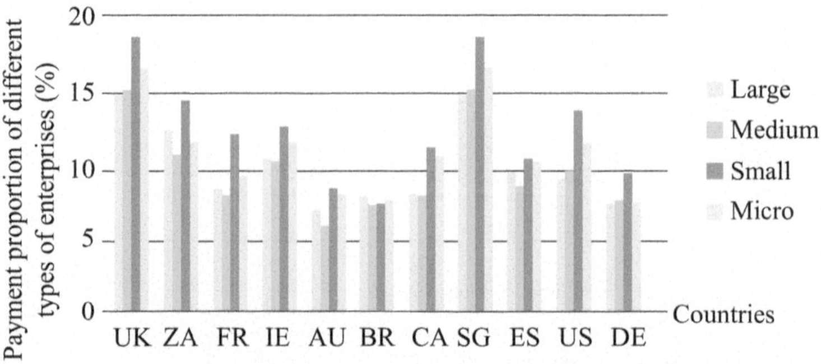

Fig. 8.3 Types of enterprises with delayed payments to small and medium-sized suppliers (Tim & Sarongrat, 2017). (Source: Tim and Sarongrat (2017))

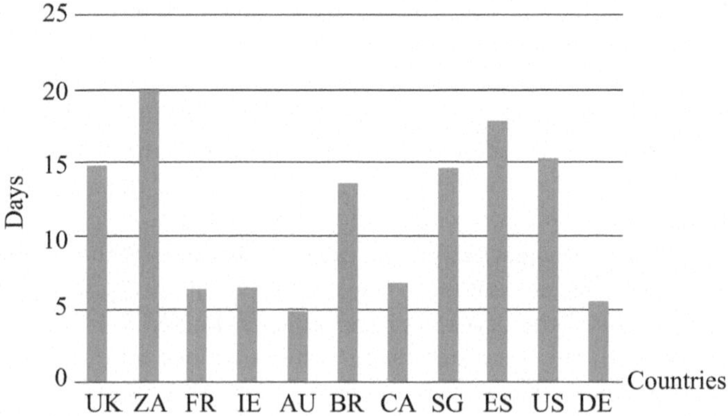

Fig. 8.4 Average man-days of small and medium-sized suppliers in 11 countries to recover overdue payments (Tim & Sarongrat, 2017). (Source: Tim and Sarongrat (2017))

manner. The survey results showed that the average number of man-days required by the SMEs to recover overdue payments is about 5–20 days (see Fig. 8.4). Second, the costs of overdue payment recovery are high. The survey reflected that the annual costs consumed by the most of the small and medium-sized suppliers in the countries surveyed for recovering overdue payments ranges from US$2000 to US$6000 (see Fig. 8.5). Third, payment delay has a negative impact on the operations of small and medium-sized suppliers, with an average of 39% of the SMEs in 11

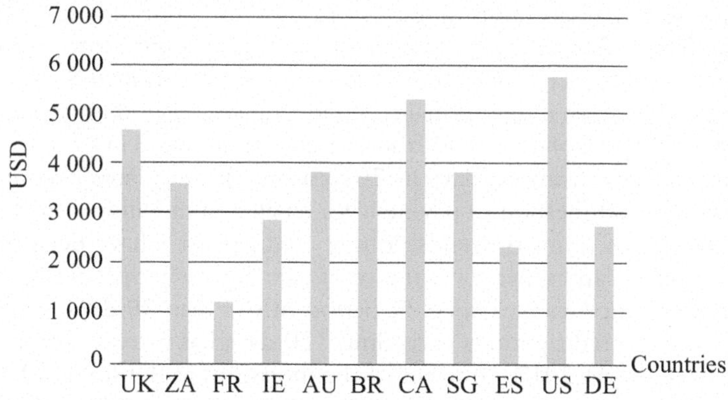

Fig. 8.5 Average costs of small and medium-sized suppliers in 1 countries spent in recovering overdue payments (Tim & Sarongrat, 2017). (Source: Tim and Sarongrat (2017))

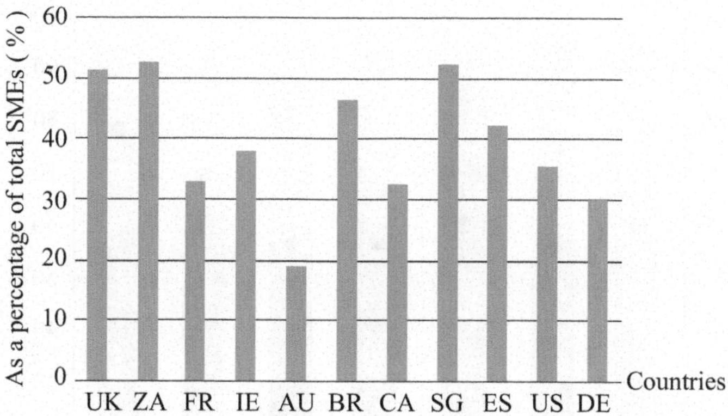

Fig. 8.6 Percentage of SMEs affected by payment delays in 11 countries (Tim & Sarongrat, 2017). (Source: Tim and Sarongrat (2017))

countries reporting challenges and threats to their daily operations because of the payment delays (see Fig. 8.6), These challenges and threats are directly reflected in their difficulties in paying employee commissions, salaries, and year-end bonuses. In addition, payment delay leads to a domino effect, creating potential challenges for these small and medium-sized suppliers to pay their upstream suppliers and worsening the development of the enterprises' own investments.

Payment delays are even more serious in China, not only in terms of serious delays after the agreed payment time but also in terms of longer payment periods. According to the *China Corporate Payment Survey 2018* issued by Coface, an international credit insurance and credit management service provider (Coface, 2018), the average credit period in China rose to 76 days in 2017 from 68 days in 2016 as credit sales have become the most widespread method of payment for small and medium-sized suppliers in China. In terms of trends, longer credit periods have been agreed between buyers and sellers over the years (see Fig. 8.7). Specifically, fewer and fewer enterprises have a credit period of less than 30 days, while the proportion of credit periods exceeding 120 days has increased from 12% in 2016 to 19% in 2017. In terms of the industries of the surveyed enterprises, the energy industry has the longest payment periods, with about one-third of the surveyed enterprises having a payment period of over

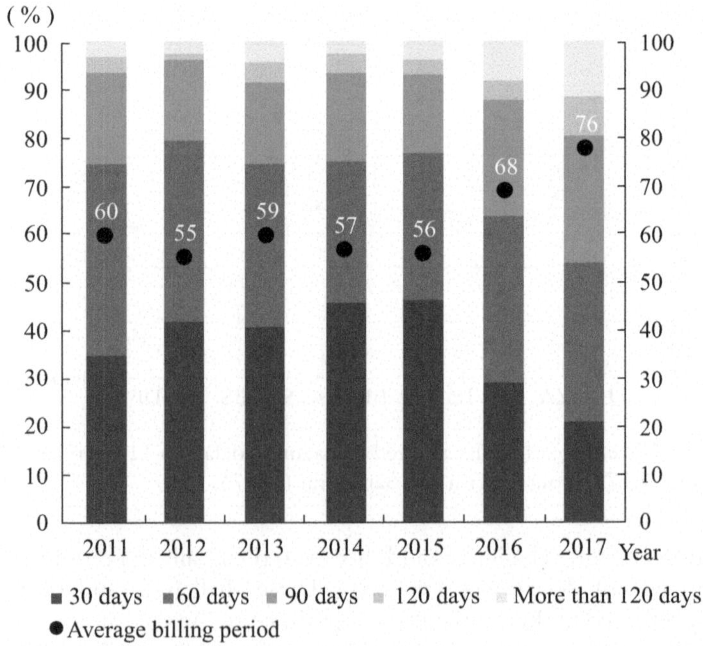

Fig. 8.7 Trends in agreed payment periods of suppliers and buyers in China (Coface, 2018). (Source: Coface (2018))

120 days. In addition, the pharmaceutical, construction, transportation, and automotive industries have above-average payment periods. The agricultural industry has shorter payment periods, with an average of 55 days in 2017, and the forestry, textile, paper, retail, and metal industries have average payment periods below the average. In addition to payment periods, another issue is payment delays. According to the survey of Coface, the percentage of rising days of payment delays in 2017 has decreased compared to the past, from 46% in 2016 to 29% in 2017 (see Fig. 8.8), but, worryingly, nearly half of the surveyed enterprises suffered payment delays of more than 90 days. The percentage of surveyed enterprises suffering payment delays of more than 120 days increased from 19% in 2016 to 26% in 2017, while the percentage of them suffering extra-long payment delays (more than 180 days) with overdue amounts exceeding 2% of their annual turnover increased from 35% in 2016 to 47% in 2017. Worse still, the percentage of surveyed enterprises suffering extra-long payment delays with an amount more than 10% of their annual turnover increased from 11% in 2016 to 21% in 2017 (see Fig. 8.9).

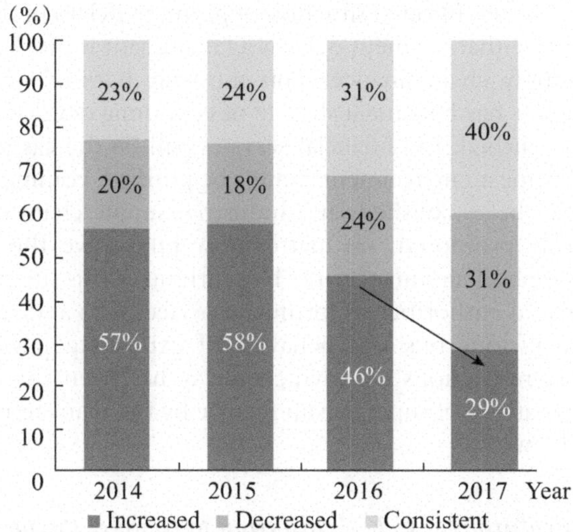

Fig. 8.8 Trend in increasing days of payment delays for SMEs in China (Coface, 2018). (Source: Coface (2018))

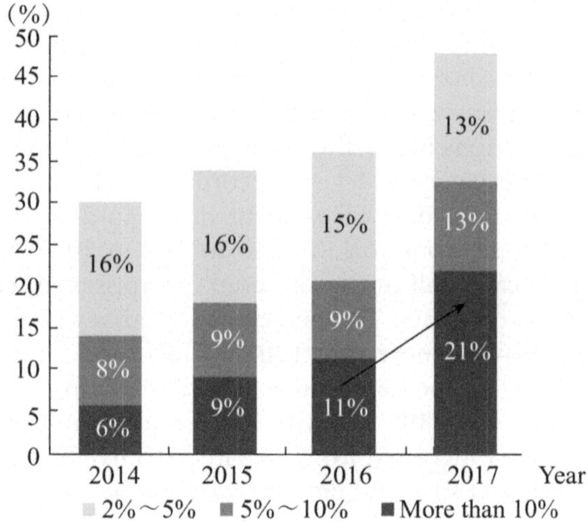

Fig. 8.9 Trends in ultra-long payment delays as a varying percentage of turnover in Chinese SMEs (Coface, 2018). (Source: Coface (2018))

From the abovementioned situation of payment delays in the world and China, we can see that payment delay is a "malignant tumor" in the development of supply chain finance. This mutually harmful and damaging business behavior has become a shackle of economic development. If it is not effectively curbed, the financial services will be the castles in the air, because the business environment cannot be purified, commercial civilization can hardly be established, and industrial supply chain development cannot be truly promoted, no matter how innovative the models and products of supply chain finance are. The curbing of this situation requires the governmental authorities to formulate perfect laws and regulations to restrict the malicious business behavior of extra-long payment delays. Therefore, the restrictions on payment delay has been the focus of the legislative regulations of supply chain finance by the management authorities all over the world.

8.2.2 Evolution of U.K. Legislation to Restrict Payment Delay

The UK's quest to restrictions on payment delays began in the 1990s, when there was a widespread problem in the UK that downstream enterprises delayed their payments to upstream small and medium-sized suppliers. As estimated by the U.K. Private Enterprise Forum held in 1993, 89% of SMEs suffered payment delays, and the average payment period for these enterprises was as high as 89 days after invoicing, while the average delay after the expiration of the payment periods was still as long as 51 days. This phenomenon has caused great concern to the U.K. government. In November 1993, then chancellor of the exchequer Kenneth Clarke announced in the budget meeting that the Conservative government was considering proposals for improving payment performance, noting, "Year after year, one issue has been at the top of the budget list submitted by small enterprises to us: payment delays. There is nothing more frustrating than delivering high-quality products on time and at the most competitive price, but not receiving payment for months. Payment delays are causing huge losses in cash flow for many small enterprises, bringing them to the brink of survival and death. The habit of payment delay is corrupting our commercial culture, so it must be solved. I would like to tell all members that there are many ways to solve this problem. Distinguished chairman of the exchange committee, two issues are highlighted here: the first is the new UK payment standards; the second and more important issue is the introduction of legislation on interest for delayed payments" (Parliament UK, 1993). In response to this proposal, the U.K. Department of Trade and Industry issued a consulting report revealing the causes of payment delays and possible solutions, including imposing interests on payment delays and U.K. prompt payment provisions. This proposal was finally incorporated into the U.K. government's White Paper 1994—*Competitiveness: Helping Businesses Succeed.*

Since then various parties in the U.K. industry have formed a divergence of views on the solutions mentioned in the government's White Paper. The Confederation of British Industry, the Federation of Small Businesses, the Credit Management Agency, and the Institute of Chartered Accountants in England and Wales have expressed qualified opinions, pointing out that a business atmosphere of prompt payment, but not legislation, should be established, as mandatory legislation would only result in large businesses signing special contracts to achieve extended payment periods, while SMEs would be afraid to resort to court for fear of losing business. On the contrary, the U.K. Private Enterprise Forum argued that voluntary action would not have any impact on the payment delay by large enterprises. The final outcome of the negotiation between the two parties was that large enterprises would need to pay interests on delayed payments to SMEs, but no regulations were formed at that time. Rather, the government took the lead. The U.K. government required all government departments and authorities to first begin complying with the CBI's prompt payment requirements and to provide information on their payment policies and specific payment status, and the U.K. government committed to a two-year review of governmental payments. After that, the UK has also put in place a series of measures to encourage prompt payment, including requiring all listed companies to state their payment policies in their directors' reports and encouraging the development of prompt payment standards.

In January 1996, Richard Page, then minister of small business of the Conservative government, announced that the government would reconsider the legislation on interests on payment delays. The reason for this reconsideration was that on September 26, 1995, John Major, then chancellor of the UK, initiated a conference themed "Your Business Matters" to seek the opinions of small businesses on payment delay and found that the SMEs were not opposed to the adoption of legislation to regulate payments delayed by large businesses. On March 20, 1996, Ian Lang, then chairman of the U.K. Trade Commission, announced that all government departments would sign up to the CBI's *Prompt Payment Code* by the end of March 1996. In June 1996, a second consulting paper was issued for the purpose of seeking comments on whether a new disclosure requirement should be introduced into the *Companies Act* requiring all public companies to publish their payment practices in their director's reports. As a result, in January 1997, a regulation was introduced requiring all public companies and their large private subsidiaries to disclose how long it takes on average to pay their bills. The actions of the Conservative government at the time were also highly supported and affirmed by the U.K. Labour Party. Even in the 1997 U.K. election campaign, the Labour Party made interests on payment delay as one of its campaign promises. After the election victory, the Labour Party proposed to pass legislation to restrict the payment delay. Against this background, the U.K. legislation on payment delay came into being.

The *Late Payment of Commercial Debts (Interest) Act* was first introduced in the UK by the House of Lords on December 10, 1997, passed on June 12, 1998, and came into force on November 1, 1998. The act provides for three phases: the first phase, from November 1, 1998, allows small businesses to claim interest from large businesses (including the public departments) on debts arising from contracts agreed after that date; the second phase, from November 1, 2000, allows small businesses to claim from other small businesses on debts arising from contracts agreed after that date; and the third phase, from August 8, 2002, allows all businesses and the public departments to claim interest from all businesses and the public departments on debts arising from contracts agreed after that date. As seen from the three phases of the act, the settlement of payment delay begins with debts owed by the government and large businesses to SMEs and then gradually extends to debts owed by all businesses or organizations to each other.

The act, which was implemented in the UK in 1998, has the following features: (1) the act clearly defines small businesses as those with less than 50 employees, which are vulnerable groups that the law needs to protect and are the focus of attention for payment delays; (2) the act provides for clear payment periods, allowing businesses to agree on credit periods (i.e., payment periods) between themselves, but generally not exceeding 30 days, and any business with a payment period of more than 30 days will need to pay interest to the supplier. Notably, the act was amended in 2015 to specify a maximum of 30 days for the public department and 60 days for the commercial institutions (except in exceptional circumstances). Therefore, despite the freedom to negotiate the payment periods between companies, the act sets a bottom line for the payment periods; (3) the act provides for the payment of delayed interest and the interest rate accordingly. The act emphasizes that the payment of interest is a legal right and is not mandatory. In other words, when a payment delay occurs, the downstream enterprise is not obliged to pay interest to the upstream supplier unconditionally, but it is up to the upstream supplier to decide whether it is required to do so. However, upon request, the interest rate for downstream enterprises to pay interest should be determined according to the formula or the rate set by the secretary of state. In practice, the interest rate set in the UK is the sum of the "statutory" rate of 8% plus the benchmark interest rate issued by Bank of England, which is usually 8.25%.

In addition to the above act, the UK enacted the *Small Business, Enterprise and Employment Act 2015*, the section 3 of which "gives the government a new power to allow the Secretary of State to require certain enterprises to publish information about payment practices." This requirement, which already existed in previous annual reports on matters such as the treatment of suppliers, is further greatly expanded by this act. In terms of its implementation, this act, together with the above act, has become an important legal basis for protecting small and medium-sized upstream suppliers.

8.2.3 EU Directive on Combating Payment Delay

The EU has also imposed regulations and restrictions on payment delays in commercial transactions and established a corresponding directive on June 15, 2000, which came into force on August 8, 2002. The directive allows countries to enact their own laws and regulations in accordance with it. Like the U.K. regulation, the directive requires enterprises to pay interest on delayed payments, but its scope of application greatly exceeds that of the U.K. regulation, mainly in the following aspects: (1) The directive should be nominally applicable to commercial transactions made after November 2002, but in fact, EU countries started to implement it since August 2002. This showed that the EU was very determined in implementing the directive and was also committed to regulating the conducts of transactions between enterprises as soon as possible; (2) the directive has introduced a new right that, unless the debtor is not responsible for the delay, the creditor should be entitled to claim reasonable compensation from the debtor for all relevant costs incurred as a result of the payment delay. This provision of the directive extends the basis for calculating the interest for payment delays. Specifically, once there is a delay in payment to the SME, the large enterprise should pay interest not only on the amount owed but also on all the costs arising from the payment delay; (3) Article 3 of the directive strictly provides that the payment of interest on payment delay is not only enforced when claimed by the SME, but even if the upstream SME does not make a claim for such an interest, the governments may enforce compensation from the large enterprise on behalf of the SME, provided that the agreement between the large enterprise and the SME is deemed unfair.

This provision of the EU Directive, later called as "reasonable compensation," provides for seven options. Each country can decide which of these options it wants to implement, depending on its own circumstances. These options include the following: (1) a fixed amount of compensation based on the size of the debt; (2) a fixed amount based on collection activity, allowing creditors to determine different amounts of compensation based on the status of collection at different stages; (3) a fixed amount of compensation based on the period of the debt, with longer periods of time corresponding to higher amounts of compensation; (4) a flat percentage of compensation, regardless of the size and period of the debt; (5) different percentages of compensation according to the period of the debt; (6) a combined option where compensation is initially paid at a fixed amount and then at the actual amount when the debt is assigned to a third party to generate recourse; (7) a combination of a fixed amount and a fixed percentage to seek compensation from large enterprises. The reasonable compensation as specified in the EU directives apparently has imposed very strict limits on payment delays of large enterprises, and this provision has encouraged all EU countries to impose effective limits on payment delays of large enterprises, as small enterprises may voluntarily waive their claims for fear of losing markets or customers, or because of the "despotic power" of large enterprises. In contrast, this provision gives third parties the right to monitor and regulate payment delays of large enterprises, effectively curbing the practice.

Based on the above directive on late payments in commercial transactions, a second directive was implemented in 2011, which further refines the payment practices between organizations or enterprises, including the following: (1) payment must be made within 30 days after the government department has a transaction with an enterprise and receives an undisputed invoice; (2) the maximum payment period for transactions between commercial enterprises is 60 days, unless the supplier expressly agrees to extend and the contract is not apparently unfair; (3) the compensation should be no less than €40 and the supplier is allowed to seek additional compensation. While the first EU directive limits payment delays by discipline (i.e., interest payment or compensation), it is clear that the second EU directive is designed to prevent payment delays of large enterprises or government departments by imposing compulsory rules on payment periods. Based on this directive, EU countries can refine or even strengthen the enforcement of these rules according to their national conditions. For example, the Netherlands has made further refinements based on this EU directive. In terms of the payment period, the Netherlands stipulates that for any transaction between a large enterprise and an SME or private owner, the payment period must never exceed 60 days for whatever reason; if it exceeds 60 days, the agreement is automatically deemed null and void and the payment period is deemed to be 30 days; if the purchaser makes payment after the 30-day period, statutory interest will be payable for the days beyond 30-day period. If a large enterprise fails to meet the above obligations, it will be required to pay a percentage of collection costs based on transaction amount, in addition to the interest that must be paid to the SME. In addition, the Dutch government provides that SMEs shall be entitled to initiate a lawsuit after five years if a large company actually delays payment. This Dutch regulation, which was introduced on a trial basis on July 1, 2017, and came into effect on August 1, 2018, aims to protect the interests of SMEs in claiming interest and compensation for payment delays, as they are often afraid to file lawsuits for claims due to their business relationships with large enterprises. This regulation in fact gives SMEs a right of recourse after the fact, which strongly protects their interests.

8.2.4 U.S. Restrictions on Payment Delay

The restrictions on payment delays have also been a major concern of the U.S. federal and state governments. As early as the 1980s, the US enacted a series of regulations and rules that limit payment delays primarily through payment periods and interest. The 31 U.S. Code § 39 provides detailed provisions for prompt payment, that is, in the case of business-to-business transactions where no specific payment date is agreed upon at the time of the transaction, the payment deadline should be always the 30th day after receipt of the invoice, while that for public departments is even shorter. For example, the payment deadline for purchases made by the U.S. Defense Logistics Agency for daily use items is ten days from the date of receipt of the invoice. In addition, with respect to statutory interest, the U.S. Code provides that penalty interest paid on any late payment beyond the 30-day period will be added to the principal amount of the debt, after which the penalty interest will be calculated on the increased amount. This provision significantly increases the cost to the late paying party. Moreover, the interest on payment delays is calculated for the period from the filing of the claim until the date of payment; interest is determined by the Treasury Department based on the five-year private commercial loan interest rate at that time. In addition to penalty interest, the US also provides for compensation. If an enterprise fails to receive the penalty interest on payment delay within the specified time, the enterprise will be entitled to additional penalty interest calculated as per the percentage set by the State Office of Management and Budget, in addition to the total penalty interest, but the interim payments for late payment cannot exempt the compensation liability. As far as the possible disputes on documents in the course of a transaction are concerned, the U.S. Code provides that each document shall be reviewed as soon as possible, and shall be returned within seven days of receipt with an explanation of the reasons if it does not fall within the criteria for a qualified document as stipulated in U.S. Code § 3901(a)(3).

Based on the U.S. Code, each state has established appropriate regulations on payment delay so as to limit the default of payments by large downstream enterprises. For example, the basic regulations for the health care industry in each U.S. state are shown in Table 8.1.

In an effort to demonstrate strong support for SMEs, the U.S. federal government has developed a series of temporary policies to spearhead its commitment to prompt payments to SMEs. For this purpose, President Barack Obama released Memorandum M-11-32, "Accelerating Payments to Small Businesses for Goods and Services," and M-12-16, "Providing Prompt Payment to Small Business Subcontractors," respectively, in 2011 and 2012. The former document requires the federal government to deliver and pay for products or services purchased from small businesses within 15 days, while the latter requires agents to expedite payments to all general contractors to the maximum extent permitted by law so that the general contractors can make prompt payments to their small business subcontractors. Besides, M-12-16 requires agencies to report semiannually on their progress in ensuring prompt payments to small business subcontractors. The effective dates specified in these memorandums (M-12-16, M-13-15, and M-14-10) were later extended to December 31, 2016. In order to further increase the support for small businesses, Obama released the Memorandum M-16-07, "Reporting of Accelerated Payments to Small Business Subcontractors," which changed the frequency of reporting to the government on the status of payments to small businesses from semiannual to quarterly, and extended the effective date of these policies to December 31, 2017. The reporting includes, among other things, (1) prompt payments by agencies to general contractors so that general contractors can make prompt payments to small business subcontractors, (2) prompt payments by agencies to small business general contractors, and (3) all measures taken to ensure prompt payments to small business general contractors or subcontractors. It is worth pointing out that this series of temporary policies formulated by Obama has not affected the implementation of the U.S. laws regarding payment delay, but has further increased the promotion of prompt payment to small businesses on the basis of the act. Such promotion is reflected in the following two main points: (1) a more stringent payment period for federal government agencies is imposed (in fact 15 days not only is the payment period but also includes all documentary transmission and payment time). In other words, the support for prompt payments to small businesses must start with government procurement; and (2) very strict process controls are

Table 8.1 U.S. state restrictions on payment delay in the health care industry

State	*Required payment period*	*Penalties*
Alabama	30 working days for electronic invoices 45 working days for paper invoices	Penalty interest at the rate set by the regulatory department
Alaska	10 working days for electronic invoices 20 working days for paper invoices	For late payments less than USD 250, the compensation shall be 5% of the amount or no more than USD 5 For late payments higher than USD 250, the compensation shall be 2% of the amount
Arizona	30 days after the order is effected, regardless of the type of transaction	Penalty interest at the legal rate
Arkansas	30 days for electronic invoices 45 days for paper invoices	Penalty interest at 12% p.a.
California	30 working days for non-HMOs 45 working days for HMOs	Penalty interest at 15% p.a., plus an additional compensation of USD 10
Colorado	45 working days after the order is effected, regardless of the type of transaction	Penalty interest at 10% p.a., payments overdue for over 90 days should be compensated at 3%
Connecticut	45 working days after the order is effected, regardless of the type of transaction	Penalty interest at 15% p.a.
Delaware	30 working days after the order is effected, regardless of the type of transaction	Penalty interest at the highest allowable loan rate
Washington D.C.	30 working days after the order is effected, regardless of the type of transaction	31–60 days: penalty interest at 1.5% 61–120 days: penalty interest at 2% Over 120 days: penalty interest at 2.5%
Florida	45 days for non-HMOs 35 days for HMOs 120 days for compensation requiring additional information	Penalty interest at 10% p.a.
Georgia	15 working days after the order is effected, regardless of the type of transaction	Penalty interest at 18% p.a.
Hawaii	15 days for electronic invoices 30 days for paper invoices	Penalty interest at 15% p.a., plus compensation after assessment

(*continued*)

Table 8.1 (continued)

State	*Required payment period*	*Penalties*
Idaho	30 working days after the order is effected, regardless of the type of transaction	Statutory interest rate
Illinois	30 days after the order is effected, regardless of the type of transaction	Penalty interest at 9% p.a.
Indiana	30 days for electronic invoices 45 days for paper invoices	Penalty interest at 2% p.a. (subject to change from year to year)
Iowa	Same time as the group health plan developed by the U.S. Department of Labor under 29 C.F.R.	Penalty interest at 10% p.a.
Kansas	30 days after the order is effected, regardless of the type of transaction	Penalty interest at 1% p.a.
Kentucky	30 days after the order is effected or direct refusal of payment, regardless of the type of transaction	31–60 days: penalty interest at 12% 61–120 days: penalty interest at 18% Over 120 days: penalty interest at 21%
Louisiana	45 days for paper invoice: both invoice delivery and payment 25 days for electronic invoice	Penalty interest of 1% p.a. on the unpaid portion, plus a compensation equal to 1% of the unpaid portion for every 25 days
Maine	30 days after the order is effected, regardless of the type of transaction	Penalty interest at 1.5% per month
Maryland	30 days after the order is effected, regardless of the type of transaction	31–60 days: penalty interest at 1.5% 61–120 days: penalty interest at 2% Over 120 days: penalty interest at 2.5%
Massachusetts	45 days after the order is effected, regardless of the type of transaction	Penalty interest at 1.5% per month
Michigan	60 days for non-contract suppliers	Penalty interest at 12% p.a.
Minnesota	30 days after the order is effected, regardless of the type of transaction	Penalty interest at 1.5% per month
Mississippi	25 days for electronic invoices 35 days for paper invoices	Penalty interest at 1.5% per month

(*continued*)

Table 8.1 (continued)

State	*Required payment period*	*Penalties*
Missouri	45 days after the order is effected or direct refusal of payment, regardless of the type of transaction	Penalty interest at 1% per month
Montana	30 days after the order is effected, regardless of the type of transaction	Penalty interest at 18% p.a.
Nebraska	45 days after the order is effected, regardless of the type of transaction	Submit "prompt payment reports" to the Nebraska Department of Insurance for consideration
Nevada	30 days after the order is effected, regardless of the type of transaction	See the government's website
New Hampshire	15 days for electronic invoices 45 days for paper invoices	Penalty interest at 1.5% per month
New Jersey	30 days for electronic invoices 40 days for paper invoices	Penalty interest at 10% p.a.
New Mexico	30 days for electronic invoices 45 days for paper invoices	Penalty interest at 1.5% per month
New York	45 days after the order is effected, regardless of the type of transaction	Penalty interest at a rate above 12% p.a. or as specified by the Commission
North Carolina	30 days after the order is effected or direct refusal of payment, regardless of the type of transaction	Penalty interest at 18% p.a.
North Dakota	15 days after the order is effected, regardless of the type of transaction	Not specified
Ohio	30 days after the order is effected, regardless of the type of transaction	Penalty interest at 18% p.a.
Oklahoma	45 days after the order is effected, regardless of the type of transaction	Penalty interest at 10% p.a., >6% same as U.S. interest rate
Oregon	30 days after the order is effected, regardless of the type of transaction	Penalty interest at 12% p.a.
Pennsylvania	45 days after the order is effected, regardless of the type of transaction	Penalty interest at 10% p.a.

(*continued*)

Table 8.1 (continued)

State	*Required payment period*	*Penalties*
Rhode Island	30 days after the order is effected, regardless of the type of transaction	Penalty interest at 12% p.a.
South Carolina	30 days for electronic invoices 45 days for paper invoices	Penalty interest at 6% p.a.
South Dakota	30 days for electronic invoices 45 days for paper invoices	Not specified
Tennessee	21 days for electronic invoices 30 days for paper invoices	Penalty interest at 1.5% per month
Texas	45 days only for HMOs	Penalty interest at 18% p.a.
Utah	30 days after the order is effected or direct refusal of payment, regardless of the type of transaction	Penalty interest may be calculated according to the formula
Vermont	45 days after the order is effected, regardless of the type of transaction	Penalty interest at 12% p.a.
Virginia	45 days after the order is effected, regardless of the type of transaction	Penalty interest shall be calculated on a daily basis based on statutory interest rate
Washington	30 days for 90% of monthly sales, payment or direct refusal	Penalty interest at 1% per month
West Virginia	30 days for electronic invoices 40 days for paper invoices	Penalty interest at 10% p.a.
Wisconsin	30 days after the order is effected, regardless of the type of transaction	Penalty interest at 12% p.a.
Wyoming	45 days after the order is effected, regardless of the type of transaction	Penalty interest at 10% p.a.

Note: "Days" refers to calendar days, not working days

imposed. In addition to the commitment to prompt payments, each government agency must also conduct self-monitoring, and report the progress and status of prompt payments made to small businesses in details so that the policy can be effectively implemented.

In addition, for the purpose of boosting prompt payments to small businesses, the U.S. government began a major push for standard electronic bills for procurement transactions in 2016. To this end, the Federal Reserve Bank released a white paper, *U.S. Adoption of Electronic Invoicing:*

Challenges and Opportunities, in 2016. As the white paper points out, in addition to reducing the cost of processing bills and more accurately capturing the status of transactions and data, the adoption of standard electronic bills can also shorten bill review cycles, promote prompt payments, and achieve dynamic discount transactions. In furtherance of this goal, the U.S. government has mandated the use of standard electronic bills for all federal government procurement by the end of fiscal year 2018, which means that 19 million bills from the U.S. federal government need to become electronic. According to the U.S. Office of Management and Budget estimates, in 2016, for example, the government procurement amounted to US$460 billion, and the full use of standard electronic bills can allow the government to accurately grasp the transaction data, monitor the status of prompt payment, and estimated to save US$260 million in costs.

8.2.5 Key Elements for Restricting Payment Delays

From the abovementioned restrictions on payment delays in several developed countries, it is clear that the rule of law is the rock upon which business civilization is built. In the absence of institutional safeguards, the profit-seeking nature of the economy will distort the rules for the normal operation of business, resulting in a situation of mutual violations and harm everywhere. As a result, on the one hand, large enterprises bully SMEs with extremely long payment terms and no repayment due; on the other hand, SMEs do not repay bank funds and use such nonrepayment as a powerful tool to threaten the government (the more bank loans an enterprise has, the more the government dares not let it close down). Worst of all, once this state of payment delays spreads, the culture of "treating delays as reasonable and bullying as customary" will become a catalyst for corrupting business civilization. Therefore, enacting laws to restrict payment delays as soon as possible is the key to truly boost the development of MSMEs and the healthy and orderly development of supply chain finance. Generally speaking, the key elements to restrict payment delays are as follows:

(1) Establishing ex ante and ex post whole process control systems. Inter-enterprise payments are a series of money flows accompanied by transactions and the agreements made between the parties in the course of transactions. Therefore, effective containment of

large enterprises using their rights to oppress upstream MSMEs requires strict control over transaction behaviors and transaction processes, and also credit policies to effectively overcome payment delays by large enterprises to small enterprises (Pike & Cheng, 2001). In terms of the transaction process, one aspect that needs to be regulated is the payment periods. Strict control over the payment periods agreed between upstream and downstream enterprises may prevent the occurrence of the phenomenon of possible appropriation of SMEs' funds. As shown in the preceding regulations in Western developed countries, such an ex ante preventive measure usually limits the maximum payment periods of downstream enterprises to upstream enterprises, which is the bottom line of laws and regulations. Moreover, in order to prevent small enterprises from acquiescing to the extension of the payment period for fear of losing their market or the power of large enterprises, many countries have established the right to recourse. In other words, after terminating a transaction with a large enterprise, SMEs can bring a lawsuit for its payment delays within a certain period of time. In addition to these ex ante measures, ex post compensation mechanisms need to be put in place. Once a delay in payment by a large enterprise or other downstream organization to an SME has occurred, the SME should be compensated for the delayed payment, which can be either in the form of penalty interest or additional compensation. Penalty interest is designed to force large businesses to compensate for the costs incurred by occupying small businesses' capital. From the practice of Western developed countries, these costs are very high, generally equivalent to the benchmark interest rate plus 8%–15% (generally, the benchmark interest rate in the US is 2.25%–2.50%, that in Europe is generally 0, and that in the UK is about 0.75%). These penalty interest rates can be considered very high in Western developed countries. Penalty interest is created out of the difficulty in obtaining capital and the high opportunity cost of capital for SMEs, so their capital being occupied hurts them very badly. For this reason, many countries have very strict control over large downstream enterprises, which is the basis of fair trade and business ethics. Apart from penalty interest, additional compensation is also a mechanism of ex post compensation. That is, on top of the penalty interest, an additional sum is added to the cost of the downstream organization defaulting on its accounts with the SMEs in order to regulate the delays. By doing so, not only are SMEs compensated, but also large downstream organizations are given a warning.

(2) Pioneering role of government agencies, public utility departments, and state-owned enterprises in prompt payment. From the practices across developed countries, government agencies, public utility departments, and state-owned enterprises are often subject to more strict prompt payment requirements. For example, the US requires the federal government to complete the review of bills, review of orders, and payment within 15 days, thus ensuring that small businesses can receive funds in a timely manner. The reason for such regulation is that government agencies, public utility departments, and state-owned enterprises represent the credit of society as a whole and of public administration, and this credit is the basis for the regulation and development of the whole society. Since government agencies, public utility departments, and state-owned enterprises are the main bodies that embody the integrity and credit of commercial transactions, restricting payment delays should start with government agencies, public utility departments, and state-owned enterprises in terms of institution building. Based on the demonstrative effect of these public sectors, all enterprises in the business community will be positively impacted.

(3) Promoting electronic invoices and electronic documents to create a fast-confirming, low-cost, and efficient payment environment. There is another infrastructure that needs to be built and promoted as soon as possible in the process of accelerating payments to SMEs, which is electronic documents and invoices. Electronic documents and invoices can not only effectively restrict irregularities in transactions and prevent tax arbitrage and other behaviors, but also accelerate the speed of document delivery, reduce the tedious works of examining and verifying paper documents and invoices, and decrease operational costs. More importantly, the adoption of electronic documents and invoices can effectively use Internet technologies to quickly and accurately confirm the rights and promote the realization of prompt payment. An important reason for the current poor flow of capital between organizations or enterprises is that large enterprises do not conform the rights to the transactions of upstream SMEs, which directly results in payment delays and also hinders financial institutions in supply chain finance

from better-serving SMEs and helping solve working capital problems. Therefore, another important factor in addressing payment delays is to limit the nonconfirmation of rights to the transactions by large firms or institutions. One solution to this problem is to promote online transactions, especially electronic documents and electronic invoices, which can set a good institutional premise for solving payment delays.

(4) Raising prompt payment to SMEs as a social responsibility of large enterprises (especially listed companies) and establishing a good business civilization. Prompt payment is not only a precautionary measure to prevent large enterprises from using their rights to harm the interests of small enterprises but also a social responsibility of large enterprises. Many developed countries have established relevant systems to require large enterprises to announce the status of payments to small enterprises. For example, the EU has required listed companies to voluntarily announce the payment periods to small businesses every two years since 2018, which is necessary for the construction of a business civilization. Therefore, incorporating the disclosure of such information into the public regulation is also an important tool for institution building.

8.3 Security Interests System in Supply Chain Finance

In addition to such basic elements as accounts receivable and payable, another basic element of the operations of supply chain finance is chattels. From the practical situation, most SMEs basically do not have real estates, but only have chattels in the forms of accounts receivable, products (inventory), equipment, and so on. Apart from using accounts receivable to obtain working capital to solve their liquidity, another element that may allow them to obtain capital is chattels. The space for this element is huge in China. With a GDP of about RMB 90 trillion and total assets of five to seven times the GDP, of which chattels account for about 75%, the total amount of chattels in China should be between RMB 350 and 500 trillion. However, despite the fact that China has such a large amount of chattels, there are huge risks in chattel financing. In particular, after the Shanghai steel trade case in 2012 and the Qingdao port case in 2014, financial institutions have a great fear of inventory financing because the inventory can be effectively supervised, but in the event of an accident, financial institutions are worried about the ability to make effective disposals to cover the corresponding risks. For this reason, in addition to strengthening the operational and monitoring capabilities of financial institutions, it is more important to establish a sound security interest management system.

8.3.1 Basic Status of the Legislation on Security Interests

Broadly speaking, there are two classifications of agreements on security interests, both of which are important in civil law system (i.e., civil law system) and common law system (i.e., Anglo-American legal system). The first classification is a true secured transaction or a transfer of ownership or goods. The former means that the creditor obtains security interests in the collateral, while the latter means that the creditor obtains not only security interests in the collateral but also a direct right in rem or ownership. Theoretically, any party should not be subject to the rules of secured transactions if it has not provided the collateral for security purposes However, under several legal systems, some transfers of ownership are also subject to such legislation. The second classification is the division between possessory security rights and nonpossessory security rights. Nonpossessory secured transactions are very clear and allow the debtor to continue to use the collateral for the duration of the loan, while the creditor obtains a security interest in the collateral. In contrast, possessory secured transactions do not allow the debtor to use the collateral for the duration of the loan until the debtor pays the debt. A very clear distinction is made in the law. Generally, in common law system, a possessory security is called a "pledge" and a nonpossessory security is called a "mortgage" or "charge." In civil law system, a possessory security is called a "pignus" and a nonpossessory security is called a "hypothec." The *Security Law of the People's Republic of China* stipulates that "mortgages are not subject to transfer of possession, while pledges must be subject to transfer of possession." It means that a possessory security is known as a pledge, while nonpossessory security is known as a mortgage.

The legal regulations of security rights play a very crucial role in guaranteeing the promotion of supply chain finance, especially the business activities of warehouse receipt pledge and chattel mortgage. Therefore, the US and the UK, which have adopted a common law system, and other countries such as Russia, which has adopted a civil law system, all have well-developed provisions in their laws in this regard. The key statute regulating security rights in the US is Chapter IX of the *Uniform Commercial Code* (commonly referred to as UCC 9), which was enacted under the *Uniform Trust Receipt Act.* The first official version of the UCC 9 was formed in 1952 and amended in 1972 to become the basis used by the states in adopting commercial laws. Currently, most states in the US have adopted the UCC 9 when engaging in security interest transactions, with Pennsylvania being the first state, in 1953, and Louisiana being the last state, in 1974. Unlike the U.S. law, which is clear and concise in its provisions, the U.K. legal system is relatively conservative and leans more toward a strictly traditional common law system (Keinan, 2000). In other words, the U.K. regulation prefers to retain the old and traditional set of rules rather than new ones. Russia had more restrictions on security interests before 1992. For example, the *Soviet Civil Code of 1964* excluded buildings, installations and equipment from the assets that could be mortgaged and pledged, which was clearly detrimental to the development of security interest transactions. Realizing that the *Soviet Civil Code of 1964* failed to promote economic development, Russia invited some scholars (including British and Russian) to draft a more advanced legal system in 1992 to accommodate the rapidly developing security interest transactions. Two and a half years later, the *Civil Code of the Russian Federation* was adopted and became the most important legal system regulating security interests.

In general, the laws governing security interests in these countries pursue four strategies to boost business activities through the expansion of commercial and consumer credit (Welsh, 2003). These strategies are as follows:

(1) Simplifying the rules of creating a security. The core of warehouse receipt pledges and chattel mortgages is the chattels in the transactions. Therefore, what things can be used as collateral or pledge for secured transactions becomes the focus of legal regulation. The laws of various countries have developed a set of simple and convenient rules for the creation of security in chattels of any nature. Overly complex rules may limit the development of security interests and impede effective commercial lending, so one of the important directions of change of the laws of various countries is how to make the collateral fully used and the procedure for creating security easy and efficient. In terms of the current regulations of secu-

rity interests, first of all, collateral for commercial credit loans has been greatly expanded to the scope that anyone can use chattels as security and anyone can accept chattel as security. Collateral can be a chattel of any nature, whether it is tangible or intangible. For example, collateral can be equipment, inventory, accounts receivable, or real property. The expansion of this scope allows for better adaptation to the financial needs of any enterprise in its daily operations. Especially for a large number of SMEs, which hardly own a large amount of real properties, but only technologies, products, and accounts receivable, the expansion of collateral allows SMEs to smoothly and quickly obtain the necessary capital for production operations from financial institutions with products, technologies, and accounts receivables. In addition, another key change in modern security interests is the significant simplification of security procedures. A single agreement is all that is required to create a security, eliminating the cost and expense of amending lending contracts under other laws. In contrast, traditional laws often required several separate contracts for the use of chattels as collateral, each with its own set of legal requirements. Besides, different chattels may be registered with different departments. As a result, modern secured transactions have reduced the cost of and removed the barriers to commercial and consumer credit loans by simplifying the rules.

(2) Clarifying the rights of competing creditors. A prerequisite for lenders in financial activities to be willing to lend funds to borrowers is that all information is symmetrical, thereby effectively reducing uncertainty. In particular, lenders want to know their rights against other competing creditors in advance of any disputes. Only when lenders are able to clearly define their rights and minimize uncertainties of all kinds, the channels and scale of financial lending can be greatly expanded. However, in modern supply chain operations, the commercial environment is characterized by constant uncertainty, while, in particular, the items used for security may be subject to various legal claims such as previous mortgages, pledges, leases, and various agreements. Under the traditional legal framework, it was very difficult to reveal the true status of encumbrance on chattels, and sometimes it was impossible for the lenders to know the true status of the collateral. Following an uncertain event, various creditors may emerge at any time in the future to claim ownership of the collateral and have priority over others. In

addition, there may be much uncertainty about the collateral itself, such as the possibility that it may be sold, leased, or even transferred with the real properties. Obviously, these uncertainties are a great obstacle to the promotion of security interests. For this reason, another focus of legal development in various countries is to estimate in advance the conflicts between competing creditors and to establish detailed and precise priority rules for the purpose of solving the possible disputes in advance. In this way, lenders are able to assess risks more prudently and minimize the risks.

(3) Public and efficient disclosure of information. Another critical element in the development of security interests is the efficient and public disclosure of information. Once a chattel is used as collateral for a loan, the borrower, the lender, and all other interested parties want an easy, fast, accurate, and inexpensive means to know the actual status of the collateral and whether any other parties have a claim to it. The laws governing secured transactions fulfills this desire by establishing a registration (filing) system. This registration system differs from the traditional registration systems. Apart from overcoming the time-consuming nature of traditional registration systems and the difficulties and costs associated with meeting compliance requirements, this modern registration system must achieve simplified and low-cost registration disclosures. In this regard, the emerging technologies such as the Internet provides a good means and avenue for efficient and convenient registration and disclosure. In other words, the registration of secured transactions can be achieved through the Internet, which is currently used as a regulatory tool by the laws of various countries. This Internet-based registration system makes it possible for any borrower to present items on the Internet the moment they are pledged or mortgaged, without delay, without uncontrollable risk, and without unnecessary formality or expense. All that is required is a simple "alert" indicating the parties to the transaction and describing the condition of the collateral. This registration system can operate on a user fee basis without the use of taxpayer money. Typically, the "alert" information recorded in the registration authority (such as the time of registration, the extent of the registered mortgage or pledge, etc.) will determine the date of the lenders' priority over the collateral in the event of competing claims to the same property. The first registrant usually has the highest priority.

(4) Efficient enforcement of security interests. In most cases, debtors are able to repay the creditors through their productive operations. However, in the event of default, the lenders will bear the financial risk that accompanies it. A well-developed security enforcement mechanism can significantly reduce the cost of this risk to the lenders; conversely, a weak enforcement mechanism can significantly increase the cost of risk to the lenders, thus discouraging the development of credit loans. For this reason, the laws and regulations of various countries also have given much attention to the enforcement of security interests. By ensuring that the lender has rights in the collateral in various default situations and that the lender can dispose of the collateral in the most economical manner and to the maximum extent possible, the laws governing secured transactions reinforce the enforcement mechanism for the security. Besides, the regulations in this regard, in fact, also favor the borrower, because the lenders are obligated to act in a commercially reasonable manner and will also be liable for any improper conduct.

8.3.2 *International Practice in the Regulations of Security Interests*

The practice of the US, the UK, Russia, and other countries with respect to security interests shows that the main regulation is focused on the legal scope, the creation of security interests, the publicity and priority of security interests, the enforcement of security interests, as well as the registration of secured transactions (Azadeh, 2018; Welsh, 2003).

(1) Legal Scope of Transactions in Security Interests

A clear definition of the scope of application is central to the establishment of laws on secured transactions in each country; otherwise, various disputes may easily arise from an unclear definition. In general, the laws of these countries have considered the following aspects in determining the scope of application:

a. the transactions covered and excluded. The laws of various countries generally cover all transactions capable of creating security over chattels, including traditional legal forms of transactions such as pledges, mortgages, and consignment sales. In addition, other legal forms used in many countries include chattel mortgages, floating charges, assignments of rights, lease-purchase agreement, financial leasing, retention-of-title sales, and title-granting security. The laws of secured transactions can effectively exchange all of these forms of transactions. In other words, while these transactions remain in their original form, they must be regulated by various provisions of secured transaction laws. The applicability of chattels that are fixed to real properties, such as wells, pumps, or generators, should also be made clear in the national security interest laws. These laws also should clearly state its applicability to the properties that are connected to land and are movable, such as crops, trees, minerals, and so on. In addition, in the case of a lease transaction, the borrower may be defrauded because the creditor may conceal the fact that it does not own the leased property. The regulation adopted in the US brings long-term leases within the legal scope of secured transactions for the purpose of alerting potential creditors and determining priority ranking. An unconditional sale of accounts receivable differs from an assignment of a security over accounts receivable in that the former sells the accounts receivable to a buyer who assumes the commercial risk of collection, while the latter, like other secured transactions, provides security support for the obligation owed, even if the rights assigned are insufficient to repay the entire debt. However, it is important to note that the sale of accounts receivable is still in the coverage of the current legal system. Similarly, potential lenders want the benefits of a registration alert system and priority rules, regardless of whether the accounts receivable are sold unconditionally or assigned as a security. For reasons of policy or practical necessity, some transactions are deemed to be best excluded from the laws on secured transactions. For example, the salaries of personnel and the rights of assignees to collect payments, and so on are generally considered to be excluded from the scope of a security interest to the extent possible.

b. Linkages with other laws are also a current regulatory concern in various countries. Existing laws may often conflict with the laws relating to secured transactions, and the abovementioned countries have suggested that existing laws should be carefully assessed and amended to eliminate conflicts. In addition, these countries believe that the possibility of conflicting provisions arising in the future should also be considered. Besides, in the process of developing other types of laws, such as those dealing with contractual capacity, agency, fraud, insolvency, and so on, there is a need to consider how to strengthen the position of the laws on secured transactions.

c. The nature of and agreement on the security interests. The laws of various countries consider that the creation of a "security interest" creates the security in chattels. The security interest should be treated as a right in rem. In other words, the true right in the collateral can be seized without unnecessary formal requirements, as long as the contracting parties agree. A security interest can arise in any present or future collateral, without subsequent amendment to the agreements or give additional alerts to the registration and filing authority.
d. Definition of the collateral. Modern secured transaction laws define collateral very broadly and include assets in the following forms: tangible chattels of any nature; intangible properties of any nature; quasi-tangible properties such as certificates of ownership, financial instruments (bills), credit sales contracts, lease agreements; chattels, tangible or intangible, that can arise in the future; chattels that are fixed or gradually fixed to real properties; properties that have been separated from the land and entered into commercial circulations such as trees, crops, and minerals; proceeds of the collateral.
e. Subjects that can provide and accept security. Generally, the laws define the subjects that can provide and accept security as natural persons and virtual persons of any nature, such as corporations, non-governmental organizations, and any entity that has the right to contract. However, in order to avoid abuses of secured transactions, many laws consider it appropriate to limit certain collateral as well as specific subjects in certain situations. For example, it is considered inappropriate for a consumer to create a general security interest in durable consumer goods as a way of credit purchase.

(2) Creation of a Security Interest in a Collateral

The laws of various countries specify when a security interest occurs after the creation of security in the collateral. If it is based on a real right in the debtor's property, the secured party has the right to take the property and dispose of it as soon as the debt is owed. However, a security interest also applies to rights that arise in the future, that is, property that does not exist until a future time. For example, after the debtor enters into a security agreement that includes future equipment and inventory, the creditor makes periodic cash advances secured by the equipment and inventory in accordance with the agreement, and the creditor subsequently purchases the goods and equipment. As the creditor makes purchases from time to time, the security interest is automatically fixed to those goods and equipment, while the goods and equipment are subject to the realization of the security interest. Therefore, the laws of various countries provides that a security interest is deemed to be created in the collateral as long as the following three conditions are met: (a) the debtor enters into a written agreement granting the security interest and describing the collateral. A waiver of the written agreement is also permitted if the secured party is in possession of the collateral; (b) the debtor has rights in the collateral; and (c) the secured party gives the debtor a certain value.

(3) Publicity and Priority of Security Interests

In pledging or charging assets to lenders for the purpose of obtaining loans, conflicts between competing claims to collateral should be taken into account. These conflicts can be resolved in advance through publicity of the collateral or pledge and clear and precise priority rules, thus giving the creditor the certainty needed to grant loans. For this reason, it is very well regulated in the laws of various countries. Publicity is a powerful tool for creditors against other third parties that also claim rights in the collateral, and is designed to maximize the protection of creditors' interests. Generally, there are three common types of publicity: (a) possession, when creditors can confirm a security interest by taking possession of most forms of tangible collateral; (b) registration, when creditors can confirm a security interest by leaving alert information with the registration authority; and (c) automatic publicity, when the security interest occurs. In the case of durable consumer goods, the common practice is that if a security interest already exists in the item, the security interest should be deemed to be automatically publicized without any registration. Publicity is also important for the protection of creditors' interests. In addition, many transactions follow the general priority rules, except in certain special or exceptional circumstances. General priority means that if no security interest has been publicized, the security interest that occurs first shall have priority. The creditor of the security interest that is registered or otherwise publicized first shall has priority among all security interests that have been publicized, so this rule is often summarized as "priority for first registrants."

In the case of a security right, the creditor' rights in the collateral may conflict with prior or future creditors. In addition, it is possible for the debtor to sell or organize the collateral. As a result, the laws of various countries provide for more detailed provisions in these aspects. Generally, after publicity of the collateral, the creditor acquires the security interests. Before accepting some goods, the buyers or lessees should search for registration and publicity information to check for the existence of a security interest in the goods, thereby avoiding disputes over the security interest. However, this principle is not always consistent with the principle of maximizing commercial interests. For example, Section 320 of the UCC 9 provides that in certain specific situations (namely, FMCG industry), a buyer's interest is protected by the law even if the buyer can discover the security interest by checking the records of the registration authority or even if the buyer knows of the existence of the security interest. Assuming that a bank has a security interest in a supermarket's inventory and the supermarket sells some groceries to a consumer who does not pay the bank, then, according to the general rules, the bank shall be entitled to get those groceries back from the consumer. However, this practice may discourage the consumer from shopping from the supermarket, thus limiting the underlying sales operations. For this reason, the laws on secured transactions protect a buyer from a security interest if the buyer is a consumer in an "ordinary course of business."

There is also a special situation under the laws of various countries, that is, the super-priority rule, or "priority for latter registrants." The super-priority rule provides that a purchase money security interest is superior to a general security interest, even if it is registered later. If a bank has a publicized security interest in all existing and future equipment acquired by a company, but a car dealer sells a truck to the company on credit and confirms its security interest in the truck by registration, the car dealer's security interest is a purchase money security interest, which is superior to the bank's general security interest, but the scope of its priority is limited to the value of the truck. This situation can also occur with respect to inventory. For example, a bank has confirmed a security interest in the existing and future inventory of a supermarket, but an appliance company provides inventory financing to the supermarket for the purchase of televisions under its brand and also publicizes its security interest in those televisions. In such a case, thanks to its position as a creditor of the credit purchaser, the appliance company has a security interest that is superior to the bank's.

In addition to collateral in the general sense as mentioned above, there is a special category of collateral that is chattels fixed on real properties, such as mortgages on land and assets on land (including wells, pumps, and generators), air conditioners and other appurtenances on buildings, and cash crops on land (including crops, trees, minerals, etc.). The ambiguity in the definition of chattels and real properties can very easily lead to disputes. Therefore, legal regulation of these issues becomes necessary. The laws of various countries make it clear that fixtures are fixed or intended to be fixed to land or buildings and that this gives rise to goods based on rights in real property. The secured transactions laws of various countries stipulate that the following: the creation of security interests in fixtures is permitted; the continuity of security interests in those goods shall be ensured when the goods become fixtures; publicity of security interests in fixtures is permitted, preferably through registration in an real property registration authority; generally, if the mortgagee registers first, the interests of the mortgagee shall be protected and they shall have priority over the interests of the holders of the security interest in the fixture; a purchase money security interest in the fixture shall be superior to previously registered mortgages. Crops to be harvested, trees to be cut, and minerals to be extracted can also give rise to a conflict between the creditor and the mortgagee. If the debtor is in possession of real property or has its own interest in the real property registered, the debtor should have priority where there is a conflict between a publicized security interest in the three types of properties mentioned above and the interest of the owner or mortgagee.

These regulations mentioned above provide a clearer picture of the competing relationships of collateral. In addition to the issue of competing creditors, another issue that is regulated in the laws of various countries is the lien, namely the claim arises from a creditor in a nonconsensual transaction. For example, if an enterprise fails to pay taxes on time, the tax authority may obtain a lien on the chattels of the enterprise. In the case of a judgment, the prevailing party has the right to seize the properties of the losing party. According to the bankruptcy law, the bankruptcy administrator has the right to control and dispose of the properties of the bankrupt enterprise. These cases also have the issue of competing claims, that is, how to configure the rights between the security interest holder (creditor) and the lien holder. The regulations of various countries provide that the priority of the tax authority is subject to the "first in time" rule, the same way as other competing claims are treated. The secured transaction laws often determine the priority of a lien in a judgment based on the time of registration of the security right holder.

As far as security interests are concerned, there is also a situation where the collateral is mixed with other collateral. For example, the issue of mixture arises when a new engine is installed in a car. If a creditor provides a loan for the purchase of a new engine and accepts a security interest in the engine, the security interest will not be lost in the installation activity. If another creditor has a security interest in the entire car, the interests of the two creditors must be separated. The engine financier has a priority in the disposal of the collateral to the extent of its value, which means that this financier can have priority in obtaining the equivalent value of its interest in the engine or can remove the engine from the car and sell it. However, another issue is the mixture of collateral from different debtors. For example, when the corn of one farmer is stored in the same granary as the corn of other farmers, it may be difficult to distinguish which corn belongs to which farmer. In such a case, the laws of various countries may recognize the continued existence of a security interest in a large pile of corn formed by the mixture of collateral and distribute the interests of competing creditors in accordance with each farmer's share in the overall mixture.

(4) Enforcement of Security Interests

Creditors need to take steps to protect their interests in the event of a debtor's default, but without a system to ensure that creditors can enforce their interests in a timely, efficient, and cost-effective manner, security interests cannot effectively support the development of supply chain finance. For this reason, the laws of various countries also pay great attention to the enforcement of security interests. In general, they regulate this issue in the following ways: (a) The right to possession and disposal of the collateral. Effective enforcement of a security interest requires that the creditor be given the power to take possession of and dispose of the collateral. The proceeds of disposal (whether from the sales of the collateral in whole or in part or from lease, royalty or other disposal) must be effectively used to pay enforcement costs and reduce the secured obligation, and there should be no conduct that prevents, or even arbitrarily terminates, the creditor' ability to obtain value from the collateral. (b) Legal proceedings are minimized or avoided. Under U.S. law, possession of tangible chattels without legal process is permitted, provided that the recovery of the chattels is conducted in a peaceful manner. For situations where the debtor's consent cannot be obtained, the law of the US and other countries provides that legal proceedings should be limited to an expedited hearing and an order depriving the debtor's possession of the collateral and giving the creditor the power to take possession in order to dispose of the collateral. The hearing may be limited to the following: (1) the agreement where a security interest is found to be provided in the collateral and (2) the fact of default. In the case of accounts receivable, the creditor should have an express, direct right to act on the accounts receivable, that is, to notify the payer to pay the creditor rather than the debtor. (c) The transfer of ownership to the buyer. The laws of various countries provide for the confirmation of the transfer of full ownership to the buyer, which means the express protection for the buyer of any collateral, even if the sale is subsequently found to be procedurally defective. (d) The creditor's responsibility for enforcement. In exercising its right to possession and disposal of the collateral, the security interest holder is obligated to act in a commercial manner. The creditor must be protected from unwarranted attacks on the manner in which it disposes of the collateral. The creditor is also liable for abuse of the right to possession and disposal of the collateral.

(5) Registration of Secured Transactions

Registration of secured transactions is an important means for protecting the interests of creditors. The purpose of the registration authority's collecting, storing, and retrieving information about security interests is alerting and establishing priority. Alerting means that the registration authority remits and publishes information about security interests to alert possible future creditors that a security interest in someone's chattel already exists. Establishing priority refers to confirming the timing of registration and determining the priority of different competing claims on the chattel. The main issues involved in registration of secured transactions are where to register, what to register, and when to register.

In terms of where to register, it is most efficient to have only one registration authority, except for land-related collateral. Crop-related alert information is best registered in a central registration authority, while other land-related collateral information is more appropriately registered in the land registration authority. Registration contents include alert information on fixations, trees to be cut, and minerals to be extracted. The registration authority is a commercial credit service whose main duties include the following: receiving alert information and amendments thereto, renewal and termination instructions; assigning a unique code to each alert information; indexing alert information by registration number and debtor name; and providing search reports upon request by the public. It is important to note that the registration authority does not have a supervisory function. Moreover, the registration authority does not have the authority to deny anyone's request for registration, except in a few cases defined by law.

In terms of what is registered, the alert information should be concise and the identity of the debtor and creditor and a description of the collateral are also required information to be registered. Although the debtor's authorization is necessary for registering the alert, the authorization need not appear in the alert. For example, if the debtor's authorization is contained in another written document, the creditor may place that document in the relevant loan file. In actual legal practice, a security agreement signed by the debtor is also considered to constitute authorization to register the alert. The alert may involve more than one debtor or more than one creditor. If the alert involves multiple creditors, each creditor is entitled to amend, survive, or terminate its security interest in this alert without affecting the security interests of the other creditors therein. The laws of various countries provide for the manner of amending the alert when information about the debtor or creditor changes or when the description of the collateral changes. If a new collateral is added at the time the alert information is amended, the effectiveness of the alert with respect to the additional collateral begins on the date of registration of the change. In addition, the laws should also provide for the duration of alerts and establish easy procedures for renewing or terminating the alerts. Once the secured obligation is repaid, the debtor should have the right to request the creditor to terminate the alert.

When to register is also a very key aspect. It is clear from the laws of each country that information about the collateral should be registered before credit loans are granted. The laws also make it clear that registration prior to the signing of the security agreement is also permitted. This pre-registration method provides creditors with greater peace of mind and a better guarantee of priority.

Besides the above provisions, along with the development of Internet technologies, Internet-based electronic registration has also become an important institutional safeguard for the implementation of chattel financing in many countries. The key to the implementation of electronic registration lies in the laws to give full validity to electronic data as a proof of registration. In other words, searchers must be able to exercise their rights by virtue of electronic data and documents, without being required to check paper documents. In addition, the laws should also address the issue of authenticity in electronic data, which requires the development of appropriate methods and rules.

8.3.3 *Current Development of Security Interests in China*

The improvement of laws and regulations regarding security interests is crucial to promote the development of supply chain finance in China. The most representative law in the development of China's systems is the *Property Law* enacted in 2007, which provides the basic legal framework for chattel financing. From the practical perspective of supply chain finance, this law has the following characteristics:

(1) The scope of collateral is expanded. Article 180 of the *Property Law* provides that the scope of collateral is expanded to include the following: (a) contractual rights to operate land such as wasteland acquired by tender, auction, public negotiation, and so on; (b) raw materials, semifinished products, and products; and (c) buildings, ships, and aircraft under construction. The last paragraph of this article provides that "other property not prohibited by laws and administrative regulations" can also be mortgaged. It can be seen that China's *Property Law* has expanded the scope of collateral, especially the scope of chattels that can be mortgaged. Similarly, in terms of pledge, in addition to bills of exchange, checks, promissory notes, bonds, certificates of deposit, warehouse receipts, and bills of lading, Article 223 of the *Property Law* expands the properties that can be pledged to: (1) fund shares and equity interests that can be transferred; (2) property rights in intellectual properties such as registered trademarks, patents, and copyrights that can be transferred; (3) accounts receivable; and (4) other property rights that can be pledged according to laws and administrative regulations.

(2) The *Property Law* introduces and establishes a registration system. Article 226 of the *Property Law* stipulates the following: "If the pledge is made with fund shares or equity interests, the parties shall enter into a written contract. If the pledge is made with fund shares or equity interests registered with the securities registration and

clearing institution, the pledge shall be established when the securities registration and clearing institution registers the pledge; if the pledge is made with other equity interests, the pledge shall be established when the administration for industry and commerce registers the pledge." Article 227 of the *Property Law* stipulates the following: "If the pledge is made with property rights in registered trademarks, patents, copyrights and other intellectual property rights, the parties shall enter into a written contract, and the pledge shall be established when it is registered by the relevant competent authorities." Article 228 of the *Property Law* stipulates the following: "in the case of pledge of accounts receivable, the parties shall enter into a written contract and the pledge shall be established from the time of registration by the credit agency."

(3) A distinction is made between the entry into force of a security contract and the creation of a security interest, reducing the likelihood of an invalid security contract. Article 15 of the *Property Law* provides the following: "Unless otherwise provided by law or agreed in the contract, contracts concluded between the parties concerning the establishment, change, transfer and extinction of real property rights shall take effect from the time the contract is established; a failure to register a property right shall not affect the effectiveness of the contract"; Article 188 of the *Property Law* provides the following: "the mortgage shall be established from the effective date of the mortgage contract; a failure to register the mortgage shall not be used against bona fide third parties"; Article 189 of the *Property Law* stipulates the following: "If an enterprise, individual businessman or agricultural producer makes a mortgage on chattels as stipulated in Article 181 herein, it shall be registered with the administration for industry and commerce of the place of residence of the mortgagor. The mortgage shall be established from the time the mortgage contract takes effect; a failure to register the mortgage shall not be used against bona fide third parties." From the above provisions, it is clear that the security contract is effective from the time the contract is established, provided that there is no invalid situation as stipulated in the *Contract Law*. Before the collateral or pledge is registered or delivered, the right holder can ask the debtor to fulfill the obligation of registration or delivery of the collateral or pledge on the basis of a valid contract.

(4) Registration compensation is incorporated. Article 19 of the *Property Law* provides that if the right holder or interested party believes that there is an error in the matter recorded in the real property register, then he or she may apply for correction of the registration. If the right holder recorded in the real property register does not agree to the correction, the interested party may apply for the registration of an objection. After the registrar has registered the objection, if the applicant does not sue within 15 days from the date of registration of the objection, the registration of the objection shall expire. In addition, Article 21 of the *Property Law* specifies compensation for two cases, providing legal remedies for financial institutions to reduce the registration compensation: (a) parties who provide false materials to apply for registration, causing damage to others, and (b) registrars who cause damage to others due to registration errors.
(5) The cost of realizing the security interest is reduced. Article 208 of the *Property Law* provides that "if the debtor fails to perform the debt due or if the circumstances agreed upon by the parties for the realization of the pledge occur, the creditor shall be entitled to priority in repayment with respect to the chattel." Article 220 of the *Property Law* provides that "the pledgor may request the pledgee to exercise the pledge in time after the expiration of the performance period of the debt; if the pledgee does not exercise it, the pledgor may request the people' court to auction or sell the pledged property."
(6) The floating mortgage system is established. Articles 181 and 189 of the *Property Law* stipulate that "enterprises, individual entrepreneurs, and agricultural producers and operators may use the chattels they own and will own, such as production equipment, raw materials, semi-finished products and products (except for ships and aircraft under construction), to establish mortgages," and specify that the mortgagee may include both existing and future properties in the mortgage, and that the mortgagee may keep the mortgage in a liquid and renewed state for its own business needs until the legal cause of curing the mortgage occurs.

It should be said that the introduction of the *Property Law* has established the system of security interests in China, which has become the most important legal basis for promoting chattel-based supply chain finance, although there are still many details and management to be further improved. In addition to the *Property Law*, another key system is the *Specification for Third Party Inventory Collateral Management* (hereinafter referred to as "Specification"), a national standard jointly drafted by China Banking Association and China Association of Warehousing and Distribution. The formulation of the Specification has undoubtedly played a positive role in promoting the standardized and orderly development of logistics finance, as the current legal system of China is still facing a series of challenges: (a) imperfect laws and regulations. On the one hand, the *Property Law* only specifies that inventory can be used for secured financing, but does not provide for the registration and publicity of financing with inventory as security; on the other hand, the *Contract Law* does not provide for the details of inventory management contracts under secured financing; (b) lack of professional and consistent standards. Unlike general warehouse management, inventory management under secured financing has its own special characteristics and is more risky than general warehouse management. The existing warehouse-related standards in terms of technology, operations, services and personnel qualifications, and so on cannot fully meet the requirements of inventory management under secured financing; (c) lack of industry regulation. The lack of comprehensive understanding of the risks of such a special warehousing business has led to the fact that China has neither introduced a relevant administrative licensing system nor developed an enterprise filing system so far. Meanwhile, the status of existing enterprises engaged in inventory management under secured financing is not clear in China, and there are no specific qualification requirements for enterprises carrying out this business. For this reason, the Specification attempts to effectively address the problem of the nonapplicability of existing regulations to security interests in practice. Specifically, the Specification has the following main characteristics:

(1) The first joint drafting by the China Banking Association, China Association of Warehousing and Distribution, lenders, and secured inventory management companies ensures that the content of the Specification is comprehensive, objective, fair and operable.
(2) The Specification provides for the first time the basic requirements for the management of the secured inventory by the three parties (namely, the lender, the third-party manager and the borrower), under the two types of security (namely, mortgage and pledge),

ensuring the connection of the responsibilities of the three parties and avoiding the entanglement of responsibilities among the three parties.

(3) The Specification distinguishes and defines two types of management (i.e., "supervision" and "monitoring") and different management responsibilities for secured inventory for the first time. In order to solve the long-standing dilemma of having only one "pledge custody agreement," the Specification provides for separate agreements for "supervision" and "monitoring," depending on the geographical location of a particular warehouse and the degree of control.

(4) The Specification clarifies for the first time that "supervision agreement" is treated as "storage contract" and "monitoring agreement" is treated as "commission contract," solving the long-standing problem of unclear nature of "pledge custody agreement" and difficulty in determining the responsibility.

(5) The Specification clarifies for the first time the prerequisites, subjects, and requirements for issuing warehouse receipts for secured inventory, distinguishes four business scenarios, namely "pledged warehouse receipts supervision," "pledged inventory supervision," "mortgaged inventory supervision," and "mortgaged inventory monitoring," gradually realizes inventory warehouse receipts and electronic warehouse receipts, and fundamentally guarantees the authenticity and uniqueness of warehouse receipts.

(6) The Specification specifies for the first time that "in the case of secured inventory management, the information about the management enterprise, secured inventory and warehouse receipts shall be registered and published in the relevant public information platform," which fully reflects the principle of process supervision and post-supervision of the secured inventory management enterprise.

Specifically, according to the provisions of the Specification, the obligations assumed by the lender under a supervision agreement include the following: appointing a third-party management enterprise for the secured inventory and confirming the specific warehouse; requiring the borrower to assume responsibility for the intrinsic quality of the secured inventory and the quantity of items in the package; giving instructions on the quantity of secured inventory to be discharged, the time of discharge, and the control quantity of the minimum inventory; entering the specific warehouse from time to time to inspect and take inventory of the secured inventory; require third-party management enterprise to provide, receive, hold, and keep warehouse receipts, documents, ledgers, records (including electronic or visual records), and other documents or other copies relating to the management of the secured inventory. The obligations of the borrower include the following: delivering the secured inventory with clear ownership to the specific warehouse; providing relevant ownership, product name, specification, model, quantity, weight, origin, and other relevant information of the secured inventory (if there are special requirements for the warehousing of the secured inventory, a written explanation should be provided to the lender and the secured inventory third-party management enterprise); being responsible for the intrinsic quality of the secured inventory and the quantity of the items in the package; cooperating with the third-party management enterprise in performing its responsibilities and cooperating with the lender in establishing, maintaining, and exercising the security interest. The obligations of the third-party management enterprise include the following: ensuring that the specific warehouse has the conditions and environment for supervising the secured inventory and maintaining the legal possession and use of the specific warehouse at all times during the supervision period; inspecting and accepting the weight, quantity, and appearance quality of the secured inventory and issuing warehouse receipts and other relevant documents (if there is any other agreement on the quality of inventory and the quantity of items in the package, the agreement shall apply); properly storing the secured inventory and mark the secured inventory (notifying the lender in a timely manner if the secured inventory is lost, damaged, in shortage, has abnormal quality change, or suffers insurance accident, judicial compulsory measures taken on the secured inventory, ownership dispute, theft, or similar circumstances that may endanger the lender's rights and interests); taking inventory and checking the inventory in a standardized and accurate manner, and shifting, moving, exchanging, and releasing secured inventory according to the lender's instructions, or controlling the minimum inventory of secured inventory, and cooperating with the lender to check inventory and reconcile accounts; standardizing and accurately issuing, preparing, updating, filing, maintaining, and submitting the documents, ledgers, records (including electronic or visual records), and reports related to secured inventory management to the lender; cooperating with the lender to establish, maintain, and exercise the security interests.

Under a monitoring agreement, the obligations of the lender include the following: designating a third-party management enterprise for the secured inventory and identifying the specific warehouse; holding the borrower liable for the quantity, quality, value, and security of the secured inventory; and supervising the payment of related expenses by the borrower (if it is the responsibility of the borrower to pay for the management of the secured inventory). The obligations of the borrower include the following: ensuring that the specific warehouse has the conditions and environment for storing the secured inventory, and being responsible for the security of the specific warehouse; assuming responsibility for the quantity, quality, and value of the secured inventory, properly storing the secured inventory and marking the secured inventory; and cooperating with the third-party management enterprise in fulfilling its responsibilities. The obligations undertaken by the third-party management enterprise include the following: counting the quantity of the secured inventory and reporting to the lender; conducting on-site monitoring of the secured inventory in the specific warehouse; inspecting and recording the borrower's secured inventory management activities and reporting to the lender; and promptly reporting to the lender if the secured inventory is shifted, moved, exchanged, or removed from the warehouse in any way without the lender's consent.

8.3.4 Key Elements for Further Improvement of the Security Interest Systems

Based on the above international and Chinese developments in security interests, we can see that a perfect legal system of security interests is an institutional guarantee to promote the development of supply chain finance based on chattels and warehouse receipts. A lack of a sound regulatory system may prevent warehouse receipts and chattels from entering into supply chain finance, which is the reason why many financial institutions currently avoid talking about chattels. Despite the great efforts made in this regard, China still needs to take the international legal construction as a reference for continuous improvement and amendment, mainly including several points:

(1) The regulation of security interests needs further refinement. As can be seen from the experience of the US and other countries, security interests involve very complex business activities and need

to take into account various possible situations and the points that need to be regulated in detail, such as the aforementioned legal scope, creation of security interests, publicity and priority of security interests, enforcement of security interests, registration, and so on. Overly general provisions may cause problems of incompatibility and nonapplicability, while unclear definitions may also give rise to many disputes in the course of financial transactions. Although China has enacted the *Property Law* in 2007, Chapter IV of which defines security interests and establishes a corresponding regulatory system, some aspects of the provisions are merely broad without detailed explanations. Therefore, a corresponding interpretation is needed to clarify the specific issues; otherwise, it is difficult for both credit institutions and judicial authorities to follow.

(2) The same registration system should be implemented for accounts receivable and inventory. In order to ensure the interests of creditors, uniform registration, publicity and search of collateral is an important aspect promoted by the laws of all countries. Currently, two major agencies are responsible for registration publicity and searching in China. One is the inventory and equipment mortgage registration of the Bureau of Industry and Commerce, but this system has not yet established a nationwide unified Internet-based public notice and search platform for security interests, as a result of which there are difficulties in searching, and there are problems in adapting to the development of security interest transactions; the other is the first national Internet-based public notice and registration system for security interests launched by the Credit Reference Center of the People's Bank of China in October 2007, and its functions have covered most security interests such as accounts receivable, inventory, warehouse receipts, and other chattels. We should say that this system is of great significance in promoting the development of security interest transactions and supply chain finance in China. Therefore, China needs to set up systems and regulatory requirements so that all transactions in security interests can be registered, publicized, and searched on the platform.

(3) The management of the third-party collateral industry should be clarified and professional collateral supervision should be promoted. The management of third-party collateral directly serves supply chain finance and is the key to protect the interests of creditors. Once there is a problem in collateral management, it will gen-

erate huge financial risks. Therefore, strengthening the management of third-party collateral supervisors becomes an important institutional guarantee in supply chain finance. All developed countries have regulatory systems in place for this industry. The World Bank Group also advocates regulation when helping developing countries to develop this industry. In contrast, China currently lacks appropriate regulation for the industry of third-party collateral management, with neither a corresponding licensing system nor a filing system and clear entry conditions, which is clearly not conducive to the development of security interest transactions. Many serious frauds and defaults in China over the years (e.g., the Shanghai Steel Trade case in 2013 and the Qingdao Port incident in 2014) were all triggered by inadequate collateral regulation. Therefore, strengthening the governance and management of this industry has become an urgent task for the development of supply chain finance.

(4) A series of other legal systems should be adopted to support the enforcement of the security interests system and to protect the rights and interests of the creditors. In supply chain finance, financial institutions usually appoint third-party collateral management enterprises to manage and monitor the collateral when they carry out inventory financing. However, in case of economic disputes, some borrowers may take advantage of the convenience of the supervised warehouse within their own factory to make malicious robbery. Even if the financial institution and the third-party management enterprise call the police, such a case will be recognized as an economic dispute. This situation undoubtedly has a significant detrimental effect on securing the transactions and discourages financial institutions from promoting this financial business. In response to this situation, many developed countries have enacted very strict regulations. For example, the U.S. law provides for criminal conviction of a borrower who is suspected of transferring inventory with a value of US$500 or more in bad faith. Accordingly, the development of security interests in China also requires other laws for support and protection.

(5) Standard electronic warehouse receipts should be vigorously developed and secured property interests transactions based on electronic warehouse receipts should be implemented. The development of security interests also needs to make full use of Internet technol-

ogy to realize online security, online financing, and online management through standard electronic warehouse receipts. The benefit is that on the one hand it can effectively reduce human errors, reduce operating costs, and avoid possible disputes; on the other hand, standard electronic warehouse receipts are more favorable to push forward the development of security interest transactions, making registration, publicity, enforcement, or supervision, be convenient, efficient, and effective and eliminating information asymmetry. Therefore, the security interest transactions based on standard electronic warehouse receipts will be an important direction for future development.

References

Azadeh, N. (2018). The Lending and Secured Finance Review – Edition 4 – The Law Reviews. Retrieved March 2, 2019, from https://thelawreviews.co.uk/edition/1001198/the-lending-and-secured-finance-review-edition-4

Coface. (2018). *China Corporate Payment Survey 2018: Payment delays increase despite rapid and robust growth.*

Dacin, M. T., Oliver, C., & Roy, J. (2007). The legitimacy of strategic alliances: An institutional perspective. *Strategic Management Journal, 28*(2), 169–187.

DiMaggio, P., & Powell, W. W. (1983). The iron cage revisited: Collective rationality and institutional isomorphism in organizational fields. *American Sociological Review, 48*(2), 147–160.

Gloria, O. P. (2014). *Regulatory issues affecting trade and supply chain finance.* APEC.

Keinan, Y. (2000). *The evolution of secured transactions.* Unpublished Working Paper, University of Michigan Law School.

North, D. C. (1987). Institutions, transaction costs and economic growth. *Economic Inquiry, 25*(3), 419–428.

Oliver, C. (1991). Strategic responses to institutional processes. *Academy of Management Review, 16*(1), 145–179.

Parliament, U. K. (1993). Capital and private finance. *Column, 938.*

Pike, R., & Cheng, N. S. (2001). Credit management: An examination of policy choices, practices and late payment in UK companies. *Journal of Business Finance & Accounting, 28*(7&8), 1013–1042.

Scott, W. R. (2008). *Institutions and organizations: Ideas and interests.* Sage.

Selznick, P. (1949). *TVA and the grass roots: A study in the sociology of formal organization* (Vol. 3). University of California Press.

Selznick, P. (1957). *Leadership in administration: A sociological interpretation.* Cal.

Song, H. (2019). The development trend of China's supply chain finance. *China Circulation Economy, 33*(03), 3–9.

Suchman, M. C. (1995). Managing legitimacy: Strategic and institutional approaches. *Academy of Management Review, 20*(3), 571–610.

Tim, M., & Sarongrat, W. (2017). *The Domino Effect: A study for Sage*. plumconsulting.co.uk.

Welsh, A. (2003). *Secured transactions law: Best practices and policy options*. University of Maryland, IRIS Center, Paper, (03/06).

CHAPTER 9

Integration of Transaction and Financial Asset: The Future of Intelligent Supply Chain

9.1 Introduction

Following the gradual development of industrial supply chains, especially the increasing emphasis on global optimization and management, supply chain finance is increasingly moving out of the edges of mere short-term capital lending and toward working capital optimization of the whole enterprises and even the entire industrial supply chains (Gelsomino et al., 2016; Tate et al., 2019). In other words, supply chain finance is not only about the act of financing but also about how to help the enterprises and the many stakeholders in the chain to optimize the capital flow therein and improve the efficiency of the capital chain based on the industrial supply chain. To this end, financial instruments, financial activities, and financial participants are also increasingly diversified and collaborated for the purpose of global capital optimization of industrial supply chains, thus forming the financial ecosystems. The global capital optimization in supply chains often involves many operational links, and different links have different operational characteristics, and their needs and uses of funds are quite different; likewise, different participants have different characteristics that result in corresponding credits and risks, and their corresponding methods of funds management also vary from participant to participant; the assets in the supply chains also have various forms, and the management and application of each form of assets are also dissimilar. Therefore, the use and management of assets in capital optimization are widely

H. Song, *Smart Supply Chain Finance*,
https://doi.org/10.1007/978-981-16-5997-3_9

different. Under such a situation, relying solely on financial tools and financial participants cannot adapt to the goal of global optimization of supply chain funds; rather, it requires the synergy of multiple financial participants, the integrated use of various financial instruments, and the close combination with industrial activities under the facilitation and management of ICT (i.e., integrated ABCD) to form systematic financial solutions. To wit, the high integration of transactions and financial assets is the next direction and the future of intelligent supply chain development, and is also a topic that needs to be explored in the development of supply chain finance today.

9.2 Financial Bullwhip Effect and Financial Supply Chain

Supply chain finance has a broad meaning and narrow meaning. In a narrow sense, supply chain finance is short-term capital lending for specific SMEs in specific links based on supply chain operations (Gelsomino et al., 2016), such as financing based on accounts receivable and payable (factoring, reverse factoring, forfaiting, etc.), financing based on chattels (warehouse receipt pledge, inventory pledge, etc.), and financing based on advance payment (confirming storage financing, etc.). The characteristics of this supply chain finance are as follows: (1) Fund providers are the lenders who supply funds, and they make independent decisions on whether to provide funds to borrowers on the basis of determining their risks. In addition, financial service providers rely on the supply chain operation information and supply chain risk control to ensure the safety of funds and effectively gain financing benefits. Therefore, their risk assessments and risk preferences determine the implementation and effectiveness of lending decisions (Chmielewski, 2005). (2) Assets owners are the borrowers that need funds and some of them are SMEs in the supply chains who apply for working capital necessary for their production operations through supply chain inventory (Pfohl & Gomm, 2009; Randall & Theodore Farris, 2009; Hoberg et al., 2017) or chattels and fixed assets (Pfohl & Gomm, 2009; Gomm, 2010) or through credit generated by being embedded in the network structure (Song et al., 2016; Caniato et al., 2016; Carnovale et al., 2018; Song et al., 2018; Zhou et al., 2018). Therefore, supply chain finance in the narrow sense is a point (lender)-to-point (borrower) relationship, but this relationship is created under a supply chain operation scenario. However, in a broader sense, supply chain finance is not exclusively for a specific SME, but for all participants in the supply chain. In addition, the purpose of supply chain finance activities is not only the act of financing but also to optimize the capital flow in the whole supply chain through various financial instruments, so as to ensure the smooth supply chain operations and to improve the efficiency of industrial operations and ultimately the competitiveness of the industry (Caniato et al., 2019). Therefore, in the broad sense of supply chain finance, the capital providers are not only the traditional financial institutions originally engaged in the lending but also various other traditional and new financial institutions. Likewise, the asset owners are not only the SMEs in certain specific links but also the participants in the whole supply chain operations, namely the supply chain operators in the N-tier supply chains. As the fund providers and asset owners become diversified and diverse, the supply chain operations and supply chain finance will undergo fundamental changes. The driving factor of such changes is that the industrial bullwhip effect and the financial bullwhip effect begin to intertwine, while the effective reduction of the impact of these two bullwhip effects requires not only the optimization of asset owners, but also the synergy and integration of fund providers. Only in that way can the overall supply chain efficiency and effectiveness be promoted.

9.2.1 Financial Bullwhip Effect

The bullwhip effect, also known as the Forrester effect (Forrester, 1961), is a phenomenon in which small changes in orders and inventories cause large fluctuations along the supply chain from the bottom to the top (Lee et al., 1997). The reason for such large fluctuations is that the separation and independent decision-making of each link in the supply chain leads to inaccurate orders and excessive inventories, which puts enormous pressure on upstream production and purchasing. This cascading of pressure creates a bullwhip effect. Metters (1997) quantitatively portrayed the existence of the bullwhip effect on producers. The author argues that to curb the bullwhip effect, it is necessary to achieve a penalty cost between production and expected holding or excess demand, as well as a minimal function of future discount costs minus revenues. The achievement of this goal can increase productivity by 10–30%:

$$f(i) = \min_{y}\{c(y-i) + \int_{0}^{y}[h(y-x) - vx]\Phi(x) \times dx$$

$$+\int_{y}^{\infty}[\Pi(x-y) - vy]\Phi(x)dx + \alpha\left[\int_{y}^{\infty} f(0)\Phi(x)dx + \int_{0}^{y} f(y-x)\Phi(x) \times dx\right]$$

$$\text{s.t.} y \geq i, y - i \leq R / r$$

Wherein, i_t is the beginning inventory; y_t is the inventory before demand and after production; $\Phi_t(x)$ is the probability that demand will be generated in the term *t*; *v* is the revenue per unit of product; *h* is the holding cost per unit; *Π* is the penalty cost in addition to the loss of revenue if demand is not met; *c* is the production cost per unit; and *r* is the scarce resources per unit used to produce a unit of product.

As opposed to the bullwhip effect among producers, there is also financial bullwhip effect. The financial bullwhip effect has not been fully studied by the theoretical community for a long time, until recently when some scholars started to pay attention to it (Torres & Maltz, 2010; Chen et al., 2013; Tate et al., 2019). In fact, the bullwhip effect arises whenever there are changes in the channels between the financial sector and the real industry, especially when there are fluctuations in the channels of capital flows (Vousinas, 2012). The financial bullwhip effect refers to a distortion reflected in the supply chain capital flow, in which the changes in the capital flow in some links of the supply chain cause large fluctuations or even disruptions in the capital flow throughout the supply chain (Tate et al., 2019). The cause of this bullwhip effect is attributed to both the enterprises in the industrial supply chain and the financial institutions that inject funds into the supply chain. In some cases, after receiving the goods, the downstream enterprise does not pay the upstream enterprise in time for internal reasons (e.g., to maintain the adequacy of its own funds and improve its financial performance) or for external reasons (e.g., due to payment cycle problems in conducting business), which directly leads to a shortage of funds for the upstream enterprise. Then, the upstream enterprise have to delay the payment to its upstream enterprise in order to maintain its own normal production and operations. Such cascading delays create a financial bullwhip effect. Also in other case, the upstream suppliers have to offer longer payment terms to the downstream enterprises or tolerate arrears of downstream enterprises in order to expand their markets, while the downstream enterprises further extend the payment periods to their downstream enterprises. Such delays layer by layer can make the downstream enterprises at higher tiers have greater financial pressure, thus creating a financial bullwhip effect. Chen et al. (2011) proposed an index to measure an enterprise's liquidity, namely the solvency ratio (SR). It is the ratio of an enterprise's available liquidity to its net payment obligations at a period of time. If the solvency ratio is defined as SR_j, the liquidity risk of a given enterprise will be ($1 - SR_j$). Below is the liquidity risk of the enterprise from customers:

$$\text{CLR} = \sum_{j=1}^{m} \left(1 - SR_j\right) \times P\_CS_j$$

Wherein, CLR is the liquidity risk from customers, m is the number of m customers the enterprise has, and P_CS_j is the percentage of sales the enterprise makes to customer j.

The supply chain operation process often creates multiple layers of business relationships. That is, customers also have their own customers. When this factor is taken into consideration, it is necessary to modify the P_CS_j:

$$MP\_CS_{jf} = P\_CS_{jf} + \sum_{\substack{i=1 \\ i \neq j}}^{m} \mathrm{I}_{\{j\text{是}i\text{的客户}\}} (P\_CS_{ji} \times P\_CS_{if}) - \sum_{\substack{i=1 \\ i \neq j}}^{m} \mathrm{I}_{\{j\text{是}i\text{的供应商}\}} (P\_CS_{ij} \times P\_CS_{jf})$$

(j is a client of i;

J is a supplier of i).

The modified CLR is: $\text{MCLR} = \sum_{j=1}^{m} \left(1 - SR_j\right) \times MP\_CS_j$.

Similarly, the enterprise's liquidity risk from suppliers is as follows:

$$\text{SLR} = \sum_{j=1}^{n} \left(1 - SR_j\right) \times P\_\text{SP}_j$$

Wherein, *SLR* is the liquidity risk from suppliers, *n* is the number of suppliers the enterprise has, and P_SP_j is the percentage of the enterprise's purchases from supplier *j*.

Similarly, considering the multitier supply system, the modified P_SP_j is:

$$MP\_SP_{fj} = P\_SP_{fj} - \sum_{\substack{i=1 \\ i \neq j}}^{n} \mathrm{I}_{\{j\text{是}i\text{的客户}\}} (P\_SP_{fj} \times P\_SP_{ji}) + \sum_{\substack{i=1 \\ i \neq j}}^{n} \mathrm{I}_{\{j\text{是}i\text{的供应商}\}} (P\_SP_{fi} \times P\_CS_{ij})$$

(j is a client of i;
J is a supplier of i).
The enterprise's liquidity risk from suppliers was modified to:

$$\text{MSLR} = \sum_{j=1}^{n} \left(1 - SR_j\right) \times MP\_SP_j$$

Therefore, the overall requirement to curb the financial bullwhip effect (o-t period) is as follows:

$$v_{(k)} = \min \int_0^t \left(\sum_{k=1}^{p} MCLR_k + \sum_{k=1}^{p} MSLR_k - \sum_{k=1}^{p} C_0 \right)$$

Wherein, K is the participants in the supply chain from 1-p; C_0 is the funds owned by the enterprise at the beginning of the period.

The factors that lead to the financial bullwhip effect are not only the direct impact of capital fluctuations of upstream and downstream enterprises but also the influence of financial institutions. In fact, the role of financial institutions can also have a huge effect on the capital movements of the industrial supply chain, mainly in three aspects: (1) Risk appetite. This is the degree to which an institution actively takes risks and prefers volatility of returns over stability. If a financial institution has a risk appetite for a higher degree of risk-taking, the liquidity it releases to enterprises will increase (Chmielewski, 2005); conversely, if its risk appetite tends to be conservative, the funds it can supply will be limited, which will have a dramatic impact on enterprises' working capital. The release of liquidity from financial institutions can reduce the financial bullwhip effect because it reduces the burden of enterprises' own funds, and with the injection of funds from financial institutions, the harm caused by the lack of funds to enterprises will be weakened even if its downstream or upstream enterprises are not able to pay in time. (2) The amount of funds supplied. If each financial institution provides sufficient funds to the enterprise within a specific time period, the pressure of the enterprise' own funds can be alleviated, and the funds required for its production and operation can be fully satisfied, and its liquidity risk can be reduced (Gomm, 2010). On the contrary, if the funds supplied are insufficient, its liquidity risk will be increased, making any shortfall in operating funds lead to sharp fluctuations in upstream and downstream funding requirements. (3) The cost of funds or interest rates, especially the level of interest rates relative to the cost of own funds or the average cost of funds available in the market. In general, if the interest rate offered by financial institutions is higher than the cost of the enterprise's own funds, or the average cost available in the market, it will be more difficult for the enterprise to obtain liquidity, making the state of capital shortage magnified and driving the financial bullwhip effect. On the contrary, if financial institutions provide lower interest rates, the enterprise can obtain funds at low cost, and the financial bullwhip effect will be well mitigated. Thus, the liquidity that can be provided by financial institutions is as follows:

$$P\_SC_t = \left(it_t - AC_t\right)Q_t\varphi_t$$

Wherein, P_SC_t is the degree of liquidity that the financial institutions can provide in period t; it_t is the interest rate offered by the financial institutions in period t; AC_t is the average cost of funds obtained by the enterprise in period t; Q_t is the amount of funds that the financial institutions can supply in period t; and φ_t is the risk appetite of the financial institutions in period t.

Taking into account the influence of financial institutions, the functional relationship that curbs the financial bullwhip effect is as follows:

$$v'_{(k)} = \min \int_0^t \left(\sum_{k=1}^{p} MCLR_k + \sum_{k=1}^{p} MSLR_k - \sum_{k=1}^{p} C_0 - \sum_{l=1}^{p} P\_SC_k \right)$$

9.2.2 *Financial Supply Chain*

From the above contributing factors to the financial bullwhip effect, it can be seen that curbing the financial bullwhip effect can be done in two directions: (1) communication and synergy among industrial enterprises in the supply chain to promote the smooth flow of funds among organizations (Torres & Maltz, 2010; Wuttke et al., 2013). For example, Wuttke et al. (2013) found in a study that supplier consolidation and cross-department synergies are effective in reducing pre-shipment cash flow risk. This means that coordination between upstream and downstream enterprises can reduce both supply-side and demand-side cash flow risks, which reflects the implication of achieving the minimum of the parameters $MSLR_K$ and $MCLR_K$; and (2) increased liquidity of financial institutions to offset the liquidity fluctuations of enterprises due to their own insufficient financial flows. In other words, the enterprises are helped to expand their credit through the parameter P_SC_K. However, the above analysis of the financial bullwhip effect has shown that the key for financial institutions to expand their liquidity is to realize the financial supply chain.

Financial supply chain is a collaborative system of financial institutions that provides optimized financial resources and processes through effective synergy and mutual multiplier effect, with the help of information and communication technologies (ICTs), to fully serve and empower the industrial supply chains and provide them with comprehensive liquidity solutions. At present, the theoretical community tends to view financial supply chain as the relationships constituted by capital flows in supply chains (Fairchild, 2005; Johnson, 2008; Gupta & Dutta, 2011; Wuttke et al., 2013), and thus considers it as the object of supply chain financial services and optimization. This understanding is obviously a narrow sense of financial supply chain. In fact, the synergy and value activities between financial institutions, as key participants or components in supply chain operations, also have a great dynamic effect on industrial supply chain operations, including capital flow optimization (i.e., supply chain finance) (Blackman et al., 2013). For example, Blackman et al. (2013) noted in a study that "financial supply chains are networks between organizations and banks that coordinate monetary and financial transaction activities through financial processes and shared information systems to support and enable the commodity flow and service flow between trading partners in the product supply chain." Apparently, financial supply chain is a unique management system different from supply chain finance, and its characteristics are mainly as follows: (1) Financial supply chain is a synergistic relationship constituted among financial institutions and between financial institutions and other organizations. The formation of this relationship can truly promote the optimization of capital flow. (2) Smooth implementation of capital and financial transactions requires the management and optimization of financial processes and the sharing of information between institutions. The management of financial processes and sharing of corresponding information is the key to promote financial efficiency and serve the industrial supply chain. These processes and activities are obviously different from the industrial supply chain activities, and they are not just based on the industrial supply chain activities to provide capital services, but involve various financial processes and corresponding information. (3) The purpose of the financial supply chain is to serve the industrial supply chain through the integration of financial resources and the synergy of financial transactions, so as to ensure the smooth operation of its commodity flow and service flow and to promote the effective movement of funds among the enterprises.

In terms of the participants and their roles in the financial supply chain, a large type of participants is the fund providers who enhance the liquidity of industrial funds by financing the industrial enterprises. Such participants include diversified traditional commercial banks of the same type and diversified nonbank financial institutions of different types that provide funds. The synergy of these institutions in enhancing liquidity is mainly reflected in three aspects: (1) Their comprehensive coordination and communication improves the overall risk-taking level. Different financial institutions do not have the same degree of risk-taking. Even for commercial banks, their perceptions of risk are highly variable. Therefore, by introducing more and diversified financial institutions, it is possible to effectively reduce the blockage of capital flow caused by the risk aversion of a particular financial institution. A study on banks by Clark et al. (2018) found that the ability of individual banks to withstand risk is enhanced when cooperative banks adopt asset diversification strategies. Therefore, if different financial institutions can work together, the degree of risk appetite will increase and the liquidity in the industrial supply chain will be enhanced by the increased risk tolerance of financial institutions. (2) The synergy of multiple financial institutions will increase the total supply of funds in the industrial supply chain. Subject to risk appetite, deposit and lending scale limitations and other policy factors, it is often difficult for a single financial institution to meet the capital demand of all industrial enterprises at any time, thus creating a liquidity gap for those enterprises. However, thanks to the cooperation among multiple financial institutions, including commercial banks of different sizes and types as well as other nonbank financial institutions (such as trust companies, fund companies, micro-finance companies, etc.), the lending channels are increasingly diversified and the corresponding supply of funds can be increased (Petropoulos & Kyriazopoulos, 2010), which helps to truly serve the industrial supply chain and alleviate the shortage of working capital of the enterprises. (3) The synergy of multiple financial institutions is also conducive to reducing the interest rate of comprehensive loans. The involvement of multiple financial institutions allows the enterprises in the industrial supply chain to choose different financing channels and amounts in a combined manner according to their own capital needs and affordable interest rates, so as to optimize the cost of funds. The principle is the same as that of investment portfolio (Markowitz, 1952; see Fig. 9.1). In supply chain finance, there is a volatility of returns due to fluctuations in the cost of funds (horizontal axis). The vertical axis is the expected rate of return on funds obtained by the enterprises. On the curve of choice of funds, there is a minimum variance point (MVP) with the lowest return volatility. The portion of this curve above the MVP is the effective boundary of the Markowit financing portfolio. Conversely, if only one financial institution is able to finance industrial enterprises, the overall interest rate will rise because the risk is not diversified.

Another type of participants in the financial supply chain are financial service providers that act as financial intermediaries, such as insurance companies, brokerage firms, derivatives, and so on. Such institutions are essential and important players in the financial supply chain. In the traditional Arrow-Debreu resource allocation model, enterprises and households interact through the market without any role for financial intermediaries. This is because when markets are perfect and complete, resource allocation is Pareto optimal and intermediaries do not improve any benefits (Allen & Santomero, 1997). However, financial intermediaries become increasingly important when markets tend to be complex and have many choices, and there is variability and volatility due to time and space. The early importance lies in overcoming information asymmetries

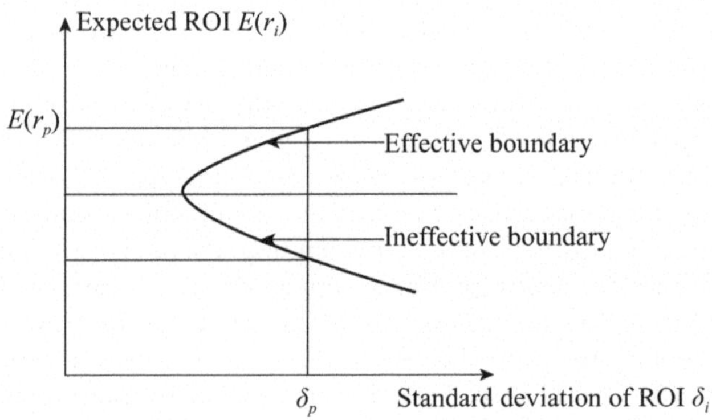

Fig. 9.1 Markowitz investment portfolio

and reducing transaction costs, which is the traditional theory of financial intermediaries. As a very classic paper on financial intermediaries (Leland & Pyle, 1977) points out, financial intermediaries can demonstrate their informed status by investing their wealth in assets about which they have special knowledge. Similarly, Diamond (1984) argued that the intermediaries overcome asymmetric information problems by acting as "delegated supervisors." Many subsequent papers on financial intermediaries have deconstructed the function or role of financial intermediaries based on the view of information asymmetry and transaction costs (Williamson, 1986). However, along with the gradual deregulation of financial markets and the development of globalization, especially the development of modern ICTs, the role of financial intermediaries as information bridges is gradually weakening. The traditional theory of financial intermediaries is no longer able to explain the fact that financial intermediaries are increasingly active and rapidly developing in the new environment and form (Allen & Santomero, 1997; Scholtens & Van Wensveen, 2003). Thus, the role of financial intermediaries is increasingly shifting from reducing information asymmetry by acting as a bridge between lenders and borrowers to providing value-creating financial services, which is the central point of modern theory of financial intermediaries. Specifically, modern financial intermediaries play two main roles: First, they help transfer risk of borrowers and lenders and other participants through various financial instruments. The risk here refers not to the risk of information asymmetries, but to the various types of uncertainty that exist when engaging in business and financial activities. The reason why financial intermediaries play an important role in this aspect is that no borrower or lender can transfer risk alone, but only through the systematic and innovative application of financial instruments by financial intermediaries and the allocation arrangements of various factors can the systematic diversification and transfer of risks be achieved. The second role played by modern financial intermediaries is to cope with the increasingly complex financial markets and activities. The changes and evolution of financial activities driven by the innovation and development of industrial activities have generated many specific service needs, and these needs are often scenario based rather than standardized financial products. Therefore, financial intermediaries are required to gain an in-depth understanding of the scenarios in which transactions take place, interpret the needs and preferences of the parties involved, and translate them into suitable, customized services and instruments (Scholtens & Van Wensveen, 2003). The main functions of a modern bank, for example, are to provide payment services, asset transformation, risk management and information processing, and borrower monitoring. Banks are less able to perform these functions entirely on their own, but often need the assistance of financial intermediaries. Therefore, the function of modern financial intermediaries is to provide value services, and the density of their value services determines the space where financial intermediaries exist and develop.

In the supply chain finance, these collaborative financial intermediaries play two roles. The first role is to effectively reduce lending rates through value services, especially financial scenario-based services. Specifically, financial intermediaries can well reveal the specific business status and financial needs of borrowers, and can effectively develop and apply financial instruments according to the scenarios to facilitate the supply of funds between the borrowers and lenders, as a result of which the lenders can more clearly know the purpose and use of the funds they have supplied, as well as the safety of the funds, and correspondingly reduce the interest rate of the funds. In other words, the lending interest rates show a Gompertz-declining curve trend as the density of value services increases, as follows:

$$it = K \bullet a_1^{bv}$$

Wherein, $k>0$; $a_1<1$; $0<b<1$; $\ln a_1>0$; v is the density of value services.

The second role played by the collaborative financial intermediaries is to increase the lenders' risk tolerance through risk disclosure and transfer functions. In the absence of risk transfer instruments and tools, commercial banks have to refuse to lend money in order to secure funds and reduce the bad debt rate, while this practice may give rise to credit rationing problems (Stiglitz & Weiss, 1981). However, financial intermediaries allow the lenders to lend funds more safely by transferring the risks and by developing various risk transfer instruments. In other words, risk preferences show an upward-downward trend on the Gompertz curve as the density of value services increases, as follows:

$$\varphi = K \bullet a_2^{bv}$$

Wherein, $k>0$; $a_2<1$; $0<b<1$; $\ln a_2<0$; v is the density of value services.

To sum up, financial supply chain is a cooperation system to comprehensively enhance the liquidity of funds through a high degree of synergy and cooperation among various fund providers and financial intermediaries to meet the characteristics of fund operations and demands in the industrial supply chain, aiming to effectively reduce the financial bullwhip effect and enhance the competitiveness of industrial supply chain operations. Therefore, it can be seen that the functions of financial supply chain and supply chain finance are different, as the latter is to bring more financial resources into the industry through industrial supply chain operations and management so as to solve the operating funds of enterprises in the industrial supply chain, while the former is to allow more financial institutions and businesses to be organically connected to systematically serve the industry and realize the optimization of the whole industrial capital flow. There are differences between these two, but they interact and promote each other. Supply chain finance is the basis and scenario for the financial supply chain to play roles, while financial supply chain is a key guarantee for the better development of supply chain finance. The interplay of the two can ultimately realize the return of finance to the real economy, while promoting the scenarios of the real economy to provide the necessary impetus for the innovation and development of finance.

9.3 Innovative Integration Models of Financial Supply Chain and Supply Chain Finance

The innovative integration of supply chain finance and financial supply chain is progressive and evolving in two aspects under the role of ICT, because the change and development of supply chain finance needs the support of ICT, and ICT can promote all kinds of financial institutions to understand and grasp the state of industry and supply chain more clearly, as well as the corresponding capital demand. In turn, the intelligence of the financial supply chain can make financial products or activities more targeted to serve the industrial supply chain operations and transaction parties. Specifically, under the role of ICT, the elements and states of both supply chain finance and financial supply chain have undergone significant changes, and these changes are what drive the innovative integration of the two.

9.3.1 *Changes of Supply Chain Finance under ICT*

In general, supply chain finance has shifted from the original financing between a single lender and SMEs to the optimization of the whole supply chain funding. Vousinas (2018) pointed out that supply chain finance is not just a financing act like reverse factoring, but a collaboration between supply chain partners and financial institutions to optimize operating funds and liquidity management in the supply chain process through the use of financial tools, practices, and various technologies. From this, we can see that the meaning of modern supply chain finance has gone far beyond short-term financing, and is to help all participants in the supply chain network to promote the overall capital flow and reduce the cost of funds therein through various financial tools and methods based on mutual synergistic relationships. In this sense, supply chain finance has changed dramatically both in the structure of operations and in the processes and elements (Blackman et al., 2013).

From the perspective of the structure of supply chain finance, the target of supply chain finance in the past was mainly specific enterprises and the industrial scenarios in which they were based. Or rather, this type of supply chain finance is a financing behavior for specific SMEs in the industrial supply chain. However, along with the development of ICT and the organization of supply chain changing from a single chain to a network ecosystem, the operation scenario of supply chain finance has moved from a single chain to a virtual e-chain, and the target of the financial services is no longer specific SMEs, but groups of interrelated and collaborative SMEs in the virtual e-chain. Virtual e-chain (VeC) is a network platform that allows all SMEs in virtual industry clusters to join at low or even zero cost through the development of high-speed communication network technologies, and these SMEs can collaborate with other participants to forecast, develop, produce, synchronize, and distribute products and services to meet the decentralized and dynamic customer demands (Folinas et al., 2004; Gunasekaran & Ngai, 2004; Manthou et al., 2004). In this scenario, integration means gathering different data sources and presenting real-time content and information to all virtual network participants. Finally, an environment is created in which every participant in the process operations and every activity is integrated (Manthou et al., 2004). Obviously, each participant in this environment is interconnected and exchanges information and resources in real time, while fully maintaining the uniqueness of its operations. This scenario and state of supply chain finance inevitably gives rise to great changes. On the one hand, the targets of financial services are not only some specific SME, but integrated SMEs, because any single point of capital optimization may not enhance the effectiveness of the entire virtual chain. Therefore, an integrated ICT platform is required to support the complex and diverse supply chain finance activities (He & Tang, 2012).

In terms of the processes of supply chain finance, the original supply chain finance relied on specific transactions and logistics in the industrial supply chain (Hofmann, 2005). Whether it is based on the receivable-payable relationship formed by the buyer-seller relationship (Dello Iacono et al., 2015; Lekkakos & Serrano, 2016; Liebl et al., 2016) or on the inventory or stock formed in the supply chain operations (Buzacott & Zhang, 2004; Hofmann, 2009; Zhang et al., 2011), the focus is on the processes formed by specific buyers and sellers in the industrial supply chain. However, under the role of modern ICT, the operational processes of the industrial supply chain have undergone dramatic changes, which are mainly reflected in the gradual shift of transaction and logistics processes from specific buyer-seller relationships to more open and wide business processes. In other words, the processes are increasingly organized in a decentralized manner, relying on Internet platforms to achieve collaboration (Ooi et al., 2011), which in turn drives crowdsourcing relationships in the supply chain operations (Wilson et al., 2018). Crowdsourcing originally refers to the practice of a company or organization outsourcing work or tasks previously performed by employees to a nonspecific (and often large) network of the general public on a free and voluntary basis (Howe, 2008). Since its introduction, the concept has become a realistic and operational business model in the industry (Massa et al., 2017). Effective supply chain operations require full integration of all suppliers and customers to achieve financial and growth goals (Tan, 2001), and enterprises can build close relationships with more customers and suppliers by crowdsourcing, so as to improve their supply chain operational performance. All the information voluntarily provided by customers and suppliers not only helps in product design but also helps in predicting the actual demand for the products before their launch (Lang et al., 2016; Ooi et al., 2011; Simula & Vuori, 2012). This change in process certainly has a huge impact on supply chain finance. First, the operations formed by crowdsourcing are becoming increasingly specialized and integrated. Any organization can integrate specialized skills and raise crowdsourced capital through a wide range of options (Prpić et al., 2015), thus making the processes that underpin the supply chain finance clearer and more competitive, and significantly reducing the risks that are more likely to exist in financial activities. Second, crowdsourcing involves open, broad-based individuals or organizations that drive organizational operations and open innovation through timely and effective interactions (Wilson et al., 2018). As a result, financial activities need to be more targeted and timely, while various financial institutions and financial products clearly need to adapt to these changes in operational processes.

In terms of the elements of supply chain finance, the information elements controlled by the supply chain finance in the past were mainly the information of specific participants and specific links, such as the operating status, credit status, and asset status of specific upstream or downstream enterprises, and so on. However, with the advent of ICT, especially network-based platforms, information not only is rising in the level of integration (Blackman et al., 2013) but also helps financial institutions to understand more transparently the accounts receivable, working capital needs, and liquidity position of enterprises (Fairchild, 2005). In addition, along with the development of Internet information platforms, information digitization for supply chain financial activities is becoming more and more significant, which is reflected in two aspects. First, the activity and popularity of online platforms have a good persuasive effect for lenders. The degree of information accessibility provides a solid basis for accessing financial resources. Besides, the availability of information about the borrowers' credits enhances the informative effect. In other words, this access to information accelerates the learning process and can help the lenders make effective investment decisions (Zhou et al., 2018). Second, ICT-enabled supply chain information platforms are increasingly dynamic, collaborative, SAAS based, and user experience rich (Sharma & Baoku, 2013), allowing for the diversification of information interaction and communication channels and a rise in information and digital density. Both of the changes in information elements present an opportunity for the development of supply chain finance, which not only reduces the risks of financial activities but also provides a good environment and foundation for various financial institutions to effectively intervene in the industrial supply chain.

9.3.2 *Changes of Financial Supply Chain under ICT*

Under the role of ICT, finance has also undergone great changes and development, as the role of finance in the supply chain finance has shifted from original capital financing to global industrial empowerment, with the aim of allowing more financial institutions and more financial tools to serve the industrial supply chain and truly realize the optimal management of global capital flow in the industrial supply chain. In this situation, the core of the changes and development of financial supply chain lies in two aspects: (a) in response to the complex value demands of the industrial supply chain, multiple financial participants collaborate to deeply serve the industrial supply chain activities and provide one-stop financial service solutions; (b) the combination of multiple financial products can reduce the cost of funds or financial risks of the whole industrial supply chain, thus optimizing the source and structure of funds. Specifically, the changes and innovations in the financial supply chain under ICT are mainly the change from limited collaborative services to integrated collaborative services. The specific effects of this shift are as follows:

1. Collaborative cooperation of fund providers leads to enhanced availability of funds, while the cost of funds decreases with the diversification of financing channels. In the supply chain operations, capital constraints have been a key problem for SMEs (Jing et al., 2012; Yan et al., 2014; Yan et al., 2016; Jin et al., 2018). In order to solve the capital problem of SMEs, traditional supply chain finance uses bank credit or trade credit provided by core enterprises to finance the SMEs. Trade credit, one of the two credit systems mentioned above, means that the core enterprises rely on the status of operations and assets to provide financial lending to their upstream suppliers and downstream customers. However, trade credit is often less attractive than bank credit because of its high cost of financing (Jing et al., 2012), while bank credit is less possible to be obtained by the SMEs because their operation characteristics (imperfect financial information, being at the start-up stage, unclear return on investment, no assets available for collateral and pledge, etc.) are prone to information asymmetry and moral hazard (Berger & Udell, 1998; Cassar, 2004; Song & Wang, 2013). For this reason, a challenge for supply chain finance is how to make funds more accessible to the SMEs on the one hand and to make the cost of financing as low as

possible on the other. With the widespread use of ICT, especially the digitized development of information between industrial enterprises and financial providers, as well as the digital connection of information between financial institutions, the accessibility and the cost of financing has been significantly reduced. This is partly attributable to the digitization of information, especially the development of internet platforms, which allows financial institutions to easily obtain the corresponding information and generates the abovementioned persuasion effect and information effect (Zhou et al., 2018). These two effects trigger the effective involvement of more financial institutions in supply chain finance, leading to the economies of scale and scope. Economies of scale in financial operations refer to the expansion of the total supply of funds due to the synergy between multiple financial institutions (including banks) and the cooperation between banks and nonbank fund providers. It should be further noted that the capital flow of the previous supply chain finance was hampered by the fact that any single financial institution, even if it had access to the relevant information, had a different understanding of asset quality due to the different degrees of information data mining and interpretation, especially the different degrees of risk appetite. However, the synergistic cooperation among financial institutions, especially the increasing efficiency of ICT, has improved the overall risk tolerance of financial institutions (Zhu et al., 2016), which in turn has expanded the overall credit lines to enterprises. Economies of scope in financial operations mean that the overall cost of financing is effectively reduced thanks to the effective involvement of multiple types of financial institutions. Under the network platform model, multiple types of financial institutions (including not only traditional commercial banks but also other nonbank financial institutions, such as VCs, trust companies, industrial funds, brokers, etc.) can easily connect to the industrial supply chain, thus jointly promoting services to enterprises in the industrial supply chain and achieving efficient and low-cost capital flows. The basis for the realization of the economies of scope lies in the synergy between multiple financial institutions, which leads to a synthetic effect. In other words, by sharing or pooling information and data, each financial institution can improve the quality of asset information, but bears lower costs of information search, as well as costs of monitoring during and after the event, compared to independent decisions of any financial institution, and also enhances the safety of capital lending (Padilla & Pagano, 2000; Jappelli & Pagano, 2002; Brown et al., 2009).

2. Another effect resulting from closer synergy among fund providers is risk transfer. Modern theory argues that the role of financial intermediaries in the networked information age is no longer to reduce information asymmetry and curb moral hazard in financial activities, but rather a comprehensive risk transfer role (Allen & Santomero, 1997; Scholtens & Van Wensveen, 2003). Traditional supply chain finance is difficult to adopt on a large scale because operations like factoring require the evaluation of historical data to control risk. The vast majority of SMEs have difficulty in presenting good data to support financial activities. Some nonbank fund providers are using IT to venture into lending, yet also face the same barriers (Nienhuis et al., 2013). Along with the development of ICT, some digital services of financial intermediaries are effectively breaking through these barriers. For example, the advent of digital invoicing, online payments, and other means have made instant financing of SMEs possible (Keifer, 2011; de Meijer & de Bruijn, 2014). In particular, third-party payment has become an important way to effectively connect various parties as well as control and transfer risks, because the self-established payment platforms are independent legal entities that provide online fund transfer channels, connecting buyers and sellers, merchants and banks, but being neutral to the buyers and sellers of online transactions, and to e-commerce merchants and banks. These platforms provide a series of application interface programs that integrate the original multiple payment methods into one interface, and is responsible for docking with banks in transaction settlement. Such an approach not only makes supply chain transactions faster and more convenient but also more completely and clearly presents the structure of payment transactions and the nature of relationships between supply chain parties, which undoubtedly plays an important role in effective risk control. Besides, insurance can be a good way to manage the risk of SMEs and reduce uncertainty (Hubbard, 2009). The cooperation between insurance companies and commercial banks can effectively enhance the quality of lending to SMEs (Terungwa, 2012), because through insurance, the risk of potential losses is fairly transferred from commercial banks or other fund providers to other risk takers, allowing fund

providers to finance SMEs more efficiently. Therefore, all these similar financial intermediary services, once combined with the fund providers, can accelerate the liquidity of funds and push down the overall risks of supply chain finance.

3. The effects of synergistic cooperation between financial institutions also include value creation and discovery. In deconstructing modern financial intermediary services, modern financial theory argues that, in addition to comprehensive risk transfer, value creation and discovery based on differentiated customer needs is a key feature in the development of modern financial intermediaries (Allen & Santomero, 1997; Scholtens & Van Wensveen, 2003). The value discovery and creation arise from the aggregation effect and functional enhancement resulting from the synergy between multiple financial institutions. The aggregation effect benefits from the synergy created by the integration of multi-finance business attributes. For example, previous studies have argued that venture capital and bank lending are substitutes, and that venture capital is only chosen when the productivity of a start-up is lower than that of venture capital (de Bettignies & Brander, 2007). In fact, both venture capital and bank lending are important financial resources for start-ups, but they play different roles. In addition to bank lending to solve their working capital problems, SMEs also need venture capital with specific market experience and management know-how to boost their growth (Keuschnigg & Nielsen, 2003). With the widespread use of ICT, the frequent interaction between venture capital and commercial banks is more likely to enhance the competitiveness of SMEs and promote capital efficiency. Similarly, the effective use of futures hedging in the industrial supply chain operations can hedge against currency and commodity price fluctuations, thus helping to reduce the vulnerability of SMEs' supply chains and improve the efficiency and effectiveness of supply chain finance (Hofmann, 2011). The functional enhancement resulting from the synergy of financial institutions refers to the enhancement of financial efficiency brought by the complementarity and interaction of different financial products, businesses or features. This enhancement not only tends to diversify the financing channels of supply chain finance, but also makes it possible to reduce the comprehensive financial risks. For example, ABS based on accounts receivable and payable and various types of assets generated among SMEs operating in the supply chain can

significantly contribute to the resolution of working capital difficulties of SMEs (Kraemer-Eis et al., 2010; Albertazzi et al., 2016). For applicants of financial services, supply chain ABS can enhance asset liquidity and reduce the financing cost, as well as facilitate applicants to move risky assets off the balance sheet and improve various financial ratios. For investors, supply chain ABS is beneficial to expand the scale of investment. In particular, in supply chain ABS transactions, securities with different levels and classes can be designed, often through the segmentation and combination of cash flows. Different classes of securities have different priority of repayment, thus "smoothing out" cash flow fluctuations. Even different types of securities can be combined to form synthetic securities, so as to better meet different investors' preferences for maturity, risk and interest rates.

9.3.3 Innovative Integration Model of Supply Chain Finance and Financial Supply Chain

Based on the above discussion, it can be seen that under the role of modern ICT, supply chain finance and financial supply chain have undergone great changes and development, which are reflected in two aspects: (a) the function of supply chain finance gradually evolves from meeting the financing needs of specific SMEs to integrating various participants, optimizing industrial capital flow, promoting more effective combination of transaction flow and logistics flow with supply chain finance, and enhancing the competitiveness of industrial supply chain; (b) the role of financial supply chain gradually evolves from the financial services of a single financial institution, to the business synergy of limited financial institutions, and eventually to the full synergy among various financial institutions and a comprehensive portfolio of financial services, thus truly guiding finance to serve the industrial supply chain in all aspects and realizing a high degree of integration of finance and industry. The combination of the above two changes has given rise to the following three types of innovative integration models of supply chain finance and financial supply chain (see Fig. 9.2).

Model I is an expanded traditional model (i.e., traditional supply chain financial business). From the perspective of supply chain finance, its service targets may be either specific SMEs, such as upstream and downstream partners of core enterprises, or broader SMEs, such as many SMEs

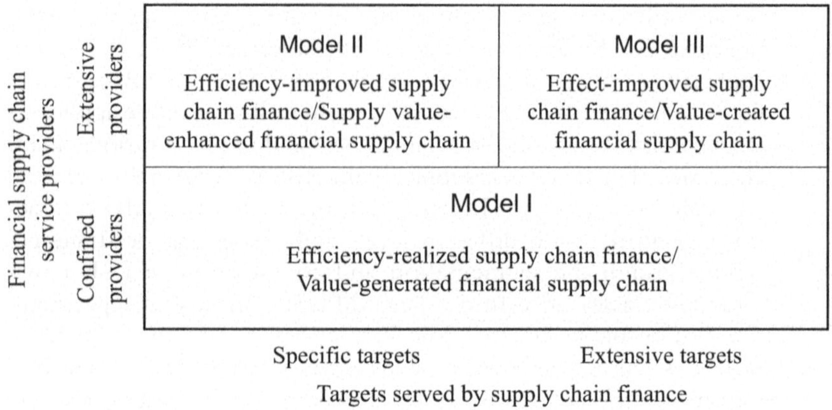

Fig. 9.2 Innovative models of supply chain finance integrated with financial supply chain

that are organically related in the industrial clusters. The goal of the supply chain financial services under this model is to solve the working capital of these specific or broader SMEs, achieve effective financing, and prevent huge risks to industrial operations due to interruption of cash flows. In this regard, the effectiveness of supply chain financial services lies in achieving efficiency, that is, helping SMEs to solve the problem of capital shortage due to information asymmetries. From the perspective of financial supply chain, limited cooperation emerges between financial institutions in this model. For example, a certain degree of synergy is formed among commercial banks, between commercial banks and nonbank financial institutions, or between fund providers and some financial intermediaries. This limited synergy facilitates the effective movement of funds to SMEs and achieves the availability of funds, thus generating value. As can be seen, this model differs from the traditional single financial service provider and financial product in that the limited cooperation between financial institutions mitigates the blockage of capital flow arising from the different understanding and control of SME risks by a single financial institution. In addition, thanks to the incipient synergy among financial institutions, financial institutions can provide a certain degree of customized financial services for the specific state of their customers, or SMEs begin to have the opportunity to choose their financial institutions. From the perspective of risk management and information technology, the basis of risk management in this model is still the industrial supply chain operations (i.e., the creditor-debtor relationships or debt structures formed by transactions between buyers and sellers) and the state of assets formed in the logistics operations of the supply chain (e.g., inventory or fixed assets). Therefore, ICT plays a role in acquiring, integrating, mining, and analyzing information in transaction and logistics flows in a timely manner for decision-making. Moreover, the ability to share this information among these financial institutions becomes a basic guarantee for their synergy.

Model II is a further upgraded and developed model, in which a more adequate interaction between financial institutions and enterprises emerges. Specifically, from the perspective of supply chain finance, although the service targets of this model are still specific SMEs in the industrial supply chain, the objectives of supply chain finance are expanded beyond solving the working capital of specific SMEs to include helping specific SMEs to achieve capital flow efficiency. The model accelerates the velocity of money on the one hand and allows SMEs to fully obtain the capital elements with appropriate comprehensive costs and achieve cost optimization on the other. Therefore, this stage of supply chain finance improves the efficiency of financial activities. From the perspective of financial supply chain, full synergy between financial institutions and between financial products and services emerges. In other words, in addition to the synergy among commercial banks or among fund providers, commercial banks, nonbank financial institutions, investment and financing institutions, and other financial intermediaries also form a wide range of alliance and cooperation to jointly serve specific enterprises in the industrial supply chain. The advantage is not only to realize the effective capital flow to specific enterprises, but also to enhance the industrial competitiveness of specific SMEs through the combination and synergy between financial institutions or services, resulting in value enhancement effect. From the perspective of risk management and information technology, thanks to the full synergy of multiple types of financial institutions serving specific SMEs, the basis of their risk management lies not only in the specific business or the creditor-debtor relationship and assets formed by SMEs in the industrial supply chain but also in the state of money flows as a result of business relationships, including payment and clearing activities. These are all the input elements for risk assessment or management. Furthermore, the credit and reputation of the partner enterprises or stakeholders with whom a given SME forms a transaction relationship are the basis for risk management of various financial institutions. Because of this situation, the role of ICT is becoming increasingly important, as it covers an increasingly wide range of areas (i.e., ICT is required to effectively link specific SMEs, related transaction parties, and different financial institutions to obtain and share digital information on commodity flow, logistics flow, and capital flow in an integrated manner), and ICT is penetrating more and more deeply. Better understanding of the capital status and operation status of specific SMEs is a prerequisite for understanding the details of capital flow and asset flow and achieving asset information penetration.

Model III truly realizes the highly innovative integration of supply chain finance and financial supply chain. Under this model, both fund providers and enterprises have achieved full synergy and cooperation, forming an integration among ecosystems. From the perspective of supply chain finance, its service targets are more extensive, often being lots of SMEs in virtual industrial clusters. These SMEs of different scales and in different links are organically linked together to form intensive competitiveness, and, based on this, various types of supply chain financial services are carried out. From the perspective of the elements of supply chain financial services, this model also not only to solve the working capital of enterprises, but also utilizes integrated supply chain finance activities, including traditional supply chain financial products (e.g., warehouse receipt pledge, inventory pledge, factoring, and reverse factoring), improved supply chain financial businesses (e.g., order financing, and credit financing), and self-financing instruments including dynamic discounts, advance payment discounts, and so on (Bhide, 1992; Winborg & Landström, 2001; Harrison et al., 2004) to optimize the mutual business relationships and transaction structures and to eventually form good business ecosystems (Brown et al., 2007). As a result, the high performance of network-based cash flow is ultimately generated. From the perspective of financial supply chain, the full synergy of multiple types of fund providers and financial intermediaries generates the superimposition and multiplier effect of financial effectiveness, forming a higher-level financial service effect and creating the financial value. This higher-level financial service effect includes the external economies of scale (financial service clustering and capacity gathering realized by the synergy among financial institutions), network effect (decrease in the cost of acquiring financial resources brought by the synergy among financial institutions), and innovation effect (innovation of financial service forms and products achieved by the synergy among financial institutions). Value creation comes from both the benefits or sustained returns generated by financial activities and the benefits brought by supply chain finance, and the potential investment returns from the formation of industrial competitiveness (i.e., the expected returns brought by the financial supply chain through offering comprehensive services to the industrial supply chain, helping realize the industrial ecosystem and enhancing the competitiveness of various industries and segments). From the perspective of risk management and information technology, the risk management under this model is systematic and fully integrates the risk management of industrial enterprises as well as the risk management of financial institutions. The risk management of industrial enterprises requires the full identification of various risk sources of industrial supply chain operations and the use of industrial operation management and modern ICT to achieve effective control of financial risks (Dyckman, 2011; Chen et al., 2018; Pellegrino et al., 2018; Tate et al., 2019; Zhu et al., 2019). At the same time, the aggregated multiple financial institutions, which provide a wide range of financial products and services, also need to adequately identify and evaluate financial resources as well as capital risks to fully meet the regulatory requirements of *Basel III Accord* regarding the capital composition, asset quality, capital adequacy ratio, and other liquidity indicators of banks. Based on the above situation, ICT needs to fully empower both enterprises and fund providers with mobile edge and cloud-based data analysis for decision-making, standard electronic invoices and documents, credit management, as well as comprehensive monitoring and management of models to achieve full digitization in terms of sensing, access and sharing of information about asset and capital flows.

The innovative integration models of supply chain finance and financial supply chain and their features are shown in Table 9.1.

9.4 Cases of Innovative Integration of Supply Chain Finance and Financial Supply Chain

The innovative integration of industrial enterprises and fund providers has become one of the key directions to promote the development of supply chain finance. Many industries and enterprises are carrying out supply chain finance to effectively address SME working capital, optimize cash flow, and even industrial capital flow. Supply chain finance has shown the synergy status of multiple financial institutions and multiple financial products, which has fully proven the features of the above three models.

Table 9.1 Innovative integration models of supply chain finance and financial supply chain and their features

Model *Key features*	*Model I*	*Model II*	*Model III*
From the perspective of supply chain finance	Serving specific or broader SMEs; solving working capital	Serving specific SMEs; solving working capital and optimizing corporate cash flow	Serving SMEs in industrial clusters, solving industry-wide working capital, and optimizing cash flow
From the perspective of financial supply chain	Limited synergy to enhance the availability of funds	Broad synergy to transfer risk and reduce overall financial costs while enhancing the availability of funds	Wide synergy to create the value of financial services for the entire industrial supply chain, combining financing returns with investment returns
Elements of risk management	Debt and assets in the industrial supply chain operations	Operational activities of industrial supply chains, corporate capital flow activities, comprehensive credit, and reputation of affiliated parties	Processes of commodity flow, logistics flow, and information flow generated in the industrial supply chain, integrated financial risk management system (capital composition, asset quality, capital adequacy ratio, and other liquidity indicators)
Results of ICT role	Digital management and sharing of business information	Capturing the information of the industrial supply chain in a wide and deep way by digitization	Full digitization of information on industrial enterprises and fund providers

9.4.1 Model I: Collaborative Supply Chain Finance of Huaxia Bank, CIPC, and Haier

Haier Group's supply chain finance started with the introduction of "Ren Dan He Yi," a business model proposed and named in 2005 by Zhang Ruimin, Chairman of the Board and CEO of Haier Group. In terms of the literal meaning of "Ren Dan He Yi," "Ren" refers to employees; "Dan" refers to user value; "He Yi" refers to the realization of the value of employees and the creation of user value. The basic meaning of "Ren Dan He Yi" is that each employee should face users directly, create user value, and realize and share their own value in creating value for users. Different from the general sense of competition and organization methods, and different from the traditional business models and profit models, the "Ren Dan He Yi" model is an innovative model for Internet enterprises that is in line with the "zero distance," "decentralization," and "non-intermediary" of the Internet era, makes systematic, continuous, and dynamic changes in strategic positioning, organizational structure, operation processes, and resource allocation from three dimensions (i.e., enterprise, employees, and users), and continuously forms and iterates in the process of exploration and practice.

In terms of Haier Group's sales, this model is mainly reflected in two aspects: (1) Haier Electronics, as the group's channel and operation center, provides a social and integrated channel service center; (2) Qingdao Haier, as the manufacturing center, creates a smart home innovation platform. The realization of the above two points requires the flattening of channels and the reduction of unnecessary intermediate links in the process of serving customers, which can make the supply chain more agile in responding to market changes while improving distribution efficiency. After the removal of the intermediate links, the original distributors under Haier's sales line directly contact with the production factories, develop the sales plans, and directly place orders to Haier factories according to their own judgment of the sales situation. This change has led to the financial problems of the distributors. In accordance with the trading practice between Haier and its distributors, the distributors are required to pay Haier an advance payment of a certain percentage of the total purchase price at the time of purchase. Only after the distributors pay this advance will Haier arrange production, and the distributors can take the products only after paying the full amount on the due date. Under the traditional distribution model, the financial problem is not significant as the distributors located at the upper tier of the multitier distribution structure are often able to meet Haier's requirements because of their larger scale of operations and more adequate own funds. However, after the removal of the intermediary links, Haier's downstream sales system has directly connected the production suppliers with the small and medium-sized distributors at the end of the supply chain. For the small and medium-sized distributors who are weak in terms of sales scale and asset status, the financial pressure is huge. In addition, these SMEs do not have sufficient assets or collateral as security, so they can hardly obtain funds from banks or have to bear high financing costs.

In response to this problem, Haier signed a strategic cooperation agreement with CITIC Bank and Ping An Bank in 2014 to realize supply chain financing support for downstream distributors based on Haier RRS official website (http://www.365rrs.com/) and in conjunction with third-party financial institutions. Therefore, industry and finance are integrated together based on the Internet (Song Hua, 2017).

However, since its implementation, Haier supply chain finance still faces huge challenges and unresolved problems, as follows: (1) Although Haier's more than 20,000 distributors are all included in the RRS official website for procurement operations, only a few enterprises can enter the commercial banks' white list. At present, only 200–300 distributors can get "goods collateral loan" and "credit loan," while such financial services cannot meet the thousands of high-quality distributors of Haier; (2) Due to the change of strategic policy, two commercial banks that provided supply chain financial services to Haier adopted a conservative posture in supply chain financial business and were not willing to further expand their business, thus preventing the new competitive distributors from getting the supply chain financial services; (3) Due to different risk control requirements, especially different risk preferences, commercial banks have different understanding of how to carry out supply chain financial business on the basis of effective risk control for industrial enterprises. Commercial banks still have doubts, even though Haier has established a B2B RRS official website and promised that the system is docked with the banks' risk control system and digital information is transmitted to the banks in real time. The reasons are as follows: (1) The data is provided by industrial enterprises, so commercial banks are still apprehensive about the data, even if Haier is a core enterprise; (2) The traditional basis for risk control analysis by commercial banks is financial data, so they do not know much about how to mine and use industrial operation data, thus causing a blockage of capital lending; (3) Due to the strict risk control requirements and the current implementation of the "lifelong accountability" system, commercial banks always stop lending to all other distributors once they find any one nonperforming loan. This capital lending practice has caused great distress to the operations of manufacturing enterprises such as Haier.

Based on the above background, Haier RRS, together with Huaxia Bank and CPIC, tried to increase the scale and percentage of financing for Haier's distributors in early 2019 by using multiple synergies and financial products. The specific business process is as follows (see Fig. 9.3).

First of all, Haier connects its distributor whitelist and B2B platform system to two financial institutions, namely Huaxia Bank and CPIC, so that the two financial institutions can acquire the distributors' operation

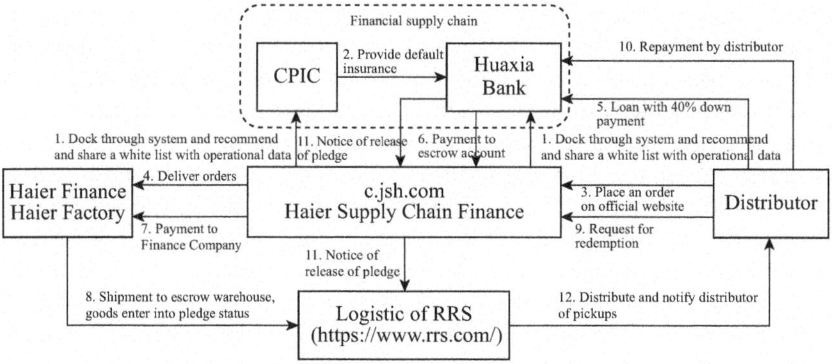

Fig. 9.3 Collaborative supply chain finance of Huaxia Bank, CPIC and Haier

status and all sales end operation data and related financial data in real time for effective risk control purpose. Based on the acquisition and analysis of the above data information, CPIC provides default insurance services to Huaxia Bank for Haier's recommended whitelisted distributors to reduce the risk of default that may arise from Huaxia Bank's credit loan. When a distributor places a purchase order on Haier's platform and needs financing, only 40% of the purchase price needs to be paid down, while Huaxia Bank provides 60% through the financing. After the Haier platform transfers the money to Haier Finance, product production is started. After that, RRS Logistics forms a pledge of the inventory. Before redeeming the goods, the distributor needs to make payment to Huaxia Bank, which notifies RRS Logistics to release the pledge. If there is a default in this process, CPIC will pay out first.

The above three-party cooperation model is beneficial to all parties. For Haier, the synergy between CPIC and Huaxia Bank makes it much more likely that its distributors are financed, thus benefiting more downstream customers and ultimately increasing sales of Haier products. In terms of specific supply chain finance performance, the previous financing scale provided to its distributors (with the cooperation of the original two banks) was about RMB 1.7–1.8 billion, supporting about RMB 4+ billion of Haier's appliance sales, while after the participation of financial institutions (including the cooperation between Huaxia Bank and CPIC, and the participation of other banks), the existing financing scale was about RMB 4+ billion, supporting RMB 10+ billion of appliance sales. About

2000–3000 distributors have been financed. For CPIC, on the one hand, by docking Haier's business platform, it grasps Haier's and distributors' business conditions in real time, effectively assess and judge risks, and design reasonable insurance products to expand insurance business and revenue (their insurance charges are about 1%); on the other hand, CPIC is better integrated into the industry operation, which promotes active participation in supply chain finance. For Huaxia Bank, the synergistic cooperation with CPIC allows it to transfer the risk of lending to SMEs, which is more conducive to supporting more competitive SMEs. In addition, because of the insurance as risk protection, their borrowing cost of capital decreases (currently 30% above the benchmark interest rate), which is more favorable to the development of industrial enterprises.

9.4.2 Model II: Xi'an Qujiang Tou Treasure and JD Supply Chain Finance ABS

9.4.2.1 Xi'an Qujiang Finance and Tou Treasure

Xi'an is a key tourist destination in China. As the first national cultural industry demonstration zone, Qujiang New District is also the main area for Xi'an trillion-level culture and tourism industry. The creation and development of tourism resources require financial support and cooperation. For this reason, under the leadership of Xi'an Qujiang Management Committee, Xi'an Qujiang Culture Finance Holding (Group) Co., Ltd. (hereinafter referred to as "Qujiang Finance") was incorporated in August 2018 with a registered capital of RMB 5 billion. The objective of Qujiang Finance is to focus on the development strategy of Qujiang New District, serve major projects and the development of cultural industry, led by financial innovation, serve the real economy, follow the road of combining industry and finance, and realize the integrated development of finance and cultural industry. Specifically, the main tasks identified by the company are as follows: (a) construction of Qujiang Culture and Finance Demonstration Zone, including the implementation of various financial services such as financial leasing and commercial factoring to support the demand of cultural and creative enterprises in the zone for financial services; (b) PreABS establishment, that is, the establishment of ABS bridge financing to support enterprises in asset securitization. In addition, Qujiang Finance makes guarantee companies to cooperate with enterprise refinancing guarantees and also has established a refinancing fund to give refinancing support to new financial enterprises. Moreover, the company set up a RMB 30 billion M&A fund to support enterprises in the zone to carry out mergers and acquisitions.

In the process of developing supply chain financial business, Qujiang Finance explores the synergy and cooperation of multiple financial institutions or financial products to support and serve industrial enterprises. Many of its financial services not only solve the operating capital of enterprises but also optimize their cash flow and realize investment income. One of the most typical financial products is Tou Treasure. With the cross-border cooperation of multiple parties in the financial field, Tou Treasure breaks the traditional financial business boundaries, realizes the linkage of equity and debt, enhances financing efficiency, reduces financing costs, and optimizes enterprise cash flow and investment returns under the premise of risk control and mutual isolation. The specific business process is as follows (see Fig. 9.4):

First, a VC/PE firm and a commercial bank conduct due diligence on an industrial enterprise, with the aim of effectively evaluating and judging the operation, business model and future development competitiveness of the enterprise. The two parties form a strategic alliance and share information in real time. The VC/PE firm makes equity investment in the enterprise. The enterprise transfers the accounts receivable generated in the process of production and operations to the commercial bank, which finances the working capital to the enterprise. After the business is

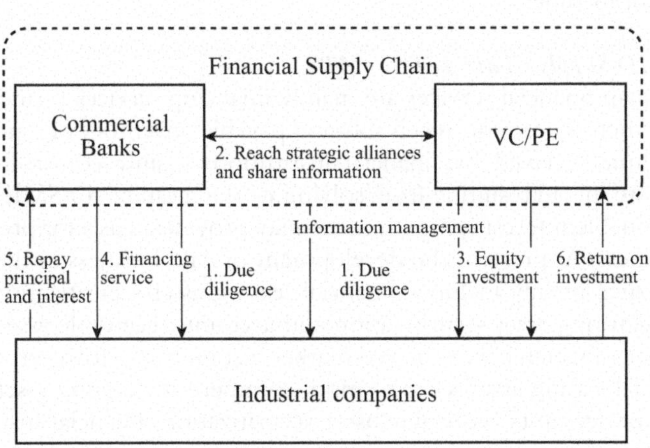

Fig. 9.4 "Tou Treasure" of Qujiang

completed, the enterprise repays the capital and interest to the commercial bank. After the enterprise keeps operating and obtains good growth and development, the VC/PE firm gets the corresponding investment income.

Qujiang Finance's Tou Treasure offers a new framework for supply chain finance development through equity and debt linkage. Through cooperation, VC/PE firms and commercial banks can grasp the situation of enterprises more comprehensively and effectively. Equity investment belongs to medium- and long-term investment and involves relatively large investment amount. Moreover, the profit margin of equity investment is relatively large, but such a lucrative return corresponds to a larger risk. Equity investors also will face the corresponding responsibilities of shareholders after becoming shareholders, and such responsibilities are often closely related to the business conditions of the enterprises. Therefore, a more comprehensive and effective assessment of the target company's business situation, business model, future growth potential and competitiveness in the industry is necessary. These information and data are undoubtedly very important for commercial banks engaged in short-term capital lending, and also help them to reduce the risk of lending funds and the probability of corporate default. In turn, the loan management and post-loan management of commercial banks are also beneficial to the realization of VC/PE firms' income. Only when enterprises maintain good operations and sufficient cash flow in the daily operation process can they ensure long-term sustainable development and obtain future investment income.

9.4.2.2 JD Supply Chain Finance ABS

Supply chain financial services are mainly financing services formed based on assets such as accounts receivable and payable, inventory or equipment. The revenue received by financial institutions mainly comes from the interest rate spread resulting from solving working capital for SMEs. Stable and sustainable interest spread income may provide a basis for promoting ABS business. At present, the development of ABS business in the supply chain finance mainly includes financial leasing asset securitization, commercial factoring asset securitization and accounts receivable asset securitization, all of which have achieved market recognition. However, whether for financial leasing asset securitization, commercial factoring asset securitization, or accounts receivable asset securitization, financial institutions have imposed strict requirements on the underlying assets and strictly limited the access assets with the aim of reducing risks. Moreover, these businesses have commonalities in the core elements of ABS (i.e., credit enhancement), which are mainly reflected in the status of the original interest owners, the senior/subordinated layering design, the overcollateralization of assets, the excess spread, the cash flow transfer and payment/credit trigger mechanism, and the deficiency payment commitment. Depending on the original interest owners and underlying assets, specific different approaches apply, which is one of the reasons why ABS as a new type of structured finance takes precedence over other traditional financial approaches.

JD Group is the largest B2C e-commerce company in China, and became the fourth-largest listed company in China after listing on NASDAQ in 2014, following Alibaba, Tencent, and Baidu. At present, JD Group has JD Mall, JD Finance, Paipai.com, JD Smart, O2O, and overseas business divisions, with over 100 million active users, over 6000 suppliers and tens of thousands of brands stationed on the platform. Relying on the advantages of its strong platform, JD Group's supply chain finance has been developing rapidly. The four financial segments have become the main profit center of the group's businesses, which also provides a good premise for ABS business. Following the successful issuance of the ABS product, JD IOU, the *Factoring Contract Debt Asset-Backed Securities Offering No. 1 of 2016 between JD Finance and Huatai Securities Asset Management* was also successfully issued, with an offering size of RMB 2 billion, behind which the corresponding assets are debt assets of Jingbaobei, and the original interest owner is Banghui Factoring. The senior annual interest rate of this offering is 4.1%, and the subordinated assets account for only 0.05%, making it the first ABS of internet factoring business in the domestic capital market.

9.4.2.3 Key Participants in JD Supply Chain Finance ABS

In addition to JD Mall and its suppliers, law firms, credit rating agencies as well as accounting, and auditing firms engaged in the supply chain finance ABS (see Fig. 9.5), the main participants also include the financial institutions involved in the ABS including the original interest owners, managers, and trustees (see Tables 9.2 and 9.3).

The original interest owner is Shanghai Banghui Commercial Factoring Co., Ltd. According to the registration information of the Industrial and Commercial Bureau, the company's business scope is accounts receivable financing, sales ledger and accounts management, accounts receivable collection, and bad debt guarantee. In order to ensure the quality of clients,

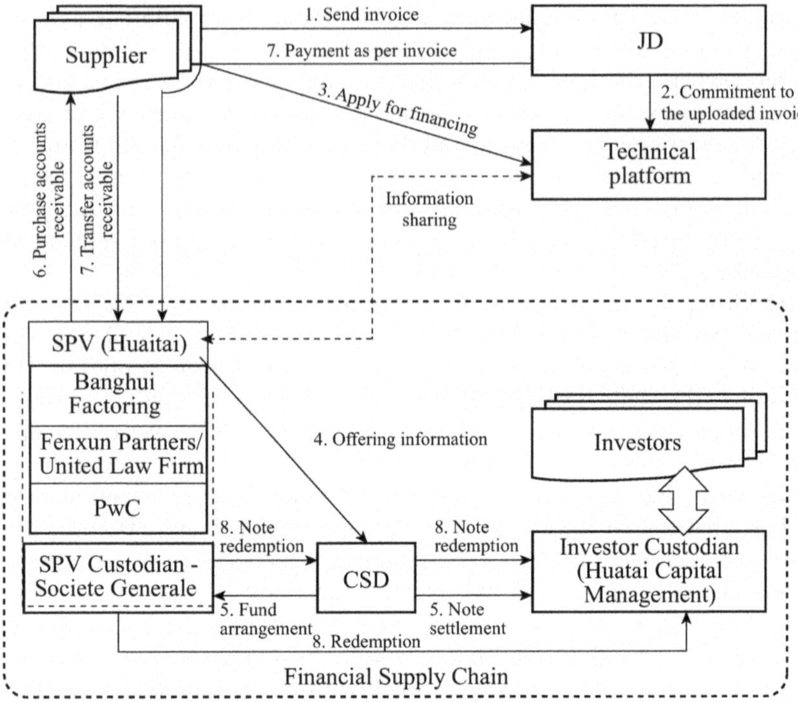

Fig. 9.5 JD supply chain finance ABS

Table 9.2 Key participants of the factoring contract debt asset-backed securities offering No. 1 of 2016 between JD Finance and Huatai Securities Asset Management

Original interest owner/ Asset service provider	*Shanghai Banghui Commercial Factoring Co., Ltd. (Banghui Factoring)*
Plan manager/Promoter	Huatai Securities Asset Management (Shanghai) Co., Ltd. ("Huatai Securities Asset Management")
Trustee	Industrial Bank Co., Ltd. ("Industrial Bank")
Law Firm	FenXun Partners ("FenXun Partners")
Credit Rating Agency	United Ratings Co., Ltd ("United Ratings")
Accountant	PricewaterhouseCoopers Zhong Tian LLP ("PwC")

Table 9.3 Main product and profile of the factoring contract debt asset-backed securities offering No. 1 of 2016 between JD Finance and Huatai Securities Asset Management

Main product	*Basic profile*
Key debtor	Beijing Jingdong Century Trading Co., Ltd. ("JD")
Underlying assets	Contractual claims of the original interest owners under the factoring documents for the provision of factoring financing services to suppliers of JD Mall, an online shopping mall
Product size and rating	The total product size is RMB 2.00 billion, of which the size of senior A securities is RMB 1.440 billion, the size of senior B securities is RMB 559 million, and the size of subordinated securities is RMB 1 million
Senior product structure	During the product revolving period (the first two years), interest is distributed annually; during the product distribution period (the last three months), principal and interest are amortized on a variable monthly basis

Banghui Factoring requires JD self-owned suppliers to have trade cooperation for more than three months before making applications, and mainly uses historical transaction records, sales of suppliers' products, suppliers' cash flow, and suppliers' purchase records from JD Mall as approval criteria. Banghui Factoring is mostly short-term financing, with the shortest financing period of 15 days and the longest financing period of 90 days. The grace period for a single factoring financing does not exceed 3 working days. If the grace period is exceeded, the penalty interest rate will be used to calculate the penalty interest. If the seller is unable to return the amount to the factoring company before the expiration of the maximum financing period, the period can be extended after the factoring company's review and approval. Meanwhile, in order to ensure the safety of the underlying assets, the factoring company has formulated the *Jingbaobei Business Process Management Procedures*, which mainly regulates the approval process, lending management, repayment management, factoring risk control system, and information authority management related to the clients of the product Jingbaobei.

The approval process of Banghui Factoring is set before lending money to clients, and is divided into active factoring and passive factoring. Banghui Factoring may initiate an offer of factoring financing business to the supplier based on the transaction records and products of JD self-owned product suppliers, or the suppliers may actively apply for factoring financing business. After receiving the *Application for Factoring Business*,

Banghui Factoring examines whether the applicant meets the relevant requirements and criteria of the *JD Self-Owned Supplier Application Approval Criteria*. Upon approval, the financing application submitted by the supplier is agreed. After consultation and no objection, both parties determine the terms and conditions of the formal contract text. The basic information of the client mainly includes basic information and data, accounts receivable data, data information under the system, information of each document, transaction history, supplier cash flow, and measurement results under the risk control system. After reviewing the basic information, Banghui Factoring allocates the product ratio to the client. The financing quota of the accounts receivable pool is the product of the effective accounts receivable balance and the financing ratio. The financing quota of the accounts receivable pool is a revolving amount, and the total amount of outstanding factoring financing within the contract period may not exceed the limit of the quota. Banghui Factoring may revoke or change the quota at its discretion.

For the financial factoring business of JD financial supply chain, Banghui Factoring has formulated a strict risk control system for factoring products, which mainly involves supplier approval criteria, basic information audit points, supplier allocation requirements, risk control guidelines, collection and bad debt management guidelines, and so on. In order to control the returned goods after the factoring financing of suppliers, ensure the real sales and reduce the risk of factoring business, Banghui Factoring strengthens the monitoring of suppliers' trade returns, designs the early warning of returns and takes corresponding measures in response to the change scenarios of the amounts of returned goods. For clients with no collection value, Banghui Factoring specifically analyzes their risk characteristics and designates a case-by-case asset preservation plan. For clients with collection value, Banghui Factoring initially determines the level of collection to be taken based on the overdue situation. After determining the collection level, the collection management personnel shall promptly allocate and implement the collection tasks. The collection methods include SMS and telephone collection, on-site collection, and collection by external agencies. If any amount is not fully settled after the collection process, the credit and risk management department will initiate a write-off and the finance department will refer to the relevant write-off laws and regulations for execution. In this way, Banghui Factoring continuously improves its risk control system.

Huatai Securities Asset Management (Shanghai) Co., Ltd. is the proposed manager of this special plan, which is responsible for using the subscription funds paid by the subscribers to purchase the underlying assets, as well as managing and distributing the asset interests of this special plan in accordance with the relevant agreement. As the manager, Huatai Securities Asset Management has the right to appoint a trustee to hold the funds of the special plan, supervise the trustee's behaviors, and take necessary measures to protect the legitimate rights and interests of the asset-backed security holders in case of the trustee's default. In addition, Huatai Securities Asset Management also has obligations, such as providing services to the asset-backed security holders. JD's ABS products, both the ABS product of JD IOU's accounts receivable and the ABS product of accounts receivable factoring, are all managed by Huatai Securities Asset Management. Through many times of cooperation, both parties have formed a tacit understanding on the issuance of products. Moreover, JD's supply chain finance, as a high-quality asset in the market, is also the object of cooperation desired by various financial institutions.

In this special plan, Industrial Bank acts as the trustee, responsible for managing the asset account, ensuring the independence and safety of the funds in the special plan, and protecting the property rights and interests of asset-backed security holders in accordance with the laws. At the same time, Industrial Bank supervises and verifies the management, application, and disposal of the special plan assets of the plan manager (i.e., Huatai Securities Asset Management), and notifies the plan manager in a timely manner to correct any violation of the above provisions. It should be noted that the platform for third-party payment is Chinabank Payments, which is a company affiliated to of JD Group, and its business types include online payment (nationwide), mobile phone payment (nationwide), fixed-line payment (nationwide), and bank card acquiring (Beijing). After several years of development, Chinabank Payments has cooperated with dozens of domestic institutions and has more than 500,000 partners, achieving industry-wide coverage. In this special plan, Chinabank Payments provides an online securitization service platform for the special plan. The plan manager opened a JD Pay merchant account number with Chinabank Payments to monitor the reserve and flow of product funds in real time through the online platform. At the same time, JD Pay has built-in withdrawal and transfer functions. The plan manager connects the JD Pay account to the escrow account of this special plan and manages the funds according to the standard terms and process agreed in advance.

Chinabank Payments only provides the front-end system for the special plan. All users' funds are held in multiple banks for excess reverses opened by them, and these banks supervise the movement of funds in the accounts. Chinabank Payments does not have the right to divert funds from the account unless ordered by the user, determined by a court, and authorized by the user. This provides security for the funds in the special plan.

9.4.2.4 Underlying Assets for ABS of Jingdong Supply Chain Finance

In the plan of Jingbaobei factoring asset securitization product, the specific underlying assets are the financing slips provided by the original interest owners to the suppliers, that is, the financing slips provided by Banghui Factoring to the suppliers of JD Mall. The internal risk control system of Banghui Factoring allows the accounts receivable to be confirmed, thus ensuring the real occurrence of the sales. The original interest owner has extracted some assets from the existing accounts receivable assets through the IT system to form a simulated asset pool. In this plan, FenXun Partners has reviewed the simulated underlying asset pool and examined the factoring financing business contracts, financing applications, opinion letters for business review and other business documents related to the sampled underlying assets as well as the data records of the business system of the original interest owner to ensure that the original interest owner truly, legally, and effectively owns the underlying assets and the ownership of the underlying assets is complete and clear. The underlying assets are specialized property rights, free of encumbrances, attached rights, and transfer restrictions, and no litigation or arbitration is involved.

From the date of establishment of the product-specific plan until the earlier of the expiration of the revolving period or the date of an accelerated liquidation event or event of default, the plan manager may use the funds of the special plan to purchase, on a revolving basis, debt assets of factoring contracts that meet the eligible criteria. The same pooling criteria as the initial purchase are used for the subsequent purchase. At the time of each subsequent purchase of underlying assets, the original interest owner should automatically screen the list of debt assets of factoring contracts that meet the eligible criteria through its IT system. The plan manager has the right to issue subsequent purchase instructions to the asset service provider, specifying the list of debt assets of factoring contracts allowed to be purchased, and authorize the asset service provider to execute subsequent purchases within the scope of such list. The asset service provider manages the subsequently purchased debt assets of factoring contracts in accordance with the agreement, including custody and collection. As of the product issuance date, the outstanding principal balance of the pool was RMB 2192.9214 million, with 1981 factoring contracts involving 514 suppliers (see Table 9.4).

As the underlying asset pool of this product plan is a dynamic asset pool, the underlying assets have not been determined on a case-by-case basis. However, since the underlying assets are purchased from the factoring contract debt assets that meet the qualified criteria in a random cycle, the distribution status of the existing factoring contract debt assets of the original interest owner reflects the distribution characteristics of the asset pool of this special plan to a certain extent.

In the simulated asset pool, we can see that the outstanding balance of factoring contracts with financing ratio (i.e., the ratio of the maximum factoring quota that Banghui Factoring can provide for suppliers to the total amount of suppliers' accounts receivable) above 80% reached 92.38% for 1747 contracts. Overall, the credit level is good.

In terms of industry distribution, Banghui Factoring makes classification according to JD's four business divisions, including IT Digital Purchase Division, Home Appliance Purchase Division, Daily Necessities Purchase Division, and Communication Purchase Division. Among the pooled assets, the daily necessities industry has the largest outstanding

Table 9.4 Asset pool details

Basic information	
Outstanding principal balance of the asset pool (RMB 10,000)	219,292.14
Number of suppliers	514.00
Number of factoring contracts	1981.00
Maximum outstanding principal balance of a single contract (RMB 10,000)	4000.00
Maximum outstanding principal balance of the contracts of a single supplier (RMB 10,000)	11,500.00
Average outstanding principal balance (RMB 10,000)	110.70
Degree of concentration	
Degree of concentration of top 10 suppliers	29.62%
Term of factoring contracts	
Weighted average term of factoring contracts (days)	42.94
Weighted average remaining term of factoring contracts (days)	47.06
Maximum remaining term of a single factoring contract (days)	59
Minimum remaining term of a single factoring contract (days)	30

Data source: Prospectus of factoring contract debt asset-backed securities no. 1 of 2016 of JD Finance balance of 39.86%, followed by the IT digital industry of 28.73%. The development trend of the industries will have a material impact on the overall credit performance of the underlying assets.

Usually, factoring companies and plan managers need to pay attention to the following points in the ABS process of factoring assets: diversification of the source of underlying assets without excessive reliance on a certain region or industry; geographical diversification, industry diversification, and debt portfolio diversification in the asset portfolio.

9.4.2.5 ABS Credit Enhancement of JD Supply Chain Finance

For ABS products, credit issues are one of the most prominent problems. Judging from the pool of funds, the suppliers are not concentrated enough and are relatively fragmented. In order to better protect against risks, the product plan arranges the layering of senior A/senior B/subordinated securities, and adopts credit enhancement measures such as excess returns, appointing the original interest owner as asset service provider, and setting up credit trigger mechanisms, as follows:

In terms of structure design, the special plan sets up a layering structure of senior A, senior B, and subordinated securities with offering size proportions of 72%, 27.95%, and 0.05%, respectively (see Table 9.5). In the event of insufficient cash flow pooling, the subordinated asset-backed securities, which are last in the cash flow payment order, will bear the initial losses, while the next ranked senior B asset-backed securities will further bear the losses for the higher ranked senior A asset-backed securities, aiming to reduce the credit risk of the high-level backed securities.

The original interest owner acts as the asset service provider. It is good at collecting information on users and is familiar with the users' habits and financial situation, thus facilitating the recovery and collection of repayments corresponding to the underlying assets. Therefore, the original interest owner, that is Banghui Factoring, is appointed as the asset service provider of the special plan and assumes the obligation to monitor the operation of the asset pool. Banghui Factoring is the largest commercial factoring company in China, with a reasonable business model and sound management system. The appointment of Banghui Factoring as the asset service provider of the special plan is also intended to reduce the risk of cash recovery of the underlying assets by leveraging its rich experience and strict risk control.

Table 9.5 Jingbaobei ABS credit enhancement

Securities layering	*Senior securities*		*Subordinated securities*
Abbreviation of securities	Jingbao 1 Senior A	Jingbao 1 Senior B	Jingbao 1 Subordinated
Offering size (RMB 0.1 billion)	14.40	5.59	0.01
Proportion	72%	27.95%	0.05%
Coupon rate	4.10%	5.90%	–
Credit rating	AAA	AA	–
Expected maturity date	2018-08-09		
Term (year)	2.28		
Interest rate	Fixed interest rate	–	
Frequency of interest payment	During the product revolving period, interest is distributed annually; during the product distribution period, principal and interest are amortized on a variable monthly basis	The remaining proceeds will be distributed after the principal of the senior A and senior B securities are repaid	

Data source: Prospectus of factoring contract debt asset-backed securities no. 1 of 2016 of JD Finance

9.4.3 Model III: Integrated Supply Chain Financial Services of UCA and YIRUN

9.4.3.1 Integrated Supply Chain Financial Services of UCA

Under the direct guidance of the government, Foshan UCA Supply Chain Service Co., Ltd. (hereinafter referred to as "UCA") is a ceramic industry chain service platform with "industry + Internet + financial capital," which is designed at the top level by Bluesource Capital, an enterprise from Zhejiang province, and embraces 15 Foshan ceramic enterprises. With "industry + Internet + financial capital" as the core path, UCA tries to build the largest platform of integrated services for ceramic industry supply chain in China. Based on the procurement needs and business characteristics of the ceramic industry, the platform actively explore new trading models and service models to improve the abilities to serve the real economy. UCA platform trading features five transaction models and procurement models on the B2B platform: deal-making transaction, centralized procurement transaction, source transaction, bidding transaction, and commissioned transaction. Based on the centralized large order procurement, the platform promotes the completion of the standardization of 108 materials in the ceramic industry, promotes the completion of the standardization of testing and inspection, and promotes the standardization of payment process for buyers, so as to achieve the goal of large order procurement, sunshine procurement, and high-quality procurement.

9.4.3.2 Overview of the Ceramic Industry and the Challenges It Faces
The architectural and sanitary ceramics industry in China has long relied on resource advantages, labor dividends, and the introduction of advanced equipment and technology from around the world to achieve rapid development. China's ceramic production has accounted for half of the world's total production, exported to more than 100 countries and regions around the world, making China the world's ceramic manufacturing power. However, as a traditional industry, the ceramic industry has increasingly serious three major problems: high energy consumption, high pollution, and nonstandardization. In the new economic normal situation, the rising costs, the increased inventory, as well as the anti-dumping policies of 38 countries and regions on Chinese ceramics result in China's ceramic industry facing a serious overcapacity. Foshan ceramic industry is experiencing a cold winter. To be more specific, the upstream and downstream enterprises in the ceramic industry supply chain are facing the following difficulties:

First, the lack of standards in the procurement process of ceramic manufacturers. Nonstandardized management of the procurement links and procurement process of ceramic manufacturers has led to unfair competition among suppliers, making it difficult to optimize the procurement costs. In addition, all kinds of raw materials and auxiliary materials procurement are subject to problems caused by the lack of standards and information asymmetry. Raw materials: Lack of standards, inefficient production, and high losses. The price has risen, leading to a serious decline in business efficiency. Energy: Due to the uneven quality of coal supply in the industry, purchasing enterprises do not know the price of coal at the mine mouth, resulting in poor quality, high cost, and unstable production of coal purchased by downstream enterprises. The lack of coal standards in the ceramic industry has also given rise to the regulatory loopholes in the production and procurement process. Hardware: most of the ceramic enterprise owners have no engineering background, and are not familiar with equipment and spare parts. As a result, the quality of the procured hardware is not guaranteed and highly counterfeit products are prevalent. Damage to hardware parts greatly affect the production. Packaging: Serious waste of resources.

Second, the production links of ceramic manufacturers are not innovative enough. Product research and development in the ceramic production relies heavily on the processes, technologies, equipment, materials, and design innovation of upstream suppliers. The suppliers possessing "new process, new technology, new equipment, new materials, new design" cannot be successfully connected with ceramic manufacturers, because, first, these suppliers are industry leaders and product prices are relatively high; second, ceramic brand procurement link is still in the rough operation, quality control and management is weak; third, ceramic enterprises do not pay enough attention to the supply chain links and do not receive timely information about the innovation capabilities of upstream suppliers, resulting in a slow pace of innovation.

Third, the production links of ceramic manufacturers are not environmentally friendly enough. If environmental friendliness is not thoroughly upgraded, pollution will affect the development space of the industry.

Fourth, ceramic manufacturers should open up new sales markets globally. In the new economic normal situation, faced with the rising costs, the increased inventory and the anti-dumping policies on Chinese ceramics by 38 countries and regions, ceramic manufacturers are in urgent need of finding new markets.

Fifth, the logistics links of the upstream and downstream enterprises of the ceramic supply chain should be optimized in terms of transport paths and return trips. On the one hand, main materials and auxiliary materials are mostly heavy, and bulk and dirty goods and transport costs account for a large proportion of the total costs (sometimes up to 50%). Therefore, there is a lot of room for logistics optimization. On the other hand, the process of transporting raw materials and finished products often results in empty boxes and empty return trips, so the comprehensive logistics costs seriously affect the efficiency and benefits.

9.4.3.3 Integrated Supply Chain Financial Services of UCA

In response to the above problems and challenges in the ceramic industry, Bluesource Capital joined forces with other financial institutions to use financial supply chain and supply chain finance to promote the industrial changes. The specific mode of operations is as follows: First, under the investment of Bluesource Capital and the guidance of the local government, 15 enterprises in Foshan, Guangdong Province, jointly established an industrial platform—UCA (see Fig. 9.6), which develops industry material standards, payment standards, and inspection standards. Standardization is a prerequisite for informationization, while information symmetry is a prerequisite for transparency and ultimately brings sunshine. As far as the production links are concerned, UCA acts as a bridge connecting suppliers and ceramic manufacturers, and has established an incubation center, a team of industry experts, a patent platform, and an environmental protection platform (dry preparation technology) to promote technological innovation, transformation of results, and industrial cooperation. In terms of sales links, first of all, UCA has built a sales platform for finished tiles, launched standard tiles excellent in five aspects, built a tile procurement platform to connect the product manufacturing, marketing channels, and other chain points, integrated tile purchase orders and ceramic manufacturers, opened up the channels of construction groups, decoration groups, property developers, major customer, as well as overseas markets, and achieved joint research and development of new products, management of quality, and plan settings to achieve a win-win

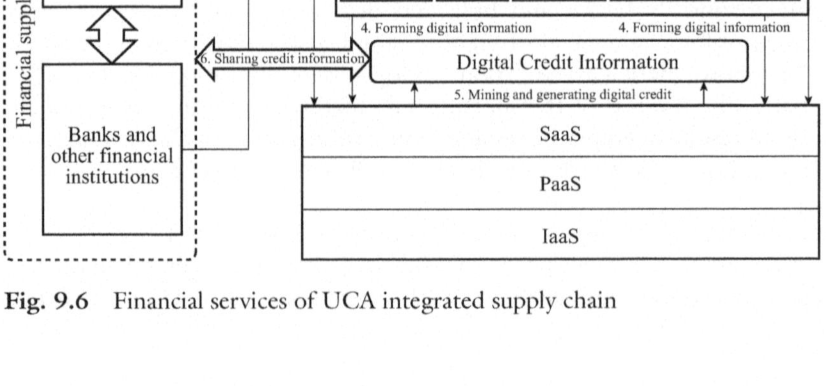

Fig. 9.6 Financial services of UCA integrated supply chain

market and mutual benefit. Second, UCA has created an overseas trade platform. UCA and Sino Great Wall has established strategic partnership with Oman Ministry of Industry, UAE Ministry of Economy and Qatar Royal Chamber of Commerce to jointly build a national cooperation platform on production capacity between China and Arabia, set up exhibition halls in Shenzhen, use bonded areas, build brand image of Foshan manufacturing, and establish a financial service system for the Belt and Road. By integrating Foshan's pan-home furnishing industries, UCA helps the enterprises go out of the country as a whole. As far as logistics is concerned, UCA has created a logistics platform for heavy goods. Unlike that for consumers' goods, this platform pursues stability, advance prediction, optimal path design, and loss control. In addition, UCA has developed return logistics solutions with logistics service providers, relying on its advantages in global procurement and sales, aiming to help logistics service providers save costs and improve efficiency, as well as to save logistics costs of UCA's customers. By virtue of the above approaches, UCA has formed a supply chain system that unites a great number of suppliers, manufacturers, and logistics service providers.

Moreover, based on the above supply chain system and the integration of resources, UCA has formed intensive supply chain operations. In terms of material segment, UCA identifies the role, origin, source procurement model, production process, reference indexes, points of concern, product advantages, development bottlenecks, and future directions for each major material. In terms of energy segment, UCA has achieved a breakthrough in three aspects. With the support of government policies, UCA carried out centralized procurement of electricity, reducing the electricity costs of ceramic enterprises by 9%. Distributed energy is carried out and the business of natural gas segment is expanded. UCA evaluated coal suppliers based on seven criteria, including source, transportation, capital, quality, bills, price, and cooperative attitude, and collected more than 100 coal samples and indexes covering 29 coal mines to develop the UCA standards for recommended "long-lasting" coals, which makes coal supply more standardized and controllable. UCA implemented retransformation from the source of the supply chain and helped enterprises monitor production through the monitoring of data such as electricity consumption, coal consumption, and finished product rate and costs. Member enterprises received assistance from scientific procurement to achieve a 10% reduction in costs, which also led to a reduction in coal consumption from 5.0 to 4.7 in one plant, creating the lowest coal consumption since the plant was built. In terms of the hardware segment, UCA has set up regional warehouses for suppliers to store accessories. UCA's guarantee of the high-quality accessories and the provisions of services allow ceramic factories to achieve zero inventory without stocking. For the packaging segment, UCA has designed standardized cartons to reduce costs.

Finally, after the formation of an integrated supply chain system and its operations, UCA uses the data and information accumulated by the platform to support the full development of supply chain financial business. Specifically, on the one hand, UCA and Dong Fang Yian Insurance Sales Co., Ltd. signed an agreement to reach cooperation with a number of insurance companies such as CIC, PICC, Ping An Insurance, and Ancheng Property & Casualty Insurance to provide a wide range of insurance services for the ceramic industry, so that insured enterprises can save 15%–40% of the costs. This is beneficial to both ceramic enterprises and insurance companies to expand their businesses. On the other hand, the Foshan Municipal Government set up a special supply-side reform fund of RMB 500 million, while the first tranche of RMB 100 million is invested in the UCA platform, which provides financial security for the industrial restructuring. Meanwhile, UCA joined hands with China Guangfa Bank, Bank of China, China Merchants Bank, rural commercial banks, and other commercial banks to provide supply chain financial services for ceramic enterprises on its platform. Currently, these commercial banks have granted UCA an overall credit line of RMB 50 million.

The effective linkage of investment, funds, insurance, and banks realized by UCA not only solves the financing problems of ceramic enterprises but also facilitates the integration of many ceramic manufacturers to form organic supply chain clusters and industrial competitiveness with intensive operations and management. As of December 31, 2018, the number of enterprises registered on the platform has increased to 563 ceramic enterprises and 3514 supplier enterprises, from 14 enterprises at the beginning. The enterprise production value has exceeded RMB 221.5 billion, and the platform's sales flow reached RMB 42.6 billion. In 2018, ceramic enterprises achieved orders of RMB 33.8 billion on the platform. In terms of resource savings, the Department of Industry and Information Technology of Guangdong Province approved 51 enterprises on the UCA platform to implement electricity reform pilot in December 2016. UCA completed the review of 29 enterprises' electricity sales information in two days, reached a centralized procurement of 1.17 billion degrees of electricity, and saved RMB 68.38 million in 2017 and RMB 140 million in 2018 for ceramic enterprises. In 2017, the cost of zirconium silicate reduced by 10%, electricity cost by 6.7%, overall coal cost by 15.3%, and the average cost of enterprises by about 10.58%. In terms of supply chain finance, the platform has obtained convenient and low-cost financing for members such as Lianshiyi, Xiaoweidai, and Shangpiaotong with the help of big data supporting and credit enhancement, and has achieved financing amount of RMB 150 million in two years.

9.4.3.4 Integrated Supply Chain Financial Services of YIRUN Agriculture

Yirun Supply Chain Management (Shanghai) Co., Ltd. (hereinafter referred to as "YIRUN") is a service provider focusing on integrated solutions for the commodity supply chain. YIRUN was founded in 2015 with a registered capital of RMB 100 million and is headquartered in Shanghai, with 51% held by AVIC Trust Co., Ltd. and 49% held by Huitonghui (Shanghai) Logistics Co., Ltd. Its branches include Jiangxi Xinrun Hangda Supply Chain Management Co., Ltd., which is engaged in steel trade business, Jiangxi Zhongherun Trade Co., Ltd., which is engaged in agricultural products and grain and oil business, and Yingtan Copper Industry Platform, which is engaged in nonferrous metals business. Led by the integration of trade, finance, and operation, based on the strategic cooperation of core enterprises, and supported by risk control innovation and information technology, YIRUN agricultural supply chain integrates all resources in the supply chain to realize the "unified" closed-loop operation of commodity flow, capital flow, logistics flow, and information flow and solve the problem of difficult risk control. Specifically, YIRUN embeds itself in the trade and distribution links and penetrates deeply into the supply chain. YIRUN integrates upstream and downstream enterprises in the supply chain, horizontal cooperative enterprises, supporting warehousing and logistics providers, and financial institutions, and so on. Through equity, debt, and strategic cooperation, YIRUN utilizes the close partnerships formed to achieve the integration of trade, financing, and operation. With the support of digital technology, financial supply chain and supply chain finance, YIRUN realizes the organic linkage of industries.

The specific process (see Fig. 9.7) is as follows: First of all, Zhongherun forms cooperation with core enterprises, futures companies, insurance companies, commercial banks, and its own insurance companies to share information and form a financial supply chain. Second, a third-party trustee manages farmers' land and appoints farmers to plant. When a

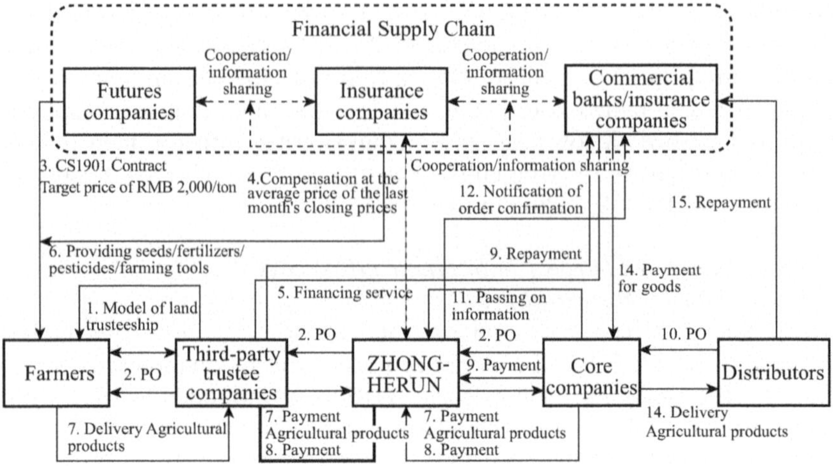

Fig. 9.7 Yirun agriculture integrated supply chain finance

supplier places an order for corn, Zhongherun places the order to the third-party trustee. Meanwhile, the futures company forms the futures product 1901 contract to guarantee the target price. The insurance company provides insurance at the average price of the last month's futures closing price. Such a linkage between the futures company and the insurance company addresses the potential losses to farmers resulting from price fluctuations of agricultural products. On the basis of a confirmed production order, the commercial bank finances a third-party trustee for the provision of seeds, fertilizers, pesticides, and farm equipment to the farmers. After the agricultural products are produced, the farmers deliver the products to the core enterprise via the third-party trustee and Zhongherun. After payment by the core enterprise, the third-party trustee repays the funds to the commercial bank.

Similarly, based on its own development needs, large core enterprises hope to obtain double-digit business growth from long-term cooperated downstream one-tier distributors and a large number of two-tier distributors, commercial supermarkets, and other small distributors every year. Therefore, YIRUN supply chain intervenes in the sales process of distributors and helps the downstream distributors of core enterprises to solve the financing problem by means of supply chain finance, which in turn helps core enterprises to achieve the purpose of expanding sales scale. The specific operation process is as follows: after the distributors place orders to the core enterprises, the core enterprises synchronize the information to YIRUN. YIRUN passes the confirmation information to the factoring company, and the latter pays the payment to the core enterprises first, forming a transfer of accounts receivable. After that, the core enterprises deliver the products to the distributors, who then repays the amount.

Through the abovementioned model, YIRUN supply chain achieved revenue of RMB 200 billion in 2019, including RMB 30 billion for the agriculture segment. By the end of 2018, the total amount of financing for the three major business segments was RMB 5,624,257,000, and YIRUN has helped small, medium, and micro enterprises to realize 1268 financing transactions. The total credit line granted by the financial institutions that Yirun is currently cooperating with has reached RMB 5500 million.

References

Albertazzi, U., Bottero, M., & Ongena, S. (2016). Asymmetric information and the securitization of SME loans. *SSRN Electronic Journal.*

Allen, F., & Santomero, A. M. (1997). The theory of financial intermediation. *Journal of Banking & Finance, 21*(11–12), 1461–1485.

Berger, A. N., & Udell, G. F. (1998). The economics of small business finance: The roles of private equity and debt markets in the financial growth cycle. *Journal of Banking & Finance, 22*(6–8), 613–673.

Bhide, A. (1992). Bootstrap finance: The art of start-ups. *Harvard Business Review, 70*(6) Retrieved from https://europepmc.org/abstract/med/10122688

Blackman, I. D., Holland, C. P., & Westcott, T. (2013). Motorola's global financial supply chain strategy. *Supply Chain Management: An International Journal, 18*(2), 132–147.

Brown, T. C., Bergstrom, J. C., & Loomis, J. B. (2007). Defining, valuing, and providing ecosystem goods and services. *Natural Resources Journal, 47*(2), 329–376. Retrieved from JSTOR.

Brown, M., Jappelli, T., & Pagano, M. (2009). Information sharing and credit: Firm-level evidence from transition countries. *Journal of Financial Intermediation, 18*(2), 151–172.

Buzacott, J. A., & Zhang, R. Q. (2004). Inventory management with asset-based financing. *Management Science, 50*(9), 1274–1292.

Caniato, F., Gelsomino, L. M., Perego, A., & Ronchi, S. (2016). Does finance solve the supply chain financing problem? *Supply Chain Management: An International Journal, 21*(5), 534–549.

Caniato, F., Henke, M., & Zsidisin, G. A. (2019). Supply chain finance: Historical foundations, current research, future developments. *Journal of Purchasing and Supply Management*. https://doi.org/10.1016/J.PURSUP.2019.02.002
Carnovale, S., Rogers, D. S., & Yeniyurt, S. (2018). Broadening the perspective of supply chain finance: The performance impacts of network power & cohesion. *Journal of Purchasing and Supply Management, 25*(2), 134–145.
Cassar, G. (2004). The financing of business start-ups. *Journal of Business Venturing, 19*(2), 261–283.
Chen, T.-K., Liao, H.-H., & Lu, C.-W. (2011). A flow-based corporate credit model. *Review of Quantitative Finance and Accounting, 36*(4), 517–532.
Chen, T.-K., Liao, H.-H., & Kuo, H.-J. (2013). Internal liquidity risk, financial bullwhip effects, and corporate bond yield spreads: Supply chain perspectives. *Journal of Banking & Finance, 37*(7), 2434–2456.
Chen, Y. J., Tsai, H., & Liu, Y.-F. (2018). Supply chain finance risk management: Payment default in tourism channels. *Tourism Economics, 24*(5), 593–614. https://doi.org/10.1177/1354816618762187
Chmielewski, T. (2005). *Bank risks, risk preferences and lending*. Munich Personal RePEc Archive. http://mpra.ub.uni-muenchen.de/5131/ Paper No. 5131, posted 07, November 2007.
Clark, E., Mare, D. S., & Radić, N. (2018). Cooperative banks: What do we know about competition and risk preferences? *Journal of International Financial Markets, Institutions and Money, 52*, 90–101.
de Bettignies, J.-E., & Brander, J. A. (2007). Financing entrepreneurship: Bank finance versus venture capital. *Journal of Business Venturing, 22*(6), 808–832.
de Meijer, C., & de Bruijn, M. (2014). Cross-border supply-chain finance: An important offering in transaction banking. *Journal of Payments Strategy & Systems, 7*(4), 304–318.
Dello Iacono, U., Reindorp, M., & Dellaert, N. (2015). Market adoption of reverse factoring. *International Journal of Physical Distribution & Logistics Management, 45*(3), 286–308.
Diamond, D. W. (1984). Financial intermediation and delegated monitoring. *The Review of Economic Studies, 51*(3), 393–414.
Dyckman, B. (2011). Supply chain finance: Risk mitigation and revenue growth. *Journal of Corporate Treasury Management, 4*(2), 168–173. Retrieved from buh.
Fairchild, A. (2005). Intelligent matching: Integrating efficiencies in the financial supply chain. *Supply Chain Management: An International Journal, 10*(4), 244–248.
Folinas, D., Manthou, V., Sigala, M., & Vlachopoulou, M. (2004). E-volution of a supply chain: Cases and best practices. *Internet Research, 14*(4), 274–283.
Forrester, J. W. (1961). *Industrial dynamics*. Pegasus Communications.
Gelsomino, L. M., Mangiaracina, R., Perego, A., & Tumino, A. (2016). Supply chain finance: A literature review. *International Journal of Physical Distribution & Logistics Management, 46*(4), 348–366.

Gomm, M. L. (2010). Supply chain finance: Applying finance theory to supply chain management to enhance finance in supply chains. *International Journal of Logistics Research and Applications, 13*(2), 133–142.

Gunasekaran, A., & Ngai, E. W. T. (2004). Virtual supply-chain management. *Production Planning & Control, 15*(6), 584–595.

Gupta, S., & Dutta, K. (2011). Modeling of financial supply chain. *European Journal of Operational Research, 211*(1), 47–56.

Harrison, R. T., Mason, C. M., & Girling, P. (2004). Financial bootstrapping and venture development in the software industry. *Entrepreneurship & Regional Development, 16*(4), 307–333.

He, X., & Tang, L. (2012). Exploration on building of visualization platform to innovate business operation pattern of supply chain finance. *Physics Procedia, 33*, 1886–1893.

Hoberg, K., Protopappa-Sieke, M., & Steinker, S. (2017). How do financial constraints and financing costs affect inventories? An empirical supply chain perspective. *International Journal of Physical Distribution & Logistics Management, 47*(6), 516–535.

Hofmann, E. (2005). Supply chain finance: Some conceptual insights. *Logistik Management—Innovative Logistikkonzepte, 80*, 203–214.

Hofmann, E. (2009). Inventory financing in supply chains: A logistics service provider-approach. *International Journal of Physical Distribution & Logistics Management, 39*(9), 716–740.

Hofmann, E. (2011). Natural hedging as a risk prophylaxis and supplier financing instrument in automotive supply chains. *Supply Chain Management: An International Journal, 16*(2), 128–141.

Howe, J. (2008). *Crowdsourcing: How the power of the crowd is driving the future of business.* Random House.

Hubbard, D. W. (2009). *The failure of risk management: Why its broken and how to fix it.* John Wiley & Sons.

Jappelli, T., & Pagano, M. (2002). Information sharing, lending and defaults: Cross-country evidence. *Journal of Banking & Finance, 26*(10), 2017–2045.

Jin, W., Zhang, Q., & Luo, J. (2018). *Non-collaborative and collaborative financing in a bilateral supply chain with capital constraints.* Omega.

Jing, B., Chen, X., & Cai, G. G. (2012). Equilibrium financing in a distribution channel with capital constraint. *Production and Operations Management, 21*(6), 1090–1101.

Johnson, M. E. (2008). Information risk of inadvertent disclosure: An analysis of file-sharing risk in the financial supply chain. *Journal of Management Information Systems, 25*(2), 97–124.

Keifer, S. (2011). E-invoicing: The catalyst for financial supply chain efficiencies. *Journal of Payments Strategy & Systems, 5*(1), 38–51.

Keuschnigg, C., & Nielsen, S. B. (2003). *Public policy for start-up entrepreneurship with venture capital and Bank finance*. CESifo Working Paper Series 850, CESifo.

Kraemer-Eis, H., Schaber, M., & Tappi, A. (2010). *SME loan securitisation—An important tool to support European SME lending* (Working Paper No. 2010/07). Retrieved from EIF Working Paper website: https://www.econstor.eu/handle/10419/176637

Lang, M., Bharadwaj, N., & Di Benedetto, C. A. (2016). How crowdsourcing improves prediction of market-oriented outcomes. *Journal of Business Research, 69*(10), 4168–4176.

Lee, H. L., Padmanabhan, V., & Whang, S. (1997). Information distortion in a supply chain: The bullwhip effect. *Management Science, 43*(4), 546–558.

Lekkakos, S. D., & Serrano, A. (2016). Supply chain finance for small and medium sized enterprises: The case of reverse factoring. *International Journal of Physical Distribution & Logistics Management, 46*(4), 367–392.

Leland, H. E., & Pyle, D. H. (1977). Informational asymmetries, financial structure, and financial intermediation. *The Journal of Finance, 32*(2), 371–387.

Liebl, J., Hartmann, E., & Feisel, E. (2016). Reverse factoring in the supply chain: Objectives, antecedents and implementation barriers. *International Journal of Physical Distribution & Logistics Management, 46*(4), 393–413.

Manthou, V., Vlachopoulou, M., & Folinas, D. (2004). Virtual e-chain (VeC) model for supply chain collaboration. *International Journal of Production Economics, 87*(3), 241–250.

Markowitz, H. (1952). Portfolio selection. *Journal of Finance, 7*(1), 77–91.

Massa, L., Tucci, C. L., & Afuah, A. (2017). A critical assessment of business model research. *Academy of Management Annals, 11*(1), 73–104.

Metters, R. (1997). Quantifying the bullwhip effect in supply chains. *Journal of Operations Management, 15*(2), 89–100.

Nienhuis, J. J., Cortet, M., & Lycklama, D. (2013). Real-time financing: Extending e-invoicing to real-time SME financing. *Journal of Payments Strategy & Systems, 7*(3), 232–245.

Ooi, K.-B., Chong, A. Y.-L., & Tan, B.-I. (2011). Application of web 2.0 in supply chain management: A brief overview. *Trends in Applied Sciences Research, 6*(4), 394–399.

Padilla, A. J., & Pagano, M. (2000). Sharing default information as a borrower discipline device. *European Economic Review, 44*(10), 1951–1980.

Pellegrino, R., Costantino, N., & Tauro, D. (2018). Supply chain finance: A supply chain-oriented perspective to mitigate commodity risk and pricing volatility. *Journal of Purchasing and Supply Management, 25*(2), 118–133.

Petropoulos, D., & Kyriazopoulos, G. (2010). Profitability, efficiency and liquidity of the co-operative banks in Greece. *Proceedings of ICOAE.*

Pfohl, H.-C., & Gomm, M. (2009). Supply chain finance: Optimizing financial flows in supply chains. *Logistics Research, 1*(3–4), 149–161.

Prpić, J., Shukla, P. P., Kietzmann, J. H., & McCarthy, I. P. (2015). How to work a crowd: Developing crowd capital through crowdsourcing. *Business Horizons, 58*(1), 77–85.

Randall, W. S., & Theodore Farris, M. (2009). Supply chain financing: Using cash-to-cash variables to strengthen the supply chain. *International Journal of Physical Distribution & Logistics Management, 39*(8), 669–689.

Scholtens, B., & Van Wensveen, D. (2003). *The theory of financial intermediation: An essay on what it does (not) explain*. SUERF Studies.

Sharma, G., & Baoku, L. (2013). Customer satisfaction in Web 2.0 and information technology development. *Information Technology & People, 26*(4), 347–367. https://doi.org/10.1108/ITP-12-2012-0157

Simula, H., & Vuori, M. (2012). Benefits and barriers of crowdsourcing in b2b firms: Generating ideas with internal and external crowds. *International Journal of Innovation Management, 16*(06), 1240011.

Song H. (2017). *Internet Supply Chain Finance*. China Renmin University Press.

Song, H., & Wang, L. (2013). The impact of private and family firms' relational strength on financing performance in clusters. *Asia Pacific Journal of Management, 30*(3), 735–748.

Song, H., Yu, K., Ganguly, A., & Turson, R. (2016). Supply chain network, information sharing and SME credit quality. *Industrial Management & Data Systems, 116*(4), 740–758.

Song, H., Lu, Q., Yu, K., & Qian, C. (2018). How do knowledge spillover and access in supply chain network enhance SMEs' credit quality? *Industrial Management & Data Systems, 119*(2), 274–291.

Stiglitz, J. E., & Weiss, A. (1981). Credit rationing in markets with imperfect information. *The American Economic Review, 71*(3), 393–410.

Tan, K. C. (2001). A framework of supply chain management literature. *European Journal of Purchasing & Supply Management, 7*(1), 39–48.

Tate, W. L., Ellram, L. M., & Bals, L. (2019). Supply chain finance: Solutions for financial sustainability, risk management and resilience in supply chain. In *Supply chain finance: Risk management, resilience and supplier*. Kogan Page.

Terungwa, A. (2012). Risk management and insurance of small and medium scale enterprises (SMEs) in Nigeria. *International Journal of Finance and Accounting, 1*(1), 8–17.

Torres, O. C., & Maltz, A. B. (2010). Understanding the financial consequences of the bullwhip effect in A multi-echelon supply chain. *Journal of Business Logistics, 31*(1), 23–41.

Vousinas, G. (2012). The transmission channels between financial sector and real economy in light of the current financial crisis: A critical survey of the literature. Available at SSRN 2159837.

Vousinas, G. (2018). Supply chain finance revisited: A critical review with future prospects. *SSRN Electronic Journal.*
Williamson, S. D. (1986). Costly monitoring, financial intermediation, and equilibrium credit rationing. *Journal of Monetary Economics, 18*(2), 159–179.
Wilson, K. B., Bhakoo, V., & Samson, D. (2018). Crowdsourcing: A contemporary form of project management with linkages to open innovation and novel operations. *International Journal of Operations & Production Management, 38*(6), 1467–1494.
Winborg, J., & Landström, H. (2001). Financial bootstrapping in small businesses. *Journal of Business Venturing, 16*(3), 235–254.
Wuttke, D. A., Blome, C., & Henke, M. (2013). Focusing the financial flow of supply chains: An empirical investigation of financial supply chain management. *International Journal of Production Economics, 145*(2), 773–789.
Yan, N., Dai, H., & Sun, B. (2014). Optimal bi-level Stackelberg strategies for supply chain financing with both capital-constrained buyers and sellers: N. Yan, H. Dai and B. Sun. *Applied Stochastic Models in Business and Industry, 30*(6), 783–796.
Yan, N., Sun, B., Zhang, H., & Liu, C. (2016). A partial credit guarantee contract in a capital-constrained supply chain: Financing equilibrium and coordinating strategy. *International Journal of Production Economics, 173*, 122–133.
Zhang, A. N., Goh, M., & Meng, F. (2011). Conceptual modelling for supply chain inventory visibility. *International Journal of Production Economics, 133*(2), 578–585.
Zhou, Z., Xiao, S., Ho, Y.-C. (Chad), & Tan, Y. (2018). The persuasive and informative effects of information disclosure: Evidence from an online supply chain finance market. *SSRN Electronic Journal.*
Zhu, N., Wang, B., Yu, Z., & Wu, Y. (2016). Technical efficiency measurement incorporating risk preferences: An empirical analysis of Chinese commercial banks. *Emerging Markets Finance and Trade, 52*(3), 610–624.
Zhu, Y., Zhou, L., Xie, C., Wang, G.-J., & Nguyen, T. V. (2019). Forecasting SMEs' credit risk in supply chain finance with an enhanced hybrid ensemble machine learning approach. *International Journal of Production Economics, 211*, 22–33.

CHAPTER 10

Risk Management in Intelligent Supply Chain Finance

10.1 Introduction

How to solve the working capital pressure of MSMEs has been an important issue of concern in academic and industrial circles. This issue arises from the inherent characteristics of SMEs that lead to information asymmetry between borrowers and lenders, generate credit issues and default risks (Berger & Udell, 2006; Irwin & Scott, 2010; Abbasi et al., 2018), and generate credit rationing problems (Stiglitz & Weiss, 1981). Besides, considering the information redundancy, how to effectively identify valid data and information, truly profile the risks, and provide appropriate financial products has now become the key to the development of supply chain finance. Supply chain finance mainly serves SMEs, while they are prone to bad debts and defaults because their risks are generally higher than those of large enterprises. For example, according to a report issued by the People's Bank of China (PBOC), the nonperforming loan rate for large enterprises in China is only 1.19%, while that for SMEs is 5.94%. Similarly, the nonperforming rate of loans to SMEs exceeds 5% (Zhu et al., 2019), as noted by the Industrial and Commercial Bank of China (ICBC). Faced with this situation, financial institutions are concerned about the credit quality of SMEs and thus fear and refuse to lend money. Therefore, an effective solution to this problem requires a systematic analysis and control of risks, so that the supply chain financial business can be carried out on a safe basis.

H. Song, *Smart Supply Chain Finance*,
https://doi.org/10.1007/978-981-16-5997-3_10

10.2 Risks in Supply Chain Finance

As far as the supply chain field is concerned, risk management has been an important topic of exploration. Usually risks are considered as unstable states or uncertain resources that lead to supply chain disruptions and usually have two characteristics: (a) these events have a small probability of occurrence, but may happen suddenly; and (b) these events, once they occur, have a continuous harmful effect on the whole system (Tang & Nurmaya Musa, 2011). Risks in supply chain finance refer to the behaviors of unstable supply chain operations or individual opportunistic and moral hazards that not only lead to the disruption of the whole supply chain but also cause substantial harm to the suppliers of funds. Supply chain financial risks may arise from supply chain operations or opportunistic and moral hazard of SMEs. The former is the disruption of the supply chain due to problems in processes or elements of supply chain operations (Tang & Nurmaya Musa, 2011; Zhao et al., 2015), which in turn makes the default risk higher. The latter is a malicious act of the financing applicant, that is, a firm with lower credit quality exploiting information asymmetry, leading to higher transaction costs and bad debts arising from the lending (Bester & Hellwig, 1987; Zhang et al., 2015; Kouvelis & Zhao, 2018). Despite their different nature (the former is arguably an objective factor, while the latter is a subjective act), both of these risks can pose significant challenges to financing.

10.2.1 Risks of Supply Chain Finance Arising from Supply Chain Operations

10.2.1.1 Sources of Risks in Supply Chain Operations

The first factor that poses a threat to the continuity and stability of supply chain finance is the disruption of supply chain operations. Therefore, the factors that lead to supply chain risks can also negatively affect supply chain finance. Among the studies on supply chain risk management, some focus on the sources of supply chain risks, which are mainly categorized into environmental factors, industry factors, organizational factors, issue-specific factors, and decision-maker-related factors (Rao & Goldsby, 2009). Clearly, the first three categories of factors span macro, meso, and micro perspectives, and are the different dimensions that affect supply chain operations and are the systemic factors of supply chain risks. The latter two categories of factors are the subject and object of supply chain operations. In other words, they refer to the decision-makers for supply chain operations and the specific contents or objects of supply chain operations, respectively. These systemic factors, together with the subject and object factors, constitute the sources of risks affecting supply chain operations.

Environmental factors refer to the external factors that affect the business scenario of each industry, or, rather, external factors that can negatively affect the industry as a whole (Ritchie & Marshall, 1993). These factors include political stability, changes in government policies, macroeconomic uncertainty, social uncertainty, and natural uncertainty (Miller, 1992). Despite their external nature, any change or uncertainty in these factors can often cause significant losses in the enterprises' supply chain operations, and these risks are often more difficult for the enterprises to control and manage.

Industry factors include variables that may not affect all sectors of the economy as a whole, but do affect specific industries (Ritchie & Marshall, 1993). These variables include input market uncertainty (i.e., the uncertainty affecting the industry's production input factors), product market uncertainty (i.e., unexpected changes in corporate or industrial demand (Miller, 1992), which can arise both from changes in customer demand and from the emergence of substitutes (Tang & Nurmaya Musa, 2011)), and competitive uncertainty (i.e., all types of risks related to market competition, covering the uncertainties associated with existing enterprises and potential competitors entering the industry).

Organizational factors are variables that are associated with specific enterprises. As pointed out by Ritchie and Marshall (1993), the third category of factors that contribute to supply chain risks are those associated with the enterprises. Although related to specific enterprises, such factors can have an impact on the entire supply chain. Organizational factors include uncertainty in corporate operations, liabilities, R&D, credits, and agency behaviors (Wu et al., 2006). Uncertainty in corporate operations includes a variety of uncertainties faced by enterprises in organizing their supply chain activities, such as labor uncertainty because of changes in employee productivity for various reasons, uncertainty in production input elements such as raw materials and components, and output uncertainty due to equipment failure (Rao & Goldsby, 2009).

Uncertainty in liabilities refers to the unforeseen and unexpected events related to the production or consumption of an enterprise's products, while the occurrence of these events may directly harm the enterprise's supply chain, thus leading, for example, to issues in product safety as well as environmental hazards.

Uncertainty in credits is often a risk to the entire supply chain due to default on the debts of the participants in the supply chain. For example, the nonperformance of a customer of an enterprise may cause financial flow pressures of the enterprise, which in turn may delay payments to other parties. Kleindorfer and Saad (2005) have pointed out that a strategic supplier with business problems or serious financial problems is likely to have a negative impact on the entire supply chain, and Finch (2004) also mentioned that if partners in the supply chain have financial problems with other enterprises, this may eventually lead to risks for the enterprise itself.

Uncertainty in agency behaviors refers to the uncertainty of agency relationships among enterprises. Agency relationships refer to the behaviors of "one or more persons authorizing another person (agent) to perform a contract for a service on their behalf, and delegating some decision-making powers to the agent" (Jensen & Meckling, 1976). If a participant in the supply chain delegates certain tasks to an agent, and the agent fails to complete the tasks or poses a moral hazard, the supply chain operations will be at great risk.

Issue-specific risk is an endogenous risk of enterprises, or a risk that is internalized when the enterprises solve a problem or perform an activity (Bettis & Hall, 1982). For example, enterprises may outsource certain business processes to others (Ang & Straub, 1998), but outsourcing not only reduces specific risk, but also increases the enterprises' vulnerability, making them lose control over the activity (Hallikas & Lintukangas, 2016; König & Spinler, 2016). According to Rao and Goldsby (2009), issue-specific risk consists of the following main aspects: first, the structure of the overall risk and the correlation between the affecting variables; second, the objectives and constraints that affect the solution of the issue; and third, the complexity of the decision tasks reflected in each dimension.

Decision-maker-related uncertainty refers to the uncertainty associated with the decision-making person or decision-making group, including the specific knowledge, skills, experience, or preferences of the decision-maker to understand the overall risk. Obviously, if the decision-maker has more of these knowledge and ability, the risk of uncertainty to the supply chain may be reduced; otherwise, the lack of corresponding knowledge and ability may magnify the local risk, and then affect the whole supply chain. The information-seeking behavior of the decision-maker is also an element that affects uncertainty. If the decision-maker is able to search for the required information in a reasonable way, the risk caused by information asymmetry can be reduced. The institutional rules and procedures that affect the decision-making process are also one of the uncertainties. These institutional rules and procedures directly impose constraints on the decision-making behaviors of the decision-maker, thus limiting the extent to which the decision-maker can avoid risk.

The bounded rationality of the decision-maker is also a factor to be considered (Simon, 1972). The bounded rationality of the decision-maker can lead to biased decisions in the presence of scarce or redundant information. The factors that generate bounded rationality are initially mainly information scarcity or information incompleteness. In other words, decision-makers are unable to make optimal choices because they do not have access to complete information. It is worth noting, however, that with the rapid development of information and communication technologies today, bounded rationality may come from information fog, or information overload (Shenk, 1997). The overload of digital information prevents the decision-makers from effectively judging what information is true and valid and what information is of lower quality or even false, thus leading to decision-making under bounded rationality.

10.2.1.2 Forms of Risks in Supply Chain Operations

In addition to exploring the sources of risks affecting supply chain operations, several theoretical studies have focused on the intrinsic forms of risks in supply chain operations, or the manifestations of risks in supply chain operations. Many studies classify supply chain operation risks into transaction flow risks, financial flow risks, and information flow risks (Tang & Nurmaya Musa, 2011; Verbano & Venturini, 2013). Obviously, these risks are mainly reflected in four aspects of supply chain operations, namely commodity flow, logistics flow, capital flow, and information flow. Uncertainty or risk in these aspects can eventually lead to supply chain disruptions, which in turn can jeopardize financial behaviors.

Transaction flow risk is a risk that results from the uncoordinated commodity flow and logistics flow of the parties in the supply chain. This type of risk is distributed in the procurement, production, and distribution phases. In the procurement phase, the choice of a single supplier or multiple suppliers in the supply chain may have an impact on the supply chain. A single supplier often has a negative impact on the smooth operations of the supply chain, as high concentration of supply can bring about instability in procurement and create a situation where upstream suppliers put pressure on the enterprises (Peck, 2005). Flexible choice of multiple suppliers allows the enterprises to break through the constraints on resource and capacity and use supply resources flexibly, but this kind of choice also generates hidden costs. Especially in the globalized operations of supply chains, there are a lot of integrated risks that generate hidden costs, such as various taxes, exchange rate fluctuations, import and export costs, transport costs, and supplier certification and audit costs (Tang & Nurmaya Musa, 2011). Therefore, supplier selection requires a comprehensive consideration of supplier stability, national risks, transport reliability, and suppliers' supply reliability (Levary, 2007). Beyond the above factors, risk factors to be considered in the procurement phase include lead time, supplied product monitoring, and mastery of supply capacity. The absence of all these factors may directly result in supply chain risks. In the production phase, the risks of supply chain operations are generally considered to include design risks for products and processes, or the inability of enterprises to adjust products or processes in a timely manner in response to rapid changes in the market (Khan et al., 2008). These risks make it costly for enterprises to position their products or processes in the market and incur losses. Another risk in the production phase is the production capacity risk, which is related to technology, skills, and quality capabilities (Korpela et al., 2002). In other words, the enterprises may fail to maintain and promote normal production and operations due to a lack of resources and capabilities. In addition to this, operational disruption is one of the important forms of risks in the production phase. As a result of various internal reasons (mismanagement, operational problems, etc.) or external reasons (business cycles, etc.), the production and operations of an enterprise cannot be carried out properly, causing huge losses to the supply chain (Mizgier et al., 2015; Wagner et al., 2017). The exploration of this risk has become an important area in supply chain risk management research. In the distribution phase, a key factor for risks is the volatility or seasonality of demand, which often causes unpredictability and thus creates great difficulties for efficient and effective distribution because it is difficult for enterprises to effectively determine the varieties and quantities of products or services to respond to changing demand and markets (Wong & Hvolby, 2007). Moreover, excess and obsolete inventory resulting from rapid changes in technologies or customer demand is a frequent risk in the distribution phase (Narayanan & Raman, 2004).

Financial flow risk often involves the inability in settlement and payments or the occurrence of improper investments. This risk may result in stress or even disruption of an enterprise's capital flow. It generally includes factors such as exchange rate risk, price risk and cost risk, financial problems of supply chain partners, and improper financial treatments. For enterprises engaged in global supply chain operations, exchange rate risk is an important factor affecting their supply chains because exchange rate fluctuations may directly affect after-tax profits, supplier selection, market development, and other related decisions (Huchzermeier & Cohen, 1996; Allayannis et al., 2001; Christopher & Holweg, 2011; Liu & Nagurney, 2011). Another financial risk factor associated with the exchange rate is the price factor and cost factor. A sudden increase in costs may lead to higher procurement costs of raw materials or inputs for the enterprises, which negatively affecting the supply chain (Papadakis, 2006; Christopher & Holweg, 2011). The financial problems of partners in the supply chain is also one of the key financial risks that cause supply chain disruptions. Financial disruptions or financial problems of any partner in the supply chain, such as equity, financial leverage, and asset risk (Hendricks & Singhal, 2005), may have adverse effects on their upstream and downstream enterprises, which in turn may affect the entire supply chain (Tang & Nurmaya Musa, 2011). Besides, specific financial operations, which include payment policies and management of the procurement-to-payment process, can also cause fluctuations in supply chain operations (Hartley-Urquhart, 2006; Nienhuis et al., 2013).

Information flow risk refers to the inefficiency or interruption of the whole supply chain operations due to the blockage or error of the supply chain information. The efficiency or effectiveness of the supply chain requires perfect information, such as demand information, inventory information, order information, and production capacity information. All these kinds of information are an important basis for decision-making to optimize supply chain operations. If the information is wrong or not available in time, the supply chain decision will be a major mistake. The risks in the information flow are mainly reflected in the correctness of information, security and disruption of information systems, intellectual property rights, and information outsourcing risks (Tang & Nurmaya Musa, 2011). The risk of information correctness mainly arises from information availability, information efficiency, and data accuracy (Lee, 2002; Nishat Faisal et al., 2007). The information availability refers to the accessibility of information. Without effective ways and means to obtain the appropriate information, the accuracy of information will be low. Information efficiency is the orientation of information, or the ability of information to reflect what is intended to be understood. If the information obtained is efficient, the accuracy of information can be improved. Data accuracy reflects the meticulousness of the data obtained. More accurate data produces more accurate data analysis results. The threat of information system security and disruption may arise from internal mismanagement, or hackers and natural disasters (Nishat Faisal et al., 2007), or application, enterprise-level, or cross-enterprise factors (Finch, 2004). Intellectual property risks may result from the inability to protect the information shared due to increased supply chain information flows, as well as from the leakage of confidential information. In particular, while enterprises can focus on core competencies when outsourcing data analysis and processing, the opportunism of information service providers would also lead to potential risks (Nishat Faisal et al., 2007).

10.2.1.3 Sources of Supply Chain Risks, Operation Risks, and Supply Chain Financial Risks

The above five sources of supply chain risks directly affect supply chain operation risks (see Fig. 10.1), and all these factors ultimately have a negative impact on decisions of supply chain finance. According to Gomm

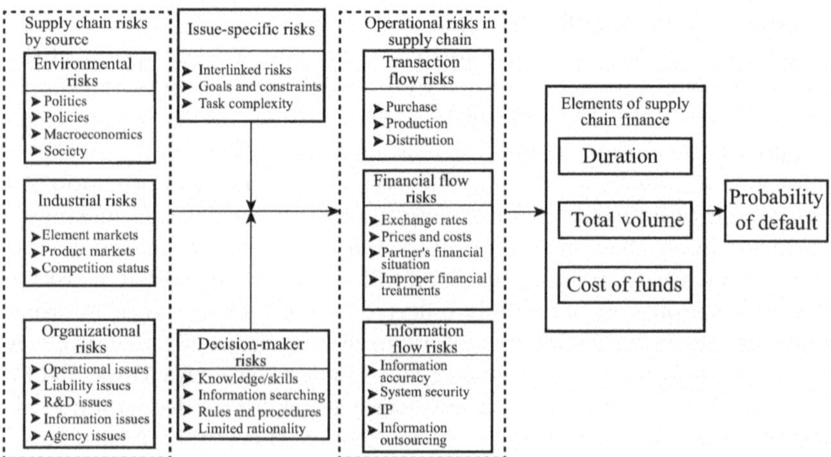

Fig. 10.1 Supply chain operations and supply chain financial risks

(2010), the main factors that lead to supply chain financial risks or high default rates are duration, total amount, and cost of funds. Duration or financing cycle refers to the length of time that the funds are occupied. A longer financing cycle implies greater financial costs and risks (Ortiz-Molina & Penas, 2008), as uncertainty in the transaction flow, finance flow, and information flow in the supply chain may lead to ineffective recovery of borrowed funds, and the interests of the borrowed funds may not be protected, leading to higher default rates. The total amount or financing volume is the degree to which the funds are occupied. Likewise, a larger volume of financing implies a greater risk. A study by Riding and Haines (2001) found that SMEs (especially start-ups) with larger financing volumes showed higher default rates. The financing rate is the cost of the funds occupied. The establishment of this cost requires consideration of various factors that affect the risks of supply chain operations. In the financial lending, higher financing rates may increase the probability of default for SMEs (Serrano-Cinca et al., 2015). These three factors mentioned above are not isolated, but interact and influence each other to determine the degree of default rate.

10.2.2 Supply Chain Financial Risks Resulting from Opportunism of Participants

Supply chain financial risks arise not only from supply chain operations, but also from opportunistic behaviors of participants. This type of risks is different from the risks of decision-makers in supply chain operations, as the latter is an objective source of risks due to the limitation of decision-makers' abilities. Opportunistic behaviors of participants are subjective, which means that the participants involved in a transaction or exchange violate the agreed rules in order to pursue their own interests to the detriment of others, which eventually leads to the creation of risks. (Williamson, 2007). A study by Karlan and Zinman (2009) concluded that 13–21% of defaults in financial lending were attributed to moral hazard and opportunism. Opportunism is an important concept in transaction cost economics. Often, influenced by environmental uncertainty as well as asset specificity, defaulting parties exploit information asymmetries or specific positions to act in their own interest to the detriment of others. For example, opportunistic behaviors of enterprises in a supply chain management environment can be reflected in their efforts to create a high level of supplier dependence and use this dependence to put pressure on suppliers

(Ketchen & Hult, 2007), or in the use of their own intermediary position to increase the potential for abuse and deliberate exploitation, such as cheating and dishonest activities (Grover & Malhotra, 2003; Ketchen & Hult, 2007). All these behaviors may have a major adverse effect on supply chain finance activities.

From a theoretical perspective, the opportunism arising from information asymmetry in credit markets is divided into two categories: opportunism resulting from ex ante and ex post information asymmetry (Donnelly et al., 2014). Ex ante information asymmetry is the asymmetry of information or the transmission of false information that occurs before a transaction or a lending business, which produces the undesirable result of adverse selection (Roberts, 2015). SMEs, as borrowers, tend to transmit positive information in their favor to lenders and conceal negative information to succeed in obtaining lending funds, which can lead to the phenomenon of "bad money driving out good money." In addition, ex ante information asymmetry may also occur in mortgages or guarantees. Mortgages, pledges, or guarantees are generally considered an effective means of preventing default risks arising from information asymmetry (Stroebel, 2016). However, financial institutions may also fail to effectively reduce default when carrying out mortgage, pledge, or guarantee business due to the lack of information about the true state or the quality. For example, a study by Ping Xinqiao and Yang Muyun found that ex post default rates for mortgages were higher than those for credit loans (2009). Ex post information asymmetry is often accompanied by moral hazard (Bubb & Kaufman, 2014). It is difficult to fully monitor the behaviors of SMEs because the true movement of funds as well as the operations, management, and other actions of the borrowing enterprises are not known after the lender provides money. Therefore, SMEs may change the use of funds without informing the lender, thus increasing the lender's financing risks.

In practice, supply chain financial risks arising from opportunism of participants has various fraud forms according to ex ante opportunism and ex post opportunism (see Fig. 10.2).

Ex ante opportunistic behavior is a fraudulent act committed by participants before lending in order to obtain funds from financial institutions, which in practice includes fictitious trade, illegal contracts with multiple parties, financing under false guarantees and other forms. An important point that distinguishes supply chain finance from other capital lending is that the lending decision is based on the transaction structure and trade relationship formed by upstream and downstream enterprises in the

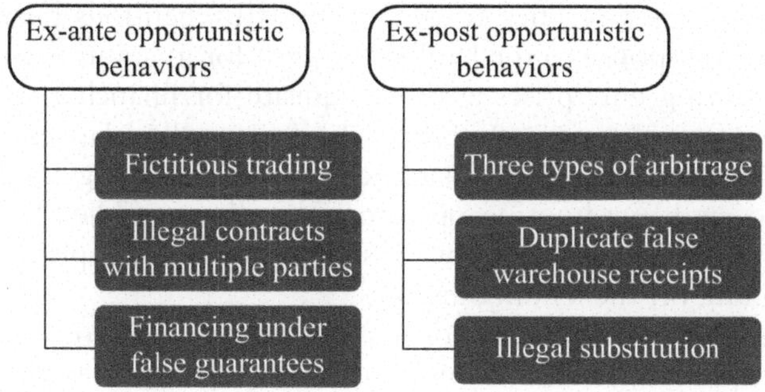

Fig. 10.2 Frauds in supply chain finance

supply chain. Therefore, for the purpose of obtaining funds, some participants use fictitious trade to implement the so-called trade financing. In other words, the participants form a false trade relationship with their related parties and fakes a series of transaction contracts and documents, so as to fraudulently obtain funds from banks or other financial institutions. Formally, it appears that there is a real transaction flow (buying and selling) and logistics flow (provision of logistics services) among different participants or service providers, and the documents and elements of the transaction are complete, but actually all these are fictitiously created by the related parties and there is no real and substantial industrial activity. The purpose of this behavior is to allow the related parties to falsify operating income and profits on the one hand and to obtain credit loan and low-cost financing from banks on the other. The behavior of signing illegal contracts with multiple parties is different from fictitious trade in that the transactions and assets formed by the latter are substantially false, while the former is based on real transactions and assets; however, the borrower obtains funds from multiple parties by virtue of the real transactions and assets formed, thus increasing the borrowing leverage and amplifying the risks of lending funds. Specifically, considering there is almost no information sharing between different financial institutions and supply chain financial service providers, coupled with the fact that the unified information and credit publicity platform of the whole society has not yet been set up, the borrowing enterprises use their transactions or logistics business or their certain assets to apply for financing from multiple institutions (especially unregulated private lending or P2P platforms) to enlarge their credit for the purpose of getting more funds. The financing under false guarantees is a practice to obtain funds by fictitious guarantors or supervisors in response to the lenders' request for guarantees and pledges of the borrowing enterprises as a prerequisite for financing. During the supply chain financing process of this behavior, usually relatives, friends, or closely related parties provide guarantee for the borrowing enterprises, or the logistics and warehousing operators actually controlled by the same person or its related parties provide supervision for the pledged goods, thus siphoning off the lending money.

Ex post opportunistic behavior is the practice of borrowers acquiring funds and siphoning off the financial proceeds through various fraudulent behaviors, as well as increasing the risks of financing. It mainly includes three types of arbitrage, duplicate false warehouse receipts, and illegal substitution. The behavior of three types of arbitrage is a typical supply chain financial fraud phenomenon in the previous years (from 2011 to 2016), which refers to interest arbitrage, exchange arbitrage, and tax arbitrage for the purpose of obtaining financial proceeds. Interest arbitrage and exchange arbitrage refers to the use of interest rate or exchange rate fluctuations and the use of fictitious trade and logistics to obtain interest rate and exchange differences and other illegal gains (e.g., fraudulent expansion of business volume to obtain credit loans from banks, and the use of small loans to purchase financial products; or fraudulent export tax rebates, etc.). Tax arbitrage refers to the use of the separation of goods and bills to obtain the corresponding tax benefits. Specifically, tax invoices that should have been sent to the end customers but were not sent because the end customers did not need them are sold to some enterprises or used to fill the tax invoice for the false sales transactions. The result is that on the one hand the invoice buyers gain the proceeds generated through the tax arbitrage and the end customers get a rebate on part of those proceeds; on the other hand, the invoice buyers can fill the gap of their false transactions.

In addition, there is a practice of tax arbitrage and fraud behavior based on the class of goods. For example, an enterprise reports Class B goods as Class A goods, thus siphoning off tax refund proceeds. It is worth noting that the early practices related to three types of arbitrage were based entirely on fictitious transaction (i.e., no real trade or logistics occurred) to obtain exchange differences, interest differences, or other gains. Nowadays, we have seen real transactions in some cases of the three types of arbitrage, resulting in "real fake transactions." In other words, the transaction or logistics activities are real, but the purpose is to expand the business falsely with the help of related transactions, so as to obtain more funds and earn a variety of corresponding proceeds. For example, some enterprises currently use domestic and offshore collusion in international trade activities to form export transactions, thus fraudulently obtaining export tax refund proceeds. Commodities are exported to foreign countries, reexported to other regions for distribution and processing, and then shipped back to China under the name of cross-border imports. Duplicate false warehouse receipts are also a common fraud phenomenon in supply chain finance, which is especially reflected in the 2013 Shanghai Steel Trade Event and the subsequent Qingdao Port Event. It refers to the malicious collusion between borrowing enterprises and warehousing enterprises or related personnel to falsely issue or repeatedly issue warehouse receipts for other people's goods or the same goods to the borrowing enterprises who repeatedly pledge the warehouse receipts to different financial institutions, thus obtaining a large number of loans and proceeds. Illegal substitution is a kind of supply chain finance fraud that has become more common in recent years. Supply chain finance is characterized by financial activities driven by the supply chain business, serving the participants in the industrial supply chains (especially SMEs), and eventually further driving and optimizing the industrial supply chain operations. Against these characteristics, illegal substitution means that the funds borrowed based on the business or assets in the supply chain are invested in other areas where the borrower can make profits, such as the stock market, real estate, financial products, and so on, or even reissue loans directly as a "second-hand bank," instead of being used in the industrial supply chain itself. Therefore, these borrowed funds do not really enter the industrial supply chain operations.

10.3 Risk Management System of Intelligent Supply Chain Finance

10.3.1 Two-Dimensional Driver of Risk Management of Intelligent Supply Chain Finance: Intelligent Credit

Corresponding to the two states that generate risks of supply chain finance (i.e., supply chain operation risks and opportunism of participants), the effective control and management of supply chain financial risks require the establishment of a risk management system and the full use of modern information and communication technologies to curb the various factors that may bring financial risks. Specifically, there are two different dimensions or directions for the control and management of supply chain financial risks. These two dimensions have different focuses, approaches, and characteristics, and have a trend of gradual integration (see Fig. 10.3).

One dimension of the control and management of supply chain financial risks is the elements in the supply chain structure and supply chain operations. Simply put, the risk of financial lending is effectively prevented based on a comprehensive grasp of the supply chain transaction process and assets. This kind of risk control and management is just the original meaning of the emergence of supply chain finance (Dyckman, 2011). Under the traditional lending cases, financial institutions were unable to know the real information of the borrowers, thus resulting in their fear and refusal to lend money. Supply chain finance is based on the real supply chain operations and the state of assets therein, allowing financial institutions to carry out financial activities directly based on the information and elements in the supply chain. Assets in the supply chain (e.g., inventory managed by a third party) provide the most direct way for financial institutions to evaluate products and values, facilitating the movement of funds in the supply chain (Buzacott & Zhang, 2004; Hofmann, 2009), or, transactions in supply chain operations generate good transaction credits, facilitating the efficiency of the movements of funds (Lee & Rhee, 2011; Casey & O'Toole, 2014; Canto-Cuevas et al., 2019). In addition, the

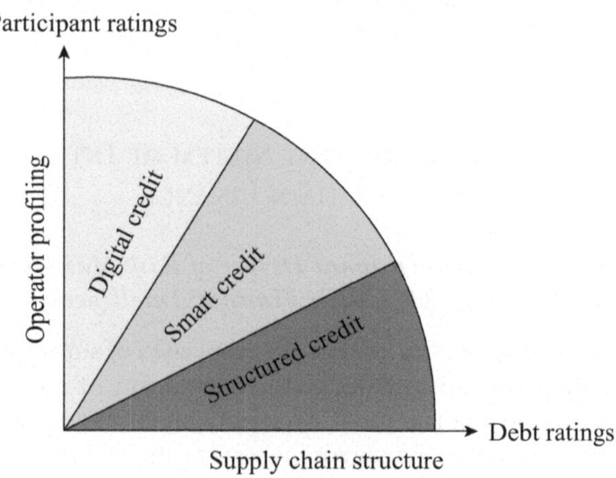

Fig. 10.3 Risk management system of intelligent supply chain finance

cooperative relationships and information sharing formed in the supply chain operations have reduced the level of information asymmetry, thus helping the effective control of risks. Financial institutions are able to control the corresponding risks while expanding the market for financial services by virtue of the systems and factors occurring in supply chain operations (He & Tang, 2012; Silvestro & Lustrato, 2014). Thus, it can be seen that the basis of this risk control is the debt rating. In other words, financial institutions can effectively control potential financial risks by controlling and managing the behavioral process based on a full grasp of the structure of the creditor-debtor relationship that generates from the transaction. After comparing it with the traditional bank lending models, Song Hua and Lu Qiang (2017) pointed out that supply chain finance effectively solves the financing problem of SMEs because it focuses more on transaction information and transaction credit before lending, and also emphasizes more on structural embedding and behavioral control after lending. Therefore, this risk control is based on structural credit, instead of focusing on the characteristics of the participants in the supply chain operations. It can be said, alternatively, that as long as the participants are well embedded in the supply chain operations, they can obtain effective financial services from financial institutions even if they are not sufficiently qualified, and the financial institutions can control their potential risks well.

Another dimension of risk management, as opposed to debt rating, is the profiling of the borrowers, or the entity rating. This kind of risk control is based on a comprehensive profile of the borrowers with a set of attributes defined for them (Middleton et al., 2004; Morey et al., 2015). Along with the development of big data analysis as well as machine learning, this approach has become the most important technical tool in the field of business intelligence. In particular, most SMEs in the financial sector are unable to provide sound financial statements and enough assets for montage or pledge, so the effective profiling can portray their operating status and creditworthiness and provide a basis for financial service decisions (Koyuncugil & Ozgulbas, 2008). For example, according to Wang Peiyuan (2018), the credit profiling of small enterprises can be described by a collection of tags, and the data source of tags is mainly based on tax data, which can dynamically reflect the business situation of enterprises. In addition, the design of the tags fully combines data from government departments such as the administrations for industry and commerce, courts, as well as the online data. Obviously, this risk control and management approach is mainly digital credit. In other words, financial institutions indirectly understand the credit status of the borrowers and obtain credit decision support through deep mining and analysis of borrower-centered data.

Following the development of intelligent supply chain finance, the integration between structured credit based on supply chain structure and operations and digital credit based on participant profiling has started to take place. Through user profiling as well as machine learning, financial institutions can better understand supply chain operations and the credit of each participant, thus effectively reducing supply chain financial risks (Zhu et al., 2019). On the one hand, relying entirely on structured credit to control supply chain financial risk does not provide a more effective understanding of the characteristics of the participants' profiles. Especially, after the supply chain operations become more and more networked and ecological, the core enterprises cannot control and understand all the operations, so the single use of structured credit cannot make supply chain financial services available to more SMEs in the supply chain, especially the N-tier suppliers or clients. On the other hand, controlling risk entirely with the help of participant profiling also limits the scale development of supply chain financial services. As mentioned in the previous section, risks come not only from the participants or borrowers but also from the supply chain operation environment, industry and business activities, as well as factors related to specific tasks. For example, sometimes supply chain financial risks do not arise directly from the credit deficiency or opportunistic behaviors of the borrowers, but from the operation issues or defaults of their upstream and downstream enterprises. Therefore, fully understanding and grasping the structure and operation of the supply chain is also a major prerequisite for effectively preventing potential risks and promoting the orderly development of financial services. The combination of structured credit and digital credit results in intelligent credit, which means fully using modern information and communication technologies such as advanced analysis technology, machine learning, and blockchain to profile the attributes of each participant in the supply chain, understand the business relationship and operational status formed between them, and then systematically control supply chain financial risks and promote the development of supply chain finance.

10.3.2 Establishment Principles and Management Elements of Intelligent Credit

The establishment of intelligent credit requires the use of modern ICT, especially big data analysis and various other analytic tools (e.g., machine learning and biometrics). It is also essential to control the business flow of the supply chain and to profile the participants, so as to reflect the real status of the supply chain operations and the real credit of the participants and to effectively control the credit risks (Wallis, 2003; Zhu et al., 2019; Bakoben et al., 2019; Petropoulos et al., 2019). In particular, as the supply chain finance becomes increasingly networked and ecological, the supply chain participants become increasingly tiered, and the Internet continues to develop with increasing information overload, a more comprehensive, detailed, and precise control over the business and participants through effective means is the key to the development of intelligent supply chain finance. More specifically, the establishment of intelligent credit requires the realization of six new principles different from the previously mentioned closed-loop business, revenue self-reimbursement, transaction informatization, management verticalization, risk structuralization, and reputation assetization (see Chapter X of *Internet-based Supply Chain Finance* written by Song Hua). The six new principles include behavior contextualization, asset penetration, management refinement, operational early warnings, information governance, and reputation digitization.

10.3.2.1 Behavior Contextualization

Contextualization is still not universally defined in the academic community. Schilit and Theimer (1994) defined it as "location, relationships with nearby persons, and behaviors that occur." Despite the lack of a uniform definition, the general consensus is that a "context" is related not only to the location at that time but also to the social identities such as network connectivity, communication costs, social situation, identity status, and social class. Behavior contextualization means a specific relationship formed by a specific group of subjects at a specific time and place. In the business sector, for example, enterprises design and develop products and services around the value demands of users, and deliver them to users through specific interactive methods, thus forming an integrated community effect. Similarly, there are also interactive community relationships in the financial services sector. According to Morrison et al. (2015), in a U-commerce environment (i.e., ubiquity, universality, unison, and uniqueness), financial service providers can only achieve effective financial services through amplification, reduction, contextualization, and transcendence. Specifically, effective control over credit risks requires a comprehensive use of data analysis and information processing to portray the structure of upstream and downstream enterprises in the supply chain, so as to truly reflect the position and status of core enterprises, borrowers, and related stakeholders in the business context. If, for example, a core enterprise is in a key coordinating and management position in the supply chain, its characteristics will determine the characteristics of the supply chain as a whole. Similarly, if two parties of the transaction have a long-run business relationship, the corresponding supply chain financial risks will be smaller. In terms of specific analysis elements, it is necessary to focus on two aspects of the status through artificial intelligence, virtual reality as well as fog computing and cloud computing. The first aspect is the status of the network constructed by the borrower and its upstream and downstream enterprises, which includes the status of the network formed among the core enterprises, SMEs as borrowers, and other affiliated parties, the closeness of the network, the position of each subject in the network, the structure of the relationship among them, and the degree of influencing and being influenced (Carnovale et al., 2018; Song et al., 2018; Song & Yang, 2018a; Carnovale et al., 2019); the other aspect is the status of business conducted by the borrower with its upstream and downstream enterprises, such as the degree of concentration and continuity of transactions with the previous suppliers and clients. In general, the degree of concentration should be neither too low nor too high. Too low means that the borrower does not have a close business relationship with the upstream and downstream enterprises, while too high means that it is more dependent on and vulnerable to the threats from the upstream and downstream enterprises. Similarly, the degree of continuity reflects the stability of the business relationship. Lack of such continuity may increase the risks of lending, while too high continuity implies that the enterprise lacks sufficient exploration in the long run.

10.3.2.2 Asset Penetration

Assets are one of the key elements of supply chain finance (Constand et al., 1991; Buzacott & Zhang, 2004). For example, inventory financing is a kind of financial business formed based on warehouse receipts, inventory, products, and so on (Buzacott & Zhang, 2004; Hofmann, 2009). However, inventory financing remains risky, both from the business cycle and price volatility of inventories (Gaur & Seshadri, 2005) and from moral hazard in inventory management (Song & Yang, 2018b). Therefore, the real promotion of asset-based supply chain finance business requires a true, detailed, and comprehensive reflection and management of assets in the supply chain. Asset penetration refers to the clear profiling and reflection of the assets and the movement of assets in the supply chain operations with the help of big data and artificial intelligence. Specifically, the profiling of assets mainly means the ability to clearly reflect the structure and the value status of assets, and the ability to penetrate into the fine-grained management of assets. The asset structure means the proportion of each type of asset to the total assets, such as the proportion of different types of fixed assets, other assets, and current assets invested. The proportions of current assets and fixed assets often determines the returns and risks of the enterprise. If the net working capital of an enterprise is lower, it means that it allocates a larger share of its capital to more profitable fixed assets, which leads to higher overall profitability; however, in terms of riskiness, lower working capital of an enterprises means smaller difference between current assets and current liabilities, and the risk of insolvency at maturity is also higher. In practice, if too much capital is invested in upfront fixed assets, it will most likely lead to tight liquidity, causing operational problems and reducing short-term solvency. Therefore, the focus of asset structure management is to determine a level of liquidity that can maintain normal business activities and bring more profit to the enterprise with less or no risk increased. Asset value reflects the price of an asset in the trading market, and is a price level that is acceptable to both buyers and sellers in the open market bidding and trading process. For example, what value the pledged inventory has at a particular time and place in supply chain finance is the basis for risk control and management. In addition to determining the asset structure and asset value statically, it is also important to dynamically profile the changes that reflect asset prices. If asset prices change drastically or are highly volatile, the risks of supply chain financial business will increase; otherwise, they will be relatively low. Therefore, the analysis of both short-term and long-term value changes of assets and the growth of corporate business are the key to risk management in supply chain finance.

10.3.2.3 Management Refinement

The management mentioned here is mainly a state of management for supply chain operations and business. Many studies have concluded that effective supply chain management, including supply chain knowledge, education, and culture, is able to trigger higher supply chain performance (Li et al., 2006; Luo et al., 2018). Organizations with more efficient management of supply chain operations are more competitive (Hult et al., 2007) and therefore significantly reduce supply chain financial risks. Although there are many indicators that reflect the level and status of supply chain management, the most direct one is still the cash conversion cycle (i.e., CCC) of the organizations. Currently, many studies have considered the CCC as an important factor reflecting the level of supply chain management of an organization (Stewart, 1995; Lai et al., 2002; Randall & Theodore Farris, 2009). It is worth noting that the components of the CCC reflect two different aspects: (a) The enterprise's ability in supply chain operation management, that is, days inventory held or inventory turnover ratio. A longer days inventory held or a smaller inventory turnover rate indicates a weaker ability of an enterprise in supply chain operations (Jones & Riley, 1985; Gunasekaran et al., 2004). Therefore, using data to analyze an enterprise's inventory turnover is the most practical way to reflect its operational ability. (b) Commercial credit, that is, DSO minus DPO. This indicator is a direct reflection of the level of credit that an enterprise offers to its clients. According to a study by Zhang et al. (2014), if a retailer delays payment in a supply chain system consisting of a manufacturer and a retailer, the upstream manufacturer will supply in small quantities and will not expect the downstream retailer to order in bulk, as expected. The upstream manufacturer will supply in bulk only if the downstream retailer adopts effective means to provide commercial credit. Thus, the status of commercial credit reflects the level of upstream and downstream capital management. In general, the lack of commercial credit makes it difficult to stabilize and develop the upstream and downstream business. On the contrary, too much commercial credit can take up the enterprise' own capital and cause cash flow problems. Therefore, commercial credit needs to be set at a reasonable range.

10.3.2.4 Operational Early Warnings

Operational early warnings are based on the perspective of income self-reimbursement. Revenue self-reimbursement reflects the fact that all potential risks in supply chain finance can be covered by the identifiable future profits (Song, 2017). In other words, once the future profitability is challenged, the risks of financing will increase. Therefore, both the bookkeeping status and operating capacity of an enterprise, among others, may affect the supply chain operation risks (Wu et al., 2006), which in turn affects financial security. Specifically, a predictive judgment of an enterprise's operating status requires the measurement of its operating performance from various aspects, including historical profitability of transactions, the coverage of product categories, interest coverage ratio, and tax-based financial data such as revenues and expenses. Historical profitability of transactions refers to the profitability of an enterprise's transactions that have occurred in the past and the persistence of profitability. This indicator reflects the operating capacity and growth potential of an enterprise. The coverage of product categories refers to the scope within which an enterprise is engaged in product operations. This indicator directly reflects the ability of an enterprise to develop and organize its products or businesses, and, indirectly, its internal ability to collaborate and innovate products. Stronger innovation ability will have a more significant contribution to supply chain finance (Song et al., 2019). Interest coverage ratio is the ratio of the earnings before interest and tax to the interest expense (the ratio of corporate EBITDA to interest expense). This indicator measures an enterprise's ability to pay its liabilities and interest (ability to repay interest on borrowed money). A larger ratio indicates a better ability of the enterprise to pay interest costs. Tax-based analysis refers to the fact that the credit profiling of a small enterprise can be described by a collection of tags, the data source of which is mainly based on tax data. This indicator can dynamically reflect the operating situation and operational capacity of the enterprise (Peiyuan Wang, 2018).

10.3.2.5 Information Governance

Information governance is a new concept that is both related to and distinct from IT governance. As a part of corporate governance, IT governance is "a way of leading and organizing IT structures and processes to ensure that an organization's IT systems can maintain and expand corporate strategies and goals." In this regard, IT governance is only a tool for corporate strategy and IT integration, but not a way to realize the value of the supply chain, and the way for information generation, use, processing, and exchange. In addition, IT governance overemphasizes the integration of IT and strategy through the control of systems, ignoring the innovative behavior, or the process of value re-creation, generated by the use of information technologies. The concept of information governance was creatively developed by Donaldson and Walker (2004). Information governance involves creating the environment, opportunities, rules, and decision-making powers to evaluate, create, collect, analyze, transmit, store, use, and control information to answer the questions of "what information do we need, how do we use it, and who is responsible for it" (Kooper et al., 2011). Of course, information governance behaviors include transaction management, rule establishment, information security, data flow management, and full life cycle management of information.

Effective information governance needs to address four questions: (a) How to establish effective information sources and information structures. In other words, in the process of value chain construction, what kind of information is needed for the realization of the efficiency of the whole value chain and the realization of the synergistic value of all interested parties? What is the relationship between this information and the common goal pursued by all parties? Where does this information come from? What means can be used to obtain this information? The answer to these questions lies in achieving the balanced relationship among information sources, receivers, and information management, and each set of triangular relationships constitutes the most basic unit of information governance. For example, when providing financing services to an SME, the financial institutions needs to obtain the real logistics information of the SME, while the realization of this goal involves the triangle of information source, receiving place and information management. The information sources may be various and diverse, such as commodity flow information formed with the help of IoT, customs clearance information from the customs department, product quantity and quality inspection information issued by the commodity inspection department, and so on. However, what the receiver needs is information about the integrity and preservation of the value of goods, and this information needs to be integrated, mined, generated, and delivered to the receiver by the organizations engaged in information management or information regulation from fragmented information from different sources. Once this triangle relationship is out of balance, various blind spots and barriers of information are easily created, making the supply chain operations disrupted. (b) How to guarantee the reliability, security, and use of information. Information reliability means that the information is reliable enough to take action accordingly. If a supply chain service integrator decides whether to provide a service based on a customer' financial statement, it must be able to confirm that the statement is true and reliable, because any distortion of information is bound to lead to disastrous results. Information security means that information is generated, transmitted, and used in a way that is accessible to the receivers, without information leakage or spillover, or violation of legal and privacy regulations. Information use means that the acquired information is able to be used to address challenges, understand situations, solve problems, and make decisions. Obviously, the realization of the above three characteristics of information requires a lot of efforts in IT construction, information form, business hierarchy, and process standard management. (c) How to realize the continuous and full life cycle management of information, or whether information can be generated, promoted, and used continuously, and more stakeholders can be involved in the process of information generation and sharing. Achieving this goal requires the information regulators to address two relationships: first, the information domain constructed by all network members through sharing, learning, and communication (i.e., collaborative parties working together to improve the quality of information, its processing, and its application); and second, information reciprocity and management improvement between network members and external management parties. Given that no business information is immune to economic, policy, and institutional influences, truly achieving information sustainability requires information interaction with institutional managers. (d) How to control of the costs of information acquisition and processing. There is always a cost to acquire information. Nobel laureate Stigler pointed out that the degree of access to information is determined by the equilibrium of marginal benefits and marginal costs. How to reduce the costs of information acquisition through more effective network construction of value chain participants has become the core issue of information governance in the era of "Internet Plus."

10.3.2.6 Reputation Digitization

Reputation is an important source of corporate competitiveness (Gu & Lu, 2014) because reputation implies the overall evaluation of the enterprises made by stakeholders in terms of beliefs, emotions, and sentiments (Dacin & Brown, 2006; Mukherjee & He, 2008). Two different dimensions of reputation definition exist in the academic circles. Some scholars view reputation as a recognition of an enterprise's abilities (Walsh et al., 2009; Low & Robins, 2014); others view reputation as a perception of an enterprise's possibilities (Love & Kraatz, 2009). Clearly, these two definitions do not have the same focus, with the former tending toward an objective perception of the current state of the enterprise and the latter tending toward an anticipatory judgment of the enterprise's behaviors. In fact, both of the above definitions profile the state of the enterprise from different aspects, so they are complementary to each other and together constitute the overall concept of corporate reputation (Raithel & Schwaiger, 2015; Song et al., 2017). As far as risk control in supply chain finance is concerned, the reputation defined by the above two dimensions is fully profiled with the help of artificial intelligence and big data analysis. Specifically, the profiling of reputation in terms of objective ability includes bank credit, industry qualifications, and transaction behaviors, while the profiling of predictive reputation can be manifested in entity profiling based on data from third parties such as the industrial and commercial bureaus, tax bureaus, and anti-money laundering agencies. The combination of the two can provide a more comprehensive picture of the overall creditworthiness of the borrower.

References

Abbasi, W. A., Wang, Z., & Alsakarneh, A. (2018). Overcoming SMEs financing and supply chain obstacles by introducing supply chain finance. *HOLISTICA—Journal of Business and Public Administration, 9*(1), 7–22.

Allayannis, G., Ihrig, J., & Weston, J. P. (2001). Exchange-rate hedging: Financial versus operational strategies. *American Economic Review, 91*(2), 391–395.

Ang, S., & Straub, D. W. (1998). Production and transaction economies and IS outsourcing: A study of the US banking industry. *MIS Quarterly, 22*(4), 535–552.

Bakoben, M., Bellotti, T., & Adams, N. (2019). Identification of credit risk based on cluster analysis of account behaviours. *Journal of the Operational Research Society*, 1–9. https://doi.org/10.1080/01605682.2019.1582586

Berger, A. N., & Udell, G. F. (2006). A more complete conceptual framework for SME finance. *Journal of Banking & Finance, 30*(11), 2945–2966.

Bester, H., & Hellwig, M. (1987). Moral hazard and equilibrium credit rationing: An overview of the issues. In *Agency theory, information, and incentives* (pp. 135–166). Springer.

Bettis, R. A., & Hall, W. K. (1982). Accounting determined risk, and accounting determined return. *The Academy of Management Journal, 25*(2), 254–264.

Bubb, R., & Kaufman, A. (2014). Securitization and moral hazard: Evidence from credit score cutoff rules. *Journal of Monetary Economics, 63*, 1–18.

Buzacott, J. A., & Zhang, R. Q. (2004). Inventory management with asset-based financing. *Management Science, 50*(9), 1274–1292.

Canto-Cuevas, F.-J., Palacín-Sánchez, M.-J., & Di Pietro, F. (2019). Trade credit as a sustainable resource during an SME's life cycle. *Sustainability, 11*(3), 670.

Carnovale, S., Rogers, D. S., & Yeniyurt, S. (2018). Broadening the perspective of supply chain finance: The performance impacts of network power & cohesion. *Journal of Purchasing and Supply Management, 25*(2), 134–145.
Carnovale, S., Rogers, D. S., & Yeniyurt, S. (2019). Broadening the perspective of supply chain finance: The performance impacts of network power and cohesion. *Journal of Purchasing and Supply Management, 25*(2), 134–145.
Casey, E., & O'Toole, C. M. (2014). Bank lending constraints, trade credit and alternative financing during the financial crisis: Evidence from European SMEs. *Journal of Corporate Finance, 27*, 173–193.
Christopher, M., & Holweg, M. (2011). 'Supply chain 2.0': Managing supply chains in the era of turbulence. *International Journal of Physical Distribution & Logistics Management, 41*(1), 63–82.
Constand, R. L., Osteryoung, J. S., & Nast, D. A. (1991). Asset-based financing and the determinants of capital structure in the small firm. In *Advances in small business finance* (pp. 29–45). Springer.
Dacin, P. A., & Brown, T. J. (2006). Corporate branding, identity, and customer response. *Journal of the Academy of Marketing Science, 34*(2), 95–98.
Donaldson, A., & Walker, P. (2004). Information governance—A view from the NHS. *International Journal of Medical Informatics, 73*(3), 281–284.
Donnelly, C., Englund, M., & Nielsen, J. P. (2014). The importance of the choice of test for finding evidence of asymmetric information. *ASTIN Bulletin: The Journal of the IAA, 44*(2), 173–195.
Dyckman, B. (2011). Supply chain finance: Risk mitigation and revenue growth. *Journal of Corporate Treasury Management, 4*(2), 168–173.
Finch, P. (2004). Supply chain risk management. *Supply Chain Management: An International Journal, 9*(2), 183–196.
Gaur, V., & Seshadri, S. (2005). Hedging inventory risk through market instruments. *Manufacturing & Service Operations Management, 7*(2), 103–120.
Gomm, M. L. (2010). Supply chain finance: Applying finance theory to supply chain management to enhance finance in supply chains. *International Journal of Logistics Research and Applications, 13*(2), 133–142.
Grover, V., & Malhotra, M. K. (2003). Transaction cost framework in operations and supply chain management research: Theory and measurement. *Journal of Operations Management, 21*(4), 457–473.
Gu, Q., & Lu, X. (2014). Unraveling the mechanisms of reputation and alliance formation: A study of venture capital syndication in China. *Strategic Management Journal, 35*(5), 739–750.
Gunasekaran, A., Patel, C., & McGaughey, R. E. (2004). A framework for supply chain performance measurement. *International Journal of Production Economics, 87*(3), 333–347.

Hallikas, J., & Lintukangas, K. (2016). Purchasing and supply: An investigation of risk management performance. *International Journal of Production Economics, 171*, 487–494.

Hartley-Urquhart, R. (2006). Managing the financial supply chain. *Supply Chain Management Review, 10*(6), 18–25.

He, X., & Tang, L. (2012). Exploration on building of visualization platform to innovate business operation pattern of supply chain finance. *Physics Procedia, 33*, 1886–1893.

Hendricks, K. B., & Singhal, V. R. (2005). An empirical analysis of the effect of supply chain disruptions on long-run stock price performance and equity risk of the firm. *Production and Operations Management, 14*(1), 35–52.

Hofmann, E. (2009). Inventory financing in supply chains: A logistics service provider-approach. *International Journal of Physical Distribution & Logistics Management, 39*(9), 716–740.

Huchzermeier, A., & Cohen, M. A. (1996). Valuing operational flexibility under exchange rate risk. *Operations Research, 44*(1), 100–113.

Hult, G. T. M., Ketchen, D. J., & Arrfelt, M. (2007). Strategic supply chain management: Improving performance through a culture of competitiveness and knowledge development. *Strategic Management Journal, 28*(10), 1035–1052.

Irwin, D., & Scott, J. M. (2010). Barriers faced by SMEs in raising bank finance. *International Journal of Entrepreneurial Behavior & Research, 16*(3), 245–259.

Jensen, M. C., & Meckling, W. H. (1976). Theory of the firm: Managerial behavior, agency costs and ownership structure. *Journal of Financial Economics, 3*(4), 305–360.

Jones, T. C., & Riley, D. W. (1985). Using inventory for competitive advantage through supply chain management. *International Journal of Physical Distribution & Materials Management, 15*(5), 16–26.

Karlan, D., & Zinman, J. (2009). Observing unobservables: Identifying information asymmetries with a consumer credit field experiment. *Econometrica, 77*(6), 1993–2008.

Ketchen, D. J., Jr., & Hult, G. T. M. (2007). Bridging organization theory and supply chain management: The case of best value supply chains. *Journal of Operations Management, 25*(2), 573–580.

Khan, O., Christopher, M., & Burnes, B. (2008). The impact of product design on supply chain risk: A case study. *International Journal of Physical Distribution & Logistics Management, 38*(5), 412–432.

Kleindorfer, P. R., & Saad, G. H. (2005). Managing disruption risks in supply chains. *Production and Operations Management, 14*(1), 53–68.

König, A., & Spinler, S. (2016). The effect of logistics outsourcing on the supply chain vulnerability of shippers: Development of a conceptual risk management framework. *The International Journal of Logistics Management, 27*(1), 122–141.

Kooper, M. N., Maes, R., & Lindgreen, E. E. O. R. (2011). On the governance of information: Introducing a new concept of governance to support the management of information. *International Journal of Information Management, 31*(3), 195–200.

Korpela, J., Kyläheiko, K., Lehmusvaara, A., & Tuominen, M. (2002). An analytic approach to production capacity allocation and supply chain design. *International Journal of Production Economics, 78*(2), 187–195.

Kouvelis, P., & Zhao, W. (2018). Who should finance the supply chain? Impact of credit ratings on supply chain decisions. *Manufacturing & Service Operations Management, 20*(1), 19–35.

Koyuncugil, A. S., & Ozgulbas, N. (2008). Financial profiling for detecting operational risk by data mining. *World Academy of Science, Engineering and Technology, 46*, 6238–6253.

Lai, K., Ngai, E. W. T., & Cheng, T. C. E. (2002). Measures for evaluating supply chain performance in transport logistics. *Transportation Research Part E: Logistics and Transportation Review, 38*(6), 439–456.

Lee, H. L. (2002). Aligning supply chain strategies with product uncertainties. *California Management Review, 44*(3), 105–119.

Lee, C. H., & Rhee, B.-D. (2011). Trade credit for supply chain coordination. *European Journal of Operational Research, 214*(1), 136–146.

Levary, R. R. (2007). Ranking foreign suppliers based on supply risk. *Supply Chain Management: An International Journal, 12*(6), 392–394.

Li, S., Ragu-Nathan, B., Ragu-Nathan, T. S., & Subba Rao, S. (2006). The impact of supply chain management practices on competitive advantage and organizational performance. *Omega, 34*(2), 107–124.

Liu, Z., & Nagurney, A. (2011). Supply chain outsourcing under exchange rate risk and competition. *Omega, 39*(5), 539–549.

Love, E. G., & Kraatz, M. (2009). Character, conformity, or the bottom line? How and why downsizing affected corporate reputation. *Academy of Management Journal, 52*(2), 314–335.

Low, K. Y. J., & Robins, J. A. (2014). Finding knowledge: The role of reputation in knowledge-transfer to chinese companies. *Long Range Planning, 47*(6), 353–364.

Luo, W., Shi, Y., & Venkatesh, V. G. (2018). Exploring the factors of achieving supply chain excellence: A New Zealand perspective. *Production Planning & Control, 29*(8), 655–667.

Middleton, S. E., Shadbolt, N. R., & De Roure, D. C. (2004). Ontological user profiling in recommender systems. *ACM Transactions on Information Systems (TOIS), 22*(1), 54–88.

Miller, K. D. (1992). A framework for integrated risk management in international business. *Journal of International Business Studies, 23*(2), 311–331.

Mizgier, K. J., Hora, M., Wagner, S. M., & Jüttner, M. P. (2015). Managing operational disruptions through capital adequacy and process improvement. *European Journal of Operational Research, 245*(1), 320–332.
Morey, T., Forbath, T., & Schoop, A. (2015). Customer data: Designing for transparency and trust. *Harvard Business Review, 93*(5), 96–105.
Morrison, S., Pitt, L., & Kietzmann, J. (2015). Technology and financial services: Marketing in times of U-commerce. *Journal of Financial Services Marketing, 20*(4), 273–281.
Mukherjee, A., & He, H. (2008). Company identity and marketing: An integrative framework. *Journal of Marketing Theory and Practice, 16*(2), 111–125.
Narayanan, V., & Raman, A. (2004). Aligning incentives in supply chains. *Harvard Business Review, 82*(11), 94–102.
Nienhuis, J. J., Cortet, M., & Lycklama, D. (2013). Real-time financing: Extending e-invoicing to real-time SME financing. *Journal of Payments Strategy & Systems, 7*(3), 232–245.
Nishat Faisal, M., Banwet, D. K., & Shankar, R. (2007). Information risks management in supply chains: An assessment and mitigation framework. *Journal of Enterprise Information Management, 20*(6), 677–699.
Ortiz-Molina, H., & Penas, M. F. (2008). Lending to small businesses: The role of loan maturity in addressing information problems. *Small Business Economics, 30*(4), 361–383.
Papadakis, I. S. (2006). Financial performance of supply chains after disruptions: An event study. *Supply Chain Management: An International Journal, 11*(1), 25–33.
Peck, H. (2005). Drivers of supply chain vulnerability: An integrated framework. *International Journal of Physical Distribution & Logistics Management, 35*(4), 210–232.
Petropoulos, A., Siakoulis, V., Stavroulakis, E., & Klamargias, A. (2019). A robust machine learning approach for credit risk analysis of large loan level datasets using deep learning and extreme gradient boosting. *IFC Bulletins* chapters 49.
Ping, X. Q., & Yang, M. Y. (2009). An Empirical study of information asymmetry in credit markets: Evidence from Chinese state-owned commercial banks. *Journal of Financial Research, 3,* 1–18.
Raithel, S., & Schwaiger, M. (2015). The effects of corporate reputation perceptions of the general public on shareholder value. *Strategic Management Journal, 36*(6), 945–956.
Randall, W. S., & Theodore Farris, M. (2009). Supply chain financing: Using cash-to-cash variables to strengthen the supply chain. *International Journal of Physical Distribution & Logistics Management, 39*(8), 669–689.
Rao, S., & Goldsby, T. J. (2009). Supply chain risks: A review and typology. *The International Journal of Logistics Management, 20*(1), 97–123.

Riding, A. L., & Haines, G. (2001). Loan guarantees. *Journal of Business Venturing, 16*(6), 595–612.

Ritchie, B., & Marshall, D. V. (1993). *Business risk management*. Chapman & Hall.

Roberts, M. R. (2015). The role of dynamic renegotiation and asymmetric information in financial contracting. *Journal of Financial Economics, 116*(1), 61–81.

Schilit, B. N., & Theimer, M. M. (1994). *Disseminating active mop infonncition to mobile hosts*. IEEE Network.

Serrano-Cinca, C., Gutiérrez-Nieto, B., & López-Palacios, L. (2015). Determinants of default in P2P lending. *PLoS One, 10*(10), e0139427.

Shenk, D. (1997). *Data smog: Surviving the information glut*. HarperCollins Publishers.

Silvestro, R., & Lustrato, P. (2014). Integrating financial and physical supply chains: The role of banks in enabling supply chain integration. *International Journal of Operations & Production Management, 34*(3), 298–324.

Simon, H. A. (1972). Theories of bounded rationality. *Decision and Organization, 1*(1), 161–176.

Song, H. (2017). *Internet supply chain finance*. China Renmin University Press.

Song, H., & Lu, Q. (2017). How industrial enterprise-led supply chain finance to help SME financing—A multi-case comparative study. *Economic Theory and Business Management, 12*, 47–58.

Song, H., & Yang, X. (2018a). Study on impact of SMEs' competitiveness and network embeddedness on performance of supply chain finance. *Chinese Journal of Management, 15*(4), 616.

Song, H., & Yang, X. (2018b). Supply chain finance risk sources and systematic management: An integrative framework. *Journal of Renmin University of China, 4*, 119–128.

Song, H., Turson, R., Ganguly, A., & Yu, K. (2017). Evaluating the effects of supply chain quality management on food firms' performance: The mediating role of food certification and reputation. *International Journal of Operations & Production Management, 37*(10), 1541–1562.

Song, H., Lu, Q., Yu, K., & Qian, C. (2018). How do knowledge spillover and access in supply chain network enhance SMEs' credit quality? *Industrial Management & Data Systems, 119*(2), 274–291.

Song, H., Chen, S., & Ganguly, A. (2019). Innovative ecosystem in enhancing Hi-Tech SME financing: Mediating role of two types of innovation capabilities. *International Journal of Innovation Management, 24*(2), 2050017. https://doi.org/10.1142/S1363919620500176

Stewart, G. (1995). Supply chain performance benchmarking study reveals keys to supply chain excellence. *Logistics Information Management, 8*(2), 38–44.

Stiglitz, J. E., & Weiss, A. (1981). Credit rationing in markets with imperfect information. *The American Economic Review, 71*(3), 393–410.

Stroebel, J. (2016). Asymmetric information about collateral values: Asymmetric information about collateral values. *The Journal of Finance, 71*(3), 1071–1112.
Tang, O., & Nurmaya Musa, S. (2011). Identifying risk issues and research advancements in supply chain risk management. *International Journal of Production Economics, 133*(1), 25–34.
Verbano, C., & Venturini, K. (2013). Managing risks in SMEs: A literature review and research agenda. *Journal of Technology Management & Innovation, 8*(3), 33–34.
Wagner, S. M., Mizgier, K. J., & Papageorgiou, S. (2017). Operational disruptions and business cycles. *International Journal of Production Economics, 183*, 66–78.
Wallis, J. (2003). Information-saturated yet ignorant: Information mediation as social empowerment in the knowledge economy. *Library Review, 52*(8), 369–372.
Walsh, G., Mitchell, V., Jackson, P. R., & Beatty, S. E. (2009). Examining the antecedents and consequences of corporate reputation: A customer perspective. *British Journal of Management, 20*(2), 187–203.
Wang P. (2018). Research on the key technologies of the bank-tax interactive platform based on credit profile. *Information Technology and Informatization*, (04), 153–156.
Williamson, O. E. (2007). The economic institutions of capitalism. Firms, markets, relational contracting. In *Das Summa Summarum des management* (pp. 61–75). Springer.
Wong, C. Y., & Hvolby, H.-H. (2007). Coordinated responsiveness for volatile toy supply chains. *Production Planning & Control, 18*(5), 407–419.
Wu, T., Blackhurst, J., & Chidambaram, V. (2006). A model for inbound supply risk analysis. *Computers in Industry, 57*(4), 350–365.
Zhang, Q., Dong, M., Luo, J., & Segerstedt, A. (2014). Supply chain coordination with trade credit and quantity discount incorporating default risk. *International Journal of Production Economics, 153*, 352–360.
Zhang, L., Hu, H., & Zhang, D. (2015). A credit risk assessment model based on SVM for small and medium enterprises in supply chain finance. *Financial Innovation, 1*(1), 14.
Zhao, X., Yeung, K., Huang, Q., & Song, X. (2015). Improving the predictability of business failure of supply chain finance clients by using external big dataset. *Industrial Management & Data Systems, 115*(9), 1683–1703.
Zhu, Y., Zhou, L., Xie, C., Wang, G.-J., & Nguyen, T. V. (2019). Forecasting SMEs' credit risk in supply chain finance with an enhanced hybrid ensemble machine learning approach. *International Journal of Production Economics, 211*, 22–33.

Printed and bound by CPI Group (UK) Ltd, Croydon CR0 4YY

[illegible]

[illegible]